GUERRILLA MARKETING

ON THE INTERNET

The Definitive Guide from the Father of Guerrilla Marketing

JAY CONRAD LEVINSON, MITCH MEYERSON,
and Mary Eule Scarborough

Jere L. Calmes, Publisher
Cover Design: Beth Hansen-Winter
Composition and Production: MillerWorks

This publication is designed to provide accurate and authoritative information
in regard to the subject matter covered. It is sold with the understanding that the
publisher is not engaged in rendering legal, accounting or other professional services.
If legal advice or other expert assistance is required, the services of a
competent professional person should be sought.

Library of Congress Cataloging-in-Publication Data

Levinson, Jay Conrad.
Guerrilla marketing on the Internet/by Jay Conrad Levinson, Mitch Meyerson,
and Mary Eule Scarborough.
   p. cm.
  ISBN-13: 978-1-59918-194-3 (alk. paper)
  ISBN-10: 1-59918-194-0
  1. Internet marketing. 2. Internet advertising. I. Meyerson, Mitch.
  II. Scarborough, Mary Eule. III. Title.
HF5415.1265.L477 2008   658.8'72—dc22
2008015789

Printed in Canada

11 10   10 9 8 7 6 5 4

CONTENTS

CHAPTER 1
The Internet: The Most Powerful Guerrilla Marketing Tool
Ever Created 1

Guerrilla Marketing Principles at a Glance 5

Guerrilla Investment: Time, Energy, Imagination,
and Knowledge 6

Guerrilla Intentionality: Marketing Includes Every
Contact with the Public 7

Guerrilla Commitment: Building Successful
Businesses One Step at a Time 8

Guerrilla Partnerships: Working Together to
Make Things Happen 9

Guerrilla Psychology: Tapping into Their Target
Audiences' Minds 10

Guerrilla Assortments 10

Guerrilla Measurement 11

Guerrilla Action 11

Guerrilla Fieldwork 15

CHAPTER 2

The 12 Biggest Internet Marketing Mistakes—And How to Avoid Them 17

    Mistake 1: Putting Up a Website With No Planning 19

    Mistake 2: Failing to Research Competitors and the Marketplace 21

    Mistake 3: Developing Poorly Designed Websites that are Difficult

        to Navigate 22

    Mistake 4: Failing to Write Effective Direct Response Copy 23

    Mistake 5: Failing to Build Permission-Based E-mail Marketing Lists 24

    Mistake 6: No Traffic Generation Strategy 24

    Mistake 7: Not Using Web 2.0 Social Media and Technology. 25

    Mistake 8: Not Using Online and Offline Marketing Combinations 26

    Mistake 9: Failing to Track Marketing Campaigns 26

    Mistake 10: Neglecting to Build Virtual Teams and Partnerships 27

    Mistake 11: Failing to Follow Up with Prospects and Customers 28

    Mistake 12: Failing to Ensure that Computer Equipment is up to the Task 29

        Hardware 30

        Software 30

        Security 30

        Disaster Recovery 30

        Maintenance 31

        Mobility 31

    Guerrilla Fieldwork 31

CHAPTER 3

Guerrilla Websites: High Impact at a Low Cost 33

    Site Design Strategy 34

        Immediate Online Sales 35

        Lead Generation for Future Online Sales 36

        Lead Generation for Future Offline Sales 36

        Hybrid. 36

    Types of Websites 36

        Squeeze Page 36

        Sales Page/Letter 38

        Blogs 38

        Continuity Websites (Membership/Subscription) 42

        Informational or Brochure Websites 42

CONTENTS

Choosing Your Domain Name and Hosting Company 42

Selecting Your Domain Name 42

Selecting Your Hosting Company 45

Developing Your Website 46

Structure First.. 46

Organizing Content for Multiple Page Websites 46

Navigation and Usability Guidelines 48

Use Clear, Simple, Logical Words and Phrases for Labeling Menus 48

Categorize your Content Logically.................................... 48

Make Speed a Priority.. 48

Adjust your Browser Settings 49

Use No-Surprise Navigation Devices 49

Outsourcing Your Web Development 50

Check Out Lots of Websites.................................... 51

Survey Current and Past Customers. 51

Finalize Your Requirements.................................... 51

Determine How Your Website Will Be Maintained 51

Professional Website Design on a Guerrilla Budget 52

Use Easy-to-Read Typefaces and Formatting 53

Use Color Carefully 54

Place Key Content Above the Fold.................................... 54

When It Comes to Design, Less Is More.................................... 55

Use Artwork and Graphics To Your Best Advantage 55

Guerrilla Fieldwork 60

CHAPTER 4
Direct Response Marketing: Turning Visitors into Customers 61

What Do Consumers Really Buy? 63

Direct Response Communication 64

How to Turn Website Visitors into Customers—Guerrilla Style 64

Talk Naturally.. 64

Grab Hold of Their Hearts and Don't Let Go 65

Personalize 65

Provide Just Enough Information to Help Them Make a Decision 65

Don't Mumble.. 65

Paint a Picture.. 65

Sales Page Outline **66**

Identify Your Visitors' Most Urgent Problem 66

Create an Attention-Grabbing Headline (and Subheadings) 66

State Their Problem 67

Offer the Solution 68

Resolve Their Concerns 68

Use Bullets That Resonate 68

Offer Something Irresistible 69

Justify the Cost and Build Value 69

Reverse The Risk 69

Call 'Em to Action 70

Remind, Repeat, Recap, and Reassure 71

Guerrilla Simplicity: The Squeeze Page **72**

Tactics for Increasing Conversions 72

Opt-In Conversions 73

Sales Conversions 74

Models for Moving from Opt-Ins to Sales 75

What Will You Measure? **77**

The Ultimate Guerrilla Web Measurement Tool 78

Guerrilla Fieldwork **79**

CHAPTER 5
Guerrilla Communications: E-Mail, Podcasts, and Feeds **81**

Promotional E-Mails **83**

Getting Your E-Mails Opened 84

Subject Lines 84

Getting Your E-Mails Read 86

Getting Your Readers to Take Action 88

Advanced Techniques for Making Your E-Mails Memorable **89**

Moving From Text to Video E-Mails 89

Audio Postcards 90

Really Simple Syndication (RSS) Feeds **91**

Ways to Use RSS Feeds 92

Gathering RSS Feeds 93

Adding RSS Feeds to Your Website 93

Podcasting **94**

What are Podcasts? 94

Why Guerrillas Use Podcasts 95

Equipment You'll Need to Publish Your Own Podcast 95

Steps for Creating Podcasts. 97

More Tips for Effective Podcasting 97

Nanocasts. **98**

The New Language of Mobile Devices **98**

Guerrilla Fieldwork **101**

CHAPTER 6
Guerrilla Traffic: Driving Visitors to Your Website **103**

Search Engine Traffic: Where It All Begins **104**

Search Engine Optimization: A Primer. **105**

Powerful Keywords and Phrases: The Heart of Search Engine

Optimization 106

Guerrillas Make Their Sites Easy to View and Use **108**

Guerrillas Link with Others **109**

Inbound Links 109

Outbound and Reciprocal Links 109

Guerrillas Add Relevant Content 110

Guerrillas Participate. **112**

Find Out Where They Gather 112

Become Part of the Community 112

Position Yourself as an Industry Expert. 113

Guerrillas Partner Using Affiliate Programs. **113**

How Are Affiliate Programs Managed? 114

Choosing Affiliate Programs. **115**

Make a List and Check It Twice 115

Research and Click 116

Assess, Compare and Sign-Up 116

Building An Affiliate Program **117**

1. Take a Page Out of Your Own Book. 117

2. Take Care of First Things First. 117

3. Affix, Invite, Promote 118

4. Continue to Deliver—Even After the Sale 118

Guerrillas Publish. **118**

Guerrillas Write Articles. 118
Guerrillas Stay in Touch with Newsletters 119
Guerrillas Use Word-of-Mouth Marketing **120**
Guerrillas Go Viral 121
Guerrillas Use Tell-A-Friend Programs 121
Guerrillas Generate Online Publicity 122
Guerrillas Set Up E-Mail Signatures 123
Guerrilla Fieldwork **124**

CHAPTER 7
Guerrilla Automation: Online Systems for Effortless Follow-Up **125**
Processing Online Payments **127**
Merchant Accounts 127
PayPal and Other Third-Party Processors 129
One-Stop Shopping Carts 129
Sequential Autoresponders: Guerrillas' Automated Workforce **131**
Using Autoresponders to Create Sublists and "Scratch Your Niches!" 134
Offline Automation for Easy Follow-Up **134**
Tracking and Measuring **135**
What Does the Future Look Like for Automation Technology? **137**
Guerrilla Fieldwork **137**

CHAPTER 8
Guerrilla Multimedia:
Using Audio and Video for Maximum Impact **139**
Guerrilla Audios **140**
Audio Equipment and Software Supply List 142
Guerrilla Videos **143**
Ten Best Guerrilla Online Video Strategies 144
Video Equipment and Software Supply List. 146
Telephone and Web-Based Seminars and Conferences **147**
Guerrilla Fieldwork **151**

CHAPTER 9
Guerrilla Internet Weapons **153**
Choosing Your Marketing Weapons **155**
Guerrilla Fieldwork **169**

CHAPTER 10
The Web 2.0 Guerrilla **171**

   Web 2.0 Simplified **173**

   The Web 2.0 Culture and Mindset Shift **174**

   Demystifying Web 2.0 Technology, Tools, and Strategies **178**

      Blogosphere. 178

      Bookmarking, Social Bookmarking 178

      Social Media 178

      Social/Business Networking Websites 178

      Bookmarklets 179

      Content Management System (CMS) 179

      Long Tail Strategy 179

      Mashups 180

      Membership Sites 180

      Open Source 181

      Syndication Feeds: RSS and ATOM. 181

      Tags 181

      User-Generated Content (UGC) 182

      Widgets. 182

      Wikis. 182

   How Guerrillas Use The Best-of-the-Best Web 2.0 Websites **183**

      Social Video Websites: YouTube. 183

      Picture Sharing Websites: Flickr.com and Facebook.com 183

      Social Networking Websites: MySpace.com and Squidoo.com. 184

      Social Bookmarking Websites: Del.icio.us and Technorati.com 184

      Community-Based User Generated Websites. 184

   Guerrilla Fieldwork **186**

CHAPTER 11
Guerrilla Internet Marketing in Action:
Four Innovative Campaigns. **187**

   Russell Brunson **188**

      Creating Large Streams of Income with Your Dream Team 188

      Creating The Dream Team 189

      Leveraging My Contacts. 190

      Multiple Income Streams 190

Rick Raddatz **193**
   The Creation and Launch of Audio Generator 193
   Guerrilla Planning. 193
   Instant Audio: Breaking the Silence on the Web 196
   The Teleseminar Affiliate and Customer Dance 197
Bo Bennett **199**
   Guerrilla Web 2.0 Membership Sites 199
   Guerrillas Stay on Top of the Latest Trends 199
   Trend or Fad? 200
   Never Fear Technology 200
   Following the Leader Is for Kids, Not for Guerrillas 201
   Viral Marketing: Get Them Talkin' 201
Mitch Meyerson **203**
   Creating the Guerrilla Marketing Coach Certification Program 203
   Guerrillas Take Action 204
   Approaching a Fusion Marketing Partner. 204
   Growing the Brand 206

CHAPTER 12
Guerrilla Momentum and People Power **207**
   Commitment **209**
   Fusion Marketing **210**
      Joint Venture Partnerships 211
      Strategic Alliances. 212
   Outsourcing: Building a Virtual Team the Smart Way **216**
   Putting Together Your Virtual Team **219**
   Guerrilla Fieldwork **222**
   Wrapping Up **222**

Glossary **223**

About the Authors **229**

Index **231**

THE INTERNET:
The Most Powerful Guerrilla Marketing Tool Ever Created

Bob Dylan wrote his famous lyrics, "the times they are a changin'" over 40 years ago, but they've never been truer than today, especially when it comes to the effects of the internet. The world is changing and the internet is changing the way marketers do business. The first Guerrilla Marketing book was published in 1984, more than 20 years ago, and it was followed by many more. The initial Guerrilla books provided small business owners with a clear vision of what marketing really means and how to make it work for them. Readers—mostly entrepreneurs, solopreneurs, and small business owners and managers operating with shoestring budgets—learned how to master the process of marketing and convert it into honest-to-goodness sustainable profits.

Since then the marketing industry as a whole has evolved and matured, and Guerrilla Marketing is no exception. As the years progressed, we gained new insights and adjusted accordingly. Guerrilla Marketing's strategies and tactics were updated to ensure that entrepreneurs worldwide were equipped with the knowledge and skills necessary to compete in the ever-changing business world at even higher levels.

And even though some of the specific tools we use to achieve success have changed dramatically, Guerrilla Marketing's fundamental precepts remain intact. They will, in fact, endure long after we're gone because they're based on the eternal nature of the human psyche. They're relevant today and will be far into the future.

Therefore, you'll find that we stay true to Guerrilla Marketing's original tenets in this book even though we will add meaningful insights into *the most powerful, exciting, and revolutionary marketing tool ever created*—the internet. We'll explain why Guerrilla Marketing and the internet are a perfect match—just like a great marriage—and convince you that there's never been a better time to get hitched.

We'll also show you how to use your scarce resources and the internet to your best advantage. We'll get to the heart of what every small business owner wants to know: How to harness the power of the internet to gain an upper hand in the marketing playing field.

If you follow along carefully, we promise that you'll walk away with valuable knowledge and a deeper understanding and appreciation for ways to increase your profits, save incredible amounts of time and money, and create multiple streams of passive income using this ultimate of marketing tools.

Additionally, you'll learn how the internet has single-handedly shifted the landscape of the business world and placed incredible power back into the hands of the world's small businesspeople.

In 1984 very few of us imagined that in just a little over 20 years, Guerrilla Marketers would be able to:

- get instant information about their prospects, customers, industry, and competitors using worldwide databases

- operate cost-effective and easy-to-use technologies to create product demonstration videos, relationship-building audios, compelling e-mail campaigns, and digital newsletters and e-books

- expand their social and business networks to likeminded groups of people regardless of their location

- participate in global conversations via blogs, forums, and wikis
- educate their prospects and customers using podcasts, seminars, and webinars
- conduct real-time audio and videoconferences with a few or many geographically diverse people
- stay connected with customers by placing their communications on autopilot using sophisticated web-based software
- track and measure their marketing efforts and obtain up-to-the-moment results with the click of a mouse
- extend their service area to prospects and clients worldwide
- use passion, energy, and know-how to get a blog or website business up and running in no time—and for very little money
- create and deliver professional branding strategies in minutes
- read and answer e-mails over cell phones, PDAs, and other mobile devices.

Back then, these everyday realities would have sounded like a far-fetched episode of *Star Trek,* but today we take for granted that they're part of our everyday lives. Guerrilla Marketers are smart to take full advantage of them, especially when you consider that over 1 billion people have access to the internet.

According to a recent Juniper Research study, the number of U.S. internet shoppers will grow at an average rate of 12 percent per year through 2010 resulting in over $144 billion in online sales.

Experts also predict that by 2010, 50 percent of traditional and e-commerce purchases will be substantially impacted by research conducted by consumers online, indicating that all retailers need to develop multiple sales channels and fully assimilate their online and offline strategies.

Over the next several years, online retail growth will not only be driven by an increase in the numbers of consumers, but by a boost in the average spending amount per buyer—predicted to be nearly $780 per consumer per year by 2008. Until now the tremendous growth of online businesses has been driven by the steady increase in new online shoppers.

> ## "Today's technology
> gives small businesses an unfair advantage. It enables them to do what the big spenders do without the necessity to spend big."
>
> —Jay Levinson

According to industry analysts that will change as the marketplace continues to mature.

These positive forecasts should be music to the ears of current, or aspiring, Guerrilla Marketers. However, if you're among the millions of small business holdouts who think that they can get by without hopping aboard the technology bandwagon, I'm afraid you're going to continue to lose ground every day and, like the dinosaurs, face extinction. So please pay attention to the following four very important facts.

1. Your competitors are smarter, more sophisticated, and even more aggressive than ever before. Therefore, you must use every potent tool at your disposal and know Guerrilla Marketing like the back of your hand.

2. The internet is here to stay and will continue to play an ever-increasing role in your lives and businesses. If you're not already techno-cozy, it's time to become so.

3. You're not a Guerrilla Marketer unless you use the internet and have a website.

4. Anyone with an interest can learn to be a Guerrilla Marketer and learn to use the Internet Guerrilla style. It involves understanding some very basic concepts, which are based on common sense rather than complicated secret solutions. They are not magic—but you'll feel like they are!

However, if you don't master Guerrilla Marketing it will be nearly impossible to master the internet. Being online doesn't grant you automatic proficiency in the online world, but it does make it easier for Guerrillas to do their best work.

In order to compete effectively, you must be competent, knowledgeable, and just as importantly, ready for anything at a moment's notice. That's how the fluid and ever-changing internet landscape works; it is in a constant state of flux.

You must be on your toes and ready for whatever comes your way because change will occur faster than you ever imagined. What works well today may not work well tomorrow. Guerrillas expect change and they prepare for it. They welcome change—because they know how to manage it. You will, too.

For example, we'll cover the basics on writing compelling promotional e-mails in Chapter 5, which contain most of the same elements found in any good sales letter. In the offline world entrepreneurs can reasonably expect to wait six weeks or more to obtain the final results from direct mail campaigns (and by that time it's often too late to adjust). The internet has changed all of that. Now you can test sales letters, headlines, landing pages, offers, and ads and receive valuable feedback in a matter of hours, not weeks. This allows businesspeople to change and fine-tune their marketing elements before they've spent thousands of dollars and wasted considerable time. What a benefit!

But with the good comes the not so good. Imagine how discouraging it was a few years ago for internet marketers to learn that their once effective pop-up ads were being blocked from their target audience by sophisticated browser software. Disappointing as this was, most adapted quickly and began using other traffic generation and conversion methods to lessen the impact and increase sales.

And just when everyone thought that was the end of pop-up ads, they're back! They're subtler, more targeted, and less intrusive, but they are there nevertheless and confident online marketers are using them in a whole new way. This would not be possible if they hadn't embraced change and made it their ally, not their enemy.

Thus, we'll begin with a crash course on Guerrilla Marketing for those of you who are just beginning your journey with us or need a quick refresher course. Please read carefully; this will serve as the foundation for all of the tips and advice we offer throughout the rest of this book.

In subsequent chapters, we'll take you by the hand and walk you through actionable steps for transforming these concepts into profit-producing action. So hang on—it's going to be a great ride!

Guerrilla Marketing Principles at a Glance

In this section, we offer a snapshot of Guerrilla Marketing's basics—its core beliefs, competencies, and actions. Since many of you are more familiar with the blockbuster advertising you see on network TV and elsewhere, it's often easier to explain Guerrilla Marketing by comparing the differences between the two. However, since we have so much new material to cover in this book, we'll hit the highlights and provide references to other Guerrilla books for those of you who wish to delve deeper into the fundamentals.

As you read through the list, use your imagination and think of ways you can apply these principles to the internet (although we'll provide you with lots of specific ideas throughout the book, we encourage you jumpstart the process using your own creativity).

Also, be sure to remember this very important fact: The Guerrilla brand evolved from a passionate belief that small businesspeople with limited resources can compete—and win— on a level playing field with other companies—regardless of their size or financial strength— as long as they're armed with the right weapons and knowledge.

And the internet has redefined and improved this reality because it affords Guerrillas the opportunity to get even more accomplished—*better, quicker, and with less.*

If you're already familiar with Guerrilla Marketing principles and practices, you'll still benefit by reviewing the following eight tenets.

Guerrilla Investment: Time, Energy, Imagination, and Knowledge

Superior marketing provides all companies with their greatest leverage, or control, and should be viewed as an investment. Unlike traditional marketers, *Guerrillas invest more time, energy, imagination, and knowledge (or information) than money.* This is probably the single most important Guerrilla Marketing principle of them all, even though it may be counter-intuitive and the opposite of what you've heard.

Simply said, Guerrillas recognize that they cannot buy their way to a successful company! They know that paying through the teeth for slick advertising does not ensure success and will never make up for shoddy products or services. So they work to achieve the best possible outcome using their limited resources wisely. As a result, they don't worry as much as traditional marketers do when money is in short supply because they have enthusiasm, know-how, talent, wisdom, skills, and creativity to spare.

While Guerrillas spend their money prudently, they understand the difference between investing in disposable

> **"None of us has** gotten where we are solely by pulling ourselves up by our own bootstraps. We got here because somebody bent down and helped us."
> —Thurgood Marshall

commodities, such as paper clips and bookkeeping services, and investing in goods and services that get closer to attaining their goals, such as reliable phone systems and company logos.

Additionally, they don't waste their precious time making penny-wise and pound-foolish purchases or throwing good money after bad. For example, Guerrillas are keenly aware that poorly designed and written marketing materials are recipes for disaster, so they hire graphic designers and copywriters—even if it means they have to barter, lease, or pare down their wish list.

Conversely, Guerrillas are also open to investing in new skills so they can do for themselves instead of hiring others, which is much easier today than it's ever been due to affordable software and internet technology. They also wouldn't consider buying expensive mass media TV advertising in lieu of low- or no-cost alternatives such as referral programs, automated promotional e-mail campaigns, or revenue-generating websites. In other words, Guerrillas understand the difference between assets and expenses. They don't confuse "least cost" with "best cost" and know that "cheap" does not mean the same as "inexpensive."

Guerrillas are also not as afraid of failure as traditional marketers. Why? First, they understand that the path to wealth and profitability is paved with "do-overs," and they don't allow themselves to fail in big ways because they don't plunge headlong into any venture without testing it on small scales initially.

In the end, Guerrillas believe in their hearts that money is not the key to joy or achievement but they sure enjoy the beautiful gold and silver keys you can buy with it.

Guerrilla Intentionality: Marketing Includes Every Contact with the Public

Superior marketing doesn't happen by mistake. It occurs when it is deliberately planned and executed. Because Guerrillas are well trained in all aspects of the marketing process, they know that "first-things-first" considerations such as the way they greet their customers, their employees' attire and demeanor, how easy their website is to navigate, and their business and domain names, are extremely critical components for success.

You'll never hear a true Guerrilla Marketer say, "That's not our fault," or "I'm sorry that my receptionist was rude. I've heard it before but there isn't much I can do about it since we work in different offices," or heaven forbid, "What do dirty bathrooms have to do with anything?" That's because Guerrillas know that every company, regardless of the products and services they offer, is in the marketing business, and prospects and customers will judge them on every single aspect of their experience. This careful attention to detail gives Guerrillas an edge over bigger businesses that often overlook little things that have a big impact on their customers.

In other words, Guerrillas do everything in their power to ensure that their prospects and customers have complete confidence in their ability to solve their most pressing problems. They accomplish this using a variety of techniques, none more important than the following:

- **Amazement.** Their marketing includes elements that inspire wonder and amazement. And by this we don't mean over-the-top, exaggerated promises. We're talking about those unique "wows" that sets a business apart from its competitors, whether it's speed of delivery, freebies, bundled service packages, or something else that's entirely unique.

- **Content.** Guerrillas value substance over glitz, so they continually over-deliver on the promised experience. They respect their target audiences' intelligence and sophistication and know their customers are looking for more than sizzle.

- **Involvement.** Guerrilla Marketers believe in inclusive marketing. That's why they are careful to converse with prospects and customers in ways that encourage them to become more engaged in the experience. They consistently solicit their opinions and encourage two-way conversations, which are very different from the classic "I-talk-you-listen" business models. They understand that their ears are the best marketing tools they own, so ask questions and really listen to the answers they receive. In later chapters, we'll show you how even internet beginners can enhance their website visitors' experiences using audio, video, surveys, tell-a-friend scripts, frequently-asked-questions, "ask" campaigns, and more.

Guerrilla Commitment: Building Successful Businesses One Step at a Time

Commitment is a word that separates Guerrilla Marketers from traditional marketers and winners from losers—an intangible trait that allows them to surpass roadblocks that would stop others dead in their tracks. It is also a hallmark principle of the brand because it's based on the belief that superior marketing requires steadfast focus and a dedication to building and maintaining long-term relationships, rather than bean-counting.

Maintaining focus may sound easy, but it's not—especially in today's cluttered world. Current and evolving technologies make it easy for entrepreneurs to be wooed down the "diversification" path where distraction and trouble lurks. And while Guerrillas welcome change, they are careful not to be lured into going after every "golden opportunity" that comes their way, because they know it's a recipe for disaster.

> **"It was character** that got us out of bed, commitment that moved us into action, and discipline that enabled us to follow through."
> —Zig Ziglar

Simply put, so-so marketers who possess a dogged commitment to their craft outperform superior marketers without this trait 100 percent of the time.

Additionally, commitment means regularity, so Guerrillas don't drop out of the public's sight for long. They don't run an ad two times and then abandon it because "it didn't work." They don't reinvent their identities whenever it suits them. Rather, Guerrillas understand that familiarity creates trust and trust creates profitable sales and lifelong customers.

But how does this play out in the real world? What do committed Guerrilla Marketers look like? How do they act? How does this behavior differ from traditional marketers?

First of all, they are **patient.** Unlike conventional marketers, Guerrillas understand that building rapport and trust take time, so they plan a phased-in strategy and execute it in a realistic timeframe.

Secondly, they demonstrate **consistent** action. Guerrillas translate marketing knowledge into action, because they understand that no one earn profits on thought alone. Although they are well prepared they don't delay progress in search of perfection.

Guerrilla Partnerships: Working Together to Make Things Happen

Unlike the "winner-take-all" mentality of conventional businesspeople, Guerrillas know that their livelihoods are dependent upon others. Therefore, they proactively seek out joint venture partnerships and strategic alliances and continually look for ways to expand their personal and professional networks. Guerrillas even look for innovative ways to work with their competitors. For instance, they might develop products that compliment their competitors' offerings and join forces with them so they both benefit. In Chapter 6 we'll provide specific details for using free and/or inexpensive internet software to reach out to like-minded individuals and groups all over the world.

Guerrilla Psychology: Tapping into Their Target Audiences' Minds

What does psychology have to do with marketing? Everything. No matter who you are, you must understand human psychology.

Traditional marketers often use guesswork, disguised as "experience" and "judgment" as a basis for making decisions. Guerrillas say, "Nonsense!" Instead, they use the laws of human psychology and behavior—ones that tap into the public's subconscious and appeal to both sides of their brains. This is why Guerrillas are so confident in their abilities to tap into their prospects' inner mind—where 90 percent of purchase decisions are made. In other words, they know that potential buyers do want to be sold anything; rather, they want to improve their current situation. If that means they must purchase a product or service to fulfill their needs and desires, they'll consider it. So Guerrillas don't sell clothes; they sell comfort and good looks. Guerrillas don't sell aspirin; they sell freedom from pain. Guerrillas don't sell books; they sell knowledge. Guerrillas don't sell lipstick; they sell beauty.

Guerrilla Assortments

For many years marketers have traditionally used one "big gun" advertising vehicle to increase sales. Guerrillas, on the other hand, believe this to be risky, expensive, and ineffective. Instead they use a variety of low-cost, high-impact marketing weapons to achieve their goals. They arm themselves with the tools, skills, and knowledge—including internet technologies—that are necessary to compete in today's rough-and-tumble global economy.

Today this means integrating online and offline weapons, such as including website addresses on business cards and providing directions to their brick-and-mortar locations on their websites. In Chapter 9 we'll introduce to over 200 weapons—online, offline, and both—that you can choose from to build your own mighty marketing arsenal.

TRY IT!

Create and sustain beneficial partnerships with like-minded people, companies, and website owners.

Guerrilla Measurement

Marketing is becoming more of a science every day as we find more accurate ways to predict human behavior and advances in technology allow us to gauge and evaluate results automatically and instantaneously. Guerrillas believe that the benchmark for success is profits, which

> **"An ounce of action**
> is worth a ton of theory."
> — Friedrich Engels

come subsequent to sales, unlike companies who measure effectiveness on revenues, orders, transactions, and the like. Guerrillas track and measure all of their marketing efforts to ensure that they receive a positive return on their investments. And nowadays, marketers can use affordable web-based automation software to put their marketing analytics on autopilot, so time-consuming manual tracking is a thing of the past.

Now that you know a little bit more about Guerrilla Marketing's central ideologies, you may be wondering how these fit into the online world and why we believe that the internet is the quintessential Guerrilla Marketing tool. Read on, because throughout the rest of the book we'll continue to reiterate why they make such a fantastic couple!

Guerrilla Action

By now you should have a better understanding of Guerrilla Marketing's basic precepts and the important role your energy, time, imagination, and knowledge play in helping you grow and sustain a thriving business. You should also recognize and be prepared to use internet technology to process payments, perform market research, conduct online meetings and seminars, offer digital products, and much more.

In order to gain mastery over your marketing and internet efforts, it's a great idea to candidly assess your own strengths and weaknesses so you can discover whether your current skills, attitudes, and behaviors will help or hurt your chances of building and sustaining a successful business.

To help you with this, we've developed a 30-question self-assessment quiz (Figure 1.1). It should take you less than 15 minutes to complete and is a worthwhile exercise, because you'll gain valuable insights into your own Guerrilla Marketing strengths and weaknesses.

After you've finished, make a list of your potential roadblocks—those that you scored 3 or less on—and over the next several weeks work on fixing them one or two at a time.

Figure 1.1 What's Your Guerrilla Marketing IQ?

	Strongly Disagree	Often Disagree	Sometimes Agree (50%)	Often Agree	Strongly Agree
1. I never compete on price alone. My customers purchase my products and services based on the value they deliver.	1	2	3	4	5
2. My customers understand how and why my products are different than my competitors.	1	2	3	4	5
3. My communication, attitudes, and actions are all intentional and based on my marketing goals.	1	2	3	4	5
4. I build strong one-to-one relationships with my prospects and customers.	1	2	3	4	5
5. I often seek advice from business experts.	1	2	3	4	5
6. I consistently use my imagination to develop marketing strategies that are unconventional.	1	2	3	4	5
7. I actively work on developing marketing partnerships with other businesses.	1	2	3	4	5
8. I look for ways to amaze my customers with exceptional service.	1	2	3	4	5
9. I focus on having a clearly defined marketing niche.	1	2	3	4	5
10. I track and measure the effectiveness of all of my marketing weapons.	1	2	3	4	5

Figure 1.1 What's Your Guerrilla Marketing IQ? (continued)					
	Strongly Disagree	**Often Disagree**	**Sometimes Agree (50%)**	**Often Agree**	**Strongly Agree**
11. I have a clear and specific written marketing plan.	1	2	3	4	5
12. I am fervently devoted to following up with my customers and prospects.	1	2	3	4	5
13. Instead of focusing on sales, I am dedicated to building long-term relationships.	1	2	3	4	5
14. Instead of thinking what I can take from others, business is built on a foundation of serving others.	1	2	3	4	5
15. It's important to deliver on your promises.	1	2	3	4	5
16. I spend time each week improving my marketing capabilities.	1	2	3	4	5
17. My marketing efforts are consistent and synergistic, not disconnected sales gimmicks.	1	2	3	4	5
18. I have a unified plan for imparting my message to others.	1	2	3	4	5
19. I know where to locate information on my target market.	1	2	3	4	5
20. My company has many different supplemental products in addition to our core offerings.	1	2	3	4	5

Figure 1.1 What's Your Guerrilla Marketing IQ? (continued)					
	Strongly Disagree	**Often Disagree**	**Sometimes Agree (50%)**	**Often Agree**	**Strongly Agree**
21. I keep information on my current customers and prospects.	1	2	3	4	5
22. I embrace change and adjust well to the changing marketplace environment.	1	2	3	4	5
23. I keep track of current trends on the internet.	1	2	3	4	5
24. I am an optimist and see possibilities in all situations.	1	2	3	4	5
25. I know what it costs me to retain a valuable customer.	1	2	3	4	5
26. I understand that I am in control of the marketing process and all of my efforts are intentional.	1	2	3	4	5
27. I make it easy and convenient for my customers to do business with my company.	1	2	3	4	5
28. I believe that every businessperson must be "techno-cozy" in order to compete effectively in today's marketplace.	1	2	3	4	5
29. I am committed to achieving my goals using sound Guerrilla Marketing strategies and tactics	1	2	3	4	5
30. I practice "you" marketing.	1	2	3	4	5

GUERRILLA FIELDWORK

1. Go to GMarketinginternet.com and download your Guerrilla Marketing IQ assessment, print it out and complete the quiz.

2. Go to GmarketingCoach.com and Gmarketing.com for more Guerrilla Marketing articles and fundamentals.

Now it's time to move on to Chapter 2, where you'll learn to avoid common internet marketing mistakes and learn some smart moves.

THE 12 BIGGEST INTERNET MARKETING MISTAKES—
And How to Avoid Them

Today's marketplace is jammed with competition, and even more so on the internet. Therefore, if your goal is to tower above your competitors and grow a profitable business, you're going to have to work smarter and arm yourself with the right insights, knowledge and tools. However, before delving deeper into the "how-tos," we've devoted this chapter to debunking the most common internet marketing misapprehensions and blunders, so you're not operating under any false illusions as you proceed through the rest of the book.

We'll begin by reiterating a point we made in the previous chapter: Internet marketing must be part of your overall marketing efforts, regardless of your business' size, industry, location, or type. If it isn't, you are severely handicapping your chances of success.

Following are three very basic tenets. Read them, understand them, write them down on post it notes, and tape one to your forehead and the other on your computer screen, because they are the underlying principles for everything that we're going to teach you in this book.

Rule 1   Every business, government agency, and non-profit organization must have some type of website or presence. There are no exceptions to this rule.

Rule 2   Guerrilla websites have one main purpose: Generate direct or indirect income.

Rule 3   Being online and/or having a website is not internet marketing. Anyone who wants to earn money using the internet must learn and use effective online marketing strategies and tactics.

But what is enough? What is the exact right way to do this thing called internet marketing? Finding the answers to these questions is similar to holding smoke in your hands. The minute you grab it, it disappears.

Online marketing's fundamental nature is fluid and unstructured, and it will continue to be that way for years to come, as innovative technologies improve and evolve, and ordinary people try to figure out to how to make it fit into their lives and businesses comfortably.

For most of us, online technology is both exhilarating and confusing. We love hearing about the latest gee-whiz gadgets and software, and can't wait to get our hands on them—only to find that we're utterly frustrated and often cursing the very things that were supposed to make our lives easier.

Sound familiar? If so, you're not alone. This is but one example of the many times we've all felt that "progress" isn't always what it's cracked up to be, and we may even be better off avoiding it all together.

That's why there are two more rules to add to your list. They are:

Rule 4   If you are going to compete in today's marketplace you must be open to learning about and using new technologies, because when used correctly they will have a dramatically positive effect on every aspect of your life.

Rule 5   Sometimes technology exists because it can. If a little is good, more is not necessarily better. Bigger, brighter, faster, new and improved software, buttons and features are worthless if you can't, don't, or won't use them.

So although this book is devoted to teaching you how to use internet equipment and technology to improve your lifestyle and your business, keep in mind that there are many, many other innovative technologies out there and we couldn't possibly cover them all. And we wouldn't even if we could, because it would be overwhelming, and more importantly, unnecessary. There are literally hundreds of ways you can use the internet to grow your business, so one of your biggest challenges will be narrowing your selections, choosing the ones that best fit you and your business, developing a prioritized plan, and implementing it.

> **"If we could sell our** experiences for what they cost us, we'd all be millionaires."
> —Oscar Wilde

Take some time now to read the next section carefully, so you can learn how to avoid the 12 most common mindset, strategy, and action mistakes that business owners make when marketing on the internet.

Mistake 1: Putting Up a Website With No Planning

Business people who choose to engage in internet marketing begin for many very good reasons, all having to do with their desire to achieve their loftiest dream. So they begin their journey down a path armed with good intentions and enthusiasm—but no plan. Their passion and energy carry them for a while, but over time their short sightedness weakens their ability to respond properly to unforeseen challenges and opportunities.

In fact, many internet marketers plan their vacations in more detail than their businesses! For example, let's assume that our friend, David, who lives in Baltimore, Maryland, has a clear objective. He wants to arrive in Boise, Idaho, in four days. He decides to drive, even though he's never done so before. Given this, David would be foolish to hop in his car and leave. If so, he would greatly increase his chances of encountering problems along the way—ones that could have a devastating effect on his ability to arrive in Boise in good shape and on time.

Most of us would agree that it would be much wiser and safer for David to carefully plan his trip and make sure that he had the resources and wherewithal to accomplish his goal before jumping into action. For instance, he might replace the bald tires on his car with new ones; have his car checked out by a mechanic; pack his clothes and toiletries; make sure he's

"If you never fail,
you never act. If you never act, it's impossible to succeed. You can only succeed by failing!"
—Procrastinator's Guide

got enough money to buy gas and food; map his route; determine how far he'll travel each day; double check that he's got a spare tire, jumper cables, driver's license, vehicle registration, credit cards, and emergency numbers, and hotel reservations.

In other words, David is thinking ahead. He understands what it will take to arrive at his final destination and is improving his chances for succeeding. Even better, he'll get there cheaper, quicker, and less stressfully.

This straightforward analogy illustrates how vitally important it is to plan backwards. Yet, small business people squander billions of dollars every year because they misunderstand the reality of marketing and rush into it headlong—particularly on the internet. And a huge amount of this wasted money is being spent on websites that are developed, posted, and ignored.

If you don't know what we're talking about, just hop online and check around. There are gobs of disjointed websites that look like they haven't been updated since 1999—replete with outdated or missing information, broken links, ear-jarring music, and annoying animation. Visitors may have no idea what to do when they arrive or what type of business is represented. They are confused, frustrated, and annoyed, so they leave quickly and never come back.

As Guerrillas know, it's hard to get prospects interested enough to visit your website, so the last thing you want to do is disappoint them once they find you. Even worse, these website owners are not only missing golden opportunities, but they're paying for services that are producing absolutely nothing.

Although we'll get into more specifics in Chapter 3, remember that it's critically important to carefully plan every aspect of your website's development—and all of your other internet marketing efforts—before it goes live, as well as how it will be maintained and updated moving forward. Trust us: The moment you know where you're going and how you're going to get there you'll feel a tremendous weight lifted off of your shoulders. And no matter where you are on the path, you can always move further along as long as you have the foresight to plan for the unexpected.

Mistake 2: Failing to Research Competitors and the Marketplace

Even though beginners are far more likely to commit this blunder, seasoned business people also fall in love with a cool product or creative idea and rush headlong into a venture without conducting objective research in advance.

In other words, it's a great idea to take a look at the things you love to do most and see if there's a way to turn those passions into viable products or services, but it's not enough. If enough other people don't share your enthusiasm and/or have no desire to purchase your products, you're sunk. Additionally, it's important to make sure the marketplace isn't oversaturated with competitors and you can create a unique niche that you can call your own.

The good news is that the internet is full of resources—way too many to list here—for obtaining free information quickly and easily. As a first step, we suggest you go to a website like inventory.overture.com and use their keyword tool to find out how many people have used specific words or phrases to search for products and services in the recent past.

Once there, type in the words or phrases you think your targeted prospects would use to find them (e.g. wedding toasts, 20-inch 14K gold chains, marriage counseling, flea shampoo for dogs, shrimp and grits recipes). You'll get back a list of keywords and phrases—the ones you entered and similar ones—and the approximate number of times they've been used to conduct a search. If you want to drill down even further, simply double-click on any word or phrase in the list. If you use more general terms, your numbers will likely be higher. For instance, a word such as "tennis" would result in much higher search numbers than "pink tennis socks," "titanium tennis rackets," or "tennis tutorials for beginners."

It's a balancing act. There needs to be enough people in your target pool but quantity is not as important as quality. If you sell "tennis bracelets" it does you no good to bring people to your website who are looking for tennis lessons. You get the idea.

And it always helps to check out your competitors. Find out what they're selling and how their websites, services,

> **"You have got to** pay attention, you have got to study and you have to do your homework. You have to score higher than everybody else. There is always somebody there waiting to take your place."
>
> —Daisy Fuentes

and prices compare with yours. Go to Google and type in the same keywords you used in step one, see what you get, and visit several. As you're looking the over their websites, jot down your answers to questions like:

- How do their products and services compare with mine?

- Are they priced similarly?

- Do they have a wider or narrower selection?

- What types of packages do they offer?

Then look for ways to make your site stand out by continuing to bore down into your niche for products that appeal to the same target market (your target audience size will be smaller, but you'll attract more qualified prospects) or uncover unfulfilled needs.

Alternatively, drill down even further and become the expert in a specific service area. For example, although your recycling consultation services might be beneficial to the entire planet, you might be better off specializing in recycling solutions in dry climates or dry cleaners.

Guerrillas take the time to find out what others are selling and/or talking about, particularly on the internet. Use websites such as ClickBank.com to find out what people are buying; news sites such as CNN.com and NYTimes.com; online magazines; chat rooms; forums (e.g., Amazon.com, eBay.com), and blogs.

Once again, an easy way to keep your finger on your target audience's pulse is to go to any search engine and type in phrases like "French bulldog blogs" or "small business marketing forums."

Mistake 3: Developing Poorly Designed Websites that are Difficult to Navigate

Online consumer research studies confirm that when visitors land on a website they experience "stay" or "go" moments within the first ten seconds. If it looks unprofessional or hard to use, they leave and usually won't be back. In other words, your target audience will judge you, your products and services, and company, in a snap—and you're likely to get only one chance to impress them.

Given this, all website owners should be doing everything they can to ensure that their online visitors are blown away by their website's look, feel, and navigability. Unfortunately, however, this is often not the case at all. Quite a few shortsighted entrepreneurs underestimate the negative impact of poorly written copy, amateurish design, and convoluted navigation. We will cover this subject in more detail in Chapter 3, and provide specific directions for overcoming this blunder. For now, however, it's enough to remember that this is one of those areas where it doesn't pay to be penny wise and pound foolish—it's just too important. Don't annoy, or worse yet alienate, prospective customers because your cousin's friend's aunt's next-door neighbor's brother volunteers to design your website on the cheap.

Mistake 4: Failing to Write Effective Direct Response Copy

Direct response messaging has one main goal: Get the intended audience to take action. Guerrillas create direct response copy almost exclusively, because it is an extremely effective form of promotional communication that can easily be adapted for all delivery vehicles.

We mention it now because, in spite of all the available help, most small business owners fail to use extremely effective direct response copy elements in their website's written, audio, or video communication.

In our opinion, most websites do not contain such things as attention-grabbing headlines, risk-free guarantee policies, and compelling customer testimonials. Instead you'll usually find something like "Welcome to Our Website" or the company's name splashed across the top of the page, exactly where a benefit-driven headline belongs.

And we all understand how cautious many consumers are about handing over money in exchange for products or services, so why not make it as easy as possible for them to do so by shifting the risk from them to you with an ironclad guarantee?

Additionally, third-party feedback is one of the fastest and most effective ways to establish credibility, yet few entrepreneurs take advantage of their immense power by showcasing customer testimonials throughout their websites (and other locations, for that matter).

Direct response explains the direction in which marketing and business is heading. Rather than shouting fuzzy messages to the masses, marketers are crafting specific messages for particular people and encouraging them to act as directed. These Guerrillas understand that interactivity is at the heart of direct response and the internet is the best direct response technique in the history of the world.

Mistake 5: Failing to Build Permission-Based E-Mail Marketing Lists

Ask any successful internet Guerrilla Marketer this question: "What is the holy grail of online marketing?" They'll tell you it's their e-mail list. Regardless of whether they're selling packaged products, giving away free information, or anything else in between, they will all be focused on obtaining their website's visitors' names and e-mail addresses. Why? Because people who "opt in" have essentially given them permission to send them promotional e-mails and/or other information.

But once again, many entrepreneurs fail to collect this invaluable information—and it's a huge mistake. One of the reasons for this is that they erroneously believe that marketing is a "one-shot" transaction. They focus their efforts on making immediate sales instead of using a sounder, relationship-building model.

Internet marketing is a lot like building a personal relationship: It takes time, effort and commitment to develop lasting bonds. In order to accomplish this, you'll need to create a system that leads your prospects down a comfortable and natural path to the first sale and many more after that. So unless you sell "impulse-buy" products or your target audience is pre-sold before landing on your site—the two exceptions to this rule of thumb—we strongly encourage you to use a **marketing funnel** approach. This solid strategy works because it addresses two fundamental consumer psyche laws: People are more apt to purchase products and services from people and companies they know, like, and trust; and it is more effective and less expensive to get more out of existing customers than it is to attract new ones.

Mistake 6: No Traffic Generation Strategy

Many entrepreneurs erroneously believe that the famous phrase "build it and they will come" applies to their websites. They're wrong. If you want to get people to your site, you need to understand the basic laws and contributory principles that govern internet traffic, and apply them.

Guerrillas understand that great marketing is a methodical and accountable process. There are no secret tricks that will effectively drive tons of qualified visitors to your website. And even though there are many things you can do to jumpstart your progress (which we'll cover in Chapter 6) you'll need to carefully plan each one if you want your site to be a not-to-be-missed feature on the internet. But for now, keep in mind two things:

1. Your goal should be to entice the *right people* to your website, not just warm bodies.

2. The *right people* don't visit your website by happenstance. They'll get there because you developed a comprehensive plan and executed it using well-thought-out strategies and tactics.

Mistake 7: Not Using Web 2.0 Social Media and Technology

During the early days of the internet, individuals were busy learning how to use their new computers and software, so they were less concerned with connecting to the World Wide Web.

Today, however, most folks have moved beyond the basics and are more focused on finding new ways to connect with people by using the internet.

And we're seeing evidence of the effects more and more each day. For instance, a major TV network used the internet's powerful technology to obtain real-time feedback and questions from viewers during a televised debate in January 2008. The show's producers set up an interactive forum on the popular website, FaceBook, which allowed viewers to submit and answer questions. Even better, the results were aired immediately and the shows' hosts could add new questions and receive answers on the spot—talk about a great marketing weapon!

Unfortunately, however, far too many entrepreneurs miss out on incredible opportunities like this because they fail to take advantage of inexpensive and easy-to-use web-based social media tools.

We will go into much greater detail on this topic in Chapter 10, but remember this for now: Marketing is never about reinventing the wheel. It's about working less and gaining more. It's about knowing what's out there and choosing the tools and weapons that will provide the greatest impact for at the best cost. And if you're not using the internet's fresh new culture and technology to your advantage, you're making a big mistake.

Mistake 8: Not Using Online and Offline Marketing Combinations

Guerrillas know that having a website is not an option nowadays. They also realize that most consumers still purchase the majority of their goods and services and obtain most of their information in the offline world—for now—so they work hard to achieve top-of-mind awareness there. Unfortunately, many small business people focus their efforts on one or the other—a big mistake. For example, they fail to put their website addresses on their business cards and signs, or provide directions to their locations on their websites.

Don't let this happen to you. Plug your site in your ads, on invoices, business cards, brochures, flyers, newspaper ads, specialty gifts, catalogs, gift certificates, newsletters, and more. Refer to it in seminars, radio and TV ads, direct mail letters, faxes, and anywhere your company's name appears. In other words, actively promote it; it should not be an afterthought. Talk enthusiastically about your website and you'll get more people there. You'll know you're doing a great job when people start asking you if your last name is "dot.com."

But don't stop there; feel free to get creative! For instance, place a small, inexpensive ad in your local paper's classified section that reads something like this:

The 7 Things Local Real Estate Agents Don't Want Homeowners to Know. Selling your house? Don't even think of it until you read this. Go to yourwebsite.com to obtain your FREE report."

Then, when interested prospects go to your website, they'll be asked to provide their names and e-mail addresses in order to download the report. Once you have this information, you can send them promotional e-mails about your mini e-course on real estate sales! You get the idea...

Mistake 9: Failing to Track Marketing Campaigns

Every type of advertising costs something—time, energy, people power, and/or money. That's why you must track everything you do. It's the only way you'll ever know what's working and what's not. This is the only way to build a successful business. Unfortunately, lots of business owners don't take the time to track and measure their activities and end up wasting thousands of dollars and precious time.

TRY IT!

Add Google's free Analytics to your web pages to track key metrics.

If you've been around marketing for a while you've probably heard the phrase, "You can't improve what you don't track." But it can also be said like this: "If you track it you will improve it." Tracking your results allows you to amend or stop whatever is not working. For instance, let's say you sent out five promotional e-mail messages; two of them worked well and three didn't. You'd simply get rid of the three that didn't do well, and keep the two that did. Then you'd continually test new ideas until you beat the winner.

You need to know key metrics such as the number of unique visitors to your website, opt-in conversion rate, how many people get to order page, and then how many of those buy.

Mistake 10: Neglecting to Build Virtual Teams and Partnerships

Too many small business people think they can do it all. So they fail to develop timesaving systems and neglect to look for ways to put routine tasks on autopilot. So what happens? They answer phones, write e-mails, purchase inventory, deal with suppliers, write sales letters, design logos, and more. Consequently, they are burned out and have to live with below-average results. There's absolutely no good reason to continue doing this when there are so many affordable resources on the internet. These days you can outsource one-time tasks or hire virtual assistants for your ongoing duties, even if your operating budget is very limited. We'll be offering specifics on how to farm out work in later chapters.

Additionally, many entrepreneurs end up going it alone another way by failing to develop beneficial fusion marketing relationships or to expand their social and business networks.

Teaming up with other people via strategic alliances, joint ventures, and affiliate partnerships is the key to online marketing because it's one of the best ways to increase traffic, build subscriber lists, grow product lines, and more.

The future of internet marketing will be based on people working together with others, so if you've got a lone ranger mindset, it's time to get rid of it.

Mistake 11: Failing to Follow Up with Prospects and Customers

Most entrepreneurs have not created a system for following up with their prospects and customers. This is a huge mistake for the following two reasons:

1. It can take up to 29 reminders before an interested prospect turns into a customer.

2. Customers who are "ignored" after a sale will take their business elsewhere.

Guerrillas know that excellent marketing requires patience and commitment and one of the best ways to get and keep lifelong customers is to communicate with them often and consistently. In the old days they wrote and mailed letters; today they use affordable web-based automation technology and stay in touch without breaking a sweat.

Let's take each one individually. First, let's assume that 40 percent of your website's visitors opt in; that is, give you their names and e-mail addresses, even if they didn't purchase anything. By providing this information, your prospects are granting you permission to market to them. (Like the description implies, this is called permission-based marketing.)

Your goal is to develop a detailed plan for utilizing automation software to send out both informational and educational e-mails to prospects that remind them of your products' benefits and features. The process might look something like:

- Day 1-10—Send an e-mail telling them how to consume and use product

- Day 11—Send reminder e-mails that begin like this: "Frankly, I'm puzzled that you haven't made a decision about _____. Is there anything more you'd like to know?"

- Day 13, 15, 17, 19, 21... Every other day for the next two weeks, send reminder e-mails that continue to educate. Be sure to include testimonials, benefit-laden bullet points, compelling subject lines, etc.

- Once a week for four weeks, and then once a month for the rest of the year, continue with the same process.

This works in much the same way for current customers. Obviously the messages will be suited to the circumstance, but the process is much the same.

Mistake 12: Failing to Ensure that Computer Equipment is Up to the Task

We decided to add this one final caution even though it doesn't really fit under the internet marketing umbrella. We felt it was still important to cover here because it's often difficult for entrepreneurs to keep up with today's fast-paced technology while they're doing a myriad of other things. If you ignore this critical aspect of your business, it's going to greatly hinder your ability to attain your goals.

Additionally, today's technology affords us the opportunity to do many things ourselves; tasks we hired specialists for in the not-too-distant past. This is a wonderful thing for small business people because it allows them more freedom of choice. It allows them to save money on some things and putting it to work for them elsewhere.

As a result, most companies have computers, and a lot of software to go with them. Some business owners only use their computers from time to time, but they're the exception. Nowadays, most entrepreneurs rely on their computers. They expect them to perform a multitude of vital tasks on demand such as tracking their marketing efforts, communicating with customers and prospects, designing marketing collateral, housing their clients' private information, and much more.

When they get to their desks each morning, they expect their computers to work. They have confidence that the documents they saved on Tuesday will be on their hard drives Wednesday. They assume that their software will work today if it worked yesterday. They don't see the need to back up important customer information because they don't anticipate problems. They think that a $400 laptop can easily handle their workload. They're usually wrong.

Do your research and make sure your computer equipment is robust enough to handle your business needs. Remember, there are lots of people who earn their livings because computers crash! It's not a question of *if* it's a question of *when*. And that's another thing: Inexpensive computers rarely come with free troubleshooting assistance. So even though you may be saving money on one end, you're surely pay for it on the other.

We consulted with Alex Morrison, computer and technology geek and founder of morrisontechnologies.com, who offered the following six guidelines to help you cope better with this area of your business.

Hardware

Many small business owners who are trying to save money purchase inexpensive computer equipment. This is often a mistake that comes back to haunt them. Computers are a lot like cars. They're machines. They have a definitive useful life and require regular maintenance and care. If you use them a lot and load them up, the wear and tear will show. You can't expect them to outperform its engineered specifications, but many entrepreneurs do just that.

This is not one of those times when cheaper is necessarily better. Yes, you can get sturdy computers for less than $500 these days. But if you rely on your computer to generate any part of your income, it's a big mistake.

We're not implying that they won't work—they're perfectly fine for light use—but don't short change yourself with a cheap computer that's not designed as a business machine. Do your research—there are many online resources—and evaluate your computer as you would the foundation of your house. Ask yourself if it can withstand the weight of your business or will it crack? A good rule of thumb is to buy twice the power and ability you think you need.

Software

Laptops and desktop computers are only as good as what they carry. The type of software you use can either make your job easier or far more difficult, so it's up to you to research what's available and choose wisely. There are two general types of software available: commercially licensed, which you must purchase; and open source, which is free. Each type has its distinct advantages and disadvantages, so do your homework. Choose software programs that fit your needs and are highly rated among current users.

Security

With all the current headlines about data theft and identity theft it's no wonder computer security has become a priority for every small business owner. Make sure your computer and business systems are equipped with the latest spam blockers and anti-virus protection

Disaster Recovery

It is quite astonishing how many business owners never back up their critical information or if they have, have never tested the recovery of their data. Millions of dollars are lost and hundreds of businesses in the U.S. are shut down because they do not have a reliable and secure backup system for the information that they process on their systems.

Maintenance

Unfortunately, the phrase "set it and forget it" does not apply when it comes to information systems. Much like a car, your computer needs to be tuned up and maintained. Get an IT pro to check yours every six months at a minimum.

Mobility

Information is power, and powerful businesses are the ones that allow customers, suppliers, employees, and others to have 24/7 access to them. Given today's smartphones, portable USB devices, and other mobile equipment, there's no reason to lose touch, and what a great way to lend big business credibility to your small business!

Now that you've learned *what not to do*, it's time to discover *what to do*. But before we move on to Chapter 3 take a moment and consider whether you're committing any of the mistakes we've identified in this chapter. If you are, put a plan in place to fix them now. You'll be glad you did.

GUERRILLA FIELDWORK

1. Go to GMarketinginternet.com, print out your workbook, and complete the section titled "The 12 Biggest Marketing Mistakes."

2. Back up the information on your computer today. Check out the system they offer on MyCarbonite.com, purchase an external back-up drive, or Google "computer backups" for more options.

In the next chapter, we'll introduce you to the various types of websites and guide you in making decisions on domain names, writing compelling sales copy, designing your website, and more. Remember, the internet is exploding with new ideas, new friendships, and new opportunities, so take advantage of it!

CHAPTER 3

GUERRILLA WEBSITES:
High Impact at a Low Cost

Twenty-five years ago, most successful businesspeople would have agreed that "location, location, location" played a big role in their ability to generate profits. And that's still true today, except it's not the best corner on Main Street anymore—it's the internet.

Yet if you're like the thousands of attorneys, medical equipment wholesalers, small town retailers, physicians, local health food store operators, piano teachers, custom art framers, residential landscapers, auto repair mechanics, and other small business owners who have convinced themselves that their business is "different" and is therefore excluded from this directive, think again. No amount of newspaper ads, direct mail campaigns, glossy business cards, radio spots, or trade shows can substitute for a website.

However, "having a website" is not enough. Remember, the internet, and more specifically, your website, *is merely a tool*—albeit it a powerful one. Aside from the obvious technology components, it's not all that dissimilar to other types of marketing communications like brochures, sales letters, and flyers. In other words, your goal is to use your website to generate income—whether it's all online, all offline, or a combination of the two.

By nature and necessity, Guerrillas know that they must use every marketing weapon available to them if they plan on competing effectively in today's rough-and-tumble marketplace. The internet is the most powerful, effective, and affordable tool out there, but it can also be the most baffling, and when you consider that the internet is still in its infancy, it's even more mind-boggling. But Guerrillas know that this is a great benefit because they're eager to grow right along with the internet.

However, due to the incredible assortment of internet marketing tools and knowledge, it can be downright overwhelming, especially in the beginning. We're going to help you cut through the clutter and focus primarily on the things you must know for certain and ones that are not likely to change overnight.

The first stage of internet marketing begins with the development of your website. During the second stage you'll let people know it's there and ensure that you're ready to convert them into customers after they arrive. In the final step, you'll update and maintain your site.

Creating websites that result in sales is not as easy as it sounds, but it's a snap compared to what you'd have to do to achieve the same results without one. Building the site is relatively easy with a little know-how and help; generating income is the more difficult part. We'll take it one step at a time and begin with helping you develop your website Guerrilla style.

Site Design Strategy

As we move through this chapter, you'll discover that there are many different ways to create a web presence. The type you choose will depend upon a variety of factors such as the types of products you offer; your target audience's age range, personality types, and preferences; any budget or time constraints; your skills; and much more.

For example, it's obviously impossible for a plumber to fix a homeowner's leaky faucet over the internet, but the plumber's website could provide tips for avoiding leaks, offer emergency instructions, or spotlight service specials. The list is endless.

Although websites can be used solely to entertain or inform, Guerrillas use them to generate income directly or indirectly. The first thing you'll need to decide is how you'll use your website to generate income so you can build the right structure to accomplish that goal. Begin by asking yourself nine important questions:

> **"Have a theme,**
> a goal, a purpose…If you don't know where you're aiming, you don't have a goal."
> —Mary Kay Ash

1. What are my short- and long-term business goals?

2. How will I use my website to achieve these goals (what do I want it to do)?

3. How will I measure my website's performance?

4. What do I want to emphasize?

5. Who are my targeted visitors?

6. How will I measure success?

7. Who is accountable for my website's success?

8. What resources (e.g., time, energy, money, people, skills, technology) do I have available for building my website?

9. What are my limitations?

Once you answer these questions and consider the other factors that will affect your website's development, you should be ready to narrow down your website's income-generating methods using one of the following four basic approaches.

Immediate Online Sales

You'll sell packaged goods, services, and/or digital products, which will be delivered immediately or sometime in the future. Although you may accept "offline" payments, like checks, you'll need a method for accepting online payments via a shopping cart.

Lead Generation for Future Online Sales

Guerrillas love this approach because it's a quicker and more economical way to build rapport and credibility with their targeted prospects—and generate substantial income over time. Although the model varies widely, the website owner asks their visitors to "opt in"—provide their names and e-mail addresses—in exchange for free information, samples, advice, service, and the like. This also serves another very important purpose in that it provides web owners with permission to market to these prospects and builds their all-important e-mail lists.

Lead Generation for Future Offline Sales

These websites are used to encourage offline sales and are most appropriate for service professionals, brick-and-mortar retailers and wholesalers, or any other business requiring face-to-face sales processes. For example, furniture retailers might include pictures of their best-selling pieces, provide directions to their store location, highlight clearance items, and offer advice on fabric choices in an effort to get their prospects to visit their location.

Hybrid

This type of site gathers leads of interested prospects for multiple products and services that can be purchased online, offline, or both.

Types of Websites

Once you've decided on your website's purpose—or how you'll use it to generate income—it's time to think about the type of website you'll build or its structure. Although you could reasonably choose any one of the five following types—all of which are appropriate for Guerrilla Marketers—you should choose the kind that best supports your income-generating goals and business category. As we walk you through each type we'll offer suggestions on how best to put them to use.

Squeeze Page

Also called single opt-ins, these are one-page "take-it-or-leave-it" landing sites, and are actually just more sophisticated versions of pop-up ads. Visitors are generally asked to do only one thing, such as opt-in, purchase right away, or obtain more information. Prospects who wish to purchase right away are either directed to a shopping cart/order page or an up-sell sales page. Those who choose to leave or opt out can be directed out of the site, to another sales page, to a download area, or just about anywhere else the web owner wants them to go.

Squeeze pages work particularly well when web owners' are proven commodities and/or their visitors are pre-sold before they arrive. Good squeeze pages contain most of the same copy and design elements other direct response sales letters and landing pages, just more concisely.

Figure 3.1 is a screenshot of an effective single opt-in website. Notice how your attention is drawn to the opt-in box because of its placement, color, and the green arrow pointing to it.

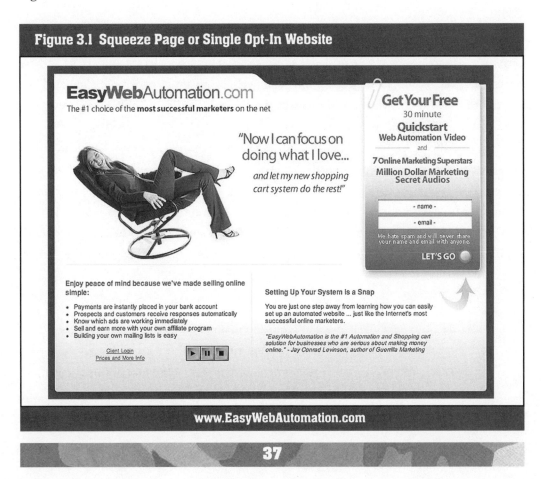

Figure 3.1 Squeeze Page or Single Opt-In Website

Sales Page/Letter

Guerrillas know traditional advertising is a waste of their time; instead, they use persuasive direct response communication. On the internet, this includes persuasive sales letter websites, which include specific direct response elements such as compelling headlines, benefit-laden bullet points, strong calls to action, and irresistible offers—all aimed at encouraging and closing online sales (see Figure 3.2).

They can offer products, services, or both. Although the sales letter may ask visitors to purchase immediately, they're usually more effective if they invite prospects to take the next logical step in the relationship-building process, also called an ascension model. The sales letter can be long or short and the site can consist of one page or several.

These websites can be used for just about any business, but may be overkill for some.

Blogs

In very simple terms, blogs (short for web logs) are websites where a series of messages, or posts, on particular subjects are posted in chronological order—newest to oldest. Most have areas where blog visitors can post comments as well. Blogs are intended to be updated and read often. Usually conversational in nature, they began as a logical vehicle for people who used them as a forum for public journaling.

Over time, however, the nature of blogs has changed dramatically and they're no longer considered little more than personal diaries. Some are solely informational, others are sales driven, and others are somewhere in between. This flexibility is just one of the reasons Guerrilla Marketers choose blogs over more traditional websites more and more often.

You may not realize the power of blogs, because on the surface it looks like nothing much is going on. However, you will soon learn that there is a lot happening under the surface. Here are some other reasons why blogs make such great sense:

- They can be up and running in no time—often in a matter of minutes.

- Blogs are extremely inexpensive to build and maintain, and there are many good, reputable companies who will host your blog for a small fee or absolutely free. (See Outsourcing Your Website's Development and Design at the end of this chapter.)

Figure 3.2 Sales Page

GUERRILLA MARKETING

The Official Program of Guerrilla Marketing International Created by Mitch Meyerson and The Father of Guerrilla Marketing Jay Conrad Levinson

Click to listen to Jay

In less than four years Morgan James Publishing has gone from a start-up to a $10 million business and was ranked number 44 on Fast Company's "Fast 50" Companies for 2006. As Morgan James' founder, I was even named a Finalist in the Best Chairman category in The 2006 American Business Awards.

My Guerrilla Marketing Coach Certification training has significantly impacted our day to day business. It shows in how we answer the phone. It shows in how we develop and maintain relationships.. My Guerrilla Marketing Coach training even teaches me how to eliminate competition by creating opportunities for collaboration.

Our efficient business model, enabled by our Guerrilla Marketing training, makes our success possible. We would never be where we are today without Mitch Meyerson, Jay Conrad Levinson and the Guerrilla Marketing Certification Program.

Now You Can Instantly Brand Your Business With The Best-Selling Marketing Series In History and Get the Competitive Edge You Need More than Ever in Today's Very Cluttered Marketplace with the Internationally acclaimed...

Guerrilla Marketing Coach Certification Program (TM)

Starting Monday January 14, 2008
7:00-8:00pm EST
Filling up quickly

"The Guerrilla Marketing Coach Certification Program had a huge impact on launching my coaching/consulting career which now includes a number of highly successful books and a column with Entrepreneur.com. My best seller, *Guerrilla Marketing In 30 Days* began when I took this course and Mitch Meyerson introduced me with Jay Conrad Levinson to co write GM30 . ... In addition to becoming an expert Guerrilla Marketer, The GM Coach Certification Program can help you in ways that may exceed your expectations" -- Al Lautenslager, Author Of Guerrilla Marketing In 30 Days

"**Guerrilla Marketing Certification has helped me gain more new business, faster**, because I now have the tools to respond better to my clients' needs." Alex Mandossian, Traffic Conversion Specialist

"Your GM Coaching Certification training changed my life... My business has grown dramatically over the past few months. My clients are in awe with my service. I have changed many of my marketing activities and received pleasing results. Finally, at the age of 48, I found myself. Thank you Mitch"

▷ Are You A Business Owner Looking **To Increase Your Yearly Revenue by Adding Guerrilla Marketing and Coaching To Your Skill Set?**

▷ Are You A Coach Looking To **Affiliate Yourself with an International Brand** and Stand Out In A Cluttered MarketPlace?

www.GMCoachCertification.com

- Search engines—and people—like them because they're wonderful vehicles for sharing ideas, showcasing videos, airing podcasts, and much more. Most provide RSS or ATOM syndication subscription feeds (see Chapter 5 for more details on these great distribution programs).

- When updated and maintained regularly, blogs are one of the best ways to move up in search engine results lists.

- Blogs can serve as central hubs (portals) for website owners with multiple products, services, and/or websites or pages.

- They can be used to quickly establish you as an industry expert.

- Blogs can generate substantial income when used as an extension of other marketing efforts.

- They can be published in many different formats, and it's easy to add video, audio, graphics, shopping carts, photos, RSS feeds, and PDF files.

- Blogs can be viewed on a variety of devices such as cell phones, iPods, and MP3 players.

Blogs are managed by software (called platforms) that runs on internet servers. There are two basic types of blog platforms: standalone or hosted.

Standalone blog platforms run on your website's server so you'll need standard platform software such as WordPress (the most flexible of them all), MovableType, PMachine, Greymatter, B2Evolution, TextPattern, or ExpressionEngine. While they are more flexible and robust than hosted web platforms, they are harder to set up, so we recommend that you stick with one-click installs like WordPress.

If you're a beginner you should consider starting with a hosted web platform like those on Blogger.com, WordPress.com, or MySpace.com. All you need to do is register and provide your URL and then follow their simple instructions.

Figure 3.3 shows a screenshot of the Guerrilla Marketing Blog's home page. Notice how clean and simple the site looks, even though it contains multiple pages.

Figure 3.3 Guerrilla Marketing Blog

Mitch Meyerson, Founder of Guerrilla Marketing Coach and
Jay Conrad Levinson, The Father of Guerrilla Marketing present the Official

GUERRILLA MARKETING BLOG

Home   About Us   Guerrilla Marketing   Online Marketing   Personal Growth   Audio/Video   Music

Guerrilla Marketing Coaching and
The Online Marketing Superstars
Bring You the Best Tips and
Strategies for Growing Your Business...

▶ Squidoo.com – A Must Use Site for Guerrillas

April 29th, 2008

By: Michael Tasner, Internet Marketing Expert, Certified Guerrilla Marketing Coach

Some of you have heard of it, others might think from the name it's some type of fish. Squidoo.com is the brainchild of expert marketer Seth Godin. It's quickly becoming one of the most trafficked web sites in the world and is a must use for any Guerrilla Marketer.

What is Squidoo?

Squidoo is simply a collection of sites, or len's as they call them. These len's can be on any topic (from the environment, to laptop bags, or web design even the upcoming elections) and both business and personal in nature.

The user fills the lens with relevant content, audios, pictures, links and even videos to make it not only informative, but attractive.

Why Should You Use Squidoo.com to market your product/service?

Do a search for laptop bags in google, check out the number 1 result – A Squidoo page. This Squidoo lens is beating out companies that have been trying to get in the top ten of the search engines for years for that phrase.

How did they do it? Simple; content on a site that Google loves. Let me repeat that statement: Google LOVES Squidoo.com because it's full of content. And if Google loves Squidoo.com, they also love lens's that were built on the Squidoo.com platform.

How Can I Get Started with Squidoo.com?

Visit Squidoo.com, sign up and create a lens. It's just that easy! You can create a nice looking lens in under an hour. The key to creating a nice lens is to keep it information driven and fresh. As guerrilla's know– if you deliver value first, people will respect you, keep coming back for more, and eventually buy from you!

Also, visit SquidU for a plethora of free information.

Happy Squidooing!

Search

Free Marketing

name

e-mail

Privacy Policy   go

Get New Guerrilla Marketing posts

enter e-mail   go

Subscribe in a reader

MY YAHOO!

Google

newsgator

BOOKMARK

RSS FEED

Guerrilla Marketing Coaching:
How To Get One
or Become One

Continuity Websites (Membership/Subscription)

These websites allow certain visitors—usually those who have paid subscription or membership fees—access to their site's best content, such as documents, forums, and audio and video downloads. They work best for companies whose visitors are looking for hard-to-find, highly focused information on specific topics, want to belong to a community of like-minded individuals, and want exclusivity.

Guerrillas love subscription websites because they understand what an important role they can play in jumpstarting their websites' profitability and maintaining it for years. Figure 3.4 is a screenshot of the Guerrilla Marketing Association's membership website. As you can see from the menu right below the banner, it contains lots of information on a variety of subjects. Membership sites are expanding rapidly on the web and are a great source of information and community at an affordable cost. Another topnotch membership site to check out is MasterBusinessBuildingClub.com.

Informational or Brochure Websites

As the name implies, these websites are used to publicize detailed information about a company's product and service selections, quality, specifications, prices, availability and more, in hopes of stimulating offline sales. They are often the best choice for service providers, such as attorneys, physicians, specialized local retailers, financial advisors, hair stylists, and nonprofits.

Once again, they should contain a well-written direct response sales letter and an opportunity for visitors to leave their e-mail address and name for follow-up in person, over the phone, and/or via e-mail.

After you've made these decisions, it's time to choose your domain name and hosting company, if you haven't already done so.

Choosing Your Domain Name and Hosting Company

Selecting Your Domain Name

Just as our world is covered with many paths to diverse destinations and alternate routes that lead to the same place, the internet has its own set of pathways and directions—called domain

Figure 3.4 Subscription/Membership Website

GUERRILLA MARKETING ASSOCIATION
A Guerrilla Marketing Support Service to Maximize
Your Small Business Profits
Created by Jay Conrad Levinson. the father of Guerrilla Marketing

> login   > support

If you join The Guerrilla Marketing Association you'll receive a PDF Jumpstart Program, an additional value of $49. Even if you cancel your membership, the Program is yours to keep forever.

Join Now!

Sign up for the FREE Guerrilla Marketing Weekly Intelligence email newsletter:

Subscribe to the GM Weekly Intelligence:
First Name:
Last Name:
Email:

Subscribe!

Download The 100 Weapons of Guerrilla Marketing for FREE!

The Guerrilla Marketing Association
A Unique Interactive Small Business Marketing Support System to Help You Succeed

"Jay is one of the foremost business marketing experts in the world. No one knows how to use the weapons of the trade better than industry expert Jay Levinson."
Entrepreneur Magazine

I'm Jay Conrad Levinson. I'm the author of the "Guerrilla Marketing" series of books. Over 15 million copies of those books have been sold. They're now in 44 languages. (Admission: I don't understand 43 editions of my own book!)

I also spent a good part of my career on the creative teams that made household names of The Marlboro Man, The Pillsbury Doughboy, Allstate's good hands, United's friendly skies, and the Sears Diehard battery, along with that Green Giant.

If you're really serious and want to boost your profits with some of the best marketing information on the planet, take a closer look at becoming a member of our **Guerrilla Marketing Association**.

Would you spend one hour a week with the world's most informed marketing experts if it would transform your business into the ultimate marketing machine? How about 90 seconds? Just select the core benefit of our resource center that can help you the most.

Don't cheat yourself or your business. Pick a time every week that you will visit this extraordinary resource for in-depth information on rocketing your way ahead of your competition. Jay is paid $50,000 for his presentations, yet you can access all his dynamic content right now for just pennies a day.

You have access 24/7 to that entire Guerrilla Marketing Association Resource Center, chock full of features to increase your profits.

Discover how you can access more and better information than anyone else offers, at a rate that is ridiculously low for what it can mean to you.

Live Teleclasses Weekly

Get brand new insights every week from first-rate brand name marketing minds. Interact with the best marketing experts alive. Past gurus include Alex Mandossian, Chet Holmes, Steven M.R. Covey. and more than 200 experts in every field of marketing.

JUST OUT!
Guerrilla Marketing, New Edition
-by Jay Conrad Levinson

In this completely revised and expanded fourth edition, Levinson offers a new arsenal of weaponry for small-business success in the next century. Filled with strategies for marketing on the Internet (explaining when and precisely how to use it), tips for putting other new technologies to work, programs for targeting prospects and cultivating repeat and referral business, and management lessons in the age of telecommuting and freelance employees, this book will be the entrepreneur's marketing bible in the twenty-first century.

JAY CONRAD LEVINSON
GUERRILLA MARKETING

Guerrilla Marketing, 4th edition
Jay Conrad Levinso...
Best Price $5.49
or Buy New $10.17
Buy from amazon.com

Privacy Information

This is the first testimonial which I have ever written which I think says a lot about how great your service and information is at Guerrilla Marketing Association. Before I joined this service I didn't know what to think, but once I logged into the member area and watched the videos of Jay Levinson I knew I had the information I needed to take things to the next level with my new business. After

www.GuerrillaMarketingAssociation.com

TIP:

Your website must instantly convey its content. Whenever you fail to enhance the two-way communication between you and your visitors, you greatly undermine your website's success.

names—that steer visitors to one location or another. It would be impossible for online visitors to find websites without using domain names—those identifiers that are typed into browser windows and usually begin with www.

And just as with a brick-and-mortar company, there's a lot in a name. You'll want to choose your domain name very carefully—after all, it's an extension of you and your business. Take into consideration the types of products you offer, your company's and target audience's personalities, and the type of message you want your domain name to convey.

Additionally, your domain name should be one that effectively brands your business whether you stick with one site, or end up creating multiple websites. That's why you may want to pick your own name (e.g., TheSmithCompanies.com, MitchMeyerson.com, or StrategicMarketingAdvisors.com

Alternatively, you might select a more descriptive generic domain name—one that includes important keywords or expresses what you do. But be careful! You don't want to end up with one that's difficult to spell, hard to remember or pronounce, or so long that it will get cut off in e-mails. (e.g., federated-amalgamated-iron-and-steel-corporation.com).

Let your creativity run wild and come up with a list of optional names. Test them out on friends and family members before registering them. Do your best to pick ones that are vivid, short, and to the point; easy to spell, speak, and remember; and contain your most popular keywords. If possible, end in a ".com" extension rather than .net, .biz, or .org.

It's also a fine idea to prepare for your future and consider purchasing more than one domain name (especially since they may not be available if you need them later on). Also, buy domain names that are very similar to yours and might be confusing to your prospects and customers or snatched up by competitors. If using different domain names—for instance, one non-specific and one branded—generates more traffic to your site, it makes complete sense to have more than one.

Finally, remember that Guerrillas hate wasting money and there's no reason to pay $20 per month to register your domain names. Some good resources are GoDaddy.com or OnlineMarketingSuperstore.com.

Selecting Your Hosting Company

There are many different hosting companies on the internet today; you'll have no trouble finding one. However, Guerrillas choose hosting companies only after they're sure that they offer outstanding services, superior tools, and ongoing support. (It's best not to try free hosting; you'll end up with banner ads on your page, which may annoy your visitors and make it harder to get others to link with you.) In this case, least cost is not always best cost, so it's best to stick with a reputable and reliable provider that gives you a lot for your money, such as SuperstarHostingAndDomains.com. Check the other resources we have listed at the end of this chapter as well.

Before you choose a hosting company, make sure to ask what safety measures they use to deter spammers from jumpstarting their illegal e-mail campaigns. This is a critical consideration, since internet service providers (ISPs) blacklist (also called "blocklist") hosting companies that do not take spam seriously (more on this in Chapter 5). What does that mean to you? Simple. If your hosting company is blacklisted, all e-mails originating from their servers—even yours—are blocked and never reach their intended destination, and you won't even know it happened—that is, until you start getting angry phone calls from colleagues and friends. However, it's easy enough to check the status of any hosting company by going to sites like spamhaus.org.

Another thing you'll want to consider before choosing a hosting company is *dependability*. Let's face it, cyberspace hiccups occur and you should expect your website to be down occasionally for very short periods of time. But, some hosting companies are famous for inconveniencing their customers (who then inconvenience *their* customers) time after time with avoidable downtimes that last for several hours or even days. Often this happens because too many people are using their servers and they are overloaded.

That's why it's wise to check out would-be hosting companies' dependability score beforehand, even though the vast majority of hosting companies do provide consistent service. One way to find out is by asking company representatives—who will, of course, swear that their servers are 100 percent reliable. We think there's a better and more objective way to uncover this information. Go online and check out their past and current reliability record by typing their name into one of the major search engines.

Developing Your Website

Structure First

"I can't find anything!" Does this sound familiar? It's because it's one of the main reasons internet users leave websites. And although there are numerous and varied reasons, such as broken links, poorly organized information, hard-to-read fonts, and clutter, it always stems from one thing: poor planning. If you construct your website without organizing its structure you will surely miss critical elements. It is similar to building a house without a blueprint!

In other words, if the structure isn't there and reinforced, your website will collapse. So once you've outlined your site's goals and objectives, selected the type of site you'll build, and picked your domain name and hosting company, it's time to take a closer look at how you'll organize your content and ensure that your site is easy to use and navigate. Look at the following screenshot (Figure 3.5) for an example of a clean look and clear structure.

Organizing Content for Multiple Page Websites

All-in-one, single-page websites are the simplest of all for website owners and visitors and work well for presentation of specific content or products. However, many of you will be developing multi-page websites and therefore will have to decide how many pages you'll need and how you'll organize its content.

As William Pollard said, "Information is a source of learning. But unless it is organized, processed, and available to the right people in a format for decision making, it is a burden, not a benefit." And since your goal is to provide information that your visitors can find quickly, it needs to be organized in a logical manner. There are two basic layout structures to consider.

Flat

Although there is one main page, all other pages are presented as equals with no "parent-child" relationship and each page can be accessed from all others. This format works well for sites with standard pages like "Home," "About Us," "FAQs," and "Our Products."

Figure 3.5 Organization and Structure in Website Design

Indexed

Although this is similar to the flat structure, the main page serves as searchable index for the entire site's content, and is usually the only page that can be accessed from all others. This layout works best for websites with more content because it can be easily and logically organized alphabetically or otherwise.

You can add multiple hierarchies to this model and customize the way content is accessed. For instance, Amazon users can search for books by title, author, or ISBN. The vast majority of small business websites do not need to be this complex, so only consider this if it's a must and then let a web developer handle it. Remember, less is more when it comes to websites.

But before you design your site, you need to decide what information you want to provide and how your visitors will find it.

Navigation and Usability Guidelines

You don't have to be a technical genius; just follow a few basic rules of thumb.

Use Clear, Simple, Logical Words and Phrases for Labeling Menus

Regardless of whether you're selling high-tech scientific equipment or e-books titled *How to Boil Water*, keep your language simple and consistent. Remember people with different needs and perspectives will visit your site, so make it easy for everyone to find what they're looking for.

Categorize your Content Logically

Categorize your website's content so it makes sense to your visitors, whether by products, services, or tasks. Then you can further organize those menus alphabetically, chronologically, or geographically. If possible, organize your content in more than one way so your visitors can use either method.

Make Speed a Priority

Your site should load in less than 10 seconds (even using a sluggish 56k modem). Use smaller, compressed images and files and don't use elements like animation, large banners, or other special effects unless they add a real "wow" or are absolutely necessary (and even then use them sparingly).

Adjust your Browser Settings

Your visitors will be viewing your site from a variety of different devices (desktop computer, laptop, PDA, iPod, etc.), which will affect the way they see your pages. Ask your web developer to optimize your site to accommodate dif-

TIP:

Respect your website visitors' time. Large graphics and photos take longer to download so make sure they're worth the wait.

ferent browsers, then double check how your pages look at anybrowser.com. You can also download a variety of browsers onto your computer to try out your pages; Internet Explorer, Firefox, Mozilla, and Netscape are commonly used.

Use No-Surprise Navigation Devices

Creativity is a wonderful thing but not when it comes to your website's navigation. Make your website's navigation intuitive for your visitors by using standard elements and placing them in expected areas. For example:

- Hyperlinks (live links to internal or external web pages) should be underlined in blue and lead to an HTML document (e.g., www.thenameofyourwebsite.com).

- Use standard phrases like "user name" and "password" to verify visitors' identities.

- A shopping cart leading to a virtual checkout process should be in place for all online purchases.

- Display main page menu links prominently on the top and/or left hand side of the page.

- Place subordinate menu links at the bottom of the page.

- Test your internal links regularly to make sure they're not broken or sending your visitors to the wrong page.

- Use favicons (small logos that are automatically picked up and displayed in your visitors' "favorites" explorer bar) and gentle reminders that make it easy for your visitors to bookmark your site.

Outsourcing Your Web Development

If you have no idea how to find someone trustworthy to build or design your website, you're not alone. But it can be much easier than you imagine, if you use the ideas in this section.

Before you begin looking, make sure you understand the difference between a web developer and web designer. A developer builds a website's under-the-hood infrastructure—its behind-the-scene elements—by assigning relevant HTML codes and Java scripting. A designer, on the other hand, creates a website's look and feel.

While you do not have to know the nitty-gritty details, it is important to understand that each will heavily influence your final product. It's okay to leave the particulars to the experts, just as long as they're up on the latest technologies, trends, and techniques.

For example, designers now take advantage of new technologies like CSS (Cascading Style Sheets) to improve the look of web pages and save time. And even though HTML (HyperText Markup Language) is the internet's official coding language, novices can now make changes to their websites using friendly web authoring programs such as Adobe's Dreamweaver or Microsoft's FrontPage. Keep these in mind as you move through the rest of this chapter.

It makes sense to start with a "not-to-do" list when it comes to building your website. So here goes. Don't:

- hire your next-door neighbor's teenager

- use a friend-of-a-friend who "knows computers"

- employ your daughter-in-law who's "always online"

- hire anyone who doesn't provide references (and make sure you check them) and can't show you websites they've built.

You may save a few bucks in the beginning but it will cost you a lot more in time, lost business, rework, and frustration in the long run.

But Guerrillas know that you don't have to pay a fortune to end up with a website that's fast, dependable, easy to use, optimized for people and search engines, well designed, and trouble free. There are literally thousands of talented web developers to choose from and we've provided web addresses for several at the end of this chapter (See Outsourcing Your Website's Development and Design). Here's how to get started.

Check Out Lots of Websites

Look at sites in your industry that look and function as you'd like your own to look and function. When you discover ones that you like, use them; click on their internal and external links, take note of the types of pages they include, look at their site maps, etc. If you're still pleased, jot down the web developer's name, which is usually located at the very bottom of the home page. Or call the website's owner. Believe it or not, even if they're your competitors, they'll usually be willing to help out.

Survey Current and Past Customers

There's no better way to learn "the real deal" about a company than to survey their current or past customers. So ask each web developer you get in touch with to provide you with the domain names of other sites they've built, and reach out to their owners. Ask them if they're pleased with the company's level of service, expertise, after-sale support, and ongoing maintenance programs. Also, make sure they're happy with their site's design and navigability. Then top it off with the following two final questions: *What does this company do best? What does this company do worst?*

Finalize Your Requirements

Begin by identifying and describing the look and functionality of your ideal website, then get at least three quotes from the top developers on your list. If cost estimates you receive are reasonable and within your allocated budget, select one based on your other important criteria (e.g., time, location, etc.). If not, start cutting costs by getting rid of nice-to-have extras—pages, animations, video, additional color—which don't impact your site's overall effectiveness and can be added later. Ask the developers to recommend other ways to cut expenses.

Determine How Your Website Will Be Maintained

Your website will never be an effective tool—and your credibility and profits will suffer—if it's not maintained and updated often and continuously. So before you settle on a web developer, make sure you consider how your site's ongoing care will be handled.

> **"Design is a plan** for arranging elements in such a way as best to accomplish a particular purpose."
> —Charles Eames

Guerrillas know that search engines—and more importantly, their visitors—expect to find fresh content, updated information, interactive discussions, and hassle-free navigation, and would never rely on web developers to make these on-the-fly improvements. You need to make a decision whether to outsource the creation and uploading of content to others or do it yourself. If you choose to do it yourself you'll need to learn a web-authoring program, like Dreamweaver or FrontPage. You will also need to learn how to upload web pages using an FTP (File Transfer Protocol) program (which are widely available for free on the internet). From our viewpoint there are great advantages for Guerrillas to take control of their websites: It's less expensive, it's faster, and it's more flexible—you can make on-the-fly changes or additions whenever you want.

Professional Website Design on a Guerrilla Budget

Are first impressions that important? Here are a few questions to think about.

- Would you return to a store where you had to rummage through box after box to find a gallon of milk?

- Would you stay long at a business if your brain were addled by eardrum-piercing music, glaring lights, and unreadable signs?

- Would you give your business to a retailer who sent you off into an endless maze of rooms to search for the product you came to purchase?

- Would you hire a management candidate whose cover letter and resume were filled with misspelled words and grammatical errors?

- Would you go back to a restaurant where the tables were dirty and the floors were covered with leftover food?

Guerrillas know that you only have one chance to make a good first impression. Just as in more traditional business locations like these, your website's look and usability play critical roles in your visitors' decisions to hang around and learn more, or leave. What makes this even more challenging is that most of them will judge your website in less than ten seconds! If it's easy on the eyes, simple to use, credible, and relevant, they'll stick around for a while longer—your first goal.

That's why your website's design—how it looks and feels—is a key element in your overall strategy. Since individual tastes vary widely, you may not know where to begin or how to tell if your current site is up to snuff. Our best advice is to approach it as Guerrillas would—armed with imagination, knowledge, and a well-thought-out plan, not a big check.

We'll assume for now that your website will consist mostly of written copy (text), artwork and/or photos (graphics), and links (connection to other internal and external web pages). Although we encourage you to include audio, video, and other interactive devices, we'll wait to cover those in later chapters.

Determining how best to generate a positive impression in the first few seconds is not as easy as some would have you believe, but if you apply the following five design rules of thumb you should do just fine.

Use Easy-to-Read Typefaces and Formatting

Some of your website's visitors will have 20-20 vision, others will not. Some may be viewing your site from cell phones and others will access it from laptops. Some of them will spend a great deal of time in front of a computer while others will be occasional users. These are just a few of the ways your visitors will differ and why your site must be easy for all of them to read.

Here are some quick tips for improving your website's readability factor.

- **Don't <u>underline</u> words or phrases.** It makes type harder to read. It may also cause confusion, since underlining is the default signal for live links.

- **Avoid *italics* and other cursive styles.** They're also harder to read so should be used sparingly and only for smaller chunks of text, such as book titles and quotes.

- **Use Bold to emphasize single words or phrases.** Don't get carried away or you'll defeat the purpose.

- **Use upper and lower case type.** ALL CAPITALIZATION creates a blocked effect and is more difficult to read. It's okay for headlines or titles, but that's about it. Also, it "sounds" like shouting, which is not a good way to make your visitors feel welcome.

- **Use no more than two typeface styles.** Try to use one serif (e.g. Times New Roman, Georgia, and Times) and one sans serif (e.g. Arial, Helvetica, and Verdana). The contrast will result in an "eye pop."

- **Avoid reverse type (light lettering on a dark background).** While it can be a great attention-grabber, reading type set up this way can be tough on the eyes and should be used infrequently.

Place Key Content "Above the Fold"

Don't make your visitors scroll down your pages to locate your most important information. Also, use devices such as headlines, bulleted and numbered lists, and call-out boxes to enhance your site's "scannabilty quotient."

Use Color Carefully

Many website owners let their imaginations run wild when selecting website colors. And while creativity usually is an admirable trait, this is one of those times when it's a good idea to err on the side of conservatism.

It's imperative to remember that colors can be used in many different ways. They can evoke emotions, set moods, emphasize or de-emphasize content, decrease eyestrain, and establish brands—making them very powerful tools. That's why it's important that you use the following guidelines to choose your website's colors carefully.

- **Limit the number.** Don't use more than three main colors (although you can add lighter shades). More than this will give your site a rainbow effect, which your visitors may view it as unprofessional, cluttered, or even childish.

- **Use complimentary or contrasting colors.** Consult a color wheel and look for colors that are opposite one another.

- **Learn the relationship between color and emotion.** For instance, use red if you want to communicate action or excitement; use yellow to convey happiness or to attract attention; green will help your visitors feel reassured and secure; and blue will increase their tranquility, relaxation, and sense of order.

> **Reminder:**
> You don't get a second chance to make a good first impression.

- **Use softer variations of white.** Light beige or grey backgrounds are more relaxing to read. And even though bright colors are entirely appropriate under certain circumstances, don't get carried away.

When It Comes to Design, Less Is More

Remember, if a little is good, more is not necessarily better. Don't assault your visitors' eyes with over-the-top animations (which will also cause your pages to load slower), embossed-bordered rules and tables, or too much clutter. Keep it simple and under-stated.

Use Artwork and Graphics To Your Best Advantage

Visual images are some of the simplest yet most effective ways to communicate a lot. Whoever coined the phrase "a picture is worth a thousand words," got it right. When used properly, good artwork will enhance your visitors' understanding, memories, and moods; grab and hold their attention; and convey positive emotions.

Photos are considered more professional than clip art, which can have a comical feel. Regardless of which type you choose, be consistent. Don't overuse artwork, especially animations, and make sure every graphic has a purpose. Be sure to check out how fast your pages load; you can go to sites such as websiteoptimization.com to test this.

Here are some other best practices for photos and clip art:

- **Apply ALT (alternative test) tags to your photos.** That way, if users can't see the image they will at least know what is there.

- **Use artwork that leads your visitors' eyes into your page.** Your photos should include images of people looking at or into your page (use head and shoulder shots for portraits) and graphics or symbols that do the same.

- **Keep the size and proportions of your artwork consistent.**

- **Show movement whenever possible;** use photos that are interesting and illustrate action of some sort.

- **Make sure there are no copyright restrictions** if you're using clip art or stock photos.

When you find websites that are particularly appealing, write down the types of components they used that captured your interest. Write down your ideas and draw a rough draft of your vision on a piece of paper and fine-tune it. You can also use graphics software like Adobe Photoshop or even a presentation program like Microsoft PowerPoint. Before finalizing your website's design, it's best to get advice from a professional unless you're trained in graphic design.

But the easiest and least expensive (free or under $100) way to get a simple, adaptable, and professional-looking site up is to purchase a ready-made design template. Then you can personalize your logo and then give it to a programmer to upload onto your server.

If you prefer a totally customized design, it will cost you quite a bit more or you'll have to do it yourself—and it's not all that easy. You'll have to buy editing software such as Macromedia's Dreamweaver, Adobe's GoLive, or Microsoft's FrontPage and download an FTP (File Transfer Protocol) program. You'll have to learn how to design and set up your pages; you can check out templates provided with the programs. But either way you can outsource some or all of your work. Sites like scriptlance.com and RentACoder.com are great places to start, and we've included many more at the end of this chapter.

Hopefully by now you're convinced that effective websites don't happen by chance and must be approached with your goals, your audience, and your technical requirements in mind. But if you take the advice you've learned in this chapter, it doesn't have to be a daunting process.

To help you out even further, we've included a list of website resources for various functions (Figure 3.6). You'll also find a web development checklist (Figure 3.7) that you can use to keep you on track. These websites offer a variety of design and development services. Check them out or conduct an online search of your own.

In the next chapter you'll learn how to turn prospects into customers—Guerrilla style!

Figure 3.6 Outsourcing Your Website's Development and Design

Blog Platforms

WordPress.org
TypePad.com
Drupal.org
Joomla.org
MovableType.com
Greymatter.com
B2Evolution.com
TextPattern.com
ExpressionEngine.com

Membership Site Software

Joomla.org
Drupal.org
MemberGate.com
VisionGatePortal.com
iGroops.com

Hosting Companies

SuperstarHostingAndDomains.com
GoDaddy.com

Logo Design

sitepoint.com
aaa-logo.com
logoworks.com
logoyes.com

Web Development and Design

Scriptlance.com
RentACoder.com
guru.com
elance.com
craigslist.com
liveperson.com
logiforms.com
brave.net
highpowersites.com
thinkbigsites.com
onepagewebdesign.com

Graphic Design for Sales Letters and Squeeze Pages

minisitegraphics.com
logodesignguru.com
ecoverdesign.com
ecoverfrog.com
ecovergeeks.com
killercovers.com

Design Templates

templatemonster.com
luckymarble.com
rocketheme.com

Spam Monitoring Websites

spamhaus.org

Figure 3.7 Web Development Checklist			
Yes or No	**Action**	**Answer**	**Ideas for Improving**
	Do I have well-defined short and long-term goals for my website? If so, what are they?		
	Do I use my website to generate income online only, offline only or both? Describe.		
	What is the type of website I'll use to achieve my goals? (e.g. squeeze page, subscription/ membership, informational, or blog).		
	Is my website's domain name descriptive and easy to remember, say and spell? My website's domain name is: _____		
	Is my website's hosting company dependable, flexible, affordable and hard on spammers? My website's hosting company is: _____		
	Is my website's developer experienced, knowledgeable, up on the lastest technologies and has a successful track record? My website's developer is: _____		
	Will I hire a designer for my site or use a template?		
	Does my website look welcoming and professional to visitors?		
	Is my website copy easy to read?		
	Do my web pages have a consistent look and feel?		
	Is my most important information in the most visible areas of my website?		

	Figure 3.7 Web Development Checklist (continued)		
Yes or No	**Action**	**Answer**	**Ideas for Improving**
	Are my site's background colors muted to make reading easier?		
	Does my website provide the information my visitors are looking for?		
	Do my web pages load quickly?		
	Are my website's directions and navigation clear, simple, and logical?		
	Have I adjusted my browser settings so my website can be viewed using many different devices?		
	Do I need/use a shopping cart? If so, is it flexible and safe?		
	Have I used special features—Flash animations, graphics, banners—carefully?		
	Are my internal and external links working correctly?		
	Are my website's primary menu page links across the top of the home page?		
	Are my visitors encouraged to bookmark my pages?		
	Is my most important information in the most visible areas of my website?		

GUERRILLA FIELDWORK

1. Go to GMarketinginternet.com and download the web development forms and checklists. Use them as a reference for your website's design and navigation strategy.

2. Research your competition. Visit ten of your top competitors and make notes on what you like and don't like. Based on this research, make improvements to your own website.

CHAPTER 4

DIRECT RESPONSE MARKETING:
Turning Visitors into Customers

Converting visitors into repeat customers takes a lot more than simply offering good products at fair prices or filling your website with celebrity testimonials. Marketing—whether it's online or offline—is far more about people than it is about things. So even though we're going to teach you lots of great Guerrilla tactics for converting your online visitors into profitable and loyal customers (and show you how direct response communication elements will make this job easier) we're also going to provide glimpses into consumers' minds—where motivation begins.

Unfortunately many online marketers underestimate the importance of this, and focus on driving traffic to their websites before they're ready. We aren't going to let you make that mistake because it will zap your energy, time, and money—and get you no closer to your goals.

Simply said, you must get into your target audience's heads if you want to market to them. The psychology of marketing requires basic knowledge of human behavior. Human beings are leery about making quick purchasing decisions and prefer to develop relationships slowly.

Since the majority of consumers have been burned in the past, they view most marketing messages with skeptics' eyes. They've been stung by too much fine print, too many phony sales, too many bait-and-switch tactics, too many high-pressure salespeople, and too little after-sale care.

Guerrillas know that consumers are sick to death of over-the-top claims, flashy animation, empty promises, baffling jargon, and poor service from websites that keep them waiting or from web owners who do not listen.

Given this, Guerrilla Marketers recognize that they must make a positive emotional impact in their target audiences' subconscious minds if they want to move them from interested prospects to profitable customers.

Most consumers base their buying decisions on emotional factors, even if they claim that they're based on logic. Yes, they also may be proactively looking for the benefits that your products and services offer, but they'll only be willing to hand over their hard-earned money if they know, like, and trust you.

Don't mistake their decision to purchase as the last step; if they encounter any pothole on their journey from prospects to customers, they're likely to change their minds. You also should not confuse one-time purchasers with loyal customers—they are not the same creatures.

So if you plan on building a profitable business you must accept that it can only be as strong as your weakest efforts and all of your stellar marketing efforts can be instantaneously derailed if you underestimate the importance of making genuine connections with your prospects and customers.

Guerrilla Marketing is not linear; it does not have a hard start and stop. Instead, it is a 360-degree commitment-building process that starts when your prospects recognize you as a problem-solver and continues long after the first sale. That's why Guerrillas' marketing efforts are designed to motivate prospects and delight customers. But this process doesn't happen overnight.

How long does it take until this happens? Try seven years on for size. That's the outside. It could happen in a month, even a week or less if the prospects are in the market right now and neglected by their former supplier. But it probably won't happen soon and it most assuredly won't happen if you ignore them after contacting them once or twice.

You have to have the fortitude and patience to hang in there and let nature take its natural course. The moral of this story? Don't give up!

What Do Consumers Really Buy?

As we alluded to earlier, people purchase products and services, but they buy dreams. Products are merely the delivery vehicles for those fantasies. In other words, consumers purchase benefits—beauty, safety, financial freedom, homes, popularity, sex appeal, and glowing health—not features—horsepower, sleek design, house color, or size.

Guerrilla Marketers recognize that their single most important goal is to help their customers achieve their dreams. If they accomplish this, all else will come. So they find out exactly what their target audience is searching for, articulate it, and then deliver on their promises. This is an important point to remember because many small business owners mistakenly talk more about themselves than their prospects! In other words, the public isn't too interested in how long you've been in business, whether you're family owned and operated, or if your warehouse is large or small.

They don't want to hear a story about *you*, they want to hear a story about *them*. They want to know how you can help them save time, make more money, find their soul mates, improve their relationships, get promoted, reduce pain, or make them laugh.

And Guerrillas know that their target audiences' desires are usually not lofty, enduring, or huge. One e-course, one shirt, one painting, or one tube of lipstick aren't likely to have significant or lasting impact on their lives—but they may have an impact for a moment or two. And that's okay, because for that brief period of time they shared a positive experience. And even though their customers might forget about the product, they will remember the feeling.

Guerrillas realize that they're not the only show in town and the main reason consumers buy from one com-

> **"The sale merely** consummates the courtship. Then the marriage begins. How good the marriage is depends on how well the relationship is managed by the seller."
> —Thomas Levitt

pany over the other is because they have confidence in the seller. They have confidence in their ability to solve their most pressing problems. They have confidence that they won't be abandoned after the sale. And they have confidence in their product's quality, value, and selection.

Yet if you can't talk to them about these things, you might as well hang up your hat because you'll just waste a lot of time, money, and energy. The good news, however, is that just about anyone can converse effectively with their intended audience, *if* they follow basic direct response copywriting guidelines. And in the next section we'll show you how.

Direct Response Communication

How to Turn Website Visitors into Customers—Guerrilla Style

If you're like many entrepreneurs, you're not an experienced or skilled writer. Getting started on your sales letter may be your most daunting challenge. You'll find if you break down the process into smaller steps and include all of the direct response elements we suggest in the following sections, you'll do just fine. And remember, even if you plan to outsource your copywriting to a professional, you must still walk through this process, otherwise, they won't have the information they need to develop a powerful sales letter!

The goal of your website's sales copy is to signal your visitors that you are a cut above the rest. They will judge your letter on how it looks, what you say, and as importantly, how you say it—your style. So make sure that your letter's tone and language fit your target audience's personalities, ages, locations, and preferences, and includes other critical style elements like the ones we've listed below.

> **"The most important** part of your web site is neither the home page nor any other individual page. Instead, the most important part of your web site is the registration incentive you offer to encourage visitors to submit their e-mail address to you."
>
> —Jay Conrad Levinson

Talk Naturally

Write informally but not carelessly. Casually conversing with your prospects, as you would a friend, is great—being sloppy is not. Don't ruin your message with avoidable mistake such as typos, misspelled words, and so forth. Edit, edit, edit! And if possible, outsource the final copywriting to a professional. You can find lots of affordable freelancers at sites such as elance.com.

Grab Hold of Their Hearts and Don't Let Go

Speak to the hard core and let others listen in. Know what your target market wants badly enough to pay money for. This may sound like obvious advice, but too many businesses try to promote what they want to sell instead of what their prospect wants to buy. You can't get people to opt into your list these days unless you truly offer them something they want badly.

Personalize

Begin with a personalized greeting like "Hi, John" not "Dear Friend." Also include familiar jargon or phrases so your audience feels like you truly know them. If you are targeting certain geographical regions, mention their sports teams, street names, or restaurants. For instance, residents in various east coast states refer to their main highways in a number of ways such as "the interstate," " Rt. 70," or "the turnpike." Californians, on the other hand, add the word "the" to their designations, so that "Rt. 10" or "Highway 10" becomes "The 10."

Provide Just Enough Information to Help Them Make a Decision

Should sales copy be long or short? The simple answer is both. In other words, there is no hard and fast rule for the length of sales letter—both work equally well as long as the most important information is conveyed.

Don't Mumble

Add some zing to your writing! Create some hullabaloo, tell stories, and use colorful language. As far as sales letters go, most ordinary is most dangerous.

Paint a Picture

Highlight benefits, not features. Put yourself in your prospects' shoes. As you write, keep asking yourself this question: "Why should they care?" This will keep you focused on communicating benefits, not features. You should also tell stories so your readers can better identify with your experiences by drawing from their own.

In the rest of the chapter we will be limiting our discussion to two very common types of website pages: sales letters and opt-in pages. However, keep in mind as you read through these that the concepts we talk about can be applied to any instance when your goal is to get your target audience to take action. Guerrillas were using effective direct response communication long before the internet was invented, so take the lessons you learn and adapt them to your situation. The "action" you request doesn't have to be "internet action." For example, brick-and-mortar retailers could invite their prospects to print out discount coupons to redeem at their stores. Or service professionals might encourage their website visitors to call for free 30-minute consultation sessions. As you can see, you can adapt your sales letters to fit your specific needs.

Sales Page Outline

Your sales efforts on your website will start with a sales letter. Let's create this one piece at a time. Here are the most important elements and devices to include in your sales letter. Learn them, memorize them, and use them.

Identify Your Visitors' Most Urgent Problem

You can't create an effective sales letter if you don't know or can't articulate your target audiences' most pressing problem. So before you do anything else, find this out. Otherwise your letter will be for naught.

Once you're sure you've captured it accurately, dig a little deeper and see if there are one or two others that are weighing on their minds and jot them down as well. And remember, you're the problem-solver, so make sure you offer the best solution.

Create an Attention-Grabbing Headline (and Subheadings)

The internet is a very crowded place and your website will either be a momentum-gathering snowball heading down a steep mountain or just another snowflake in the blizzard. If you don't want your website to get lost in the crowd, your headline must instantly call out to your visitors and pique their interest. If it doesn't, they'll leave. If it does, you're over the first copy hurdle and they'll stay a bit longer.

Simply put, your sales letter's headline must contain your most compelling benefit, and worded in a way that arouses curiosity and triggers the visitors' "hot buttons." The headline can be short or long and can include a sub-heading or not. Your headline should be positioned at the top and center of the web page and be immediately noticeable. You can accomplish this in a number of ways like using bigger font sizes, different colors, and bolding key words and phrases.

Your headline must be powerful enough to stand on its own—that is, you should be able to add your URL or toll-free number and use it as a small ad.

People love cliffhangers, inside secrets, how-tos, and persuasive questions so use them to your advantage, as in the following paint-by-numbers headline templates.

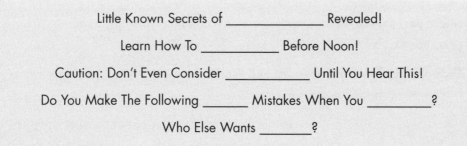

Little Known Secrets of _____ Revealed!

Learn How To _____ Before Noon!

Caution: Don't Even Consider _____ Until You Hear This!

Do You Make The Following _____ Mistakes When You _____?

Who Else Wants _____?

State Their Problem

Now that you have the visitors' attention, you need to keep their interest. Affirm their problem and describe in colorful language how it feels to have that problem. Your visitors should be nodding and thinking, "You got it! That's exactly how I feel!" Keep in mind that Guerrilla Marketing is based on the science of human psychology. The truth is that most people are content with the status quo and need to be inspired to do something out of their comfort zone—so paint a vivid picture of their pain and inject a sense of urgency.

> **TRY IT!**
> Add a soft pop-up message to your website that announces special discounts, new products, and the like.

Offer the Solution

After you've accurately stated their problem, tell them why you're the best person to solve it and offer your solution. Explain to them why it's unnecessary for them to keep struggling with their problem when your product or service will alleviate it. You should begin with an introduction like this: "Hi, I'm John Smith and I've discovered a great way to _____."

Resolve Their Concerns

Even after you've correctly communicated their problem and your solution, your visitors may still be thinking, "Why should I believe him?" Therefore, it's important to tell them why they should trust you. The best way to accomplish this is by listing your credentials, offering social proof, relating your "been-there-done-that" story, providing privacy pledges, calming their fears about buying online, citing verifiable facts and/or alleviating their after-sale troubleshooting worries. For example, you can provide:

- **Credentials.** Copies of industry certifications or licenses, college degrees, years of experience, list of notable companies you've done business with, or books you've written.

- **Social proof.** Customer testimonials, association memberships, write-ups in newspapers and magazines.

- **Indisputable data.** Verifiable facts and data that back up your claims, objective reviews or assessment from industry experts.

- **Privacy policy.** Your pledge not to share their personal information with anyone outside of your company.

- **After-sale support.** Set expectations for after-sale support and customer care.

> **TIP:**
> If there is nothing that distinguishes your business from others, you have two choices:
> 1. Come up with a unique twist to an existing service or something completely new and different.
> 2. Consider another career.

Use Bullets That Resonate

Include a benefit-laden bullet-pointed list of the additional benefits they'll receive. Don't make the mistake of focusing on features—stick with the benefits. Unfortunately, many entrepreneurs have difficulty putting benefits into words. For example, check out websites for ergonomic office chairs. By and large, you'll see a picture of the product and descriptions like *all leather, multi-functional chairs; ergonomic high back;* and *adjustable padded arms.*

These are fine attributes, but they don't speak to the benefits. In other words, they don't answer prospects' most pressing question, "Why should I care?" But there's an easy way to list important features and turn them right into benefits, using the transitional phrase, "*which means that.*" In this case, it might read, "*We sell all leather, high-back ergonomic office chairs, which means that your office will look great and your back will thank you!*" The types of bullet points that work well in sales copy are "top secrets," big benefits in less time, how-tos, and "exclusives."

> **TIP:**
> Discounts are designed to have an immediate positive impact on sales for a predetermined, and limited, period of time. Use them wisely.

Offer Something Irresistible

This is where the rubber meets the road in your sales letter—the moment when your visitors think they would be foolish not to accept your invitation to act or just the opposite. The best online offers include valuable digital freebies, discounts, or add-ons such as newsletters, e-courses, members-only area access, surveys, software downloads, white papers, e-books, and the like.

Justify the Cost and Build Value

Demonstrate the exceptional value your prospects are receiving by doing an apple-to-apple or even apple-to-oranges comparison of competitive offerings. The more specific you are, the better. Also, add bonuses that are related to your offerings, but don't over-inflate their value or you'll set off the hooey alarms.

Reverse The Risk

Spell out your guarantee and provide them a risk-free way out. Even better, find out what's standard in your industry and go one or two better. Contrary to what many believe, the more restrictive the guarantee, the more returns. So be as liberal with yours as possible! Then state it clearly and spell it out exactly.

Call 'Em to Action

Do not assume that your prospects know what you want them to do; tell them using a very clear, complete, and definitive invitation. This is not the place to be vague or subtle. For example, "Pick Up Your Phone and Call Our Toll-Free Number 1-800-000-0000 Now!" is much more effective than, "Call us to find out more."

However, even if they're sold on your company, offer, and products, there's a better than even chance that they'll do nothing. The fact is that people procrastinate for a host of different reasons—they're too busy, too tired, or too distracted. But they're less likely to put things off if they're given a good reason to act immediately. That's where you come in.

Use these other effective techniques to motivate your visitors to act, now!

- **Give them a head's up.** Let your prospects know that you're about to tell them what to do with phrases like, "Here's how to opt-in..."

- **Make it easy and convenient.** Provide a live link to your order pages, toll-free number, directions to your location, and a speedy checkout process.

- **Remind them.** Pepper obvious "Buy Now" or "I'm ready to order" buttons throughout your page.

- **Inject scarcity.** Limit quantities, invoke deadlines for discounts, offer add-ons or freebies on orders placed before a certain date, place quantity or time deadlines, or state a "first-come-first-serve" policy. Offers that expire after a brief time period work especially well, particularly when consumers feel that it's attached to a real bargain or free gift.

Use your call to action as a motivator, not a scam. Never underestimate the intelligence of consumers—they know frauds when they see them. There's a big difference between inspiration and hucksterism.

Here are some examples of effective calls to action:

"If you sign up for our tele-seminar before _____(future date) we'll give you access to the MP3 recordings and transcripts, free."

"We've only got 40 CDs left and when they're gone, that's it—there will be no more."

"We will honor this price on all orders placed by 11:59 pm _____ (future date). At midnight _____ (future date) our _____ (product or service) will return to its original price."

"I have room for _____ more students."

Remind, Repeat, Recap, and Reassure

Remember, your visitors are skeptical, even if they've read through your entire sales letter and are thinking about taking the next step. So offer them additional reassurance that they're about to make a wise choice and/or that they did make smart decision, because many online shoppers get cold feet while they're on a website's order page!

Here's are some tips for making them feel more comfortable:

- **Always add a postscript (P.S.).** Reiterate your offer and guarantee, remind them to act now, and tell them exactly what to do.

- **Keep your order page consistent.** Brand your order page and shopping cart with your logo and maintain your site's look and feel. Also, reaffirm your prospects' decisions to buy, remind them of your risk-free guarantee, and most importantly, offer clear instructions on what they should do next and what they should expect from you.

> "**Repetition of the same** thought or physical action develops into a habit which, repeated frequently enough, becomes an automatic reflex."
> —Norman Vincent Peale

Guerrilla Simplicity: The Squeeze Page

If you recall from the last chapter, squeeze pages—also called flycatchers, opt-ins, and "shy yes" pages—are condensed versions of dedicated online sales pages. They get right to the point and usually contain a "take-it-or-leave-it" offer. Although they can be used to generate direct sales, most website owners use them as a first step for building their permission-based e-mail marketing lists using a compelling opt-in offer.

guerrillas love squeeze pages, because they're simple, inexpensive, and flexible direct response communication vehicles. And they're extremely effective vehicles for generating direct or indirect income over the internet.

Successful squeeze pages use the same effective direct response elements such as attention-getting headlines, bulleted lists of benefits, clear calls to action, and compelling offers just like full-blown sales pages. The biggest difference is that squeeze pages generally cut to the chase sooner and therefore are much shorter. That's all there is to it. As you can see, once you know the elements, you can use them in all forms of direct response messaging.

And although some website owners use both squeeze and sales pages as standalone websites, savvy Guerrilla Marketers know that they work best together. We'll cover this, and other solid conversion tactics, in the next section.

Tactics for Increasing Conversions

Since your website's purpose is to create direct or indirect income you need to be ready to convert your visitors into profitable customers. And, as you learned in the previous chapter a well designed and easy-to-navigate website is a must, it's only the first step. Now, it's time to dig deeper and learn strategies and tactics for increasing the odds that your prospects will say "yes!" to your invitation once they arrive.

In other words, conversion is a process for turning your website guests into interested prospects. It turns interested prospects into purchasers and turns purchasers into lifelong customers!

Basically, you'll invite your visitors to take action and do everything in your power to ensure that they take you up on your offer. This is the essence of direct response communication. For some of you, the conversion journey will be a straight and speedy highway directly to a sale, but most of you will take a slower more methodical road, such as:

- the dance instructor who invites her visitors to sign up for a free tango class

- the weaver who wants his prospects to send for a free fabric sample

- the computer instructor who instructs her visitors to download her free e-book, titled *The Ins and Outs of Search Engine Optimization*

- the attorney who asks prospective clients to call her office to schedule a free 30-minute consultation

- the landscaper who invites his website guests to sign up for a free tree-pruning workshop

- the computer technician who invites visitors to schedule a free systems assessment

- the non-profit service professional asks her prospects to subscribe to her organization's monthly newsletter

- the software developer who offers a free 30-day trial of his new software program.

Before deciding on your own best route, consider factors like your target audiences' level of knowledge or previous experience regarding your products and price points, your competitors' offerings, the brand's top-of-mind awareness, and the average length of your products' sales cycle.

Opt-In Conversions

Building lists of qualified and interested prospects is a prime objective for all types of businesses, but even more so for companies that market online and one of the reasons that "opt-in" conversions are a must for serious internet marketers.

As you probably recall from previous chapters, an opt-in is a permission-based market tactic that occurs when website visitors voluntarily submit their names and e-mail addresses in exchange for something of value such as free information, software, CDs, or newsletter subscriptions. By doing so, they are in essence giving web owners permission to market to them.

(You're not allowed to send promotional e-mails to anyone unless they've granted you permission. It's called spamming and it's a crime.)

You can see why your database list of prospects and customers will become one of your website's most valuable assets. Every time it grows, your leads grow.

But in this case, quantity is not as important as quality. Fewer qualified and interested prospects are more valuable than warm bodies. Your goal is to get the right people on the bus, not fill the bus. For example, if you're selling e-books on boats, having a list filled with people who live in the desert and are searching for cars will do you no good.

Sales Conversions

While opt-ins are wonderful, they're just the beginning. If you've been around the internet for a while, you've certainly heard many online marketers say, "The money is in the list." Don't believe them.

E-mail lists don't generate a cent unless they contain names and e-mail addresses of buyers. In other words, if your list doesn't result in sales it's not doing you a bit of good. The money isn't in the list, it's in the purchases made by people on the list!

Guerrilla Marketers closely monitor the folks on their e-mail lists and look for patterns of behavior that help them move from opt-ins to single sales, and from single sales to multiple purchases. In the sections that follow we'll suggest tactics you can use to accomplish this. If you want to increase your opt-in and sales conversions be sure to do the following:

- **Position your opt-in box in a prominent location,** above the fold (the section of your website that can be seen without scrolling up or down).

- **Use interactive involvement devices** like quizzes, surveys, blogs, and "ask" campaigns to engage your visitors.

- **Encourage your visitors to consume** the information or products they've downloaded or purchased.

- **Combine products and offer add-ons and bounce-backs.** Look for common sense products or services that you can add, bundle, or use to improve your core offering and invite your new customers to take advantage of them on your order page.

- **Follow up.** Once you have your new subscriber, stay in touch. One of the biggest mistakes marketers make is not mailing often enough.

- **Set expectations up front.** If you have a daily tip newsletter, tell your subscriber that's what they'll get. If you only mail out once a week or a month, let them know that, too. Just make sure that you send them what they are expecting to get.

- **Remind them on the way out** by using automated pop-up generator software that opens up when your visitors click to leave your website.

Models for Moving from Opt-Ins to Sales

Many website owners mistakenly assume that people will find them and buy immediately. Although there are the occasional exceptions, this usually doesn't work, because marketing is about building relationships, and hard sell pressure tactics don't improve relationships.

That's why online marketing superstars approach it another way, using a **marketing funnel** or **ascension conversion model**. Simply put, visitors are encouraged to opt-in little bits at a time, which makes the buying process much more comfortable. Figure 4.1 is a simple illustration of how this might look for a chef interested in getting people to sign up for a private Thai cooking class.

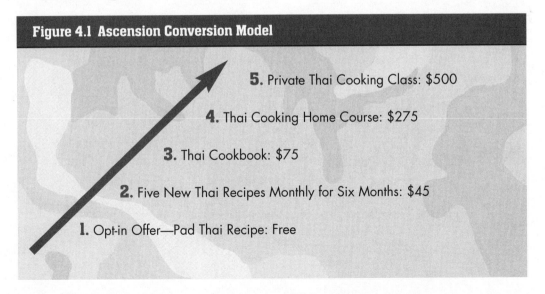

Figure 4.1 Ascension Conversion Model

5. Private Thai Cooking Class: $500

4. Thai Cooking Home Course: $275

3. Thai Cookbook: $75

2. Five New Thai Recipes Monthly for Six Months: $45

1. Opt-in Offer—Pad Thai Recipe: Free

Who says you have to use squeeze pages and sales letters alone? Why not use them together and cover all of your bases? For instance, let's say you drive targeted traffic to a squeeze page that encourages visitors to opt-in and reserve their spot on your free tele-seminar classes. Once there, they have only two options: Opt-in or exit.

If they opt-in, great! That's means they're interested in joining you on the call. They might also be happy to know that they can get MP3 recordings of the calls—in case they miss one or more—for $10. So why not offer them that option by sending them to your sales letter, especially if the price will increase to $20 once the classes begin? If they do take you up on it, you can send them to your shopping cart (where they can also reserve their spot on the free calls) and if not, they're sent to the sign-up page.

Either way, you win. You either have their opt-in information so you can continue marketing to them *or* you have their opt-in information and $20!

Figure 4.2 shows how this might look.

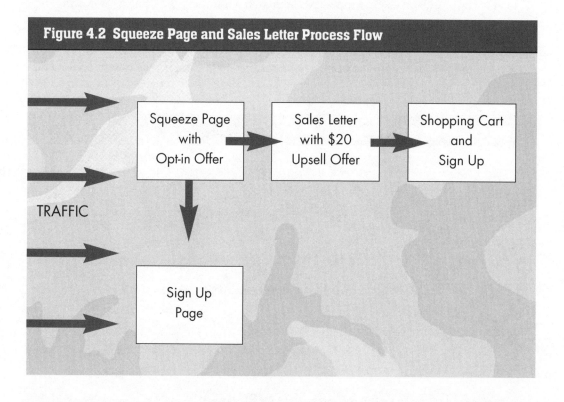

Figure 4.2 Squeeze Page and Sales Letter Process Flow

TRAFFIC

Squeeze Page with Opt-in Offer

Sales Letter with $20 Upsell Offer

Shopping Cart and Sign Up

Sign Up Page

More and more online marketers are using this basic model and going one step further in order to immediately qualify and further narrow down their traffic by placing them into one of three categories—**browsers** (visitors who leave without opting-in), **opt-ins,** and **buyers**. Here's how this might work:

1. Internet users click on links that take them to a squeeze page.

2. Once they arrive on the squeeze page they are invited to do one thing only: Provide their names and e-mail addresses in exchange for access to a free downloadable e-book.

3. The people who choose not to opt-in will exit the site.

4. Visitors who opt-in are sent to a sales page where they're encouraged to go one or two better and purchase the e-book, a 10-week e-course, and a 12-month newsletter subscription for $1. Yes, that's right—$1.

This accomplishes several things. First, visitors are happy because not only have they received valuable information in exchange for their names and e-mail addresses, but they've also purchased an entire package of digital products for a buck—a real bargain. Talk about relationship building!

Second, web owners receive constructive information about the people on their lists, such as which ones are willing to take out their credit cards and spend money. Lastly, in order for prospects to complete the purchase they must provide their credit card information, shipping addresses, and phone numbers.

And what do you think Guerrillas do with this information? You guessed it—they use it to market aggressively to their new customers. They pick up the phone and call them, conduct a direct mail campaign, or ship them a thank-you gift.

The possible ways you can qualify your prospects and use the information are endless, so let your creativity run wild.

What Will You Measure?

As we've said in previous chapters, measurement is a must. You should track, monitor, and analyze your key website metrics such as page views, unique visitors, referrals, downloads, and the like. You should check these indicators often—at least once a week—and use the information to update and tailor your website to comply with your target audiences' requirements.

Remember, metrics like number of overall hits are very misleading because they won't provide you with enough data to make informed decisions. For example, you won't know how many people landed on your web page accidentally or how many times others returned to the same pages.

Most importantly you'll want to measure your **visitor value** so you know how what percentage of visitors are converting and what you could reasonably spend to acquire new ones. You'll get to this number by multiplying the price of your product or service by your conversion percentage. So if you have a product that sells for $50 and you convert 2 percent of your visitors, your visitor value would be 2 percent x $50 or $1.

Don't worry about calculating this manually; these days, most shopping carts come with automated conversion trackers and there are lots of free programs like Google Analytics that will perform these calculations.

You'll also want to test various marketing elements like headlines, photos, squeeze pages, offers, and more using **split testing.** It works like this: Every time a visitor clicks a link in an e-mail you have sent them, they will be alternately directed to one of two or three differently designed sales pages that you will have set up in advance.

Each page will be identical except for one element—the one you want to test. Using your ad-tracking program, you'll quickly be able to determine which web page resulted in the most conversions—sales and/or opt-ins.

Once you have a "winner," retire the others and continue to use that as the benchmark for testing other elements. But remember, you should only change one element at a time or you'll never be sure what's driving the results!

The Ultimate Guerrilla Web Measurement Tool

Just two years ago you would have had to pay $20-$30 per month for a good metrics program for your web pages. But then Google, our favorite Guerrilla company, released a free analytics program that has all of the features of the competitors and more. They've made it even easier for advertisers, website owners, and publishers to compose better ad copy, add power to their marketing efforts, and convert more prospects into customers.

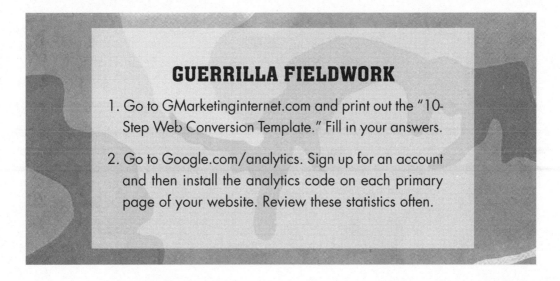

GUERRILLA FIELDWORK

1. Go to GMarketinginternet.com and print out the "10-Step Web Conversion Template." Fill in your answers.

2. Go to Google.com/analytics. Sign up for an account and then install the analytics code on each primary page of your website. Review these statistics often.

Now that you've learned how to get your website visitors to take action, it's time to move on to Chapter 5, where we'll show you how to use other low or no-cost internet marketing tools to jumpstart your online efforts and much more.

GUERRILLA COMMUNICATIONS:
E-mail, Podcasts, and Feeds

It's easy to get bogged down with ever-changing technology tools and file formats, but when you really look at it, you'll see something that never changes—human nature at work. Guerrillas understand this and know how important it is to connect with their prospects and customers. And that means communicating with them meaningfully in the manner they find most appealing. It's the only way to build sustainable relationships.

In the past, Guerrillas wrote letters and post cards using pens or typewriters, placed them in an envelope, affixed a stamp, and dropped them in the mail—then waited three or more days for them to arrive at their designated location, a very time-consuming and expensive process.

While this worked okay for the most part, it wasn't a viable solution when Guerrillas needed critical information or immediate decisions and deadlines were looming. During those times, Guerrillas were forced to call or page their contacts or use pricey courier services. Once again, it worked okay, unless the person they were calling was on the line (remember busy signals?), away from their phone (i.e. in their car, at lunch, or on the golf course) and/or not near a pay phone. Snafus such as these often resulted in missed opportunities and frustrating delays. Even worse, many business people used suppliers in different states and countries and paid exorbitant long-distance and postage fees, making frequent communication cost prohibitive.

Thankfully, those days are over and Guerrillas now have a mountain of great tools they can use to control how, when, and where they stay in touch with others. We now have devices such as laptops, cell phones, iPods, and MP3 players, and state-of-the-art communication technologies like instant and text messaging, Voice Over IP (VoIP), e-mail, webinars, video-conferences, RSS feeds, and pod and nanocasting. Guerrillas can move seamlessly between video, text and voice conversations and alter their device and type whenever their location and communication sharing needs change.

Some folks are understandably confused and overwhelmed by the number of choices available and their seeming complexity. As a result, they avoid using any "new gadgets" and end up wasting time unnecessarily and frustrating others.

Then there are people who are just the opposite and want every new-fangled toy. They either never learn to use them properly, or use them too well and drive themselves and every-one else crazy. Because they're constantly multi-tasking (e.g., text messaging while they're on the phone with someone else, checking e-mails during business meetings, or instant mes-saging five people at once) their attention spans can be measured in nanoseconds and they're usually suffering from a bad case of information overload.

That's why it's important to understand how to use these powerful tools and technolo-gies to make your life easier, not more complicated. In this chapter you'll learn the basics on five of the best, and most affordable, communication tools: e-mail, RSS feeds, podcasts, nanocasts, and text messaging. These will allow you to:

- stay in constant contact with others when you need to be

- control the way you receive information and connect with others

- screen out unwanted messages and callers

- get real-time, customized information delivered automatically

- publish information to worldwide audiences, just like Fortune 500 companies

- broadcast key messages to thousands of people when and where they want it.

We'll begin with the most popular form of internet communication—e-mail—and show you how Guerrillas use it to grow their businesses.

> **"E-mails deserve** as much attention as the most expensively printed brochure or newsletter. Every e-mail offers clients another opportunity to judge your competence and professionalism."
>
> —Jay Conrad Levinson

Promotional E-Mails

Because e-mail allows instant communication, costs nothing, and saves precious resources (i.e. paper), promotional e-mails are quickly replacing business letters. As the internet evolves and grows, e-mail will continue to act as one of its most important applications.

Consider the following findings of 2007 research study by E-mail Data Source:

- 88 percent of adults have personal e-mail accounts

- 46 percent of adults have e-mail accounts at work

- 147 million Americans use e-mail each day (Juniper research)

- 2007 "Cyber Monday" (Monday after Thanksgiving) e-mail activity increased by 55 percent over 2006

- 68 percent of the US's largest retailers sent promotional e-mails in 2007, up from 44 percent in 2006

- 25 percent of the largest online retailers sent at least one promotional e-mail on the Sunday directly preceding Cyber Monday (up from 12 percent in 2006).

These numbers point to the obvious: e-mail usage, promotional and otherwise, will continue to grow in the foreseeable future and should be added to your marketing arsenal.

But there's more to it than merely sending e-mails. As we discussed in the last chapter, you'll first need to build your permission-based e-mail list, via an opt-in offer. Next, you need

TIP:

Composing your e-mails in HTML —which allows you to add color and graphics— will increase your response rates. Just remember not to overdo.

to compose an e-mail inviting recipients to visit your website, and you'll need to decide what you'll ask your visitors to do once they get there. Last but not least, you'll need to figure out the best way to ensure that your e-mails are **opened** and **read** and that your recipients accept your invitation to **take action**.

Getting Your E-mails Opened

Although specific estimates vary, online researchers agree that e-mail recipients make quick decisions on whether or not they will open and read promotional e-mails and if they'll "act" as requested by their senders. Additionally, they indicate that there are four main factors they use to make these decisions:

1. **Products or Services Featured.**

2. **Copy.**

3. **The Subject Line.**

4. **The Offer.**

Obviously, if they like, want, need, and/or are actively seeking the products being offered, they're far more likely to open the e-mail. Also, as we discussed in Chapter 4, all effective direct response communication requires well-written copy and a compelling offer. But e-mails come with their own special challenge: The subject line, which is a short, information burst that can make you or break you.

Subject Lines

Like direct mail envelope "teasers," e-mail subject lines must grab the recipients' interests and increase the chances that they'll open the messages. That's why you'll want to work on getting yours just right.

Start getting ideas by scanning your own inbox! Jot down any that catch your interest and then see how you can tweak them to suit your needs. You can also look at headlines in your local newspaper, magazines, websites, and the like and see if you can covert any of those into intriguing subject lines.

Then use these tips to fine-tune your choices.

- **Keep subject lines short and to the point.** Less is definitely more in this instance, especially since overly long subject lines will get cut off from view anyhow.

- **Don't divulge too much information.** Add intrigue. Build curiosity. Make them want to open your e-mail to find out more. For example:

> Zach, have you heard this yet?
>
> The psychology behind the $40 Pet Rock craze
>
> When $100 per hour is just okay

- **Use your recipients' first names**, unless it's awkward or sounds forced. (This can be done using automated mail merge found in most e-mail delivery systems.) For example:

> John, will you help me?
>
> Mary, you'll want to print this e-mail.

- **Ask questions,** such as:

> Is procrastination killing your business?
>
> Do you believe in this deadly marketing myth?

- **Include your product or service's number one benefit** and make sure it's relevant to your target audience:

> One Tip for Losing Ten Pounds in One Week
>
> 5 Free Ways to Sell More Houses

- **Avoid sending off "hooey" and spam alarms** with exaggerations or hints of high pressure sales tactics, such as:

Earn thousands at home	My dear so-and-so	Your e-commerce business
Triple your...	Making money the easy way	Immediate action required

TRY IT!

Send a personal "no-sales" e-mail to two customers every day and text message a friend, just for fun.

Getting Your E-Mails Read

Once you've seen to it that your recipients open your e-mails, you're over the first hurdle. Next, you'll want to make sure they're read and this requires careful thought, planning and practice. If you don't have experience with this, begin by copying the experts. Seek out respected online marketers' copy and use them as guides for developing your own.

Conversely, you can start from scratch by asking and answering the following questions. They'll help keep you focused and can be used as the foundation for your message. Many of these should sound familiar because they're the direct response elements we covered in the last chapter, but we added a few extra tips.

1. **What is the goal of your e-mail?** Why are you writing it? What is your intent?

2. **What is your audiences' most pressing problem?** For example, maybe they're worried about rising interest rates, increasing fuel costs, their children's safety, or global warming. Whatever their concerns, this must be stated accurately and right away.

3. **Who are you and why are you the best person or company to help them solve their problem?** What types of experiences, degrees, credentials, observations, or past results do you have that suggests they should trust you? What makes you and/or your products, policies, procedures, systems, or company different from your competitors?

4. **Why is it important to solve this problem immediately?** What negative effects will they experience if the problem persists? For example, they might:

   - endure more sleepless nights

   - lose their homes

   - risk preventable health problems

   - cause irreversible damage to the earth's atmosphere

5. **What are the benefits they'll experience when you solve their problem,** such as:

- greater sex appeal

- increased wealth

- financial freedom

- popularity

- less stress

- more free time.

6. **How do you want your readers to act?** How about:

- click on a link to your website

- call your toll-free number

- visit your store

- pass the e-mail along to ten friends.

Following are some additional dos and don'ts for increasing your chances of getting your e-mails read.

- **Open the e-mail with a personal greeting.** "Hi, Friend" is not acceptable. "Good Morning, Jack!" is much better.

- **Make it easy for your audience to continue reading** using logical transition phrases, such as:

Here's how…	Even better,
And one more thing…	That's because…
Want to know why?	And remember,

- **Write casually,** as if you're having a one-on-one conversation with each recipient, using language that is familiar and friendly, but not sloppy.

- **Don't beat around the bush.** Get to the point already and stay there. If it's not relevant, it's not necessary.

- **Use bulleted lists.** Highlight the most important information and cut back on unnecessary words. Use short paragraphs, sentences, and words.

- **Introduce yourself, but don't go overboard.** Your warehouse's square footage and the fact that your company is family owned and operated means nothing to them. They're concerned only about how you can help them. Period.

- **Don't be too pitchy.** Good copy doesn't need a hard sell. Solve their problems and they will willingly buy from you.

- **Space out your text.** Use subheadings and/or leave extra space between paragraphs to make them easier to read.

- **Provide a postscript message.** Write a P.S. that reiterates your most important point.

Once you've written your e-mail, it's time to schedule when you'll send it. Use the following study findings to guide your decision.

- Tuesdays are the most popular day for reading e-mails; Wednesdays are a close second.

- The majority of Americans check their e-mails first thing in the morning.

- 75 percent of e-mails are sent between 7 am and 4 pm, weekdays.

- Only a small minority of e-mail users read messages on Saturdays and Sundays.

Based on this, it's a good idea to send your promotional e-mails early Tuesday morning, before 7 am—but not too early since spammers are most active from midnight to 5 am.

Now, last but certainly not least, it's time to learn how you'll get your readers to take you up on your invitation to act in some way.

Getting Your Readers to Take Action

As we said in the last chapter, you need to give recipients a reason to take action. Even interested and well-intentioned prospects are far less likely to become customers if they don't act as requested right away. In addition to making sure that your letter is compelling, well written, and relevant you must also convince them that it's in their best interest to act right away. How, you ask?

- **Don't make them guess.** Never assume anything. Tell you readers exactly what you want them to do in clear and concise language. If you want them to call you, say so.

- **Introduce scarcity.** For example:

> "We have only 50 left to sell at this price. When they're gone, that's it. "

> "We understand that many of you would love to purchase larger quantities of our ____. However, in order to be fair, we will limit purchases to two per family on a first-come, first-served basis."

- **Impose time limits.** For example:

> "We will honor this discounted price on every order we receive on or before 11:59pm, Friday, December 14th. At the stroke of midnight, Saturday, December 15th, the new price will be $xx."

> "This price is good for the next 24 hours only. Get in now, or wait 'til next year."

Advanced Techniques for Making Your E-Mails Memorable

Moving From Text to Video E-Mails

Can you imagine the entire world moving from text e-mails to video? If not, you may want to rethink it because that's where it's headed. Think about it: Ten years ago most of us couldn't imagine that there would come a day when millions of ordinary people would be creating and uploading homemade videos onto sites like YouTube each month, and this is just the tip of the iceberg! This is not some flash-in-the-pan fad; it is a symbol of the growing clout of online users who expect to get information delivered the way they want it—in video.

Since Guerrillas are famous for finding innovative, affordable, and effective ways to stand out from the crowd, they are using web-based technologies to send video e-mails and post-cards. Moreover, they are using them in extremely creative ways and even integrating them

TIP:

On December 16, 2003, President George Bush signed the CAN-SPAM Act, which is a law that outlines specific standards for promotional communication. While most people associate spamming with emails, it can also be applied to similar misuse in other media such as newsgroups, blogs, and fax transmissions.

into their automatically generated promotional e-mail campaigns. Talk about cool!

Since many of us struggle with writing, it often takes us a lot longer to write e-mails than to explain things verbally. Imagine how much time it would save to video product demonstrations and instructions, sales messages, mini-e-courses, and marketing tips!

Even better, creating videos for distribution via e-mail is now a relatively easy process, since most new computers come with built-in video cameras (and if yours doesn't you can purchase an inexpensive web cam from any electronics store or online). It essentially involves two main steps—creating a video file and attaching it to an e-mail message.

These days, you can add video to e-mails using most browsers' free applications, but the technology isn't quite ready for primetime yet and the process can get cumbersome and frustrating. So for now we suggest that you check out websites like HelloWorld.com. They offer a very affordable system that you can use to upload and send e-mail files and manage them all in one place.

As technology continues to advance, these types of systems will become more available, more popular, and more adaptable. Before you know it, you'll be receiving video e-mail messages on your cell phone!

Audio Postcards

Looking for another way to become memorable? If so, consider e-mailing audio postcards to your prospects and customers. It's a great and easy way to add pizzazz to your messages. Once again, you'll be better off—at least for now—using web-based applications. They're more flexible and robust and you'll save space on your computers' hard drive. Websites like InstantFlashAudio.com use programs that allow you to send audio presentations as well as still photos. Not only is it fun, but it is a great way to add profits!

Really Simple Syndication (RSS) Feeds

Surfing the internet for the latest blog postings and updated website content can be enjoyable, but wouldn't it be even more fun if the information you wanted came directly to you? Guerrillas think so and that's why they love RSS feeds.

RSS stands for Really Simple Syndication or Rich Site Summary. Regardless of the name you use, RSS feeds are groups of internet distribution programs that allow anyone to monitor and collect information in one place and receive alerts when updated blog, news, and podcast content is added. Think of it this way—subscribing to an RSS feed is like having a personal assistant who scours the internet, sifts through mounds of information, pulls out what you've requested, and delivers it to you exactly the way you like it. Talk about convenient! Why do you think NetFlix's business model has worked so well? Simple. It's more convenient to get DVDs delivered than having to go out and find them at video stores!

Guerrillas use RSS feeds to find out what people are saying about their names, products, partners, affiliates, industry, marketplace trends, company names, competitors, and interests! Here how it works: Let's say you regularly visit ten websites to obtain the latest information on trends in your industry. Given this, you'd first have to go to each of the websites—a time-consuming process and just the beginning. Once there, you'd have to do more searching to find the specific content you want. This is a major waste of time!

An RSS document, known as a **feed, web feed,** or **channel,** provides complete content or summaries from particular websites. The content is read using software called **RSS readers, feed readers,** or **aggregators,** which we'll tell you more about in the following pages.

When users subscribe to feeds, these readers continually search the internet for new content and whenever they locate it, they send it to specified locations, chosen by subscribers.

RSS feeds are quickly becoming internet mainstays because they make it possible for people to receive specifically requested information in the format they choose. Literally anyone with an internet connection can request an RSS feed; they cost nothing to set up and the information is sent automatically.

These are a far cry from the days when the best you could do was "personalize" your browser pages (e.g. Yahoo, MSN or Google) with information feeds from official news sources like CNN, *The Wall Street Journal,* or *The New York Times,* and check them manually for updates. Now you can get feeds from news sites such as *Drudge Report, The Smoking Gun,* and *The New Yorker* in a matter of minutes.

For example, if you are looking for hot blog topics you can get up-to-the-minute information from web services such as BlogLines.com, NetVibes.com, or Google Reader (Reader.google.com). Think of the time this saves!

Ways to Use RSS Feeds

Guerrillas use RSS Feeds because they are free, effective, and easy-to-use alternatives to pricey online advertising and complicated content sharing partnerships. Now anyone, even solopreneurs with limited marketing budgets, can use syndication feeds to promote their websites, products, content, and companies to thousands of people without spending a cent.

Additionally Guerrillas use RSS feeds to send e-mails to their prospects and customers to keep them up-to-date on product, pricing, and content changes.

They understand that RSS feeds are great relationship-building tools because they allow their subscribers to filter out unwanted information and receive only what they've specifically requested. And what's more, these feeds bypass onerous spam filters so Guerrillas know that their content was actually received.

As an alternative, you can bypass the need for a reader by subscribing to free services such as Google Alerts. It takes less than five minutes to set up an alert on just about any topic or keywords you can think of. Then, whenever Google obtains updated content, you'll receive an e-mail with a link to the source. But walk before you run; begin by monitoring one thing as a time, or you may end up with information overload.

They're also wonderful tools for:

- driving targeted traffic to their websites

- increasing their newsletter, e-zine, and membership subscriptions

- attracting new blog readers

- sharing news, articles, and topics of interest with others

- promoting products, services, and affiliate links

- achieving higher search engine page rankings.

Gathering RSS Feeds

As we said earlier, if you want all of your information delivered to one spot, you'll need software—a reader or aggregator—that translates cyberspace coding into readable text. There are many to choose from; some are free, and others are not. You can download free software at sites like Reader.google.com, RSSreader.com, or Newsgator.com. Google has three choices for adding RSS feeds:

1. You can add one to your Google Home page.

2. You can add one to Google Reader.

3. You can do both.

And for the more advanced, there is a resource called RSS Compendium that offers even more options. However, the latest versions of Internet Explorer (7.0 or later), Outlook 2007, Firefox, or Opera have built-in readers so if you're using these you're good to go.

After you've installed your reader, it's easy to subscribe to particular feeds; it's not much different than signing up for online newsletters. First, visit any website and look for the RSS feed icon. Next, click on the icon and follow the directions for subscribing. If the website has more than one feed, you'll probably have to sign up for each one individually. However, in some instances web owners consolidate all of their feeds into one, so you may be subscribing to more than you really want.

Adding RSS Feeds to Your Website

It's fairly easy to add one or many RSS feeds to your website. We suggest using tools like the one you find at RSStojavascript.com. You'll be asked to enter the RSS source's URL, answer a few questions, and then they'll provide you with the HTML code you'll need to activate your feed. You'll also be able to preview and test your feed and make sure it's working properly. There's not much more involved than that.

However, just adding a feed to your website isn't enough. If you want it to be an effective tool, you'll need to make sure that your visitors and search engines know it's available and that it contains relevant and useful information.

Following are some tips you can use to get the most out of your RSS feeds.

- **Regularly add fresh content using articles and blogs.** This is one of the easiest ways to ensure that your subscribers get updates immediately. Also if your website is new, this is a great strategy for getting it indexed faster.

- **Include Google's AdSense ads to your syndication content** to earn extra cash.

- **Position your RSS button "above the fold"**—in the part of your web page that's visible without scrolling up or down, and preferably at the very top of your landing page.

Podcasting

What are Podcasts?

Podcasts are recorded audios, videos, or both that are posted to web servers. Usually created in MP3 formatting, they include radio and TV shows, homegrown movies, commercial videos, narrative and music audios, and more.

Podcasts can be downloaded into many different devices such as desktop computers, iPods, MP3 players, and laptops. Most people manually download podcasts one at a time, but podcast series subscribers are increasing in number. When people subscribe to designated series, each new episode is automatically downloaded and subscribers can view them whenever and wherever they choose.

As broadband connectivity continues to rise, technology becomes easier to use, more content becomes available, and equipment becomes more sophisticated and affordable, podcasts will become more and more popular communication vehicles, especially among adults "on the go." Consider this:

- 20 percent of American adults and 26 percent of all internet users own iPods or MP3 players.

- As of August, 2006, 12 percent of all internet users had downloaded at least one podcast.

- 14 percent of internet users between 18 and 29 years of age, say they have downloaded podcasts.

Why Guerrillas Use Podcasts

Podcasting is as easy as blogging and great fun, since it allows anyone to host their own radio or TV show. Better yet, it's more than affordable and can be used by anyone looking to stand out in an overcrowded marketplace, from giant companies to mom-and-pop retailers.

These are just a couple of reasons that Guerrillas love podcasts and are already using them to generate leads, attract new customers, increase their company's visibility, expand their reach to worldwide audiences, build customer loyalty, and more. They understand that consumers are moving here and there at the speed of sound and have no interest in doing business with companies that make it less convenient for them to get the information they like, delivered where and when they want it. And podcasts are powerful vehicles for making this happen. In summary, podcasting offers tremendous benefits to both creators and users, such as:

- **Instant access to information.** As the podcast barriers (e.g., costs, lack of connectivity, and limited device choices) continue to lower they will increasingly be seen as viable alternatives for disseminating real time information.

- **Place shifting.** Podcasts are extremely versatile, and can be downloaded onto almost any device that accepts audio feeds, which allows users greater flexibility than more traditional audio types.

- **Time shifting.** Often described as the internet's audio versions of TiVo, podcasts allow users to save content digitally, and replay it at their convenience.

- **Affordable citizen journalism.** Podcasting is a wonderful way for anyone to produce and publish digital audio and video inexpensively and easily, making it a viable tool for even the smallest businesses.

Equipment You'll Need to Publish Your Own Podcast

All you'll need to produce your own podcast is a few hundred dollars, a decent computer (just about any computer that's less than three years old should work just fine), some inexpensive equipment and software, and a little bit of know-how. Since the quality of your finished product depends, in part, on the equipment you use, let's get your supply list covered first.

First, you'll need a **microphone** for recording your audio unless your computer has one built in. You'll find many options, from the most basic to the most sophisticated, and lots in between. Good ones will run you over $100, but you can find them as low as 20 bucks. But as you know, least cost is not always best cost, and this is one of those instances.

You can buy a good, mid-range, USB-cabled microphone at most electronics stores (*do not* purchase the less expensive ones that plug into your sound card—you'll be disappointed in the quality). Once purchased, plug it into your computer's USB port (every computer manufactured within the last three to five years comes equipped with multiple ports) and wait a bit until the computer automatically recognizes the new hardware (you'll receive an "alert" when it's ready). Although any microphone will suffice, we like the simplicity (true plug-and-play capability), comfort (ear buds), and clarity of the headset models.

While it's not necessary to spend a bundle, you do want to make sure that your audio is clear and static-free. The quality of recordings produced with inexpensive microphones is almost never good enough, because they don't filter out room noise, including your computer's fan.

Since the sheer number of choices can be downright confusing, make it easy on yourself and consider buying your equipment from websites that specialize in audio equipment and software, like m-audio.com. They offer all-in-one podcasting starter kit, which includes a microphone with a desk stand, audio interface, editing software, and other features for under $200. For excellent recording gear, visit WebAudioVideoTools.com.

Next, you'll need **editing software.** Editing software essentially allows you to take a basic video and modify or customize it. The most common edits are trimming the length, adjusting the sequencing of content, and adding titles, cool transitions, and music.

If you're on a PC, you can use the built-in program called MovieMaker; if you're on a Mac, you can use the built-in program called iMovie. There are also a number of higher-end video editing programs on the market such as Final Cut Pro and Sony Videomaker. A good step would be to Google "video editing software" and do some research.

Finally, you'll need **audio uploading software.** In order to upload your podcast from your computer's hard drive to the internet, you'll need either blogging software like WordPress or TypePad, a web-based system like iTunes, or a file transfer protocol (FTP) program.

Steps for Creating Podcasts

Step 1   **Record.** If you can use a VCR, you can record audio.

Step 2   **Edit.** Get rid of anything you don't want and tighten up your recording using your editing software.

Step 3   **Produce.** If you'd like, you can go one better by jazzing up your podcast with radio-style extras such as music and sound effects.

Step 4   **Save and Upload.** Save your recording as an RSS file and upload it to your website. Adding a podcast to your website is easy: You simply put the link to your server where the podcast is kept and allow others to download it.

Step 5   **Syndicate.** It's a good idea to broadcast and distribute your podcasts through syndication feeds at sites like Odeo.com, FeedBurner.com, and FeedDemon.com. Then post your feeds to directory sites such as PodcastAlley.com, Podcasts. Yahoo.com, or iTunes at Apple.com/podcasting. You can also request to be given a searchable category on websites like iTunes.com, Podcastingnews.com, Podcastcentral.com, and Podcasting-station.com.

More Tips for Effective Podcasting

- **Don't forget bandwidth.** Check in with your web hosting company to make sure that there's enough space and bandwidth available so your subscribers won't have problems downloading your podcasts.

- **Plan ahead.** Decide in advance how you'll structure and use your podcasts. Ideas include interviews, panel discussions, and monologues.

- **Keep it brief.** Five to 30 minutes is standard.

- **Write a script.** This is the best way to avoid awkward pauses, long-winded tangents, and confusing segues.

- **Promote your podcast** on your website's front and interior pages.

- **Mention your podcast(s) in your blog postings.** This will increase the chance that Google searchers will find it.

- **Converse, don't recite.** No one wants to hear someone reading copy, so keep your podcast conversational. It sounds much more natural.

- **Avoid the temptation to sell.** People want to be informed and educated, not pitched. Don't jeopardize their trust in you by using your podcast as a cheap advertising tool.

Nanocasts

Since nanocasts are much like podcasts in most ways, you'll learn more if we highlight their differences rather than repeat what's included in the previous section.

So here it is: Nanocasts are the commercial versions of podcasts. In other words, they produce audios and/or videos specifically designed to reach pre-determined and narrowly niched consumer groups, in order to achieve very specific business and/or revenue goals, using feeds called Really Targeted Syndication, or RTS.

These business models are on the cutting edge of the marketing industry because they appeal to smaller target market sub-segments who have traditionally been ignored by mass advertisers.

If you think that nanocasts are nothing more than product and service advertisements, think again. In reality, nanocasts are far more like TV programming than overt commercials. For instance, a nanocast documentary on climbing Mt. Everest might include commercials for mountain climbing equipment or vacation packages to Mt. Everest.

All in all, internet radio, podcasting, and nanocasting are rapidly growing (albeit, still unconventional) methods for disseminating information, education, and entertainment—which is precisely why Guerrillas use them as much as possible. If you'd like learn more about nanocasting go to the International Nanocasting Alliance's website at Nanocasting.org.

The New Language of Mobile Devices

The world is changing and the internet is not just on your desktop anymore; it can be in your pocket, on mobile devices such as iPhones, Blackberries, PDAs, and more. People are consuming internet-based information in new ways and Guerrillas are poised to take advantage of new trends that make it easier for them to communicate with prospects and customers. A common scenario may look like this: A consumer downloads a podcast off of iTunes onto their desktop computer in their office. Then they sync their iPod to their computers and transfer audio or video to the mobile device. And then they listen to music while working out or view a video at a remote location. This is Guerrilla communication in the 21st century.

This has spawned a new abbreviated language. The ability to send text messages over mobile phones relies on a system called SMS (Short Message Service). All that's needed to send and receive text messages is subscription from a cell phone carrier like AT&T, Verizon, or Sprint.

Since the technology only allows for transmissions with a maximum of 160 text characters per message (or 224 if using a 5-bit mode), a new shorthand language has been created to say more, with less. Figure 5.1 shows the most common shortcuts.

Guerrillas use text messaging because it provides a fun and flexible way to communicate with others, especially when they're in situations or places where:

- discretion is important

- there is a lot of noise, making hearing difficult

- talking on a cell phone would be considered inappropriate or disturb others

- there's a need to send information to others (such as phone numbers or directions) who are not able to write it down.

And most importantly, Guerrillas learn and use text messaging because they understand how important it is to correspond with others in ways they find most acceptable. And since more and more people are using text messaging as their primary mobile phone communication style, it's another valuable Guerrilla weapon.

Additionally, many companies now transmit text messages to users who have requested alerts and updates. For example, you can get local text message traffic updates sent directly to your cell phone from sites such as traffic.com. And as time goes on there will be more and more innovative uses for IM and text messaging.

In order to save space and time, most text messagers use their own brand of shorthand. If you're a beginner, use the translation chart below to get started—it's a whole new language!

Figure 5.1 Instant Messaging Shorthand

ABBREVIATION	TRANSLATION	ABBREVIATION	TRANSLATION
NETHING	Anything	RUOK?	Are you okay?
R	Are	8	Ate
B	Be	B4	Before
BCNU	Be seeing you	QT	Cutie
D8	Date	DNR	Dinner
EZ	Easy	A?	Eh?
XLNT	Excellent	F8	Fate
4	For	FYI	For your information
GR8	Great	L8	Late
L8R	Later	LUV	Love
M8	Mate	PLS	Please
PCM	Please call me	Q	Queue/cue
R8	Rate	C	See/sea
CU L8R	See you later	SPK	Speak
T	Tea	THX	Thanks
THNQ	Thank you	2	To/too
2MORO	Tomorrow	2DAY	Today
2B	To be	WAN2	Want to
WOT	What?	WRK	Work
Y	Why?	U	You
:-)	Happy/Smiley	:-||	Angry
:-))	I'm very happy	%-)	Confused
;-)	Winking	:-&	Tongue tied
:-(	I'm Sad	O:-)	Saintly
:-D	I'm Laughing	:'-(	I'm Crying
:-O	I'm surprised/shocked	:-@	I'm Screaming
:-*	Kiss	:-P	Tongue in cheek
:@)	Pig	*:-)	Clown
d:-)	Baseball cap man	:O)	Big nose smiley

Can internet marketing really be made this simple? Guerrillas think so. Even though they stay true to their fundamental principles, they don't fight change and instead adapt their marketing delivery and research methods to suit the times. And their bank accounts attest to the wisdom of this mindset. They understand that their marketing communication style should be memorable and leave their prospects thinking, "Wow, that was innovative!" because the next thing they're going to think is "I want that product!"

GUERRILLA FIELDWORK

1. Sign up for two to three e-mail newsletters in your industry. When you receive your first e-mail newsletter, study the subject line, copy, and calls to action. Use the best ones as guides for crafting your own promotional e-mails.

2. Visit iTunes.com, PodcastAlley.com, or your favorite podcast sites. Listen to at least five audios and watch as many videos. Jot down what you like and use them as models for creating your own.

In the next chapter we'll get your creative juices flowing again as we share the Guerrilla secrets for driving targeted traffic to your website.

GUERRILLA TRAFFIC:
Driving Visitors to Your Website

You've developed an attractive and easy-to-use website and are all set to convert your prospects into customers when they arrive. Now the real fun begins. It's time to learn how to increase your website's traffic by making sure that people who are actively looking for your products and services—and are willing to pay for them—find you.

Many entrepreneurs believe that only a select few internet gurus know the secret for stimulating website traffic. They assume that they've created magical formulas for driving hordes of people to websites, and they're far too complicated for ordinary folks. They're wrong.

Increasing website traffic is not about smoke and mirrors. Rather, it's about learning and applying the fundamental set of rules and principles that govern why people visit websites. As we walk you through the traffic-generating strategies and tactics in this chapter, keep in mind that there are many, many ways to attract people to your website; so many in fact, that we couldn't possibly cover them all in this limited space.

Since we're Guerrillas, we'll focus our exploration on very effective techniques that require more time, energy, imagination, and knowledge than money. In other words, you don't have to pay out the wazoo to get people to your website! There are many low- or no-cost methods for driving hordes of targeted visitors to your site, so put your wallets back in your pockets!

We'll begin with an overview on search engines because these are the first places online surfers go to when they're looking for information or products—and if the search engines don't know you exist, people won't either.

Search Engine Traffic: Where It All Begins

According to a recent Georgia Institute of Technology research study, 87 percent of online surfers use search engines as their primary means of finding new websites, resulting in over 100 million searches each day.

They also concluded that:

- Most people assume that websites listed first are better than those that come after.

- By and large, online consumers prefer to do business with websites listed in the top 20 results, and 80 to 90 percent rarely look beyond the first page of results.

- Visitors sent to websites by search engines are ten times more likely to become customers than those who arrive by other means.

What does this all mean? Simple. The higher your website appears in the search engine listings, the better! And that's where **search engine optimization** comes in. Although the phrase sounds onerous, search engine optimization (SEO) is merely a process for improving the quantity and quality of traffic sent to websites from search engines.

Even better, search engine traffic is the most affordable and most effective strategy to ensure that your website continues to generate income for years, not months. Optimization will drive traffic to your website directly and indirectly, but it won't happen over night.

Although SEO involves several different elements such as your website's design, development, and submission techniques, you don't have to be a techno-junkie to move your website up the search-engine chains over time. However, you do have to know a few fundamentals, so we're going to explain search engine optimization in Guerrilla language—simply, clearly, and briefly!

Search Engine Optimization: A Primer

At the time of this writing there are many search engines but the most powerful are the big three: Google (Google.com), MSN (msn.com), and Yahoo! (Yahoo.com).

Companies all over the world pay search engines large sums of money to expose their products and services to as many people as possible in the form of online advertisements. Given this, it's in the search engines' best interest to attract and keep large numbers of users, and this is best accomplished by ensuring that they're happy with the results they receive. In other words, search engines are in the "trust" business.

In spite of what you may believe, search engines do not perform live internet queries. Instead they establish their own set of mathematical rules called algorithms, and send out electronic "spiders" that scan the internet's pages daily. These spiders collect information and bring it back to their respective engines, where the data is sorted and stored in directories (also called indexes). In other words, the information search engine users receive depends solely upon what's stored in their databases.

How does this affect you? First, it explains why it takes a while for search engines to find new websites. And that's just the beginning. Once the search engines find your site, it can take months, even years, before it moves up to a respectable place on their results list. Regardless of what you may hear, there are no "quick fixes" that will land your website in the top spots. And if you're thinking about trying to "trick" the search engines into placing you up front, forget it; many have tried, and none have succeeded.

Even after you've done as we suggest, you must still be patient; Guerrillas understand that slow and steady wins this race. They also know how to jumpstart the process using some very basic under-the-hood web development and front end web page techniques, which we'll discuss shortly. But first, nothing plays more of a major role in getting search engine traffic than keywords, so this is where we'll begin. After that, we'll

TIP:
Want to save time conducting searches on "the big three?" If so, check out Dogpile.com. It's the search engine for search engines and combines results from major and minor search engines.

teach you Guerrilla tactics that are sure to please the search engines—and real, live human beings!

Powerful Keywords and Phrases: The Heart of Search Engine Optimization

Like a concrete foundation is to a building, so are keywords and phrases to your traffic generation strategy. These are the terms your visitors will use to find your website; where and how they're used will play a tremendous role in your ability to attract new visitors. And if you use the right keywords, not only will people and search engines find you, but they'll also consider you "relevant" and that alone can make all the difference in how well you do. If not, they'll be disappointed when they arrive and leave or miss your site all together.

That's why you should choose your keywords carefully and make sure they'll be able to draw targeted traffic that's ready, willing, and able to become your customers.

Your keywords will be included in visible areas of your web pages—your URL, headlines, copy, titles, and the like—and non-visible places such as meta description tags (paragraph description for your website on search engines). This can get a little confusing but just remember that people read words and search engines read cyberspace language called HTML code.

And while it's not critical that you understand the nitty-gritty details, it is important to keep in mind that search engine spiders don't "see" web page graphics or actually "read" content. Instead, they scan and count the total number of words and keywords. That's why it's so important to place your keywords in areas that aren't visible to people, but are to search engines.

Use the following tips to help choose your keywords and tags.

- Put your most powerful keywords on your web pages' copy, headings, alongside graphics, anchor and footer text, domain names, bulleted lists, and internal and external links.

- Use only one or two different keywords on any given page and don't overdo them (you can check your keyword density for free at Keyworddensity.com). If you use too few keywords on your web pages, the search engines will ignore you, and therefore place you further down on their results lists, or exclude you all together. Conversely, if you overstuff your pages with keywords, they'll assume you're trying to "trick" them, so that will work against you. A safe bet is to aim for a 2 to 5 percent keyword density. Said another way: Use your keywords 2 to 5 times every 100 words.

Tip:

Keywords are the building blocks of every online marketing strategy.

- Since search engines scan text documents, it's a good idea to make your keywords the very last words on a page. For example, let's assume that one of your website's landing pages is a sales letter for "dog grooming products" and those are the keywords you've chosen to drive traffic there. The very last sentence of your sales letter might say, "As you can see, there's no need to look any further... because you've come to the right place for the very best and most affordable dog grooming products." This is a simple and easy way to get noticed quickly by the search engines.

- Conduct your own searches using keyword variations (e.g., synonyms, abbreviations, plurals, and misspellings) and see what you get back.

- Take advantage of online tools. Find which keywords are most popular at sites like KeywordDiscovery.com and Wordtracker.com.

- Avoid using one-word keywords, tags, and page titles and make sure they're not overly generic. For example, "pruning bonsai trees" is a much better keyword phrase than "trees." And a page titled "Home Page" is not as descriptive as, "Bonsai Tree Pruning Home Page."

- Check out your competitors, especially those at the top of the list. Read their copy carefully and find out what keywords they're using. A fast and easy way to get this information is to go online and type in your competitor's URL (for example, mycompetitor.com). This will take you to their website. To view the source code, go to the View Menu and look for View Source or View Page Source. A new window will open that contains the actual HTML code for the URL (in this case, mycompetitor.com). At the top of the page you should see the following two tags: **<head>** and **</head>**. Once you locate both you're going to focus your attention on what's **contained between them**.

Look for:

<title>

These are the **keywords** your competitors are using for their page titles. These words appear in the top bar of the browser when the page is viewed.

<meta name="description" content= "_____" >

These keywords or phrases are the **tags** your competitor is using to describe the content of their page. Web crawlers use these tags as a source of information about the page.

<meta name="keywords" content= "_____" >

These are the **meta keywords.** Again, see which ones are listed here. These provide additional text for crawlers to index, though many crawlers (including Google) no longer use this tag.

Guerrillas Make Their Sites Easy to View and Use

In Chapter 3 we provided strategies and tactics for enhancing your website's look, feel, and usability, so we won't rehash that detailed information here. However, there are several specific design and navigation elements that the search engines weigh and therefore, you should pay particular attention to them.

First, make sure that your site's internal links, or "hyperlinks"—those clickable references to other pages on your website—are all working properly. Search engines, and people, don't appreciate links that go nowhere.

Second, provide plenty of links to and from all of the pages on your website and make sure that your visitors can get back to your "Home" page from all others. Most of us know what it feels like to get lost in a website's maze. It's frustrating and annoying to say the least, and the quickest remedy is simply to exit the site. So why risk losing your visitors when it's quite simple to incorporate enough links when your site is developed? It's also smart to include multiple and regular internal hyperlinks from longer pages to others.

Finally, be sure to give your links descriptive names so that scanners and search engine spiders know exactly where they lead, without having to read more text. For instance "Frequently Asked Questions" is better than "Click Here." If that's not possible, use footers (text links found at the bottom of the page) to explain more about your links.

Guerrillas Link with Others

There's an old adage, "You're judged by the company you keep." In other words, people evaluate others based on how they assess their friends. If they deem the friends worthy and credible, they'll view you similarly—and vice versa. This applies to the internet as well; your website acts as the cyberspace version of "you" and other websites are your "friends." It also helps explain why search engines weigh a website's inbound links so heavily.

Inbound Links

Also called "**backlinks**," inbound links are direct one-way links from other websites into yours. Because they act as a kind of objective vote for your website, they are one of the best things you can do to improve your standing with search engines. As you might expect, they are can also be tough to get, since other web owners may see no advantage in non-reciprocal links.

But this doesn't stop Guerrillas, because they know how to improve the odds that other web owners will agree to provide backlinks into their websites. Checking out competitors is a great way to get started because you'll find out which, and how many, websites link into them. Once armed with this information, you can contact the web owners and ask them to link to your site as well—and chances are they will!

All you have to do is go to Google (or one of the other search engines) and type in the word "link:" before your competitors' domain name, like this: link:yourcompetitorswebsite.com. After you hit "Search" you'll get back a list of websites that link into theirs. You also can get the same information for free at websites such as BacklinkWatch.com. It's that simple!

Writing and submitting online articles and blog postings are other good ways to build links and gain exposure. You can even ask other blog owners to review yours—especially those with large followings—if you want to jumpstart your linking efforts even more.

Outbound and Reciprocal Links

Outbound links are the exact opposite of inbound links. In other words, they are one-way links from your site to others. Even though outbound links have no direct effect on your search engine ranking, they are a great vehicles for enhancing your credibility, since they're viewed as sincere value-added resources.

You can also exchange links with other website owners. Even though it probably won't provide a direct positive effect on your search engine listing, it's still a good strategy if you're careful; otherwise, it can do more harm than good. Search engines take a dim view of web owners who provide outbound links and/or exchange links with questionable websites. Remember that your website visitors (and search engines) are relying on you to provide trustworthy and reputable information and nothing will harm your credibility—and rankings—more than endorsing shoddy products, services, people, companies, or websites by linking with them.

That's why Guerrillas link with online marketers and business owners who share their core philosophies and with websites that enhance their customers' experience such as information-rich news sites, blogs, portals, and forums.

Moreover, it's wise to link with companies that offer compatible products and services or have a logical connection with yours so that the relationship doesn't appear forced.

Guerrillas Add Relevant Content

As we said earlier in this chapter, the search engines are in the trust business. Their visitors rely on them for great results; their lifeblood is quality, fresh, popular, and relevant content. Simply put, if their users are to remain happy—and loyal—the search engines must consistently decode keywords and phrases that result in content links that they deem appropriate and applicable. If searchers are disappointed with the choices they're given, they're far more likely to go elsewhere.

Therefore, using the right keywords to get people to your website is only half of the battle. For example, it's logical to assume that people searching for "free medical help for emphysema sufferers" are seeking information on where they—or their loved ones—can go to obtain free medical treatment.

So how do you think they'd feel if they clicked on a link and landed on an attorney's website—one offering free 30-minute consultations for emphysema sufferers willing to consider suing tobacco companies—instead of getting the kind of information they wanted? At the very least they'd be annoyed. Remember, search engines are in the "trust" business; each time they disappoint one of their users, their credibility suffers. That's why they reward websites that provide the most appropriate content for specific keywords and phrases.

Therefore, even though the attorney in our example technically used relevant keywords to attract visitors to his site, the search engines would probably view them as deceptive and

penalize him accordingly. Our attorney would be far better off if he used keywords such as "legal representation for
emphysema sufferers" or something similar. Moreover, the
search engines would be even happier if his site contained
additional relevant and useful content such as, background
reports and white papers, industry news, answers to frequently asked questions, and the like. The information can
be on most any topic as long as its intended audience finds it useful and pertinent, and not
a thinly veiled sales pitch.

> **"Either write**
> something worth reading, or
> do something worth writing."
> —Benjamin Franklin

For instance, you can create content that challenges commonly held beliefs or assumptions; discusses business trends; provide instructions and troubleshooting advice, expresses
opinions on newsworthy events or stories, and even leverages newspaper editorials by re-
printing them online.

What's more, you don't have to limit yourself by providing content you created. It's perfectly acceptable—and smart—to provide excellent information from other sources such as
articles written by others (as long as you have proper permission and attribution), free software, syndicated columns, public domain documents, and links to open source and local,
state, and federal government websites, just to name a few. However, we do offer tips for
writing great articles later in this chapter.

Search engines reward websites and blogs that regularly offer new and updated content—
not one-shot efforts. Search engine spiders prefer non-static pages and over time visitors will
type in an almost unlimited number of keywords just to find you! Therefore, if you know the
keywords they use (which you can find in your website's logs or stats software), you can add
information that includes them, which will drive even more traffic to your site.

What's more, over time your site will become recognized as a trusted industry resource.
This alone will give you an edge with the search engines so the more pages on good content you add, the better.

Now that you know some simple ways to optimize your site for search engines, it's time
to learn other techniques for driving traffic, Guerrilla style. As we indicated earlier, there are
many ways to accomplish this but we'll stick to the methods that are most affordable and
appropriate for small businesspeople—the kind Guerrillas like best.

TIP:

Looking for data that applies to your industry? You just may be able to locate the information on site such as BizStats.com, SBA.gov, MarketingSherpa.com, and StartupInernational.com.

So in addition to optimizing their websites, what types of methods do Guerrillas use to jumpstart traffic to their websites? Simple. Guerrillas participate, partner, publish, and use people power to get the job done!

Guerrillas Participate

The internet is made up of thousands of communities where people with similar interests, lifestyles, occupations, values, and beliefs gather to exchange ideas, share information, and expand their business and social networks. That's why Guerrillas hang out where their prospects gather online—in blogs, forums, and other discussion groups.

Three of the best places to find groups of people with similar interests are blogs, forums, and other social media websites such as Squidoo.com, YouTube.com, and MySpace.com. Although they're very similar, blogs are usually owned by one person, while forums are owned by many and anyone can start a new discussion thread. That's why participating in online conversations is an interesting, successful, and free (or very inexpensive) way to bring more traffic to your website. Here are three easy steps for getting started.

Find Out Where They Gather

Your biggest challenge lies in finding groups that fit well. You can simplify the process by conducting online searches where you type in appropriate keywords and then add "blogs," "discussion groups," "forums," right after. For instance, if you wanted to connect with other cocker spaniel breeders, you might enter, "cocker spaniel breeder forums" or "cocker spaniel discussion boards." You get the idea.

Become Part of the Community

Once you've located several good groups, participate! Post thoughtful comments, questions, and advice. And remember, most groups have very strict guidelines that prohibit overselling, so resist the temptation to brag about your latest product or service. However, you can add a signature file with a live link to your site in the resource box under your comments.

Position Yourself as an Industry Expert

Let people know that you're an expert in your field (if you are) and offer to answer their questions or provide them with useful information.

But this is just the tip of the iceberg because state-of-the-art technologies and the fresh new Web 2.0 internet culture is making it even easier for entrepreneurs to connect with others. And since Chapter 10 is devoted to teaching you how to take advantage of powerful Web 2.0 social networking tools, websites, and other resources, we'll save further discussion of these until then.

Guerrillas Partner Using Affiliate Programs

Guerrillas understand that people build great businesses. It doesn't matter if they're brick-and-mortar companies, e-commerce businesses, or anything in between. Entrepreneurs need each other. It's that simple.

Therefore, Guerrillas join forces with others whenever it makes sense, especially if it helps them increase the numbers of targeted visitors to their websites. And one of their favorite ways for accomplishing this is using affiliate programs. Therefore, in the next sections we'll provide you with details on setting up your own affiliate program, and becoming an affiliate seller.

Affiliate programs are one of the least complicated and underrated forms of online partnerships—probably because many assume they're more complex than they really are.

Also called "revenue sharing" and "associate programs," they are the internet's version of commission-based sales. Basically, one person pays another person an agreed-upon fee for selling his or her products to others.

This marketing model has worked beautifully for hundreds of years and will continue to do so because it allows both partners to contribute their individual assets—for example, manufacturing capabilities versus salesmanship—to benefit themselves and each other.

Years ago it used to take miles of red tape, pages of legal documents, and a cadre of professionals to put together these types of arrangements, but this is no longer the case. Now, any smart small business owner with a website—even if they're just starting out—can earn additional income quickly, without spending one red cent in advance, selling other, more established companies' products and services.

Alternatively, business owners now have the opportunity to dramatically grow their revenues using an army of motivated salespeople who are eager to sell their products and services all over the world. What's more, they can use sophisticated and user-friendly automation software to place the entire management of the process on autopilot (if this sounds unfamiliar refer to Chapter 7).

The bottom line is, you don't need to buy, create, or inventory your own products and services to make money on the internet nor do you have to pay large salaries to get your products and services sold there.

Savvy Guerrillas often take this one step further and offer a new twist on affiliate partnerships: Contests. For example, in a recent promotion, we offered prizes (MasteringOnline Marketing.com/affiliatecontest.htm) to the affiliate who sold the most products during a three-month period. This, of course, created healthy competition between affiliates and dramatically increased sales. The winner of this contest was Michael Tasner (Tazsol.com), an excellent online strategist and Web 2.0 specialist.

While this may sound inviting, it may not be something you've considered before—especially if your product line is large and/or your current sales channels are humming along just fine. However, true Guerrillas recognize that time and circumstance alter many things, and they prepare themselves for unexpected, but inevitable, downturns in their businesses. Instead of putting all of their eggs in one basket, they thoughtfully create multiple streams of income to ensure that they're less vulnerable if one of their revenue generators hit hard times.

Thus, affiliate programs—yours and others'—are not only ways to add security to your earning potential, but they're also some of the most effective and affordable weapons for squeezing more profits out of your website.

How Are Affiliate Programs Managed?

Affiliate programs are usually supported and managed by database software programs such as EasyWebAutomation. A program such as this:

- identifies all affiliates (those selling the product)
- documents the appropriate commission percentage per sale

- monitors each affiliate's sales
- tracks each affiliate's preferred payment method.

All affiliates are assigned unique alphanumeric codes, which are imbedded into web links and e-mailed to them. They can then add the links to any of their communication pieces—e-mails, articles, ad, etc.

Whenever a recipient of the promotional content clicks on the affiliate link, it opens the product's promotional web page or shopping cart. If they purchase, the automated system documents and assigns the sale to the appropriate affiliate member.

Choosing Affiliate Programs

Before setting up your own affiliate programs, it's a great idea to learn the ropes first. That's why we heartily recommend that you try your hand at selling other people's products and services first. This way, you'll be able to draw from your own experiences to make more informed decisions.

Signing up as an affiliate is easy. Sifting through mounds of websites and narrowing down your choices is much harder, but if you pay attention to the following instructions, you'll do just fine.

Make a List and Check It Twice

If you currently have a product or service line, think of other products that you would like to sell. They should compliment but not compete with your current offerings and appeal to the same target audience. If you already have an established product line, look for natural add-ons. For example, if your company specializes in dog grooming supplies you might become an affiliate for websites that offer gourmet doggie treats, dog leashes and bedding supplies, dog rescue sites, and breeders. If you sell grooming products for longhaired dogs, it would be even better to become an affiliate for companies that cater to longhaired dog lovers as well. Opt for quality over quantity. If you get too many products, your site will looked cluttered and your visitors may view your offerings as irrelevant.

However, if you're a start-up with no products or services but would like to try your hand at this, pick a "theme" that interests you and then think about creating a website that offered nothing but other companies' products. For example, let's say you're a passionate Atlantic Coast Conference (ACC) college basketball fan. If so, you might build an entire "affiliate website" where you sell nothing but other companies' ACC sports memorabilia—hats, mugs, sweat shirts, photographs, and the like.

If you want a quick and easy way to find affiliate merchants and products, create a free account on websites like ClickBank.com, cj.com, and PayDotCom.com. There you'll find comprehensive lists of all kinds of products, services, and web owners to choose from.

Research and Click

Once you've created your list, it's time to go online and look for websites that sell the types of products you have in mind and if they have affiliate programs. They're easy to find. Just look for phrases like, "Make Money," "Reselling Programs," "Associates," or "Affiliates." They will usually lead you to another page where you'll find more information on their payment amounts and policies, support programs, and marketing materials as well as instructions for signing up.

Assess, Compare and Sign-Up

Before signing up, make sure you're pleased with the commission you'll earn; you've checked out the other services they offer, and that they're comparable—or better—than others on your list. In other words, choose your affiliate programs carefully and make sure they:

- use unique codes that automatically track your sales

- are reputable companies with quality products and services

- reward "super affiliates" with additional spiffs

- employ an independent company to monitor sales activity

- pay incentives quickly and allow you to continue earning commissions on recurring monthly fees like subscriptions, membership renewals, etc.

- provide links that stay active indefinitely (versus ones with expiration dates)

- offer extras such as marketing tips, training, graphics, and copy

- allow you to terminate the agreement at any time

- do not charge you a fee to join.

After you've done all this, sign up! Enrollment forms come in all shapes and sizes but they'll all request the same basic information.

Finally, don't forget to store your affiliate code in a safe place (or several) on your computer's hard drive and remember to imbed it into any promotions you run—otherwise, you won't get paid!

Now that you know how to become an affiliate, it's time to learn how to set up your own affiliate program.

Building An Affiliate Program

So how do you go about recruiting, paying and rewarding affiliates? Simple. Follow these three easy steps.

1. Take a Page Out of Your Own Book.

There was more than one reason we suggested that you try your hand at becoming an affiliate before setting up your own program. Aside from the obvious educational benefits, you should design your own program so that it measures up in every way—commission percentages, additional rewards for super affiliates, links that don't expire, etc. (If this sounds unfamiliar reread the previous section.)

2. Take Care of First Things First.

Before launching your affiliate program, make sure you're ready to communicate how much you value your affiliates, and that you've prepared promotional materials that will make their jobs easier. These include:

- welcome letters

- sales collateral that they can use right away—letters, graphics, e-mails, testimonials, FAQs, images, tips—with easy downloading instructions

- sequential autoresponders that contain updates, encouragement, reminders, etc.

- a support page that includes such things as contact information, after-hours help, and discussion forum.

3. Affix, Invite, Promote.

After you place your sign-up link in a prominent spot on your website, invite others to sign up by promoting your program through e-mails, newsletters, store signs, seminars, and the like. Let your imagination be your guide.

4. Continue to Deliver—Even After the Sale.

There are thousands of affiliate programs on the internet so you'll be competing with many others to attract and retain quality salespeople. So in addition to tending to pre-sale matters, you'll have to be extra diligent after sales. For instance, use autoresponders to generate and send out a congratulatory e-mail each time a sale has been made. Also, be sure to pay commission on time all the time. No one wants to chase money—it's one of the quickest ways to lose affiliates.

As Guerrillas know, Pareto's 80-20 rule (80 percent of your affiliate income will come from 20 percent of your affiliates) is alive and well, so use it to enhance your affiliate sales. That is, offer extra rewards, such as higher commission percentages, iPods, steeper product discounts, stellar testimonials, leadership opportunities, cell phones, or laptops to encourage healthy competition between your affiliates and to reward your top 20 percent performers. This group of super affiliates should also be among the first you consider when you're looking for a joint venture or strategic alliance.

Guerrillas Publish

Guerrillas Write Articles

Remember, the number one thing that people look for on the internet is information—news, products, and services, resources, technology, and much more. That's why writing and posting informative online articles to your website as well as submitting them to others is one of the best methods for increasing your website's traffic quickly and dramatically. And even if you don't like to write or have poor writing skills, you should still give it a try. You'll find plenty of affordable freelance ghostwriters on websites like elance.com and craigslist.com. Also, you can place other people's articles on your site (as long as you give credit to the author and a link back to their site). So this is a great tactic for just about anyone!

TIP:

Before writing articles, make a list of your favorite topics and create a rough drafts first. You'll save lots of time and achieve a better result.

And don't worry, your articles don't have to be long—500 to 700 words are ideal—but they do have to be meaty. It's best to choose topics related to your website, industry, products, or company. Offer useful tips, solutions to common problems, or how-tos, and don't forget to pepper your major keywords and phrases throughout.

Also, be sure to enter your contact information in the "resource box" at the end of your article. Introduce yourself, provide a brief bio, and include a direct link to your site, an opt-in invitation, and a clear call to action. There are literally hundreds of online submission sites, so in order not to get overwhelmed, focus only on ones that make sense for your industry and/or use one of the affordable online distribution services like SubmitYourArticles.com. For a small monthly fee, they'll distribute your articles to a number of reputable websites.

Guerrillas Stay in Touch with Newsletters

Writing and sending regular online newsletters, also called e-zines, is one of the most effective strategies for getting repeat website traffic.

Remember, your mailing list can be a goldmine, *if* you use it to correspond regularly with your opt-in subscribers and customer by providing them with high-value content combined with compelling promotional offers. In order to get the most out of newsletters they need to be sent regularly—at least every two weeks and more often, if possible.

Once again, they don't have to be long but they should be filled with great information such as cool resources, hot tips, top 10 lists, surveys, and FAQs. As long as you provide this first, it's perfectly okay to toot your own horn—as long as it doesn't take up more than 25 percent of the newsletter. Your promos should contain the same basic direct response elements we pre-

> **"Here's what's good**
> about publicity: it's free. It's
> believable. It gives you and
> your company credibility and
> stature. It helps establish the
> identity of your business. It
> gives you authority. It's read
> by a large number of people.
> It's remembered."
>
> —Jay Conrad Levinson

sented in Chapter 4, such as attention-grabbing headlines, compelling offers, and strong and clear calls to action.

Most online marketers e-mail their newsletters and publish them in HTML format, which means they retain color, typefaces, and graphics. For the most part, this works well and you should do the same—it results in higher response rates, as long as you don't get carried away and overdo it! Remember, less is more.

Guerrillas Use Word-of-Mouth Marketing

Is your message, product or service worth talking about? We certainly hope so, because a recent study conducted by eMarketer.com concluded that 53 percent of online traffic comes from recommendations made by family members and/or friends. This confirms what Guerrillas have always known: **positive word-of-mouth "buzz" is the best advertising money can't buy**—whether offline or online! So every single business person in the world should be spending a great deal of their time strategizing ways to acquire and retain profitable customers using word-of-mouth marketing—especially since the internet makes it so much easier!

It wasn't too long ago that it took several months and even years before entrepreneurs derived the benefits that their positive word-of-mouth referrals generated. Before the advent of the internet, it simply took longer for news to spread because we relied on phone or in-person conversations and handwritten correspondence. Additionally, business owners depended in large part on their happy customers' willingness (and memory) to refer them to others—not a very efficient or effective system.

But fortunately, thanks to the internet, those days are gone. Nowadays news travels at lightning speeds via instant messaging, e-mail, desktop computers and laptops, mobile phones, and SMS text messaging. In addition to more traditional forms, social media websites like MySpace.com, YouTube.com and many others allow Guerrillas to spread their message to potentially millions of people at the click of a mouse.

Guerrillas are particularly fond of using three of the very best online word-of-mouth tactics—**viral marketing, tell-a-friend programs,** and **online publicity.**

Guerrillas Go Viral

You've probably heard of viral marketing but may not know exactly what it means. If so, you're not alone. However, viral marketing is nothing more than a method for encouraging large numbers of people to spread marketing materials to family members, friends, and associates. It's like planting seeds, adding water, and watching them grow! Because so many of the best internet distribution channels are free or extremely low-cost, viral marketing is a Guerrilla's best friend and should be an integral part of your online marketing efforts.

And how do you "go viral" quickly? Simple. Give something valuable away for free. Please understand that there's a big difference between valuable and expensive, so don't misinterpret what we're suggesting. People have a natural tendency to help others, especially their close friends and relatives. Therefore, if they're given something really special and encouraged to share it, they will. So before you choose your "freebie," answer these types of questions:

- What do my target prospects value?
- Are they looking for instructions on how to build something?
- Do they crave inspiration?
- Are they in need of inspiration?
- Are they seeking comfort?
- Do they just want a good laugh?

Once you know this, you're on your way; the sky's the limit on what you can give away. It can be as elaborate as an original video or something like a photo slideshow set to music. You can give away e-books, software programs, or daily jokes. Or if you're a designer, why not offer free graphics, photos, or banners? Regardless of what you choose, just be sure to include your name and website address (and live link if applicable) so interested people can find you! If you'd like to see a good example of a viral e-book go to GMarketingCoach.com/HotMarketingTips.pdf.

Guerrillas Use Tell-A-Friend Programs

If you've spent any time at all on the internet you've certainly been asked to provide the names and e-mail addresses of others you know who would also be interested in visiting websites. This is a great way to make it easy for people to recommend your site to their family members and friends! All visitors have to do is enter the requested information and an e-mail with your website's URL and a short message is generated. And since the e-mails' "from" lines are from recognizable e-mail addresses, they're not likely to get blocked by spam filters and are not considered spam.

So why not save your visitors a phone call and make it simple and convenient for them to suggest your site to others? You'll only need two things to get started: a tell-a-friend form and script.

Most shopping carts include scripts and forms in their packages, but if you need one, go to Google and type in: "tell a friend forms" or "tell a friend scripts" and you'll have lots to choose from.

Guerrillas Generate Online Publicity

As an alternative to utilizing traditional advertising, Guerrillas love using the internet to create buzz about themselves, their products and services, and their companies. That's why so many smart online entrepreneurs take advantage of free and/or low-cost and highly effective traffic generation strategies, such as online press releases (PR).

There are a number of websites that offer free resources and guidance on writing press releases and how to use them to generate traffic to your website and obtain inbound links. To find them, go to Google (or any of the other big search engines) and search for "online press releases" or "free press release information."

If you've never written a press release, we also strongly suggest that you use online services such as PRweb.com. Not only do they provide tips for creating your press release, but they'll also distribute your release for you and have various "contribution" levels depending upon the amount of exposure you want.

If you want to get the biggest bang out of your online PR efforts, let the following rules of thumb guide you.

- **Use an assortment of weapons.** It's hard to get anyone's attention using one channel. So mix it up! Use a combination of online and offline strategies and tactics such as recording a radio interview and putting it on your website. Put your web address on your business cards, mention it in your voice mail greeting, and include it in every one of your offline ads.

- **Find out what people are talking about.** Then write a press release that ties you, your company, or your products and services to the story or topic. Just pick up any national newspaper like USA Today, or visit online news sites to find out what subjects are hot.

- **Send out press releases often.** One-shot attempts won't get you anywhere, so any time you have news worth mentioning send out press releases.

- **Add a little controversy.** Nothing is worse than a boring story, so go ahead and add a little pizzazz to your press releases. There's nothing wrong with controversy, as long as you don't go overboard. So stick your neck out, stand up for something, and shout it to the world.

Guerrillas Set Up E-Mail Signatures

Here's a strategy that's so simple you can have it up and running in less than ten minutes! Open your e-mail program (e.g. Microsoft Outlook, Entourage, GMail, Thunderbird) and go to the "Tools" tab (or "Preferences" on Macs) and set up a signature file—or "sig file." Once there, enter whatever information you'd like to appear at the end of all of the e-mails you send, like your name, e-mail address, contact information, active link to your website, graphic, and/or marketing message.

This is a wonderful way to capitalize on every e-mail you send! It doesn't get much better than that! And who says you can't get creative? Just put on your Guerrilla Marketing hat and go for it. As long as it's easy to read (no fancy fonts, please) and contains a live link to your website, you'll be okay. Here are a couple of examples of good signatures:

Mitch Meyerson, author, speaker and consultant
Get Your Free Online Marketing Toolkit with
The #1 Multi-Media Mini Course on the Web
www.MitchMeyerson.com

David A. Scarborough
What's Your Big Idea Worth? Millions...
www.members.Ideas-to-Income.com

As you can see, this is another wonderfully effective, fast, flexible, and free method for getting more and more people to your website.

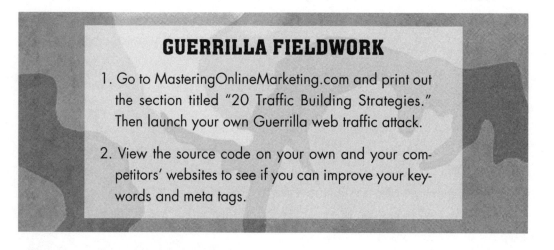

GUERRILLA FIELDWORK

1. Go to MasteringOnlineMarketing.com and print out the section titled "20 Traffic Building Strategies." Then launch your own Guerrilla web traffic attack.

2. View the source code on your own and your competitors' websites to see if you can improve your keywords and meta tags.

We've talked about a lot of different strategies in this chapter and hope you'll begin using them as soon as possible. The internet is moving like a tidal wave and you need to get your feet wet as soon as possible. But don't try everything at once or you're likely to become overwhelmed. Begin with a few, then try others and get ready to soar!

GUERRILLA AUTOMATION:
Online Systems for Effortless Follow-Up

By their very nature, entrepreneurs are doers. They love challenges and are eager to roll up their sleeves and take on the day-to-day responsibilities of running their businesses. However, given the increased complexities of today's market place and the explosion of worldwide competition, many small businesspeople are trying to operate on too many levels and simply cannot manage it all.

In addition to their traditional tasks—dealing with employees and suppliers, handling customer complaints, making payroll, and more—they now contend with additional duties that they may not have bargained for when they started their business. Many entrepreneurs—particularly those born before 1960—didn't know they'd be responsible for putting up websites, answering hundreds of e-mails each week, vying with competitors in distant lands, and/or fixing regular computer glitches.

And even if they have exceptional time management skills, keeping up with it all can be a daunting job. But for people who have a tendency to jump at every opportunity and reinvent the wheel every time they do something new, it's usually disastrous.

Simply said, time—our most precious asset—is more valuable than ever before and if you're in business today you'll need to work intelligently or face extinction. Your livelihood (and sanity) depends upon it.

Yes, computers can be frustrating. They don't always work they way we think they should and sometimes stop for no apparent reason. "Simple" software installations are not always simple. Web developers and internet geeks have their own indecipherable language filled with bits, bytes, and bots. And many of us have, on one or more occasions, considered throwing our computers out the window of a ten-story building just to see it shatter into millions of tiny cyberspace pieces. (That's usually after losing something—a document, file, or program—that was "just there!")

It's no wonder that there are pockets of small business owners who still refuse to use a computer, let alone put up a website. After all, who needs this? The answer is: you do. Yes, computers and software can be frustrating, but if you believe that technology is your enemy, you're not only jeopardizing the health of your business but you're wasting gobs of valuable time!

Savvy entrepreneurs understand this and use state-of-the-art software and web-based programs to perform a multitude of ongoing tasks, such as communicate with customers, process credit card and electronic payments remotely, manage multiple e-mail lists, segment target market into smaller groups, respond to prospects' questions, monitor sales activity, and offer downloadable digital products. Even better, once they've set up their programs this can all happen without lifting another finger!

However, if you're like many small businesspeople you have fallen prey to the unproductive "work-harder-stay-longer" rut. But if you're really serious about growing a profitable company you're going to have to accept your need for help and look for ways to use your limited time more effectively. And using powerful web-based automation tools is one of the best ways to begin working smarter, not harder.

Have we convinced you that automation is a must-have? We hope so. But acknowledging this is one thing; slogging through mounds of information to find affordable, reliable, easy-to-use, and relevant automation programs is another. But fear not, because even beginners can afford and use powerful, state-of-the-art automation programs, which will pay for themselves in no time and continue to provide incredible benefits year after year.

Please understand that there are hundreds of ways to perform the work of your business more efficiently—too many, in fact, to cover in this limited space. So in true Guerrilla fashion, we're going to focus our attention on covering the basics on automation software that will help you:

- take money

- communicate with prospects and customers

- track and measure your marketing efforts.

Processing Online Payments

Some of the very best automation tools in existence today are all-in-one shopping carts—cyberspace versions of the ones in retail locations. However, unlike your local grocery store's carts, the online kinds do much, much more. We'll talk more about the particulars of shopping carts in the next section, but for now let's step back and cover several fundamental first steps for any of you who are just beginning this process.

Merchant Accounts

In order to transact business on your website you'll need a method for processing your customers' payments. You could do this the hard way (i.e., wait for your customers to mail a check or take credit cards over the phone) or do it the right way and set up automatic payment processes. We'll assume that you've chosen the latter.

In order to accept credit cards and other forms of online payments you'll need an internet merchant account. Essentially, merchant accounts are nothing more than payment "gateways." In other words, they are vehicles that enable funds to be transferred from purchasers' credit cards to sellers' bank accounts.

Some banks and many web-based service companies offer these types of accounts and can have your account activated in a few days. You'll usually pay a one-time set-up fee, a percentage of every transaction, and ongoing monthly maintenance charges.

> **"Being busy does not** always mean real work. The object of all work is production or accomplishment and to either of these ends there must be forethought, system, planning, intelligence, and honest purpose, as well as perspiration. Seeming to do is not doing."
>
> —Thomas A. Edison

> ## "The number one benefit
> of information technology is that it empowers people to do what they want to do. It lets people be creative. It lets people be productive. It lets people learn things they didn't think they could learn before, and so in a sense it is all about potential."
>
> —Steve Ballmer

The good news is that you have lots of choices available (visit your favorite search engine and type in "merchant accounts") so you can shop around for the best deal. The bad news is that there are lots of choices available, so it can be downright confusing if you don't know what to look for. We like EasyWebMerchant.com and MerchantWarehouse.com, but check out as many as you'd like.

In any event, in addition to checking prices, you'll want to make sure that your payment gateway—merchants' account—supports your shopping cart's functionality. Huh, you say?

Think of it this way: The process that allows customers to submit online payments and transfer monies elsewhere is orchestrated by several entities that provide only one link in the chain. And since their interests lie in just their part, it's up to you to make sure they all work together.

For example, in order to prevent fraud and process payments instantly, many e-commerce marketers add another layer of security to their payment processes, in the form of secure payment gateways. Companies such as VeriSign and Authorize.net offer these fee-paid services as add-ons to standard internet merchant accounts and shopping carts. The important point here is to make sure that each provider is aware of the others and that all pieces work well together.

Therefore, check ahead of time to make sure that your internet merchant account:

- integrates well with your shopping cart

- explains all of their fees carefully and you understand them —especially watch out for outrageous set-up and application fees

- offers the ability to charge customers' credit cards for ongoing services such as monthly subscription fees

- has 24/7 technical support

- provides a variety of security measures that protect you from fraud

- offers virtual terminals: add-ons that allow you to take credit card and electronic check payments over the phone and in-person as well.

PayPal and Other Third-Party Processors

If you're looking for a quicker solution to taking online payments consider setting up a PayPal account, owned by eBay (there are other third-party processors, but PayPal is the largest and most familiar). For a fee they'll process your payments and deposit the money—almost instantly—into your PayPal account. After that, you'll need to go online and transfer your money into your bank account, thus alleviating the need to set up an internet merchant account.

And while speed is an obvious benefit there are also some drawbacks, such as:

- PayPal's transaction fees are usually higher, but there are no set-up or monthly fees, so your overall costs may actually be less.

- You'll be working within the constraints of PayPal's environment, so you'll have less flexibility when it comes to customizing your customers' ordering experiences.

- It may take up to three days for funds transferred from PayPal to your bank account to become available.

- PayPal doesn't allow you to accept credit cards over the phone.

As you see, integrating features and service providers can be confusing and expensive. That's why we strongly suggest that you avoid using standalone applications in favor of a better solution: the all-in-one shopping cart.

One-Stop Shopping Carts

Your shopping cart is your website's workhorse and the path to earning you money, so you'll want to make sure it is robust enough to handle everything you need to have done. And given the fact that today's web-based all-in-one shopping cart programs are inexpensive, reliable, and easy-to-use, there's simply no need to over complicate this vital process using standalone solutions—especially if you offer more than one product.

Although you will find free shopping cart programs, this is one of those times when least cost is not always best cost, so we encourage you to select one that is fully functioning, stable, and affordable. Although you'll find lots of choices available we are partial to EasyWebAutomation.com.

However, no matter what shopping cart program you choose, at a minimum they should contain all of your automation, tracking, and communication needs and include:

- **Added security features.** Remember, many people are still uncomfortable when it comes to paying and/or sharing personal information online (even though it is a very secure payment method). So make sure your shopping cart uses "digital converters" which encrypt information and make it nearly impossible for anyone else to access.

- **Upsell modules.** Good shopping carts retain customers' data so they're able to recommend related products to them based on previous purchases or what's currently in their shopping cart. If you've purchased a book on Amazon.com you've probably noticed that there's a "Customers Who Bought This Item Also Bought," area on each of their books' pages.

- **Ad trackers.** This is a quick and accurate way to find out the results of testing offers, headlines, copy, etc. Although Google offers a great free tracking tool, many shopping carts come with their own versions.

- **Special offer management.** One-stop shopping cart should allow users to offer and manage special volume offers, such as "buy one, get one free" discounts.

- **Good instructions and simple set up.** Your cart should come with clear instructions; you shouldn't have to download or install anything

- **Flexibility.** It should be able to handle sales of packaged as well as downloadable digital products and services in the same transaction. Also, it should offer security for downloadable products (so they aren't passed from person to person all over the internet).

- **Superior post-sale support.** You're going to be especially grateful for this during the early stages because you're likely to have questions.

- **A method for calculating taxes and shipping costs.** Your cart should automatically calculate applicable sales taxes and include several shipping options for your customers, including next day air services.

- **Web-based administration interfaces.** Online interface should be provided so that you can log in and add products, change prices, generate special offers, etc., from anywhere in the world.

- **Affiliate program management capabilities.** You shouldn't have to buy separate software in order to manage your affiliate programs. Instead, your shopping cart system should include one that can be managed from their web-based administration page

- **Autoresponders.** Sequential autoresponders are some of the best online tools you'll ever use. Therefore, make sure your shopping cart is equipped with an integrated system so you can take advantage of their incredible power, which we'll discuss in detail in the next section.

Sequential Autoresponders: Guerrillas' Automated Workforce

Guerrillas know how important it is to stay in touch with customers and prospects. That's why they love autoresponders—those technology gems that put their correspondence on autopilot.

Don't let the name scare you. Autoresponders are merely tools that you can use to design, create, and send one or many e-mails to prospects and customers who have given you permission to contact them by opting into your e-mail list.

Although we believe in regular and ongoing communication, there are times when it's appropriate to send out only one e-mail response. For instance, when you want to

- provide new customers instructions for consuming your products

- convey exclusive, detailed and/or time-sensitive information, such as conference call-in numbers, user names and passwords, emergency contact information, answers to frequently asked questions, and the like

- alert your e-mail list about upcoming special discounts, sales, or promotions.

For the most part, however, you'll use **sequential autoresponders**. These are tools that will help you send portions of information to multiple and separate groups of people over a prolonged period of time. In the world of marketing these make the most sense since they provide an easy way to stay in touch with customers and prospects regularly. Once you set them up they run on autopilot.

Here are the basic steps you'll follow to set up your autoresponders.

Step 1   **Identify the purpose of your e-mail campaign.** How will you use your series of e-mails? What types of information do you want to convey? (For example, weekly tips, mini e-courses, inspirational quotes, etc.)

As you begin this process, remember that your visitors signed up because they're looking for pertinent and valuable information, so deliver it. For instance, decide what you'll give in exchange for your visitors' name and e-mail address (e.g. white paper, e-book, newsletter, teleseminar, etc.).

Step 2   **Set up your automated e-mail delivery system.** This will send your opt-in responders' contact information to a database, which you'll create and name. This is easier than you would imagine with the technologies available today.

Step 3   **Compose your e-mails.** Decide exactly what you want to say, to whom you'll say it, and then write it. If you need help, refer back to Chapter 4 on direct response marketing.

Step 4   **Program and schedule your e-mails.** Give each e-mail a different title. For example: Day One: "The Three Biggest Mistakes Guerrilla Marketers Make and How to Avoid Them"; Day Two: "The Two Things Guerrilla Marketers Should Do Every Day"; Day Three: "The Ins and Outs of Newspaper Ads," etc. Then schedule your series. Make sure you send them out regularly and consistently, but don't risk becoming a pest by overdoing. Balance is everything.

And, as they say, that's it in a nutshell. It's probably not as difficult as you thought. Just remember to follow directions carefully, ask for help when you need it, and use your own creativity to put your unique stamp on yours.

If you'd if you'd like more exacting "under-the-hood" details for programming your database(s) you can view a video at: EasyWebAutomationVideos.com.

Here's a tip on Guerrilla automation in action by co-authors Mitch Meyerson and Mary Eule Scarborough, which Mitch included in his book, *Mastering Online Marketing* (2007, Entrepreneur Press).

The average person

living in a metropolitan area is exposed to more than 3,700 marketing messages a day. Studies also indicate that it can take as many as nine exposures for online consumers to become customers. Thus, follow-up is critical, and the best way to accomplish this is with automation.

"When I first decided to write my first marketing book, Success Secrets of the Online Marketing Superstars, *a compilation of personal interviews I conducted with 24 of the world's most successful e-commerce marketers (Dearborn 2005), I recognized I had a lot of work ahead of me before I'd ever see it in a bookstore.*

Yet I realized early on that the content I was collecting was perfect for a mini-course even before the book was written.

Now here's where it gets fun. I used my shopping cart/autoresponder system to create a sequential autoresponder-based mini-course that contained audio excerpts of the interviews I had completed (with permission, of course, from the experts). Each e-mail featured one superstar who provided solid and actionable tips.

I set up a good-looking web page explaining what they would get featuring all the benefits of the content in the audios. Within one year I had over 16,000 sign-ups! I subsequently used this list to mail announcements for my book when it was completed.

I still use this strategy to build my e-mail lists."

Once you get really good at this, you should consider creating autoresponders for products that they have purchased from you to get them to consume them as well as other offers, services, and the like. When you're ready, you'll want to set up targeted sub lists, which we'll discuss in the next section.

Using Autoresponders to Create Sublists and "Scratch Your Niches!"

As Guerrillas know, small businesses are more successful when they appeal to smaller segments rather than the masses. Keep this in mind, and try to carve out niches within your industry. Look for smaller pockets of interested consumers in narrower subgroups (particularly ones who may be finding it difficult to find the products or services they're looking for).

For instance, you'll do better if you reach out to "African violet growers" than "people who grow flowers." Remember this as you craft your opt-in offers; while it's okay to offer multiple distinct products to the same people, it's not a good idea to offer all of your products to the same people.

Moreover, you could reasonably assume that mothers of toddlers might be interested in potty training techniques (such as AskThePottyTrainer.com), innovative educational toys, and personalized musical CDs for kids. However, there's no reason to believe that this same group of consumers want tips on how to brew beer.

In cases like these you'd want to build a targeted sublist for each product or service. This is particularly critical for business people who operate multiple websites, which is becoming more and more common these days.

The power here is that you can send individual announcements to a targeted group of people interested in a specific topic. For example, I don't send marketing tips to someone who asked for songs! It makes each mailing more relevant which make the list more responsive. You'll want to do this even if you start with one list.

Offline Automation for Easy Follow-Up

If you're not quite ready for e-mail autoresponders or would like to stay in touch with your customers and prospects in multiple ways, consider placing your offline communication on autopilot as well.

Let's face it: It's difficult to automate offline communication even though most of us start with the best of intentions. We send out a batch of holiday greeting cards, welcome letters, or thank-you notes, and then stop after one mailing. However, nowadays there are very affordable web-based systems that work exactly like autoresponders except they generate postcards and greeting cards, instead of e-mails. Check out MomentsOfMagicCards.com. You can even send one for free, so give it a try. It's got one of the most powerful and user-friendly systems out there. They have loads of designs and you can even add custom touches such as your signature, photos and graphics, and personalized greetings. They even have a feature that allows you "write" messages in your own handwriting.

The most important thing to remember—regardless of the automation method you use—is this: Your customers are far more likely to remain loyal to your business and your prospects are far more likely to become your customers if you reach out to them consistently and frequently. And, if you fail to automate these vital communication streams, you're also far more likely to stop all together!

Now it's time for you to learn how to monitor your marketing efforts using state-of-the-art analytics technologies.

Tracking and Measuring

Guerrillas understand the importance of tracking, measuring, and analyzing all of their marketing efforts to ensure that they get a positive return on their investments and so they can double up on things that are working and discard ones that are not.

You can use automation software to track offline campaigns but it requires that you conduct some form of direct response advertising, which invites people to visit various landing pages that you've set up in advance. This process can get complicated so if you're a beginner take it slow and start with one or two at a time.

However, as we discussed in Chapter 5, it's imperative that you keep tabs on your website's key metrics. You should know how many people visit your site once and/or return two or more times, and the numbers who opt into your e-mail list. Then you'll want to compare with the numbers who instantly, or eventually, become customers and which communication messages and vehicles worked best. When armed with this type of information your odds of succeeding are significantly improved, because your decisions are based on actual behaviors—the best predictors of future behaviors—not random guesswork and

Tip:

Try using e-mail management programs such as Microsoft's Outlook or Entourage, Google's GMail, or Mozilla's Thunderbird to set up rules for managing and filing e-mails automatically.

intuition. This moves your marketing efforts out of the realm of "crapshoot" and into the much preferred "calculated risk" arena.

For example, years ago e-commerce marketers had a heck of time figuring out how many people opened their promotional e-mails and clicked through to their websites. Needless to say, this made it extremely difficult for them to know what, if anything, they needed to do to improve their results.

Nowadays, problems like this are easily solved using automated ad trackers that perform just what their name implies. Traditionally, ad trackers are software programs that are integrated into shopping cart programs or purchased as standalone products. Today, however, we strongly advise you to use Google's free Analytics tracking program—the same one we mentioned in Chapter 3.

Aside from the obvious cost-saving benefits you'll also be able to take advantage of their robust tracking and calculation tools, and much more.

Even better, they're simple to set up and quite easy to use—even for novices. Based on your individual needs, your first step will be to determine what to track. For example, let's assume that you have two great subject lines for the same e-mail and want to find out which one resonates better with your target audience. In this case, you'd set your trackers up to count the numbers of people who opened each and compare your results.

And this is just the beginning. After this you'd want to know how many people in each group converted to customers or opted into your list. Now imagine that you have three completely different e-mail campaigns going at the same time. Do you see how easy it would be to keep track of them all without going crazy?

By the way, it will be next to impossible for you to attract good online fusion partners unless you can provide them this type of objective and detailed information. Understandably, successful e-commerce entrepreneurs are increasingly protective over their coveted e-mail lists and are more reluctant than ever to risk their credibility by joint venturing with anyone who doesn't have their act together.

What Does the Future Look Like for Automation Technology?

The simple answer to this question is that none of us can be sure. However, we should keep in mind that online shopping carts and other types of automation technology are still relatively new. And if the recent past has taught us anything, it's a safe bet to assume that automation technology will continue to evolve and improve rapidly in the very near future. Before you know it, we'll be using these powerful resources in whole new ways.

GUERRILLA FIELDWORK

1. Decide what areas of your business can be automated, such as your payment system, customer communication, or product delivery process. Check out one of the one-stop shopping carts recommended in this chapter.

2. Go to EasyWebAutomationVideos.com and view the two videos to see how automation is done from the inside out.

In the next chapter, we'll show you how to add audio and video to your website and communicate with small or large groups of people combining inexpensive state-of-the-art technology with a little bit of creativity!

GUERRILLA MULTIMEDIA:
Using Audio and Video for Maximum Impact

Guerrillas have long known that excellent marketers focus on building long-term relationships with their customers. They also know that in order to accomplish this lofty goal they must make sincere emotional connections with their target audience, by appealing to both their right and left brains. These connections are enhanced when multiple senses are involved. That's why Guerrillas always take advantage of opportunities to dialogue with prospects and customers using visual and verbal media—especially on the internet.

It wasn't that long ago when large corporations were the only businesses that could afford audio and video commercials. Smaller companies simply could not afford to pay the exorbitant production and broadcasting costs, and therefore used other, less expensive communication vehicles. And even when cable TV made video commercials more affordable they were still out of reach for many small businesses.

Things have changed, however, and Guerrillas all over the world are using simple, inexpensive, and cutting-edge interfaces to reach out more effectively to

> ## "The world is
> but a canvas to the
> imagination."
> —Henry David Thoreau

their target audience. They are combining the internet and multi-media elements—audio and video—to add emotional impact to their marketing messages, demonstrate their products, hold meetings with people in far-away lands, showcase before-and-after transformations, teach classes to geographically diverse groups of students, and much more.

Also, due to the expansion of worldwide broadband connectivity, increased availability of powerful mobile devices, and innovative website formatting, they use web-based multimedia messaging to obtain real time information in record time, expand their business and social networks, and even entertain one another.

The term "multimedia" has been used to describe such communication vehicles as radio, animation, TV, graphics, and more. And while these are all valid forms of multimedia, we have narrowed our discussion in this chapter to audiovisual media used on the internet—namely **web audios, videos,** and **conferencing**. As you read through this chapter, think about all of the different ways you can use these affordable and flexible tools to drive more targeted traffic to your website, increase your website's visitors experiences, gather with small or large groups of people, educate your prospects and customers, and more. Also, keep in mind that today's internet users want information delivered how, when, and where they prefer—and increasing numbers of them are demanding audio and video delivery. Therefore, if you think that you can avoid adding audio and/or video to your website—or others—think again. The good news is that uploading multimedia files is painless, as long as you know what you're doing. We'll begin by walking you through the steps for creating your own audios, Guerrilla style.

Guerrilla Audios

Adding audio—narrative, voice-overs, music, and sound effects—to your website is a brilliant way to get your visitors excited about your company and its products and services. It's no secret that people are more emotionally engaged when they make use of multiple senses, instead of just one. If you needed more proof, just take a look at the skyrocketing popularity of multimedia websites such as YouTube, Squidoo, Google Video, and MySpace.

Guerrillas know that consumers have always preferred to do business with people they know, like, and trust, so the more you can do to let them know that you're a real flesh-and-blood person, the better. And for many it's far easier to converse verbally, than through the written word—especially when you let your passion, energy, and enthusiasm shine through.

Let your creativity run wild and think of ways audio can make your website visitors feel more welcomed and stay longer. Here are a few ideas to get you started.

- Record and upload customer testimonials (go to MitchMeyerson.com/consulting.htm if you'd like to listen to a sample of some).

- Point out areas of particular interest.

- Provide directions for navigating between pages.

- Reiterate your risk-free guarantee and privacy policies.

- Add music to energize or relax your guests or demo musical CDs (check out MitchSongs.com if you'd like to see this at work).

- Provide special messages such as holiday greetings, after-hours help, emergency instructions, or reminders.

- Publicize upcoming events and sales.

- Create streamable online recordings of teleseminars that students can download onto MP3 players and iPods.

- Add a personal audio greeting to your e-mails for extra pizzazz using video and audio postcards.

Once you've decided how you use your audio, your next steps will involve planning, creating, and uploading it to the internet. As we said earlier in this chapter, it's relatively simple process as long as you're armed with some practical knowledge and a few good tools. If you're a beginner, you'll maneuver the audio landscape more easily if you're armed with the following high-level background information.

First, there are two types of audio formats that are considered global standards: MP3 and Flash. Without going into unnecessary detail, each type takes huge audio files, like ones contained on a CD, and compresses them into much smaller ones, so they can be uploaded onto the internet easily and quickly.

MP3 is the most common audio format on the web; however, there are some limitations to posting audio on your website using this format. On some computers you will need a plug-in to play MP3 files, although most computers purchased in the last few years come loaded with players, such as Microsoft's Windows Media Player or Apple's iTunes. Conversely, Adobe's Flash formatting is as close as you can come to a foolproof audio—and video—delivery system. Even better, it's web-based technology that's imbedded into every major browser. What does that mean to you? Simply that nearly 100 percent of your website's visitors can use it instantly—without having to download anything—and will enjoy its instant playback feature and more reliable sound.

But don't worry if you're already using MP3-formatted audios. They can be converted to Flash format, which is something you should definitely consider. Websites such as InstantFlashAudio.com and AudioAcrobat.com can help you convert your MP3 files to Flash quickly—plus they have lots of other cool stuff you can check out while you're there.

Audio Equipment and Software Supply List

In order to get started, you'll need the following basic equipment and software:

1. **A microphone.** As we discussed in Chapter 5, you'll need a good medium-range USB-cable microphone, which are widely available in electronic and some department stores and online retailers.

2. **Recording software.** You'll find lots of inexpensive software all over the internet. Look for one that allows you to save your recording to an MP3 player or a computer. Make sure it comes with simple instructions, and a single-button recording option. Check out Sony's SoundForge if you own a PC or Apple's Garageband if you use a Mac. We

also like the software you can purchase at FiveMinuteWebAudio.com. It's really easy to use and you can get a great sounding audio up in less than ten minutes.

3. **Uploading software.** You'll need file transfer protocol (FTP) software to transfer your audio from your computer's hard drive to your website's hosting server. Software programs like Microsoft's FrontPage or Adobe's Dreamweaver come with FTP capabili-

> **Tip:**
> Using audio and video on your website will enhance your ability to meet the needs of all of your visitors. Merely hearing and seeing web copy is not enough.

ties. However, these software programs can be tricky for beginners, so if this is your situation you may want to hand this task off to your web developer or outsource it to a freelancer.

For the best recording equipment designed exclusively for the internet, visit OnlineMarketingSuperstore.com.

Alternatively, you can use web-based audio services like those found on websites like AudioAcrobat.com. Since audio files are stored on their servers, you can easily include live links in your e-mails and web pages, which lead "clickers" to the file's location where they can listen to the audio.

But Guerrillas know there's an even easier way to upload their audios onto the internet, and you don't have to know a thing about programming or have to download any special software. All you have to do is go to one of the bigger blog websites such as WordPress.com or Drupal.org. Once there you'll find tools in their administration sections that allow you to add audio or video to your blog or website instantly. You'll be asked to select the correct file from your computer's hard drive, and submit it. That's about all there is to it. Just think, its possible to have audio capability with just a couple of clicks of your mouse!

Guerrilla Videos

Once you've gotten the hang of audio, kick it up a notch and add digital video to your website. Given today's extraordinarily easy and inexpensive alternatives, there's no reason to avoid it. When you use web videos you add another compelling dimension to your communication. Not only will your visitors hear you, but they'll be able to see your warm smile and enthusiastic body language (we hope).

And don't assume that you have to be the one in front of the camera! As a matter of fact, if you want to create a great online video you must first objectively assess your presentation skills to determine if your "performance" will help, or hurt, you achieve your goals.

Even if you come up on the short end of the stick on this one, don't let that stop you, because you have lots of other options. For instance, you can shoot videos that demonstrate products, offer "real person" testimonials, present PowerPoint slides, conduct interviews, showcase action footage, address heartfelt issues, take visitors on exotic trips to faraway places, and much more. The goal is to share a part of yourself with your audience.

The list is endless; so after you learn and apply a few fundamental strategies, let your imagination run wild. And don't think that you have to be George Lucas. A single camera shot of you speaking in a room is perfectly fine. Here are just some of the ways you can use digital video to generate income on your website or upload it to one of the popular video websites such as YouTube, Joost, Revver, DailyMotion, Stickam, or Jumpcut.

Ten Best Guerrilla Online Video Strategies

If you adhere to the following ten video rules of thumb you'll be well on your way to an internet Oscar!

Rule 1 **Go viral.** The more people who view your video, the better. That's why your first goal is to get folks to pass it along to others. That means it must be entertaining and memorable (e.g., Lynn Jericho's theinnerchristmasmovie.com) because if it's boring, even your mom will be too embarrassed to pass it along. It also means that you need to clearly ask family, friends, and co-workers to send it to others.

Rule 2 **Make your video's meaning clear and keep it short.** If your viewers have to guess at your meaning, you're in trouble. Keep videos short and to the point. Don't create a mini-series; communicate what you want in laser fashion, preferably in less than five minutes if possible. It's better to produce a greater number of smaller videos than fewer longer ones.

Rule 3 — **Be your unassuming self.** Let "you" shine through. If you're funny, be funny. If you're warm and caring, act warm and caring. If you care passionately about something, say so. Don't hold back on what makes you unique. Will all of your viewers appreciate it? Most will, some won't. But don't worry about that too much because you'll have made a lifelong connection with the folks who do.

Rule 4 — **Include your website or blog's URL.** Take a page out of the book of TV's major networks and place your website's address in the lower right hand corner of your video screen and keep it there throughout. Also, add a larger version of it at the end and remind your viewers that they can "get more" there.

Rule 5 — **Make sure your viewers see themselves, not you.** We've said this many times before, but it's so important that it bears repeating. Your viewers don't care much about your impressive credentials (unless it means you're better able to help them), computer skills, or past jobs. They are concerned with their success, their problems, their lifestyle, their health, their sex appeal, and their relationships. That's why you must convincingly persuade them that they'd be foolish not to take you up on your offer to solve their most pressing problems.

Rule 6 — **Package your videos in with other informational products.** This is a wonderful way to add tremendous value, without adding tremendous costs. For example, if you sell an educational toy for children, why not include an instructional DVD as well? Alternatively, you might offer a password-protected video that can be streamed and downloaded directly from your website.

Rule 7 — **Capture your audience's attention from the get-go.** You have 15 to 30 seconds (tops!) to interest viewers in your online video. Give your audience a reason to stay right off the bat, or they won't hang around long. Video is not about telling your prospects everything about you. It's simply about capturing their attention, and THEN getting them to take the next step. So capture their fancy immediately, then let them know where and how to get more of you.

Rule 8 **Show them, don't tell them.** Don't pontificate! If you want to turn people off, tell them about your five-step process for nirvana. If you want to *excite people* (and my guess is that's why you're using video), give them a vivid, emotional, compelling vision of nirvana, and then invite them in.

Rule 9 **Jump on the YouTube bandwagon.** Tens of thousands of beginners and experts are using this Google website to showcase or hone their video skills, entertain or inform each other, and much more. And since access to the site is free and it's already attracted a captured audience, it's a great tool to add to your marketing weapons arsenal. What's more, YouTube's videos are categorized using keyword "tags" (we'll discuss these in more detail in the next chapter). This makes it easier for visitors to locate videos on specific topics, and means that you can expect an increase in targeted traffic to your website if you take advantage of this feature. Also, make sure you place a "share" button at the bottom of your video. This way, others can do the sharing for you!

Rule 10 **Grab your viewers' heartstrings, and never let go.** Don't just deliver information. Make sure your viewers *feel* something. Make them laugh. Make them cry. Make them outraged. Make them curious. Just don't make them numb.

Video Equipment and Software Supply List

1. **Video camcorder.** Unless your computer is relatively new—in which case it may have a camera installed already—you'll need an inexpensive camcorder. You can purchase a decent webcam for $50 or less. Since videos are also compressed and formatted for internet use, you'll lose the enhanced picture and sound quality that high-end cameras allow, so don't waste money buying the pricier versions.

2. **Microphone.** Use the same we provided earlier in this chapter under *Audio Equipment and Software Supply List*.

3. **Editing software.** There are plenty of video and audio editing software packages available, both high end and shareware. Try Windows' Movie Maker or the Macintosh equivalent, iMovie. Visit OnlineMarketingSuperstore.com for hardware and software options.

4. **Uploading software.** Use the guidelines we provided previously in this chapter under *Audio Equipment and Software Supply List.*

Telephone and Web-Based Seminars and Conferences

Teleseminars and teleconferences are growing in popularity, especially among Guerrillas, because they simply make great sense! However, since they're very similar, the terms themselves can be confusing so we'll begin by clearing away any lingering fog that may exist regarding their definitions.

For starters, both teleseminars and teleconferences are conducted over telephones (thus the "tele" prefix). And as their names further imply, teleseminars are live training sessions—classes, workshops, and the like—and teleconferences are live group meetings. It's that simple.

In either case, small or large groups of participants from just about anywhere in the world dial into predetermined conference bridge numbers and take part in real-time sessions which may, or may not, include additional visual internet support, making them a great alternative to in-person get-togethers.

And if you're assuming that conference calls are too pricey for small businesspeople, think again. There are several good free services available (check out FreeConferenceCall.com). For more options, go to Google and search under "free conference" calls.

If you need more versatility, we recommend that you choose from one of the many affordable but extremely reliable companies, such as EasyLiveConference.com. These companies build in fantastic "credibility-building" convenience features and options into their basic plans, many of

Tip:
It's a good idea to use landline phones for teleconferences. You'll experience fewer sound quality and connection problems.

which they include free. These features include expanded web conferencing capabilities (for adding PowerPoint presentations and monitoring callers online), desktop controls for managing individual callers, reduced international phone rates, toll-free number access, and question-and-answer tools.

Most services provide dial-in numbers with separate access codes for moderators and participants for added security. Additionally, participants are usually placed on hold until the moderator(s) arrive. All you'll need to get started is a service provider and phone—although a good quality headset is also great to have. Also, make sure that your provider offers real-time support in case you have problems during a call, provides instructions for getting around firewall barriers, and uses software that works equally well with Macs and PCs.

And while teleseminars and teleconferences are viable alternatives for many face-to-face gatherings, they are not a one-size-fits-all solution for every occasion. Simply said, there will be times when you'll want to go one step better and add additional layers of interactivity and intimacy and host **web conferences**—real time web-based audio-visual meetings— or **webinars**—teacher-led seminars that use the same internet technology.

Today's state-of-the-art internet technologies and software make it effortless for groups of people to convene "face-to-face" anytime, any place.

Guerrillas love web-based meetings because they can share files and presentations, demonstrate how to use products, hold question and answer sessions and the like. Imagine the power of bringing remote work teams together to collaborate, plan, and brainstorm, on the spot. That is the clout of web conferencing technology.

If you'd like to see web conferencing in action, visit easyliveconference.com and take a look at their demo video.

Why pack bags, rush to the airport, and wait in long security lines when you can teach or take classes, deliver instructional materials, and/or train employees from the comfort of your own home, or anywhere else you might be? Guerrillas love this kind of flexibility and convenience—and they also love saving money and increasing profits. So audio and/or video meetings make great Guerrilla Marketing weapons, which can help you:

- **Generate more income.** Transform older products such as e-books, workshops, and/or other instructional materials into fee-paid interactive teleseminars.

- **Build your e-mail list.** Offer free mini-teleseminars to prospects who provide their names and e-mail addresses on your website.

- **Enhance your customers' experiences.** Host live question and answer sessions with customers looking for additional support, troubleshooting advice, and/or more detailed instructions on your product and service offerings.

- **Avoid last-minute stress.** The days of reserving space and scheduling conference calls weeks or months in advance are over. These days you can schedule calls instantly, which can be accessed by anyone with a landline or cell phone. Your conference bridge is available for use 24/7 so there's no stress involved in setting up emergency conference calls.

- **Improve efficiency.** It doesn't make sense to wait weeks to communicate important information to groups of people when it can be accomplished right away using teleseminars and teleconferences.

- **Record your classes and/or meetings.** Most conference calling services include recording capabilities in their basic product packages. This makes it easy for participants who missed meetings or classes to hear what they've missed. Plus you can add your teleseminar recordings to your marketing kit to show off your teaching skills.

> **Be sure to test**
> all phone lines, access codes, and recording capabilities prior to hosting a teleconference or teleseminar. It's far easier to prevent problems beforehand than to try and fix them during the call.

As you can see, affordable state-of-the-art technologies allow Guerrillas to gather with groups of people for just about any reason. Also, use your imagination and come up with ways to take advantage of incredible software and web-based programs to add pizzazz to your website, demonstrate your products, stay in touch with clients, and make genuine connections with likeminded people.

On the next page is a summary of the website resources we cited in this chapter, as well as several more (Figure 7.1). Use this resource to help you create audios and videos, and conduct teleconferences and teleseminars.

Figure 8.1 Web Resources for Audio and Video

Audio Creation, Recording, Editing, and/or Sharing Software and Equipment

OnlineMarketingSuperstore.com

InstantFlashAudio.com

CopyTalk.com

SonicMemo.com

SonyCreativeSoftware.com

Plantronics.com

Audio Uploading Software

Microsoft.com—FrontPage

Adobe.com—Dreamweaver

Audio Editing

Adobe.com/special

Audacity.Sourceforge.net

GigaVox.com

Audio Equipment

WebAudioVideoTools.com

Real.com

Audio Recording

SoundForge.com

Garageband.com (for Macs)

AudioStrategies.com

TelephoneRecording.com

Audio Sharing

iTunes.com

Rhapsody.com

Video Equipment and Software

OnlineMarketingSuperstore.com

InstantVideoGenerator.com

Microsoft.com—Windows' Movie Maker

Apple.com—Macintosh's iMovie

Video Websites

YouTube.com

Squidoo.com

Joost.com

Revver.com

DailyMotion.com

Stickam.com

Jumpcut.com

GoogleVideo.com

MySpace.com

Teleconferencing Tools and Bridges

Camtasia.com

Moodle.com

EasyLiveConference.com

FreeConferenceCall.com

teleconferenceline.com

GUERRILLA FIELDWORK

1. Go to YouTube.com and view videos in your niche. Create and upload one of your own.

2. Go to WebAudioVideoTools.com and get more information on the best audio and video tools for the internet.

In the next chapter, we'll spill the beans on the top 20 Guerrilla online marketing weapons—as well as divulge our first-ever list of over 150 more!

CHAPTER 9

GUERRILLA
Internet Weapons

Since 1984, untold numbers of entrepreneurs all over the world have learned Guerrilla Marketing principles and applied them to grow their businesses profitably. The brand has earned their trust principally because its tenets fly in the face of old school, traditional marketing mindsets and actions that simply don't resonate, or work, for small businesspeople.

Therefore, unlike many entrepreneurs, Guerrillas do not believe in conventional and widely accepted marketing myths such as "advertising works," "websites work," "direct mail works," or "radio works." Rather, they know that advertising doesn't work, websites don't work, direct mail doesn't work, and business cards don't work.

You're probably wondering if we're serious. We are. But now that we've got you completely confused, we'll explain. Simply put, no single form of online or offline advertising works; it is **marketing combinations** that work. And while

> **"Be daring,
> be different,**
> be impractical, be anything
> that will assert integrity of
> purpose and imaginative
> vision against the play-it-safers,
> the creatures of the common-
> place, the slaves of the
> ordinary."
> —Cecil Beaton

this has always been the case, it's even more important in today's fast-paced internet world.

Think of it this way: Regardless of whether your business is solely online, offline, or somewhere in between, you should use an assortment of weapons to reach your target audience. To do otherwise is foolish.

For instance, online marketers can use classified ads and billboards to drive traffic to their websites. Brick-and-mortar companies can use their websites to showcase their products and service, provide directions to their location, and/or advertise sales. Or how about retailers who run newspaper and radio ads directing people to their website, and use their website to encourage guests to visit their store locations? Talk about combining efforts!

These are just two of the hundreds of low-cost and highly effective techniques that we'll discuss in this chapter. Up to this point we've focused on teaching you ways to use the internet and state-of-the-art technology to help you generate income. We've talked about blogs, e-mails, website design and navigation, podcasting, opt-ins, and much more. But now it's time to get creative and learn how to generate even more income by combining hundreds of affordable online and offline weapons such as referral programs, fusion marketing partnerships, advertising vehicles, involvement devices, and more.

And while we suggest that you consider each and every one of the marketing weapons we include in this chapter, you'll ultimately have to cut the list down to those that are most appropriate for you and your business, target audience, and resources. But once you've done this, act; because when you experience the synergistic effect that combining two surefire marketing methods with two other surefire marketing methods, you'll quickly learn that it adds up to a lot more than four.

The secret to growing business profitability lies in understanding and applying time-tested marketing concepts, developing a plan that effectively uses limited resources for maximum results, and combining the right marketing message with the best marketing media. This is the Guerrilla truth. That's why we've devoted this chapter to going over the very best online Guerrilla Marketing weapons. So let's get started.

Choosing Your Marketing Weapons

First and foremost, you should be looking for online and offline communication vehicles that make the most sense for your business. For example, retailers might use newspaper ads that direct readers to their websites for product demonstration and directions, but lawyers might do better with online directories.

Regardless of the specific method you choose, it's vitally important that you select ones that offer you the highest return on your investment. This means that you want to choose a medium that delivers your marketing message to your target audience at the lowest possible cost.

So before you do anything, you must have intimate knowledge of your target audience, a compelling message and offer, and products and services they want. After that, it's time to think about how you'll reach them.

Here are some fundamental tips for choosing the right weapons for your business.

- **Select low-cost or free weapons first.** Why spend money when you don't have to? There are hundreds of ways to promote your business without spending a dime (and we've included many of them in the checklist at the end of this chapter).

- **Choose weapons that are suitable for your target audience.** For instance, it makes no sense to advertise your retirement community using a fast-paced, loud, radio spot on a hip-hop station—no matter what the salesperson says!

- **Understand that quality is more important than quantity.** Unless your target audience is broad, it's best to choose 1-2 primary weapons—especially if you're paying for them.

Tip:

Guerrillas launch their attack confidently, but not too fast. Their attack is deep and broad, but they're more interested in control than speed. Guerrillas do not have trigger fingers.

- **Check out other companies in your industry.** Find out what your competitors are using. If you see the same methods over and over again, it's a safe bet that they're working well.

- **Choose methods according to cost, targeting, and response.** Any campaign can be broken down into costs per thousand. If you're using direct response advertising (which you should) benchmark your success using costs per sale. Your expenses include cost of design (also known as creative), producing or printing your ad (production), and placement (radio, print ads, direct mail, list purchase, etc.), and postage.

If you find the number of choices overwhelming, begin with the following 20 best online marketing weapons (Figure 9.1). Most of them have already been covered in other chapters of this book but they're worth mentioning again. Others, such as Web 2.0 weapons, will be discussed in the next chapter.

Keep in mind that these are only 20—albeit the most important—internet marketing weapons that you can use to help you generate substantial income, even if you're operating on a tight budget. They will save you a great deal of time, money and stress.

There are hundreds more. Figure 9.2 is a quick-reference list of over 150 additional valuable and low-cost Guerrilla internet marketing weapons that you can include in your arsenal. Some will save you money, some will save you time, some will save you stress, and some will be just plain fun. Others will have an immediate and direct result on your ability to generate cash, while some will work to increase your visibility and generate leads. And still others will do several things all at once. However, all of them will help you use the internet to improve the way you do business and increase your profits.

So look over this list carefully and choose the ones that are most interesting, relevant and actionable for your situation. Then, after prioritizing (high, medium, or low), pick ones that have the most relevance to your business and try them! You have nothing to lose and much to gain, so go for it.

Tip:

Some of the weapons you use will hit dead center of the bull's eye. Others will miss the target by a mile. But if you keep track, you'll know how to get twice as much out of the winners and stop wasting time and money on the losers.

Figure 9.1 The Top 20 Internet Guerrilla Marketing Weapons

INTERNET WEAPONS	BENEFITS
1. Guerrilla Marketing internet knowledge and mindset	Grow and maintain profitable business using more time, knowledge, and imagination, and less money.
2. A well-researched written plan for marketing on the internet	Your odds for achieving your goals will increase substantially.
3. A professional-looking and easy-to-use website	Generates income—online, offline, or both.
4. Keyword-rich domain name(s)	Makes it easy for people and search engines to find, and remember, your website.
5. Effective Search Engine Optimization (SEO) strategies	Moves your website closer to the top of search engine results' lists.
6. Compelling and well-written direct response sales letter	Makes it more likely that prospects will act as invited.
7. Ad-tracking software to measure opt-in and sales conversions	Tells you what's working well and what isn't so you can earn—and save—more money.
8. Blogs	Search engines—and people—love these affordable, flexible, self-publishing additions (or replacements) to traditional websites.
9. Autoresponders	Follow up and stay in touch with large, and diverse, groups of people without lifting a finger.
10. All-in-one shopping carts	Eliminates the need to purchase and set up separate payment, communication, and tracking automation software and ensures that all elements work in harmony with each other.
11. E-mail campaigns	Highly effective and free way to get more people to visit your site—especially if you add cool elements like video.
12. E-mail list-building strategies that combine opt-in opportunities with compelling offers	Increases the pool of interested prospects and begins the relationship building process.

Figure 9.1 The Top 20 Internet Guerrilla Marketing Weapons (continued)	
INTERNET WEAPONS	**BENEFITS**
13. Multimedia: Audio and video to enhance communication	Enhances visitors' experiences by engaging multiple senses, makes product demonstrations more effective.
14. Fusion marketing partnerships—joint venture and strategic alliances	Allows people to share the work and wealth by joining forces.
15. Podcasts and nanocasts	Cost-effective vehicles for repurposing and repackaging existing products and increasing brand awareness and visibility.
16. Teleseminars, teleconferences, and webinars	Offers many of the same benefits as face-to-face communication far less expensively; allows global participation in meetings and classes.
17. Involvement Devices: wikis, surveys, polls, forums, blogs	Enhances the relationship-building process by transforming traditional one-way web conversations into two-way dialogues.
18. Affiliate Programs—Yours and others'	Allows website owners to hire an army of salespeople without hiring employees and allows website owners to earn money on other people's products and services.
19. Web 2.0 Social Media	Provides everyone the opportunity to expand their personal and business networks globally.
20. Outsourcing—Building a Virtual Team	Cost effective to outsource routine administrative duties to ensure that business owners are free to spend time where it counts most.

Figure 9.2 Guerrilla Marketing on the Internet Weapons

TACTIC/ACTION	PRIORITY
1. Place a classified ad that directs people to your website to obtain value-added information.	
2. Open a PayPal account (PayPal.com).	
3. Create two-sided business cards with your website's address in big, bold letters.	
4. Have your logo designed inexpensively (check out scriptlance.com).	
5. Produce a podcast and upload it to iTunes.	
6. Develop a bumper sticker with your website address emblazoned in bold letters.	
7. Join your local Chamber of Commerce and offer a one-hour presentation on what you learned in *Guerrilla Marketing on the Internet*.	
9. Visit websites such as Affiliatescout.com and Affiliateprograms.com to learn more about affiliate programs.	
10. Offer discount coupon codes for online purchases.	
11. Subscribe to your industry's online newsletters and trade magazines.	
12. Write and upload a "tell-a-friend" script and offer incentive for customers who refer others.	
13. Go to TeleClass.com and check out their list of free classes.	
14. Gather customer testimonials and include them on all of your website pages.	
15. Go to Skype.com and download their program so you can call anyone in the world computer-to-computer for free (and national and international landlines for as low as two cents/minute).	
16. Tie your company to a local or national story and issue an online press release (check out: PRWeb.com).	
17. Visit Technocrati.com and find out what people are blogging about.	
18. Add a frequently asked questions page to your web site.	

Figure 9.2 Guerrilla Marketing on the Internet Weapons (continued)	
TACTIC/ACTION	**PRIORITY**
19. Collect your website's visitors' e-mail addresses using an opt-in box.	
20. Visit websites such as ClickBank.com, cj.com, or PayDotCom.com to find cool affiliate products.	
21. Create company t-shirts, hats, and name tags and put your website address on them.	
22. Provide directions to your location easily by adding a link to Google maps (maps.google.com).	
23. Offer to write columns for relevant associations' websites.	
24. Write and submit online articles with links to your website (SubmitYourArticle.com).	
25. Use free internet e-mail management programs such as Google's Gmail or Firefox's Thunderbird.	
26. Opt-in to your competitors' websites and see what they're offering.	
27. Write a customer welcome e-mail and automate deliveries using your shopping cart software.	
28. Take photos of your products and upload them to your website.	
29. Add your photo to your website.	
30. Pick one day a week to add two articles with great content to your website.	
31. Download letter writing, planning, and financial templates to help with repetitive work. (Check out TheProcrastinatorsGuideToMarketing.com)	
32. Outsource projects and task through Elance.com, Scriptlance.com, Contentdivas.com, or Rentacoder.com.	
33. Automate your website using a one-stop-shop shopping cart. (Check out EasyWebAutomation.com)	
34. Send video e-mails to customers and prospects (Check out Helloworld.com.)	
35. Enroll in a business or marketing tele-seminar or webinar (Check out Ideas-to-Income.com)	

| Figure 9.2 Guerrilla Marketing on the Internet Weapons (continued) ||
TACTIC/ACTION	PRIORITY
36. Write at least one personal e-mail to a high-value customer each day.	
37. Create a product demonstration video and upload it onto YouTube.com.	
38. Repackage and/or repurpose digital content for supplemental sales (e.g., MP3 audios, seminars, e-books).	
39. Create a marketing calendar that includes your offline and online marketing activities.	
40. Follow up promotional e-mails with phone calls.	
41. Expand your social network by opening a FaceBook.com, Squidoo.com or MySpace.com account.	
42. Place an ad that invites readers to visit your website in the local or regional section of a national magazine.	
43. Let prospects test before they buy—provide free product samples.	
44. Participate in online forums or blogs.	
45. Bundle "natural" products or services and offer discounts.	
46. Use billboards to broadcast your website's address.	
47. Update the look and feel of your website.	
48. Organize your work area so you can be more efficient—this includes your computer's desktop.	
49. Learn ways to master the clock and calendar, set a time for 1-3 hrs a day of priority productive time.	
50. Use web-based programs such as SendOutCards.com to have birthday, holiday, and/or general greeting cards mailed automatically to friends, family members, colleagues, and customers.	
51. Hire a virtual assistant.	
52. Go to Roboform.com and check into purchasing software that will fill in your passwords and personal information on websites.	
53. Minimize stress by exercising daily.	

Figure 9.2 Guerrilla Marketing on the Internet Weapons (continued)	
TACTIC/ACTION	**PRIORITY**
54. Enroll in a computer class at your local community college to improve your efficiency with programs such as Microsoft Excel, PowerPoint, or Adobe Acrobat.	
55. Get inspired—take a break from your computer to read, meditate, walk, etc.	
56. Find relevant e-zine directories for your business at sites such as EZineseek.com and Topica.com.	
57. Auction something on eBay.com.	
58. Visit BCentral.com—they have lots of great free tools and information for small businesses.	
59. Conduct a search on Dogpile.com—it's the search engine for search engines!	
60. Redesign your website for easier navigation.	
61. Document your business processes using software like SmartDraw (SmartDraw.com).	
62. View and download PDF files—Try Adobe.com.	
63. Check into software that allows your customers to pay their bills online.	
64. Get free downloads for Windows operating system at Downloads.com.	
65. Use an affordable template to redesign your website (Luckymarble.com or Bigwebmaster.com).	
66. Convert a newspaper or magazine ad into a JPG graphic and post it on your website.	
67. Use commuter signage—on buses, streets, and subway stations—to advertise your website's URL.	
68. Ask other reputable website owners to link into yours to get back links.	
69. Go to Bizstats.com to obtain retail benchmarks for your industry.	
70. Check out the blog platforms at Drupal.org, Joomla.org, and WordPress.com.	

Figure 9.2 Guerrilla Marketing on the Internet Weapons (continued)	
TACTIC/ACTION	**PRIORITY**
71. Ask customers how they heard about your business and track their answers.	
72. Create a podcast and upload it to ichat.com.	
73. Offer online gift certificates.	
74. Use content voting sites such as Diggs.com and Shoutwire.com	
75. Analyze the effectiveness of your Yellow Page ad and make adjustments.	
76. Conduct video sales training.	
77. Text message a friend just for fun.	
78. Check out open source Content Management Systems such as Joomla.org, and Drupal.org.	
79. Submit your website to appropriate internet directories.	
80. Go to Sketchcast.com and download their free webinar software tool.	
81. Develop and maintain strategic partnerships with like-minded people and companies.	
82. Conduct regular weekly sales training with your employees to increase online and offline sales.	
83. Create your company's USP, slogan, and elevator speech.	
84. Create product price sheets and upload them onto your website.	
85. Have a sign made for your vehicle with your website's address on it.	
86. Write relevant industry white papers for your target audience and upload them to your website.	
87. Barter for products and services you want or need.	
88. Add a product discount coupon to your newspaper ad for customers who purchase online.	
89. Sponsor a local community or charitable event and publicize it on your website.	
90. Create buzz and expand your mailing list using contests.	

Figure 9.2 Guerrilla Marketing on the Internet Weapons (continued)	
TACTIC/ACTION	**PRIORITY**
91. Check out the free widgets on Apple.com and add some to your website.	
92. Create a product demonstration video and add it to your web site.	
93. Serve on a local company or organization's Board of Directors.	
94. Organize a local leads group with like-minded professionals.	
95. Back up your entire computer using affordable software at Carbonite.com.	
96. Provide outbound links from your website to others.	
97. Update your computer system every two to three years.	
98. Offer free 30-minute "no-sales-pitch" consultations to interested prospects.	
99. E-mail useful tips to your customers and prospects regularly.	
100. Have your web site optimized for search engines and visitors.	
101. Ask your customers what they want using online surveys.	
102. Create a tell-a-friend script and upload it onto your website.	
103. Replace your traditional website with a free blog site.	
104. Use Google's free analytics program.	
105. Join your college alumni association.	
106. Use anywho.com to find people and businesses.	
107. Create a perception map to see where you stand with prospects and customers.	
108. Visit DnB.com to find affordable business reports and check out their small business section while you're there.	
109. Check out the free office suite on OpenOffice.org.	
110. Conduct an internet radio interview with a well-known person in your industry, then upload it to your website and others.	
111. Create your own online affiliate program and participate in others.	
112. Write an e-book.	

Figure 9.2 Guerrilla Marketing on the Internet Weapons (continued)	
TACTIC/ACTION	**PRIORITY**
113. Listen to educational tapes or CDs during your commute to and from work.	
114. Submit a press release to PRWeb.com.	
115. Check out recording equipment for the web at WebAudioVideoTools.com.	
116. Conduct customer polls using web-based software on AskDatabase.com or SurveyMonkey.com.	
117. Have a super-duper one-day sale and advertise it on your website.	
118. Read a good internet marketing book every six months.	
119. Update your phone system to take advantage of new technologies.	
120. Choose two family members, friends, or colleagues to call or e-mail each day.	
121. Put a portable magnetic sign—with your website's URL—on your vehicle.	
122. Go online and learn more about the Web 2.0 technologies and culture—you'll be amazed.	
123. Offer spiffs for online referrals.	
124. Use soft pop-ups on your website to announce specials.	
125. Learn more about online marketing strategies at MasteringOnlineMarketing.com.	
126. Frame and hang your credentials on your wall—and include them on your website—to continually remind yourself that you are the expert.	
127. Add a shopping cart to your website (check out EasyWebAutomation.com).	
128. Barter!	
129. Offer an automatic payment option to your customers using web-based software.	
130. Develop and communicate your company's ironclad guarantee on your website.	

Figure 9.2 Guerrilla Marketing on the Internet Weapons (continued)	
TACTIC/ACTION	**PRIORITY**
131. Conduct ongoing "lessons learned" debriefing sessions with employees.	
132. Join a local health club and exercise often.	
133. Participate in your prospects' and customers' trade organizations, not just your own.	
134. Write and implement a strategic and tactical marketing plan.	
135. Conduct web-based seminars or teleconferences.	
136. Go to Skype.com and download their software that allows you to call computer-to-computer for free.	
137. Join a local Toastmasters International group to improve your presentation skills (Toastmasters.org).	
138. Offer logical supplemental products or services to your existing customers.	
139. Deliver on your promised customer experience.	
140. Surprise your best customers with a no-strings-attached gift.	
141. Reach out to smaller groups (niches) along with your targeted market.	
142. Use internet viral marketing to increase traffic to your website.	
143. Record and combine soothing on-hold music with useful marketing messages.	
144. Provide employees with customer-care scripts and job aids.	
145. Traveling on business? Save time by downloading your boarding pass before you leave home.	
146. Subscribe to Audible.com and listen to books while you're exercising, commuting, or cooking.	
147. Advertise your services on elance.com, guru.com, or kasamba.com.	
148. Offer a teleseminar on a subject your target audience would like.	

Figure 9.2 Guerrilla Marketing on the Internet Weapons (continued)	
TACTIC/ACTION	**PRIORITY**
149. Whenever possible, use environmentally friendly products, services, and processes—go green!	
150. Use an automated keep-in-touch strategy.	
151. Download some of the cool extension tools offered on Firefox.	
152. Donate used computer equipment to a local charity.	
153. Go to alexa.com and see how your website ranks.	
154. Visit Backlinks.com and see how many other websites link into yours.	
155. Go to link building sites like Outpost-earth.com and MyBlogLog.com.	
156. Upload photos to FaceBook.com or PhotoBucket.com.	
157. Create a "lens" on Squidoo.com.	
158. Create and execute an online mystery shopper's program.	
159. Provide online discount coupon codes.	
160. Develop a FAQ resource library on your website.	
161. Use conference calling services to connect with vendors, suppliers, franchisees, etc.	
162. Get help with driving traffic to your website at OnlineTrafficNow.com.	
163. Check out hosting companies like SuperstarHostingandDomains.com, NetworkSolutions.com, and BlackWireHosting.com.	
164. Use open source software as a free alternative.	
165. Submit articles to SubmitYourArticle.com, Ezine.com, GoArticles.com, or ArticlesAlley.com.	
166. Use the free web-meeting software at dimdim.com.	
167. Repackage and repurpose existing online products.	
168. Subscribe to your competitors' newsletters.	
169. Subscribe to a book summary club that summarizes business books (executivebooksummaries.com).	

Figure 9.2 Guerrilla Marketing on the Internet Weapons (continued)	
TACTIC/ACTION	**PRIORITY**
170. Add Google Page Rank to your browser tool bar (Google-pagerank.net)	
171. Visit several sites that use audio and make notes about what you like or dislike about them. Start with Ezinequeen.com, MitchSongs.com, and AudaciousAudio.com.	
172. Check out the audio creation services at InstantFlashAudio.com and AudioAcrobat.com.	
173. Visit InternetVideoGuy.com and CarpetDepotDecatur.com. Check out their videos and make notes about what you like and dislike about them.	
174. Learn more about teleconferencing by visiting FreeConferenceCall.com, EasyLiveConference.com, or Google "teleconferencing."	
175. Research your competitors' websites, keywords, and meta tags.	

As you can see, we've provided a multitude of effective Guerrilla tactics and strategies that you can use right this very minute (but not all at once, please!) to jumpstart your internet marketing efforts. Your most challenging task will be to stay focused, so don't take on too many. It's a good idea to start with one or two a day until you get comfortable. Remember, Rome wasn't built in a day. Be patient and take it one logical step at a time.

GUERRILLA FIELDWORK

1. Go to GMarketingInternet.com and print out the Guerrilla Marketing weapons listed above. Use this list as a tracking system for your own internet marketing efforts.

2. Use your imagination to create five to ten additional online marketing weapons that are appropriate for your industry niche.

In the next chapter, we'll expand our discussion on Guerrilla internet marketing weapons and zero in on Web 2.0 technologies and culture. We'll show you how to use social media to expand your business and personal networks, introduce you to new websites, and explore the fresh new internet culture.

THE WEB 2.0
Guerrilla

Internet technology and software continue to change at a dizzying pace, leaving more than just few of the 1 billion global internet users confused and overwhelmed. Why it wasn't more than a few years ago—or so it seems—that many of us purchased our first computers and began integrating them into our daily lives. This was particularly daunting for those of us who were used to writing with pen and paper or typewriters, and talking in person or over the phone.

If you can identify with this, you may also remember how thrilling it was to perform mundane tasks, such as sending and receiving e-mails, creating PowerPoint presentations and Excel spreadsheets, downloading software, and connecting to the internet without too many problems. However, just as soon as some of us conquered the basics we realized that we were three years behind some others who were already creating more robust websites, adding video and audio, using autoresponders, blogging, and the like.

And for Guerrilla Marketers, it wasn't much different. Many of us were happy to get our websites up and running, publish an online article or two, and have

"A journey
of a thousand sites begins
with a single click."
—Author Unknown

an operational shopping cart. The fact that Guerrillas gained proficiency in these types of techniques placed them way ahead of the curve. In other words, during the World Wide Web's infancy, which we'll call Web 1.0, most of us were focused on learning how to connect with technology and equipment—software programs, computers, and the internet.

But this isn't good enough anymore. Guerrillas say "Bring it on!" They understand that the seismic advances in internet technology have made possible the social revolution known as "Web 2.0." Guerrillas have always believed in the collective power of the everyman and everywoman, and now they are witnessing a cultural phenomenon where ordinary citizens use state-of-the-art technologies to participate in global discussions, expand their personal and professional networks, share information and opinions worldwide, create and publish books, videos, and audios, and much more. We are experiencing a sizable and growing shift in the ways people relate to their computers and most importantly, the internet. Simply put, growing numbers of people are using the internet to connect with people, not technology.

Let's face it, human beings are social creatures; we have been for thousands of years and will be so for all of eternity. So it was inevitable that the internet would evolve more and more into a social medium. Today's Web 2.0 social media culture, which has put the development, advertising, and allocation of information, products and services into a tailspin—is really just human nature at work (even though extremely sophisticated and very cool under-the-hood technology make it possible).

There was a time when the internet was dominated by one-way conversations; web owners talked, visitors listened. Hollywood advertised its blockbuster movies on the internet and elsewhere and the public had only two choices: Take them or leave them. Politicians and VIPs felt free to say one thing on camera, and something completely different after the cameras stopped rolling—as long as a journalist wasn't within ear shot. Big companies catered to the masses; if your likes and dislikes were outside of the norm, you were ignored.

But Web 2.0 is changing the status quo person by person. Now blasts of user-generated information are transforming the business, media, and marketing landscapes and creating brighter opportunities for entrepreneurs and individuals all over the world. Consider this:

- According to a June 2007 eMarketer report, approximately $1 billion in online revenues were generated in 2007—up from $450 million in 2006—and projected to exceed $43 billion by 2011.

- 40 percent of Rhapsody sales come from products not in retail stores.

- According to Technorati.com, there are over 55 million blogs today.

If you're serious about growing a profitable business, you must be ready to embrace this fresh new internet culture and use emerging state-of-the-art tools and strategies to stay one step ahead of your prospects, customers, and competition.

This is such an important point that it deserves its own chapter—and could very well be an entire book. So given our space limitations, we'll only hit the highlights of Web 2.0 culture and technology but also provide lots of additional resources for those of you who want to learn more. But first, what exactly is Web 2.0?

Web 2.0 Simplified

If you're like many entrepreneurs, you've probably heard the term but are still not sure of its precise definition. That's entirely understandable. Pundits still debate its meaning in magazines, newspapers, talk shows, and blogs, keeping it a hot topic of conversation and a moving target.

Therefore, it may be clearer if we begin with what Web 2.0 *is not*, first. Web 2.0 is not:

- a piece of software
- a particular type of technology
- a website
- a company
- a think tank
- computer program upgrade
- a club
- a product
- a person
- a fad

So, now that you know what Web 2.0 *isn't*, you're probably wondering what it *is*. Well, it's not that easy because a precise definition doesn't exist. Instead, Web 2.0 can best be described as the second iteration of internet technologies and human interaction—one where people are encouraged to move beyond standard ways of communicating on the internet and use widely available, affordable, and interactive web-hosted services to share and collaborate with likeminded individuals and groups.

The name was first used during a 2003 O'Reilly Media and MediaLive International brainstorming meeting. The following year it became the name for a landmark industry conference.

According to company CEO Tim O'Reilly, "Web 2.0 is the business revolution in the computer industry caused by the move to the internet as platform, and an attempt to understand the rules for success on that new platform."

But don't mistake this to mean that "Web 1.0" is a thing of the past. Everything you're currently doing and experiencing on the internet will not become obsolete any time soon and you'll be right back at square one. Web 2.0 isn't better than Web 1.0, it just makes it easier and less expensive for Guerrilla Marketers—and others—to use the internet in the ways they choose.

In the following sections, we provide a crash course in Web 2.0's social media culture and focus on three key areas:

1. Web 2.0 Culture and Mindset Shifts

2. Using Web 2.0 Tools to Grow Your Business

3. The Best-of-the-Best Web 2.0 Sites

As we go through them, keep in mind that each are intertwined and dependent upon the others. But one thing is for sure: They all begin in our minds.

The Web 2.0 Culture and Mindset Shift

All positive cultural changes begin when growing numbers of people challenge their old way of thinking, articulate a healthier philosophy, and empower themselves and others to achieve significant paradigm shifts. This is exactly how the internet's fresh new culture started and why it continues to grow. But remember, Web 1.0 hasn't disappeared altogether—it's merely fading into the background. And while there are still millions of people that believe in the older "winner take all" business model, many are tossing it aside in favor of something better. And since Guerrillas have embraced these tenets since 1984, they're eager to expand their collaborative marketing efforts with the rest of the world!

Try It!
Pick at least two social media websites and reach out to two new "friends" at least three times a week. You'll be surprised at how quickly your network will grow.

One of the best ways to visualize this new mindset is by demonstrating how it's changed what real people see, and how they interact and use the internet. That's why we created the chart on the next page (Figure 10.1). It provides a straightforward comparison between "what was then" and "what is now."

As the saying goes, "What's old is new again." The innovative, technology-driven Web 2.0 internet culture is in large part a return to a kinder, more collaborative time where:

- genuine relationships are valued over bean counting

- substance is valued over glitz

- honesty is valued over hucksterism

- time, energy, imagination, and knowledge are valued over money

- cooperation is valued over competition

- collaboration, teamwork, and sharing are valued over going it alone.

Now that you have a better understanding of the new internet culture, it's time to learn more about its tools— the technology, strategies, and websites you can use to help achieve your goals.

We'll begin by providing a high-level tutorial on basic Web 2.0 jargon. Some of these strange-sounding words and phrases are types of web-based technology and others are theories and strategies. There are many more, but we've chosen to hit the highlights on the most common terms and the ones that are most appropriate for small business owners.

Figure 10.1. Web 1.0 vs. Web 2.0	
WEB 1.0 MINDSET	**WEB 2.0 GUERRILLA MINDSET**
Online users receive internet communication by reading one-way conversations. Web owners talk, visitors "listen."	Collective intelligence is valued. People want to share their ideas and opinions. Internet users are tired of listening; they want to talk and be heard.
Build it and they will come. Get something up and people will find you.	With millions of websites on the internet, just putting up a website is not enough. You must provide relevant products and services, develop and execute plan for increasing targeted traffic, maintain your website and update it often.
Get as many warm bodies to your website as possible using paid-for internet advertising such as banner ads, pop-ups, and pay-per-clicks.	Use effective free—or inexpensive—social media tools and vehicles, such as blogging, viral marketing, and online referrals to drive targeted traffic to your website and convert them to customers.
Ask website visitors to purchase as soon as they arrive on your website.	People buy from companies they trust. Give before you take. Allow your visitors to get to know you before asking them to buy.
Target Markets: Hunt for large groups of people and "tell" them what they want. The more popular, the better. If you want specialized information, get it from fringe magazines or catalogs.	The hunted become the hunters. Ordinary people are banding together to determine what is created and consumed. The cream will rise to the top.
Products, Services, and Content: If it's not a big hit, it's a big dud. True success is mass success. Create products and services with mass appeal.	Products, Services, and Content: Selling less of more is better. Find a niche and scratch it. People with specific interests will spend a great deal of money on non-mainstream products. Look for smaller groups of rabid consumers who are underserved by traditional businesses.
Every man or woman for themselves. You can make a fortune on the internet sitting at your computer by yourself.	You can't go it alone. You need others. Website owners engage and involve their visitors using audio, video, surveys, wikis, and more.

Figure 10.1. Web 1.0 vs. Web 2.0 (continued)	
WEB 1.0 MINDSET	**WEB 2.0 GUERRILLA MINDSET**
The vast majority of people access the internet from their homes or offices using desk- or laptop computers. When traveling, expect limited access to e-mails and websites.	Internet users expect to receive the information they want, delivered how (audio, video, or both), when (on demand), and where they want it (iPods, cell phones, and MP3 players).
Higher-cost technology and software implies higher quality.	Savvy internet users take advantage of high-quality open source (free) web-based applications and software programs.
If you're looking for specific information, your best bet is one of the major search engines. But be prepared to slog through mounds of information to find what's relevant.	Online users want specific information delivered to them using tools such as syndication feeds, Google Alerts, and podcasts. They rely on each other—via tagging—to catalog and find the information they're seeking.
In order to upgrade your computer's software you have to buy new versions and download them	Download want you want and need directly from websites using widely available open source (free) applications, operating systems, and utilities (without installations, upgrades, or "versions") that continue to evolve and improve.
It's best to rely on a web developer to make changes to websites.	Easy-to-use programs and software make it simple for web owners to make their own "on-the-fly" changes to their websites. They can add new content and update or delete information as necessary.

Demystifying Web 2.0 Technology, Tools, and Strategies

Culture and technologies are not the only things new about the Web 2.0 revolution. It also brings with it a brand new language that can, at first, seem baffling. Therefore, we've provided the following Web 2.0 word and phrase glossary that you can use as a reference when words escape you.

Blogosphere

The word is used to describe regular bloggers—a very big and diverse group of internet users. Since various communities of bloggers are increasingly influential in the marketplace growing numbers of companies, large and small, are devoting more resources to monitoring blogs.

Bookmarking, Social Bookmarking

These browser tools store web page links and make it easier for internet users to return to their favorite pages. Social bookmarking websites like del.icio.us and Digg.com let visitors tag, store, and share their favorite internet links with the public or specified groups of people.

Social Media

This is a universal term that describes tools and technologies that increase internet users' abilities to expand their business and professional networks. If you want to attract repeat visitors and make them stay longer, you will have to focus on the social aspects of your website.

Social/Business Networking Websites

These websites are devoted to helping people expand their personal and/or professional networks. Although dating sites such as Match.com have been around for years, newer ones spring up all the time. The undisputed king of social networking is MySpace, followed by sites such as Friendster.com, FaceBook.com, Twitter.com, and others like Mashable.com, one of the leading social networking news blogs. On the business side, websites like LinkedIn.com and Spock.com lead the pack.

Bookmarklets

Like bookmarks, bookmarklets are active web links that help people return to specific spots. However, instead of getting them back to a particular web page, they are direct links to precise functions within a page. For instance, internet users who click on their bookmarks for Wikipedia are taken to one of the website's pages. However, those same folks can use bookmarklets to look for specific terms within the Wikipedia site.

> **"You can make** more friends in two months by becoming interested in other people than you can in two years by trying to get other people interested in you."
>
> —Dale Carnegie

Content Management System (CMS)

Content Management Systems are applications that allow website owners to add content and make changes to their website by accessing a backend administration application.

Long Tail Strategy

First coined by Wired magazine editor-in-chief Chris Anderson, this is a statistical concept used to describe—and support—a nicheing strategy used by many web businesses. The "long tail" represents consumers on the outermost areas of traditional bell curves—those who have typically been ignored by large companies that offered products and services aimed at the masses. Anderson maintained that seeking out these smaller groups of hardcore fans—selling more to less—was the wave of the future for companies, particularly given nearly unilateral broadband deployment and internet companies' abilities to deliver an unlimited supply of digital products (e.g., iTunes, Rhapsody.com, and audio.com).

For example, he demonstrated how frontrunners like eBay and Amazon—merchandise warehouses without physical warehouses or inventory—proved that selling specialized products to smaller groups of likeminded people could result in seriously large profits, and suggested that this model was the wave of the future.

And while this idea of micro segmentation is not a new concept, Web 2.0 technology and culture make it easier for business owners to locate smaller segments of enthusiastic fans and reach out to them.

Mashups

Mashups are web applications that make it easy for software developers to grab digital data from a variety of sources and combine them with each other to develop new products and/or enhance current ones. For example, Google Maps has teamed up with the Chicago Police Department to create a new web experience on ChicagoCrime.org. Visitors to that site can now obtain information regarding criminal activity by location.

Google Map's other famous mashup collaboration with Craigslist.com occurred when the two companies married their databases using application programming interfaces (APIs) so Craigslist buyers would have instant access to neighbor maps and directions.

Membership Sites

With the advent of Web 2.0 technology, membership sites are beginning to actively use social media principles and technology. Only a few years ago online communities and membership sites consisted primarily of discussion boards and uploaded audios. While useful it was limited from the member standpoint as it only allowed participants to post e-mail-based communications in the form of questions and comments while the leaders shared audios and sometimes videos. Web 2.0 technology has changed all that.

With the proliferation of broadband connections, virtually unlimited hosting space, and increased bandwidth for an extremely low cost, two-way multimedia communications are now easily achieved. In Web 2.0 membership sites, participants are now easily able to:

- communicate with audio and video postcards and share with anyone in the club or on the web

- upload their own videos and ones from sites like YouTube

- create their own blogs and podcasts within the community

- have real time web audio and video chats with other members

- send private messages and post to discussion boards

- earn affiliate revenue with embedded links into each postcard.

These 2.0 technologies let members control the show as much as the leaders. And this level of involvement not only enhances the community excitement and creative interaction, it deepens the commitment of the members. Plus it is more fun. For an example of cutting-edge 2.0 membership environment visit MasterBusinessBuildingClub.com

Open Source

The term open source is used to describe free, web-based, ownerless technology protocols that allow users to import, export, share, publish, and download documents, software, and applications. Because the files are imbedded in the web's platform, they can be used by everyone, regardless of the type of operating system stored on their computers. Good examples of open source network sites are Drupal.org, OpenOffice.org, Joomla.org, and Moodle.com.

Syndication Feeds: RSS and ATOM

As we said in Chapter 5, syndication feeds are XML files that code web content and enable subscribers to read updated information from readers on their computers or browsers, websites, or other mobile devices.

Tags

Tags are informal, user-generated keyword descriptors for classifying internet content including word documents, videos, and audios. Tagging allows online visitors to sort through internet clutter by categorizing information using logical and personal words and phrases.

For example, let's say that Susan Smith went on to YouTube.com and uploaded a funny video of her potbelly pig, Sparky, doing tricks. Since she wants as many people as possible to see her clip, she tries to come up with all of the possible things an average person would enter into the search field to locate her video, and includes "funny pig video," "Sparky, the pig," "Susan Smith and Sparky, the pig," "pig doing tricks," "Sparky video," and "hilarious pig Sparky." You get the idea.

Now, whenever anyone types in those keywords, they'll be offered Susan's video as a choice. If she's the only one who's used a particular tag such as "Susan Smith and Sparky, the pig" her video might be their only option. However, if thousands of other people also tagged their videos "funny pig video," people using those keywords to search on that site would have thousands of choices. That's why it's best to be as descriptive—and narrow—as possible when tagging content.

So how do tags benefit online marketers? Simply put, they're wonderful tools for finding out what's going on in the marketplace and what people are saying about them, their company, and/or their products and services.

Popular tagging websites: Flickr.com, YouTube.com, Amazon.com, and Del.icio.us.

User-Generated Content (UGC)

UGC is a very general term that describes a group of Web 2.0 internet tools that allow users to add, delete, and edit website and blog content. Some good examples of user-generate websites are Wikipedia.org, YouTube.com, Digg.com, and Craigslist.com.

Widgets

Widgets are moveable and reusable swatches of HTML software programs that are imbedded into web pages. They are small parts of compete applications and are designed to perform very specific functions.

For instance, internet users can go to sites such as Widgetbox.com and grab free widgets to use on their websites, send text messages, merge syndication feeds, and more.

Wikis

Wikis are actually web-based software that allow users to produce, delete, amend or add website content. Many people use the word, however, to describe collaborative, "authorless" websites, like Wikipedia.org (online user-generated encyclopedia), which uses wiki technology to leverage the world's collective intelligence.

Wiki software is extremely flexible. It can be password protected for limited access and the system automatically stores every document iteration, so users can view how and when it was changed and snatch earlier versions if they want.

Guerrillas use wikis to improve their internal and external communications. They add wikis to their websites to involve their visitors and encourage them to "leave their mark," by making content changes, providing suggestions, and adding new information. Wikis are also wonderful tools for updating internal training and instructional materials.

You can get started using hosted software on sites such as Guerrillapedia.com, Pbwiki.com, or with software you'll install on your site at MediaWiki.com.

How Guerrillas Use The Best-of-the-Best Web 2.0 Websites

Social Video Websites: YouTube

As of this writing, YouTube.com—the hottest user-generated video sharing website on the internet—serves up over 100 million videos per day to it users. As we discussed in Chapter 8, internet users are flocking to YouTube (and other video-sharing websites like GoogleVideo, MiniClip.com, Joost.com, Revver.com, and DailyMotion.com) to add their own videos and/or view others.

After users upload their own videos onto the site's servers, YouTube converts the clips into "streaming" formats, which can be viewed on YouTube and their websites.

Getting started on YouTube is free and a snap—that is, once you've produced your video. Here's how:

1. Visit the site and register.

2. Create your profile page and brief bio. Those pages will link to all of your YouTube videos and back to your website.

3. Follow their directions for uploading your video from your computer to the website.

4. Use intriguing and interesting titles and descriptive tags to make your video easier for others to find.

Picture Sharing Websites: Flickr.com and Facebook.com

Flickr.com, owned by Yahoo!, and Facebook.com currently sit on the top of the photo-sharing website heap, although sites like SmugMug.com are coming into their own as well.

Guerrillas love using these sites to add another layer of credibility to their businesses, share interesting experiences and meetings, highlight photos of themselves and their customers, and showcase their products and services.

You can set up and use a basic account for free, but if you're looking for more advanced features, you can expect to pay something—although the costs are still very reasonable.

Once again, it's easy to get started—even for beginners—and the drill is pretty much the same. Go online, register and follow their directions for uploading. If you know how to attach photos to e-mails, you'll do just fine.

Social Networking Websites: MySpace.com and Squidoo.com

As we said previously in this chapter social networking websites are designed to expand their users personal (and often, professional) networks. Today's champion is MySpace.com. And regardless of what you may have heard, it ain't just for kids anymore!

According to a recent ComScore.com study, 40 percent of MySpace's 200+ million users are 35-45 years old (the average user age is 35). This makes it a great choice for Guerrillas who want to leave more "traces" of themselves all over the internet!

But here's a bit of extra advice: After you register, create your profile and MySpace page, and link them back to your website, your job is just beginning! Remember, this is a "social" networking website and that means being "social," so spend at least one hour every week reaching out to others. Then ask your new acquaintances to contribute to your blogs, check out your website, and become more involved in promoting your business.

Squidoo.com is another social networking website that's gaining popularity by leaps and bounds, in large part because of its tremendous flexibility. Users can create as many accounts as they like and upload audios, videos, photos; host and participate in blogs; and bookmark their favorite web pages.

Social Bookmarking Websites: Del.icio.us and Technorati.com

Today's premier social bookmarking website is del.icio.us—a one-stop site for storing links to your favorite articles, blogs, music, reviews, web pages and more. It's also a great place to organize information.

Technorati.com is a website that, like search engines, sends out spiders that track and monitor millions of blogs. It's a great place to find out what topics, tags, and social media sites are the hottest. You can also register your blog on technorati and then add an action button—a wonderful social bookmarking tool—for every posting on your blog.

Community-Based User Generated Websites

There are thousands of wonderful community-based, user-generated websites, but we'll discuss three here: Digg.com, Twitter.com, and Craigslist.com. We've chosen these because each is different from the others in key ways.

First, Digg.com's content (articles, blog postings, audios, and videos) is entirely submitted by its users. Visitors to the website view the submissions and "digg," or vote for, the ones they like best. If enough people "digg" yours, it gets pushed further to the top, which means it's visible to more people.

> **"Always remember** that the future comes one day at a time."
> —Dean Acheson

Twitter.com allows its users to send short 10-character messages to designated mobile phones or other instant message devices that essentially answer the question "What are you doing?" Although many people use them to stay in touch with close friends and family, savvy entrepreneurs are going one better. For instance, websites like Mashable.com use this technology to send headlines and links to new blog postings. We've even heard of a restaurant that uses twitter to send customers its daily specials.

Craigslist.com, founded in 1995 by Craig Newmark, is one of the frontrunners of the Web 2.0 world. Originally created as a free classified ad and job-posting site for San Franciscans, it now has postings in over 450 cities worldwide and is owned by eBay.com. Guerrillas use Craigslist to post announcements, find employees and contractors, sell products, and much more.

What does this mean to Guerrilla Marketers? A lot. Simply put, today's Guerrilla Marketers can:

- create new products and get them to market faster using mash ups, keyword search tools, joint ventures, and strategic alliances

- obtain real time and quick info and/or monitor word-of-mouth buzz on just about any topic

- keep websites up to date using free or affordable web-based Content Management Systems

- use long tail strategy, and strive to become an expert in a very narrow field (the days of "generalists" are over, so there's little profit in trying to be everything to everybody)

- use tags to find and attract more targeted traffic and buy cheaper, more niched pay-per-click keywords

- use wikis to obtain instant feedback and suggestions from prospects and customers

- deliver information the way their target audience prefers using podcasting, audio, and video

- attract more targeted visitors to their websites by participating in social media dialogues

- conduct free or low-cost webinars and seminars.

Remember, websites will come and go, but the technology will not. If you're going to compete effectively in today's internet marketplace you must reach out to the virtual places where your target audience congregates and communicate with them the way they communicate with each other. Don't get left behind—get out there and mingle with the world!

We have a very special treat for you in the next chapter. We've asked five of the world's most successful online superstars to share their recipes for success on the internet—Guerrilla style. Hang on to your hats, it going to be a fun ride!

GUERRILLA FIELDWORK

1. Create a profile on MySpace.com, Facebook.com, Squidoo.com, or any of the other social media websites listed in this chapter.

2. Visit MasterBusinessBuildingClub.com to experience a leading edge Web 2.0 community.

GUERRILLA INTERNET MARKETING IN ACTION:
Four Innovative Campaigns

In the last ten chapters, we've introduced you to the most important principles, tactics, and strategies for creating a successful business on the internet using more time, energy, and imagination than marketing dollars.

Now it's time to see Guerrilla Marketing in action and learn from four of the internet's premier online marketing experts, who will each share—in their own words— their personal stories on how to achieve maximum impact using minimum expense. Our four superstars are:

1. **Russell Brunson**, a young wrestler from Idaho who turned $50 into a multi-million-dollar online business.

2. **Rick Raddatz,** a software innovator who broke the silence of the internet by creating one of the first audio generator programs.

3. **Bo Bennett**, a best selling author and developer of cutting-edge Web 2.0 software that is helping transform social media membership websites.

4. **Mitch Meyerson**, a best-selling author and online program developer who is also the creator of the Guerrilla Marketing Coaching program.

Russell Brunson

Creating Large Streams of Income with Your Dream Team

Russell Brunson, one of the top e-commerce marketers on the internet, is also an author, speaker, software developer, and is the president and founder of DotComSecrets.com.

He has been extremely successful in helping companies of all sizes—including his own— grow their businesses profitably using online Guerrilla Marketing strategies and tactics. His website is DotComSecrets.com.

I started marketing online back in 2002 while wrestling at Boise State University. I had just married my beautiful wife Collette, and wanted to figure out a way to make some money to help support our new family.

Because of NCAA regulations I wasn't allowed to have a full-time job (not that I would have had time anyway between wrestling and classes), so I had to figure out other ways to start and build a business. I had an idea for a simple software program and decided to give it a try. I found a programmer in Romania who built the program for just $20 and I was able to turn my tiny investment into a company that grossed over $1 million in sales within a year of my graduation and is currently nearing our eight-figure-a-year sales target.

I wanted to share that with you to show you how the internet has made it possible for people like me and you to not only make money, but to build a successful business without much startup capital.

During the past few years, I've had a chance to put together some amazing Guerrilla Marketing, list building, and traffic generation campaigns.

In my first campaign, I earned the $5,500 I needed to build my first website. The second campaign raised over $70,000 in just 14 days. A campaign this year added over 60,000 new subscribers to our list and generated just short of $1,000,000 in sales in just 7 days.

But the Guerrilla campaign that I will tell you about in this chapter is probably the most dynamic that we have put together. It had so many facets and profit streams that I thought it could be very beneficial to everyone. It was called our 2007 Online Marketer of the Year promotion.

The concept was to run a contest to name the greatest online marketer of the year. The first thing we needed to do was to create our "Dream Team" list of marketers for our contest.

> **"I'm a great believer** in luck, and I find the harder I work the more I have of it."
>
> —Thomas Jefferson

Creating The Dream Team

There is a movie called *Never Been Kissed*. In it, a girl named Josie, a newspaper reporter had an assignment to go back to her old high school and pretend to be a student to try to get a great story. The problem was she was a nerd when she was in high school, and immediately started to hang out with the same group she did when she was younger.

Her boss almost fired her because he wanted her to be around the cool crowd. So she tried and tried, but just couldn't fit in. Then one day her brother decided to go back to school too to re-live his old baseball days. He instantly fit in with the cool kids, and when she asked him why, he said something very profound: "Josie, all you need is one cool kid to think you're cool, and you're in."

He then went around the school and told everyone how cool Josie was, and she instantly became popular. Now I knew this concept going in, so because I wanted to get the best people possible as part of our group, I had to get a "cool kid" to say yes, then I could leverage my way into the other relationships.

I set my sights on one of my marketing heroes, Dan Kennedy. I signed up for all of his programs and ended up paying his company a lot of money to be part of his mastermind group. Was it worth it? Yes, because when he agreed to be in our contest, I knew I had my "cool kid."

We then setup a secret page that had Dan's picture at the top, and under it we wrote out in big red letters CONFIRMED. We then put the pictures everyone else in our dream team under his with the words "UNCONFIRMED" below it.

Then, I contacted everyone I knew and told them that I was doing a project with Dan Kennedy, and asked if they would like to be involved. Immediately almost everyone said yes. I'd show them the page with everyone's pictures, and if they said yes, I'd change them to CONFIRMED!

The more people we got, the easier it was because everyone saw who else was involved. If someone said no, we quickly deleted their picture, and replaced it with someone else on our list! Soon everyone said yes and we had a group of close to 60 marketers who would be part of our contest.

Leveraging My Contacts

Now, having 60 people on your dream team is great, but that alone wouldn't make us any money. We had to figure out ways to leverage this contest to build our lists, generate buyer leads, and make us money. We decided to put a few rules into the contest that would make everyone compete, not only for the trophy but also to build our business.

The rules we set for winning were simple. Everyone was graded on three things.

1. The number of people that they could get to sign up for the contest (and, in return, our list). This would show how strong their relationship was with their lists, and how many active subscribers they actually had.

2. Each participant had a chance to be on a webinar and teach their best content—and the attendees voted on their favorite.

3. Each participant had the chance to sell their products and services at the end of their webinar—so we could see how good of a salesperson they were.

Their three points gave us the fuel for our fire. When we launched, everyone was fighting to see how many people they could add to our lists. When we conducted the webinars, everyone was fighting to give the best content possible. And at the end of the webinars, they were using their best skills to sell their products to our new subscribers' lists (which we split with each participant 50/50).

Multiple Income Streams

During this promotion we received a ton of traffic to our sites. We had hundreds of thousands of visitors coming every day and we had to figure out as many ways to monetize this as possible. (I can't stand to waste marketing campaign opportunities.)

As a matter of fact, we found 12 hidden income streams throughout the promotion that most people didn't even know existed! Here they are:

"To profit from good advice requires more wisdom than to give it."
—John Churtip Collins

Stream 1   This was, hands down, the most valuable. When people joined the contest, they also subscribed to our e-mail newsletter. We added almost 50,000 NEW subscribers to our e-mail lists. We have since sold millions of dollars worth of products to these folks and will continue to realize profits for years to come.

Stream 2   We knew that you have peoples' rapt attention when they make their first purchase or register for something, since they are anxious to find out what is "behind that door." So what happened immediately after they registered? We offered them a one-time deal for a DVD, which had copies of all 60 of the webinars from our series. Close to 18 percent of those people who registered ordered this DVD.

Stream 3   We ran a DVD and Newsletter of the Month Club and added it as an option for those who ordered the DVD. Almost 3,000 people signed up for our print continuity program. They were charged $39.97 a month.

Stream 4   After they had finished the signup process, we conducted a cross sell on the "Thank You" page for three of our other affiliate products. We picked products that had free or very low priced trial offers with large upsells, backend commissions, or continuity programs.

Stream 5   Each person who ordered one of the DVDs received a phone call from someone on our sales staff who offered them backend coaching.

Stream 6   We promoted each webinar to our list prior to its start date. After people would registered for their webinar, we offered them an upsell for one of the speakers products.

Stream 7   Each participant in the contest was asked to present a 60-90 minute webinar. At the end of each webinar, they were provided an opportunity to sell their products or services. We earned well over an additional six figures just from these webinars!

Stream 8   We also offered resale rights to each webinar for those who wanted to purchase them. They could then sell the webinar to their customers and keep 100 percent of the profits.

Stream 9   When the resellers sold any of the webinars, their customers saw the same offer and we received the revenue for anything they purchased.

Stream 10   At the end of the webinar series, we mailed a hard copy sales letter to purchasers of the DVD, and offered them resale rights to the full DVD. They would get the sales letter, graphics and all!

Stream 11   When the DVD resellers sold them to their customers and they bought the resale rights, we received profits.

Stream 12   Many people who ordered from the contest also received tickets to one of our seminars, where a few speakers sell their products after their presentations. We receive commissions from those sales.

One of the biggest mistakes I see marketers make is not having as many income streams as possible on each of their promotions. When you limit yourself by selling just the front-end product, you are losing all of your real profits.

This promotion was so successful that we actually took the same model and copied it for the real estate niche and also the network marketing industry. We currently have plans to move it forward into other markets as well.

Rick Raddatz

The Creation and Launch of Audio Generator

Rick Raddatz is the founder and CEO of three companies, all designed to help small business owners. His companies include Xiosoft.com, creator of web-marketing tools; EntrepreneursRetreatNetwork.com, getaways for small business owners; and BrevityMarketingSeminar.com, a virtual marketing seminar. But it all started in his basement with a desire for something more than a salary.

Your first business is the hardest because everything is working against you. In your first business, you are

- missing the knowledge, experience, and wisdom you will have later

- missing a reputation in the marketplace that can create instant sales

- missing relationships with peers who can accelerate your growth and reduce risk

- possibly experiencing tension at home, because your spouse may have concerns and fears (both real and imagined)

- underfunded and probably financing your business the wrong way

- running the risk of partnering with the wrong people.

That's why the key to building a successful first-business is to have a plan that allows lots of mistakes. That's where the Guerrilla Marketing mindset comes in. It's all about preserving cash, and preserving hope.

Guerrilla Planning

Before I started my first business, I compiled a list of all the elements I was looking for in a business—nothing costs less and nothing is more valuable.

> **"Mistakes are painful**
> when they happen, but years later a collection of mistakes is what is called experience."
> —Denis Waitley

Here's the actual business criteria I came up with in 2002:

Business Criteria 1	Inexpensive to create.
Business Criteria 2	Inexpensive to market.
Business Criteria 3	High profit margins.
Business Criteria 4	Can be profitable and small.
Business Criteria 5	Can grow big.
Business Criteria 6	Not tied to a location.
Business Criteria 7	Can make money on autopilot—without me too involved.
Business Criteria 8	A real business—not Multi-Level Marketing or get-rich-quick.

That's a Guerrilla business! But is it too much to ask for?

I could think of only two businesses that met all those criteria: information publishing and software/web-services. Both those businesses share one thing in common: Once you create the product, the cost to create a second copy of it is almost zero, but you can still charge full price. That's pretty cool and very Guerrilla! Those kinds of profit margins allow you to make all kinds of mistakes while you are learning, yet still succeed in the end.

Since I knew more about programming than I did about information publishing, I decided to create a web-based service.

If I had the choice again, I would choose information products because people expect the price of web services to constantly shrink, sometimes even to zero. But the value of information—when properly marketed—keeps going up! And information products are so much easier to create and support.

But I chose to create a web service, and so I moonlighted for nine months to build my first business. It was a specialized voice-mail service for divorcing couples. It gave both spouses a 30-minute cooling off period before their voice-mail was sent—a chance to cancel their messages before they were delivered. The companion e-mail service had a "psychology checker." It caught agitating or offensive words and phrases like "always," "never," and "you money-grubber." Additionally, all the voice-mails and e-mails were archived on the web for easy access—away from business or personal communication, which kept negative energy from creeping into the divorcees' efforts to rebuild and move on.

Super product, right? Everyone I talked to said they loved my business idea; everyone except the marketing guru I hired to review my sales letter. (It's much more cost effective to hire them to review your work instead of do your work.)

Here's what he said, "Hmmm... You're targeting consumers, so they won't pay a lot, but not all divorcing couples need this. And those that do might not need it very long. So how are you going to know which couples will use your service for a while and which ones will not? The best potential affiliates for you (therapists and attorneys) may have ethical and legal reasons why they can't promote your service."

"So," he concluded, "you have a wonderfully inventive idea here, but I don't think you have a business."

After thinking about it, I knew he was right. But what went wrong? After all, the business met all eight of my criteria. There's was only one answer: I was missing the ninth criteria:

Business Criteria 9	Choose a market that is hungry for your product and can be reached easily.

I went back to the drawing board and came up with a new business idea. It took me six additional months of moonlighting, but I ended up with a product that met all nine criteria. I took my voice-mail service and turned it into a service that helped small businesses add audio on their websites. They could call in by phone, record their message, and BOOM— it was on their website in a matter of minutes.

Instant Audio: Breaking the Silence on the Web

On April 1st, 2003, I launched InstantAudio.com. My first Guerrilla campaign was to search Google and Yahoo! for businesses that I thought could use my service. Then I sent an e-mail saying "Hey... I visited your website and I noticed you don't have any audio on it. I think audio could help you sell more. Check out my new service—it makes it really easy. All you need is a phone."

This first Guerrilla campaign worked well and resulted in some sales. However, it was time consuming and not leveraged. But I had time and I needed customers and it got me going.

Leverage Gurus and Peers

To accelerate things, I joined an inexpensive mentor program with a mid-level marketing expert who not only gave me knowledge and wisdom, but also saw the value in my product and introduced me to other gurus. I never spent better money. For less than the price of a decent sized TV, I had access to a network of people who could make me millions.

Some of them promoted my product to their list in exchange for a 33 percent sales-commission. This is what they call affiliate marketing—a powerful Guerrilla Marketing technique. These affiliate partners produced enough sales so my business was cash flow positive within a month of launch. That's a big milestone for a new business.

Realizing the power of getting affiliates to promote my service to their list, I accelerated it more. But I also realized it would take a while for me to build all the relationships it would take to really get this product to market.

Creating Powerful Partnerships

So I pulled out my magic calculator. I thought, "What if I partner with someone who already has all the relationships? What impact would that have on my business?" I saw two big advantages. First, I would accelerate my growth by a factor of at least five times. Second, if I partnered with the right people, they would help me make a name for myself, and that would help me in the future.

The cost? Most partnerships between technology partners and marketing partners end up being 50/50. So by giving up 50 percent of the revenue, I get an estimated 250 percent increase in bottom-line income, and I get a chance to become a name in the industry myself.

I started putting the word out into the guru networks that I was looking for a marketing partner. And I ended up partnering with Armand Morin and Alex Mandossian, two luminaries in the online marketing space with excellent reputations.

We agreed to relaunch InstantAudio.com under a parallel brand name called AudioGenerator.com. It took them just three weeks. They rewrote my sales letter, they updated my graphics, and they prepared a masterful Guerrilla Marketing campaign using affiliates and teleseminars.

The Teleseminar Affiliate and Customer Dance

A teleseminar is just a conference call where hundreds or thousands of potential customers call in to learn from experts about a product or topic. Here's how you can use powerful sales strategy works:

Step 1   Invite all of your potential affiliate partners to attend an affiliate-training teleseminar.

Step 2   On that call, ask your affiliates to promote a sales teleseminar a week or two in the future. Their job is to get people on the call; your job is to close sales, and your affiliates get the commission.

Step 3   Send lots of e-mail to your affiliates reminding them to promote. Provide them with a basic e-mail template that they can enhance or send as-is.

Step 4   Conduct the sales call. Make sure it's educational and entertaining, and then make an irresistible offer with quantity-limited special offer available only for 30 minutes after the call is over.

Step 5   Invite your new customers to attend the next affiliate training call.

Step 6   Repeat.

That's the only marketing Armand and Alex did. But they got me ten times the sales I got on my own. So by giving away 50 percent of the revenue to the right partners, I earned five times more than if I had stayed on my own.

That teleseminar technique worked so well and cost so little that I have used it for all of my product launches for the last four years. And I even created a product to make it easy for beginners: XiosoftPresenter.com

My products for small business have produced tens of millions of dollars in revenue, and none it was generated from advertising; it was all Guerrilla Marketing in action.

Bo Bennett

Guerrilla Web 2.0 Membership Sites

Bo Bennett is the founder and CEO of iGrOOps, LLC and the author of the book Year To Success, *a book that Donald Trump calls "an inspiration to every person who reads it." He has been involved in internet marketing since 1995, creating one of the very first online affiliate programs. Today, he runs iGrOOps.com, a business that provides organizations with the tools they need to have a dynamic and interactive website that allows them to charge membership fees to their site, thus creating residual income.*

In 1995, I started a web hosting company called Adgrafix with nothing more than a few hundred dollars and an elementary understanding of computers and the internet. In 2001, I sold that company for 20 million dollars. In 2002, I started another web hosting company. This time, I had virtually unlimited funds, in-depth knowledge of computers and the internet, and an ego the size of Manhattan. In 2004, after two years of doing everything I thought was right, the company was practically worthless. Times changed, but my thinking did not. I realized that in the current marketplace, to succeed and succeed big, it takes unconventional ways of using creativity, imagination, and energy to achieve maximum profits with minimum money, or it takes Guerrilla Marketing.

Guerrillas Stay on Top of the Latest Trends

When I started my first web hosting company I was fortunate enough to pick up a trend that was very obvious to me—the internet and the "website revolution." Even though I was well aware of the internet bust of the early 21st century (that's what it will be called by our grandkids), I knew deep inside that people and companies would continue to need websites, and at an increasing rate. What I didn't know was that the website of yesteryear was not the website of today. The old school website of the '90s is about as hot as the public pay phone. It isn't enough to spot just one trend; you need to consider all the trends in your market.

In 2005, when I started spending more time on the internet than with my offline ventures, that elusive trend that was partly responsible for my two-year web hosting failure (I

> ## "We can reach
> our potential, but to do so, we must reach within ourselves. We must summon the strength, the will, and the faith to move forward... to be bold... to invest in our future."
>
> —John Hoeven

was ultimately responsible, but it feels good to share the blame) became very clear to me. People didn't want static websites anymore; they wanted *dynamic* websites that use cutting edge technology, websites that give users the power to contribute content, websites that generate buzz and, of course, they wanted all this at an affordable price. They wanted *Web 2.0*.

Trend or Fad?

One of the biggest traps in business is allowing clever marketers to lead you to believe a fad is actually a trend. There is so much hype on the internet today and everyone is looking to act on the "latest and greatest." Ignore the hype, use common sense business principles, and identify the trends from the fads. The term "Web 2.0" itself is a fad—a soon-to-be (if not already) term that holds the same wow factor as "Pentium processor" or "presented in Technicolor." However, the concept behind Web 2.0, specifically making the most use of the latest tools the internet has to offer, is a trend.

Never Fear Technology

I have to admit, I do get a little annoyed when people brush off technology, say something like "Oh, I don't understand that stuff," and don't make any attempt to learn it. Technology drives business today, and without a good understanding of the technologies out there, you will spend your life sitting in the back seat—in the middle, with your legs on the hump.

Certain types of technology can be a Guerrilla's best friend. It is this technology that allows your marketing efforts to return phenomenal results. Take for example e-mail marketing. Back in the day, a legitimate marketer could send a text-based e-mail to a qualified list and get amazing results. Today, with spam flooding every home and office inbox, your "important marketing message" is more likely to be read by your dog than a prospect. But what if you could send a "video postcard" to a prospect, with a video of you sharing your message? How much more effective do you think that would be? Even if people are not interested in your message, they are impressed with the technology, and will listen to what you have to say. By staying ahead of the technology curve, you have a huge advantage over other marketers by knowing how to use certain technologies in a creative way.

Following the Leader Is for Kids, Not for Guerrillas

It is interesting how so many "grown ups" still play follow the leader. It is not hard to understand why, after all, it is easy, mindless, and by logical thinking, should result in at least some of the same success of the leader. However, it rarely does. The market does not need more followers, it needs more leaders. It needs more individuals who use creativity and ingenuity to make a better product at a more affordable price.

In building iGrOOps, I knew in my head exactly what I wanted to build. It was a combination of a social network, community website, corporate Intranet, and membership site. There was nothing like it out there, so how did I know there would be a demand for it? The fact is I did not know. Leaders rarely know the outcomes of their chosen course of action ahead of time, this is why it is so much easier to follow. But there were some things I did know.

I did know that the trend was moving away from static, difficult to manage, expensive to build websites to dynamic sites that were built to generate revenue for the owners. I knew that technologies such as podcasting, blogs, video chat, forums, audio/video postcards, multi-media galleries, and other similar productivity, communication, and marketing tools were on the rise and sought after by online business owners. This was all I needed to know to build my vision of the ideal membership site platform.

Viral Marketing: Get Them Talkin'

When getting ready to launch iGrOOps, I started thinking about more traditional marketing—Google Adwords, press releases, and ads in trade publications. But I then remembered a universal truth in marketing: if you have a product or service that is so amazing that it actually excites people to talk about it and share it with others, you will find that you have created a viral marketing campaign that costs you virtually nothing. Now, what if you also compensated people for sharing your business with others? The viral marketing effects could be explosive.

This concept works extremely well for iGrOOps, so I figured, why not allow our membership site administrators to use the same great concept? We built in an affiliate program that allows administrators to compensate their members for referring other members to their site. The overall concept behind an affiliate program is to let others do the marketing for you, and you pay only for results. It is a perfect example of a true win-win situation.

In just one year, we have experienced phenomenal growth at iGrOOps. Not because of advertising or dumping a boatload of money into our business, but because of the product itself and the Guerrilla Marketing techniques and philosophies used. Best of all, our customers are experiencing the same success using the tools we provide them though iGrOOps. We encourage our customers to continue to use unconventional ways of using creativity, imagination, and energy to achieve maximum profits with minimum money. We promote Guerrilla Marketing.

Mitch Meyerson

Creating the Guerrilla Marketing Coach Certification Program

Mitch Meyerson is the founder of Guerrilla Marketing Coaching and author of eight books includ-ing Mastering Online Marketing, Success Secrets of the Online Marketing Superstars, Six Keys To Creating The Life You Desire, When Is Enough Enough, *and* Guerrilla Marketing on the Frontlines, *as well a three groundbreaking internet programs. His website is MitchMeyerson.com.*

The Guerrilla Marketing Coach Certification Program is now one of the leading coach training programs in the world. And in keeping with the principles of the brand, this 12-week training program was created and marketed using time, energy, imagination and the power of a good idea at the right time in the right marketplace.

In the 1990s I was living in Chicago. Although it was a vibrant city, I was very unhappy with the cold winter weather and wanted to move to a warm sunny climate. The biggest challenge, however, was that I had a thriving counseling practice that was based on clients coming locally to my downtown office. The thought of starting over in a new city and build-ing a business from the ground up sounded daunting.

In early 1999, I spent more and more time online and noticed that a small number of counselors and coaches were moving their businesses on to the internet and advising clients over the telephone. As I began to study this new trend it sounded like a great way to take my current skills and make my business "virtual," earning revenue that would allow me to grow my business from any location.

The big idea came one day as I was reading a Guerrilla Marketing book by author Jay Conrad Levinson. When I first studied it, I found myself wondering if readers were actu-ally putting what they learned into action. I intuitively knew that many people buy books but don't follow up with the action exercises without some kind of structure and support.

Then it occurred to me that the trend of the emerging coaching market would be a per-fect marriage with Guerrilla Marketing, which had dozens of books published and hun-dreds of thousands of followers all over the world. Having already written a few books in the psychology area and having skills in program development this seemed like a business concept that I was uniquely qualified to create.

Guerrillas Take Action

Taking immediate and consistent action is a hallmark of Guerrilla Marketing. Jay Conrad Levinson says Guerrilla Marketers have two-way brains instead of one-way brains. One-way brains acquire information and two-way brains take action on that information.

Knowing this idea had enormous potential, I spent a lot of focused time formulating my ideas for a 12-week Guerrilla Marketing Certification Program and created a proposal for the Father of Guerrilla Marketing himself, Jay Conrad Levinson.

As I developed my vision for this new program I asked myself what kind of online environment and structures would move people to take action on the powerful set of ideas contained in the Guerrilla Marketing series. In my mind, the answer was to combine a tele-seminar series with a teaching guide, interactive coaching, and a strong community environment.

All of the content and interactivity would be web- and telephone-based so that entrepreneurs all over the world could participate. Knowing that Guerrillas are never technophobic, I began learning the new technologies of the internet by researching other programs and exploring newer options. I needed to create a strong web presence (GmarketingCoach.com) with excellent sales copy that clearly articulated the benefits of becoming a Certified Guerrilla Marketing Coach.

By using the Guerrilla concept of leveraging existing material, I knew I could repurpose the existing content of the bestselling marketing series in history and turn it into a coaching model. My goal was to impact thousands of coaches and potentially millions of small business owners. But a good idea was not enough. I had to take action and get the green light from the Father of Guerrilla Marketing.

Approaching a Fusion Marketing Partner

Fusion Marketing is a Guerrilla Marketing concept based on the idea that we can geometrically increase exposure and profits by partnering with others in joint ventures. When partners come together they bring separate sets of resources that strengthen their product or service.

I knew that if I partnered with Levinson, I would not have to reinvent the wheel by creating new content and building a new brand. The Guerrilla Marketing series was (and still is) the bestselling marketing series in history. Even so I knew that, with time, energy, and imagination, I could increase sales of the Guerrilla Marketing books, extend the brand into the coaching industry, offer something new and useful to Levinson's customer base, and increase his exposure to new markets.

I approached Levinson in the same way he advises in his books: The best way to pursue a partner is to lead with *what's in it for them*. I explained that he could geometrically grow his Guerrilla Marketing brand through a coaching certification program and he wouldn't have to spend any time creating new content—I would do everything. After speaking with him, he quickly enrolled in a joint venture concept that would combine his marketing models with my coaching expertise to build an army of Guerrilla Marketing experts all over the world.

Here were some points I kept in mind when approaching Jay Levinson:

- Do your research ahead of time to find out about your potential partner and what is most important to him or her.

- Be specific and don't leave anything vague.

- Develop simple deals, especially ones that don't require either of you to look over the others' shoulders.

- Give before you get, particularly if you're just starting out.

- Avoid using a sales pitch with a prospective partner.

- Don't obsess over who is getting more out the deal; make your best deal and forget about it.

These are some of the principles I used when I approached Levinson with my partnership idea. Within a few short months, we were partners developing the Guerrilla Marketing Coaching Program: a 12-week class, curriculum materials, and group training sessions.

Growing the Brand

Since 1999, the Guerrilla Marketing Coach Certification program has certified over 250 coaches worldwide with students located in Australia, US, UK, Japan, Singapore, South Africa, France, Canada, Brazil, Iceland, Spain, and New Zealand, to mention only a few countries. There have been countless success stories of businesses owners worldwide who have been coached in Guerrilla Marketing.

In May 2008 we featured 35 Guerrilla Marketing coaches and authors and their success stories in *Guerrilla Marketing on the Front Lines (*Morgan James, 2008) by Jay Levinson and Mitch Meyerson.

In the last five years I have continued to expand the Guerrilla Marketing Coaching brand by co-authoring *Guerrilla Marketing on the Internet* with Jay Levinson and Mary Eule Scarborough, and also providing leading edge internet tools (EasyWebAutomation.com) and online environments (MasterBusinessBuildingClub.com).

The Guerrilla Marketing Coaching program continues to grow every year, not from marketing dollars, but from the basic keys to Guerrilla Marketing: using time, energy, imagination, and knowledge and, of course, a good idea.

GUERRILLA MOMENTUM
and People Power

This book is quickly drawing to a close. However, your internet marketing efforts may just be starting. We've covered a lot of material in the last eleven chapters and hope that you'll use it to compete more successfully in the internet's rough-and-tumble landscape.

We introduced you to the most powerful Guerrilla Marketing tool in history and gave you the tools and techniques you need to achieve your goals more quickly, build positive, long-term relationships with others, and grow your online and offline businesses profitably. Now the rest is up to you.

Still, you may be asking, "Where and when will this all come together for me?" The first answer is "the internet." The second answer is "the minute you act."

Reading this book is not enough. Understanding Guerrilla Marketing concepts is not enough. Putting up a website is not enough. Uploading a video onto YouTube.com is not enough. Thinking about taking a computer class is not

> ## "It doesn't matter
> how slowly you go as
> long as you do not stop."
> —Confucius

enough. Adding your website address to your business cards is not enough. *Doing it right is enough.*

And while we are confident that the solid internet marketing strategies and tactics presented in this book can help Guerrillas worldwide grow their businesses more profitably, this is not a get-rich-overnight program. Like the tooth fairy, there is no such thing.

This is, however, a get-rich-over-time program as long as you have the work ethic, tenacity and perseverance to see it through to a successful conclusion. If not, you should consider another career, because this is a lot of work.

Ask yourself these questions: Do I have "the stuff" to keep going in the face of rejection? Am I ready to craft a plan of attack for my internet marketing efforts? Am I willing to keep track of everything I do and analyze my results? Can I see myself intimately involved in updating and maintaining my website? And most importantly, am I ready to embark on an exciting journey—one that will help me achieve my ultimate goals, which may be to

- do work that is pleasant, interesting, and challenging?

- earn sufficient income, enough to free up worry over money?

- enjoy a healthy lifestyle?

- sustain loving, supportive, give-and-take connections with friends and family members?

- have time for fun, and relish in life's pleasures?

- live a long life and glory in the wisdom that it brings?

If you're ready, it's time to act and continue doing so even when the going gets tough—or worse yet, boring and mundane. If you want to use the power of the internet to assist you in growing a profitable business, you must continue to expand your marketing knowledge; update your products, services, and websites; add and update content; and improve your skills. And this process begins with a serious commitment to seeing it through to its logical conclusion.

Commitment

As we said in Chapter 1, commitment is the attribute that divides winners from losers, and keeps some people moving when others stop dead in their tracks. It is the characteristic that keeps successful people optimistic in the midst of crushing disappointments. It is the quality that allows champions to learn from their losses and move on. Commitment keeps victors energized when the newness wears off. How do you recognize committed souls from others? Simple. People who are committed do the following:

- They keep their promises. They do what they say, long after the moment they said it in has passed.

- They are in it for the long haul. They are willing to exchange short-term luxuries for a brighter future.

- They have their eye on the finish line, but enjoy the ride there.

- They demonstrate a minute-after-minute, day-after-day, month-after-month, and year-after-year attention to ensuring that "mundane" tasks are accomplished, because they know that excellence isn't in the details, it is the details.

- They don't build walls, they learn how to surpass them.

Yet, while most businesspeople agree that commitment is an admirable trait, they may not know exactly what it means to put into action—especially as it relates to internet marketing. If you don't believe this, go online and take a look. You'll find gobs of abandoned and/or poorly maintained websites and blogs all over the place. Then, consider how much time, energy, know-how, and money their owners wasted, because neglected websites and blogs do not generate income!

Unfortunately, this is an all-too-common fate for entrepreneurs—who by their very nature, are generally much more action-oriented than others. So why do so many well-intentioned and intelligent small businesspeople lack the commitment needed to grow and maintain a profitable

> **"Productivity is** never an accident. It is always the result of a commitment to excellence, intelligent planning and focused effort."
>
> —Paul Meyer

business? If you're assuming that the answer to this question is that these folks lack solid work ethics, you couldn't be more wrong. Rather, it's usually just the opposite. That is, many entrepreneurs become paralyzed because they're overworked, over committed, and overwhelmed! For example:

- They're eager to take advantage of new opportunities, so say "yes" to more than they can handle.

- They're reluctant to delegate tasks to employees or outsource work because they're convinced that their product or service quality will suffer—or it will cost them a fortune.

- They grossly underestimated how much time and energy it would take them to run their businesses smoothly.

- They fail to document key processes and systems, which makes it very difficult for them to train others to take over.

And the list goes on... Yet even if you don't identify with entrepreneurs who suffer from these, your plate is probably still full and you haven't a clue where you'll find the time to add more responsibilities to your burgeoning to-do lists. All of us have times when we want to shout, "Will somebody please help me?!"

That's just the point. We all need someone to help us. We've said this many times before throughout this book, but it bears repeating. Yes, Guerrillas accomplish many things using only their time, energy, and know-how, but they also know when and how to get help.

Therefore, in the next sections, we'll show you how to use "people power"—or fusion marketing—to expand your product line, share resources, and increase sales. Then we'll offer valuable tips in ways to reduce your workload using virtual teams.

Fusion Marketing

Fusion marketing has been around since the Stone Age. But back then it was called "you-scratch-my-back-and-I'll-scratch-yours." However, no matter what form it takes or what it's called, it's about people helping people. Guerrillas know that they can't go it alone so they welcome the opportunity to team up with the right people and see it as one of the smartest and most effective ways to market their businesses. For many years Guerrillas have been advocating cooperation instead of fierce competition; openness and honesty instead of hucksterism; and relationship building over bean counting. Now, due to the fresh Web 2.0 internet culture, more and more people are shedding their "win at all cost" attitudes in favor of a smarter, less stressful, and more profitable mindset. And incredible technology allows every entrepreneur the opportunity to share resources and partner with likeminded individuals all over the globe and continue to reap the benefits for years to come.

> **Tip:**
> There are many things that even beginners can do. You don't have to hire an expert for everything. But smart marketers know the difference between least cost and best cost.

Even the smallest business owners no longer have to rely on friends, colleagues, and family members in their local communities to act as their suppliers, supporters, alliances, or contractors. These days they can outsource jobs to companies in faraway lands and join forces with people at opposite ends of the country from the comfort of their own homes. So while people helping people is nothing new, it's taken on a whole new look thanks to the internet.

And today's savvy Guerrilla Marketers know that partnering with others to expand their product lines, test working relationships, and share resources is a smart way to do business, and a great way to increase their influence and awareness. That's why they enter into joint venture partnerships and strategic alliances.

Joint Venture Partnerships

Joint ventures (JVs) are usually temporary partnerships where two or more people combine their resources and skills to achieve the goals of a single project. Because they are short-term in nature and people can have one or many JV partners, they are wonderful vehicles for testing working relationships before entering into more formalized business relationships, such as strategic alliances, which we'll talk about in the next section.

Each JV partnership is as unique as the individuals involved and can be set up in many different ways. For example, Jane is a freelance writer who, after many years of experience,

> ## "The best teamwork
> comes from men who are
> working independently toward
> one goal in unison."
> —James Cash Penney

understands that many people agonize when they have to write anything—letters, sales copy, brochures, etc. It's the reason she's stayed so busy over the years and she's confident that easy-to-use writing template software would be a great product to sell online. However, Jane has a limited budget and no idea how to transform her Word documents into a software package, design the packaging, or bring it to market. So Jane does the smart thing and looks for partners who can each perform various duties, pay their share of the development costs, and co-own the software copyrights. Once developed, each partner can choose to market the product independently and keep 100 percent of the profit they earn, or join forces and market the product together or with others.

Strategic Alliances

After you've gotten your feet wet with a couple of joint ventures, it may be time to kick it up a notch by entering into one or more strategic alliance partnerships, where you'll work on multiple projects with one or several people on a regular basis.

Strategic alliance partners often work side-by-side for many years and rely on each other to help generate most of their revenues, which make them quite similar to more conventional partnerships. Yet, in most cases they are far more flexible, because either partner can "opt out" of the arrangement at any time.

Now, however, you may be wondering which type of internet partnership—joint venture or strategic alliance—works best. The answer is: both. In other words, there is no one-size-fits-all solution. But one thing is certain regardless of the kind you choose: Partnerships work best when everyone involved clearly communicates their goals and expectations, concurs that the work arrangement benefits all parties, and agrees to a fair distribution of duties and compensation.

More importantly, truly successful partnerships occur when each partner is genuinely interested in the success of the others.

Therefore, before you approach a prospective partner learn as much as you can about them, their company, their values, and the like. Remember, partnerships are a lot like marriages—some work out fantastically but a whole lot of them end in disaster. So don't be fooled into thinking that anyone who knows how to make a few bucks will make a great partner. Instead, list the traits that you'd like your ideal partners to possess—skill set, work style, experience, expertise, reputation, and the like. Then rate them according to how important they are and use it to narrow down your choices.

And if you're just starting out and looking to join forces with others who may be more established, be sure to approach them in a careful, considerate, and "what's-in-it-for-them" (not you) manner. And always:

- Demonstrate that you value their time as much as your own by presenting your ideas clearly, specifically, and concisely.

- Give before you get. People are understandably nervous about partnering with folks they don't know, so offer to prove yourself before they are required to risk too much.

- Get off on the right foot by communicating the benefits of your give-and-take proposal, without subjecting them to an exaggerated sales pitch.

And one more thing, don't overlook the value of cause marketing partnerships. Team up with associations, alumni groups, government agencies (e.g., Service Corps of Retired Executives—or SCORE—and the Small Business Development Center—or SBDC), charities, and other affinity groups to reach motivated niche markets.

In the past, large corporations donated the largest chunk of dollars to charities. But this is changing rapidly. Nowadays, small businesspeople—who previously could not afford large charitable outlays—are giving a portion of their proceeds to worthwhile causes.

And it isn't all about charity either. A recent consumer study conducted by Cone, Inc., in 2002, suggests that 84 percent of consumers would be willing to switch brands if one supported a cause that they supported, and that "cause-marketing" spending will continue to rise in the near future.

Sometimes the best thing to do is pay for some help! You'll squander far more of your precious resources if you take on every job that comes your way. Consider this: Experts estimate that in a typical eight-hour day, most business owners spend less than two hours on revenue-generating activities. The remaining six hours are spent on administrative and operational tasks that don't add to the bottom line, and in reality cost them more in the long run.

Are we suggesting you hire an army of employees? Hardly. But we are recommending that you gradually start to outsource work and begin building your "virtual" team of assistants. Don't panic—even if you're operating with the tiniest of budgets, you can find extremely inexpensive and excellent help at hundreds of internet sites, which we'll cover later in this chapter.

For now, your biggest challenge will be in coming up with your list of duties, and deciding which ones to tackle yourself and which ones to farm out.

Obviously, your list will be as unique as your businesses, personalities, industries, talents, and interests, so there is no right or wrong answer. However, we strongly suggest that you take an objective look at how you're spending your time and consider outsourcing work that:

- **Doesn't play to your strengths or skills.** For instance, if you're not a trained graphic designer, don't create your own logos!

- **Takes you twice as long to complete.** It's better to pay someone five dollars to FTP files for you than try to figure it out yourself.

- **Is repetitive and can be systematized.** Hand off ongoing routine work—answering e-mails, scheduling appointments, etc.—to others, and free your time up for more important things.

- **Requires specialized knowledge or certification.**

- **Could seriously jeopardize your business if done incorrectly.** For example, let an IT professional set up your computer's security system. Why risk losing invaluable customer data when it can be avoided?

Keep in mind that business people who work hard on the wrong things wind up in the same place as lazy business people—nowhere.

If you're still left wondering where to begin, you probably need to step back and spend some time documenting everything that you do, or should do, in a week's time and placing them into appropriate categories, such as:

1. Customer/Prospect Communication That Can Be Automated

- Thank you letters to new customers
- Weekly tips e-mails
- Newsletters

2. Ongoing Marketing and/or Administrative Duties That Can Be Systematized and Outsourced

- Writing and submitting blog postings and articles
- Updating website's pricing information
- Adding new content to website
- Scheduling teleconferences and communicating details to participants
- Uploading videos, graphics, and audio to various internet sites
- Answering customer care e-mails
- Monitoring affiliate programs and other marketing efforts

3. Projects Requiring Specialized Skills

- Logo creation
- Graphic design and sales copywriting
- Website development and SEO techniques

4. Ongoing Functions That Require Specialized Skills

- Bookkeeping
- IT troubleshooting
- Blog, article, and newsletter writing
- Marketing research

5. "Owner Jobs"—Ones to Keep Doing

- Strategic planning
- Face-to-face coaching sessions
- Seminar delivery

The goal is to come up with practical and effective ways to perform at the highest level possible, without overloading yourself with work. First, list the action steps required to complete each job and *cross off any that can be automated*. (If this doesn't sound familiar, refer to

Chapter 7, where you'll find detailed information on ways to put time-consuming business and marketing jobs on autopilot.)

Next, take a closer look at your routine jobs and processes, particularly ones that can be "boiler-plated" and/or systematized. In other words, if you can document the steps needed to complete a particular job, you should. Also, when you find yourself reinventing the wheel when you answer prospects' questions, it's time to rethink your process.

The specifics aren't as important as the approach—at least right now. The goal is to create systems—recipes—and tools for successfully completing given tasks. You decide what "successfully" looks like by setting measurable benchmark standards ahead of time.

Sounds like a lot of work, doesn't it? The truth is, it will take some time, but not as much as you think AND you'll end up getting those hours back thirty-fold with the time you'll save in the long run. And it will be much easier to document your business' processes using process maps. Because each step is illustrated in order using simple geometric shapes, such as circles, squares, and triangles, they are great tools for designing, analyzing and documenting processes. Even better, you won't have to get out a ruler, paper, or gel pens to create yours, since there are several good software programs that you can use to get started, at websites such as MindJet.com.

Once you have one system in place it will be far easier to repeat the process for any task at any time. What's more, once you've got these sorted through you'll be amazed at the benefits you and your business will experience. You'll be spending your time where it counts the most. As a result, you'll naturally generate more income, make your business less vulnerable to downtimes, decrease your virtual team's learning curves, find it easier for everyone to stay focused and on track, reduce rework, duplication and stress, and most importantly, have more time to spend enjoying life's simple pleasures.

Even better, you can achieve all this with very little money—and we're about to show you how.

Outsourcing: Building a Virtual Team the Smart Way

Once you've decided what tasks you'll automate and documented your systems and processes, it's time to begin building your all-important team. Even if you're not quite ready to delegate work, you should still identify and prioritize the jobs you'd like to delegate, and conduct research on where you'll find qualified help, and how much it will cost you, so you're ready when the time is right.

But don't wait too long to get help. If you're already experiencing burn-out there's a better than even chance that your customers are feeling your pain as well. Also, before putting it off another minute, go through your list and add up what you're losing—in real dollars and opportunity costs—when you perform tasks that could and should be outsourced. This is something very few entrepreneurs calculate, and one of the reasons they find themselves in terrible binds. If you've heard the saying "penny wise and pound foolish," you'll know what we mean.

For examples, let's say John is a freelance copy editor—a soloprenuer—whose clients pay him $50 per hour to edit books, papers, and the like. Business is good—so good in fact, that he is working at maximum capacity and has had to turn away a couple of would-be clients in the recent past. This has caused him considerable angst because he genuinely wants to grow his business and knows that he'll remain in place unless he comes up with a way to increase his client base.

In his mind, he has only three choices:

1. **Increase his average workweek from 40 to 50 hours**. However, given his responsibilities at home, John knows this is not a realistic option.

2. **Find, hire, and train one or more employees.** John knows he needs help, but feels as though even one employee would result in more, not less, stress for several reasons. First, his workload is often unpredictably cyclical and he worries that he'll end up paying out more than he brings in during slower periods. Second, John is concerned that he doesn't have what it takes—time, energy, and know-how—to find and train top-notch copy editors.

3. **Keep doing what he's doing.** John feels that this is not an acceptable solution either, because even though things are moving along okay, he's smart enough to realize that he is putting himself and his family at considerable risk, because he is "the business." That is, if something unexpected were to happen—his clients took their business elsewhere or he became too sick to work—they would all be in big trouble.

"To get what

you want, stop doing what isn't working."

—Dennis Weaver

In short, John doesn't view any of these as viable options—a conundrum. He's stuck. And because he doesn't want to make a bad decision, he makes none at all. He just "keeps on keeping on" and promises himself that he will think about it later.

If this is true, the only other way John can make more money is by increasing his prices. A price increase is risky at this stage, because he doesn't have the momentum necessary to sustain a potential loss of business.

But we think John is avoidably paralyzed. He has limited his thinking and therefore his possibilities. He doesn't understand that he is building a product, not a business. In other words, John should have approached his problem using the following very simple process.

Step 1 Track and document all daily work tasks during a typical month.

Step 2 Calculate the number of hours spent during that time period on specific duties not related to copy editing.

If he had done this, he would have discovered that in addition to the two hours a week he spent answering phone calls and invoicing customers, he spent another five hours working on his website's logo design, returning e-mail messages, blogging, and submitting online articles. In total, John he spent seven hours each week taking care of jobs that are not copy editing. No big deal in the scheme of things, right? Wrong.

Consider this. John's clients pay him $50 an hour when he edits their copy. They pay him nothing when he works on anything else but copyediting. Therefore, John is being paid for 33 hours of work or $1,650 each week, totalling $6,600 per month. However, he's losing 7 hours of pay every week (and 28 hours each month), which means he's leaving $1,400 on the table every month—a lot of money!

But as John would say, these things have to get done, and his chances of hiring anyone to work seven hours a week are slim to none; so he's left with paying an employee more than they're worth or performing the tasks himself. In truth, he doesn't have to do either.

John can outsource the work and receive trustworthy, reliable, and knowledgeable help in the form of a virtual assistant, graphic designer, and/or web developer, for far less per hour than it's currently costing him. And this is just for starters. As his business grows and his needs change, he will have the flexibility of adding and deleting duties as necessary. (John should also be using timesaving business forms, and letter and report templates, etc. like you'll find at BusinessTemplatesInABox.com).

As with many things, the toughest parts are learning where to find reputable help and taking that first step. However, it's probably not nearly as difficult as you imagine; there are literally armies of talented people all over the world ready and waiting to help support your efforts affordably. So don't put it off another minute!

Putting Together Your Virtual Team

In order to locate good help you'll need to be clear about your goals and expectations, how you'll measure results, and any specialized skills required to perform at a satisfactory level. You should also document things such as your standards, values, working style, and the like to use as a guide when interviewing candidates.

What types of tasks should you consider outsourcing? These days it's fairly easy to find help with just most common business tasks, such as:

- Website design and maintenance
- Affiliate program management
- Customer support
- Content creation and editing
- Link building
- Copywriting
- Graphic design
- Payment processing and merchant account management
- Fulfillment
- Traffic generation
- Product creation

Once you've decided what you'd like to outsource, it's time to start spreading the word. Before going online, some people prefer to ask friends, relatives, and colleagues for referrals first. This is a great way to begin, but don't be discouraged if you come up empty handed, because you'll find lots of help online.

The best way to get started is by visiting several of the websites we've listed in Figure 12.1 and seeing what they have to offer. We've categorized them by task, but as you'll see, many overlap with others. There are hundreds more—so if you don't find what you're looking for, use your favorite search engine to locate other websites.

Figure 12.1 Web Resources for Outsourcing

General/Multiple Services
- ELance.com
- Liveperson.com
- Craigslist.com
- AskSunday.com
- Guru.com
- ContentDivas.com
- WorkaholicsForHire.com

Website Development and/or Design
- ScriptLance.com
- SitePoint.com
- AgentsOfValue.com
- RentACoder.com
- Guru.com
- Elance.com
- NetStudio.com
- eLance.com

Traffic Generation
- OnlineTrafficNow.com

Administrative Support
- Kayako.com
- PerlDesk.com
- OutsourceIncubator.com

Copywriting
- CopywritersBoard.com
- Guru.com
- Kendare.com

Graphic Design
- GotLogos.com
- Scriptlance.com
- 800MyLogos.com
- eCoverDesign.com
- PulpMiniSites.com
- KillerCovers.com

Fulfillment
- Disk.com
- 48HrBooks.com
- SpeakerFulfillmentServices.com
- DoctorDuplicator.com
- ViaTechPub.com

Link Building
- PayPerPost.com
- ReviewMe.com
- LoudLaunch.com
- Blogsvertise.com

Once you're ready to take the plunge, write a job description and post it on one or more websites. Don't know what to say? It's really quite easy. Keep it short, concise, and clear. Tell them exactly what you want done and if at all possible, provide specific examples of work that you like. (Trust us, this will save you tons of headaches later on!)

Be sure to also include the maximum dollar amount you're willing to pay. And remember, never, ever, ever pay one penny—no matter how pushy they are—until you are 100 percent delighted with their work, it's in your possession, and you've changed your site's FTP password (an extra safety measure to ensure that outsiders don't have continued access to your site).

Here is a sample of a job posting for a graphic designer.

SUBJECT: WordPress Blog Design

TYPE OF PROJECT/WORK: Graphic Design

Hi—

I'm looking for someone to customize a design for my new blog site.

I like the following three blog designs and would like my site to have a similar look and feel.

whatever1.com

whatever2.com

whatever3.com

In addition to the design, I will need you to provide my web developer with the HTML coding so it can be plugged into my site.

Please e-mail me no more than five samples of other blog designs you've done in the past so I can get a better idea of your skill and style. Please choose ones that are closest to the look and feel of three examples I've provided above.

This is a straightforward and simple project for someone with the right skill set and experience.

I look forward to hearing from you soon. My contact information is provided below.

Price: Maximum bid should be no higher than $100.

GUERRILLA FIELDWORK

1. Make a list of the jobs that you can outsource and use some of the online services mentioned in this chapter to find the best possible virtual team for your business.

2. Guerrillas know that they can't get the best results alone, so your mission is to reach out to at least two possible joint venture partners and discuss how you might work together to grow both of your businesses.

Wrapping Up

It's impossible to grow your business and keep the momentum going without leveraging your most important asset—time. Nobody gets more than 24 hours a day, so be sure to use yours to help you get closer and closer to achieving your dreams.

Now, it's your turn to get out there and prove to yourself and the rest of the world that superior Guerrilla internet marketing has more to do with time, imagination, knowledge, and energy than money. So go get 'em, Guerrillas!

GLOSSARY

A

Affiliate programs: the internet's version of commission-based sales, where one person pays another an agreed-upon fee for selling his or her products or services.

Anchor tag: hyperlinks that point to a to a specific resource (HTML page, image, audio, video, etc.)

Autoresponder: software that allows people to schedule and send prewritten e-mails automatically at regular intervals.

B

Back-end marketing: generating sales by introducing additional products and services to existing customers.

Bandwidth: the amount of data that can be sent through a broadband connection, usually measured in bits-per-second (*bps.*)

Benefits: the advantage, gain, or improvement derived from products and/or services

Blog (Web Log): web sites, usually owned by one person, where a series of messages, or posts, on particular subjects are posted in chronological order, newest to oldest. Usually conversational in nature, they are meant to be updated and read often.

Blogsphere: a group of regular bloggers.

Bookmarklets: active web links that help people return to specific functions within a web page.

Bookmarks: browser tools that store web page links and make it easier for internet users to return to web pages.

Bonus: an additional benefit received when purchasing products or services.

C

CMS (Content Management System): applications that allow website owners to add content and make changes to their sites via administrative control panels.

Cookies: pieces of information sent to browsers by web servers.

Copywriting: the art of writing sales pages and content.

D

Domain name: a unique name that identifies an internet site.

Downloading: transferring data (usually a file) from one computer (or website) to another.

DSL (Digital Subscriber Line): a method for moving data more quickly over regular phone lines. It also allows for faster downloads and surfing on the internet.

E

E-mail (Electronic Mail): messages, usually text, sent from one person to another via computers.

Ethical bribes: usually giveaways that website owners offer their visitors in exchange for their names and e-mail address. They are most often used to build e-mail lists.

F

FTP (File Transfer Protocol): a common method of moving files between two internet sites. It is a way to *login* to another internet site for the purposes of retrieving and/or sending files and most often used to upload files on to servers which host internet sites.

H

HTML (Hyper Text Markup Language): a programming language that allows web sites to display the text, images, and graphics you see on the internet.

L

Landing page: web page where visitors are sent after clicking on a live internet link.

Linking: a process and strategy for connecting one web page with another that usually involves placing HTML code into images and/or text.

List: a collection of names and e-mail addresses for permission-based marketing efforts.

List building: collecting names and e-mail addresses of people for marketing purposes.

Long tail: statistical concept used to describe and support niching strategies.

M

Mashups: web applications that make it easy for software developers to grab digital data from a variety of sources and combine them together to create new, or enhanced, products.

Meta tags: group of page definitions coded into a website.

MP3: a popular digital audio compression format that substantially reduces the amount of data required to create audio without sacrificing the quality of the original audio.

Monetize: using different strategies and tactics to obtain money for products and services.

O

Open source: term used to describe free, web-based "ownerless" technology and applications.

Opt-in box (or page): an area on a website used to collect visitors' names and e-mail addresses.

P

Pay-per-click: internet advertisement system where web owners pay fees when internet users click through to their websites from placed ads.

Podcasting or pod-casting: a form of internet audio broadcasting.

R

RSS (Rich Site Summary or Real Simple Syndication): a commonly used protocol for syndicating and sharing content, originally developed to facilitate the syndication of news articles.

S

Search engines: programs that search web pages for specified keywords and return a list of the links where the specified keywords were found in order of relevance.

Search engine optimization (SEO): describes techniques and tools for improving websites' visibility, and quality and quantity of website traffic.

Social media/networking: universal term that describes tools, technology, techniques, and websites that help internet users expand their personal and/or professional networks.

Split testing: a technique that allows internet advertisers to test copy, headlines, graphics, and the like.

Spam (or Spamming): illegal promotional e-mails sent to people who have not provided senders permission to contact them.

Squeeze page: a landing page, usually shorter than most web pages, where visitors are required to perform a specific action (call, opt-in, purchase, etc.) to access the web site, or leave. It is use to build e-mail list and to pre-qualify visitors about your product or service offerings.

Syndication feeds: XML files that code web content to allow subscribers to read updated information from readers on their computers or other devices. RSS and Atom are the most common systems.

T

Tags: informal user-generated keyword descriptors for internet content.

Templates: patterns used to create documents. Used to save time and provide consistent results, templates can be tables, forms, tutorials, spread sheets, letters, etc.

Testimonial: A statement, given by a customer, affirming the value of a product or service. It can be in written, audio or video format.

Tracking: methods used to measure the results of your marketing efforts. You can track sales, click-through rates, opt-ins, etc.

U

User Generated Content (UGC): general term that describes a group of Web 2.0 internet tools that allow users to add, delete, and edit web page content.

Upsell: invite current customers to purchase additional or supplemental products or services.

V

Value per visitor: a key website formula that measures what one website visitor is "worth" in dollars. Price of the Product multiplied by the Number of Sales divided by the Number of Visitors equals Average Visitor Value. For example, if 100 prospects visited a website and 5 became customers who spent an average of $37, each visitor would be worth $1.85.

Viral marketing: a word-of-mouth advertising method for spreading marketing messages via the internet using e-mail, social networking sites, blogs, etc.

Virus: Computer programming code that makes copies of itself without any conscious human intervention. Some viruses are annoying but not harmful, but others replicate themselves and install other software or files, delete software or files, or crash hard drives. They can also be used to steal information from a computer by attaching programs that allow intruders to gain access to a computer via the internet.

W

Web 2.0: often thought of as the second iteration of internet technologies and culture.

Widgets: moveable and reusable swatches of HTML software programs that are imbedded into web pages.

Wikis: web-based software that allow users to produce, delete, amend, or add website content.

Word of Mouth: grassroots marketing that occurs when people refer companies, websites, products, or services to others. It is often considered the most effective form of advertising because it is considered an objective vote of confidence.

ABOUT
THE AUTHORS

Jay Conrad Levinson is the author of the highest-selling marketing series in history, Guerrilla Marketing. The series includes 58 books that appear in 52 languages and have sold 20 million copies worldwide, as well as audiotapes, videotapes, a CD-ROM, an Internet website, and an online marketing advancement called The Guerrilla Marketing Association, which is an interactive marketing support system for small business owners. He has written a monthly column for *Entrepreneur* magazine, articles for *Inc. Magazine,* and online columns for Microsoft, Netscape, America Online, Fortune Small Business, and Hewlett-Packard. He has given presentations extensively worldwide, and his Guerrilla concepts have influenced marketing so much that today they are required reading in many MBA programs worldwide.

Jay Conrad Levinson taught Guerrilla Marketing for ten years at the extension division of the University of California in Berkeley.

He was a practitioner of it in the United States as Senior Vice-President at J. Walter Thompson, and in Europe as Creative Director and Board Member at Leo Burnett Advertising. He is the Chairman of Guerrilla Marketing International, a marketing partner of Adobe and Apple, and he has served on the Microsoft Small Business Council.

Mitch Meyerson has been a visionary, trainer, and author since his first book was featured on the Oprah Winfrey show in 1990. On the internet, he is the founder of three groundbreaking programs including the much-acclaimed Guerrilla Marketing Coaching Program, The 90 Day Product Factory, and Online Traffic School.

Mitch has personally trained and certified over 260 Guerrilla Marketing coaches worldwide and has provided consulting and coaching services to thousands of businesses, helping them grow their customer base and market share effectively and affordably.

Mitch is also the author or co-author of *Success Secrets of the Online Marketing Superstars*, *Guerrilla Marketing on the Frontlines*, *Guerrilla Marketing on the Internet*, *Mastering Online Marketing*, *When Is Enough Enough? Six Keys to Creating the Life You Desire*, and *When Parents Love Too Much*. His books have been translated into 25 different languages.

Mitch is a strategic thinker and is committed to achieving measurable results for himself and his clients. He is passionate about working with projects in the arts and has been an accomplished musician for over 30 years. He lives in Scottsdale, Arizona. Learn more about his companies and get free business building resources at MitchMeyerson.com.

Mary Eule Scarborough, an unassailable marketing expert and thought leader, helps businesses of all sizes get and keep more profitable customers. A former Fortune 500 marketing executive, she is also the founder of two successful small businesses; an award-winning speaker; certified Guerrilla Marketing coach; and the co-author of the books *The Procrastinator's Guide to Marketing* (Entrepreneur Press), *Mastering Online Marketing*, and *Guerrilla Marketing on the Internet*. She has a BA in Journalism/English from the University of Maryland and a master's degree in marketing from The Johns Hopkins University. Log onto her web site (StrategicMarketingAdvisors.com) for free marketing articles, tools, tips, and templates, or to learn more about her books and services.

INDEX

A

Action, Guerrilla, 11
Affiliate
    partnerships, 9–10, 27
    programs, 27, 113–118
Amazement, inspiring, 8
Analytics, marketing, 11, 27,
    78–79
Articles, writing and publish-
    ing, 118–119
Artwork and graphics, best use
    of, 55–56
Ascension conversion model,
    Figure 4.1, 75, 100
Assets and expenses, under-
    standing the difference
    between, 7
Attention to detail, 8
Audios, 140–143
    equipment and software
    supply list, 142–143
    uploading software, 143
    web resources for, Figure
    7.1, 150
Automation technology, 125–
    137
    future of, 137
Autoresponders, sequential,
    131–134

B

Bennett, Bo, 199–202
Blogs, 38, 40–41, 112, 178
Bookmarking, 178
Bookmarklets, 179
Brunson, Russell, 188–192

C

Coach certification program,
    Guerrilla Marketing,

203–206

Color, careful use of, 54–55

Commitment, 8–9, 209–210

Communications, e-mail, podcasts, and feeds, 81–101, 181

Communities, marketing through Internet, 112–113

Community-based user generated websites, 184–185

Competition, working with your, 9–10

Competitive research, 21–22

Computer equipment, six guidelines for procuring and maintaining, 29–31

Consistent action, 9

Content
above the fold, 54
management system (CMS), 179
overdelivering on promised experience, 8
relevant, 110–112
user-generated (UGC), 182

Continuity Website (membership/subscription), 42, 43–44

Conversions
opt-in, 73–74
sales, 74–75
tactics for increasing, 72–73

Copy, importance of writing effective interactive, 23–24

Craiglist.com, 180, 182, 184, 185

Creation and launch of Audio Generator, 193–198

D

Del.icio.us, 184

Design strategy, 34–36

and easy navigation as essential for success, 22–23
four basic, 35–36
nine questions to ask, 35
on a Guerrilla budget, 52–56

Digg.com, 182, 184

Direct response marketing
communication, 64–65
copy, importance of writing effective interactive, 23–24
sales page outline, 66–72
turning visitors into customers, 61–79
what do consumers really buy, 63–64

Discussion groups, 112

Do-overs, path to wealth and profitability paved with, 7

E

E-mail
advanced techniques for making memorable, 89–90
audio postcards, 90
marketing lists, building permission-based, 24
moving from text to video, 89–90
promotional, 83–89
signatures, 123–124

F

Facebook.com, 183

Feeds, syndication, RSS and ATOM, 181

Figure 01.1, What's Your Guerrilla Marketing IQ?, 11, 12–14

Figure 03.1, Squeeze Page or Single Opt-In Website, 37

Figure 03.2, Single Page/Letter, 39

Figure 03.3, Guerrilla Marketing Blog, 41

Figure 03.4, Subscription/Membership Website, 43

Figure 03.5, Organization and Structure in Website Design, 47

Figure 03.6, Outsourcing Your Website's Development and Design, 57

Figure 03.7, Web Development Checklist, 58–59

Figure 04.1, Ascension Conversion Model, 75, 100

Figure 04.2, Squeeze Page and Sales Letter Process Flow, 76

Figure 07.1, Web Resources for Audio and Video, 150

Figure 09.1, Top 20 Internet Guerrilla Marketing Weapons, 157–158

Figure 09.2, Guerrilla Marketing on the Internet Weapons, 159–168

Figure 10.1, Web 1.0 vs. Web 2.0, 176–177

Figure 12.1, Web Resources for Outsourcing, 220

Flickr.com, 183

Follow-up systems, 28

Forums, 112

Fusion marketing, 210–211
    relationships, developing beneficial, 27

G

Glossary, 223–228

Google Analytics, 27, 78–79

Google Map's mashup collaborations, 180

Guerrilla Marketing on the Internet Weapons, Figure 9.2, 159–168

H

Hosting company, selecting your, 45

Hybrid website, 36

I

Immediate online sales, 35

Inclusive marketing, encouraging, 8

Income, creating large streams of, 188–192

Innovative campaigns, Guerrilla Internet marketing in action, 187–206

Intentionality, marketing includes every contact with the public, 7–8

Internet as most powerful Guerrilla Marketing tool ever created, 1–15

Investing in time, energy, imagination and knowledge, 6–7

J

Joint ventures, 9–10, 27, 211–212

K

Keywords and phrases, powerful, 106–108

L

Lead generation for future online and offline sales, 36

Less is more design, 55

Links, internal and external, 108–110

Long Tail Strategy, 179

Long-term relationships, building, 8–9

M

Marketing
    business, every business is in the, 8

funnel approach, 24
mistakes on the Internet,12 most common, 17–31
Mashups, 180
Measurement, 11, 77–79, 135–136
Membership sites, 180–181
Guerrilla Web 2.0 for, 199–202
Merchant accounts, 127–129
Mistakes
1, putting up a website with no planning, 19–20
2, failing to research competitors and the marketplace, 21–22
3, developing poorly designed websites that are difficult to navigate, 22–23
4, failing to write effective direct response copy, 23–24
5, failing to build permission-based e-mail marketing lists, 24
6, no traffic generation strategy, 24–25
7, not using Web 2.0 social media and technology, 25–26
8, not using online and offline marketing combinations, 26
9, failing to track marketing campaigns, 26–27
10, neglecting to build virtual teams and partnerships, 27
11, failing to follow up with prospects and customers, 28
12, failing to ensure that computer equipment is up to the task, 29–31
Mobile devices, new language of, 98–99
Multimedia, 139–150
Multiple page websites, organizing content

for, 46–48
Myerson, Mitch, 203–206
Myspace.com, 184

N

Nanocasts, 98
Navigation and usability guidelines, 48–49
Networking, social and business, 27
Newsletters, online, 119–120

O

Offline automation for easy follow-up, 134–135
One step at a time, building a successful business, 8–9
Online and offline marketing, combining, 26
Open source, 181
Opt-ins to sales, models for moving, 75–77
Organization and structure in website design, Figure 3.5, 47
Outsourcing, 27, 50–52, 57
building a virtual team the smart way, 216–221
job posting for graphic designer, 221
web resources for, Figure 12.1, 220
your website's development and design, Figure 3.6, 57

P

Partnerships, 211–212
affiliate, 9–10, 27
Patience, 9
Payments, processing online, 127–129
PayPal and other third-party processors,

129–131
People power, Guerrilla Marketing and, 207–222
Picture sharing websites, 183
Podcasts, 94–98
Principles of Guerrilla Marketing, 5–11, 18
Profits as benchmark for success, 11
Prospects, creating a system for following up with, 28
Psychology, Guerrilla, 10
Publicity, generating online, 122–123

R

Raddatz, Rich, 193–198
RSS Feeds (Really Simple Syndication), 91–94, 181
Rules 1-5, underlying principles of Internet Guerrilla Marketing, 18

S

Search engine
    and usability of your website, 105–108
    optimization, 105–108
    traffic, 104–105
Self-assessment quiz, 11, 12–14
Selling needs and desires not products or services, 10
Seminars and conferences, web-based and telephone, 147–149
Shopping carts, 129–131
Single page/letter, 38, 39
    Figure 3.2, 39
Social bookmarking, 178, 184
Social media, 178
Social networking, 27, 112–113, 178, 184

Social video websites, 183
Squeeze Page or Single Opt-In Website, 36–37, 72–77
    Figure 3.1, 37
Squidoo.com, 184
Strategic alliances, 9–10, 27, 212–216
Structure of your website, 46
Subscription/membership website, Figure 3.4, 43
Syndication feeds, RSS and ATOM, 91–94, 181

T

Tags, 181–182
Technorati.com, 184
Tell-a-friend programs, 121–122
Templates, ready-made, 56
Tenets of Guerrilla Marketing, 6–11
Top 20 Internet Guerrilla Marketing weapons, Figure 9.1, 157–158
Tracking, 11, 77–79
    and measuring with automation software, 135–136
    marketing campaigns, 26–27
Traffic
    driving visitors to your website, 103–124
    generation strategy, 24–25
Twitter.com, 185
Typeface and formatting, easy-to-read, 53–54

U

Unique quality that sets a business apart from its competitors, 8
User-generated content (UGC), 182

V

Videos, 143–147
    equipment and software supply list, 146–147
    ten best online strategies, 144–146
    uploading software, 147
    web resources for, Figure 7.1, 150
Viral marketing, 120–122

W

Weapons, Guerrilla Internet, 153–169
    Figure 9.1, Top 20 Internet Guerrilla Marketing weapons, 157–158
    Figure 9.2, Guerrilla Marketing on the Internet weapons, 159–168
Weapons, utilizing a variety of low-cost, high-impact marketing, 10–11
Web 2.0
    culture and mindset shift, 174–175
    demystifying technology, tools and strategies, 178–182
    Guerrilla, 171–186
    simplified, 173–174
    social media and technology, utilizing, 25–26

web 1.0 vs. web 2.0, Figure 10.1, 176–177
Web development checklist, Figure 3.7, 58–59
Web resources for outsourcing, Figure 12.1, 220
Website
    development, 46, 48
    high impact at a low cost, 33–60
    hybrid, 36
    organizing content for multiple page, 46–48
    planning every aspect of, 19–20
    types of, 36–42
    well designed and easily navigable as essential for success, 22–23
What's your Guerrilla Marketing IQ?, Figure 1.1, 11, 12–14
Widgets, 182
Wikipedia.org, 182
Wikis, 182
Word-of-mouth marketing, 120–123
Wow factor, 8

Y

YouTube.com, 182, 183

MORE
GUERRILLA MARKETING RESOURCES

Become a Certified Guerrilla Marketing Coach
www.GMarketingCoach.com

Guerrilla Marketing International
www.GMarketing.com

MORE
MARKETING RESOURCES

www.StrategicMarketingAdvisors.com

www.Ideas-to-Income.com

www.MasterBusinessBuildingClub.com

As promised on the front cover...

YOUR FREE
GUERRILLA MARKETING
ON THE INTERNET
JUMPSTART KIT

Instantly Download Your
Action Manual for This Book and Get

MORE FREE
GUERRILLA MARKETING RESOURCES

($97.00 value)

Go to:
www.GMarketingInternet.com

Jeremy Harmer

how to

teach english

new edition

with DVD

PEARSON

Longman

Pearson Education Limited
Edinburgh Gate
Harlow
Essex
CM20 2JE
England
and Associated Companies throughout the world.

www.longman.com

Seventh impression 2011

Printed in China   CTPSC/07

Produced for the publishers by Stenton Associates, Saffron Walden, Essex, UK. Text design by Keith Rigley. Illustrations by Jackie Harland and Sarah Kelly.

Editorial development by Ocelot Publishing, Oxford, with Helena Gomm.

ISBN 978-1-4058-4774-2

Acknowledgements
The Roald Dahl Estate for extract from *George's Marvellous Medicine* by Roald Dahl published by Jonathan Cape © The Roald Dahl Estate, and for extract from *Matilda* by Roald Dahl, published by Jonathan Cape © The Roald Dahl Estate; and Pearson Education for extract from *How to Teach English* by J Harmer © Pearson Education; and for extracts from *Energy 4, Student Book* by Steve Elsworth and Jim Rose © Pearson Education; and extracts from *New Cutting Edge (Intermediate workbook)* by J Comyns Carr and F Eales © Pearson Education; and extracts from 'Business Opportunities for Women in the UK and the USA' from *Opportunities Upper Intermediate* by M Harris, D Mower, A Sikorzynska © Pearson Education; extracts from *Total English Pre-intermediate* by R Acklam and A Crace © Pearson Education and for extracts from *New Cutting Edge* by S Cunningham and P Moor; extracts from *New Cutting Edge Elementary Student Book* by J Harmer, D Adrian-Vallance, O Johnston © Pearson Education; and for extracts from *now* by Jeremy Harmer & Richard Rossner © Pearson Education and extracts from *Energy 2* by Steve Elsworth & Jim Rose © Pearson Education, extract from *Sky 3* by Brian Abbs and Ingrid Freebairn © Pearson Education; extract from *How to Teach Writing* by Jeremy Harmer © Pearson Education and an extract from *Cutting Edge Pre-Intermediate* by S Cunningham and P Moore © Pearson Education; extract from *The Practice of ELT* by Jeremy Harmer © Pearson Education 2001; extract from *Total English* by Mark Foley & Diane Hall © Pearson Education; Oxford University Press for an extract from *English File Upper Intermediate* by Clive Oxenden and Christina Latham-Koenig © Oxford University Press 2001; Guardian Newspapers for *Q&A Neil Gaiman* by Rosanne Greenstreet first published in *The Guardian* 18 June 2005 and extracts from 'We are at risk of losing our imagination' by Susan Greenfield, *The Guardian* 25 April 2006 © Guardian News and Media 2006; Regina Schools, Regina SK Canada for *Six Traits Writing Rubric* published by Regina Schools adapted from original by Vicki Spandel; and Marshall Cavendish for an extracts from *Just Right Intermediate Students' Book* (Mini Grammar) by Jeremy Harmer © Marshall Cavendish 2004

We are grateful to the following for permission to reproduce photographs: Page 88: (Thinkstock/Alamy; page 103: (all) Royalty-free; page 104: Royalty-free; page 114: Royalty-free; page 115: Royalty-free; page 124: (Paul M Thompson/Alamy (left), (GOODSHOOT-JUPITERIMAGES FRANCE/Alamy(middle-left), (Bubbles Photolibrary/Alamy (middle-right), (STOCKIMAGE/PIXLAND/Alamy (right); page 127: The Portrait of Giovanni Arnolfini and his Wife Giovanna Cenami (The Arnolfini Marriage) 1434 (oil on panel), Eyck, Jan van (c.1390-1441)/National Gallery, London, UK,/The Bridgeman Art Library; page 140: (AMET JEAN PIERRE/Corbis Sygma; page 210: Royalty-free; page 213: Royalty-free; page 217: (both) (Jeremy Harmer; page 221: (all) (Royalty-free); page 256: © Michael Booth / Alamy. We have been unable to trace the copyright holders for the photographs on page 151. We apologise for this and any other unintentional omissions. We would be pleased to insert the appropriate acknowledgement in any subsequent edition of this publication.

This is for the students that readers of this book may teach.
(But most especially for Tanya and Jessy.)

Contents

		Page
Acknowledgements		8
Introduction		9
1	Learners	11

• Reasons for learning
• Different contexts for learning
• Learner differences
• The importance of student motivation
• Responsibility for learning

| 2 | Teachers | 23 |

• Describing good teachers
• Who teachers are in class
• Rapport
• Teacher tasks
• Teacher skills
• Teacher knowledge
• Art or science?

| 3 | Managing the classroom | 34 |

• Classroom management
• The teacher in the classroom
• Using the voice
• Talking to students
• Giving instructions
• Student talk and teacher talk
• Using the L1
• Creating lesson stages
• Different seating arrangements
• Different student groupings

| 4 | Describing learning and teaching | 46 |

• Children and language
• Acquisition and learning
• Different times, different methods
• Elements for successful language learning (ESA)
• ESA lesson sequences
• ESA and planning

5   Describing language   59
    • Meaning in context
    • The elements of language
    • Forms and meanings
    • Parts of speech
    • Hypothetical meaning
    • Words together
    • Language functions
    • Text and discourse
    • Language variables

6   Teaching the language system   81
    • Teaching specific aspects of language
    • Explaining meaning
    • Explaining language construction
    • Practice and controlled practice
    • Examples of language system teaching
    • Mistakes, slips, errors and attempts
    • Correcting students

7   Teaching reading   99
    • Reasons for reading
    • Different kinds of reading
    • Reading levels
    • Reading skills
    • Reading principles
    • Reading sequences
    • More reading suggestions
    • Encouraging students to read extensively

8   Teaching writing   112
    • Reasons for teaching writing
    • Writing issues
    • Writing sequences
    • More writing suggestions
    • Correcting written work
    • Handwriting

9   Teaching speaking   123
    • Reasons for teaching speaking
    • Speaking sequences
    • Discussion
    • More speaking suggestions
    • Correcting speaking
    • What teachers do during a speaking activity

10 Teaching listening   133
- Reasons for listening
- Different kinds of listening
- Listening levels
- Listening skills
- Listening principles
- Listening sequences
- More listening suggestions
- Audio and video

11 Using coursebooks   146
- Options for coursebook use
- Adding, adapting and replacing
- Reasons for (and against) coursebook use
- Choosing coursebooks

12 Planning lessons   156
- Reasons for planning
- A proposal for action
- Lesson shapes
- Planning questions
- Plan formats
- Planning a sequence of lessons
- After the lesson (and before the next)

13 Testing   166
- Reasons for testing students
- Good tests
- Test types
- Marking tests
- Designing tests

14 What if?   176
- What if students are all at different levels?
- What if the class is very big?
- What if students keep using their own language?
- What if students don't do homework?
- What if students are uncooperative?
- What if students don't want to talk?
- What if students don't understand the audio track?
- What if some students finish before everybody else?

Task File   186

Task File Key   233

DVD Task File   245

Appendices   252
  • Appendix A: Classroom equipment, classroom technology
  • Appendix B: Useful organisations and websites
  • Appendix C: Chapter notes and further reading
  • Appendix D: Phonemic symbols

Glossary   268

Index   286

Acknowledgements

In the first edition of *How to Teach English*, I acknowledged the contributions made to the development of the book by Richard Rossner, Anita Harmer, Gill Stacey, Sue Jones, Rodney Blakeston amd Martin Parrott. I was especially thrilled with the reactions of students being taught by Maggy McNorton (at the University of Glamorgan) and David Ridell (at Kingsway College, London). I paid tribute to Melanie Butler's role in getting the whole project going. I should also, back then, have acknowledged Kate Goldrick's support and help at Pearson Education, especially during one particular phase of development.

With the development of this new edition I need to offer thanks to a whole lot of other people. At the start of the project in one truly wonderful day of meetings which included Katy Wright (the inspiring methodology publisher at Pearson Education to whom I owe an increasing debt of gratitude) many issues were confronted, and new directions suggested. And since then the clear head and firm editing of Helena Gomm have made putting thoughts into finished words a real joy.

This new edition has benefited enormously from some stunning reporting by Hilary Rees-Parnell, Katie Head and Jeremy Pearman in the UK, Gabriel Diaz Maggioli in Uruguay, Adriana Gil in Brazil, Mitsuyo Ohta in Japan and Maria Pujak in Poland. I hope they all know how seriously I looked at their suggestions and criticisms, and how tough it was, sometimes, to decide how far to agree or disagree with them. They feel, to me, like real collaborators in this enterprise (and special thanks to Adriana, Gabriel and Jeremy for their input on planning). And it is thanks to Jacqui Hiddleston at Pearson that their thoughts came through so clearly. Jane Reeve has handled the production process with her usual exemplary skill.

But it would be wrong of me to forget to mention countless others – the teachers and trainers I meet and listen to at training sessions and conferences around the world. It is amazing how much you can learn, and how the process of reflection is enhanced by hearing other professionals describe their experiences and expound their beliefs.

Finally, I want to thank Jane Dancaster (principal) and especially Fiona Dunlop (director of studies) at the Wimbledon School of English for letting us invade their school with a film crew, and for helping us to organise two fascinating days of filming. But it is to six teachers that I want to offer thanks from the bottom of my heart for their cheerfulness, cooperation and friendliness. They planned lessons for us, allowed themselves to be filmed delivering those lessons (a nerve-wracking experience!) and were prepared to be interviewed about their teaching on camera. When you watch Chris McDermott, Louise Russell, Mark Smith, Philip Harmer, Pip Stallard and Pip Titley you will only see a fraction of their fabulous teaching, but it is worth every minute of the time they and we invested in it!

Of course, none of the people I have mentioned should be held to account for the final version you have in your hands. In the end that is entirely my responsibility. But I hope that they (and you) will enjoy how it has all turned out.

Jeremy Harmer
Cambridge, UK

Introduction

A friend of mine who is an orchestral conductor was asking me (early in our acquaintance) about what I did for a living. When I told him that, apart from other activities, I wrote books about how to teach English he said 'Books in the plural? Surely once you've written one, there's nothing more to say!' I wanted to reply that he had just argued himself out of a job (I mean, how many performances of Beethoven symphonies have there been in the twenty-first century alone?), but someone else laughed at his question, another musician made a different comment, the conversation moved on, and so Martin-the-conductor's flippant enquiry evaporated in the convivial atmosphere of a British pub.

But his question was a good one. Surely we know how to teach languages? After all, people have been doing it successfully for two thousand years or more, and some aspects of teaching in the past have probably not changed that much. But other things have, and continue to change. Which is (I suppose) why every time I re-examine past assumptions about teaching, I find myself questioning and reinterpreting things I thought were fixed. And of course, I am not alone in this. We all do it all the time – or at least we do if we haven't closed our minds off from the possibility of change and renewal.

Language teaching, perhaps more than many other activities, reflects the times it takes place in. Language is about communication, after all, and perhaps that is why philosophies and techniques for learning languages seem to develop and change in tune with the societies which give rise to them. Teaching and learning are very human activities; they are social just as much as they are (in our case) linguistic.

But it's not just society that changes and evolves. The last decades have seen what feels like unprecedented technological change. The Internet has seen to that and other educational technology has not lagged behind. New software and hardware has appeared which we could hardly have imagined possible when the first edition of *How to Teach English* was published as recently as 1998. And it's exciting stuff. There are so many wonderful possibilities open to us now (not least the ability to write and edit books electronically!). I've tried to reflect that excitement and newness in parts of this new edition. But we need to be careful, too. In the words of Baroness Greenfield, speaking in Britain's House of Lords, 'We must choose to adopt appropriate technologies that will ensure the classroom will fit the child, and buck the growing trend for technologies … to be used to make the twenty-first-century child fit the classroom.'

But finally, there is the sheer joy – and frustration, and disbelief and (in the words of the playwright Dennis Potter) 'tender contempt' – you experience when you look again at what you wrote a few years back; the challenge is to see, in the light of what has happened, what has been said and what has been written, the things that need to be changed, excised or added to.

Readers of the first version of *How to Teach English* will notice a change of chapter order and see a new chapter to introduce the subject of testing. There are new materials and techniques on offer – and quite a few old ones too because they have stood the test of time. There's a more up-to-date set of references at the end of the book, and a glossary to help new teachers through parts of the mighty jargon swamp that our profession generates just like any other.

And so – I want to say to my conductor friend – thank heavens for new developments, new technologies and new interpretations. They keep us alive; they make us better teachers. We shall not, of course, cease from exploration in T S Eliot's famous words, but even if we do end up back where we started, the journey is all.

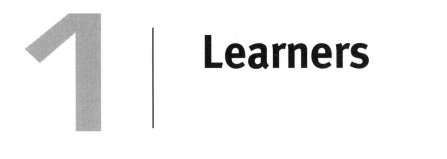

Learners

- ■ Reasons for learning
- ■ Different contexts for learning
- ■ Learner differences
- ■ The importance of student motivation
- ■ Responsibility for learning

Reasons for learning

All around the world, students of all ages are learning to speak English, but their reasons for wanting to study English can differ greatly. Some students, of course, only learn English because it is on the curriculum at primary or secondary level, but for others, studying the language reflects some kind of a choice.

Many people learn English because they have moved into a **target-language community** and they need to be able to operate successfully within that community. A target-language community is a place where English is the national language – e.g. Britain, Canada, New Zealand, etc – or where it is one of the main languages of culture and commerce – e.g. India, Pakistan, Nigeria.

Some students need English for a Specific Purpose (**ESP**). Such students of ESP (sometimes also called English for Special Purposes) may need to learn legal language, or the language of tourism, banking or nursing, for example. An extremely popular strand of ESP is the teaching of **business English**, where students learn about how to operate in English in the business world. Many students need English for Academic Purposes (**EAP**) in order to study at an English-speaking university or college, or because they need to access English-language academic texts.

Many people learn English because they think it will be useful in some way for international communication and travel. Such students of **general English** often do not have a particular reason for going to English classes, but simply wish to learn to speak (and read and write) the language effectively for wherever and whenever this might be useful for them.

The purposes students have for learning will have an effect on what it is they want and need to learn – and as a result will influence what they are taught. Business English students, for example, will want to spend a lot of time concentrating on the language needed for specific business transactions and situations. Students living in a target-language community will need to use English to achieve their immediate practical and social needs. A group of nurses will want to study the kind of English that they are likely to have to use while they nurse. Students of general English (including those studying the language as part of their primary and secondary education) will not have such specific needs, of course, and so their lessons (and the materials which the teachers use) will almost certainly look different from those for students with more clearly identifiable needs.

Consideration of our students' different reasons for learning is just one of many different learner variables, as we shall see below.

Different contexts for learning

English is learnt and taught in many different contexts, and in many different class arrangements. Such differences will have a considerable effect on how and what it is we teach.

EFL, ESL and ESOL

For many years we have made a distinction between people who study English as a foreign language and those who study it as a second or other language. It has been suggested that students of **EFL** (English as a Foreign Language) tend to be learning so that they can use English when travelling or to communicate with other people, from whatever country, who also speak English. **ESL** (English as a Second Language) students, on the other hand, are usually living in the target-language community. The latter may need to learn the particular language variety of that community (Scottish English, southern English from England, Australian English, Texan English, etc) rather than a more general language variety (see page 79). They may need to combine their learning of English with knowledge of how to do things in the target-language community – such as going to a bank, renting a flat, accessing health services, etc. The English they learn, therefore, may differ from that studied by EFL students, whose needs are not so specific to a particular time and place.

However, this distinction begins to look less satisfactory when we look at the way people use English in a global context. The use of English for international communication, especially with the Internet, means that many 'EFL students' are in effect living in a global target-language community and so might be thought of as 'ESL students' instead! Partly as a result of this we now tend to use the term **ESOL** (English for Speakers of Other Languages) to describe both situations. Nevertheless, the context in which the language is learnt (what community they wish to be part of) is still of considerable relevance to the kind of English they will want and need to study, and the skills they will need to acquire.

Schools and language schools

A huge number of students learn English in primary and secondary classrooms around the world. They have not chosen to do this themselves, but learn because English is on the curriculum. Depending on the country, area and the school itself, they may have the advantage of the latest classroom equipment and information technology (**IT**), or they may, as in many parts of the world, be sitting in rows in classrooms with a blackboard and no other teaching aid.

Private language schools, on the other hand, tend to be better equipped than some government schools (though this is not always the case). They will frequently have smaller class sizes, and, crucially, the students in them may well have chosen to come and study. This will affect their motivation (see page 20) at the beginning of the process.

Large classes and one-to-one teaching

Some students prefer to have a private session with just them on their own and a teacher. This is commonly referred to as **one-to-one teaching**. At the other end of the scale, English is taught in some environments to groups of over 100 students at a time. Government school classes in many countries have up to 30 students, whereas a typical number in a private language school lies somewhere between 8 and 15 learners.

Clearly the size of the class will affect how we teach. **Pairwork** and **groupwork** (see pages 43–44) are often used in large classes to give students more chances for interaction than they would otherwise get with whole-class teaching. In a one-to-one setting the teacher is able to tailor the lesson to an individual's specific needs, whereas with larger groups compromises have to be reached between the group and the individuals within it. In large classes the teacher may well teach from the front more often than with smaller groups, where mingling with students when they work in pairs, etc may be much more feasible and time-efficient.

In-school and in-company

The vast majority of language classes in the world take place in educational institutions such as the schools and language schools we have already mentioned, and, in addition, colleges and universities. In such situations teachers have to be aware of school policy and conform to syllabus and curriculum decisions taken by whoever is responsible for the academic running of the school. There may well be learning outcomes which students are expected to achieve, and students may be preparing for specific exams.

A number of companies also offer language classes and expect teachers to go to the company office or factory to teach. Here the 'classroom' may not be quite as appropriate as those which are specially designed for teaching and learning. But more importantly, the teacher may need to negotiate the class content, not only with the students, but also with whoever is paying for the tuition.

Real and virtual learning environments

Language learning has traditionally involved a teacher and a student or students being in the same physical space. However, the development of high-speed Internet access has helped to bring about new virtual learning environments in which students can learn even when they are literally thousands of miles away (and in a different time zone) from a teacher or other classmates.

Some of the issues for both real and **virtual learning** environments are the same. Students still need to be motivated (see page 20) and we still need to offer help in that area. As a result, the best virtual learning sites have online tutors who interact with their students via email or online chat forums. It is also possible to create groups of students who are all following the same online program – and who can therefore 'talk' to each other in the same way (i.e. electronically). But despite these interpersonal elements, some students find it more difficult to sustain their motivation online than they might as part of a real learning group.

Virtual learning is significantly different from face-to-face classes for a number of reasons. Firstly, students can attend lessons when *they* want for the most part (though real-time chat forums have to be scheduled), rather than when lessons are timetabled (as in schools). Secondly, it no longer matters where the students are since they can log on from any location in the world.

Online learning may have these advantages, but some of the benefits of real learning environments are less easy to replicate electronically. These include the physical reality of having teachers and students around you when you are learning so that you can see their expressions and get messages from their gestures, tone of voice, etc. Many learners will prefer the presence of real people to the sight of a screen, with or without pictures and video. Some communication software (such as MSN Messenger and Skype) allows users to see each other on the screen as they communicate, but this is still less attractive – and considerably more jerky – than being face to face with the teacher and fellow students. Of course, whereas in real learning environments learning can take place with very little technical equipment, virtual learning relies on good hardware and software, and effective and reliable Internet connections.

Although this book will certainly look at uses of the Internet and other IT applications, it is not primarily concerned with the virtual learning environment, preferring instead to concentrate on situations where the teachers and learners are usually in the same place, at the same time.

Learner differences

Whatever their reasons for learning (or the circumstances in which it takes place), it is sometimes tempting to see all students as being more or less the same. Yet there are marked differences, not only in terms of their age and level, but also in terms of different individual abilities, knowledge and preferences. We will examine some of these differences in this section.

Age

Learners are often described as children, young learners, adolescents, young adults or adults. Within education, the term *children* is generally used for learners between the ages of about 2 to about 14. Students are generally described as *young learners* between the ages of about 5 to 9, and *very young learners* are usually between 2 and 5. At what ages it is safe to call students *adolescents* is often uncertain, since the onset of adolescence is bound up with physical and emotional changes rather than chronological age. However, this term tends to refer to students from the ages of about 12 to 17, whereas *young adults* are generally thought to be between 16 and 20.

We will look at three ages: children, adolescents and adults. However, we need to remember that there is a large degree of individual variation in the ways in which different children develop. The descriptions that follow, therefore, must be seen as generalisations only.

Children

We know that children don't just focus on what is being taught, but also learn all sorts of other things at the same time, taking information from whatever is going on around them. We know that seeing, hearing and touching are just as important for understanding as the teacher's explanation. We are conscious, too, that the abstraction of, say, grammar rules, will be less effective the younger the students are. But we also know that children respond well to individual attention from the teacher and are usually pleased to receive teacher approval.

Children usually respond well to activities that focus on their lives and experiences. But a child's attention span – their willingness to stay rooted in one activity – is often fairly short.

A crucial characteristic of young children is their ability to become competent speakers of a new language with remarkable facility, provided they get enough exposure to it. They forget languages, it seems, with equal ease. This language-acquiring ability is steadily compromised as they head towards adolescence.

Adolescents

One of the greatest differences between adolescents and young children is that these older children have developed a greater capacity for abstract thought as they have grown up. In other words, their intellects are kicking in, and they can talk about more abstract ideas, teasing out concepts in a way that younger children find difficult. Many adolescents readily understand and accept the need for learning of a more intellectual type.

At their best, adolescent students have a great capacity for learning, enormous potential for creative thought and a passionate commitment to things which interest them.

Adolescence is bound up with a search for identity and a need for self-esteem. This is often the result of the students' position within their peer group rather than being the consequence of teacher approval.

Adults

Older learners often (but not always) have a wider range of life experiences to draw on, both as individuals and as learners, than younger students do. They are often more disciplined than adolescents and apply themselves to the task of learning even when it seems fairly boring. They often have a clear understanding of why they are learning things, and can sustain their motivation (see pages 20–21) by perceiving (and holding on to) long-term learning goals.

On the other hand, adult learners come with a lot of previous learning experience which may hamper their progress. Students who have had negative learning experiences in the past may be nervous of new learning. Students used to failure may be consciously or subconsciously prepared for more failure. Older students who have got out of the habit of study may find classrooms daunting places. They may also have strong views about teaching methods from their past, which the teacher will have to take into account.

Because students at different ages have different characteristics, the way we teach them will differ too. With younger children we may offer a greater variety of games, songs and puzzles than we would do with older students. We may want to ensure that there are more frequent changes of activity. With a group of adolescents we will try to keep in mind the importance of a student's place within his or her peer group and take special care when correcting or assigning roles within an activity, etc. Our choice of topics will reflect their emerging interests.

One of the recurring nightmares for teachers of adolescents, in particular, is that we might lose control of the class. We worry about lessons that slip away from us, and which we can't manage because the students don't like the subject, each other, the teacher or the school – or sometimes just because they feel like misbehaving, or because issues in their life outside the classroom are affecting their behaviour and outlook on life. Yet teenagers are not the only students who sometimes exhibit problem behaviour (that is behaviour which causes a problem for the teacher, the student him- or herself, and, perhaps, the others in the classroom). Younger children can, of course, cause difficulties for the teacher and class, too. Adults can also be disruptive and exhausting. They may not do it in the same way as younger learners, but teachers of adults can experience a range of behaviours such as students who resist the teacher's attempts to focus their attention on the topic of the lesson and spend the lesson talking to their neighbours, or who disagree vocally with much of what the teacher or their classmates are saying. They may arrive late for class or fail to do any homework. And, whatever the causes of this behaviour, a problem is created.

Teachers need to work both to prevent problem behaviour, and to respond to it appropriately if it occurs. We will discuss how the teacher's behaviour can inspire the students' confidence and cooperation on pages 25–27, and we will discuss what to do if students exhibit problem behaviour on pages 180–182.

Learning styles

All students respond to various stimuli (such as pictures, sounds, music, movement, etc), but for most of them (and us) some things stimulate them into learning more than other things do. The **Neuro-Linguistic Programming** model (often called **NLP**) takes account of this by showing how some students are especially influenced by *visual* stimuli and are therefore likely to remember things better if they see them. Some students, on the other hand, are especially affected by *auditory* input and, as a result, respond very well to things they hear. *Kinaesthetic* activity is especially effective for other learners, who seem to learn best when they are involved in some kind of physical activity, such as moving around, or rearranging things with their hands. The point is that although we all respond to all of these stimuli, for most of us, one or other of them (visual, auditory, kinaesthetic) is more powerful than the others in enabling us to learn and remember what we have learnt.

Another way of looking at student variation is offered by the concept of **Multiple Intelligences**, first articulated by Howard Gardner. In his formulation (and that of people who have followed and expanded his theories), we all have a number of different intelligences (mathematical, musical, interpersonal, spatial, emotional, etc). However, while one person's mathematical intelligence might be highly developed, their interpersonal intelligence (the ability to interact with and relate to other people) might be less advanced, whereas another person might have good spatial awareness and musical intelligence, but might be weak mathematically. Thus it is inappropriate to describe someone as being 'intelligent' or 'unintelligent', because while we may not have much of a knack for, say, music, that does not mean our abilities are similarly limited in other areas.

What these two theories tell us (from their different standpoints) is that in any one classroom we have a number of different individuals with different learning styles and preferences. Experienced teachers know this and try to ensure that different learning styles are catered for as often as is possible. In effect, this means offering a wide range of different activity types in our lessons in order to cater for individual differences and needs.

Nevertheless, we need to find out whether there are any generalisations which will help us to encourage habits in students which will help *all* of them. We might say, for example, that **homework** is good for everyone and so is **reading for pleasure** (see Chapter 7). Certain activities – such as many of the speaking activities in Chapter 9 – are good for all the students in the class, though the way we organise them (and the precise things we ask students to do) may vary for exactly the reasons we have been discussing.

Levels

Teachers of English generally make three basic distinctions to categorise the language knowledge of their students: **beginner**, **intermediate** and **advanced**. Broadly speaking, beginners are those who don't know any English and advanced students are those whose level of English is competent, allowing them to read unsimplified factual and fictional texts and communicate fluently. Between these two extremes, *intermediate* suggests a basic competence in speaking and writing and an ability to comprehend fairly straightforward listening and reading. However, as we shall see, these are rough and ready labels whose exact meaning can vary from institution to institution.

Other descriptive terms are also used in an attempt to be more specific about exactly what kind of beginner, intermediate or advanced students we are talking about. A distinction is made between beginners (students who start a beginners' course having heard virtually no English) and **false beginners** to reflect the fact that the latter can't really use any English but actually know quite a lot which can be quickly activated; they're not real beginners. **Elementary** students are no longer beginners and are able to communicate in a basic way. They can string some sentences together, construct a simple story, or take part in simple spoken interactions.

Pre-intermediate students have not yet achieved intermediate competence, which involves greater fluency and general comprehension of some general authentic English. However, they have come across most of the basic structures and lexis of the language. Upper-intermediate students, on the other hand, have the competence of intermediate students plus an extended knowledge of grammatical construction and skill use. However, they may not have achieved the accuracy or depth of knowledge which their advanced colleagues have acquired, and as a result are less able to operate at different levels of subtlety.

In recent years, the Council of Europe and the Association of Language Testers of Europe (**ALTE**) have worked to define language competency levels for learners of a number of different languages. The result of these efforts is the Common European Framework of Reference for languages (CEFR), with levels ranging from A1 (roughly equivalent to the elementary level) to C2 (very advanced). The following diagram shows the different levels in sequence:

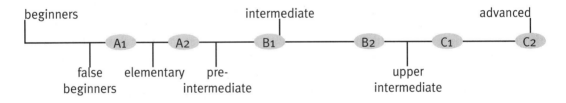

Terms for different student levels (and CEFR levels)

What do these levels mean, in practice, for the students? If they are at level B1, for example, how can their abilities be described? ALTE produced 'can do' statements to try to make this clear, as the example on page 18 for the skill of writing demonstrates (A1 is at the left, C2 at the right).

CEFR levels and 'can do' statements (alongside the more traditional terms we have mentioned) are being used increasingly by coursebook writers and curriculum designers, not only in Europe but across much of the language-learning world.

Can complete basic forms and write notes including times, dates and places.	Can complete forms and write short simple letters or postcards related to personal information.	Can write letters or make notes on familiar or predictable matters.	Can make notes while someone is talking or write a letter including non-standard questions.	Can prepare/ draft professional correspondence, take reasonably accurate notes in meetings or write an essay which shows an ability to communicate.	Can write letters on any subject and full notes of meetings or seminars with good expression or accuracy.

ALTE 'can do' statements for writing

However, two points are worth making: the ALTE standards are just one way of measuring proficiency. ESL standards were developed by the **TESOL** organisation in the US (see chapter notes), and many exam systems have their own level descriptors. We also need to remember that students' abilities within any particular level may be varied too (i.e. they may be much better at speaking than writing, for example).

If we remind ourselves that terms such as *beginner* and *intermediate* are rough guides only (in other words, unlike the ALTE levels, they do not say exactly what the students can do), then we are in a position to make broad generalisations about the different levels:

Beginners

Success is easy to see at this level, and easy for the teacher to arrange. But then so is failure! Some adult beginners find that language learning is more stressful than they expected and reluctantly give up. However, if things are going well, teaching beginners can be incredibly stimulating. The pleasure of being able to see our part in our students' success is invigorating.

Intermediate students

Success is less obvious at intermediate level. Intermediate students have already achieved a lot, but they are less likely to be able to recognise an almost daily progress. On the contrary, it may sometimes seem to them that they don't improve that much or that fast anymore. We often call this the **plateau effect**, and the teacher has to make strenuous attempts to show students what they still need to learn without being discouraging. One of the ways of doing this is to make the tasks we give them more challenging, and to get them to analyse language more thoroughly. We need to help them set clear goals for themselves so that they have something to measure their achievement by.

Advanced students

Students at this level already know a lot of English. There is still the danger of the plateau effect (even if the plateau itself is higher up!) so we have to create a classroom culture where students understand what still has to be done, and we need to provide good, clear evidence of progress. We can do this through a concentration not so much on grammatical accuracy, but on style and perceptions of, for example, **appropriacy** (using the right language in the right situation), **connotation** (whether words have a negative or positive tinge, for example) and **inference** (how we can read behind the words to get a writer's true meaning). In these areas, we can enable students to use language with more subtlety. It is also at this level, especially, that we have to encourage students to take more and more responsibility for their own learning.

Although many activities can clearly be used at more than one level (designing newspaper front pages, writing radio commercials, etc), others are not so universally appropriate. With beginners, for example, we will not suggest abstract discussions or the writing of **discursive essays**. For advanced students, a **drill** (where students repeat in chorus and individually – see pages 86–87) focusing on simple past tense questions will almost certainly be inappropriate. Where a simple role-play with ordinary information questions ('What time does the next train to London leave?', 'What's the platform for the London train?', etc) may be a good target for beginners to aim at, the focus for advanced students will have to be richer and more subtle, for example, 'What's the best way to persuade someone of your opinion in an argument?', 'How can we structure writing to hold the reader's attention?', 'What different devices do English speakers use to give emphasis to the bits of information they want you to notice?'

Another obvious difference in the way we teach different levels is language. Beginners need to be exposed to fairly simple grammar and vocabulary which they can understand. In their language work, they may get pleasure (and good learning) from concentrating on straightforward questions like 'What's your name?', 'What's your telephone number?', 'Hello', 'Goodbye', etc. Intermediate students know all this language already and so we will not ask them to concentrate on it.

The level of language also affects the teacher's behaviour. At beginner levels, the need for us to rough-tune our speech (see page 37) is very great: we can exaggerate our voice tone and use gesture to help us to get our meaning across. But at higher levels, such extreme behaviour is not so important. Indeed, it will probably come across to the students as patronising.

At all levels, teachers need to ascertain what students know before deciding what to focus on. At higher levels, we can use what the students already know as the basis for our work; at lower levels we will, for example, always try to **elicit** the language (that is, try to get the language from the students rather than giving it to them) we are going to focus on. That way we know whether to continue with our plan or whether to amend it then and there because students, perhaps, know more than we expected.

Educational and cultural background

We have already discussed how students at different ages present different characteristics in the classroom. Another aspect of individual variation lies in the students' **cultural** (and **educational**) **background**.

Some children come from homes where education is highly valued, and where parental help is readily available. Other children, however, may come from less supportive backgrounds where no such backup is on offer. Older students – especially adults – may come from a variety of backgrounds and, as a result, have very different expectations of what teaching and learning involves.

Where students have different cultural backgrounds from the teacher or from each other, they may feel differently from their classmates about topics in the curriculum. They may have different responses to classroom practices from the ones the teacher expected or the ones which the writers of the coursebook they are using had anticipated. In some educational cultures, for example, students are expected to be articulate and question (or even challenge) their teachers, whereas in others, the students' quietness and modesty are more highly prized. Some educational cultures find **learning by rote** (memorising facts and figures) more attractive than **learning by doing** (where students are involved in project work and experimentation in order to arrive at knowledge). And it is worth remembering that even where students all live in the same town or area, it is often the case that they come from a variety of cultural backgrounds.

In many English-speaking countries such as Britain, the US, Australia, etc, **multilingual classes** (classes where students come from different countries and therefore have different **mother tongues**) are the norm, especially in private language schools. As a result, students are likely to represent a range of educational and cultural backgrounds.

As teachers, we need to be sensitive to these different backgrounds. We need to be able to explain what we are doing and why; we need to use material, offer topics and employ teaching techniques which, even when engaging and challenging, will not offend anyone in the group. Where possible, we need to be able to offer different material, topics and teaching techniques (at different times) to suit the different individual expectations and tastes.

The importance of student motivation

A variety of factors can create a desire to learn. Perhaps the learners love the subject they have chosen, or maybe they are simply interested in seeing what it is like. Perhaps, as with young children, they just happen to be curious about everything, including learning.

Some students have a practical reason for their study: they want to learn an instrument so they can play in an orchestra, learn English so they can watch American TV or understand manuals written in English, study T'ai Chi so that they can become fitter and more relaxed, or go to cookery classes so that they can prepare better meals.

This desire to achieve some goal is the bedrock of motivation and, if it is strong enough, it provokes a decision to act. For an adult this may involve enrolling in an English class. For a teenager it may be choosing one subject over another for special study. This kind of motivation – which comes from outside the classroom and may be influenced by a number of external factors such as the attitude of society, family and peers to the subject in question – is often referred to as **extrinsic** motivation, the motivation that students bring into the classroom from outside. **Intrinsic** motivation, on the other hand, is the kind of motivation that is generated by what happens inside the classroom; this could be the teacher's methods, the activities that students take part in, or their perception of their success or failure.

While it may be relatively easy to be extrinsically motivated (that is to have a desire to do something), **sustaining** that motivation can be more problematic. As students we can become bored, or we may find the subject more difficult than we thought it was going to be.

One of the teacher's main aims should be to help students to sustain their motivation. We can do this in a number of ways. The activities we ask students to take part in will, if they involve the students or excite their curiosity – and provoke their participation – help them to stay interested in the subject. We need, as well, to select an appropriate **level of challenge** so that things are neither too difficult nor too easy. We need to display appropriate teacher qualities so that students can have confidence in our abilities and professionalism (see Chapter 2). We need to consider the issue of **affect** – that is, how the students feel about the learning process. Students need to feel that the teacher really cares about them; if students feel supported and valued, they are far more likely to be motivated to learn.

One way of helping students to sustain their motivation is to give them, as far as is feasible, some **agency** (a term borrowed from the social sciences) which means that students should take some responsibility for themselves, and that they should (like the agent of a passive sentence) be the 'doers' in class. This means that they will have some decision-making power, perhaps, over the choice of which activity to do next, or how they want to be corrected, for example (see page 97). If students feel they have some influence over what is happening, rather than always being told exactly what to do, they are often more motivated to take part in the lesson.

But however much we do to foster and sustain student motivation, we can only, in the end, encourage by word and deed, offering our support and guidance. Real motivation comes from within each individual, from the students themselves.

Responsibility for learning

If giving students agency is seen as a key component in sustaining motivation, then such agency is not just about giving students more decision-making power. It is also about encouraging them to take more responsibility for their own learning. We need to tell them that unless they are prepared to take some of the strain, their learning is likely to be less successful than if they themselves become active learners (rather than passive recipients of teaching).

This message may be difficult for some students from certain educational backgrounds and cultures who have been led to believe that it is the teacher's job to provide learning. In such cases, teachers will not be successful if they merely try to impose a pattern of **learner autonomy**. Instead of imposing autonomy, therefore, we need to gradually extend the students' role in learning. At first we will expect them, for example, to make their own dialogues after they have listened to a model on an audio track. Such standard practice (getting students to try out new language) is one small way of encouraging student involvement in learning. We might go on to try to get individual students to investigate a grammar issue or solve a reading puzzle on their own, rather than having things explained to them by the teacher. We might get them to look for the meanings of words and how they are used in their dictionaries (see below) rather than telling them what the words mean. As students get used to working things out for themselves and/or doing work at home, so they can gradually start to become more autonomous.

Getting students to do various kinds of homework, such as written exercises, compositions or further study is one of the best ways to encourage student autonomy. What is important is that teachers should choose the right kind of task for the students. It should be within their grasp, and not take up too much of their time – or occupy too little of it by being trivial. Even more importantly than this, teachers should follow up homework when they say they are going to, imposing the same deadlines upon themselves as they do on their students. Other ways of promoting student self-reliance include having them read for pleasure in their own time (see pages 99–100) and find their own resources for language practice (in books or on the Internet, for example).

Apart from homework, teachers will help students to become autonomous if they encourage them to use **monolingual learners' dictionaries** (dictionaries written only in

English, but which are designed especially for learners) and then help them to understand how and when to use them. At earlier stages of learning, good **bilingual dictionaries** serve the same function and allow the students a large measure of independence from the teacher.

We will help students to be responsible for their learning if we show them where (either in books, in self-access centres or online) they can continue studying outside the classroom. For example, we can point them in the direction of suitable websites (if they have computer access), or recommend good CD or DVD resources. If students are lucky, their institution will have a **self-access centre** with a range of resources comprising books (including readers – see page 100), newspapers, magazines, worksheets, listening material, videos and DVDs, and computers with access to the Internet. Students can decide if and when to visit such centres and what they want to do there. Self-access centres should help students to make appropriate choices by having good cataloguing systems and ensuring that people are on hand to help students find their way around. However, the object of a self-access centre is that students should themselves take responsibility for what they do and make their own decisions about what is most appropriate for them.

Of course, many schools do not have self-access centres, and even where they do, many students do not make full use of them. This is because not all students, as we have said, are equally capable of being (or wanting to be) autonomous learners. Despite this fact, we should do our best to encourage them to have agency without forcing it upon them.

Conclusions | *In this chapter we have:*

- discussed different reasons for learning, including students living in a target-language community, or studying English for specific or academic purposes, or because they want to improve their English generally.

- looked at different learning contexts, including English as a Foreign or Second Language (now both generally called English for Speakers of Other Languages), the world of schools and language schools, different class sizes, in-company teaching and virtual learning (via information technology).

- detailed student differences in age, learning styles, language level and cultural/educational background, and how we should cater for such differences.

- talked about the importance of motivation and how to foster it.

- discussed the students' responsibility for their own learning, and how we can encourage this.

Teachers

- **Describing good teachers**
- **Who teachers are in class**
- **Rapport**
- **Teacher tasks**
- **Teacher skills**
- **Teacher knowledge**
- **Art or science?**

Describing good teachers

Most people can look back at their own schooldays and identify teachers they thought were good. But generally they find it quite hard to say *why* certain teachers struck them as special. Perhaps it was because of their personality. Possibly it was because they had interesting things to say. Maybe the reason was that they looked as if they loved their job, or perhaps their interest in their students' progress was compelling. Sometimes, it seems, it was just because the teacher was a fascinating person!

One of the reasons that it is difficult to give general descriptions of good teachers is that different teachers are often successful in different ways. Some teachers are more extrovert or introvert than others, for example, and different teachers have different strengths and weaknesses. A lot will depend, too, on how students view individual teachers and here again, not all students will share the same opinions.

It is often said that 'good teachers are born, not made' and it does seem that some people have a natural affinity for the job. But there are also others, perhaps, who do not have what appears to be a natural gift but who are still effective and popular teachers. Such teachers learn their craft through a mixture of personality, intelligence, knowledge and experience (and how they reflect on it). And even some of the teachers who are apparently 'born teachers' weren't like that at the beginning at all, but grew into the role as they learnt their craft.

Teaching is not an easy job, but it is a necessary one, and can be very rewarding when we see our students' progress and know that we have helped to make it happen. It is true that some lessons and students can be difficult and stressful at times, but it is also worth remembering that at its best teaching can also be extremely enjoyable.

In this chapter we will look at what is necessary for effective teaching and how that can help to provoke success – so that for both students and teachers learning English can be rewarding and enjoyable.

Who teachers are in class

When we walk into a lesson, students get an idea of who we are as a result of what we look like (how we dress, how we present ourselves) and the way we behave and react to what is going on. They take note, either consciously or subconsciously, of whether we are always the same or whether we can be flexible, depending on what is happening at a particular point in the lesson.

As we have said, teachers, like any other group of human beings, have individual differences. However, one of the things, perhaps, that differentiates us from some other professions, is that we become different people, in a way, when we are in front of a class from the people we are in other situations, such as at home or at a party. Everyone switches roles like this in their daily lives to some extent, but for teachers, who we are (or appear to be) when we are at work is especially important.

Personality

Some years ago, in preparation for a presentation to colleagues, I recorded interviews with a large number of teachers and students. I asked them 'What makes a good teacher?' and was interested in what their instant responses would be. A number of the people I questioned answered by talking about the teacher's character. As one of them told me, 'I like the teacher who has his own personality and doesn't hide it from the students so he is not only a teacher but a person as well – and it comes through in the lesson.'

Discussing teacher personality is difficult for two reasons: in the first place there is no one ideal teacher personality. Some teachers are effective because they are 'larger than life', while others persuade through their quiet authority. But the other problem – as the respondent seemed to be saying to me in the comment above – is that students want not only to see a professional who has come to teach them, but also to glimpse the 'person as well'.

Effective teacher personality is a blend between who we really are, and who we are as teachers. In other words, teaching is much more than just 'being ourselves', however much some students want to see the real person. We have to be able to present a professional face to the students which they find both interesting and effective. When we walk into the classroom, we want them to see someone who looks like a teacher whatever else they look like. This does not mean conforming to some kind of teacher stereotype, but rather finding, each in our own way, a persona that we adopt when we cross the threshold. We need to ask ourselves what kind of personality we want our students to encounter, and the decisions we take before and during lessons should help to demonstrate that personality. This is not to suggest that we are in any way dishonest about who we are – teaching is not acting, after all – but we do need to think carefully about how we appear. One 12-year-old interviewee I talked to (see above) answered my question by saying that 'the teacher needs to have dress sense – not always the same old boring suits and ties!' However flippant this comment seems to be, it reminds us that the way we present ourselves to our students matters, whether this involves our real clothes (as in the student's comments) or the personality we 'put on' in our lessons.

Adaptability

What often marks one teacher out from another is how they react to different events in the classroom as the lesson proceeds. This is important, because however well we have prepared, the chances are that things will not go exactly to plan. Unexpected events happen in lessons and part of a teacher's skill is to decide what the response should be when they do. We will discuss such **magic moments** and unforeseen problems on page 157.

Good teachers are able to absorb the unexpected and to use it to their and the students' advantage. This is especially important when the learning outcomes we had planned for look as if they may not succeed because of what is happening. We have to be flexible enough to work with this and change our destination accordingly (if this has to be done) or find some other way to get there. Or perhaps we have to take a decision to continue what we are doing despite the interruption to the way we imagined things were going to proceed. In other words, teachers need to be able to 'think on their feet' and act quickly and decisively at various points in the lesson. When students see that they can do this, their confidence in their teachers is greatly enhanced.

Teacher roles

Part of a good teacher's art is the ability to adopt a number of different roles in the class, depending on what the students are doing. If, for example, the teacher always acts as a **controller**, standing at the front of the class, dictating everything that happens and being the focus of attention, there will be little chance for students to take much responsibility for their own learning, in other words, for them to have **agency** (see page 21). Being a controller may work for grammar explanations and other information presentation, for instance, but it is less effective for activities where students are working together cooperatively on a project, for example. In such situations we may need to be **prompters**, encouraging students, pushing them to achieve more, feeding in a bit of information or language to help them proceed. At other times, we may need to act as feedback providers (helping students to evaluate their performance) or as **assessors** (telling students how well they have done or giving them grades, etc). We also need to be able to function as a **resource** (for language information, etc) when students need to consult us and, at times, as a language **tutor** (that is, an advisor who responds to what the student is doing and advises them on what to do next).

The way we act when we are controlling a class is very different from the listening and advising behaviour we will exhibit when we are tutoring students or responding to a presentation or a piece of writing (something that is different, again, from the way we assess a piece of work). Part of our teacher personality, therefore, is our ability to perform all these roles at different times, but with the same care and ease whichever role we are involved with. This flexibility will help us to facilitate the many different stages and facets of learning.

Rapport

A significant feature in the intrinsic motivation of students (see page 20) will depend on their perception of what the teacher thinks of them, and how they are treated. It is no surprise, therefore, to find that what many people look for when they observe other people's lessons, is evidence of good **rapport** between the teacher and the class.

Rapport means, in essence, the relationship that the students have with the teacher, and vice versa. In the best lessons we will always see a positive, enjoyable and respectful relationship. Rapport is established in part when students become aware of our professionalism (see above), but it also occurs as a result of the way we listen to and treat the students in our classrooms.

Recognising students

One of the students I talked to in my research said that a good teacher was 'someone who knows our names'. This comment is revealing both literally and metaphorically. In the first place, students want teachers to know their names rather than, say, just pointing at them. But this is extremely difficult for teachers who see eight or nine groups a week. How can they remember all their students?

Teachers have developed a number of strategies to help them remember students' names. One method is to ask the students (at least in the first week or two) to put name cards on the desk in front of them or stick name badges on to their sweaters or jackets. We can also draw up a seating plan and ask students always to sit in the same place until we have learnt their names. However, this means we can't move students around when we want to, and students – especially younger students – sometimes take pleasure in sitting in the wrong place just to confuse us.

Many teachers use the register to make notes about individual students (Do they wear glasses? Are they tall?, etc) and others keep separate notes about the individuals in their classes.

There is no easy way of remembering students' names, yet it is extremely important that we do so if good rapport is to be established with individuals. We need, therefore, to find ways of doing this that suit us best.

But 'knowing our names' is also about knowing *about* students. At any age, they will be pleased when they realise that their teacher has remembered things about them, and has some understanding of who they are. Once again, this is extremely difficult in large classes, especially when we have a number of different groups, but part of a teacher's skill is to persuade students that we recognise them, and who and what they are.

Listening to students

Students respond very well to teachers who listen to them. Another respondent in my research said that 'It's important that you can talk to the teacher when you have problems and you don't get along with the subject'. Although there are many calls on a teacher's time, nevertheless we need to make ourselves as available as we can to listen to individual students.

But we need to listen properly to students in lessons too. And we need to show that we are interested in what they have to say. Of course, no one can force us to be genuinely interested in absolutely everything and everyone, but it is part of a teacher's professional personality (see page 24) that we should be able to convince students that we are listening to what they say with every sign of attention.

As far as possible we also need to listen to the students' comments on how they are getting on, and which activities and techniques they respond well or badly to. If we just go on teaching the same thing day after day without being aware of our students' reactions, it will become more and more difficult to maintain the rapport that is so important for successful classes.

Respecting students

One student I interviewed had absolutely no doubt about the key quality of good teachers. 'They should be able to correct people without offending them', he said with feeling.

Correcting students (see page 97) is always a delicate event. If we are too critical, we risk demotivating them, yet if we are constantly praising them, we risk turning them into 'praise junkies', who begin to need approval all the time. The problem we face, however, is that while some students are happy to be corrected robustly, others need more support and positive reinforcement. In speaking activities (see Chapter 9), some students want to be corrected the moment they make any mistake, whereas others would like to be corrected later. In other words, just as students have different learning styles and intelligences, so, too, they have different preferences when it comes to being corrected. But whichever method of correction we choose, and whoever we are working with, students need to know that we are treating them with respect, and not using mockery or sarcasm – or expressing despair at their efforts!

Respect is vital, too, when we deal with any kind of problem behaviour. We could, of course, respond to indiscipline or awkwardness by being biting in our criticism of the student who has done something we do not approve of. Yet this will be counterproductive. It is the behaviour we want to criticise, not the character of the student in question.

Teachers who respect students do their best to see them in a positive light. They are not negative about their learners or in the way they deal with them in class. They do not react with anger or ridicule when students do unplanned things, but instead use a respectful professionalism to solve the problem.

Being even-handed

Most teachers have some students that they like more than others. For example, we all tend to react well to those who take part, are cheerful and cooperative, take responsibility for their own learning, and do what we ask of them without complaint. Sometimes we are less enthusiastic about those who are less forthcoming, and who find **learner autonomy**, for example, more of a challenge. Yet, as one of the students in my research said, 'a good teacher should try to draw out the quiet ones and control the more talkative ones', and one of her colleagues echoed this by saying that 'a good teacher is … someone who asks the people who don't always put their hands up'.

Students will generally respect teachers who show impartiality and who do their best to reach all the students in a group rather than just concentrating on the ones who 'always put their hands up'. The reasons that some students are not forthcoming may be many and varied, ranging from shyness to their cultural or family backgrounds. Sometimes students are reluctant to take part overtly because of other stronger characters in the group. And these quiet students will only be negatively affected when they see far more attention being paid to their more robust classmates. At the same time, giving some students more attention than others may make those students more difficult to deal with later since they will come to expect special treatment, and may take our interest as a licence to become overdominant in the classroom. Moreover, it is not just teenage students who can suffer from being the 'teacher's pet'.

Treating all students equally not only helps to establish and maintain rapport, but is also a mark of professionalism.

Teacher tasks

Teaching doesn't just involve the relationship we have with students, of course. As professionals we are also asked to perform certain tasks.

Preparation

Effective teachers are well-prepared. Part of this **preparation** resides in the knowledge they have of their subject and the skill of teaching, something we will discuss in detail on pages 30–32. But another feature of being well-prepared is having thought *in advance* of what we are going to do in our lessons. As we walk towards our classroom, in other words, we need to have some idea of what the students are going to achieve in the lesson; we should have some **learning outcomes** in our head. Of course, what happens in a lesson does not always conform to our plans for it, as we shall discuss on pages 156–157, but students always take comfort from the perception that their teacher has thought about what will be appropriate for their particular class on that particular day.

The degree to which we plan our lessons differs from teacher to teacher. It will often depend, among other things, on whether we have taught this lesson (or something like it) before. We will discuss planning in detail in Chapter 12.

Keeping records

Many teachers find the administrative features of their job (taking the register, filling forms, writing report cards) irksome, yet such **record keeping** is a necessary adjunct to the classroom experience.

There is one particularly good reason for keeping a record of what we have taught. It works as a way of looking back at what we have done in order to decide what to do next. And if we keep a record of how well things have gone (what has been more or less successful), we will begin to come to conclusions about what works and what doesn't. It is important for professional teachers to try to evaluate how successful an activity has been in terms of student engagement and learning outcomes. If we do this, we will start to amend our teaching practice in the light of experience, rather than getting stuck in sterile routines. It is one of the characteristics of good teachers that they are constantly changing and developing their teaching practice as a result of reflecting on their teaching experiences.

Being reliable

Professional teachers are reliable about things like timekeeping and homework. It is very difficult to berate students for being late for lessons if we get into the habit (for whatever reason) of turning up late ourselves. It is unsatisfactory to insist on the prompt delivery of homework if it takes us weeks to correct it and give it back.

Being reliable in this way is simply a matter of following the old idiom of 'practising what we preach'.

Teacher skills

As we have suggested, who we are and the way we interact with our students are vital components in successful teaching, as are the tasks which we are obliged to undertake. But these will not make us effective teachers unless we possess certain teacher skills.

Managing classes

Effective teachers see classroom management as a separate aspect of their skill. In other words, whatever activity we ask our students to be involved in, or whether they are working with a board, a tape recorder or a computer, we will have thought of (and be able to carry out) procedures to make the activity successful. We will know how to put students into groups, or when to start and finish an activity. We will have worked out what kinds of instructions to give, and what order to do things in. We will have decided whether students should work in groups, in pairs or as a whole class. We will have considered whether we want to move them around the class, or move the chairs into a different seating pattern (see pages 40–43). We will discuss classroom management in more detail in Chapter 3.

Successful class management also involves being able to prevent disruptive behaviour and reacting to it effectively when it occurs (see pages 180–182).

Matching tasks and groups

Students will learn more successfully if they enjoy the activities they are involved in and are interested or stimulated by the topics we (or they) bring into the classroom. 'Teachers', I was told when I conducted my interviews (see above), 'should make their lessons interesting, so you don't fall asleep in them!' Of course, in many institutions, topics and activities are decreed to some extent by the material in the coursebook that is being used. But even in such situations there is a lot we can do to make sure we cater for the range of needs and interests of the students in our classes (see pages 14–20).

Many teachers have the unsettling experience of using an activity with, say, two or three groups and having considerable success only to find that it completely fails in the next class. There could be many reasons for this, including the students, the time of day, a mismatch between the task and the level or just the fact that the group weren't 'in the mood'.

However, what such experiences clearly suggest is that we need to think carefully about matching activities and topics to the different groups we teach. Whereas, for example, some groups seem happy to work creatively on their own, others need more help and guidance. Where some students respond well to teacher presentation (with the teacher acting as a controller), others are much happier when they investigate language issues on their own.

Variety

Good teachers vary activities and topics over a period of time. The best activity type will be less motivating the sixth time we ask the students to take part in it than it was when they first came across it. Much of the value of an activity, in other words, resides in its freshness.

But even where we use the same activity types for some reason (because the curriculum expects this or because it is a feature of the materials we are using), it is important to try to ensure that **learner roles** are not always the same. If we use a lot of group discussion, for example, we want to be sure that the same student isn't always given the role of taking notes, rather than actually participating in the discussion themselves. When we get students to read texts, we won't always have them work on comprehension questions in the same way. Sometimes they might compare answers in pairs; sometimes they might interview each other about the text; sometimes they might do all the work on their own.

Variety works within lessons, too. It is not just children who can become bored by doing the same thing all the time. Thus, although there may be considerable advantages in using language **drills** for beginner students, we won't want to keep a drill running for half an hour because it would exhaust both students and teacher. However, we might make a different kind of activity, such as a role-play, last for longer than this. A lot depends on exactly what we are asking students to do.

Where we are using a coursebook for a large part of the time, it is advisable to vary the ways in which we use certain repetitive activity types. Just because reading comprehension exercises always look the same in a book, for example, it doesn't mean we always have to approach them in the same way. We will discuss ways of using and adapting coursebooks in more detail in Chapter 11.

Destinations

When we take learning activities into the classroom, we need to persuade our students of their usefulness. Good activities should have some kind of destination or **learning outcome**, and it is the job of the teacher to make this destination apparent. Students need to have an idea of where they are going, and more importantly, to recognise when they have got there.

Of course, some activities, such as **discussions**, don't have a fixed end. Nevertheless, even in such circumstances, it will be helpful if we can make sure that students leave the class with some tangible result. That is why a summing-up, or feedback session at the end of a discussion, for example, is so valuable.

Teacher knowledge

Apart from the ability to create and foster good teacher–student rapport and the possession of skills necessary for organising successful lessons, teachers need to know a lot about the subject they are teaching (the English language). They will need to know what equipment is available in their school and how to use it. They need to know what materials are available for teachers and students. They should also do their best to keep abreast of new developments in teaching approaches and techniques by consulting a range of print material, online resources, and by attending, where possible, development sessions and teacher seminars.

The language system

Language teachers need to know how the language works. This means having a knowledge of the **grammar** system and understanding the **lexical** system: how words change their shape depending on their grammatical function, and how they group together into phrases. They need to be aware of pronunciation features such as **sounds**, **stress** and **intonation**. These different features of the language system are explained in Chapter 5.

Students have a right to expect that teachers of the English language can explain straightforward grammar concepts, including how and when they are used. They expect their teachers to know the difference between the colloquial language that people use in informal conversation and the more formal language required in more formal settings. They also expect teachers to be able to demonstrate and help them to pronounce words correctly and with appropriate intonation.

When students have doubts about the language, they frequently ask their teachers to explain things. They ask 'What's the difference between … and …?' or 'Why can't we say …?' Sometimes the answer is clear and easy to explain. But at other times the issue is one of great complexity and even the most experienced teacher will have difficulty giving an instant answer. In other words, our knowledge of the language system may not be adequate for certain kinds of on-the-spot questions about subtleties. Moreover, sometimes the question is not especially relevant – it is a distraction from what is going on in the lesson.

In such situations, teachers need to be able to say things like 'That's a very interesting question. I think the answer is X, but I will check to make sure and I will bring you a more complete answer tomorrow' or 'That's a very interesting question. I don't want to answer it now because we are doing something else. But you can find the answer yourself if you go to this book. We'll discuss it tomorrow'. Students will realise that these answers are perfectly appropriate when the teacher does indeed return for the next lesson with the information that they have promised. This will demonstrate the teacher's knowledge of the language and reference materials. But if, on the other hand, we forget to find the information and never mention the question again, students will gradually start to think we just don't know enough about the language to find what we are looking for – or that we just don't care.

Materials and resources

When students ask the kind of complicated questions mentioned above, good teachers know where to find the answers. We need, in other words, to know about books and websites where such technical information is available. However, this is quite a challenge in today's world, where the sheer number of coursebook titles released every year can sometimes seem overwhelming, and where there are quite a significant number of grammar books and **monolingual learners' dictionaries** (**MLDs**) to choose from – to say nothing of the multitude of useful websites on the Internet. No one expects teachers to be all-knowing in this respect: what colleagues and students can expect, however, is that teachers know where to find at least one good reference grammar at the appropriate level, or a good MLD, or can direct them to a library or a website where *they* can find these things.

If teachers are using a coursebook, students expect them, of course, to know how the materials work. Their confidence will be greatly enhanced if they can see that the teacher has looked at the material they are using before the lesson, and has worked out a way of dealing with it.

Classroom equipment

Over the last few decades the growth in different types of classroom equipment has been incredible. Once upon a time we only had pens, board and chalk to work with. But then along came the tape recorder, the **language laboratory**, video machines, the **overhead projector**, computers, **data projectors** and **interactive whiteboards** (these are all described in Appendix A on page 252).

Some teachers are more comfortable with these various pieces of educational technology than others. This will always be the case. There is no reason why everyone should be equally proficient at everything. However, students will expect that teachers should know how to use the equipment that they have elected to use. Learning how to use various types of equipment is a major part of modern teacher training.

However, we should do everything in our power to avoid being overzealous about the equipment itself. It is only worth using if it can do things that other equipment or routines cannot. The essentials of good teaching – i.e. rapport, professionalism, using good activities – will always be more important than the actual means of delivery. What has changed recently, though, is that students can do things they were unable to do before thanks to technical innovation. Thus modern **podcasts** (downloadable listening which can be played on individual MP3 players) give students many more listening opportunities than ever before. They can also write their own **blogs** (Internet diaries) and put them on the web. They can burn CDs with examples of their work and the materials used in class to take home when a course has finished. They can search for a wide range of language and information resources in a way that would have been impossible a few years ago.

As teachers, we need to do everything we can to keep abreast of technological change in educational resources. But we should never let technology drive our decisions about teaching and learning. We should, instead, decide what our learners want to achieve and only then see what kind of techniques and technology will help them to do this.

Keeping up-to-date

Teachers need to know how to use a variety of activities in the classroom, of course, but they also need to be constantly finding out about new ways of doing things.

A good way of learning about new activities and techniques is to read the various teachers' magazines and journals that are available (see Appendix B on page 259). There is now a wealth of information about teaching on the Internet, too. Magazines, books and websites often contain good descriptions of new activities and how to use them. We can also learn a lot from attending seminars and teachers' conferences, and listening to other teachers describing new activities and the successes they have had with them.

Two things need to be said about the various 'knowledges' we have been describing. In the first place, it is difficult for newly qualified teachers to keep everything in their heads at the same time as they struggle with the demands of a new job. Nevertheless, as they learn their craft, we would expect them to be hungry for as much knowledge in these areas as possible since this will make them better teachers. Secondly, this kind of knowledge is not static, hence the need to keep up-to-date. Things change almost daily. New books, classroom equipment and computer software are being produced all the time, just as teachers keep coming up with wonderful new ways of doing old things (such as grammar presentation or discussion activities). Staying in touch with these developments can seem daunting, of course, because of the pace of change, but it is worth remembering how deadly it would be if things always stayed the same.

Art or science?

Is teaching language an art, then, or is it a science? As this chapter has shown, there are good grounds for focusing on its almost-scientific attributes. Understanding the language system and finding the best ways to explain it is some kind of a scientific endeavour, especially when we continue to research its changes and evolution. In the same way, some of the technical skills that are required of teachers (procedures for how to do things, a constant attention to innovation in educational technology and materials design) need to be almost scientific in their rigour.

Yet teaching is an art, too. It works when the relationship that is created between teacher and students, and between the students in a group, is at its best. If we have managed to establish a good rapport with a group, almost anything is possible. We have discussed some of the key requirements in creating such a rapport, yet behind everything we have said lurks the possibility of magic – or a lack of it. Because the way some teachers are able to establish fantastic rapport, or get students really interested in a new activity may be observable, but trying to work out exactly how it was done or why it happened may be more difficult. In the same way, the instant decision-making we have been discussing can happen on supposedly scientific grounds, but its success, and the creativity that can be unleashed, is often the result of the teacher's feelings or judgment at that very moment. For as we have said, good teachers listen and watch, and use both professional and personal skills to respond to what they see and hear. Good teachers have a knack of responding by doing things 'right', and that is most definitely an art.

Conclusions | *In this chapter we have:*

- discussed the personality that teachers show to the students. We have said this has to be in some way different (and more 'teacher-like') from our normal selves.
- talked about the need for teachers to be both adaptable and able to perform different roles at different lesson stages.
- seen the necessity of creating good teacher–student rapport as a result of listening to students, respecting them and being totally even-handed in our treatment of individuals and groups.
- mentioned the need for preparation, record keeping and reliability.
- said that among the skills teachers need to acquire are the ability to manage classes, match tasks to different groups and circumstances, provide variety in lessons and offer students clear learning outcomes.
- discussed the knowledge that teachers need to acquire, including knowledge of the language system, available materials, resources and classroom equipment, and knowledge about the latest developments in the field.
- said that teaching is both a science and an art.

# Managing
the classroom

- **Classroom management**
- **The teacher in the classroom**
- **Using the voice**
- **Talking to students**
- **Giving instructions**
- **Student talk and teacher talk**

- **Using the L1**
- **Creating lesson stages**
- **Different seating arrangements**
- **Different student groupings**

Classroom management

If we want to manage classrooms effectively, we have to be able to handle a range of variables. These include how the classroom space is organised, whether the students are working on their own or in groups and how we organise classroom time. We also need to consider how we appear to the students, and how we use our most valuable asset – our voice. The way we talk to students – and who talks most in the lesson – is another key factor in classroom management. We also need to think about what role, if any, there may be for the use of the students' **mother tongue** in lessons. Successful classroom management also involves being able to deal with difficult situations – an issue we will discuss on pages 180–182.

The teacher in the classroom

Our physical presence can play a large part in our management of the classroom environment. And it's not just appearance either (though that was clearly an issue for the secondary student in Chapter 2 – page 24). The way we move and stand, and the degree to which we are physically demonstrative can have a clear effect on the management of the class. Most importantly, the way we are able to respond to what happens in class, the degree to which we are aware of what is going on, often marks the difference between successful teaching and less satisfactory lessons.

All teachers, like all people, have their own physical characteristics and habits, and they will take these into the classroom with them. But there are a number of issues to consider which are not just matters of personality or style and which have a direct bearing on the students' perception of us.

Proximity

Teachers need to consider how close they should be to the students they are working with. Some students are uncomfortable if their teacher stands or sits close to them. For some, on the other hand, distance is a sign of coldness. Teachers should be conscious of how close they are to their students, should take this into account when assessing their students' reactions and should, if necessary, modify their behaviour.

Appropriacy

Deciding how close to the students you should be when you work with them is a matter of appropriacy. So is the general way in which teachers sit or stand in classrooms. Many teachers create an extremely friendly atmosphere by crouching down when they work with students in pairs. In this way, they are at the same level as their seated students. However, some students find this informality worrying. Some teachers are even happy to sit on the floor, and in certain situations this may be appropriate. But in others it may well lead to a situation where students are put off concentrating.

All the positions teachers take – sitting on the edge of tables, standing behind a lectern, standing on a raised dais, etc – make strong statements about the kind of person the teacher is. It is important, therefore, to consider what kind of effect such physical behaviour has so that we can behave in a way which is appropriate to the students we are teaching and the relationship we wish to create with them. If we want to manage a class effectively, such a relationship is crucial.

Movement

Some teachers tend to spend most of their class time in one place – at the front of the class, for example, or to the side, or in the middle. Others spend a great deal of time walking from side to side, or striding up and down the aisles between the chairs. Although this, again, is to some extent a matter of personal preference, it is worth remembering that motionless teachers can bore students, while teachers who are constantly in motion can turn their students into tennis spectators, their heads moving from side to side until they become exhausted.

Most successful teachers move around the classroom to some extent. That way they can retain their students' interest (if they are leading an activity) or work more closely with smaller groups (when they go to help a pair or group).

How much we move around in the classroom will depend on our personal style, where we feel most comfortable for the management of the class and whether or not we want to work with smaller groups.

Awareness

In order to manage a class successfully, the teacher has to be aware of what students are doing and, where possible, how they are feeling. This means watching and listening just as carefully as teaching. This will be difficult if we keep too much distance or if we are perceived by the students to be cold and aloof because then we will find it difficult to establish the kind of rapport we mentioned in Chapter 2.

Awareness means assessing what students have said and responding appropriately. According to the writer Michael Lewis, a colleague of his, Peter Wilberg, put this perfectly when he said that 'the teacher's primary responsibility is response-ability'! This means being able to perceive the success or failure of what is taking place in the classroom, and being flexible enough (see page 157) to respond to what is going on. We need to be as conscious as possible of what is going on in the students' heads.

It is almost impossible to help students to learn a language in a classroom setting without making contact with them in this way. The exact nature of this contact will vary from teacher to teacher and from class to class.

Finally, it is not just awareness of the students that is important. We also need to be self-aware, in order to try to gauge the success (or otherwise) of our behaviour and to gain an understanding of how our students see us.

The teacher's physical approach and personality in the class is one aspect of class management to consider. Another is one of the teacher's chief tools: the voice.

Using the voice

Perhaps our most important instrument as teachers is our voice. How we speak and what our voice sounds like have a crucial impact on classes. When considering the use of the voice in the management of teaching, there are three issues to think about.

Audibility

Clearly, teachers need to be audible. They must be sure that the students at the back of the class can hear them just as well as those at the front. But audibility cannot be divorced from voice quality: a rasping shout is always unpleasant.

Teachers do not have to shout to be audible. Good voice projection is more important than volume (though the two are, of course, connected). Speaking too softly or unpleasantly loudly are both irritating and unhelpful for students.

Variety

It is important for teachers to vary the quality of their voices – and the volume they speak at – according to the type of lesson and the type of activity. The kind of voice we use to give instructions or introduce a new activity will be different from the voice which is most appropriate for conversation or an informal exchange of views or information.

In one particular situation, teachers often use very loud voices, and that is when they want students to be quiet or stop doing something (see the next section). But it is worth pointing out that speaking quietly is often just as effective a way of getting the students' attention since, when they realise that you are talking, they will want to stop and listen in case you are saying something important or interesting. However, for teachers who almost never raise their voices, the occasional shouted interjection may have an extremely dramatic effect, and this can sometimes be beneficial.

Conservation

Just like opera singers, teachers have to take great care of their voices. It is important that they breathe correctly so that they don't strain their larynxes. Breathing properly means being relaxed (in the shoulders, for example, and not slumped backwards or forwards), and using the lower abdomen to help expand the rib cage, thus filling the lungs with air. It is important too that teachers vary their voices throughout the day, avoiding shouting wherever possible, so that they can conserve their vocal energy. Conserving the voice is one of the things teachers will want to take into account when planning a day's or a week's work.

Talking to students

The way that teachers talk to students – the manner in which they interact with them – is one of the crucial teacher skills, but it does not demand technical expertise. It does, however, require teachers to empathise with the people they are talking to by establishing a good rapport with them.

One group of people who seem to find it fairly natural to adapt their language to their audience are parents when they talk to their young children. Studies show that they use more exaggerated tones of voice and speak with less complex grammatical structures than they would if they were talking to adults. Their vocabulary is generally more restricted, they make more frequent attempts to establish eye contact and they use other forms of physical contact. They generally do these things unconsciously.

Though the teacher–student relationship is not the same as that between a parent and child, this subconscious ability to **rough-tune** the language is a skill that teachers and parents have in common. Rough-tuning is the simplification of language which both parents and teachers make in order to increase the chances of their being understood. Neither group sets out to get the level of language exactly correct for their audience. They rely, instead, on a general perception of what is being understood and what is not. Because they are constantly aware of the effect that their words are having, they are able to adjust their language use – in terms of grammatical complexity, vocabulary use and voice tone – when their listener shows signs of incomprehension.

In order to rough-tune their language, teachers need to be aware of three things. Firstly, they should consider the kind of language that students are likely to understand. Secondly, they need to think about what they wish to say to the students and how best to do it. And thirdly, they need to consider the manner in which they will speak (in terms of intonation, tone of voice, etc). But these considerations need not be detailed. To be successful at rough-tuning, all we have to do is speak at a level which is more or less appropriate.

Experienced teachers rough-tune the way they speak to students as a matter of course. Newer teachers need to pay attention to their students' comprehension and use it as the yardstick by which to measure their own speaking style in the classroom.

Apart from adapting their language, teachers also use physical movements and **gestures** (these are often quite exaggerated), such as shrugging the shoulders for 'who cares?' or scratching the head to show puzzlement. Many teachers also use gestures to demonstrate things like the past tense (pointing back over their shoulders). They use facial expressions to show emotions such as happiness and sadness, and mime to demonstrate actions such as opening a book or filling a glass and drinking. Gesture, expression and mime should become a natural adjunct to the language we use, especially with students at lower levels.

Giving instructions

This issue of how to talk to students becomes crucial when we give them instructions. The best activity in the world is a waste of time if the students don't understand what it is they are supposed to do.

There are two general rules for giving instructions: they must be kept as simple as possible, and they must be logical. Before giving instructions, therefore, teachers must ask themselves the following questions: What is the important information I am trying to convey? What must the students know if they are to complete this activity successfully?

What information do they need first? Which should come next?

When teachers give instructions, it is important for them to **check** that the students have understood what they are being asked to do. This can be achieved either by asking a student to explain the activity after the teacher has given the instruction or by getting someone to show the other people in the class how the exercise works. Where students all share the same mother tongue (which the teacher also understands), a member of the class can be asked to translate the instructions into their mother tongue as a check that they have understood them.

Student talk and teacher talk

There is a continuing debate about the amount of time teachers should spend talking in class. Classes are sometimes criticised because there is too much **TTT** (Teacher Talking Time) and not enough **STT** (Student Talking Time).

Overuse of TTT is inappropriate because the more a teacher talks, the less chance there is for the students to practise their own speaking – and it is the students who need the practice, not the teacher. If a teacher talks and talks, the students will have less time for other things, too, such as reading and writing. For these reasons, a good teacher maximises STT and minimises TTT.

Good TTT may have beneficial qualities, however. If teachers know how to talk to students, if they know *how* to rough-tune their language to the students' level as discussed above, then the students get a chance to hear language which is certainly above their own productive level, but which they can more or less understand. Such **comprehensible input** – where students receive rough-tuned input in a relaxed and unthreatening way – is an important feature in language acquisition.

Perhaps, therefore, we should not talk simply about the difference between STT and TTT, but also consider **TTQ** (Teacher Talking Quality). In other words, teachers who just go on and on, using language which is not especially useful or appropriate, are not offering students the right kind of talking, whereas teachers who engage students with their stories and interaction, using appropriate comprehensible input will be helping them to understand and acquire the language.

The best lessons, therefore, are ones where STT is maximised, but where at appropriate moments during the lesson the teacher is not afraid to summarise what is happening, tell a story or enter into discussion, etc. Good teachers use their common sense and experience to get the balance right.

Using the L1

All learners of English, whatever their situation, come to the classroom with at least one other language, their mother tongue (often called their **L1**). We need to ask ourselves, therefore, whether it is appropriate for them to use the L1 in class when their main object is, after all to learn an **L2** (in our case English).

The first thing to remember is that, especially at beginner levels, students are going to translate what is happening into their L1 whether teachers want them to or not. It is a natural process of learning a foreign language. On the other hand, an English-language classroom should have English in it, and as far as possible, there should be an English environment in the room, where English is heard and used as much of the time as possible. For that reason, it is advisable for teachers to use English as often as possible, and not to spend a long time talking in the students' L1.

However, where teacher and students share the same L1 it would be foolish to deny its existence and potential value. Once we have given instructions for an activity, for example, we can ask students to repeat the instructions back to us in the L1 – and this will tell us whether they have understood what they have to do. When we have complicated instructions to explain, we may want to do this in the L1, and where students need individual help or encouragement, the use of the L1 may have very beneficial effects.

Since students translate in their heads anyway, it makes sense to use this translation process in an active way. For example, we can ask students to translate words, phrases or sentences into their L1, and then, perhaps, back into English without looking at the original. This helps them to think carefully about meaning and construction. Teachers may translate particular words, especially those for concepts and abstractions, when other ways of explaining their meaning are ineffective. At a more advanced level, we can have students read a text, say, in their L1, but get them to ask and answer questions about it, or summarise it, in English.

When teaching pronunciation, it is often useful if students can find an equivalent sound in the L1 for the English one they are trying to produce. We may want to explain to them how English has two different sounds where the L1 does not make such a distinction (e.g. /b/ and /v/ for Spanish speakers, /l/ and /r/ for Japanese speakers).

Some teachers like to use films in the L1 with English subtitles; judging whether the subtitles offer an adequate version of the original can offer considerable insight for higher-level students. Alternatively, with switch-on/off subtitles, students can be asked to write their own English subtitles for a scene before watching how the filmmakers have done it.

However, using the translation process in the ways described above does not mean a return to a traditional **Grammar–translation method** (see page 48), but rather that, from time to time, using the students' L1 may help them to see connections and differences between the L1 and the L2, and that, occasionally, the teacher's use of the L1 may help them to understand things that they are finding difficult to grasp.

However, in many classrooms around the world there are students with a variety of different L1s and, as a result, the use of L1 becomes more problematic. In such situations, it is still useful to get students to think of similarities and differences between their L1 and the L2, but they will have to explain these differences in English.

Making use of the students' L1 (where possible) does not mean we should abandon the commitment (mentioned above) to creating an English environment. Although we have seen that the L1 can be used as an enabling tool, English should predominate in an English lesson, especially where the teacher is concerned since, as we have seen, he or she is the best provider of comprehensible input that the students have got. Not only that, but English is the language they are learning, not their L1. However, despite our best efforts, some students find it difficult to use English in the classroom, and we will discuss that issue on pages 178–179.

Creating lesson stages

Since, as we said in Chapter 2, teachers needs to provide variety, then clearly we have to include different stages in our lessons.

When we arrive in the classroom, we need to start the lesson off in such a way that the students' interest is aroused so that they become engaged. Where possible and appropriate, we will tell the students what they will be doing or, in a different kind of lesson, discuss with them what they can achieve as a result of what they are going to do.

We do not always need to explain exactly what we are going to do, however, particularly if we want to maintain an element of surprise. But even in such cases, a clear start to the lesson is necessary, just as a good play starts with the rise of a curtain, or a visit to the doctor starts when he or she asks you, 'Now then, what seems to be the problem?' or 'How can I help you?'.

When an activity has finished and/or another one is about to start, it helps if teachers make this clear through the way they behave and the things they say. It helps students if they are made clearly aware of the end of something and the beginning of what is coming next. Frequently, teachers need to re-focus the students' attention, or point it in some new direction.

In order for such changes of direction to be effective, the teacher first needs to get the students' attention. This can sometimes be difficult, especially when teachers try to draw a speaking activity to a conclusion, or when students are working in groups. Some teachers clap their hands to get the students' attention. Some speak loudly, saying things like, 'Thank you … now can I have your attention, please?' or 'OK … thanks … let's all face the front, shall we?'. Sometimes when teachers speak loudly, the students just speak louder in order not to be bothered by the interruption. To counter this, some teachers speak quietly in order to force the students to listen to them. Another method is for the teacher to raise his or her hand. When individual students see this, they raise their hands briefly in reply to indicate that they are now going to be quiet and wait for the next stage.

When we have brought an activity or a lesson to a finish, it helps if we provide some kind of closure: a summary of what has happened, perhaps, or a prediction of what will take place in the next lesson. Sometimes, teachers find themselves in the middle of something when the bell goes. This is unfortunate because it leaves unfinished business behind and a sense of incompleteness. It is much better to round the lesson off successfully. Ideally, too, we will be able to give the students some idea of what they will be doing next, and create enthusiasm for it so that they come to their next lesson with a positive attitude.

The stages of a lesson will be a particular concern when planning lessons (see Chapter 12).

Different seating arrangements

In many classrooms around the world students sit in orderly rows. Sometimes, their chairs have little wooden palettes on one of the arms to provide a surface to write on. Sometimes, the students will have desks in front of them. At the front of such classrooms, often on a raised platform (so that all the students can see them), stands the teacher. In contrast, there are other institutions where you can find students sitting in a large circle around the walls of the classroom. Or you may see small groups of them working in different parts of the room. Sometimes, they are arranged in a horseshoe shape around the teacher. Sometimes, in a class of adults, it is not immediately obvious who the teacher is.

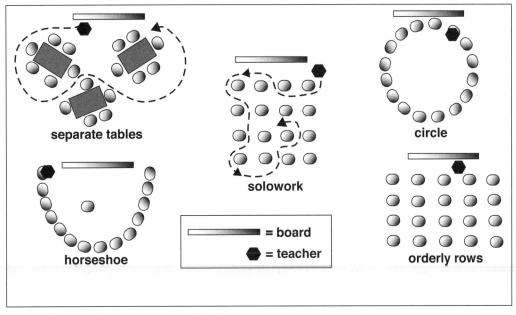

Different seating arrangements in class

Clearly, the different arrangements of chairs and tables indicate a number of different approaches and this raises a number of questions. Are schools which use a variety of seating plans progressive or merely modish, for example? Is there something intrinsically superior about rigid seating arrangements – or are such classrooms the product of a particular methodological orthodoxy? Is one kind of seating arrangement better than another? What are the advantages of each? We will look at the advantages and disadvantages of various seating arrangements.

Orderly rows

Having the students sit in rows can appear somewhat restrictive, but there are advantages to this arrangement. The teacher has a clear view of all the students and the students can all see the teacher – in whose direction they are facing. It makes lecturing easier, enabling the teacher to maintain eye contact with the people he or she is talking to. If there are aisles in the classroom, the teacher can easily walk up and down making more personal contact with individual students and watching what they are doing.

Orderly rows imply teachers working with the whole class. Some activities are especially suited to this kind of organisation such as explaining a grammar point, watching a video/DVD or a PowerPoint (or other computer-based) presentation, using the **board** (whether or not it is **interactive**) or showing student work on an **overhead transparency** (see Appendix A on page 252 for descriptions of these and other classroom technologies). It is also useful when students are involved in certain kinds of language practice (as we shall see in Chapter 6). If all the students are focused on a task at the same time, the whole class gets the same messages.

When we are teaching a whole class of students who are sitting in orderly rows, it is vitally important to make sure that we keep everyone involved in what we are doing. So, if we are asking the class questions, we must remember to ask the students at the back – the quiet ones, perhaps – rather than just the ones nearest us. We must move round so that we can see all the students and gauge their reactions to what's going on.

One trick that many teachers use is to keep their students guessing. Especially where teachers need to ask individual students questions, it is important that they do not do so in a predictable sequence, student after student, line by line. That way, the procedure becomes very tedious and each student knows when they are going to be asked and, once this has happened, that they are not going to be asked again. It is much better to talk to students from all parts of the room in random order. It keeps everyone on their toes!

In many classrooms around the world, teachers are faced with classes of anywhere between 40 and 200 students at a time. In such circumstances, orderly rows may well be the best or only solution.

Pairwork and groupwork (see page 43) are possible even when the class is seated in orderly rows; students can work with people next to them or in front of them or behind them.

Circles and horseshoes

In smaller classes, many teachers and students prefer circles or horseshoes. In a horseshoe, the teacher will probably be at the open end of the arrangement since that may well be where the board, overhead projector and/or computer are situated. In a circle, the teacher's position – where the board is situated – is less dominating.

Classes which are arranged in a circle make quite a strong statement about what the teacher and the students believe in. The Round Table in the British and French legends about King Arthur was specially designed so that there would not be arguments about who was more important than who – and that included the king himself when they were in a meeting. So it is in classrooms. With all the people in the room sitting in a circle, there is a far greater feeling of equality than when the teacher stays out at the front. This may not be quite so true of the horseshoe shape where the teacher is often located in a commanding position but, even here, the rigidity that comes with orderly rows, for example, is lessened.

If, therefore, teachers believe in lowering the barriers between themselves and their students, this kind of seating arrangement will help. There are other advantages too, chief among which is the fact that all the students can see each other. In an 'orderly row' class-room, you have to turn round – that is, away from the teacher – if you want to make eye contact with someone behind you. In a circle or a horseshoe, no such disruption is necessary. The classroom is thus a more intimate place and the potential for students to share feelings and information through talking, eye contact or expressive body movements (eyebrow-raising, shoulder-shrugging, etc) is far greater.

Separate tables

Even circles and horseshoes seem rather formal compared to classes where students are seated in small groups at individual tables. In such classrooms, you might see the teacher walking around checking the students' work and helping out if they are having difficulties – prompting the students at this table, or explaining something to the students at that table in the corner.

When students sit in small groups at individual tables, it is much easier for the teacher to work at one table while the others get on with their own work. This is especially useful in **mixed-ability** classes where different groups of students can benefit from concentrating on different tasks (designed for different ability levels). Separate table seating is also appropriate if students are working around a computer screen, for example where students are engaged in **collaborative writing** (see Chapter 8) or where they are listening to different audio tracks in a jigsaw listening exercise (see Chapter 10).

However, this arrangement is not without its own problems. In the first place, students may not always want to be with the same colleagues; indeed, their preferences may change over time. Secondly, it makes 'whole-class' teaching more difficult, since the students are more diffuse and separated.

Different student groupings

Whatever the seating arrangements in a classroom, students can be organised in different ways: they can work as a whole class, in groups, in pairs or individually.

Whole class

There are many occasions when the best type of classroom organisation is a teacher working with the class as a whole group. However, this does not always mean the class sitting in orderly rows; whatever the seating arrangement, we can have the students focus on us and the task in hand. This is useful for presenting information and for controlled practice (such as repetition and drilling) which is often used, especially at lower levels (see Chapter 6, pages 85–87).

Whole-class teaching can be dynamic and motivating and, by treating everyone as part of the same group, we can build a great sense of belonging – of being part of a team. However, when a class is working as a whole group, it is necessarily the case that individual students get fewer individual opportunities either to speak or to reflect. Whole-class teaching is less effective if we want to encourage individual contributions and discussion, since speaking out in front of a whole class is often more demanding – and therefore more inhibiting – than speaking in smaller groups.

Groupwork and pairwork

Groupwork and pairwork have been popular in language teaching for many years and have many advantages. They both foster **cooperative activity** in that the students involved work together to complete a task. They may be discussing a topic, doing a role-play or working at a computer in order to find information from a website for a webquest (see page 105) or they may be writing up a report. In pairs and groups, students tend to participate more actively, and they also have more chance to experiment with the language than is possible in a whole-class arrangement.

The moment students get into pairs or groups and start working on a problem or talking about something, many more of them will be doing the activity than if the teacher was working with the whole class, where, in most cases, only one student can talk at a time.

Both pairwork and groupwork give the students chances for greater independence. Because the students are working together without the teacher controlling every move, they take some of their own learning decisions (see page 21), they decide what language to use to complete a certain task and they can work without the pressure of the whole class listening to what they are doing.

Another great advantage of groupwork and pairwork (but especially of groupwork) is that they give the teacher more opportunity to focus attention on particular students. While groups A and C are doing one task, the teacher can spend some time with group B who need special help.

Neither groupwork or pairwork are without their problems. As with 'separate table' seating, students may not like the people they are grouped or paired with. Some students are ill-at-ease with the idea of working without constant teacher supervision, and may be unconvinced by the student-centred nature of these groupings. In such situations we may want to discuss the advantages of pair- and groupwork with the class, but we should not insist on endless pairwork where students are seriously opposed to it.

In any one group or pair, one student may dominate while the others stay silent or engage, in William Littlewood's wonderful phrase, in 'social loafing'. But we can counteract this by structuring the task so that everyone's participation is mandatory or we can employ tricks such as Littlewood's *numbered heads*. Here the teacher asks the groups to number themselves from 1 to 5 (if there are five-student groups). They don't tell the teacher who has which number. At the end of the activity the teacher can then say, 'OK, let's hear from number 3 in group C', and because the teacher doesn't know who that student is, and the students don't know who the teacher may call (but do know that the call will, in some senses, be random) they are all more motivated to take part and don't leave it all up to the others.

In difficult classes, groupwork can sometimes encourage students to be more disruptive than they would be in a whole-class setting, and, especially in a class where students share the same first language, they may revert to that language, rather than English, when the teacher is not working with them. Ways of dealing with this are discussed on pages 178–179.

Apart from groupwork and pairwork, the other alternative to whole-class teaching is solo (or individual) work.

Solowork

This can have many advantages: it allows students to work at their own speed, allows them thinking time, and allows them to be individuals. It often provides welcome relief from the group-centred nature of much language teaching. For the time that solowork takes place, students can relax their public faces and go back to considering their own individual needs and progress.

Class-to-class

One last grouping should be mentioned, and that is when we are able to join two classes so that they can interact with each other. Where different-level classes are concerned, higher-level students often feel positive about being able to help students from other classes, just as lower-level students can feel motivated by being able to engage with people whose language is better than theirs.

Class-to-class interactions are good for surveys (where students can work with students they do not normally interact with in the English lesson), discussions and lectures and presentations. They can be time-consuming to organise, but, at their best, can often give students a huge sense of satisfaction.

How much use we make of groupwork, pairwork or solowork depends to a large extent on our style and on the preferences of our students. But it also depends to a large extent on what kind of learning task is involved. Good teachers are able to be flexible, using different class groupings for different activities. As they do this, they can assess which ones are the most successful for which types of activity, so that they can always seek to use the most effective grouping for the task in hand.

Conclusions | *In this chapter we have:*

- discussed the teacher's physical presence and behaviour in the classroom, suggesting that how we move and how close to the students we stand are matters of appropriacy.

- suggested that we need to be self-aware enough to be able to assess the effect of how we act in the classroom.

- examined the need for audibility and variety in the way we use our voice in the classroom – and emphasised the need to conserve our voice.

- introduced the concept of rough-tuning, that is adapting the way we speak especially for students so that they can more or less understand what they are hearing. We have said that rough-tuning is an inexact process.

- talked about the usefulness of gestures, facial expression and mime.

- discussed the need for clear and effective instructions – including checking that students have understood them.

- measured the relative merits of Teacher Talking Time (TTT) and Student Talking Time (STT). We have suggested that the quality of what teachers say may be more important than whether or not TTT predominates.

- discussed the natural phenomenon of student translation (both conscious and unconscious). The students' L1 can be very useful, but we should try to emphasise the use of English.

- suggested that teachers need to indicate clearly the different stages of a lesson.

- talked about different seating possibilities in the classroom (orderly rows, horseshoes, circles and separate tables) and discussed the relative merits of each.

- discussed the relative merits of groupwork, pairwork, solowork, whole-class and class-to-class groupings.

Describing learning and teaching

- ■ Children and language
- ■ Acquisition and learning
- ■ Different times, different methods
- ■ Elements for successful language learning (ESA)
- ■ ESA lesson sequences
- ■ ESA and planning

Children and language

Almost all children acquire a language, apparently without effort. In many parts of the world, children grow up speaking two or more languages. And if young children move to a new country and go to school there, they seem to 'pick up' the new language with incredible ease.

Language **acquisition** seems to be almost guaranteed for children up to about the age of six. They seem to be able to learn languages with incredible facility. They are also capable of forgetting a language just as easily. It is almost as if they can put on and take off different languages like items of clothing! However, this ease of acquisition becomes gradually less noticeable as children move towards puberty, and after that, language acquisition is much more difficult.

Acquisition here describes the way in which people 'get' language with no real conscious effort – in other words, without thinking about grammar or vocabulary, or worrying about which bits of language go where. When children start vocalising their mother tongue at around the age of two, we do not expect them to study it; we expect to just watch it emerge, first at the level of one-word utterances, then two-word utterances, until the phrases and sentences they use become gradually more complex as they grow older.

In order for acquisition to take place, certain conditions need to be met. In the first place, the children need to hear a lot of language. Such **exposure** is absolutely vital. Secondly, it is clear that the nature of the language they hear matters, too. When parents talk to their children, they simplify what they say, both consciously and unconsciously. They don't use complex sentences, or technical vocabulary; they use language which fits the situation, **rough-tuning** what they say to match the child's age and situation. Parents' language is marked by other features, too. They often exaggerate the intonation they use so that their voices sound higher and more enthusiastic than they would if they were talking to friend, colleague or partner.

During childhood we get an enormous amount of such language exposure. Furthermore, most of the language we hear – especially from our parents – is given to us in typical social and emotional interactions so that as we hear language, we also hear the ways in which that language is used. Finally, children have a strong motivational urge to communicate in order to be fed and understood. Together with their parents (and later other adults) they make language together. And then they try it out and use it. This 'trying out' is shown by the way children repeat words and phrases, talk to themselves and generally play with language. But in the end it is their desire to communicate needs, wants and feelings that seems to matter most. And throughout childhood and beyond, most people have a great many opportunities and inducements to use the language they have been acquiring.

It sounds, then, as if three features need to be present in order for children to acquire a language: exposure to it, motivation to communicate with it and opportunities to use it.

Acquisition and learning

If, as we have said, children acquire language subconsciously, what does this tell us about how students should get a second language? Can we (indeed, *should* we) attempt to replicate the child's experience in the language classroom?

Some theorists, notably the American applied linguist Stephen Krashen in the 1980s, have suggested that we can make a distinction between acquisition and **learning**. Whereas the former is subconscious and anxiety free, learning is a conscious process where separate items from the language are studied and practised in turn. Krashen, among others, suggested that teachers should concentrate on acquisition rather than learning and that the role of the language teacher should be to provide the right kind of language exposure, namely **comprehensible input** (that is, language that the students understand more or less, even if it is a bit above their own level of production). Provided that students experience such language in an anxiety-free atmosphere, the argument goes, they will acquire it just as children do, and, more importantly, when they want to say something, they will be able to retrieve the language they need from their acquired-language store. Language which has been learnt, on the other hand, is not available for use in the same way, according to this argument, because the learner has to think much more consciously about what they want to say. The principal function of learnt language is to **monitor** what is coming from our acquired store to check that it is OK. As a result, learnt language tends to 'get in the way' of acquired-language production and may inhibit spontaneous communication.

This apparently convoluted discussion becomes relevant when we consider what we should do with students in class. If we believe that acquisition is superior to learning, we will spend all our time providing comprehensible input. What we will not do is to ask the students to focus on how the language works. Yet there are problems with this approach. In the first place, the ability to acquire language easily tends to deteriorate with age. Secondly, as we saw in Chapter 1, teenagers and adults have perfectly good reasoning powers and may want to think consciously about how language works. To suggest that they should not think about language if they want to (that is, learn it consciously), would seem absurd. And we should remember that for many language learners, one of the biggest differences between them and children acquiring their first language is the amount of exposure they get (in terms of hours), and the situation in which this language is used. Learners in foreign language classrooms are in a very different situation from that of children of loving parents.

Perhaps, mere exposure to comprehensible input is not enough, therefore, for older children and adults. Perhaps, as some claim, they should have their attention drawn to aspects of language so that they can **notice** these aspects; as a result they will recognise them when they come across them again, and this recognition will be the first stage in their 'knowing' of the language which, once known in this way, will be available for them to use.

We can go further and say that a rich classroom environment would not only expose students to language (of course), but also give them opportunities to **activate** their language knowledge. Furthermore, we should offer them chances to **study** language and the way it works too, since for some learners this will be the key to their success, and for all others (apart from young children) it will be an added bonus to the other activities which we take into the classroom. In other words, both acquisition *and* learning have their part to play in language getting for students after childhood.

Different times, different methods

The acquisition-versus-learning debate may seem to be a relatively recent argument, yet for as long as languages have been taught people have argued about the best way of doing it, and how to help students to learn more effectively. The great linguist Harold Palmer made a similar distinction between *spontaneous* and *studial* capacities in a book published in 1921. And this was just one of many writings before and since which have tried to pin down what makes a good language lesson or an effective method.

Current teaching practice is the direct result of such argument and discussion, and not only on the subject of acquisition and learning. Both abstract theory and practical techniques have been debated, have gone in and out of fashion, and have influenced what was and is included in classrooms and teaching materials. In the 1990s, for example, there was considerable discussion about the **Lexical Approach**, where it was suggested that we should structure our curriculum around **language chunks**. These are the various phrases of two or more words which we use as units of meaning to communicate with (see page 75–76 for a fuller explanation). In the 1970s, methods such as the **Silent Way** (where teachers do little talking and the onus is put on the students), or **Community Language Learning** (where bilingual teachers help students to translate what they want to say from their first language into the language they are learning) were advocated, and although they may not be used much any more – certainly not as they were originally envisaged – still some of the techniques they included have been incorporated into modern teaching practice.

Amongst the plethora of ideas and techniques which have been offered over the years, some trends have had – and continue to have – a significant impact on how languages are taught today.

Grammar–translation

The Grammar–translation method (which was first named as such in Germany in the 1780s) introduced the idea of presenting students with short grammar rules and word lists, and then translation exercises in which they had to make use of the same rules and words. It was introduced in a reform of the German secondary school system and soon, with changes and expansions, spread much further afield.

Grammar–translation still has relevance today, though it is not practised as a method in the same way. But most language learners translate in their heads at various stages anyway, and they (and we) can learn a lot about a foreign language by comparing parts of it with parts of our own **mother tongue**. However, a total concentration on grammar–translation stops students from getting the kind of natural language input that will help them acquire language (since they are always looking at L1 equivalents), and it fails to give them opportunities to activate their language knowledge. If they are always translating the language, they are not using the L2 for communication. The danger with Grammar–translation, in other words, is that it teaches people *about* language but doesn't really help them to communicate effectively with it.

Audio-lingualism

The audio-lingual method originated in army education in the 1940s. It was then developed in the 1950s and enhanced by the arrival of the language laboratory in the 1960s. It capitalised on the suggestion that if we describe the grammatical patterns of English, we can have students repeat and learn them. In such **structural-situational** teaching, grammatical structures were presented in simple situations which exemplified their usage. Crucially, too, the structures were carefully graded so that students learnt the easy ones first before moving onto things that were more complex.

Audio-lingualism marries this emphasis on grammatical patterns with **behaviourist** theories of learning. These theories suggested that much learning is the result of habit-formation, where performing the correct **response** to a **stimulus** means that a **reward** is given; constant repetition of this reward makes the response automatic. This procedure is referred to as **conditioning**. In effect, audio-lingual classes made extensive use of drilling, in which students produced the same grammatical pattern but were prompted to use different words within the pattern, in the hope that they would acquire good language habits. By rewarding correct production during these repetition phases, students could be conditioned into learning the language. Early language laboratory tapes used this procedure with students spending hours wearing headphones and responding to prompts or cues in so-called **cue-response drills**. It was only later that people realised all the other uses to which laboratories could be put (such as exposing students to a variety of listening materials), and the laboratory drill 'regime' went out of fashion.

Audio-lingualism (and behaviourism) lost popularity because commentators argued that language learning was far more subtle than just the formation of habits. For example, students are quickly able to produce their own combinations of words, whether or not they have heard them before. This is because all humans have the power to be creative in language, basing what they say on the underlying knowledge they have acquired, including rules of construction and a knowledge of when a certain kind or form of language is appropriate. Methodologists were also concerned that in Audio-lingualism students were not exposed to real or realistic language, and were therefore unlikely to produce natural-sounding language themselves.

However, it is interesting to note that **drilling** (choral and individual repetition and cue-response drilling – see Chapter 6, especially) is still considered a useful technique to use, especially with low-level students.

PPP

Both Audio-lingualism and its assimilation into structural-situationalism have their modern equivalent in the procedure which is often referred to as **PPP**. This stands for

Presentation, Practice and Production. In PPP lessons or sequences, the teacher presents the context and situation for the language (e.g. describing someone's holiday plans) and both explains and demonstrates the meaning and form of the new language (for example, the 'going to' future – e.g. 'He's going to visit the Hermitage Museum'). The students then practise making sentences with 'going to' (this is often called **controlled practice** and may involve drilling – see above) before going on to the production stage in which they talk more freely about themselves ('Next week I'm going to see that new film') or other people in the real world ('My cousin's going to buy a new car', etc). The same procedure can also be used for teaching students functions, such as how to invite people, or for teaching vocabulary. We can teach **pronunciation**, too, using the PPP procedure. After an explanation of how a sound is produced, for example, students are involved in the controlled practice of words using the sound before they are asked to come up with their own words in which the sound is present.

The PPP procedure is still widely used in language classrooms around the world, especially for teaching simple language at lower levels. Most modern coursebooks include examples of PPP grammar and vocabulary teaching which have retained elements of structural-situation methodology and Audio-lingualism. But the general consensus is that PPP is just one procedure among many, and takes no account of other ways of learning and understanding; it is very learning-based (see above) and takes little account of students' acquisition abilities.

Communicative Language Teaching (CLT)

CLT was a 1970s reaction to much that had gone before – namely the grammatical patterning of structural-situationalism and the rigidity of the drill-type methodology that Audio-lingualism (and later PPP) made varying use of.

CLT has two main guiding principles: the first is that language is not just patterns of grammar with vocabulary items slotted in, but also involves **language functions** such as inviting, agreeing and disagreeing, suggesting, etc (see page 76), which students should learn how to perform using a variety of **language exponents** (e.g. we can invite by saying 'Would you like to come to the cinema?', 'D'you fancy coming to the cinema?', 'What about coming to the cinema?', 'How about a film?', 'Are you on for a film?', etc). Students also need to be aware of the need for appropriacy when talking and writing to people in terms of the kind of language they use (formal, informal, tentative, technical, etc). CLT is not just about the language, in other words, it is about how it is used.

The second principle of Communicative Language Teaching is that if students get enough **exposure** to language, and opportunities for language **use** – and if they are motivated – then language learning will take care of itself. Thus CLT has a lot in common with the acquisition view of language absorption that we discussed above. As a result, the focus of much CLT has been on students communicating real messages, and not just grammatically controlled language. The deployment of many **communicative activities**, where students use all and any language they know to communicate, shows this aspect of CLT at work.

Communicative Language Teaching has had a thoroughly beneficial effect since it reminded teachers that people learn languages not so that they know *about* them, but so that they can communicate *with* them. Giving students different kinds of language, pointing them towards aspects of style and appropriacy, and above all giving them opportunities to try out real language within the classroom humanised what had sometimes been too rigidly controlled.

Task-Based Learning (TBL)

TBL is a natural extension of communicative language teaching. In TBL, the emphasis is on the task rather than the language. For example, students perform real-life tasks such as getting information about bus timetables, or making a presentation on a certain topic. Later, after the task has been completed, they can look at the language they have used and work on any imperfections that have arisen, correcting grammatical mistakes or thinking about aspects of style. In other words, instead of language study leading to a task, the task itself is the main focus and jumping-off point for (possible) subsequent study later. This approach puts communicative activities (see above) at the heart of learning, and as a result a TBL syllabus might well be a list of tasks and activities, not a list of language.

A typical TBL sequence starts with a **pre-task** (where students are introduced to the topic and told what the task will be). This is followed by a **task cycle** where the students plan the task, gathering language and information to do it, and then produce the piece of writing or oral performance that the task demands. In the final **language focus** phase, students analyse the language they used for the task, making improvements and practising any language that needs repair or development.

TBL, like a communicative methodology, has allowed teachers and students to concentrate on how we achieve things with language, and how we can use language for certain tasks. It is a significant departure from the original PPP sequence, since it takes the third element (production) as the starting point, not the end-point of the procedure.

Elements for successful language learning (ESA)

Most current language teaching tries to offer a judicious blend of many of the ideas and elements discussed above. It recognises the value of language exposure through comprehensible input, while still believing that most people (apart from young children) find chances to concentrate on language forms and how they can be used extremely helpful. Current language teaching practice generally gives students the opportunity to think about how a piece of grammar works (or which words group together, for example), while at the same time providing opportunities for language use in communicative activities and task-based procedures. It offers students the security of appropriate controlled practice (depending on variables such as the students' age, personal learning styles and the language in question), while also letting them have a go at using all and any language they know.

Such eclecticism – choosing between the best elements of a number of different ideas and methods – is a proper response to the competing claims of the various trends we have described. However, the danger of eclecticism is the possible conclusion that since we can use bits and pieces from different theories and methods, 'anything goes'. Our lessons can then become a disorganised ragbag of different activities with no obvious coherence or philosophy to underpin them. This can be just as damaging as the methodological rigidity that eclecticism aims to replace.

However, eclecticism that makes use of an underlying philosophy and structure, in other words, a **principled eclecticism** avoids these risks. Believing that students need exposure, motivation and opportunities for language use, and acknowledging that different students may respond more or less well to different stimuli, it suggests that most teaching sequences need to have certain characteristics or elements, whether they take place over a few minutes, half an hour, a lesson or a sequence of lessons. These elements are **Engage**,

Study and **Activate**. Having discussed what they mean, we will go on to look at how they can occur within three typical sequences (out of many).

Engage (E)

Most of us can remember lessons at school which were uninvolving and where we 'switched off' from what was being taught. We may also remember lessons where we were more or less paying attention, but where we were not really 'hooked'. We were not **engaged** emotionally with what was going on; we were not curious, passionate or involved. Yet things are learnt much better if both our minds *and* our hearts are brought into service. Engagement of this type is one of the vital ingredients for successful learning.

Activities and materials which frequently engage students include: games (depending on the age of the learners and the type of game), music, discussions (when handled challengingly), stimulating pictures, dramatic stories, amusing anecdotes, etc. Even where such activities and materials are not used, teachers can do their best to ensure that their students engage with the topic, exercise or language they are going to be dealing with by asking them to make **predictions**, or relate classroom materials to their own lives. A lot will depend, of course, on what the individual students are like, as we saw in Chapter 1, and how well the teacher provokes and encourages engagement.

The reason why this element is so important in teaching sequences, therefore, is that when students are properly engaged, their involvement in the study and activation stages is likely to be far more pronounced, and, as a result, the benefit they get from these will be considerably greater.

Study (S)

Study activities are those where the students are asked to focus on the **construction** of something, whether it is the language itself, the ways in which it is used or how it sounds and looks. Study activities can range from the focus on and practice of a single sound to an investigation of how a writer achieves a particular effect in a long text; from the examination and practice of a verb tense to the study of a transcript of informal speech in order to discuss spoken style. In the PPP procedure described above, both presentation and practice (the first two stages) are focusing on the construction of an element of grammar or lexis; after all, controlled practice (where students repeat many phrases using the language they are focusing on) is designed to make students think about language construction. When we have students repeat words with the correct pronunciation (or say the words we want them to say based on **cues** we give them), it is because we want them to think about the best way to say the words. We want them to think of the construction of the words' pronunciation.

But study here means more than the PPP procedure – although PPP is, of course, one kind of study. Students can study in a variety of different ways. Sometimes we may show them a new grammar pattern, repeating each element separately or putting a diagram on the board before getting them to repeat sentences, and that is very much like a PPP procedure. But at other times, we may show students examples of language and ask them to try to work out the rules. Such **discovery activities** ask the students to do all the intellectual work, rather than leaving it to the teacher. Sometimes students can read a text together and find words and phrases they want to concentrate on for later study. At other times, they may spend time, with the teacher, listening to or looking at the language they have used to see when it has been more or less successful. All of these (and many other possibilities) are examples of the study of language construction.

Some typical language areas for study might be the study and practice of the vowel sound in 'ship' and 'sheep' (e.g. 'chip', 'cheap', 'dip', 'deep', 'bit', 'beat', etc), the study and practice of the third person singular of the present simple ('He sleeps', 'she laughs', 'it works', etc), the study and practice of lexical phrases for inviting ('*Would you like to* come to the cinema/to a concert?', etc), the study and practice of the way we use pronouns in written discourse (e.g. 'A man entered a house in Brixton. *He* was tall with an unusual hat. *It* was multicoloured …', etc), the study and practice of paragraph organisation (topic sentence, development, conclusion) or of the rules for using 'make' and 'do'.

Activate (A)

This element describes exercises and activities which are designed to get students using language as freely and communicatively as they can (as in CLT – see page 50). We will not be asking them to focus on the use of a particular structure, or to try to use words from a list we give them. That would make what they are doing more like a study activity, where they are expected to focus on the accuracy of specific bits of language, rather than on the message they are trying to convey or the task that needs to be performed. The objective in an activate activity is for them to use *all* and *any* language which may be appropriate for a given situation or topic. In this way, students get a chance to try out real language use with little or no restriction – a kind of rehearsal for the real world.

Personalisation (where students use language they have studied to talk about themselves, or to make their own original dialogues, often as the third or production phase of PPP) provides a bridge between the study and activate stages. But more genuinely activate exercises include role-plays (where students act out, as realistically as possible, an exchange between a travel agent and a client, for example), advertisement design (where students write and then record a radio commercial, for example), debates and discussions, *Describe and draw* (where one student tries to get another to draw a picture without that other student being able to see the original), story and poem writing, email exchanges, writing in groups, etc.

Activation is not just about producing language in speech and writing, however. When students read or listen for pleasure (or when they are listening or reading to understand the message rather than thinking about the form of the language they are seeing or hearing), they are involved in language activation. They are using all and any language at their disposal to comprehend the reading or listening text.

But, of course, students may, once they have been through an activation stage, go back to what they have said or to the text they have read, and focus upon its construction. Activation can be a prelude to study, rather than necessarily the other way round.

All three ESA elements need to be present in most lessons or teaching sequences. Whatever the main focus of the lesson (e.g. a grammar topic or a reading skills exercise), students always need to be *engaged*, if possible, so that they can get the maximum benefit from the learning experience. Most students will readily appreciate opportunities to activate their language knowledge, but for many of them the inclusion of study elements, however small or of short duration these are, will persuade them of the usefulness of the lesson.

Some events, for example a **debate** or a **role-play**, a prolonged Internet-based search or a piece of extended writing take a lot of time and so, in one lesson, teachers may not want to interrupt the flow of activation with a study stage. But they may want to use the exercise as a basis for study (perhaps in a different lesson). The same might be true of an extended study period where chances for activation are few. But, in both these cases, the only limitation is time. The missing elements will appear at some other time.

The majority of teaching and learning at lower levels is not made up of such long activities, however. Instead, it is far more likely that there will be more than one ESA sequence in a given lesson sequence or period.

ESA lesson sequences

Just because the three elements of ESA need to be present in lesson sequences, this does not mean that they should always occur in the same order. In the first place, the order is bound to change depending on what we want to achieve. If we are running a task-based lesson, the study event may well come after activation. On the other hand, if we are introducing a piece of grammar, we may study the language first before the students are asked to try to use it.

Secondly, there is a danger that if we always do things in the same order, students will become bored; predictability can diminish students' enthusiasm and motivation – and ours, as teachers, too.

Many different teaching sequences (using the ESA elements in a number of different ways) are possible. We can look at just three possibilities to sense how varied the sequences can be.

One type of teaching sequence takes students in a straight line and, as a result, is called **straight arrows**: first the teacher gets the class interested and engaged; then they study something; then they try to activate it by putting it into production. Here is an example of such a sequence designed for elementary-level students to teach 'can' and 'can't':

1 **Engage:** students and teacher look at a picture, website or DVD of new generation robots. Perhaps they can watch a brief clip of the movie *I, Robot* or some other contemporary film with a similar theme. They say whether they like or don't like the idea of robots.

2 **Study:** the teacher shows students (the picture of) a particular robot. Students are introduced to 'can' and 'can't' (how they are pronounced and constructed) and say things like 'It can use a cash machine' and 'It can't play the piano'. The teacher tries to make sure the sentences are pronounced correctly and that the students use accurate grammar.

3 **Activate:** students work in groups to design and describe their dream robot. They make a presentation to the class saying what their robot can and can't do.

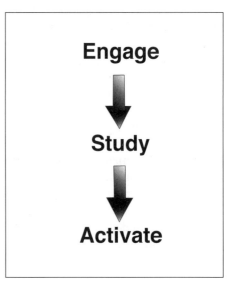

We can represent this kind of lesson like this:

ESA straight arrows sequence

Straight arrows lessons, much like PPP procedures (see page 49), work very well for certain structures. The robot example clearly shows how 'can' and 'can't' are constructed and how they are used. It gives students a chance to practise the language in a controlled way (during the study phase) and then gives them the chance to begin to activate the 'new' language in an enjoyable way.

However, if we teach all our lessons like this, we may not be giving our students' own learning styles (see page 16) a fair chance. Such a procedure may work at lower levels for straightforward language, but it might not be so appropriate for more advanced learners with more complex language. It won't be of much use if we want students to get involved with a reading text or have a discussion about something. It wouldn't be terribly useful either if most of the students already know how to use 'can' and 'can't'.

Thus, while there is nothing wrong with using the straight arrows sequence – for the right students at the right level, learning the right language – it is not always appropriate. Instead, there are other possibilities for the sequence of the ESA elements. Here, for example, is a **boomerang** procedure:

1 Engage: students and teacher discuss issues surrounding job interviews. What makes a good interviewee? What sort of thing does the interviewer want to find out? Hopefully, the students get interested in the topic.

2 Activate: the teacher describes an interview situation which the students are going to act out in a role-play. The students plan the kind of questions they are going to ask and the kind of answers they might want to give (not focusing specifically on language construction, etc, but treating it as a real-life task). They then role-play the interviews. While they are doing this, the teacher makes a note of language difficulties they have and particular mistakes that can be worked on later.

3 Study: when the role-plays are over, the teacher works with the students on the grammar and vocabulary which caused them trouble. For example, students can compare their language with more correct usage and try to work out (discover) for themselves where they went wrong. The teacher may explain what the problems were or refer students to grammar books, etc. They might do some controlled practice of the language (see pages 85–87).

4 Activate: some time later, students role-play another job interview, having absorbed the corrections to the language they used last time round.

A diagram for boomerang lessons can show this procedure like this:

EAS(A) boomerang sequence

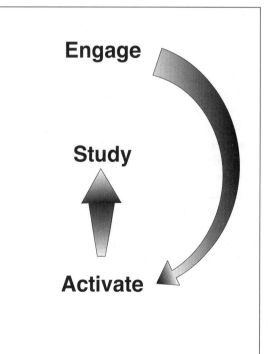

Engage

Study

Activate

In this sequence the teacher is answering the needs of the students. They are not taught language until and unless they have shown (in the activate phase) that they have a need for it. In some ways, this makes much better sense because the connection between what students need to learn and what they are taught is more transparent. However, it places a greater burden on the teacher since he or she will have to be able to find good teaching material based on the (often unforeseen) problems thrown up at the first activate stage. It may also be more appropriate for students at intermediate and advanced levels since they have quite a lot of language already available to them to use in an activate stage.

Boomerang sequences feel much more like the kind of TBL procedures we discussed on page 51; the task came first, not a specific language point. But then the boomerang comes back (if we need it) to remind us to study some of the language used, more or less successfully, in the task. A more specific type of boomerang sequence is sometimes called **test–teach–test** where the students are first asked to use language in an activation stage, and are then taught how to deal with things they made mistakes with before trying the testing part of it again.

Many lessons aren't quite as clear-cut as this, however. Instead, they are a mixture of procedures and mini-procedures, a variety of short episodes building up to a whole. Here is an example of this kind of **patchwork** lesson:

1 Engage → Activate: students look at a picture of sunbathers and respond to it by commenting on the people and the activity they are taking part in. Maybe they look at each other's holiday photos, etc. Then they act out a dialogue between a doctor and a sunburn victim after a day at the beach.

2 Activate: students look at a text describing different people (with different skin types) and the effects the sun has on their skin (see page 103). They say how they feel about the effects of the sun.

3 Study: the teacher does vocabulary work on words such as 'pale', 'fair-skinned', 'freckles', 'tan', etc, ensuring that students understand the meaning and the hyphenated compound nature of some of them, and that they are able to say them with the correct pronunciation in appropriate contexts.

4 Activate: students describe themselves or people they know in the same kind of ways as the reading text.

5 Study: the teacher focuses the students' attention on the relative clause construction used in the text (e.g. 'I'm the type of person who always burns' and 'I'm the type of person who burns easily'). The use of the 'who' clause is discussed and students practise sentences, saying things like 'They're the kind of people who enjoy movies', etc.

6 Engage: the teacher discusses advertisements with the students. What are they for? What different ways do they try to achieve their effect? What are the most effective ads the students can think of? Perhaps the teacher plays some radio commercials or puts some striking visual ads on an overhead projector.

7 Activate: the students write a radio commercial for a sunscreen. The teacher lets them record it, using sound effects and music.

We can represent a (version of a) patchwork lesson sequence in the following way:

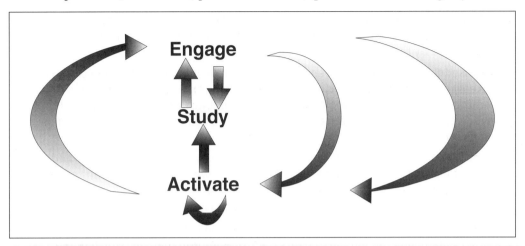

EAASASEA (etc) patchwork sequence

Such classes are very common, especially at intermediate and advanced levels. Not only do they probably reflect the way we learn – rather chaotically, not always in a straight line – but they also provide an appealing balance between study and activation, and between language and topic.

Engage, Study and Activate are the basic building blocks for successful language teaching and learning. By using them in different and varied sequences, teachers will be doing their best to promote their students' success since various theories and procedures which have informed debates about language learning are reflected in sequences such as straight arrows, boomerang and patchwork lessons.

ESA and planning

When we think of what to do in our lessons, we have to decide what it is we hope our students will achieve by the end of a lesson (or the end of a week or month, for example). We then try to plan how to get there (see Chapter 12). In this context, balancing up the three ESA elements reminds us of the need for student engagement; it prompts us to ensure that there are study events built into the plan; it ensures that in almost all lessons there are also opportunities for students to have a go at using the language they are learning (or learnt yesterday, last week or last month). When they try to use language (whether for interacting with other people's texts and conversation or in order to produce language themselves) they get a chance for the kind of mental processing that makes all that learning and acquisition worthwhile. We will remember, too, that is important to vary the sequence of events for the reasons we stated on page 29.

Many teachers have to plan around a coursebook (see Chapter 11) which has been chosen for their classes. But even where lessons are based on coursebook pages, it is important to manipulate the activities in the book so that the three elements, engage, study and activate are evident in appropriate sequences.

Conclusions | *In this chapter we have:*

■ looked at how children acquire language with little effort provided they have exposure to it and opportunities to use it. But the language they are exposed to is rough-tuned by their parents, etc.

■ discussed the difference between the concepts of acquisition (a subconscious process) and learning (a conscious study of language). Despite some claims that learning is only useful for monitoring our own language output, we said that for anyone post-puberty the chance to study language construction should not be in some way 'disallowed'!

■ talked about the fact that different times have thrown up different theories and different methods, including the Lexical Approach (which argues that language consists of a series of lexical phrases and that these should be the object of study) and methods from the 1970s which purported to have a humanistic emphasis.

■ looked at Grammar–translation (which depended on contrasts between the mother tongue and the language being learnt), Audio-lingualism (which relied on behaviourist views of learning, and thus involved a lot of drilling), structural-situational teaching – and its more modern equivalent P(resentation), P(ractice) and P(roduction). We also looked at Communicative Language Teaching (with its twin strands of a focus on how language is used and on communicative activities), and Task-Based Learning (which takes CLT one stage further and uses tasks as the organising units in a curriculum).

■ argued that a 'principled eclecticism' mixes elements from all these approaches, but says that all (or most) lesson sequences should have three elements, Engage, Study and Activate.

■ said that the three elements (ESA) can occur in a different order, depending on the main focus of the lesson. We saw three different sequences: 'straight arrows', 'boomerang' and 'patchwork'.

Describing language

- Meaning in context
- The elements of language
- Forms and meanings
- Parts of speech
- Hypothetical meaning

- Words together
- Language functions
- Text and discourse
- Language variables

Meaning in context

No one who speaks English has any difficulty understanding the meaning of a sentence like 'It's warm in here'. We all recognise that it is a comment on the temperature in some place or other. But why it is being said, and what the speaker wishes to convey by saying it, depends entirely on two things: the **context** in which it is said and what the speaker wants people to understand.

Suppose, for example, that the words are spoken by someone who is either lazy, ill or in some position of power. 'It's warm in here' might then be either a request or an order for someone to open a window. If, however, two people come in out of the cold, 'It's warm in here' might well be an expression of satisfaction or pleasure. If, to give a third example, two people are trying to decide which room to use as their bedroom, the sentence 'It's warm in here' might serve as a suggestion to choose or not to choose the room. In each case, the sentence is performing a different **language function** (see page 76), e.g. requesting, suggesting, etc.

The meaning of language depends on where it occurs within a larger stretch of **discourse** (see pages 76–78), and thus the relationship that the different language elements have with what comes before and after them. In other words, speakers and writers have to be able to operate with more than just words and grammar; they have to be able to string utterances together. The following conversation takes place in the context of two people getting ready for their party:

A We can leave the ice here till we need it.
B It's warm in here.
A Is it? OK, then, let's find somewhere else.

The utterance 'It's warm in here' acts as a rejection of **A**'s suggestion. **A** can then use 'it' to refer to the whole of **B**'s proposition ('It's warm in here'). And 'OK' suggests that **A** has absorbed all of the discourse so far (suggestion – rejection – agreement with the rejection) and can then move the conversation on with a further suggestion.

Our ability to function properly in conversation or writing, in other words, depends not only on reacting to the context in which we are using the language, but also on the relationship between words and ideas in longer texts.

The elements of language

Whatever the sentence 'It's warm in here' is used to mean, the speaker has put together a number of elements in order to get that meaning across:

Grammar

Our sentence depends, for its success, on putting a number of elements in the correct order, in this case **subject** (it), **verb** (is), **complement** ('warm' – called a complement because it adds information about the subject), and **adverbial** ('in here' – called adverbial because it further exemplifies the verb). The elements have to go in the right order for the sentence to work. If we tried to say '*It here in warm is', the sentence would not work. In the same way, we have to be careful about the types of words we can put in the slots (subject, verb, etc). We can't, for example, put an adjective or an adverb in the subject slot ('*stealthily is warm in here/inhospitable is warm in here'), or a verb in the adverbial position ('*It's warm go').

However, there are some changes we are allowed to make to our sentence elements, and these will alter the meaning of the sentence. For example, a simple element-order change (subject–verb → verb–subject) will make our sentence into a question ('Is it warm in here?').

Unlike the example we have used so far, some sentences only have two elements, subject and verb (e.g. 'He laughed', 'They disagreed', 'It rained!'). Verbs such as these which don't take an object are called intransitive. Some verbs can be either transitive (i.e. they do take an object) or intransitive, e.g. 'She *opened* the door/The door *opened*'.

The one sentence element we have not mentioned so far is the **object**, exemplified in sentences such as 'He opened *the door*', 'He entered *the warm room*'. Once again, the sequence of sentence elements is crucial, so we cannot say '*The room entered he'. But the situation is complicated by the fact that some sentences have two objects, a direct object and an indirect object. Direct objects refer to things or persons affected by the verb, e.g. 'He sang a *song*', 'Pizarro conquered *Peru*', 'She loved *him*'.

An indirect object refers to the person or thing that (in one grammarian's phrase) 'benefits' from the action, e.g. 'He sang *me* a song', 'She painted *him* a picture', 'I gave a ring *to my girlfriend*', 'Why should we pay taxes to *the government*?'.

Not all sentences consist of just one **clause** (e.g. subject–verb–adverbial or subject–verb–object) in this way. We can make things considerably more complex by joining and amalgamating a number of different clauses. For example, the following sentences:

'The girl met the woman.'
'The woman was standing by the canal.'
'They went to a café.'
'They had a meal.'
'They enjoyed it very much.'

can be amalgamated into a multi-clause sentence such as:

> 'The girl met the woman who was standing by the canal and they went to a café and had a meal, which they enjoyed very much.'

It is possible also to convert some elements of the separate sentences into phrases, e.g. 'The girl met the woman *standing by the canal* …', etc. But whether we are dealing with a single-clause or multi-clause sentence, our choice of what we can say is governed by what is appropriate or permissible in the various slots that make up the sentence.

Vocabulary

The sentence 'It is warm in here' is made up of the words 'it', 'is', 'warm', 'in' and 'here'. The speaker has chosen these words on purpose to express a particular meaning. He or she could have chosen 'hot' or 'cold' instead of 'warm' and, as a result, the sentence would mean something different.

What a word means is also defined by its relationship to other words. For example, we can say that the word 'hot' is the **antonym** (opposite) of the word 'cold' – and this fact helps us understand the meaning of each word. When words mean the same thing (e.g. 'hold-up' and 'delay') we call them **synonyms** – though since one word can have many meanings (see page 63), it will depend on which meaning is being used. Whereas 'cold' may be an antonym of 'hot' when talking about temperature, it is more likely the antonym of 'warm' if the words are being used to describe someone's character.

A speaker's knowledge of a word also includes an understanding of how the shape of that word can be altered so that its grammatical meaning can be changed. We call the system of rules that determine how these changes can be made **morphology**. For example, a simple morphological change will make the sentence which started this section less categorical ('It's warmish in here') whereas adding '-er' to the adjective ('It's warmer in here') makes it a comparative adjective. In the same way adding '-ed' to a regular verb ('he walk<u>ed</u>', 'she play<u>ed</u>') makes it a past tense verb.

Using words appropriately means knowing these things and, crucially, knowing which grammatical slots (see above) they can go into. In order to do this, we need to know what part of speech a word is (see pages 64–65).

Pronunciation

The way the sentence is spoken will also determine exactly what it means. For example, while reading this chapter so far you may have heard the speaker's voice (in your head) drop on the word 'warm'. However, if we change the speaker's **intonation** (the way the voice goes up or down as we speak) so that voice rises on the word 'warm', our statement becomes a question, e.g. 'It's warm in here?'.

Intonation (sometimes described as the music of speech) encompasses the moments at which we change the **pitch** of our voices in order to give certain messages. Pitch describes the level (high or low) at which we speak. Changing our pitch in an utterance is absolutely crucial for getting our meaning across. The word 'Yes', for example, can be said with a falling voice, a rising voice or a combination of the two. By changing the direction of the voice we can make 'Yes' mean 'I agree' or 'Perhaps it's true' or 'You can't be serious' or 'Wow, you are so right', or any number of other things.

Teachers often use arrows or wavy lines to show intonation tunes (pitch change), like this:

It's warm in here. (sentence)   It's warm in here? (question)

As you read the question, you probably hear the **stress** on the word 'warm', e.g. 'It's WARM in here?' (where the speaker sounds as if he or she is contesting this description of the temperature). It is on this stressed syllable that the speaker's pitch changes. But if we move the stress to the first syllable of the word 'here', e.g. 'It's warm in HERE?' the question is now an exclamation or challenge to the notion that this room or place is warm – rather than questioning the warmth itself.

Words of more than one syllable have both stressed and unstressed syllables (we say 'photographer' not '*photographer'). Frequently, the stress is different when the word acts as different parts of speech, e.g. 'import' (verb) but 'import' (noun).

Teachers use a variety of symbols to show stress, e.g.

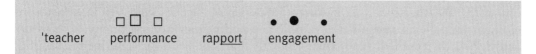

Our sentence works, too, because the speaker has used a collection of sounds – or **phonemes** – to get the meaning across. For example, the word 'warm', though it has four letters, has only three sounds, /w/, /ɔː/ (like 'or') and /m/. Just by changing one sound (e.g. saying /n/ instead of /m/) we can change the word so that now our speaker, perhaps referring to the carpet, is saying 'It's worn in here'.

The fact that 'warm' has four letters, but only three sounds (in British English) is a demonstration of the fact that there is no one-to-one correspondence between sounds and spelling. Thus, for example, the 'c' of 'cat' is pronounced differently from the 'c' of 'cease', but is the same as the 'c' of 'coffee'. 'Though', 'trough' and 'rough' all have the letter combination 'ou', but it is pronounced differently in every case. Different spellings can have the same sound, too: 'plane' and 'gain' both have the same vowel sound, but they are spelt differently.

There are two main categories of sounds: **vowel** sounds (like /ɔː/ in 'warm', /æ/ in 'cat', /ɒ/ and /iː/ in 'coffee', etc) and **consonant** sounds (like /m/ in 'warm', /t/ in 'trough' and /f/ in 'rough' and 'trough').

Vowel sounds can either be single (like /ɔː/ and /iː/) or combinations of two or more sounds (diphthongs – like /eɪ/ in 'late', /aʊ/ in 'now', /ɪə/ in 'real', or triphthongs – like /aʊə/ in 'power').

Consonants can sometimes be joined together to make sounds like /tʃ/ in 'child' and 'church', and /dʒ/ in 'judge' (the sound is used twice) and 'John'.

Consonants can be either **voiced** or **voiceless**. Voiced consonants are those where we close the **vocal cords** in our throat (see page 63) and they vibrate as the air from the lungs passes between them. Consonants like /b/, /d/, /v/ and /g/are all voiced in this way, whereas when we say the consonants /p/, /t/, /f/ and /k/, the vocal cords are left open and so there is no vibration, and therefore no voice. Thus, while, for example, we use exactly the same parts of the mouth to make the sounds /d/ and /t/, the first is voiced while the second is not. The same is true of the pairs /b/ and /p/, /v/ and /f/, and /g/ and /k/.

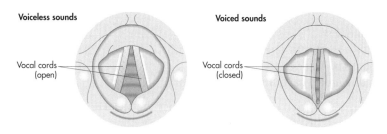

Voiceless sounds   Voiced sounds

Vocal cords
(open)

Vocal cords
(closed)

Position of the vocal cords for voiceless and voiced sounds (seen from above – the Adam's apple at the front is at the top of each diagram)

Note that vowels are always voiced.

A complete list of phonemic symbols is given in Appendix D on page 267.

Forms and meanings

Just as in English there is sometimes no readily discernible correspondence between sounds and spelling, there are frequent instances, too, where the same language forms can be used to express different meanings, or where a meaning can be expressed by many different forms.

One form, many meanings

The present continuous verb form ('is/are doing' – see page 70) can refer to both the present ('I'm not listening') and the future ('I'm seeing him tomorrow'). It can be used to refer to a temporary uncompleted event ('They are enjoying the weather') or to a series of completed events ('He's always putting his foot in it'). The same basic form is being used to express a number of different concepts of time and duration. The same is true of, for example, the present simple. 'He goes to work at 7 every day' to describe a habit, versus 'Thierry Henry scores!' to describe something taking place now are just two of its many uses. Other verb forms behave in the same way.

Words can also mean more than one thing, for example, 'book' (= something to read, to reserve, a list of bets, etc), 'beat' (= to win, to hit, to mix, e.g. an egg, the 'pulse' of music/a heart) and 'can' (= ability, permission, probability – and a container made of metal). Notice that, in these examples, not only can the same form have many meanings, but it can also be different parts of speech.

With so many available meanings for words and grammatical forms, it is the **context** the word occurs in which determines which of these meanings is being referred to. If we say, 'I beat him because I ran faster than he did', 'beat' is likely to mean won rather than physically assaulted or mixed (though there is always the possibility of ambiguity, of course). Likewise, the sentence 'I'm talking to the president' changes dramatically if we use these different expressions: 'at this very minute' or 'tomorrow at noon'.

One meaning, many forms

A meaning or concept can be expressed in many different ways. Consider, for example, the concept of the future. Different forms can be used to express the same basic concept (though each form does have a slightly different meaning).

EXAMPLES
I'll see you tomorrow.
I'm going to see you tomorrow.
I'm seeing you tomorrow – that's the arrangement, isn't it?
I can get to you by about six o'clock.
I see you at six, and afterwards I have a meeting with John.

The choice of which way to express futurity depends on whether the speaker wants to talk about fixed arrangements, plans, schedules, offers, or just a simple concept of the future with none of these overtones.

Word meaning can also be expressed in different ways. Even where words appear to have the same meaning – to be synonyms – they are usually distinct from each other. For example, we can describe an intelligent person by using a number of different words: 'intelligent', 'bright', 'brainy', 'clever', 'smart', etc. But each of these words has a different **connotation** (shade of meaning). 'Brainy' is an informal word and might well have a negative connotation when used by a schoolchild about a classmate. 'Bright' carries the connotation of lively and young. 'Smart' is commonly used in American English and has a slight connotation of tricksiness, and 'clever' is often used in phrases with negative connotations, e.g. 'too clever by half', 'He may be clever but he's not going to get away with it'.

Parts of speech

The chart on page 65 shows the different parts of speech. These are the categories which help us determine how grammatical sequences are put together, and which words can go in which slots (see page 60).

We will consider the parts of speech in terms of the noun phrase, verbs, adverbs and prepositions, and discourse.

The noun phrase

A noun phrase may consist of just a noun ('John') or a pronoun ('he', 'they'). The noun may be preceded by a determiner ('this woman', 'a man'). There may be one or more adjectives before the noun ('a young woman', 'a handsome old man'), and the noun may be post-modified in some way (e.g. 'a woman with a computer', 'the man wearing a hat').

Nouns

The way nouns behave depends upon a number of grammatical and morphological variables.

Countable and uncountable

A distinction needs to be made between countable nouns and uncountable nouns. As their name implies, with countable nouns you can 'count' what the words refer to (e.g. 'apple', 'table', 'horse', 'cottage', 'novel') and therefore you can make them plural ('apples', 'tables', etc), but you can't count what uncountable words refer to (e.g. 'furniture' and 'comfort') and you can't make them plural – we can't say '*two furnitures', '*eight comforts').

part of speech	description	examples (words)	examples (sentences, etc)
noun (noun phrase)	a word (or group of words) that is the name of a person, a place, a thing or activity or a quality or idea; nouns can be used as the subject or object of a verb	Rachel New York book sense walking stick town hall	Rachel arrives tomorrow. I love New York. I recommend this book. I can't get any sense out of her. I don't need a walking stick. They met outside the town hall.
pronoun	a word that is used in place of a noun or noun phrase	her she him they	He met her on the Internet. She is a famous dancer. Look at him! They don't talk much.
adjective	a word that gives more information about a noun or pronoun	kind better impetuous best	What a kind person! We all want a better life. She's so impetuous. That's the best thing about her.
verb	a word (or group of words) which is used in describing an action, experience or state	write watch believe have	Pushkin wrote *Eugene Onegin*. I like to watch TV. I don't believe you! Have you eaten yet?
adverb (adverbial phrase)	a word (or group of words) that describes or adds to the meaning of a verb, adjective, another adverb or a whole sentence	sensibly carefully at home in half an hour	Please act sensibly this evening. She walked across the bridge carefully. I checked my emails at home. See you in half an hour.
preposition (prepositional phrase)	a word (or group of words) which is used to show the way which other words are connected	for of in on top of	a plan for life Bring me two bottles of wine. Put that in the box. I think I put it on top of the cupboard.
determiner	definite article indefinite article possessives demonstratives quantifiers	the a an my, your, etc. this, that, these those some, many, few, etc	The composer of that theme tune A beautiful new daughter An appalling mistake My secret life Look at those buildings. Few people believed him.
conjunction	a word that connects sentences, phrases or clauses	and so but	Full of energy and ready to go I lost my mobile phone, so I couldn't call you. It's great but I can't afford it.

EXAMPLES
The *weather* is terrible today. (uncountable)
He hasn't got much *money*. (uncountable)
She's got a lot of *friends* to help her through this. (countable)
I've only got a few *coins* in my pocket. (countable)

A number of words are sometimes countable when they mean one thing but uncountable when they mean something different. For example, the word 'sugar' is uncountable when we say 'I like sugar', 'I'd like some sugar', but countable if we say 'One sugar or two?' (where 'sugar' = spoonful/cube of sugar).

Plural nouns, singular verbs
There are some nouns that appear to be plural, but which behave as if they are singular – you can only use them with singular verbs, e.g. '*Darts* is a game played by large men', 'The *news* is depressing'.

Collective nouns
Nouns which describe groups or organisations (e.g. 'family', 'team', 'government') are called *collective* nouns. They can either be singular or plural depending on whether we are describing the unit or its members. We can say 'The army *are* advancing' or 'The army *is* advancing'. This choice isn't usually available in American English, however, where you would expect speakers to use singular verbs only.

Some collective nouns are formed by making adjectives behave like nouns and in this case they are always plural, e.g. 'The poor live in terrible conditions', 'The good die young'.

Whether a noun is countable, uncountable, plural or collective affects the construction of the sentences it occurs in. Uncountable nouns are used with singular verbs, and **quantifiers** like 'much', 'a lot of' and 'some'. Countable nouns, on the other hand, are used with singular or plural verbs and with words like 'many'.

Compound nouns
We are used to nouns being one word. But English also has many compound nouns, constructed from more than one word, e.g. 'walking stick', 'cherry tree', 'town hall', 'boyfriend'.

Not all compound words are nouns, however. We can also have compound adjectives, for example, 'fair-skinned', 'neat-looking'.

Pronouns
There are three basic types of pronoun: personal pronouns, reflexive (personal) pronouns and relative pronouns.

Personal pronouns
Personal pronouns are 'I', 'you', 'he', 'she', 'we' and 'they' – and 'it' which isn't really personal at all! Not only do they have these **subject** realisations, however, but they can be **object pronouns** ('me', 'you', 'him', 'her', 'it', 'us' and 'them' in sentences like 'I saw him'), **reflexive pronouns** ('myself', 'yourself', 'himself', 'herself', 'itself', 'ourselves', 'yourselves' and 'themselves' in sentences like 'I cut myself'), and **possessive pronouns** ('mine', 'yours', 'his', 'hers', 'its', 'his', 'hers', 'ours' and 'theirs' in sentences like 'They're not yours, they're mine!').

Relative pronouns

The pronouns 'who', 'whose', 'where', 'which' and 'that' are used to introduce **relative clauses**. In the sentences, 'I photographed a dancer who was wearing national costume' and 'I stood at the door of the house where I used to live', 'who was wearing national costume' and 'where I used to live' are relative clauses. Relative pronouns are necessary if the noun in the relative clause is the subject of that clause. In the sentence, 'I found the man whose grandfather started the revolution', the grandfather is the subject of the clause 'started the revolution'. Relative pronouns are not necessary, however, if the noun is the object of the clause. In the sentence, 'I filmed the man I met', 'the man' is the object of the clause ('I met the man').

Articles and determiners

Articles ('the', 'a' and 'an') belong to a class of words called **determiners**. These identify – or indicate the type of reference of – the noun phrase, telling us whether it is general or specific, or whether it is known about or is new. Other examples of determiners are 'this', 'that', 'these', 'those', 'some' and 'all of'. Determiners usually come before a noun or at the beginning of a noun phrase, e.g. 'an apple', 'the red bus', 'some of my best friends', 'these fresh oranges'.

Definite article

We use the definite article ('the') when we think that the reader or listener knows which particular thing or person we are talking about, perhaps because we have already mentioned it (e.g. 'I met a woman in the park … the woman was alone.'), or when there can only be one, e.g. 'the Pope' (we know which one because there is only one), 'the book I read' (= we both know which one I'm talking about), 'the oldest man in the world' (because there can only be one 'oldest' man), etc.

We do not use the definite article when we are talking about people and things in general, using plural or uncountable nouns, e.g. 'Teachers should establish a good rapport with their students', 'Trumpet players tend to make a lot of noise', 'Money doesn't grow on trees', etc. This is often referred to as the zero article.

However, just to confuse things, we do sometimes make general statements with the definite article and a singular noun, e.g. 'The great white shark is a dangerous creature in the wrong situation' (see also the indefinite article below).

Indefinite article

The indefinite article ('a/an') is used to refer to a particular person or thing when the listener/reader doesn't know which one is being described, e.g. 'A man was reading the paper', 'I saw a plane take off', 'I'm going to buy a new mobile phone'.

As with the definite article (see above), we can also use 'a/an' to refer to a member of a group – in order to refer to the whole group, e.g. 'A man's gotta do what a man's gotta do', 'A good nurse will always spend time with her patients', etc.

Adjectives

Adjectives describe and modify the nouns they come before or after. They can have many forms.

Comparative and superlative forms

Adjectives can have comparative forms ('big – bigger', 'nice – nicer', 'noisy – noisier', 'young – younger') and superlative forms ('biggest', 'nicest', 'noisiest', 'youngest'). Sometimes this change is indicated by the addition of '-er' and '-est', sometimes with an additional spelling change (e.g. 'biggest', 'noisier'), sometimes not (e.g. 'younger', 'youngest'). With longer words, we use 'more' ('more colourful', 'more enjoyable') and 'most' ('most colourful', 'most enjoyable'). A few adjectives have their own comparative and superlative forms which do not conform to these patterns (e.g. 'good – better – best', 'bad – worse – worst').

Adjective sequence

When we use a string of adjectives, there is a generally accepted sequence.

	size	colour	origin	material	purpose	noun
the	small	purple	German	silk	evening	gown
the	large	( )	( )	wooden	( )	crate

Notice that if only some of the categories are present, the order is usually retained, e.g. 'the large wooden crate'.

Adjective and preposition

Many adjectives are followed by specific prepositions, e.g. 'interested <u>in</u>', 'keen <u>on</u>', 'happy <u>about</u>', etc.

Adjectives as nouns

We can use some adjectives as if they were nouns, e.g. 'the blind', 'the poor', etc (see also collective nouns on page 66).

Adjective or adverb?

Some words can be both adjectives and adverbs, depending on whether they modify nouns or verbs. When we say 'I had a late lunch', 'late' is an adjective, but when we say 'He arrived late', it is an adverb. Although many adverbs end in '-ly', a word like 'deadly' ('a deadly disease') is functioning as an adjective.

The verb phrase

In any discussion of verbs we need to bear in mind two main parameters, **tense** and **aspect**. A verb tense is the form of the verb we choose when we want to say what time (past, present, future, etc) the verb is referring to. However, this is complicated by the fact that we can use the same tense (or form) to talk about more than one time, as we saw on page 63. The form of the verb also depends on whether we want to say the action is ongoing or whether it is complete. The aspect (continuous, simple, perfect, etc) which we choose for the verb describes this.

This section looks at three different types of verb: auxiliary verbs, main verbs and **phrasal (multi-word) verbs**, before going on to look at different verb forms, and verb complementation. We will then look at adverbs and adverbial phrases.

Auxiliary verbs

Auxiliary verbs are 'be', 'do' and 'have' and the modal auxiliary verbs 'shall', 'should', 'will', 'would', 'can', 'could', 'may', 'might', 'must' and 'ought to'. They are used with main verbs (see page 69) in affirmative sentences, negative sentences and question formation.

EXAMPLES

We *are* staying at a friend's house.
We*'ve* only just got our new computer.
She *doesn't* expect to be here very long.
You *can't* afford to pay for a hotel like that, *can* you?
He *ought to* find a place of his own at his age.
Could you text me when you arrive?
Did you live in Dubai once?
I *would* never *have* guessed if I *hadn't* seen him.

Notice that we often use contractions with auxiliaries, e.g. 'do<u>n't</u>' instead of 'do not', 'we<u>'re</u>' instead of 'we are'.

Modal verbs are used to express the speaker's judgment about something ('you shouldn't smoke') or the likelihood of it happening ('It might rain'). Modals are often used in conditional sentences (see page 74).

Main verbs

Main verbs can stand alone (e.g. 'She shouted', 'They arrived'). However, where more than one verb is used, they express the main idea (e.g. 'She was <u>swimming</u>', 'Have you <u>seen</u> her?'). This makes them different from auxiliary verbs since, as their name suggests, auxiliary verbs occur when main verbs are also present. However, some auxiliary verbs like 'have' and 'do', can also take on main-verb status, e.g. 'You've <u>had</u> your chance', 'Have you <u>done</u> your homework?'. Notice that 'have' is the auxiliary in the last example, but 'do' has the status of a main verb.

EXAMPLES

I don't *believe* you. You're always *telling* stories.
He *texted* his friend about the party.
He *shouted* at us because we were *laughing* at him.
I *had* three cups of coffee.

Phrasal (multi-word) verbs

Phrasal verbs are formed by adding a particle (adverb or preposition – or an adverb *and* a preposition) to a verb to create new meanings. Thus 'set out' ('We set out the following day' or 'He set out his agenda for the meeting') has a completely different meaning from 'set' (e.g. 'set an exam', 'set the table'); 'put up with' ('I'm not going to put up with this any more') has a completely different meaning from 'put' (e.g. 'He put her photographs with the letters'). There are four basic types of phrasal verbs:

Type 1: intransitive
The verb does not take a direct object. These are verbs like 'take off' ('The plane took off'), 'slow down' ('Slow down at the corner'), 'stand up' ('She stood up when I came into the room').

Type 2: transitive and inseparable
These are verbs which take an object, and where the object must come after the complete verb (the verb and the particle cannot be separated). Examples include 'go on' ('to go on a diet'), 'look after' ('Will you look after the children?'), 'see about' ('I'm going to see about a new car').

Type 3: transitive and separable
With these verbs the object can come between the verb and the particle (or go after it). Examples include 'give back' ('He gave the present back', 'He gave back the present') and 'work out' ('We're going to work the problem out somehow', 'We're going to work out the problem somehow'). However, if the object is a pronoun, it must come between the verb and the particle ('He gave it back', 'We're going to work it out').

Type 4: transitive, 2+ particles, inseparable
Where there is more than one particle, the object has to come at the end. Examples include 'run out of' ('We've run out of petrol'), 'break up with' ('He's broken up with his girlfriend'), 'cut down on' ('I'm trying to cut down on my chocolate intake').

Verb forms
We describe the form (and meaning) of main verbs in the following ways.

Present
'Your brother is upstairs', 'I love it here', 'What's happening?', 'I'm not missing that plane'.

Past
'Eleanor said goodnight', 'She cried', 'Her parents were packing their suitcases'.

Simple
This is the **base form** of a verb (e.g. 'walk', 'do', 'run') often inflected to agree with the subject ('He walk<u>s</u>', 'She doe<u>s</u>', 'It run<u>s</u>') or to indicate time and tense ('They walk<u>ed</u>', 'It was d<u>one</u>', 'He r<u>a</u>n as fast as possible').

Continuous
Continuous verbs (also called progressive) are formed by adding '-ing' to the base form and using it with the verb 'to be', e.g. 'She is writing a letter', 'She was looking out of the window'.

Present and past verb forms can therefore be described as present simple or present continuous, past simple or past continuous. We can summarise these verb forms in the following table.

	simple	continuous
present	John is in the kitchen. I love it here.	What's happening? I'm not listening.
past	She said goodbye. He cried. She didn't buy a new cellphone.	He was waiting at the gate. They weren't listening.

Participles
There are two participle forms in English – present participles, e.g. 'taking', 'talking', 'happening', 'going', and past participles, e.g. 'taken', 'talked', 'happened', 'gone'.

Regular and irregular verbs
We can talk about verbs as regular or irregular. Regular verbs take the '-ed' ending in the past, e.g. 'talked', 'happened', 'laughed' and past participle forms (which are the same). Irregular verbs have different past tense forms, e.g. 'ran', 'went', 'bought', 'saw' and different past participles (e.g. 'run', 'gone', 'bought', 'seen', etc).

Perfect verbs

Perfect verbs are those made with 'have/had' + the past participle (or 'been' + the '-ing' form of the verb, e.g. 'I have lived here for six years', 'They had just arrived', 'She will have been to six countries', 'He's been jogging', 'He hadn't been listening', 'They'll have been travelling for sixteen hours').

People have struggled for years to explain exactly what concept present perfect verbs express. It has been variously described as suggesting the idea of an action started in the past but continuing up until the present, the idea of an action started in the past which has present relevance, or the idea of an action on a continuum which has not yet finished. Thus, we can say 'I've been to Santiago' and, although we are talking about an event in the past, we don't use the past simple (see above) perhaps because we wish to stress the present relevance of having been to Santiago or because it occurred on the unfinished continuum of 'my life'.

Apart from present perfect verb forms with 'have', e.g. 'She's studied Portuguese', we can also have past perfect verb forms with 'had', e.g. 'He had been asleep', 'They had been laughing all the way home'. In this case, the verb describes an action before the past and continuing up until that point in the past – or at least having a kind of 'past relevance'.

The future perfect refers to the period between now and some point in the future when we will be able to look back and describe an action taking place up until that point in the future (e.g. 'If he wins the gold medal this year, he will have won it five times in succession').

As with past verb forms, there are both simple and continuous perfect verb forms as the following table shows.

	simple	continuous
present perfect	I've read his new book. They haven't arrived yet.	I've been reading his new book. They haven't been travelling for long.
past perfect	He had studied English as a child. I had never worked with a robot before.	He had been waiting for about half an hour. They hadn't been talking for more than a minute when ...
future perfect	I'll have finished this homework by tomorrow. By this time next year, I will have been to the gym about 160 times.	In August we'll have been living here for twenty-six years. When you get back, I'll have been working on this chapter for six hours.

Active and passive

Another distinction to be made about verbs is that between active and passive. Active sentences have a subject (S), a verb (V) and an object (O), e.g.

A scene of utter chaos confronted her.

       S   V   O

If we flip things around, however, starting with the object (and, in effect, making it the subject) we get a passive sentence, e.g.

> She was confronted by a scene of utter chaos.

Passives are formed by the auxiliary + past participle of the verb in question, e.g. 'It's made in Taiwan', 'They're being processed right now' (present), 'He was met by the president', 'The plan was being worked on' (past), 'You'll be taken to the airport', 'She's going to be offered a new job' (future), etc.

Passive constructions are often used when we don't know or we don't want to say who did something (e.g. 'It's been destroyed', 'It was decided that you should leave'), or when we want to give a different emphasis to the subject and object of an action ('The prime minister opened the new bridge' versus 'The new bridge was opened by the prime minister').

Verb complementation

This describes what words and kinds of words we can use after particular verbs. Some verbs, for example, are followed by infinitives ('I can swim', 'He should go'), some are followed by 'to' + infinitive ('I like to swim', 'He tried to save her'), some are followed by participles ('I don't enjoy running'), and some by 'that' + a new clause ('He promised that he would finish the work on time'). There are many other complementation patterns, too. Some verbs can be followed by more than one grammatical pattern.

> EXAMPLES
> I <u>like</u> *to watch* TV/I <u>like</u> *watching* TV.
> I <u>enjoy</u> *watching* TV. (not *I enjoy to watch TV)
> I <u>must</u> *go*. (not *I must to go)
> I <u>explained</u> the problem *to* him. (not *I explained him the problem)
> She <u>suggested</u> *that I train* as a teacher. (not *She suggested me to train as a teacher)

Adverbs

Adverbs and adverbial phrases (phrases of more than one word that act like adverbs) modify verbs. Thus time adverbs ('early', 'late', 'yesterday morning') say when the action takes place, adverbs of manner ('He played <u>well</u>', 'She ran <u>quickly</u>', 'He spoke <u>fiercely</u>') say how the action happens, adverbs of place ('They work <u>upstairs</u>', 'I live <u>in Cambridge</u>', 'I'll see you <u>at home</u>') say where the action happens, and adverbs of frequency ('sometimes', 'often', 'never', 'every now and then', 'twice a week') say how often the action happens.

Adverb position

It is important to know which slots (see page 60) adverbs can fit into. They usually appear at the end of sentences, but they can sometimes be used at the beginning or in the middle.

Most frequency adverbs ('always', 'usually', 'often', 'sometimes', etc) can usually go at the beginning, middle or end of a sentence, e.g. 'Sometimes he rings me up in the morning', 'He sometimes rings me up in the morning', 'He rings me up in the morning sometimes'. However, 'never' is an exception since it can only occur in the middle position (except when starting more literary sentences, in which case it provokes a subject–verb order change, e.g. 'Never have I been in such a difficult situation').

Adverbs do not usually come between a verb and its object. We say 'I usually have sandwiches for lunch', but not '*I have usually sandwiches for lunch'.

Adverbs of degree

Adverbs can modify adjectives, e.g. 'a wonderfully physical performance', 'an unusually large cucumber', 'a really fascinating film', etc. Other adverbs of this type are words like 'extremely', 'rather' and 'very'.

Comparative and superlative adverbs

The comparative and superlative forms of adverbs follow the same pattern as those of adjectives. One-syllable adverbs add '-er' and '-est' ('loud → louder → loudest'; 'hard → harder → hardest'). Adverbs ending in '-ly' use 'more' and 'most' (e.g. 'quickly → more quickly → most quickly'). There are also irregular forms (e.g. 'well → better → best'; 'badly → worse → worst').

Joining words

Two parts of speech (prepositions and conjunctions) are concerned with how words, phrases or sentences are connected.

Prepositions

Prepositions express a time relationship between two events ('He left *before* I got there'), or a spatial relationship between two things or people (e.g. 'I saw him *at* the cinema', 'Put the projector *in* the office when you have finished with it'). They usually come before a noun but can also come at the end of a clause with certain structures. For example, we can say 'The book's on the shelf' or 'It's not something I'm very interested in'.

Particular prepositions

Many words and expressions can only be followed by particular prepositions, e.g. 'anxious about', 'dream about/of', 'good at', 'kind to', etc.

Prepositions and adverbs

Some words can be both prepositions and also adverbs (often called adverbial particles). In the sentence, 'She climbed down the ladder', 'down' is a preposition because it has an object ('the ladder'). In 'She sat down', it is an adverb because it does not have an object.

Conjunctions

Conjunctions join two clauses, e.g. 'Nicky said goodnight *and* walked out of the house with a heavy heart', 'She was going to be away for a fortnight *so* she took a large suitcase', 'I can sing *but* I can't play the guitar', 'I'm a teacher *because* I like working with people', etc.

We only use one conjunction for two clauses. We say 'Although it was early he jumped out of bed', not '*Although it was early but he jumped out of bed'.

Hypothetical meaning

When we talk about something that is not real, but that might be the case, we are talking hypothetically. English has many ways of expressing hypothetical meaning.

Modal verbs

As we saw on page 69, modals are auxiliary verbs which we use to comment on the likelihood of something. Thus, if we say 'It might rain' we are saying that it is a hypothetical possibility. If we say 'Perhaps I could be persuaded' or 'I would if I could' we are hypothesising situations in which such eventualities are possible.

However, not all modal verbs express hypothetical meaning. 'It will rain' is a statement of fact, and 'I can't go' makes no concessions to the possibility of not going.

Conditional sentences

Conditional sentences are formed when the conjunction 'if' is used to preface a condition, e.g. 'If it rains (condition), you'll get wet (result)'. In this case, it is quite likely that it will rain, and therefore the result is possible. However, if we change the sentence to 'If it rained, you would get wet' we are suggesting that the chance of it raining is unlikely – in other words, we are talking hypothetically – and this is signalled by the use of 'would' rather than 'will'. A further change of verb tense/form (using the past perfect) will produce an impossible condition, e.g. 'If it had rained, you would have got wet'. But it didn't so you were spared!

These three conditional forms are often called first, second and third conditionals. It is useful to understand whether they are real (= possible/likely) or hypothetical (= unlikely/impossible) and whether they refer to the present, future or past. The following table gives some examples of this.

	real	hypothetical
talking about the present	If you pay online, you get a discount. You get a discount if you pay online.	If I had a dog, I'd take it for walks. I'd take a dog for walks if I had one.
talking about the future	If you work hard, you'll pass the exam. You'll pass the exam if you work hard.	If I won the lottery, I'd travel round the world. If I were you I'd get a new jacket.
talking about the past	If it was very warm, we ate outside. We ate outside if it was very warm.	If I'd known about the rail strike, I would have come by car. I would have come by car if I'd known about the rail strike.

The chart shows how the order of the clauses can be reversed with little change in meaning. We also need to remember that many conditional sentences are variations on these basic patterns, using a wide range of different tenses and verb types, e.g. 'If you finish before time, hand your papers in and go', 'If it rains like it looks like it's going to rain, we're going to get soaked', 'If I'd been informed about this, I could solve the problem' – and, in American English sometimes, 'If I would have met her earlier, I would have married her', though this use of 'would' in both clauses (instead of only in the result clause) is considered unacceptable by many speakers of British English.

Words together

Students frequently worry about the meaning of individual words. Yet a marked feature of the way we construct and understand language is that far from putting together strings of individual words, we actually use collections of vocabulary items that frequently occur together in pairs of groups, as this excerpt from the novel *Small Island* by Andrea Levy (about Jamaican immigrants to Britain) makes clear:

> Louis now believed bloodyforeigner to be all one word. For, like bosom pals, he only ever heard those words spoken together.

We will look at three specific instances of words that group together: collocations, lexical chunks and idiom.

Collocations

If any two words occur together more often than just by chance, we often call them collocations. In other words, when you hear the word 'asleep' there is a good chance that the word 'fast' will be used with it ('fast asleep'). In the example above, Louis has worked out that if he hears the word 'pals', the word 'bosom' will be hovering around, too, and he never hears the word 'foreigner' occurring without 'bloody' in front of it.

Knowledge of collocation is an important part of knowing a word. For example, the *Longman Dictionary of Contemporary English* (*LDOCE*) lists the following collocations for the word 'heavy', when it means 'great in amount, degree or severity': heavy traffic, heavy rain/snow, heavy fighting, heavy drinker, heavy smoking, heavy smoker, heavy burden, heavy demands, heavy pressure, heavy fine, heavy casualties, heavy losses, heavy defeat, heavy cold, heavy use. The reason for this listing is that even though 'heavy' (with this meaning) may sometimes be used with other words, a study of language shows that it is most often found in the company of the words indicated (traffic, demands, casualties, etc). Furthermore, even though this meaning of 'heavy' is not unlike the word 'big', we do not often find 'big' collocating with words like 'smoker' and 'casualties'.

The compilers of *LDOCE* (and other dictionaries) can be confident about these issues because they have studied large computer **corpuses** (collections of articles, novels, recorded speech, journals, etc stored electronically). These corpuses (and the software which allows them to be analysed) were developed towards the end of the twentieth century – and this development process is still ongoing. Corpuses allow us to have a much clearer idea of when and how often word collocations occur.

Lexical chunks

Corpuses have shown us something else we have always been aware of – but which is now more demonstrably the case. This is that words group together into longer **lexical phrases** or **lexical chunks**. Lexical chunks are strings of words which behave almost as one unit. Some of these are fixed (which means you can't change any of the words, e.g. *over the moon, out of the blue*), and some of them are semi-fixed (which means you can change some of the words, e.g. *nice to see you/good to see you/great to see you*, etc).

Our ability to use the language effectively depends largely on a knowledge of lexical chunking of this kind. In certain varieties of English, for example, speakers may well use phrases like 'It's a safe bet that …' to preface a strong speculation, or 'I wouldn't go that far' to show only partial agreement.

Lexical chunks become more or less problematic depending on how idiomatic they are. An **idiom** is a lexical phrase where the meaning of the whole phrase may not be comprehensible even if we know the meaning of each individual word (e.g. 'full of beans' = energetic, 'as plain as the nose on your face' = obvious). Many phrasal and multi-word verbs cause problems for learners precisely because they are idiomatic in this way. We should note, however, that many idioms are extremely culture-specific and so may not be that useful anyway in international contexts.

Language functions

An exasperated teacher tells a habitually late student 'You'd better get here on time next class!' She is making a recommendation, something which is between advice and an order.

There are other ways in which the teacher can make recommendations, too, and her choice may well depend on exactly how exasperated she is and how formal, informal, direct or indirect she wishes to be – what tone she wishes to adopt (see page 79).

> EXAMPLES
> Get here on time next class if you know what's good for you.
> I strongly recommend that you get here on time next class.
> I suggest you get here on time next class.
> I think it would be a really good idea if you got here on time next class.
> It would be a good idea if you tried to get here on time next class.
> Next class? On time, OK?

A language function is a purpose you wish to achieve when you say or write something. By 'performing' the function, you are performing an act of communication. If you say 'I apologise', you are performing the function of apologising; if you say 'I promise', you are performing the function of promising. But functions are more often performed without using verbs like this at all. We can apologise by saying 'sorry' and invite someone not by saying 'I invite you' but by saying things like 'D'you fancy coming round for a meal?'. As we have seen above, there are many ways of recommending a course of action. Many functional **exponents** (patterns or phrases) are exactly the kind of lexical phrases we discussed above.

If our students want to express themselves in speaking or writing, they need to know how to perform these functions. A key feature of specific functional exponents is to know which are more or less appropriate in given situations (depending on who is being talked to, what the situation is and how determined or tentative the speaker wishes to be). Issues of register (see page 79) are crucial here.

Text and discourse

Much of this chapter has dealt with language at the level of words and **utterances** (sentences, questions, etc in speech). However, as we saw at the very beginning, utterances are generally part of a longer stretch of spoken discourse. In writing, sentences are usually part of a longer text. In order to be an effective language user, therefore, speakers and writers need to be able to operate with longer texts (stretches of discourse) as well as with words, phrases, sentences and questions.

We will now look at cohesion, coherence and the special features of spoken face-to-face discourse.

Cohesion

Cohesion refers to the devices we use to stick text together – the way we connect ideas and sentences together. **Lexical cohesion** involves using words and groups of words throughout a text to bind a topic together. **Grammatical cohesion**, on the other hand, uses pronouns, articles and tense agreement, among other devices, for the same purpose. In the following passage, describing a primary teacher's first day with a new class, lexical cohesion is achieved by the use of a group of related topic-words ('thuglets', 'boys', 'girls', 'young lad', 'children').

> Clare knew that her class had a high proportion of 'thuglets' (the word she used for boys and girls whose behaviour could cause problems). They had acquired a fearsome reputation in the previous two years. But this did not stop her from walking towards the classroom with a feeling of eager anticipation. She was a teacher, after all. This is what she did.
>
> The children were waiting for her. Some of them were sitting quietly at their desks, but one young lad was standing at the back of the room, his arms crossed and a look of sulky petulance on his face.
>
> This is how it starts, she thought as she said 'Good morning, children,' and waited for them to reply.

Grammatical cohesion is achieved by the placing of the account in the past tense, but also by the use of words like 'her' in sentence 1 referring back to 'Clare', 'they' at the beginning of sentence 2 to refer to the 'thuglets', and 'she' at the beginning of sentence 4 referring back to Clare again. Such **anaphoric reference** is present in the second and third paragraphs, too, with words like 'her', 'them', 'his', 'she', etc. But the writer also asks us to make stronger connections too. 'This' at the beginning of sentence 3 refers back to the whole situation – the fact that the 'thuglets had acquired a fearsome reputation'. 'This' in sentence 5 of paragraph 1, however, refers to both the first day of a new year and Clare's job. 'This' in the first sentence of the last paragraph refers to the experience of walking into a new class – in other words it refers to everything that has gone before.

In many longer texts we also use **linkers** ('In the first place', 'On the one hand ...', 'Furthermore ...', 'In conclusion ...', etc) to show the progress of a text.

Coherence

Cohesion will make no difference to the success of a text if it is not coherent. The following four sentences (about the same teacher working on notions of perception) are perfectly well formed, but the text makes no sense because it has no internal logic: the ideas are in the wrong order.

> She opened it and took a large spoonful. She held up the tin. Ignoring the children's shocked faces, she put the spoon into her mouth. It was marked 'Dog food'.

When a text is coherent – when it has some internal logic – the readers should be able to perceive the writer's purpose and follow their line of thought.

Conversational discourse

Many of the same elements of cohesion and coherence apply to face-to-face spoken discourse as well. But in speech we can also use ellipsis (see page 78) for grammatical cohesion, and participants need to be proficient at turn-taking, the conversational convention that requires that only one person speak at any one time. Moreover, if the conversation is to be successful, speakers should avoid long silences, and should listen when someone else is speaking.

The skill of turn-taking involves such attributes as recognising when you can take a turn, knowing how to keep your turn (or hold the floor), knowing how to signal that someone else can take their turn, and knowing how to show that you are listening. This kind of knowledge is not specific to English, of course, since such conversational skills are almost universal. However, speakers of English need to know typical **discourse markers** (that is, linguistic ways of performing these skills – much like linkers in more writing-like text) in order to operate effectively. Phrases such as 'You may be right, but …' or 'Hold on, I'd just like to say that …' or 'Yes, but …' can help speakers take a turn. 'And another thing …', 'and that reminds me …', 'I've nearly finished, but just before I do …' help to keep a turn, whereas 'uh uh', 'right' and 'yeah' show that we are listening. Speakers of English need to recognise these discourse markers and be able to use them if they are to be successful conversationalists.

Language variables

The way English speakers use systems of grammar, vocabulary and pronunciation is dependent upon a number of variables. We will look at speaking and writing, register and language varieties.

Speaking and writing

The way we put words together in correct sequences is often influenced by whether or not we are doing it in speech or writing. For example, we find that in conversation we tend to use more contractions (e.g. 'it is' contracted to 'it's', 'I have' contracted to 'I've') than in writing. In speech we might well shorten 'It's warm in here' to 'Warm in here' or even 'Warm', though such **ellipsis** is less likely in writing. However, the choice of whether something is more or less speaking-like or writing-like may depend on the register the speaker is using.

Students of English need to be able to recognise the difference between more speaking-like and writing-like language, and to use these differences creatively.

Recent computer research has also shown that words are used differently in speech and writing. 'However' is more common in writing than speaking, for example, but 'started' is much more common than 'began' in speaking. People use 'go' and 'be like' to mean 'said' ('She goes/She's like "How are you feeling?" and I go/I'm like "Not so bad" …') in speech but almost never in writing.

Because speaking is often face-to-face and interactive, speakers can use **paralinguistic** (or non-language) features, such as changing their **tone of voice**, giving added emphasis, whispering and shouting or speaking faster or slower. They can use gesture and expression to modify their meanings, too.

However, writers have their own bag of tricks:

– dashes
! exclamations marks
new paragraphs
, commas
CAPITAL letters, etc.

These can be used to create rhythm and effect. But whereas in speech the participants can clarify what they are saying as they go along, depending on who they are talking to, in writing it's much more important to get it right the first time.

Writers are likely to write full grammatical sentences and use writing-specific language. In addition, research shows that they use a higher percentage of **content words** (words that carry meaning like 'flower', 'car', 'hot', 'sun', 'feel') relative to **function words** (grammar words like 'which', 'to' or 'was'), than speakers do. With speakers, the proportion of function words is often much higher.

Register

Our choice of words is also determined by the register we are speaking in. Register refers to both the **topic** we are speaking about and the **tone** (for example **formal** or **informal**) that we wish to adopt. Thus, for example, in a weather forecast we would expect to hear topic words such as 'depression', 'cold front', 'moving in from …', 'temperatures' and 'hot', 'cool' and 'warm'.

However, if we revert to the sentence at the beginning of this chapter ('It's warm in here') and imagine that the conversation was taking place between two friends, one of them might change it to 'Pretty warm in here'. Here the use of 'pretty' (which is much more common in speech than in writing) indicates an informal tone. But if we use the word 'extremely' instead (e.g. 'It's extremely warm in here'), the tone of the speaker is considerably more formal.

Students of English need to be able to recognise register differences so that they can choose their words appropriately, depending on who they are speaking or writing to, and on the topic in question.

Language varieties

English is not just one language, of course. There are many different varieties. Even if we take just British English for example, we will find that whereas a speaker from southern England might say 'It's really warm in here', someone from Newcastle in the north of England might say 'It's right warm in here' (where 'right' is pronounced 'reet'). There are regional variations in Britain in pronunciation, word choice and grammar.

There are differences between varieties of British English and the English used in other countries too. An Australian speaker, using an informal tone, might well change our sentence to 'Bloody warm in here, mate', and many American speakers of English will say /wɔːrm/ rather than /wɔːm/ – i.e. with the /r/ sound clearly audible. There are other marked differences between British and American English, too. Whereas a British speaker may use the present perfect (see page 71) to ask a question such as 'Have you been to Venice?', American speakers might use the past simple (see page 71), e.g. 'Did you go to Venice?'. Indian and Pakistani speakers of English often use the present continuous (see page 70), e.g. 'We are not having that problem here', where British speakers, for example, would use the present simple (see page 70) to say 'We don't have that problem here'. And now that English is becoming so much more widely used as a second language than by first-language English speakers, the number of varieties (e.g. Singapore English, Korean English, Mexican English, etc) will gradually increase, even if the majority of people in some countries (e.g. Korea and Mexico) do not yet speak English with any confidence.

The status of English as one language is challenged by the many different 'Englishes' being used around the world, and notions of the ownership of English have shifted dramatically. Although there are still many people who advocate using a native-speaker model to teach English, there is growing acceptance of the concept of an International English, used as a common language of communication by people whose native language is not English. This International English belongs to everyone who speaks it, but it is no one's mother tongue.

Students should be aware of the difference in language varieties and should be given opportunities to experience different Englishes, though not in such a way as to make things incomprehensible to them. Furthermore, they need to be aware that there is much more that is similar about different Englishes than is different.

Conclusions | *In this chapter we have:*

- discussed the nature of meaning in context – and how what we say may have a different function from the actual words used.
- explained grammar as a system whereby certain parts of speech fit into certain 'slots', such as subject, verb, etc.
- briefly discussed the nature of words and their morphology.
- looked at elements of pronunciation: sounds, stress, pitch and intonation.
- investigated the fact that there is no one-to-one relationship between a language form and one meaning, but that different forms can express the same meaning, while different meanings can be expressed by one form.
- looked at aspects of the noun phrase, and at adjectives, prepositions, determiners, the verb phrase, adverbs and connecting words.
- discussed the concept of hypothetical meaning in relation to modal verbs and conditional sentences.
- detailed the way that words group together in collocations, lexical phrases and idioms.
- briefly mentioned language functions.
- discussed text and discourse (and cohesion and coherence).
- made reference to language variables, such as speech versus written English, different registers and different language varieties.

Teaching the language system

- Teaching specific aspects of language
- Explaining meaning
- Explaining language construction
- Practice and controlled practice

- Examples of language system teaching
- Mistakes, slips, errors and attempts
- Correcting students

Teaching specific aspects of language

When we ask students to concentrate on specific aspects of language, we will usually choose some way of explaining the form and meaning of that language before asking for student **repetition** as part of a **controlled practice** phase of the lesson sequence. This explanation, repetition and practice is a form of what we have called *study* (see Chapter 4, page 52). Sometimes we will spend a lot of time on this language focus, and students will be involved in quite a few minutes of repetition. At other times, once our students' attention has been drawn to the language in question, they may well be able to move fairly quickly to a stage of **personalisation** (where they use the language to talk about their lives – see page 53) or even full *activation*. In such cases, the study element has been brief because it has met with almost instant success.

How long we have to spend on language study will depend on who the students are, what their level is and what elements of language we are asking them to study.

Many people have contrasted two approaches (called, rather unhelpfully, **deductive** and **inductive**) for introducing students to specific aspects of language.

The deductive approach

In a deductive approach, students are given explanations or grammar rules, for example, and then, based on these explanations or rules, they make phrases and sentences using the new language.

In the following example, elementary students are going to focus on the present continuous tense.

The teacher starts by showing them pictures of people doing certain actions (painting a house, fixing the roof, cutting the grass, etc). He or she then **models** a sentence about one of the pictures ('He's painting the house') before using a series of devices to draw the students' attention to the grammar of the present continuous ('Listen … he's … he's … he is … he is [*using a gesture, perhaps fingers or hands coming together to show* 'he' *and* 'is' *joined together to make the contracted form*] … he's … he's … painting … listen … paint … ing … paint … ing … he's painting the house'). Students then repeat the sentence, before moving on to the next one ('He's fixing the roof'), where the teacher once again models the sentence, and again draws the students' attention to the construction of the present continuous by **isolating** parts of it ('he's', 'fixing'). The students then repeat the second sentence. The teacher now **cues** the students with a prompt ('paint') and the students have to say 'He's painting the house', or 'fix' and they say 'He's fixing the roof'. They then use what they are learning to make sentences about the other pictures, and as they do so, the teacher corrects where necessary (see pages 97–98).

It can be seen that this **explain and practise** approach to teaching aspects of the language system looks very much like a **straight arrows** sequence (see page 54) in which the order of elements is engage → study → activate. It suits some students and language points very well. We will see an example of this kind of procedure on page 88.

The inductive approach

In a so-called **inductive approach**, things happen the other way round. In other words, instead of going from the rules to the examples, students see examples of language and try to work out the rules. Thus, for example, after students have read a text, we might ask them to find examples of different past tenses and say how and why they are used. This **boomerang**-type lesson (where the elements occur in the sequence engage → activate → study) is especially appropriate where language study arises out of skills work on reading and listening texts.

If we want students to understand how speakers in informal conversation use certain phrases as delaying tactics (or to buy 'thinking' time) we might – after letting them listen and respond to someone speaking spontaneously – get them to listen again, but this time reading a transcript of what is being said. The task we give them is to find language used for buying time – hoping that they will identify phrases like 'you know', 'I mean', 'yeah', 'mmm', etc.

If we want students to understand how certain words collocate (see page 75), we can, if we want, tell them about the words and their collocations. That is what we would do in an explain and practise sequence. But in an inductive approach we prefer the students to find this information out. If we are teaching 'body language', therefore, instead of telling students which verbs like 'wave', 'clench', 'wag', etc collocate with which nouns such as 'hand', 'arm', 'teeth', 'fist', etc, we can send them to **monolingual learners' dictionaries** (**MLDs**) or computer **corpuses** to see if they can work it out for themselves. Such **discovery activities** ask students to do the work rather than having everything handed to them on a plate by the teacher or a grammar/vocabulary book.

Discovery activities suit some students very well; they enjoy working things out. Many people think that the language they understand in this way is more powerfully learnt (because they had to make some **cognitive effort** as they uncovered its patterns) than it would have been if they were told the grammar rules first and didn't have to make such an effort. However, not all students feel comfortable with this approach and would still prefer to be 'spoon-fed'. A lot will depend on their level. It is generally easier for more advanced students to analyse language using discovery procedures than it is for complete beginners. The boomerang sequence is often more appropriate with students who already have a certain amount of language available to them for the first activation stage than it is with students who can say very little. Discovery activities are especially useful when students are looking at the construction of specific language for the second or third time. When we ask them to look at the use of different past tenses in a story and to work out how they are used and why, we assume that they 'know' the individual tenses. The detective work they are doing now is intended to expand their knowledge and revise things they are already familiar with.

Explaining meaning

One of the clearest ways of explaining the meaning of something is to show it. If we hold up a book, point to it and say 'book ... book', its meaning will be instantly clear. For actions we can use mime: if we are teaching 'He is running', we can mime someone running. At other times we can use gesture. We can demonstrate superlative adjectives, by using hand and arm movements to show 'big ... bigger ... biggest', and many teachers have standard gestures to explain such things as the past (a hand pointing backwards over the shoulder), or the future (a hand pointing forwards). We can also use facial expressions to explain the meaning of sad, happy, frightened, etc.

We can use pictures to explain situations and concepts (for example, a picture of someone coming away from a swimming pool with dripping wet hair to show 'She's just been swimming'). We can use diagrams too. Many teachers use **time lines** to explain time, simple versus continuous and aspect (e.g. perfect tenses). For example, if we want to explain the present perfect continuous tense, we can use a time line to demonstrate 'I've been living here since 2004'.

If we can't show something in one of the ways mentioned above, we can *describe* the meaning of the word. For example, a 'generous' person is someone who shares their time and their money/possessions with you. 'Nasty' is the opposite of 'nice'. A 'radish' is a kind of vegetable.

If describing meaning isn't appropriate, we can list vocabulary items to explain concepts. For example, if we want students to understand the idea of the 'caring professions' (perhaps because the phrase came up in a text), we can list a number of jobs such as 'doctor', 'nurse', 'social worker' and 'counsellor' to explain the phrase. We can also use **check questions** to make sure students have understood correctly. If they are learning how to make third conditional sentences (see page 74) and one of the examples is 'If she'd missed the bus, she would have been late for work', we can ask the students questions such as 'Did she miss the bus?' and 'Was she late for work?'.

A way of making meaning absolutely clear, of course, is to translate words and phrases. Sometimes this is easy; all languages have a word for 'book'. Sometimes, however, it is more complex; many languages do not have an absolute equivalent for the English phrase 'devil-may-care attitude' and translating idioms such as 'to pull the wool over someone's eyes' means having to find an L1 equivalent, even though it may be constructed completely differently.

The trick of explaining meaning effectively is to choose the best method to fit the meaning that needs to be explained. In actual fact, most teachers use a mixture of some or all of these techniques. However, check questions are especially important since they allow us to determine if our explanations have been effective.

Explaining language construction

We have already seen (on page 81) how the teacher can model a sentence such as 'He's painting the house', isolating the features ('he's' and 'painting') which are essential parts of its grammatical construction. We can use fingers or hands, too, to show how 'he is' turns into 'he's' in speech or how 'fast' and 'er' are joined together to make a comparative adjective. We can also demonstrate word and sentence **stress** by beating time with our arms. We can show **intonation patterns** by 'drawing' the tune in the air.

Some students will find such graphic gestures sufficient, but others like to see written explanations, or diagrams on boards and overhead projectors. If we are teaching the third conditional (see page 74), we might write the following on the board:

If + had + past participle → would + have + past participle

With an overhead projector, the teacher can write on overhead transparencies to draw attention to grammatical construction, as in the example on page 85 where the two main language areas of interest are the way headlines are written, and the use of pronouns for reference within a text (see anaphoric reference on page 77):

The same can be done with technology such as an interactive whiteboard (see page 252). This has the added advantage that the end result can be saved or printed out for students to keep.

Another way of demonstrating grammatical sequence is to write words on individual cards which can then be moved around (to show the difference between affirmative sentence order and the syntax of questions, for example). We can also manipulate a set of **Cuisenaire rods** (small blocks of wood of different colours and lengths). They can be used to show parts of speech, stress patterns and sentence construction.

Finally, it is often easiest to explain language construction. For example, if we want students to understand the rule about the third person singular of the present simple, we can say:

> 'Listen ... we say I play, you play, we play, they play, but with he, she and it we add an s. Listen, I play, she plays ... you play, he plays ... we play, it plays.'

However, we will need to be careful that (a) explaining the construction of the language is fairly easy to do, and (b) that we can do it in language which the students we are teaching will find easy to understand.

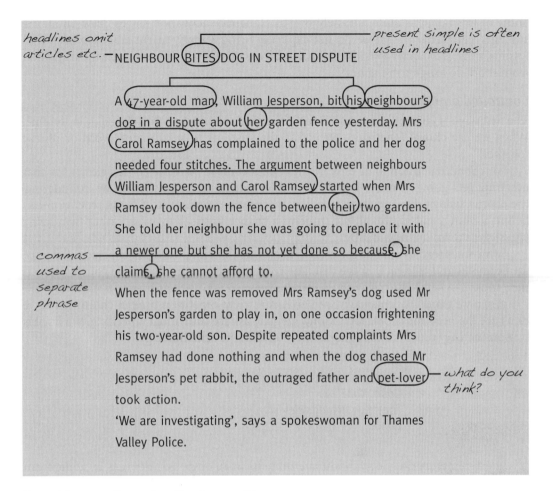

headlines omit articles etc. — NEIGHBOUR (BITES) DOG IN STREET DISPUTE — *present simple is often used in headlines*

A (47-year-old man), William Jesperson, bit (his) (neighbour's) dog in a dispute about (her) garden fence yesterday. Mrs (Carol Ramsey) has complained to the police and her dog needed four stitches. The argument between neighbours (William Jesperson and Carol Ramsey) started when Mrs Ramsey took down the fence between (their) two gardens. She told her neighbour she was going to replace it with a newer one but she has not yet done so because, she claims, she cannot afford to.

commas used to separate phrase

When the fence was removed Mrs Ramsey's dog used Mr Jesperson's garden to play in, on one occasion frightening his two-year-old son. Despite repeated complaints Mrs Ramsey had done nothing and when the dog chased Mr Jesperson's pet rabbit, the outraged father and (pet-lover) took action. — *what do you think?*

'We are investigating', says a spokeswoman for Thames Valley Police.

Practice and controlled practice

We ask students to practise the language they are studying so that they can try it out and get used to saying it or writing it. As they do this, we may well correct them if they make mistakes (see pages 97–98) so that they are clear about how it works. This practice helps them to internalise how the language is constructed so that when it passes from their **short-term memory** to their **long-term memory**, they know how it is put together.

Short-term memory is where things are stored only for as long as they are needed. For example, we may remember a house number because we have been invited to a party, but a week later we may have forgotten it because we don't need it anymore. Long-term memory, on the other hand, is for things that we want to 'keep'. We remember PIN numbers for credit cards, our own car licence plates, and passwords for bank accounts or computers because we need to use them all the time.

If we want specific language items to be part of our students' long-term memory, a once-only study session will not be enough. We need to ensure that students see new words, phrases and grammar again and again. **Repetition** works, in other words, but this does not just mean the repetition that takes place in a controlled practice session when students first meet the language. Rather, it suggests that we need to bring the language back over time and at spaced intervals so that it gradually becomes part of our students' language store.

Some of this happens quite naturally because language activation stages draw on all the students' knowledge; but if we do not explicitly bring recently learnt language back into lessons, there is a danger that, like the party-house number, it will not make the transition from short- to long-term memory.

Controlled practice

The first stage of controlled practice is repetition and this can be either choral or individual. When we use **choral repetition**, we get all the students to say the new word or phrase together.

For choral repetition to be effective, it is important to start the chorus clearly (so that everyone gets going at once) and to help the students with the rhythm by 'conducting' the chorus, using arms and hands to show where stress occurs, etc. Choral repetition can be invigorating, and it gives all the students a chance to speak together rather than being (possibly) shown up individually.

Sometimes teachers divide the class in half (when working with a two-person dialogue, for example) and give each of the dialogue roles to one or other half. The conversation is then spoken in **semi-chorus**, with the two halves each taking their turn to speak.

When we think students have been given sufficient repetition time in chorus (or if we don't see the need for choral repetition), we may ask for individual repetition. We do this by **nominating** students and asking them to give us the sentence, e.g.

TEACHER:	*OK. Sam?*
STUDENT 1 (Sam):	*They're watching television.*
TEACHER:	*Good. Kim?*
STUDENT 2 (Kim):	*They're watching television.*
TEACHER:	*Good.*
etc	

It is worth remembering not to nominate students in an obvious order (e.g. by going from one end of a row to the other) since this will make the activity predictable and, as a result, will not keep students 'on their toes'.

A form of individual practice which some teachers and students find useful occurs when teachers tell their students that they can say the word or phrase quietly to themselves, **murmuring** it a few times as they get used to saying it. It may sound strange to hear everyone speaking the phrase quietly to themselves at the same time, but it gives them all a chance for individual repetition, a chance once again to see how it feels to say the new language.

If we feel that students have done enough repetition of the phrase or phrases (or if we don't think such repetition is necessary), we might organise a quick **cue-response** session to encourage controlled practice of the new language. Suppose, for example, that we have taught a group of beginner students a series of vocabulary items such as 'nurse', 'fireman', 'doctor', 'teacher', 'policeman', etc, and that we have pictures of these people on cards. We can use these cards as a cue, which we hope will then elicit the appropriate **response**, e.g.

TEACHER (*holds up picture of a policeman*):	Sam?
STUDENT 1 (*Sam*):	Policeman.
TEACHER:	Good. (*holds up picture of a nurse*) Kim?
STUDENT 2 (*Kim*):	Nurse.
TEACHER:	Good.

Cues can also be verbal (e.g. 'Question … Flight 36' to get the response 'What time does Flight 36 leave?') or non-verbal (e.g. the teacher shrugs their shoulders to elicit 'I don't know').

Cue-response drills are an efficient way of getting the students to say the new language in a way that can be invigorating and challenging. If we think students need more controlled practice of this type, we can put them in pairs and ask them to continue saying the new words and phrases to each other. Perhaps they can take turns miming one of the professions or showing/drawing pictures of policemen, nurses, etc so that they are, in effect, conducting cue-response drills of their own.

Freer practice

Sometimes we may decide that students do not need very much controlled practice of the new language. This is often the case at higher levels where not only will they probably have understood our explanations of meaning and language construction, but they may be slightly familiar with the language anyway. In such situations we might just say something like 'OK, can anyone tell me what would have happened if they'd overslept this morning?' to provoke examples of the third conditional (see page 74). As students use personalised sentences in this way, we can point out any mistakes they might be making and encourage correct pronunciation.

If, when we try to bypass controlled practice in this way, we find that students are having more problems than we thought, we might have to return to our explanations of meaning and construction and then organise controlled practice after all. But hopefully this will not happen, and our students will be able to try using the language in this more relaxed and less formal setting.

Freer practice – especially where personalisation is concerned (see page 53) – is a kind of transition stage between language study and activation. It is still concerned with the correct construction of language and so it is part of study; it is also concerned with language use and so it is moving towards activation.

The decision about whether or not students need explanation or controlled practice will depend, as we have suggested, on whether we think they are already familiar with the new language or not. It would, after all, be inappropriate to force students to concentrate on studying language they were already perfectly capable of using. Our decision about how to proceed should, therefore, be based on what the students know already, and we will need to adapt our plan immediately if we find that the majority of them are more aware of the 'new' language than we thought they were.

Examples of language system teaching

We can now look at a few ideas for teaching grammar, pronunciation, vocabulary and language functions. These lesson sequences and ideas will include both student discovery-type moments and explain and practise examples (see pages 81–82). There will be a mixture of straight arrows and boomerang procedures. However, there are many more ways of approaching this kind of teaching than there is room for here. Readers should consult the books listed on page 263 for more ideas.

Teaching grammar

One way of teaching grammar is to use an explain and practise procedure such as we have described above. So, for example, if we want to teach the present simple (see page 70) for habitual actions, we can show elementary students pictures of someone with an interesting occupation (in this case a marathon runner). After talking about running ('Would you like to run?', 'Do you take exercise?', etc), the students see the following pictures.

We point to the first picture and model the sentence 'She gets up at half past five'. We use check questions ('Does she get up at half past five on Monday?, on Thursday?', etc) to make sure they understand the concept of habitual actions. We isolate the word 'gets' and show how an 's' is added to the verb for 'she', 'he' and 'it' (we can say 'Listen, get … s …' indicating 'get' with one hand and 's' with the other. Now we draw the

two hands together and say 'gets … gets … listen, she gets …'). Then we model the sentence again and get the students to repeat it chorally and individually.

Students now look at the second picture and we try to **elicit** the sentence (that is get them to produce it, rather than give it to them) 'She has breakfast at six o'clock'. If necessary, we model this sentence too, isolating 'has'. Students repeat this second sentence chorally and individually. We now start a cue-response drill where we say 'half past five' and the students say 'She gets up' or 'six o'clock', for them to say 'She has breakfast'. We elicit 'She leaves home at six thirty', and once again get repetition of this new sentence before conducting more elaborate cue-response stages. We correct (and perhaps re-explain) where students are having difficulties. Finally, students tell the class about their own daily routine and about the routines of people they know (members of their families, etc). Over subsequent lessons, we make sure they have more opportunities to use the present simple in this way.

If we use a discovery approach to teaching grammar, our lesson sequence will look rather different – as in the following example for upper-intermediate students studying conditional if-sentences.

We can start the sequence by asking students to think about grandparents. In pairs or groups, they discuss what adjectives ('wise', 'kind', 'old', etc) they would use to describe a typical grandmother. They write their words down. We then ask them to read the following extract (from a book for children, but which is equally appropriate for adults and young adults in this context). Their task is to see if any of the adjectives they chose fit George's grandmother, and if not, how they would choose to describe her.

'You know what's the matter with you?' the old woman said, staring at George over the rim of the teacup with those bright wicked little eyes. 'You're *growing* too fast. Boys who grow too fast become stupid and lazy.'

'But I can't help it if I'm growing fast, Grandma,' George said.

'Of course you can,' she snapped. 'Growing's a nasty childish habit.'

'But we *have* to grow, Grandma. If we didn't grow, we'd never be grown-ups.'

'Rubbish, boy, rubbish,' she said. 'Look at me. Am I growing? Certainly not.'

'But you did once, Grandma.'

'Only *very little*,' the old woman answered. 'I gave up growing when I was extremely small, along with other nasty childish habits like laziness and disobedience and greed and sloppiness and untidiness and stupidity. You haven't given up any of those things, have you?'

'I'm still only a little boy, Grandma.'

'You're eight years old,' she snorted. 'That's old enough to know better. If you don't stop growing soon, it'll be too late.'

'Too late for what, Grandma?'

'It's ridiculous,' she went on. 'You're nearly as tall as me already.'

George took a good look at grandma. She certainly was a very tiny person. Her legs were so short she had to have a footstool to put her feet on, and her head only came half-way up the back of the armchair.

'Daddy says it's fine for a man to be tall,' George said.

'Don't listen to your daddy,' Grandma said. 'Listen to me.'

'But how do I stop growing?' George asked her.

'Eat less chocolate,' Grandma said.

'Does chocolate make you grow?'

'It makes you grow the *wrong way*,' she snapped. 'Up instead of down.'

Grandma sipped some tea but never took her eyes from the little boy who stood before her. 'Never grow up,' she said. 'Always down.'

'Yes, Grandma.'

'And stop eating chocolate. Eat cabbage instead.'

'Cabbage! Oh no, I don't like cabbage,' George said.

'It's not what you like or don't like,' Grandma snapped. 'It's what's good for you that counts. From now on, you must eat cabbage three times a day, Mountains of cabbage! And if it's got caterpillars on it, so much the better!'

We can ask the students whether they liked the text or not. Did they find it funny or outrageous? Students can check any words they don't understand by working in groups with dictionaries or by asking us.

Now we ask them to look at the text and find any sentences which have the word 'if' in them. They will come up with the following:

1 'But I can't help it if I'm growing fast, Grandma,' George said.
2 'If we didn't grow, we'd never be grown-ups.'
3 'If you don't stop growing soon, it'll be too late.'
4 'And if it's got caterpillars on it, so much the better!'

We ask the students to analyse the sentences (perhaps in pairs or groups). Which sentence is hypothetical (sentence 2) and how do we know this? (Because it uses past tenses about a present/timeless situation.) Which sentence is about the future (sentence 3)? And what are the differences between the two 'present' sentences (the use of the present continuous in a clause in sentence 1; the verbless clause in sentence 4)? They need to notice that in sentences 1 and 4 there are variations from the conditional patterns which they have probably usually studied.

Students now try to make their own sentences using exactly the same grammar patterns ('I can't stop it if it's happening already' or 'If people didn't like spending money, they'd never buy expensive clothes', etc). We can then show them more texts which they have to search in the same way, looking for 'if' sentences to see if they used the same or different patterns (and to determine how different they are).

Later, students can be asked to imagine a new situation featuring George's grandmother (perhaps when she is questioned by the police, or goes to a party or can't find what she wants in a shop). They have to write a conversation in which she uses 'if' sentences like the ones in the original text. Finally, they can role-play a scene with the grandmother, or, instead, have a discussion about the depiction of old people on the TV or in the media.

The point about this kind of language study is that instead of the teacher explaining something which the students then have to practise, it is the students themselves who look at the language and come to their own conclusions (with the teacher's help). Using real text extracts (from books or the Internet, or listening to tracks from the radio or other recorded material) will always provide grammar for the students to read and study.

Teaching pronunciation

In the following lesson excerpt (for teenage and adult students at intermediate level or above), we tell the students they are going to hear conversations in which a woman asks a man to do something, and the man replies by saying things like 'Well …' or 'I'd rather not' or 'That depends on what it is' (if the woman says something general like 'Could you give me a hand?').

Students listen to an audio track in which the woman asks (for example) 'Could you give me a hand with hanging out the washing?' and the man says 'Well …'. All the students have to do is decide whether or not the man is going to help, and the only clue they have to this is the **intonation** he uses and the pitch of his voice. After each exchange, we pause the audio track and the students discuss whether the man sounded as if he was saying 'Definitely no', 'Maybe' or 'All right, I suppose so'. The class discuss and analyse the different intonation patterns the man uses.

Later, students can ask us to do things and we can answer using different intonation patterns so that the students have to work out which of the three answers it is. Students then ask each other to do things and, using the phrases 'Well …', 'That depends on what it is', etc, the answering students have to indicate (using intonation) what their answer means.

We can teach intonation (and stress) in many other ways, too:

🖼 **Punctuation:** one activity is to show pre-intermediate students a range of unpunctuated phrases such as 'You bought a lottery ticket', 'You don't like my hat' or 'You want a pizza'. The teacher plays an audio track (or says the phrases out loud), and the students have to decide whether they should put a full stop, a question mark or an exclamation mark at the end of them depending on what they have heard. Students can then practise saying the phrases in the three different ways (statement, question, exclamation).

🖼 **Same sentence, different situations:** a variation on these activities is to get students to think about how they would say the same sentence in different situations. For example, we can ask them to say, 'Good morning, Mr Jones' as if (a) they've never met him before, (b) he owes them money, (c) they really like him but don't want to be too obvious, etc.

We can practise **stress** in words by modelling the words and exaggerating the stressed syllable (e.g the second syllable of 'comPUTer' or the third syllable of 'impoSITion') and maybe beating time with our hands. We can give students a list of three- and four-syllable words which they have to put in different boxes depending on whether the stress comes on the first, second or third syllable (as in the example below):

Put the following words in the correct columns:

accompanist audience audition composer conductor double bass
interview manager percussion photographer receptionist remember
saxophone songwriter therapist violin

A ●●●	B ●●●	C ●●●	D ●●●●

Perhaps we can write the words on cards which students have to stick up on a board in the appropriate column. Or they could drag-and-drop words into the columns on a computer screen or interactive whiteboard.

There are many other ways of teaching stress and rhythm – the following are just two examples.

🖼 **Stress in phrases:** for stress in phrases, we can, for example, show intermediate students a range of phrases such as 'Come at ten', 'I lost my voice', 'Sing your song', 'The weather's awful', 'This can't go on', 'You must be joking'. The phrases can be written on individual cards. Each student has one of the cards and they have to find their 'stress pair' (the student who has a card which has a phrase with the same stress pattern as the one they are holding). 'Come at ten' is matched with 'Sing your song'; 'I lost my voice' is paired with 'This can't go on'; 'You must be joking' is paired with 'The weather's awful'.

🖼 **Songs and chants:** songs and chants are good for rhythm, and for young children, especially, they make the business of stress easy and uncomplicated since it doesn't even have to be explained. Songs like 'The wheels on the bus' have a strong rhythmic pattern which, through constant repetition, become part of the child's rhythmic sense:

> The wheels on the bus go round and round, round and round,
> round and round.
> The wheels on the bus go round and round, all through the town.
>
> The wipers on the bus go swish, swish, swish; swish, swish, swish;
> swish, swish, swish.
> The wipers on the bus go swish, swish, swish all through the town.

(There are further verses about the horn on the bus – beep, beep, beep; the mums on the bus – chatter, chatter, chatter; the dads on the bus – snore, snore, snore, etc).

Some teachers use jazz chants for rhythm. Words are spoken rhythmically to the accompaniment of clapping and stamping. Imagine, for example, putting a beat to the following lines:

> I dropped into my neighbourhood and what did I see
> A hundred happy faces smiling up at me.
> etc

When we teach **sounds**, we want students not only to speak correctly, but also to recognise sound and spelling correspondence. We also want them to be able to discriminate between similar-sounding phonemes. We can, for example, do **minimal pair** exercises (minimal pairs are pairs of words such as 'ship' and 'sheep', 'hat' and 'hut', 'sin' and 'sing', 'wash' and 'watch', which are differentiated by only one sound – the other sounds stay the same). Students can be given pairs of words, e.g.

1 ship sheep
2 heart hard

For each number, they hear a sentence and they have to circle the word they hear in each case. (For example, **1** 'Yesterday I saw a large *sheep* in the field', **2** 'Being in love is so *hard*'). We can then model the words. In the case of the vowels, we will make sure the students take note of the lip position for 'ship' (spread loosely) and 'sheep' (stretched). With the two consonants, they need to know that whereas /t/ (e.g. 'two', 'touch', 'heart') is said with the vocal chords open, /d/ (e.g. 'do', 'hard') is said with the vocal chords closed. The result is that /d/ is a **voiced** consonant (because the air vibrates as it passes though the closed chords) whereas /t/ is **voiceless** because there is no such constriction (see page 62). Students then say the words and their classmates have to decide which sound they were using.

Minimal pair exercises like this can be used with any age and, depending on what particular words, sentences and phrases are used, at any level. Once again, drawings and cards will help young children, just as getting them to stand in different groups depending on the sounds in words which they have written on cards may help the more **kinaesthetic learners** (see page 16).

Sounds and spelling: a major cause of difficulty for some students of English is the apparent lack of correspondence between sounds and spelling. The following procedures show ways of dealing with this. In the first, we give students lists of words with a certain spelling (e.g. the letter combination 'ou' in 'rough', 'tough', 'ought', 'bought', 'though', 'through', etc). They have to group the words according to the different ways 'ou' is pronounced. A second idea is to give students a list of words (e.g. 'won', 'summer', 'son', 'plunge', 'under', etc) and ask them to say which sound (in this case /ʌ/) occurs in all of them, before getting them to repeat the words and then think of others which contain the same sound.

 Tongue twisters: we can design rhymes and tongue twisters which use a particular sound or sounds and have students repeat them – for example, 'George judges jewels jealously' for the sound /dʒ/, or 'awful orphans ought to organise' for the sound /ɔː/ (at least in many varieties of British English).

The most important thing to remember about pronunciation teaching is that students should have as much opportunity as possible to listen to spoken English. When teaching different sounds, we will try to help them hear the difference between confusing **phonemes**. When teaching stress and intonation, we will ask them to recognise what different intonation patterns mean (e.g. enthusiasm, lack of enthusiasm); we will model words and phrases indicating appropriate stress and intonation (using hand and arm movements and vocal exaggeration, perhaps) and get students to try to imitate us. A lot of this occurs naturally when we are teaching grammar or vocabulary. It is important to remember that when we write new language on the board, we should indicate where the word or phrase is stressed, using one of the methods we saw on page 62.

Teaching vocabulary

At beginner levels, teachers frequently use explain and practise procedures. For example, we might have individual pictures on **flashcards** showing people who are tired, sad, happy, frightened, exhausted, etc. We hold up a picture, point to it and say 'tired … she's tired', while miming a yawn. Then we model 'tired' and get the students to repeat it. Next, we hold up (or point to) the next picture and model 'sad'. As the students learn more words, we conduct a cue-response drill, holding up different flashcards (or pointing to different pictures) so that the students give the correct word. Students can then use the words in their own sentences.

For any classes above the complete beginner level we can assume that different students will know a range of different lexical items. A way of exploiting this is to get the class (with our help) to build their own vocabulary tree. For example, suppose that intermediate students are working on a unit about homes and houses, we might put this diagram on the board.

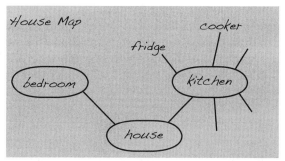

The students are asked to add to the diagram as extensively as they can. Perhaps we put them in different groups, one for each room (kitchen, bedroom, dining room, etc) and they have to come up with as many words as possible for their room. Or perhaps they just come up to the board, one by one, to add to the diagram, using chalk or marker pens. While they are doing this, we can help out with spellings and pronunciation – and when the diagram is as complete as the students can make it, we can do pronunciation work and/or add any important words which we think are missing.

This kind of activity draws on the students' existing knowledge (which is why it is appropriate for elementary levels onwards); the students are involved; there is movement and discussion, and the teacher is on hand to explain and practise when it is necessary.

At higher levels, we can ask students to take even more responsibility for decision-making about how words are used. The following example is all about vocabulary associated with the weather, including the metaphorical uses we have for weather lexis.

The activity starts when students are asked to say what their favourite kind of weather is. When they have done this, we tell them they are going to do some language research.

Students are given a series of weather phrases, e.g.

blazing sun   blizzard   breeze   downpour   gale   heavy shower   heavy snowfall light shower   light breeze   light snowfall   strong breeze   strong sunshine strong wind   sunshine   torrential rain

They are told to use the words to complete the middle column of the following table by looking for the words in a dictionary, on a CD-ROM, by using a search engine on the Internet and/or by talking to each other.

	least severe <----------> most severe	associated verbs
rain	light shower, heavy shower ...	
snow		
sun		
wind		

When they have done this (and we have checked through their tables), we can ask them to put the following weather-related verbs in the right-hand column of the chart:

blow   drizzle   fall   howl   pour   roar   scorch   settle   shine   whistle

Once again, they do this by researching the words for themselves. We only help them if they get stuck or when the activity finishes and we check through what they have found out (we can draw the chart on the board and have the students come and fill it in).

Students are then asked to tell each other about the worst weather they have ever been in – or to describe a day they remember that was particularly memorable because of the weather.

Finally, the students are asked to read a text in which various weather metaphors occur (e.g. 'sunny disposition', 'shower with presents', 'gales of laughter', 'thunder' (as a verb), 'storm out of a room', 'thunderstruck', 'thunderous applause', 'storm of protest'). They have to find the weather metaphors and say what they think they mean. We will then go through the metaphors to make sure they are comfortable with them before asking them to use them in their own invented stories.

Two things need to be said about this sequence. Firstly, when we stray into metaphorical and idiomatic usage of any kind, the language we teach is often specific to a particular variety of English (in this case British English), and so we will have to decide how genuinely useful it is for our students to learn. But secondly, and more importantly in the context of approaches to vocabulary teaching and learning, the whole sequence has involved students in doing much of the study themselves, without having to be told and taught by us – although we will, of course, confirm the students' right choices, and make sure they are using the words and phrases correctly.

Teaching language functions

In the following explain and practise sequence for elementary students, the teacher engages the students by drawing a picture of a boy and a girl on the board. She mimes the boy's nervousness. She indicates that the boy likes the girl (she can draw a think bubble coming from his head with a heart in it). She makes students aware that the boy speaks first. He says, 'Would you like to come to the cinema?' She checks the students understand 'cinema' (she draws a picture or mimes watching a big screen, etc). She models 'Would you like to come to the cinema?' She isolates 'come to the cinema?' maintaining the appropriate intonation. Students then repeat this phrase in chorus. She then models 'Would you like to …' and the students repeat that. Now she joins the two halves of the question together so that she models 'Would you like to come to the cinema?' and the students repeat it. This kind of **back-chaining** – where the teacher builds up phrases from the end – is especially useful for longer questions and sentences.

The teacher then models the answer 'Yes, please. That would be great', paying special attention to the use of appropriate stress and intonation. Students repeat the phrase. Now she cues a student with the word 'question' so that they ask 'Would you like to come to the cinema?'. She nominates another student to answer and he says, 'Yes, please. That would be great'.

After some controlled practice of this kind, the teacher elicits and models the answer 'I'm afraid I can't. Sorry'. When the students have repeated it, the teacher conducts a further cue-response session where she indicates whether the students should give a yes or no answer. Finally, she gets them to substitute other words and phrases so that they can say things like 'Would you like to come to dinner?', 'Would you like to come to my house?'.

The students practise making these two-line invitation dialogues in pairs. Finally, the teacher listens to some of these pairs, making any last-minute corrections or adjustments.

At higher levels, we can move towards a more discovery-type sequence, and build language activation into the study section of the lesson. For example, students can be shown a picture and dialogue with the lines in the wrong order, as in this example which is for upper-intermediate students.

☐ … and on top of that, the vegetables are undercooked.
☐ Excuse me!
☐ I'm not very happy with my meal.
☐ I'm sorry, madam …
☐ I'm sorry to hear that, madam. I'll take it back to the kitchen.
☐ I'm sorry to hear that, madam. What seems to be the problem?
☐ Thank you. I would appreciate it.
☐ Well, to start with the meat is too well-done …
☐ Yes, madam?

Students listen to an audio track to see if they have got the order right. They then listen again and work on aspects of stress and intonation in particular phrases. If appropriate, the teacher can ask them to repeat these phrases in the same way. Working in pairs, they then identify which phrases (a) expressed a complaint, (b) expressed regret and apology, (c) gave details of the complaint, (d) suggested ways of dealing with the complaint and (e) expressed appreciation. They are now asked to come up with any other phrases or restaurant complaints they can think of for categories a–e. The teacher can feed in more examples, too. Finally, in pairs, students make their own dialogues while the teacher goes round the room helping them and offering advice. The pairs then perform their dialogues for the rest of the class and the teacher and students discuss the good points of the dialogues they hear, while at the same time correcting any serious mistakes that have crept in.

Mistakes, slips, errors and attempts

In language study phases such as those described in this chapter, students will not always use correct English. They will make mistakes, too, when writing or speaking more freely (as we shall see in Chapters 8 and 9).

We can divide mistakes into three categories. **Slips** are mistakes which students can correct themselves, once the mistake has been pointed out to them. **Errors** are mistakes which they can't correct themselves – and which, therefore, need explanation. **Attempts** are mistakes that students make when they try to say something but do not yet know how to say it. The way we give feedback and correct such mistakes will be heavily influenced by which type we think the students are making.

There are many reasons why students might make mistakes, whichever kind of mistakes they are. Perhaps – especially in a study session – they haven't quite grasped the new information and so continue to make errors. Perhaps their own language gets in the way because the way English expresses an idea or uses a grammatical construction is either very different or tantalisingly similar to how it is done in their first language. As a result they might make a slip, produce a deeply ingrained error, or just rely on their first language when making an attempt. Japanese students frequently have trouble with article usage, for example; Germans have to get used to positioning the verb correctly; Turkish students have to deal with different sentence structure, while Arab students have to deal with a completely different written system. **False friends** (words that sound the same but have different meanings) can also cause trouble, especially for speakers of Romance languages which share a common heritage with English.

Another 'problem' category is often described as **developmental errors**. These occur naturally as the students' language knowledge develops, and are the result of the students making apparently sensible (but mistaken) assumptions about the way language works. Suppose, for example, that a student, has learnt to say things like 'I have to go', 'I want to go' or 'I would like to go'. That might lead them on to say – with perfectly appropriate logic – things like '*I must to go', not realising that the use of 'to' is not permitted with 'must'.

Whatever the reason for the students 'getting it wrong', it is vital for the teacher to realise that all students make mistakes as a natural part of the process of learning. By working out when and why things have gone wrong, students learn more about the language they are studying.

Correcting students

When students are involved in a speaking activity such as a role-play or conversation (see Chapter 9), instant and intrusive **correction** is often not appropriate since it can interfere with the flow of the activity and inhibit students just at the moment when they should be trying hardest to activate their language knowledge. But during study sessions, we will probably use correction more as it helps to clarify the language in the students' minds.

Because correction involves pointing out people's mistakes, we have to tread carefully. If we do it in an insensitive way, we can upset our students and dent their confidence. Moreover, what is appropriate for one student may be quite wrong for another.

In general, the teacher's job is to point out when something has gone wrong – and see if the students can correct themselves. Maybe what they said or wrote was just a slip and they are able to put it right straightaway.

Sometimes, however, students can't put mistakes right on their own (because they fall into the categories of errors or attempts), so we have to help them. We can do this by asking if one of their **peers** (fellow students) can help out, or by explaining the problem ourselves.

If we get other students in the class to help out, we have to make sure that the student who made the mistake in the first place isn't going to be humiliated by this ('How come they all know the answer? I must be stupid!'). Sometimes, students prefer correction directly from the teacher. On the other hand, in the right kind of atmosphere students enjoy helping each other – and being helped in return.

The following example shows students being corrected during a practice phase in which they are making sentences using the comparative form of adjectives (comparing trains and planes).

MONICA:	Trains are safer planes.
TEACHER:	Safer planes? (*with surprised questioning intonation*)
MONICA:	Oh ... Trains are safer than planes.
TEACHER:	Good, Monica. Now, 'comfortable' ... Simon?
SIMON:	Trains more comfortable. Planes are.
TEACHER:	Hmm. Can you help Simon, Bruno?
BRUNO:	Er ... Trains are more comfortable than planes.
TEACHER:	Thank you. Simon?
SIMON:	Trains are more comfortable than planes.
TEACHER:	That's right, Simon. Great. What about 'fast', Matilde?
MATILDE:	Trains faster planes.
TEACHER:	Trains are faster?
MATILDE:	Trains faster planes? I don't know.
TEACHER:	OK. Look. Trains go at a hundred miles an hour, planes go at 500 miles an hour, so planes are faster than trains. Yes?
MATILDE:	Planes are faster than trains.
TEACHER:	Well done, Matilde.

With Monica, all the teacher had to do was point out that something was wrong (by **echoing** what she said with a questioning intonation) and she immediately corrected herself. Simon was not able to do this, however, so the teacher got Bruno to help him. When Matilde made a mistake, however (and was not able to correct herself), the teacher judged that she would be unhappy to have correction from her peers so she helped her out herself.

When organising practice, then, teachers need to listen out for mistakes, identify the problem and put it right in the most efficient and tactful way.

Before leaving the subject of errors, it is worth remembering that correction is just one response that teachers can make to student language production. It is just as important – perhaps more so – to praise students for their success, as it is to correct them as they struggle towards accuracy. Teachers can show through the use of expression, encouraging words and noises ('good', 'well done', 'fantastic', 'mmm', etc) that students are doing really well. But praise should not be overused because when it is, it becomes devalued, and therefore meaningless. Praise is only effective if students know what they are being praised for – and when they themselves believe it is merited.

Conclusions | *In this chapter we have:*

- said that repetition and controlled practice are part of many study sequences.

- made a distinction between deductive approaches ('explain and practise') and inductive approaches ('discovery' activities), where students find things out for themselves.

- detailed various ways of explaining meaning – including mime, gesture, listing, translation, using pictures, etc.

- looked at various ways of organising controlled practice, including cue-response drills and choral and individual repetition.

- discussed freer practice, where students use 'new' language in a more creative way.

- detailed lesson sequences for teaching grammar, pronunciation, vocabulary and functions. In each case we have shown 'explain and practise' sequences as well as more 'discovery' focused examples.

- identified slips, errors and attempts as three different kinds of student mistake, and discussed why students make such mistakes.

- looked at different ways of correcting students, such as echoing, reformulation, using a student's peers, etc. We have stressed that we need to be especially sensitive about how we correct.

- ended by saying that praise (when it is merited) is also an important part of teacher feedback.

Teaching reading

- ■ **Reasons for reading**
- ■ **Different kinds of reading**
- ■ **Reading levels**
- ■ **Reading skills**
- ■ **Reading principles**
- ■ **Reading sequences**
- ■ **More reading suggestions**
- ■ **Encouraging students to read extensively**

Reasons for reading

There are many reasons why getting students to read English texts is an important part of the teacher's job. In the first place, many students want to be able to read texts in English either for their careers, for study purposes or simply for pleasure. Anything we can do to make it easier for them to do these things must be a good idea.

Reading is useful for language acquisition. Provided that students more or less understand what they read, the more they read, the better they get at it. Reading also has a positive effect on students' vocabulary knowledge, on their spelling and on their writing.

Reading texts also provide good models for English writing. At different times we can encourage students to focus on vocabulary, grammar or punctuation. We can also use reading material to demonstrate the way we construct sentences, paragraphs and whole texts. Students then have good models for their own writing (see Chapter 8).

Lastly, good reading texts can introduce interesting **topics**, stimulate **discussion**, excite imaginative responses and provide the springboard for well-rounded, fascinating lessons.

Different kinds of reading

We need to make a distinction between **extensive** and **intensive** reading. The term *extensive reading* refers to reading which students do often (but not exclusively) away from the classroom. They may read novels, web pages, newspapers, magazines or any other reference material. Where possible, extensive reading should involve **reading for pleasure** – what Richard Day calls *joyful reading*. This is enhanced if students have a chance to choose what they want to read, if they are encouraged to read by the teacher, and if some opportunity is given for them to share their reading experiences. Although not all students are equally keen on this kind of reading, we can say with certainty that the ones who read most progress fastest.

The term *intensive reading*, on the other hand, refers to the detailed focus on the construction of reading texts which takes place usually (but not always) in classrooms.

Teachers may ask students to look at extracts from magazines, poems, Internet websites, novels, newspapers, plays and a wide range of other text **genres** (that is, styles or types of text, see page 113). The exact choice of genres and topics may be determined by the specific purposes that students are studying for (such as business, science or nursing). In such cases, we may well want to concentrate on texts within their specialities. But if, as is often the case, they are a mixed group with differing interests and careers, a more varied diet is appropriate, as the reading sequences in this chapter will demonstrate.

Intensive reading is usually accompanied by study activities. We may ask students to work out what kind of text they are reading, tease out details of meaning, look at particular uses of grammar and vocabulary, and then use the information in the text to move on to other learning activities. We will also encourage them to reflect on different reading skills.

Reading levels

When we ask students to read, the success of the activity will often depend on the level of the text we are asking them to work with.

Ideally, we would like students to read **authentic** texts – in other words, texts which are not written especially for language learners, but which are intended for any competent user of the language. However, at lower levels this can often present insuperable problems since the amount of difficult and unknown language may make the texts impenetrable for the students. A balance has to be struck between real English on the one hand and the students' capabilities and interests on the other. There is some authentic written material which beginner students can understand to some degree: menus, timetables, signs and basic instructions, for example, and, where appropriate, we can use these. But for longer prose, we may want to offer our students texts which are written or adapted especially for their level. The important thing, however, is that such texts are as much like real English as possible.

How well the students are able to deal with reading material will depend on whether the texts are designed for intensive or extensive reading. Where students read with the support of a teacher and other students, they are usually able to deal with higher-level material than if they are reading on their own. If we want them to read for pleasure, therefore, we will try to ensure that they do not attempt material that is just too difficult for them – as a result of which they may be put off reading. This is why lower-level students are encouraged to use **simplified** or **graded readers** for extensive reading. The readers are graded so that at different levels they use language appropriate for that level – very much like the **comprehensible input** we mentioned on page 47. As a result, the students can take pleasure in reading the books even when there is no teacher there to help them.

Reading skills

Students, like the rest of us, need to be able to do a number of things with a reading text. They need to be able to **scan** the text for particular bits of information they are searching for (as, for example, when we look for a telephone number, what's on television at a certain time or search quickly through an article looking for a name or other detail). This skill means that they do not have to read every word and line; on the contrary, such an approach would stop them scanning successfully.

Students also need to be able to **skim** a text – as if they were casting their eyes over its surface – to get a general idea of what it is about (as, for example, when we run our eyes over a film review to see what the film is about and what the reviewer thought about it, or when we look quickly at a report to get a feel for the topic and what its conclusions are). Just as with scanning, if students try to gather all the details at this stage, they will get bogged down and may not be able to identify the general idea because they are concentrating too hard on specifics.

Whether readers scan or skim depends on what kind of text they are reading and what they want or need to get out of it. They may scan a computer 'Help' window to find the one piece of information they need to get them out of a difficulty, and they may skim a newspaper article to pick up a general idea of what's been happening in the world.

Reading for detailed comprehension, whether this entails looking for detailed information or picking out particular examples of language use, should be seen by students as something very different from the skills mentioned above.

Many students are perfectly capable of doing all these things in other languages, of course, though some may not read much at all in their daily lives. For both types of student, we should do our best to offer a mixture of materials and activities so that they can practise using these various skills with English text.

Reading principles

Principle 1: Encourage students to read as often and as much as possible.

The more students read, the better. Everything we do should encourage them to read extensively as well as – if not more than – intensively. It is a good idea to discuss this principle with students.

Principle 2: Students need to be engaged with what they are reading.

Outside normal lesson time, when students are reading extensively, they should be involved in joyful reading – that is, we should try to help them get as much pleasure from it as possible. But during lessons, too, we will do our best to ensure that they are *engaged* with the topic of a reading text and the activities they are asked to do while dealing with it.

Principle 3: Encourage students to respond to the content of a text (and explore their feelings about it), not just concentrate on its construction.

Of course, it is important for students to study reading texts in class in order to find out such things as the way they use language, the number of paragraphs they contain and how many times they use relative clauses. But the meaning, the message of the text, is just as important as this. As a result, we must give students a chance to respond to that message in some way. It is especially important that they should be allowed to show their feelings about the topic – thus provoking personal engagement with it and the language. With extensive reading this is even more important. Reading for pleasure is – and should be – different from reading for study.

Principle 4: Prediction is a major factor in reading.

When we read texts in our own language, we frequently have a good idea of the content before we actually start reading. Book covers give us a clue about what is in the book; photographs and headlines hint at what articles are about; we can identify reports as reports from their appearance before we read a single word. The moment we get these clues – the book cover, the headline, the web-page banner – our brain starts predicting what we are going to read. Expectations are set up and the active process of reading is ready to begin. In class, teachers should give students 'hints' so that they also have a chance to predict what is coming. In the case of extensive reading – when students are choosing what to read for pleasure – we should encourage them to look at covers and back cover copy to help them select what to read and then to help them 'get into' a book.

Principle 5: Match the task to the topic when using intensive reading texts.

Once a decision has been taken about what reading text the students are going to read (based on their level, the topic of the text and its linguistic and activation potential), we need to choose good reading **tasks** – the right kind of questions, appropriate activities before during and after reading, and useful study exploitation, etc.

The most useful and interesting text can be undermined by boring and inappropriate tasks; the most commonplace passage can be made really exciting with imaginative and challenging activities, especially if the **level of challenge** (i.e. how easy it is for students to complete a task) is exactly right for the class.

Principle 6: Good teachers exploit reading texts to the full.

Any reading text is full of sentences, words, ideas, descriptions, etc. It doesn't make sense, in class, just to get students to read it and then drop it and move on to something else. Good teachers integrate the reading text into interesting lesson sequences, using the topic for discussion and further tasks, using the language for study and then activation (or, of course, activation and then study) and using a range of activities to bring the text to life. Where students have been doing extensive reading, we should use whatever opportunities present themselves to provoke useful feedback.

Reading sequences

In the following three examples, we are going to look at three different kinds of reading text and several different kinds of reading task. As with all other skills work, it will be seen that reading often follows on from – or is followed by – work on other skills, such as speaking and writing.

Example 1: sunscreen (pre-intermediate)

In this example for pre-intermediate students, the students first look at a picture of people sunbathing and say whether it is a positive, safe and attractive image – or whether it is the opposite. They might discuss how people should protect themselves from the sun. The teacher then asks the students to read the text and identify where they think it comes from. They should do this fairly quickly.

When the class has agreed that the text is from a magazine for teenage girls (this is obvious, partly because of the format – photos combined with short texts – and also because of the language: 'and let's face it', 'gorgeous guys', 'babes', 'not only really cool'), the teacher asks them to read it again and put skin, hair and eye colour in order of least vulnerable to the sun to most vulnerable. They can do this individually or in pairs.

The class can now study some of the language in the text – including 'SPF', physical descriptions ('freckles', 'fair hair', 'dark-skinned', etc) – and the teenage language mentioned above.

POLLY GRIFFITHS GOES DOWN TO THE SEA FOR ADVICE ON HOW TO LOOK GOOD AND STAY SAFE.

So you think you're too pale and want to get a good suntan this summer? Why not? Except that unless you're careful the sun can make your skin old and leathery and can even give you skin cancer.

If you must sunbathe (and let's face it, lots of us think it's a good idea), then have a look at these gorgeous guys and babes I found on the beach and see which of them is like you.

ROGER

I'm the type who always burns. It's because I'm fair-skinned – and I've got red hair and freckles. That's why I'm so good-looking! But I still burn unless I use a really high SPF (sun protection factor) – about 20 in strong sun.

MIKE

Yeah I tan easily. People like me who are dark-skinned (with dark hair and brown eyes) are not only really cool but we go even browner in the sun. I still use sunscreen though, something light with an SPF of about 6 …

MELINDA

I have to be careful 'cause I'm the type who burns easily. But I do tan in the end. If you've got fair hair and blue eyes like me you'd better use quite a strong sunscreen (an SPF of 15 to start with) …

ALICE

Me, I've got built-in protection! I don't burn, but I don't sunbathe anyway. I mean what for? I like messing around on the beach though.

SO THE MESSAGE IS: CHECK OUT WHAT KIND OF SKIN YOU'VE GOT AND THEN BE SAFE AND SENSIBLE – AND HAVE A GOOD TIME! SEE YOU AT THE POOLSIDE BAR!

There are any number of activation possibilities with this text: students can write descriptions of themselves for the same page in the magazine. They can decide which of the four people they would most like to meet and why. They can role-play an interview with the characters in the article (see page 125), or they can prepare a short talk on how people should protect themselves against the sun, depending on skin type.

Many magazines have articles like this which we can bring into class. However, we will need to make sure that the language is not too complex for our students' levels, and we will need to think carefully about the kinds of tasks we ask students to do with them.

Example 2: campaigns (intermediate)

The following reading sequence is designed for teenage students. After doing comprehension work on the reading text, students are involved in a role-play which follows on from the reading they have done.

The sequence starts when students are asked to look quickly at the reading text and say where they think it comes from and what – at a first glance – they think it is likely to be about. They may do this in pairs, or in response to the teacher's prompting. This 'first glance' should both engage students and also allow them to start predicting what they are going to read. The teacher listens to their predictions but does not confirm or deny them at this stage.

Students are now asked to read the text fairly quickly in order to answer the following questions:

1 What's the important news?
2 Why did the council change its mind?

Once again, they can discuss their answers to these questions in pairs before the teacher solicits answers from the whole class.

The teacher can now ask students for their reactions to the story before getting them to do some study work. First of all, they are asked to match words (from the text) and meanings:

1	at the last moment	**a**	fight as hard as you can
2	funding	**b**	at the end of a period of time
3	fight tooth and nail	**c**	continue to exist
4	to persuade	**d**	your thoughts about an event

5 achievement   e work out your opinion again
6 reaction   f money for an event or place
7 survive   g to help someone decide to do something
8 think twice   h a difficult thing that you do successfully

When they have worked through this exercise successfully (and as a result cleared up doubts about the meaning of certain words), students are asked to read the text in detail again in order to correct sentences such as 'Most young people aren't interested in the youth centre', 'The council is going to pay all the money for The Grove', and 'Johnny ran the campaign alone'.

Finally, students are involved in an activation role-play (see page 125). They are told to work in groups of five in order to have a radio discussion. They are told that the council wants to close their school and open a new shopping centre. One student in each group is the radio presenter, two represent the council and two represent the school. Each student is given a role-card. For example, the presenter is told: 'Prepare your ideas with presenters from other groups. Plan what to say and how to control the discussion'. The presenter is also given some appropriate language such as 'Good evening and welcome to ...', 'I'd like to introduce ...', etc. The council representatives are told: 'Plan your ideas. Practise expressing your ideas and opinions politely', and they are given some language to help them do this. The school representatives are told to think about why they want to keep the school open (and are given some useful language such as 'Our school is special because ...'). The groups now have their 'radio discussion'. While they are doing this, the teacher can go round helping out with any difficulties. The groups can then report back on what they discussed.

This sequence will appeal to teenage students because of the topic and the fact that it is presented as a web page. The sequence demonstrates very clearly how work on one skill can lead naturally to work on another.

Example 3: webquest (intermediate to advanced)

The previous activity asked students to read a text (from a book) that pretended to be a snapshot of a web page. However, a lot of reading activities can use the Internet itself (where both teacher and students have easy access to it). One type of activity using the Internet is a **webquest**.

In a webquest, students visit various websites (pre-determined by the teacher) in order to find information to use in a class project. And because we have determined (in advance) the websites the students are going to visit, we can be confident that they will not spend endless hours in fruitless searching of the entire Internet. The quest is, as its name suggests, a search for information.

According to Gavin Dudeney and Nicky Hockly, webquests normally have four basic stages: the *introduction stage* (where the overall theme of the webquest is presented with appropriate background information. Sometimes key vocabulary is offered at this stage), the *task section* (in which the task is explained, and the students are engaged with it), the *process stage* (in which students are given web links to click on to get the information they need) and the *evaluation stage* (where students and teachers evaluate what they have learnt – and perhaps do some study work on language they have encountered and used during the quest). It can be seen, therefore, that much of the webquest procedure is concerned with *activation*. However, both at the introduction stage and the evaluation stage there may be many opportunities for language *study*.

In this webquest sequence about UFOs (unidentified flying objects), designed by JoAnn Miller, the process stage includes not only the quest itself, but also a role-play discussion based on what students have found.

The students are first given the introduction to the quest.

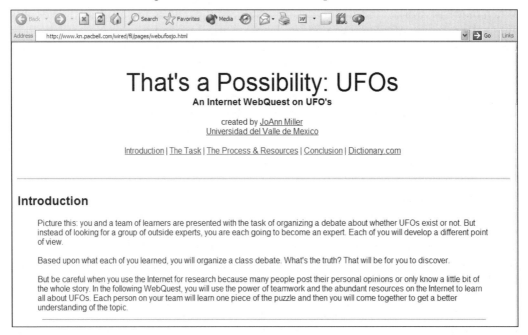

When they are clear about the information given here, they are told that the quest is to find out (a) if UFOs really exist, (b) whether people have really been abducted by extraterrestrials and (c) whether there is life on other planets. For the task, students will be divided into groups, and each group will prepare a different aspect of the debate. The students are told that because the web pages they will be visiting are real, and not designed just for schools, they may find the reading level challenging. They are reassured that they are free to use an online dictionary or any paper dictionary that is available in the classroom.

Students now begin their quest with background web links for everyone: All the students have to do is click on the links, and they will be taken to the relevant website.

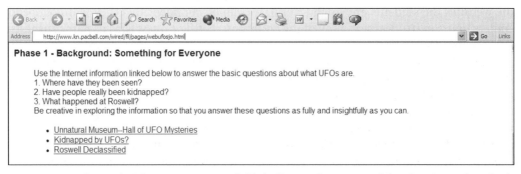

Now, students divide into groups of (i) believers in UFOs, (ii) scientists who don't believe in UFOs, (iii) members of the SETI (search for extraterrestrial intelligence) project and (iv) people who've been abducted by aliens. Each group is provided with web links like the ones above, and has to answer certain questions. For example, the alien abductees have the following tasks:

When the students have visited their websites, collected their opinions (and downloaded any images they might need), the groups then debate the original questions (a–c above), using the arguments they found in their own quests.

Finally, in the evaluation phase, the whole class tries to come up with a statement about UFOs that they can agree with, and JoAnn Miller suggests that they post their opinions on a website which discusses the topic (this provides real-world interaction which should be highly motivating).

The UFO webquest obviously depends on the class having easy and instant access to computers. It also requires a certain level of English from the students. Furthermore, it takes a long time to complete (quite apart from whatever preparation time the webquest designer has to put into it). But if time is available, this kind of reading – with the teacher on hand to help if things are especially difficult for the students – is highly motivating and yields great results.

More reading suggestions

Jigsaw reading: students read a short text which sets up a problem and then, in three groups, they read three different texts, all of which are about the same thing (different aspects of behaviour such as anger, or different reports on a problem, or different parts of a story or strange event). When they have read their texts, they come together in groups where each student has read a different text, and they try to work out the whole story, or describe the whole situation. JoAnn Miller's UFO webquest employs jigsaw reading on a large scale, but it is still a highly motivating technique, despite – or perhaps because of – the time it takes. Above all, this kind of jigsaw technique gives students a reason for reading – and then sharing what they have found out.

Reading puzzles: apart from jigsaw reading, there are many other kinds of puzzle which involve students in motivating reading tasks. For example, we can give them texts which have been chopped up so that each paragraph is on a different piece of paper. Students have to reassemble the text (see poetry below).

We can give students a series of emails between two people which are out of sequence. The students have to work out the order of the emails. We can mix up two stories and students have to prise them apart.

Using newspapers: there is almost no limit to the kinds of activity which can be done with newspapers (or their online equivalents). We can do all kinds of **matching exercises**, such as ones where students have to match articles with their headlines or with relevant pictures. At higher levels, we can have students read three accounts of the same incident and ask them to find the differences between them. We can use newspaper articles as a stimulus for speaking or writing (students can write letters in reply to what they read).

We can ask students to read small ads (advertisements) for holidays, partners, things for sale, etc, in order to make a choice about which holiday, person or thing they would choose. Later, they can use their choices to role-play descriptions, contact the service providers or say what happened when they made their choice.

We can get students to read the letters page from a newspaper and try to imagine what the writers look like, and what kinds of lives they have. They can reply to the letters.

Following instructions: students read instructions for a simple operation (using a public phonebox, etc) and have to put the instructions in the correct order. They might also match instructions about, for example, unpacking a printer or inserting a new ink cartridge with the little pictures that normally accompany such instructions in manuals. We can also get students to read instructions in order to follow them.

Recipes are a particular kind of instruction genre, but can be used in much the same way as the examples above – e.g. students read a recipe and match the instructions with pictures. We can then get them to cook the food!

Poetry: in groups, students are each given a line from a poem. They can't show the line to the other members of the group, though they can read it out loud. They have to **reassemble** the poem by putting the lines in order. A poem I have used like this with some success – at upper-intermediate levels – is 'Fire and Ice' by Robert Frost:

Some say the world will end in fire,
Some say in ice.
From what I've tasted of desire
I hold with those who favour fire.
But if it had to perish twice
I think I know enough of hate
To know that for destruction ice
Is also great
And would suffice.

We can get students to read different poems and then, without actually showing their poem to anyone else, they have to go round the class finding similarities and differences between their poem and other people's.

Another way of using poems with the whole class is to show the students a poem line by line (on an overhead projector or a computer screen) with words blanked out. The first time they see these blanks, they have to make a wild guess at what the words could be. When they see the lines for the second time, the first letter is included. When they see the poem for the third time, the first two letters are included, and so on. This is a great activity for getting students to really search in their minds for contextualised **lexis**.

Play extracts: students read an extract from a play or film and, after ensuring that they understand it and analysing its construction, they have to work on acting it out. This means thinking about how lines are said, concentrating on stress, intonation, speed, etc.

We can use many different text genres for this kind of activity since reading aloud – a speaking skill – is only successful when students have really studied a text, worked out what it means, and thought about how to make sense of it when it is spoken.

Predicting from words and pictures: students are given a number of words from a text. Working in groups, they have to predict what kind of a text they are going to read – or what story the text tells. They then read the text to see if their original predictions were correct. We don't have to give them individual words, of course. We can give them whole phrases and get them to try to make a story using them. For example, the phrases 'knock on the door', 'Go away!', 'They find a man the next morning', 'He is dead', 'James is in the lighthouse' will help students to predict (perhaps wrongly, of course!) some kind of story about a lighthouse keeper, some sort of threat and a dead person. (They then read a ghost story with these phrases in it.)

We can also give students pictures to predict from, or slightly bigger fragments from the text.

Different responses: there are many things students can do with a reading text apart from answering comprehension questions with sentences, saying whether something is true or false or finding particular words in the text. For example, when a text is full of facts and figures, we can get students to put the information into graphs, tables or diagrams. We can also ask them to describe the people in the text (where no physical description is given). This will encourage them to visualise what they are reading. We can let students read stories, but leave off the ending for them to guess. Alternatively, they can read stories in stages, stopping every now and then to predict what will happen next.

At higher levels, we can get students to infer the writer's attitude from a text. We can also get the students involved in **genre analysis** – where they look at the construction of a number of different examples of, say, magazine advertisements in order to work out how they are typically constructed.

Encouraging students to read extensively

If, as we said at the beginning of this chapter, we want students to read extensively, using simplified readers at pre-advanced levels, then we need to have systems in place to help them do this. There are four factors which contribute to the success of this kind of extensive reading:

Library

Students need to have access to a collection of readers, both at their own level and above and below it. Sometimes the library will be in a fixed place in a school, but we can also carry collections of books around to different classes. The library should have a range of different genres (factual, novels, adaptations of films, etc).

Choice

A major aspect of joyful reading (see page 99) is that students should be able to choose what they read – both in terms of genre but also, crucially, level. They are much more likely to read with enthusiasm if they have made the decision about what they read.

Feedback

Students should have an opportunity to give feedback on what they have read, either verbally or in written form. This does not mean formal reports, however, since that might take the pleasure away from reading. Instead, there might be a quick comment form on the inside cover of a book, or a folder with different forms for different titles. Students can then record their reactions to a book they have read. Other students looking for a new book to read can use those comments to help them make their choice.

Time

We need to give students time for reading in addition to those occasions when they read on their own. It is a good idea to leave a ten-minute reading period at various times during a course just to get students comfortable with the activity. It is vitally important that when we do this, we should be reading ourselves in order to underline the attractiveness of the activity.

Not all students become active readers. While some are highly motivated and consume books avidly, others don't have the same appetite. We can't force students to read, of course, but we should do everything we can to encourage them to do so.

Conclusions | *In this chapter we have:*

- talked about the fact that the more students read, the better they get at reading. We suggested that reading is good for language acquisition in general, provides good models for future writing and offers opportunities for language study.

- made a distinction between intensive and extensive reading, stressing the beneficial effects of the latter (especially in relation to simplified readers).

- said that teachers should encourage students to read in a variety of genres and that, where possible, the language of the texts should be authentic, unless it is too difficult for students (in which case we will offer authentic-like language).

- said that students need to realise how to read for different purposes – including skimming, scanning, reading for pleasure and reading for detailed comprehension.

- come up with six reading 'principles': read as often and as much as possible; students need to be engaged while they are reading; students should be encouraged to respond to the content of a text (and explore their feelings about it), not just concentrate on its construction; prediction is a major factor in reading; match the task to the topic when using intensive reading texts; and good teachers exploit reading texts to the full.

- looked at three reading sequences comprising a newspaper article, a magazine article and an extended Internet-based webquest.
- listed a number of other reading possibilities.
- discussed ways in which students can be encouraged to read extensively by providing libraries and time, letting students have choice and getting them to give feedback.

Teaching writing

- ■ **Reasons for teaching writing**
- ■ **Writing issues**
- ■ **Writing sequences**
- ■ **More writing suggestions**
- ■ **Correcting written work**
- ■ **Handwriting**

Reasons for teaching writing

There are many reasons for getting students to write, both in and outside class. Firstly, writing gives them more 'thinking time' than they get when they attempt spontaneous conversation. This allows them more opportunity for **language processing** – that is thinking *about* the language – whether they are involved in study or activation.

When thinking about writing, it is helpful to make a distinction between **writing-for-learning** and **writing-for-writing**. In the case of the former, writing is used as an aide-mémoire or practice tool to help students practise and work with language they have been studying. We might, for example, ask a class to write five sentences using a given structure, or using five of the new words or phrases they have been learning. Writing activities like this are designed to give reinforcement to students. This is particularly useful for those who need a mix of visual and kinaesthetic activity (see page 16). Another kind of writing-for-learning occurs when we have students write sentences in preparation for some other activity. Here, writing is an enabling activity.

Writing-for-writing, on the other hand, is directed at developing the students' skills *as writers*. In other words, the main purpose for activities of this type is that students should become better at writing, whatever kind of writing that might be. There are good 'real-life' reasons for getting students to write such things as emails, letters and reports. And whereas in writing-for-learning activities it is usually the language itself that is the main focus of attention, in writing-for-writing we look at the whole text. This will include not just appropriate language use, but also text construction, layout, style and effectiveness.

It is clear that the way we organise our students' writing – and the way we offer advice and correction – will be different, depending on what kind of writing they are involved in.

Writing issues

The kind of writing we ask students to do (and the way we ask them to do it) will depend, as most other things do, on their age, level, learning styles and interests. We won't get beginners to try to put together a complex narrative composition in English; we probably won't ask a class of advanced business students to write a poem about their mothers (unless we have specific reasons for doing this).

In order to help students write successfully and enthusiastically in different styles, we need to consider three separate issues:

Genre

One of our decisions about what to get students to write will depend on what **genres** we think they need to write in (or which will be useful to them). A genre is a type of writing which members of a **discourse community** would instantly recognise for what it was. Thus, we recognise a small ad in a newspaper the moment we see it because, being members of a particular group, or community, we have seen many such texts before and are familiar with the way they are constructed. We know what a poem looks like, a theatre listing or the function and appearance of the cover copy on the back of a book. One of the decisions that we will need to make, therefore, is which genres are important and/or engaging for our students. Once we have done this, we can show them examples of texts within a genre (for example, a variety of different kinds of written invitations) so that they get a feel for the conventions of that genre. Such **genre analysis** will help students see how typical texts within a genre are constructed, and this knowledge will help them construct appropriate texts of their own. At lower levels, we may give them clear models to follow, and they will write something that looks very much like the original. Such **guided writing** will help students produce appropriate texts even with fairly limited English. However, as their language level improves, we need to make sure that their writing begins to express their own creativity within a genre, rather than merely imitating it.

The writing process

When students are writing-for-writing, we will want to involve them in the **process** of writing. In the 'real world', this typically involves **planning** what we are going to write, **drafting** it, **reviewing** and **editing** what we have written and then producing a final (and satisfactory) version. Many people have thought that this is a linear process, but a closer examination of how writers of all different kinds are involved in the writing process suggests that we do all of these things again and again, sometimes in a chaotic order. Thus we may plan, draft, re-plan, draft, edit, re-edit, re-plan, etc before we produce our final version.

We will need to encourage students to plan, draft and edit in this way, even though this may be time-consuming and may meet, initially, with some resistance on their part. By doing so, we will help them to be better writers both in exams, for example, and in their post-class English lives.

Building the writing habit

One other issue, which we can refer to as *building the writing habit*, deserves mention here. Many students either think or say that they cannot, or do not want to write. This may be because they lack confidence, think it's boring or believe they have 'nothing to say'. We need to engage them, from early levels, with activities which are easy and enjoyable to take part in, so that writing activities not only become a normal part of classroom life but also present opportunities for students to achieve almost instant success. It is when students have acquired this writing habit that they are able to look at written genres and involve themselves in the writing process with enthusiasm.

Writing sequences

The three examples of writing we are going to look at show a range of level and complexity. As with almost all the skills sequences in Chapters 7–10, it will be seen that work on one skill (in this case writing) is often preceded by – or leads on to – work in another (e.g. speaking or reading).

Example 1: postcards (pre-intermediate/intermediate)

This guided writing sequence shows how students at a fairly early level can be helped to write within a certain genre so that when they do the final writing task, they have everything they need to do it successfully.

Students are told that when we write postcards, we often leave out a lot of words to save space (e.g. '~~We're~~ having a great time', '~~The~~ food is wonderful'). They then read the following postcard and decide where the words in the box should go:

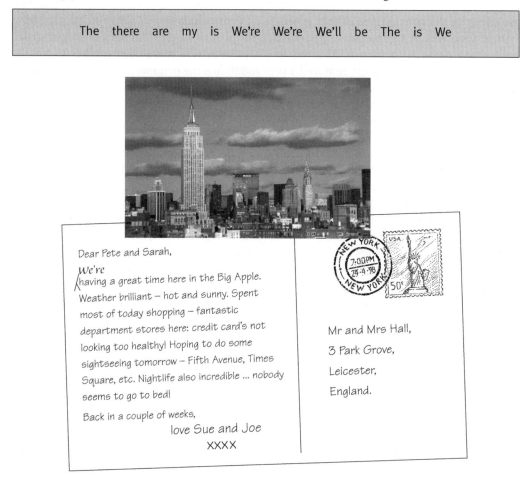

> The   there   are   my   is   We're   We're   We'll   be   The   is   We

Dear Pete and Sarah,

We're
having a great time here in the Big Apple.
Weather brilliant – hot and sunny. Spent
most of today shopping – fantastic
department stores here: credit card's not
looking too healthy! Hoping to do some
sightseeing tomorrow – Fifth Avenue, Times
Square, etc. Nightlife also incredible ... nobody
seems to go to bed!

Back in a couple of weeks,
love Sue and Joe
XXXX

Mr and Mrs Hall,
3 Park Grove,
Leicester,
England.

The students now look at another postcard, but this time they have to circle the words that can be left out.

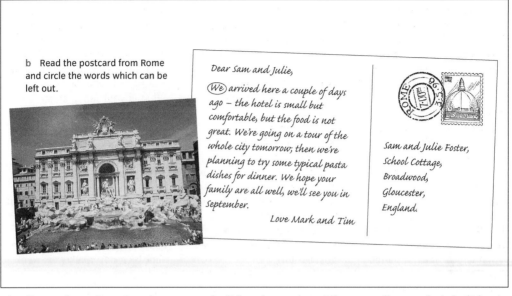

b   Read the postcard from Rome and circle the words which can be left out.

Dear Sam and Julie,

We arrived here a couple of days ago – the hotel is small but comfortable, but the food is not great. We're going on a tour of the whole city tomorrow, then we're planning to try some typical pasta dishes for dinner. We hope your family are all well, we'll see you in September.

Love Mark and Tim

Sam and Julie Foster,
School Cottage,
Broadwood,
Gloucester,
England.

Finally, students imagine they are on holiday themselves. They can discuss their holiday in pairs or small groups, deciding where they will send the postcard from and what they want to say. We will ask them to pay special attention to the kinds of words they can leave out.

We could also get them to look at how postcards are structured. For example: description of where the writer is; activities the writer is involved in; exhortation to the reader ('Hope you are well/Get well soon', etc); sign off ('Wish you were here, Love P'). We can then get them to write something similar. At beginner levels, some teachers give students 'postcard phrases' for them to arrange into a postcard.

Example 2: email interview (pre-intermediate upwards)

Many magazines and colour supplements contain short celebrity interviews in which people answer a series of inconsequential questions designed to be revealing, amusing and entertaining in equal measure. This genre is a highly effective way of getting students to write communicatively.

The excerpt from an interview with Neil Gaiman (a cartoonist and graphic novelist) on page 116 is a typical example of this kind of writing.

To use this writing genre in class, we will first show students an example (real or invented) of this kind of interview and discuss how it is put together (a whole variety of questions are emailed to the interviewee, who can answer as many of them as they want). We can elicit a whole range of possible questions from students and write them up on the board – and as we do so, modify them so that they emerge in good appropriate English.

Students now work in pairs or groups choosing the questions they want to use and adding their own. We will stress that these questions should be sufficiently general to be answered by anybody (e.g. 'When and where were you happiest?'). While students are working on these questions, we will go round the class suggestions modifications, if appropriate.

Students now write a fair copy of their questions and send them to one of the other students in the class. They can do this on pieces of paper, perhaps designed to look like email screens, or, if they have email access, they can send real emails.

Neil Gaiman was born in Hampshire in 1960. He was a journalist before becoming a graphic novelist, and his breakthrough came with The Sandman, a hugely successful cartoon strip. In 2001, he produced the bestselling adult novel American Gods. He recently published a new adult novel, Anansi Boys. His children's book, The Wolves In The Walls, has been adapted for the stage and is on tour until May 20. He is married, has three children and lives in Minneapolis.

What is your idea of perfect happiness?
Reading under a tree on a summer's day.

What is your greatest fear?
Something dreadful but unspecified happening to my children.

What is the trait you most deplore in yourself?
I'm utterly disorganised and I wish I wasn't.

What makes you depressed?
Not writing. I get moody and roody and irritable if I'm not making stuff up.

What has been your most embarrassing moment?
School – it was a long moment, but an embarrassing one.

What is your greatest extravagance?
Buying books I'll never read, in the vague hope that if I'm stranded on a desert island I'll have remembered to pack a trunk with unread books.

What is your most treasured possession?
My iPod – the idea of it, having all my music when I need it, rather than the rather battered object.

What is your favourite smell?
November evenings: the frost and leaf-mould and woodsmoke. The smell of coming winter.

What is your favourite book?
A huge leather-bound, 150-year-old accounts book, with 500 numbered pages, all blank. I keep promising myself I'll write a story in it one day.

What is your fancy dress costume of choice?
Pirate.

What is your guiltiest pleasure?
Wasting time.

What is your greatest regret?
I wish I'd enjoyed the journey more, rather than worried about it.

What single thing would improve the quality of your life?
Time. Ten-day weeks, six-week months, 20-month years. Things like that.

What do you consider your greatest achievement?
My children.

What keeps you awake at night?
Silence.

Rosanna Greenstreet

The interviewees now answer as many questions as they want to. Once again we can go round the room helping them with any difficulties they might have. They then 'send' the replies back to the questioners, whose job is to write up the interviews appropriately.

We can vary the activity by asking the questioners to turn the questions and answers into 'questionless' prose. For example, the first two utterances in the example above might be written as:

> **My idea of perfect happiness** is reading under a tree on a summer's day.
> **My greatest fear** is of something dreadful but unspecified happening to my children.

This kind of writing activity is a typical boomerang lesson sequence (see page 55) since once students are engaged, they have to activate their language knowledge before, at various stages, they modify what has been said or what they have written, and in so doing find themselves studying the construction of their texts.

There is no reason why the interviewees should be the students' classmates; if they can find other people to interview in this way, so much the better.

Example 3: writing a report (upper intermediate)

The following report-writing sequence is detailed, and will take some time. As the sequence progresses, students analyse the report genre, look at some language points, gather information, draft their report, check it and produce a final version (thus immersing themselves not only in the writing product, but in the process of writing).

When they have listened to an interview about the position of women around the world, students are asked to read a report and match sections A–D in it with the following headings:

> Positive comments
> Conclusion and recommendations
> Negative facts
> Aim of the report

Subject: Business Opportunities for Women in the UK and the USA.

A This report aims to assess the opportunities for women in top jobs in the world of business. It will examine statistics from the UK and the USA.

B In many ways, the present situation is not very positive for women in the workplace.
a) The number of women directors with companies in the UK has fallen since 1999, and fewer than 3% of directors in public companies are female.
(1) _____ , if you are a woman and want to get on, it helps to have a title.
(2) _____ a recent survey, about one-third of female directors are women with titles such as lady, professor or doctor.
b) Many women feel let down by the world of big business. They believe their work is not regarded as valuable as the work of male colleagues.
(3) _____ , they perceive they need to work harder than men in the same job to get a top position in a company. (4) _____ , women with young children often feel unsupported by company policies.

For example, a lot of companies are inflexible and make no allowance for the responsibilities of mothers (or fathers).
c) The Internet, with a few notable exceptions, is still a male-dominated world. (5) _____ , only 8% of computer engineers are women. The statistics are more encouraging for computer analysts and programmers, where 20% are female. (6) _____ , another estimate puts women working in information technology at 24% – much lower than the figures in 1994.

C (7) _____ , the future is not all gloomy.
a) More women are beginning to use e-mail and new technology to develop their own businesses from home. (8) _____ , they can avoid the discrimination of a traditional workplace and the big companies' lack of flexibility. (9) _____ , they can balance work and family responsibilities.
b) In the USA, 70% of new jobs are being set up in the small business sector where women predominate.

D (10) _____ , there are some positive developments, (11) _____ the world of business is still dominated by men. Governments should encourage more girls in the education system to follow courses in business or computer studies. (12) _____ , companies need to be more flexible with working timetables for women with family responsibilities.

Students then complete the report with the linking words 'according to', 'also', 'although', 'as a result', 'for example', 'furthermore', 'however', 'in addition', 'moreover', 'on the other hand', 'in this way' and 'to sum up'. They then move on to do some work on using synonyms.

Now that students have been prepared they write a report in six stages:

Stage 1: students are asked to choose one from a list of topics such as the benefits/dangers of mass tourism, whether banning things ever works (such as gangster rap lyrics, etc), answers to world poverty, freedom to choose (e.g. smoking, gun ownership, etc) or whether parents should be liable for the actions of their children. Alternatively, they can choose a topic of their own.

Stage 2: students are asked to gather information from a variety of sources including – in the case of the example above – the module of the coursebook the text occurs in, a library, the Internet (the teacher can give students lists of websites – rather as happened in the webquest on page 105), CD-ROM encyclopedias, magazine articles, TV and radio programmes, and anyone they would like to interview.

Stage 3: students plan their reports. They should decide what to include, what order to put it in (after looking back at the report they studied) and what their conclusions will be.

Stage 4: students write a draft of their report.

Stage 5: students check through the report in order to decide how effective it is and correct any language mistakes.

Stage 6: students write their final report (they may have repeated stages 4 and 5 more than once).

During stages 4 and 5, it is important for the teacher to be on hand to suggest changes, question parts of the report and be a useful resource for students so that they can improve their writing as they continue. When the reports are finished, the teacher can collect them for correction, or they can be assembled on a class noticeboard or put up on a class website.

More writing suggestions

Instant writing: one way of building the writing habit (see above) is to use instant writing activities as often as possible with both children/teenagers and adults who are reluctant writers. Instant writing activities are those where students are asked to write immediately in response to a teacher request. We can, for example, dictate half sentences for students to complete (e.g. 'My favourite relative is …' or 'I will never forget the time I …'). We can ask students to write two sentences about a topic 'right now'. We can give them three words and tell them to put them into a sentence as quickly as possible.

Instant writing is designed both to make students comfortable when writing, and also to give them thinking time before they say the sentences they have written aloud.

Using music and pictures: music and pictures are excellent stimuli for both writing and speaking. For example, we can play a piece of music and the students have to imagine and then write out the film scene they think it could accompany (this can be done after they have looked at a film script model). We can dictate the first sentence of a story and then have the students complete the story, based on the music we play them. We can then dictate the first sentence again and have them write a different story (because the music they hear is very different). They can then read out one of their stories and the class has to guess which music excerpt inspired it.

Pictures offer a wealth of possibilities. We can ask students to write descriptions of one of a group of pictures; their classmates then have to guess which one it is. They can write postcards based on pictures we give them. We can get them to look at portraits and write the inner thoughts of the characters or their diaries, or an article about them.

All of these activities are designed to get students writing freely, in an *engaging* way.

Newspapers and magazines: the different kinds of text found in newspapers and magazines offer a range of possibilities for **genre analysis** (see page 113), followed by writing within that genre. For example, we can get students to look at a range of different articles and ask them to analyse how headlines are constructed, and how articles are normally arranged (e.g. the first paragraph often – but not always – offers a summary of the whole article). They then write an article about a real or imaginary news story that interests them. At advanced levels, we can get students to look at the same story dealt with by different kinds of publication and ask them to write specifically for one or the other.

We can do the same kind of genre analysis in newspaper and magazine advertisements. 'Lonely hearts' entries, for example, always conform to a genre frame. Our students can learn a lot from analysing the genre and being able to imitate it. In the same vein, agony column letters (where people write in to ask for help with a problem) offer engaging writing practice.

Finally, we can show students a story and have them respond to it in a variety of different genres, and for different audiences (e.g. the report of a long traffic delay can prompt letters to the newspaper, emails, text messages, letters of apology, etc).

Brochures and guides: we can get students to look at a variety of brochures (e.g. for a town, entertainment venue, health club or leisure complex) to analyse how they are put together. They can then write their own brochure or town guide, using this analysis to help them.

Younger learners may enjoy writing brochures and guides for their areas which give completely wrong information (e.g. 'Sending postcards home: Look for the bins marked "Rubbish" or "Litter" and your postcards will be delivered next day; Travelling by bus: The buses in London are similar to taxis. Tell the drivers where you want to go and they'll drive you home!'). This is potentially just as engaging for children and teenagers as writing serious pieces of work.

Poetry: many teachers like getting students to write poems because it allows them to express themselves in a way that other genres, perhaps, do not. But we will have to give students models to help them write (to start with, anyway), since many of them will be unused to this kind of writing.

We can ask them to write acrostic poems (where the letters which start each line, when read downwards, form a word which is the topic of the poem). They can write a poetry alphabet (a line for each letter), or we can give them sentence frames to write with 'I like … because …' x 3, and then 'But I hate …'). We can get them to write lines about someone they like with instructions such as 'Write about this person as if they were a kind of weather'. We can give them models of real poems which they have to imitate.

Poetry writing is especially appropriate for younger learners who are usually not afraid to have a go in the ways suggested above; but it is appropriate for older learners, too, since it allows them to be more creative than is permitted in some other activities.

Collaborative writing: students gain a lot from constructing texts together. For example, we can have them build up a letter on the board, where each line is written by a different student (with help from the class, the group and/or the teacher). We can tell a story which students then have to try to reproduce in groups (a version of this activity goes by the name **dictogloss**, where, when students have tried to recreate what they have heard, they compare their versions with the original as a way of increasing their language awareness).

We can set up a **story circle** in which each student in the group has a piece of paper on which they write the first line of a story (which we dictate to them). They then have to write the next sentence. After that, they pass their papers to the person next to them, and they write the next sentence of the story they now have in front of them. They then pass the paper to the next student and again write the next sentence of the (new) story they have. Finally, when the papers get back to their original owners, those students write the conclusion.

Students can also engage in collaborative writing around a computer screen.

Writing to each other: the email interview (see above) is an example of getting students to write to each other. They can also write emails, or any other kind of message (the teacher can act as a postal worker) which has to be answered. They can be involved, under our supervision, in **live chat** sessions on the Internet, or we can organise **pen pal** exchanges with students in other countries (often called mousepals or **keypals** when done via the Internet).

Writing in other genres: there are countless different genres that students can write in apart from those mentioned so far. We can have students write personal **narratives** and other stories. We can prepare them for this by looking at the way other writers do it. We can analyse first lines of novels and then have students write their own attention-grabbing lines. We can get students to complete stories that are only half told. For many of these activities, getting the students to think together before they attempt the task – **brainstorming** ideas – will be a major factor in their success.

Students can write discursive essays in which they assemble arguments both **for and against** a proposition, work out a coherent order for their arguments, study various models for such an essay and then write their own. The procedures we follow may be similar to the spoken discussion ideas outlined on page 128.

All these ideas depend for their success on students having a chance to share ideas, look at examples of the genre, plan their writing and then draft and edit it.

Correcting written work

Most students find it very dispiriting if they get a piece of written work back and it is covered in red ink, underlinings and crossings-out. It is a powerful visual statement of the fact that their written English is terrible.

Of course, some pieces of written work are completely full of mistakes, but even in these cases, **over-correction** can have a very demotivating effect. Rather than this, the teacher has to achieve a balance between being accurate and truthful, on the one hand, and treating students sensitively and sympathetically, on the other.

One way of avoiding the 'over-correction' problem is for teachers to tell their students that for a particular piece of work they are only going to correct mistakes of punctuation, or only spelling or only grammar, etc. This has two advantages: it makes students concentrate on that particular aspect, and it cuts down on the **correction**.

Another technique which many teachers use is to agree on a list of written symbols (S = spelling, WO = word order, etc). When they come across a mistake, they underline it discreetly and write the symbol in the margin. This makes correction look less damaging. Where students write with electronic media, teachers can use editing tools such as Track Changes. These make it easier for students to write correct versions of their originals. However, such applications should be used carefully since they, too, can be very discouraging.

The way we react to students' writing will depend on what kind of writing it is. When students hand us final pieces of work, we may correct it using techniques such as the ones above. However, while students are actually involved in the writing process, correction will not help them learn to edit their own work, whereas **responding** (telling students what you think, teasing out alternatives and making suggestions) will. But whatever kind of writing students have been doing, we need to react not just to the form of what they have written, but also to the content (what they have written about). We also need to make sure that students do not just put corrected work into their folders without fully understanding why we have reacted as we have, and without doing their best to put things right.

Handwriting

Now that so much writing is done with electronic media, it may seem perverse to worry about handwriting. Nevertheless, many people around the world still write with pens and pencils, and so we will need to help any students who have problems of legibility.

Many nationalities do not use the same kind of script as English, so for students from those cultures, writing in English is doubly difficult: they are fighting to express themselves at the same time as trying (when they are not using a computer keyboard) to work out a completely new writing system.

Teachers cannot ask students to change their handwriting style, but they can encourage neatness and legibility. Especially when students are intending to take pen-and-paper exams, such things are crucial. Special classes or group sessions may have to be arranged to help students who are having problems with English script. They can be shown examples of certain letters, and the teacher can demonstrate the strokes necessary for making those shapes. They may also need to be shown where to start the first stroke of a letter as writing from left to right is difficult for some students. They can be asked to write in the air to give them confidence or to trace letters on lined paper which demonstrates the position and height of letters, before going on to imitate them, e.g.

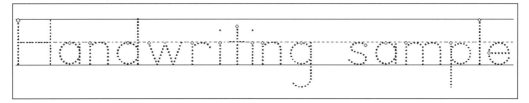

(This example was generated online at http://handwritingworksheets.com.)

Conclusions | *In this chapter we have:*

- looked at the reasons for teaching writing, which include a chance for students to process language in a more considered way than they may sometimes do when speaking. We showed how writing for learning (e.g. language reinforcement) is different from writing as a skill in its own right.

- discussed how different genres operate within a discourse community.

- looked briefly at the writing process itself and said how important it is to build the writing habit.

- looked in detail at three writing sequences.

- tackled the difficult subject of correcting writing, suggesting that over-correction should be avoided and that teachers should always strive to be encouraging.

- pointed out that, while handwriting is a matter of style, teachers should expect students to write clearly and legibly. In some cases, they may need special help with forming letters.

Teaching speaking

- ■ **Reasons for teaching speaking**
- ■ **Speaking sequences**
- ■ **Discussion**

- ■ **More speaking suggestions**
- ■ **Correcting speaking**
- ■ **What teachers do during a speaking activity**

Reasons for teaching speaking

There are three main reasons for getting students to speak in the classroom. Firstly, speaking activities provide **rehearsal** opportunities – chances to practise real-life speaking in the safety of the classroom. Secondly, speaking tasks in which students try to use any or all of the language they know provide feedback for both teacher and students. Everyone can see how well they are doing: both how successful they are, and also what language problems they are experiencing. (This is a good reason for boomerang lessons, see page 55.) And finally, the more students have opportunities to *activate* the various elements of language they have stored in their brains, the more automatic their use of these elements become. As a result, students gradually become autonomous language users. This means that they will be able to use words and phrases fluently without very much conscious thought.

Good speaking activities can and should be extremely engaging for the students. If they are all participating fully – and if the teacher has set up the activity properly and can then give sympathetic and useful feedback – they will get tremendous satisfaction from it.

We need to be clear that the kinds of speaking activities we are looking at here are not the same as controlled language practice, where, for example, students say a lot of sentences using a particular piece of grammar or a particular function. That kind of speaking is part of *study* and is covered in Chapter 6. The kind of speaking we are talking about here almost always involves the *activate* element in our ESA trilogy (see Chapter 4). In other words, the students are using *any* and *all* of the language at their command to achieve some kind of **purpose** which is not purely linguistic. They are practising what Scott Thornbury, in his book *How to Teach Speaking*, calls **speaking-as-skill**, where there is a task to complete and speaking is the way to complete it. In the same way that 'writing-for-writing' is designed to help the student get better at the skill of writing (see page 112), so the activities in this chapter are designed to foster better speaking, rather than having students speak only to focus on (and practise) specific language constructions. As with any sequence, however, we may use what happens in a speaking activity as a focus for future *study*, especially where the speaking activity throws up some language problems that subsequently need fixing.

Scott Thornbury suggests that the teaching of speaking depends on there being a classroom culture of speaking, and that classrooms need to become '*talking* classrooms'. In other words, students will be much more confident speakers (and their speaking abilities will improve) if this kind of speaking *activation* is a regular feature of lessons.

Speaking sequences

In the following three examples, we are going to look at very different speaking activities. All the activities satisfy the three reasons for using speaking tasks which we mentioned above. As with all other skills, what starts as a speaking activity may very well lead on to writing – or the speaking activity itself may develop from a reading text, or after listening to an audio track.

Example 1: photographic competition (upper intermediate to advanced)

In the following activity, students have to discuss criteria before reaching a final decision. They also have to be able to give reasons for their decision.

The activity begins when students, working in groups, are told that they are going to be the judges of a photographic competition in which all the images are of men. Before they see the four finalists, they have to decide the criteria they are going to use to make their choice. Each group should come up with five criteria. While they are discussing this, we can circulate, listening in on the groups' discussions, helping them out of any difficulties and feeding in words and phrases such as 'contrast' and 'make a strong impression', if this is necessary. We will also make a note of any language problems we may want to study later in remedial exercises.

The students are then shown the four finalists for the competition. In their groups, they have to choose the winning photograph. But they cannot do this just on the basis of which one they like best. They have to use the criteria they have previously agreed. Once again, we can go round the groups helping out, cajoling or sometimes correcting (see page 131) where this is appropriate.

Finally, the groups have to report back on their choices and say exactly why they have chosen them – which criteria made them choose one above the others. This can develop into a longer whole-class discussion about what masculinity means, or about photography and how it has been changed by the invention of digitised images, etc.

This speaking activity works because students are activating any and all of the language they know to talk about something other than learning English. They have a purpose for their speaking (designing criteria, making a choice). But the activity also allows us to feed

useful words and phrases into the discussion while, at the same time, giving us a lot of examples of student language. We can use these later in study sequences, where we both look at some of the mistakes the students made, and also help them to say things better or more appropriately.

Example 2: role-play (intermediate to upper intermediate)

Many teachers ask students to become involved in **simulations** and **role-plays**. In simulations, students act as if they were in a real-life situation. We can ask them to simulate a check-in encounter at an airport, for example, or a job interview, or a presentation to a conference. Role-plays simulate the real world in the same kind of way, but the students are given particular roles – they are told who they are and often what they think about a certain subject. They have to speak and act from their new character's point of view.

The following role-play sets up a dramatic situation and then gives the participants **role-cards** which tell them how they feel and what they want to achieve.

The teacher presents the class with the following situation:

> Last night the Wolverhampton Trophy was stolen from the Wolverhampton Football Club Headquarters at around 9.30 in the evening. The police have brought in a youth for questioning; they believe this youth stole the trophy.
>
> The suspect is being interviewed by two police officers. The suspect's lawyer is also present. But because the suspect is not yet eighteen, a parent is also present.

When the teacher is sure the students understand the situation (including, for example, the meaning of 'trophy'), the class is divided into five groups: suspect, police officer 1, police officer 2, lawyer and parent. Each member of the group is given the role-card for the part they are to play. The role-cards are as follows:

> **The suspect**
> - You are seventeen and a half years old.
> - You did steal the trophy, of course, but you don't think the police have any proof.
> - You want to know where the police got their information. When they ask you what you were doing last night, you'll say you were with a friend.
> - You enjoy being silly when the police ask you questions. You get angry when the lawyer tries to stop you doing this.

> **Police officer 1**
> - The suspect was seen leaving the club house at around 9.30 by two other criminals, Ben and Joey, but you can't tell the suspect this, because that would put Ben and Joey in danger. So the only thing you can do is to keep asking the suspect different questions about what they were doing last night in the hope that they'll get confused and in the end confess.
> - You have had enough of teenage crime in your area. It makes you really mad. Anyway, you want to get home. Unfortunately, you get angry rather quickly. When your police colleague tells you to calm down, you get really angry.

Police officer 2
- The suspect was seen taking the trophy by two other criminals, Ben and Joey, but you can't tell the suspect this, because that would put Ben and Joey in danger. So the only thing you can do is keep asking the suspect different questions about what they were doing last night in the hope that they'll get confused and in the end confess.
- You like your partner, but you get really worried when they start getting angry since this doesn't help in a police interview situation, so you try to calm your partner down. But whenever a suspect's mother or father tries to say that their beautiful child is not really to blame for something, you get really irritated.

Lawyer
- Your job is to protect the suspect.
- You try to stop the police asking difficult questions – and you try to stop the suspect saying too much.

Parent
- You think your child is a good person and that if they have got into any trouble it isn't their fault. Your partner (the suspect's mother or father) was sent to prison and the suspect is very upset about this.
- If you think the police are being unfair to your child, you should tell them so – and make sure they realise it isn't really your child's fault.

In their groups, students discuss the role they are going to play. What kind of questions will they ask if they are police officers? What will they say if they are lawyers (e.g. 'You don't have to answer that question')?, etc. They discuss what the other people in the situation are likely to do or say. While they are doing this, the teacher goes round the class clearing up any doubts the students might have and giving them language they think they might need. This pre-stage is vital for getting students in the mood for the activity.

Students are now put in new groups of suspect, two police officers, lawyer and parent, and the role-play gets going. The teacher goes from group to group, helping out and noting down any language that is worth commenting on later. When the activity is finished, the teacher tells the class what he or she witnessed and works on any persistent mistakes that occurred during the role-play.

A variation of this kind of detective activity is the game *Alibi*. The teacher invents a crime – probably related to grammar or vocabulary the students have been learning – and, say, three students are sent out of the classroom to concoct an alibi about what they were doing when the crime was committed.

The three students are now called back one by one and questioned by the rest of the class. When the second student comes in, the class try to find inconsistencies with the alibi of the first of the three. The same happens when the third student of the three turns up. The class then highlights the inconsistencies and guesses who the 'criminal' is. Of course, it doesn't actually matter who they decide on since the game is simply designed to have students ask and answer, using their questions and answers as fluently as possible.

There are differing views about whether students gain more or less benefit from simulating reality as themselves or, conversely, playing the role of someone else in the same situation. When students simulate reality as themselves, they get a chance for real-life rehearsal, seeing how they themselves would cope (linguistically) in such a situation. Giving students a role, on the other hand, allows them to 'hide behind' the character they are playing, and this can sometimes allow them to express themselves more freely than they would if they were voicing their own opinions or feelings. The best thing to do is to try simulations with and without roles and see which works best with a particular group.

Example 3: the portrait interview (almost any level)

The following speaking sequence shows how portraits can be used to provoke questions and answers which can then develop into a very involved conversation. The amount of conversation will, of course, depend to a large extent on the level of the students: at lower levels they may ask questions like 'How old are you?' to the people in the portrait (see below), whereas at higher levels the questions (and answers) may be significantly more complex. This kind of activity can work well with both children and adults. The activity develops in the following way:

Stage 1 – students are put into three groups. Each group gets a copy of 'The Arnolfini Marriage' by Jan van Eyck – or a large version of the painting is projected onto a screen.

Stage 2 – each group selects either the man, the woman or the dog. They have to look at the picture carefully and then come up with as many questions for their character as possible. Every student in the group must make a copy of all the questions produced by the group. (One group of advanced students produced questions for the man such as, 'How long did it take to have your picture done?' and 'What is written on the wall?'. For the woman they put, 'Why don't you replace the missing candles in the chandelier?' and 'Why is your room so untidy?' and for the dog, 'Why don't you run from such a dark room?' and 'How did they manage to keep you in that position for such a long time?')

Stage 3 – students are put in new groups of three (one from each of the original three groups). Each student in the group takes on the identity of one of the two characters they did *not* prepare questions for. The student with the questions for them interviews them, and the other student has to follow up each answer with a subsequent question.

Stage 4 – three students are chosen to play the different characters. They come to the front of the class and are interviewed in the same way.

Quite apart from its intrinsic appeal as an activity which provokes students into looking more closely at a work of art (which is satisfyingly ambiguous in many respects), this speaking sequence works extremely well because of the speaking and interaction it provokes. In the first place, the original groups *activate* their English knowledge as they talk to each other to plan and negotiate the questions they want to ask. In the second place, when playing one of the characters in the picture (in small groups), the students have to come up with answers (however profound or amusing), and think of follow-up questions when they have heard an answer from one of the others. This acts as a rehearsal for the interview in front of the whole class. The teacher will now have a lot of language use to comment on, and can work on the questions or any of the answers that came up if appropriate.

This kind of activity is suitable for almost any age group, including younger learners, who often find imaginative role-play like this very enjoyable. And there are many other possibilities: for example, we can have students react to anything that is said to them as if they were one of the characters in the picture. We can get them to talk about their typical day (as one of the pictured characters). We can ask them to have the conversation that two portraits have with each other when the museum lights are turned off and the doors are shut!

This interview technique can work with any pictures of people – including portraits and photographs – or, for children, puppets or computer-generated characters. It can also be employed when students have worked with a reading text: they can interview the people they have read about, asking them how they feel, what they do, etc. And of course these interviews can be turned into written profiles.

Discussion

When students suddenly want to talk about something in a lesson and discussion occurs spontaneously, the results are often highly gratifying (see 'magic moments' on page 157). Spontaneous conversation of this type can be rare, yet discussion, whether spontaneous or planned, has the great advantage of provoking fluent language use. As a result, most teachers would like to organise discussion sessions on a more formal basis. Many of them find, however, that planned discussion sessions are less successful than they had hoped.

Something we should always remember is that people need time to assemble their thoughts before any discussion. After all, it is challenging to have to give immediate and articulate opinions in our own language, let alone in a language we are struggling to learn. Consequently, it is important to give students pre-discussion rehearsal time. For example, we can put them in small **buzz groups** to explore the discussion topic before organising a discussion with the whole class. On a more formal basis, we can put students into 'opposing' groups and give them quite a lot of time for one group to prepare arguments against a proposition (e.g. 'Tourism is bad for the world'), while the other assembles arguments in favour.

We can help students in other ways too. We can, for example, give them cards containing brief statements of arguments about the topic (for them to use if they get stuck), or we can make the discussion the end of a lengthier process (such as the webquest on page 105). We can get students to rewrite statements (such as 'Boys don't like shopping' or 'Football is a man's game') so that they represent the group's opinion, and when students are speaking, we can help and encourage them by suggesting things they can say in order to push the discussion along.

More speaking suggestions

The following activities are also helpful in getting students to practise 'speaking-as-a-skill'. Although they are not level-specific, the last four will be more successful with higher-level students (upper intermediate plus), whereas the first two, in particular, are highly appropriate at lower levels (but can also be used satisfactorily with more advanced classes).

Information-gap activities: an information gap is where two speakers have different bits of information, and they can only complete the whole picture by sharing that information – because they have different information, there is a 'gap' between them.

One popular information-gap activity is called *Describe and draw*. In this activity, one student has a picture which they must not show their partner (teachers sometimes like to use surrealist paintings – empty doorways on beaches, trains coming out of fireplaces, etc). All the partner has to do is draw the picture without looking at the original, so the one with the picture will give instructions and descriptions, and the 'artist' will ask questions.

A variation on *Describe and draw* is an activity called *Find the differences* – popular in puzzle books and newspaper entertainment sections all over the world. In pairs, students each look at a picture which is very similar (though they do not know this) to the one their partner has. They have to find, say, ten differences between their pictures without showing their pictures to each other. This means they will have to do a lot of describing – and questioning and answering – to find the differences.

For information-gap activities to work, it is vitally important that students understand the details of the task (for example, that they should not show each other their pictures). It is often a good idea for teachers to **demonstrate** how an activity works by getting a student up to the front of the class and doing the activity (or a similar one) with that student, so that everyone can see exactly how it is meant to go.

Telling stories: we spend a lot of our time telling other people stories and anecdotes about what happened to us and other people. Students need to be able to tell stories in English, too.

One way of getting students to tell stories is to use the information-gap principle (see above) to give them something to talk about. Students are put in groups. Each group is given one of a sequence of pictures which tell a story. Once they have had a chance to look at the pictures, the pictures are taken away. New groups are formed which consist of one student from each of the original groups. The new groups have to work out what story the original picture sequence told. For the **story reconstruction** to be successful, they have to describe the pictures they have seen, talk about them, work out what order they should be in, etc. The different groups then tell the class their stories to see if everyone came up with the same versions.

We can, alternatively, give students six objects, or pictures of objects. In groups, they have to invent a story which connects the objects.

We can encourage students to **retell stories** which they have read in their books or found in newspapers or on the Internet (such retelling is a valuable way of provoking the *activation* of previously learnt or acquired language).

The best stories, of course, are those which the students tell about themselves and their family or friends. We can also offer them chances to be creative by asking them to talk about a scar they have, or to tell the story of their hair, or to describe the previous day in either a positive way or a negative way. When students tell stories based on personal experience, their classmates can ask them questions in order to find out more about what happened.

Storytelling like this often happens spontaneously (because a certain topic comes up in the lesson – see 'magic moments' on page 157). But at other times, students need time to think about what they are going to say.

Favourite objects: a variation on getting students to tell personal stories (but which may also involve a lot of storytelling) is an activity in which students are asked to talk about their favourite objects (things like MP3 players, objects with sentimental value, instruments, clothes, jewellery, pictures, etc). They think about how they would describe their favourite objects in terms of when they got them, why they got them, what they do with them, why they are so important to them and whether there are any stories associated with them. In groups, they then tell each other about their objects, and the groups tell the class about which was the most unusual/interesting, etc in their group.

Meeting and greeting: students role-play a formal/business social occasion where they meet a number of people and introduce themselves.

Surveys: surveys can be used to get students interviewing each other. For example, they can design a questionnaire about people's sleeping habits with questions like 'How many hours do you normally sleep?', 'Have you ever walked in your sleep or talked in your sleep?', 'Have you ever fallen out of bed?', etc. They then go round the class asking each other their questions.

A variation of this is a popular activity called *Find someone who …* . In this activity, students list activities (e.g. climb a mountain, do a bungee jump, swim in the Pacific, act in a play, etc) and they then go round the class asking 'Have you ever climbed a mountain?', 'Have you ever done a bungee jump?', etc.

Both activities are good for getting students to 'mill about' in the class, talking and interacting with others in a way that is different from many other activities. There is no reason, either, why they should not go outside the classroom to conduct surveys.

Famous people: students think of five famous people. They have to decide on the perfect gift for each person. We can also get groups of students to decide on which five famous people (living or dead) they would most like to invite for dinner, what they would talk about and what food they would give them.

Student presentations: individual students give a talk on a given topic or person. In order for this to work for the individual (and for the rest of the class), time must be given for the student to gather information and structure it accordingly. We may want to offer models to help individuals to do this. The students listening to presentations must be given some kind of listening tasks too – including, perhaps, giving feedback.

Balloon debate: a group of students are in the basket of a balloon which is losing air. Only one person can stay in the balloon and survive (the others have to jump out). Individual students representing famous characters (Napoleon, Gandhi, Cleopatra, etc) or professions (teacher, doctor, lawyer, etc) have to argue why they should be allowed to survive.

 Moral dilemmas: students are presented with a 'moral dilemma' and asked to come to a decision about how to resolve it. For example, they are told that a student has been caught cheating in an important exam. They are then given the student's (far-from-ideal) circumstances, and offered five possible courses of action – from exposing the student publicly to ignoring the incident – which they have to choose between.

Correcting speaking

It will probably be necessary for teachers to correct mistakes made during speaking activities in a different way from those made during a study exercise. When students are repeating sentences, trying to get their pronunciation exactly right, then the teacher will often correct (appropriately) every time there's a problem (see pages 97–98). But if the same teacher did this while students were involved in a passionate discussion about whether smoking should be banned on tourist beaches, for example, the effect might well be to destroy the conversational flow. If, just at the moment one of the students is making an important point, the teacher says 'Hey wait, you said "is" but it should be "are", beaches are … repeat', the point will quickly be lost. Constant interruption from the teacher will destroy the purpose of the speaking activity.

Many teachers watch and listen while speaking activities are taking place. They note down things that seemed to go well and times when students couldn't make themselves understood or made important mistakes. When the activity has finished, they then ask the students how they thought it went before giving their own feedback. They may say that they liked the way Student A said this, and the way Student B was able to disagree with her. They will then say that they did hear one or two mistakes, and they can either discuss them with the class, write them on the board or give them individually to the students concerned. In each case, they will ask the students to see if they can identify the problem and correct it.

As with any kind of correction, it is important not to single students out for particular criticism. Many teachers deal with the mistakes they heard without saying who was responsible for them.

Of course, there are no hard and fast rules about correcting. Some teachers who have a good relationship with their students can intervene appropriately during a speaking activity if they do it in a quiet non-obtrusive way. This kind of **gentle correction** might take the form of **reformulation** where the teacher repeats what the student has said, but correctly this time, and does not ask for student repetition of the corrected form. Some students do prefer to be told at exactly the moment they make a mistake; but we always have to be careful to make sure that our actions do not compromise the activity in question.

Perhaps the best way of correcting speaking activities appropriately is to talk to students about it. You can ask them how and when they would prefer to be corrected; you can explain how you intend to correct during these stages, and show them how different activities may mean different correction behaviour on your part.

What teachers do during a speaking activity

Some teachers get very involved with their students during a speaking activity and want to **participate** in the activity themselves! They may argue forcefully in a discussion or get fascinated by a role-play and start 'playing' themselves.

There's nothing wrong with teachers getting involved, of course, provided they don't start to dominate. Although it is probably better to stand back so that you can watch and listen to what's going on, students can also appreciate teacher participation at the appropriate level – in other words, not too much!

Sometimes, however, teachers will have to intervene in some way if the activity is not going smoothly. If someone in a role-play can't think of what to say, or if a discussion begins to dry up, the teacher will have to decide if the activity should be stopped – because the topic has run out of steam – or if careful prompting can get it going again. That's where the teacher may make a point in a discussion or quickly take on a role to push a role-play forward. Prompting is often necessary but, as with correction, teachers should do it sympathetically and sensitively.

Conclusions | *In this chapter we have:*

- said that speaking activities are designed to provoke 'speaking-as-a-skill', where there is a purpose for talking which is not just linguistic.

- seen how speaking activities provide opportunities for rehearsal, give both teacher and students feedback and motivate students because of their engaging qualities. Above all, they help students to be able to produce language automatically – a crucial stage on the way to autonomy.

- looked at examples of three types of speaking activity: decision-making (choosing the winner in a photographic competition), role-play and an interview 'game'.

- looked at how to get students involved in successful discussions, emphasising that they need a chance for pre-discussion rehearsal.

- discussed the way teachers should correct in speaking activities, not interrupting while they are going on, but giving feedback later.

- suggested that there may be times when teachers need to help an activity along through prompting (and perhaps participation), provided it is done sensitively.

Teaching listening

- ■ **Reasons for listening**
- ■ **Different kinds of listening**
- ■ **Listening levels**
- ■ **Listening skills**

- ■ **Listening principles**
- ■ **Listening sequences**
- ■ **More listening suggestions**
- ■ **Audio and video**

Reasons for listening

Most students want to be able to understand what people are saying to them in English, either face-to-face, on TV or on the radio, in theatres and cinemas, or on tape, CDs or other recorded media. Anything we can do to make that easier will be useful for them. This is especially important since, as we said on page 78, the way people speak is often significantly different from the way they write.

Listening is good for our students' pronunciation, too, in that the more they hear and understand English being spoken, the more they absorb appropriate pitch and intonation, stress and the sounds of both individual words and those which blend together in connected speech. Listening texts are good pronunciation models, in other words, and the more students listen, the better they get, not only at understanding speech, but also at speaking themselves. Indeed, it is worth remembering that successful spoken communication depends not just on our ability to speak, but also on the effectiveness of the way we listen.

One of the main sources of listening for students is the voice of their teacher (see page 37 for a discussion of the way teachers should talk to students). However, it is important, where possible, for students to be exposed to more than just that one voice, with all its idiosyncrasies. There is nothing wrong with an individual teacher's voice, of course, but as we saw on page 79, there are significant regional variations in the way people speak English in a country like Britain. For example, the 'a' of 'bath' is pronounced like the vowel sound in 'park' in some parts of Britain, but like the 'a' in 'cat' in others. In grammar, certain varieties of English within the British Isles use 'done' in sentences like 'I done it yesterday' where other varieties would find such tense usage unacceptable. In vocabulary, 'happen' is a verb in standard southern English, but in parts of Yorkshire (in northern England) it is often used as an adverb to mean 'maybe' or 'perhaps' in sentences such as 'Happen it'll rain'. And if there are many **regional varieties** in just one country, it is obvious that the different Englishes around the world will be many and varied.

Students need to be exposed to different Englishes, but teachers need to exercise judgment about the number (and degree) of the varieties which they hear. A lot will depend on the students' level of competence, and on what variety or varieties they have so far been exposed to.

Different kinds of listening

A distinction can be drawn between **intensive** and **extensive** listening. As with reading, the latter refers to listening which the students often do away from the classroom, for pleasure or some other reason. The audio material they consume in this way – often on CDs in their cars, on MP3 players, DVDs, videos or on the Internet – should consist of texts that they can enjoy listening to because they more or less understand them without the intervention of a teacher or course materials to help them. It is true that there is not at present a body of material developed for extensive listening as there is for extensive reading, but this looks set to change in the foreseeable future. Already, many simplified readers (see page 100) come with accompanying CDs on which the books are read or dramatised. Students can also use tapes and CDs to listen to their coursebook dialogues again after they have studied them in class. There is a growing number of podcast sites from where students can download free materials. And another way of getting students involved in a form of extensive listening is to encourage them to go to English language films with subtitles; as they hear the English dialogue, the subtitles help them understand; as they understand, they will, to some extent, absorb the language they hear.

Intensive listening is different from extensive listening in that students listen specifically in order to work on listening skills, and in order to study the way in which English is spoken. It usually takes place in classrooms or language laboratories, and typically occurs when teachers are present to guide students through any listening difficulties, and point them to areas of interest.

Listening sources

A lot of listening is experienced from **recorded extracts** – on CD, tape or via MP3 players of some kind. Frequently this is commercially produced, either as part of a coursebook or as supplementary material. But there is no reason why teachers should not record their own listening materials, using themselves or their friends or colleagues. With modern recording technology available through a range of media, it is quite possible to produce recordings of reasonable quality. We can download a huge amount of extremely useful listening material from the Internet, too, provided that we are not breaking any rules of copyright.

Recorded extracts are quite distinct from **live listening**, the name given to real-life face-to-face encounters in the classroom. To some extent all teacher talk is live listening, but in particular the term *live listening* is used to refer to situations in which the teacher brings visitors into the class or, if this is not possible, role-plays different characters for the students to talk and listen to. The main advantage of live listening over recorded extracts is that the students can interact with the speaker on the basis of what they are saying, making the whole listening experience far more dynamic and exciting.

Listening levels

We will want our students to hear listening material in a number of different **genres** (that is, styles or types of text – see page 113) and registers. This may include news broadcasts, public announcements, recorded messages, lectures, phone conversations, dramatic dialogue, etc). But we will also have to decide whether what they listen to should be **authentic** or not. Authentic speech is speech not spoken just for language learners – in other words, it is language spoken for native- or competent speakers of English, with no concessions made for the learner. Much recorded speech on the radio or on the Internet, for example, is of this type. However, it is often far too difficult for lower-level students, and is, therefore, inappropriate for use with them. But we don't want to give our lower-level students inauthentic language (which doesn't sound at all like the real thing) either. What we aim for instead is realistic language use which, while roughly-tuned to match the students' level, nevertheless approximates to real-life language. But we will aim to get our students to listen to (and understand) authentic English as soon and as often as they can.

Listening skills

Students need to be able to listen to a variety of things in a number of different ways. In the first place, they need to be able to recognise **paralinguistic clues** such as intonation in order to understand mood and meaning. They also need to be able to **listen** for **specific information** (such as times, platform numbers, etc), and sometimes for more **general understanding** (when they are listening to a story or interacting in a social conversation). A lot will depend on the particular genres they are working with.

Most students are perfectly capable of listening to different things in different ways in their own language(s). Our job is to help them become adept at this kind of multiskilling when listening to English. However, sometimes they find this exceptionally difficult. We will discuss what to do if this happens in Chapter 14 (page 183).

Listening principles

Principle 1: Encourage students to listen as often and as much as possible.
The more students listen, the better they get at listening – and the better they get at understanding pronunciation and at using it appropriately themselves. One of our main tasks, therefore, will be to use as much listening in class as possible, and to encourage students to listen to as much English as they can (via the Internet, podcasts, CDs, tapes, etc).

Principle 2: Help students prepare to listen.
Students need to be made ready to listen. This means that they will need to look at pictures, discuss the topic, or read the questions first, for example, in order to be in a position to predict what is coming. This is not just so that they are in the right frame of mind (and are thinking about the topic), but also so that they are *engaged* with the topic and the task and really want to listen.

Principle 3: Once may not be enough.
There are almost no occasions when the teacher will play an audio track only once. Students will want to hear it again to pick up the things they missed the first time – and we may well want them to have a chance to *study* some of the language features on the tape.

In the case of live listening, students should be encouraged to ask for repetition and clarification when they need it.

The first listening to a text is often used just to give students an idea of what the speakers sound like, and what the general topic is (see *Principle 5*) so that subsequent listenings are easier for them. For subsequent listenings, we may stop the audio track at various points, or only play extracts from it. However, we will have to ensure that we don't go on and on working with the same audio track.

Principle 4: Encourage students to respond to the content of a listening, not just to the language.

An important part of a listening sequence is for teachers to draw out the meaning of what is being said, discern what is intended and find out what impression it makes on the students. Questions such as 'Do you agree with what they say?' and 'Did you find the listening interesting? Why?' are just as important as questions like 'What language did she use to invite him?' However, any listening material is also useful for studying language use and a range of pronunciation issues.

Principle 5: Different listening stages demand different listening tasks.

Because there are different things we want to do with a listening text, we need to set different tasks for different listening stages. This means that, for a first listening, the task(s) may need to be fairly straightforward and general. That way, the students' general understanding and response can be successful – and the stress associated with listening can be reduced.

Later listenings, however, may focus in on detailed information, language use or pronunciation, etc. It will be the teacher's job to help students to focus in on what they are listening for.

Principle 6: Good teachers exploit listening texts to the full.

If teachers ask students to invest time and emotional energy in a listening text – and if they themselves have spent time choosing and preparing the listening sequence – then it makes sense to use the audio track or live listening experience for as many different applications as possible. Thus, after an initial listening, the teacher can play a track again for various kinds of *study* before using the subject matter, situation or audioscript for a new activity. The listening then becomes an important event in a teaching sequence rather than just an exercise by itself.

Listening sequences

The following listening sequences are pitched at different levels. As with all other skill-based sequences, they will often lead into work on other skills or present opportunities for language study and further activation of some kind.

Example 1: live interview (beginner onwards)

The following sequence works when teachers can bring visitors to the classroom (or when they themselves play a role as if they were a visitor).

The teacher primes a visitor to the class by giving them an idea of the students' level and what they may or may not understand. The visitor should be aware that they may have to modify the way they normally speak – but that speaking slowly and shouting (as people often do when confronted with people whose English is not high level) will not be appropriate!

The students are told that a visitor is coming to the lesson, and that they should think of a number of questions to ask which will tell them as much as possible about who the person is. Their questions are checked by the teacher to make sure that the students are really asking what they want to ask.

When the visitor comes to the lesson, students ask their questions and take notes of the answers. A key feature of such an exchange is the **follow-up question** – a question which follows on from the interviewee's first answer. This means that students are forced to listen carefully to the first answer. But it also gives them more opportunity to interact with the visitor, and it means that the visitor will say more.

For live listening to work well, students need to have phrases to help them such as 'I'm sorry, I don't understand what X means …', 'Could you repeat what you just said?', 'Are you saying that …?'. The actual questions they use will depend on their level.

Sometimes it is a good idea for students to find out who the visitor is through their questioning (we keep their identity a secret), but at other times they will prepare their questions more efficiently if they know who is coming and what their occupation is, or what kind of story they have to tell.

It is not always easy to find visitors. However, for those schools which are well equipped, it is now possible to replicate such interviews with the help of a webcam. As the technology improves, this will become more and more feasible. But if this is not possible, teachers can pretend to be someone else for the students to interview. With younger children, teachers can use puppets or wear masks to show that they are someone different.

Students can use their notes to write a profile of the visitor, to write to or about them, or to discuss with the class what they thought about the visitor's opinions.

Example 2: buying tickets (pre-intermediate)

The following coursebook sequence is an example of how work on one skill (listening) leads naturally into work on another (speaking). As suggested on page 135, it allows the students to predict what they will hear and involves both general and detailed comprehension work. Students look at the following pictures:

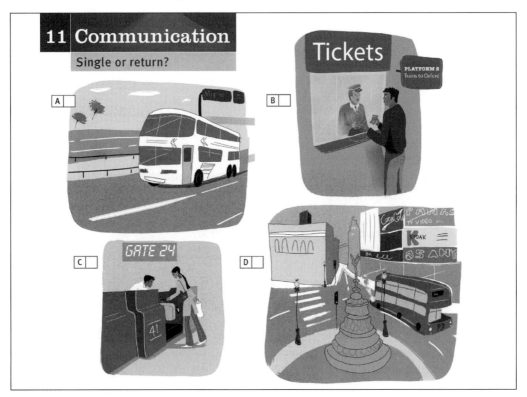

The teacher encourages them to describe what is going on in each picture. Words like 'ticket', 'check-in' and 'coach' are bound to occur naturally here, but more importantly, students have an idea of what the conversations they are going to hear are about.

Students now hear the following four conversations which they have to match with the four pictures:

1

PASSENGER:	I'd like a return to Oxford, please.
ASSISTANT:	Yes, of course. Are you coming back today?
PASSENGER:	Yes, I am.
ASSISTANT:	That's £18.50, please.
PASSENGER:	Thank you.

2

CHECK-IN:	How many pieces of luggage have you got?
PASSENGER:	One suitcase and one handbag.
CHECK-IN:	Did you pack your suitcase yourself?
PASSENGER:	Yes, I did.
CHECK-IN:	Does it contain any knives or scissors?
PASSENGER:	No.
CHECK-IN:	Fine. Could you put it on here, please? OK ... 15 kilos.

3

PASSENGER:	Piccadilly Circus, please.
BUS DRIVER:	One pound, please.
PASSENGER:	Thanks.
BUS DRIVER:	Thank you.

4

ASSISTANT:	Victoria Coach Station. Can I help you?
PASSENGER:	I'd like to book a single ticket to Edinburgh, please.
ASSISTANT:	Yes ... when would you like to travel?
PASSENGER:	Friday 14th March in the afternoon.
ASSISTANT:	OK ... uh ... there's a coach at 5.45 pm.
PASSENGER:	Yes, that's fine. How much is it?
ASSISTANT:	£45 for a single ticket. How would you like to pay?
PASSENGER:	By Visa, please.
ASSISTANT:	OK.

After this general listening task, students listen again to slot in various key language items in blanks from the audioscript, e.g.

PASSENGER:	_____ to Oxford, please.
ASSISTANT:	Yes, of course. Are you coming back today?
PASSENGER:	Yes, I am.
ASSISTANT:	_____, please.
PASSENGER:	Thank you.

This study section encourages students to focus in on the construction of the specific language which the coursebook writers have selected.

Finally, students try to *activate* the language they know for this kind of interaction. In pairs, students A and B look at different information (see page 139) in order to have exchanges which are similar to the ones they have just listened to.

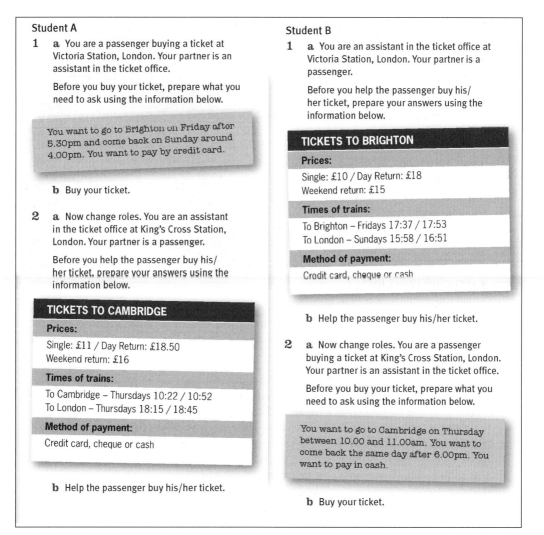

Student A

1 **a** You are a passenger buying a ticket at Victoria Station, London. Your partner is an assistant in the ticket office.

   Before you buy your ticket, prepare what you need to ask using the information below.

   > You want to go to Brighton on Friday after 5.30pm and come back on Sunday around 4.00pm. You want to pay by credit card.

   b Buy your ticket.

2 **a** Now change roles. You are an assistant in the ticket office at King's Cross Station, London. Your partner is a passenger.

   Before you help the passenger buy his/her ticket, prepare your answers using the information below.

   TICKETS TO CAMBRIDGE

   Prices:
   Single: £11 / Day Return: £18.50
   Weekend return: £16

   Times of trains:
   To Cambridge – Thursdays 10:22 / 10:52
   To London – Thursdays 18:15 / 18:45

   Method of payment:
   Credit card, cheque or cash

   b Help the passenger buy his/her ticket.

Student B

1 **a** You are an assistant in the ticket office at Victoria Station, London. Your partner is a passenger.

   Before you help the passenger buy his/her ticket, prepare your answers using the information below.

   TICKETS TO BRIGHTON

   Prices:
   Single: £10 / Day Return: £18
   Weekend return: £15

   Times of trains:
   To Brighton – Fridays 17:37 / 17:53
   To London – Sundays 15:58 / 16:51

   Method of payment:
   Credit card, cheque or cash

   b Help the passenger buy his/her ticket.

2 **a** Now change roles. You are a passenger buying a ticket at King's Cross Station, London. Your partner is an assistant in the ticket office.

   Before you buy your ticket, prepare what you need to ask using the information below.

   > You want to go to Cambridge on Thursday between 10.00 and 11.00am. You want to come back the same day after 6.00pm. You want to pay in cash.

   b Buy your ticket.

Although this particular example is culture-specific (British English, using English locations and destinations), the technique of matching what students hear to pictures can be used in many different ways at many different levels. Booking and buying tickets take place in all languages and cultures, too.

Example 3: prerecorded authentic interview-narrative (upper intermediate)

In this example, for upper-intermediate level, students are going to hear two excerpts from a recorded authentic interview. However, in both cases the interviewee often replies to the interviewer by telling stories rather than just giving short answers. These excerpts are considerably longer than lower-level listening texts – and unlike the live listening in Example 1, students will not have the opportunity to interact with the interviewee. It is, therefore, especially important that they are both fully engaged with what is going on and also ready to listen.

This interview is notable, too, in that the interviewee is a speaker of Indian English – an important world variety, and therefore one which students of English as an International Language (see page 80) should be comfortable with.

Students are first shown the picture on the right and asked to speculate about who the person is, where she's from, what she does, etc. They then look at the following questions before they hear her speak:

a What happened at the station in Mumbai (then called Bombay), and how much money did Diana have with her?

b How did Diana try to get accommodation in Mumbai?

c What time was it on Diana's watch when she knocked on the lady's door?

d Why do you think the lady said 'Come inside'?

e What lesson does Diana draw from this experience in her life?

They discuss the questions, perhaps in pairs, and try to predict the answers. The teacher now plays the following audio track (after they have been told that Diana comes from Hyderabad in southern India and that at the age of 18 she went to Mumbai, then called Bombay, to look for work):

DIANA: I had 250 rupees in my pocket. Now 250 rupees is the equivalent of about umm four pounds, and the person who was a family friend who was supposed to meet me at the station wasn't there, and then I went knocking from one door to the other looking for accommodation and umm it's a very bizarre story but I did get accommodation. Someone sent me to somebody else and they said – like you call them 'bedsits' here, in India you call them paying guests and they said 'oh so-and-so person keeps paying guests, go there', and I got sent from one place to the other off this main road and umm I knocked on this lady's door and my watch said 7.30 and she opened the door and I said 'Look, someone told me – can't remember where down the line – someone said you keep, you know, paying guests,' and she said 'No, I don't, not any more, I've stopped for the last three years,' and then I heard the English news in the background. Now the English news is from 9.30 to 9.45 and I said 'Is that the English news?' She said 'Yes, and what is a young girl like you doing on your own on the streets at this time?' and I said 'But it can't be because the English news is at 9.30'. She said, 'Yes, a quarter to ten,' and I showed her my watch and it stopped at 7.30 and she said, 'Come inside.' She was a Pakistani woman. She was married to an Englishman. She said, 'Come inside.' She says, 'My hair's standing and I just think God has sent you to me,' and she took me in. She said, 'Bring all your stuff and come tomorrow and umm go and get a job. When you get a job, then you can start paying me.' So that's the ... it's it's just everything. I believe that everything you try to do, if you put yourself out there and give it your all ... you will ... you will achieve it. I think it's very important that you look back and you connect with those experiences and you remember them as clearly as yesterday because if not, the superficial nonsense that goes on in your life like today can very easily take over you and you can lose perspective.

Students go through the questions again in pairs to see if they agree with the answers. The teacher may decide to play the audio track again if they have had difficulty catching the main points of her story.

The teacher now tells the students that Diana went on to become quite famous because she won something. They are invited to speculate what that was – though they are not told if they are right. Instead, the teacher plays the next audio track for them to see if their speculations were correct:

DIANA: ... I think it's very important that you look back and you connect with those experiences and you remember them as clearly as yesterday because if not, the superficial nonsense that goes on in your life like today can very easily take over you and you can lose perspective.

PRESENTER: But Diana didn't lose perspective. After a succession of jobs – including managing two of India's most famous pop stars – she was entered into the Miss India beauty competition and she won it. Next she found herself representing her country in the Miss World competition, something that must have been quite daunting for the 23-year-old.

DIANA: Your biggest fear is 'I shouldn't trip' and because you've got these really high heels and these long, long gowns and you've got all these steps that you're walking up and down and it's live on television you've got ...

INTERVIEWER: Watched by ...

DIANA: ... thousands of people watching ...

INTERVIEWER: Watched by ...

DIANA: ... by millions. It is huge. Everybody watches it. You have more people watching them in India than you'd have them watching the Wimbledon finals or something, you know, or the Olympic Games or something. Yeah. Umm and your biggest fear is 'I should not go blank' because you're asked questions on stage and yeah, you can just freeze.

PRESENTER: But Diana didn't freeze. In front of a huge worldwide audience she heard a voice announce that Miss India, Diana Hayden, was the new Miss World.

DIANA: Oooh you feel numb. The ... you know, it's it's a saturation point. It's too much for you to digest that your grin is stuck on your face. It was stuck on my face for weeks. I would position that crown in such a way that as soon as I opened my eyes I would see my crown. I did that for weeks. Ha ha. It was such a great feeling. You just, you're just grinning and you are just numb. If that's what euphoria is, you know, umm you, you can't speak very clearly. You speak but you're just so excited you're tripping over your own words, and immediately there was a press conference on stage itself and it's like ooh ooh ooh because you go from being nobody, a regular person. That's not fair. It's not a nobody. You go from being a regular person to being in every newspaper around the world and everyone knows. It went from going in a bus with 87 other girls to 'and Miss World is Miss India' to a stretch limousine, with bodyguards, where the heads of the company moved out of the presidential suite and I took over and chaperones and that's what it was like since then. You sit in the cockpits for take-offs and landings. You're treated like a queen you, you know, you have private planes, and all these flights and umm the red carpet and it's just Lights! Camera! Action!

Having established that Diana was Miss World, students then listen to the second audio track again to answer more straightforward information questions such as what Diana was afraid of and why, how many people were watching the second competition, how she felt when she won Miss World, what she did with her crown and what happened immediately after she won. Once again, the students will have the opportunity to listen to the audio track one or two more times.

The two audio tracks and the audioscripts provide ample opportunity for various kinds of study. For example, it is worth drawing the students' attention to some of the vocabulary that Diana uses ('bedsit', 'hair standing' – and how Diana says the phrase – 'give your all', 'trip over your words', 'mind goes blank', 'chaperone', 'cockpit', etc). We might also get the students to listen to the audio track while they read the audioscript and identify moments when Diana repeats words and phrases (and why she does this), find when she uses meaningless sounds (and why she does this) and see where she starts speaking with one grammatical construction and then changes it.

Another useful activity is to get students to retell Diana's story, trying to use as many of her expressions as they can. Retelling is a good way of fixing some of the language in their minds. We could also move on to a discussion about the ethos of the Miss World competition.

This last example of listening is highly elaborate and takes some time. But the advantages of hearing real English spoken normally – and an English that is somewhat different from the usual British and American varieties which have been the staple of listening texts for many years (though that is changing) – outweigh the potential pitfalls of length.

More listening suggestions

Jigsaw listening: in three groups, students listen to three different tapes, all of which are about the same thing (witness reports after an accident or a crime, phone conversations arranging a meeting, different news stories which explain a strange event, etc). Students have to assemble all the facts by comparing notes. In this way, they may find out what actually happened, solve a mystery or get a rounded account of a situation or topic.

Jigsaw listening works because it gives students a purpose for listening, and a goal to aim for (solving the 'mystery', or understanding all the facts). However, it obviously depends on whether students have access to three different tape or CD players, or computer-delivered listening material.

Message-taking: students listen to a phone message being given. They have to write down the message on a message pad.

There are many other kinds of message that students can listen to. For example, they may hear a recorded message about what films are on at a cinema, when they're on, what rating they have and whether there are still tickets. They then have to decide which film to go to. They might hear the message on an answerphone, or a gallery guide (where they have to identify which pictures are being talked about), or messages about how to place an order. In each case, they have to respond in some way.

It is also appropriate for students to listen to announcements in airports and on railway stations which they can match with pictures or respond to by saying what they are going to do next.

Music and sound effects: although most audio tracks consist of speech, we can also use music and **sound effects**. Songs are very useful because, if we choose them well, they can be very engaging. Students can fill in blanks in song lyrics, rearrange lines or verses, or listen to songs and say what mood or message they convey.

We can use instrumental music to get students in the right mood, or as a stimulus for any number of creative tasks (imagining film scenes, responding to mood and atmosphere, saying what the music is describing, etc). The same is true of sound effects, which students can listen to in order to build up a story.

News and other radio genres: students listen to a news broadcast and have to say which topics from a list occur in the bulletin and in which order. They then have to listen for details about individual stories. If the news contains a lot of facts and figures, students may be asked to convert them into chart or graph form.

Other genres which students get benefit from are radio commercials (they have to match commercials with pictures or say why one – on safety – is different from the rest – which are trying to sell things), radio phone-ins (where they can match speakers to topics) and any number of games and quizzes. In all of the above cases, the degree of authenticity will depend on the level of the radio extract and the level of the students.

Poetry: poetry can be used in a number of ways. Students can listen to poems being read aloud and say what mood they convey (or what colour they suggest to them). They can hear a poem and then try to come up with an appropriate title. They can listen to a poem which has no punctuation and put in commas and full stops where they think they should occur.

One way of getting students to predict what they are going to hear is to give them the titles of three poems and then ask them to guess what words the poems will contain. As a result, when they listen, they are eager to see if they are right, and awake to the possibilities of what the poem might be like.

Stories: a major speaking genre is storytelling. When students listen to people telling stories, there are a number of things we can have them do. Perhaps they can put pictures in the order in which the story is told. Sometimes we can let students listen to a story but not tell them the end. They have to guess what it is and then, perhaps, we play them the recorded version. A variation on this technique is to stop the story at various points and say 'What do you think happens next?' before continuing. These techniques are appropriate for children and adults alike.

Some of the best stories for students to listen to are when people are talking more or less informally (like Diana Hayden on pages 140–141). But it is also good to let them hear well-read extracts from books; we can get them to say which book they think the extract comes from, or decide what kind of book it is (horror, romance, thriller, etc).

Monologues: various monologue genres can be used for different listening tasks. For example, we can ask students to listen to lectures and take notes. We can get them to listen to 'vox-pop' interviews where five different speakers say what they think about a topic and the students have to match the different speakers with different opinions. We can listen to dramatic or comic monologues and ask the students to say how the speaker feels. We can have them listen to speeches (at weddings, farewells, openings, etc) and get them to identify what the subject is and what the speaker thinks about it.

Audio and video

Almost everything we have said about listening applies to video, too (or any other film platform, such as DVDs or other digitally delivered film; we will use the term *video* to include all of these – see Appendix A on page 252 for more on technology for listening and watching). We have to choose video material according to the level and interests of our students. If we make it too difficult or too easy, the students will not be motivated. If the content is irrelevant to the students' interests, it may fail to engage them.

Video is richer than audio: speakers can be seen; their body movements give clues as to meaning; so do the clothes they wear, their location, etc. Background information can be filled in visually.

Some teachers, however, think that video is less useful for teaching listening than audio precisely because, with the visual senses engaged as well as the audio senses, students pay less attention to what they are actually hearing.

A danger of video is that students may treat it rather as they treat watching television – e.g. uncritically and lazily. There may well be occasions when it is entirely appropriate for them to watch video in a relaxed way, but more often we will want them to engage, not only with the content of what they are seeing, but also the language and other features.

Four particular techniques are especially appropriate for language learners, and are often used with video footage:

Play the video without sound: students and teacher discuss what they see and what clues it gives them, and then they guess what the characters are actually saying. Once they have predicted the conversation, the teacher rewinds the video and plays it with sound. Were they right?

A variation on this technique is to fast forward the excerpt. The students say what they think was happening. The teacher can then play the extract with sound, or play it, again, without sound, but this time at normal speed.

Play the audio without the picture: this reverses the previous procedure. While the students listen, they try to judge where the speakers are, what they look like, what's going on, etc. When they have predicted this, they listen again, this time with the visual images as well. Were they correct?

Freeze frame: the teacher presses the pause button and asks the students what's going to happen next. Can they predict the action – and the language that will be used?

Dividing the class in half: half the class face the screen. The other half sit with their backs to it. The 'screen' half describe the visual images to the 'wall' half.

Conclusions | *In this chapter we have:*

- discussed the reasons for using listening in the classroom. These include the effect on the students' acquisition of good pronunciation and other speaking habits. We also need to expose students to different varieties of English, and different kinds of listening.

- identified the difference between intensive (detailed) listening and extensive listening, saying that in the case of extensive listening students should listen to things they can more or less understand, mostly for pleasure.

- talked about the difference between live listening and prerecorded extracts, saying that whereas live listening allows students to interact with speakers, they cannot do this with speakers on audio tracks. Nevertheless, the latter provide ample opportunities for hearing speakers of different language varieties.

- said that students need to hear people speaking in different genres, and that while we want them all to hear authentic English, at lower levels this may not be feasible; nevertheless, the language they hear should be as much like the 'real thing' as possible.

- discussed the fact that students need to be able to deploy different skills for listening in order to understand general meaning or, alternatively, to get specific details.

- provided six principles for listening: listen as often and as much as possible, preparation is vital, once may not be enough, students should be encouraged to respond to the content of the listening, not just the language, different listening stages demand different listening tasks, good teachers exploit listening texts to the full.

- looked at three listening sequences showing how preparation is a major part of the sequence, and showing how listening leads on to follow-up tasks.

- offered a range of other listening genres and activities.

- discussed where video (or digitally delivered images) fits in, mentioning some video techniques and stressing that using video is not an excuse for TV watching.

Using coursebooks

- ■ **Options for coursebook use**
- ■ **Adding, adapting and replacing**
- ■ **Reasons for (and against) coursebook use**
- ■ **Choosing coursebooks**

Options for coursebook use

When teachers open a page in their **coursebook**, they have to decide whether or not they should use the lesson on that page with their class. Is the language at the right level? Is the topic/content suitable for the students? Are there the right kind of activities in the book? Is the sequencing of the lesson logical?

With a good coursebook, there is a strong possibility that the language, content and sequencing in the book will be appropriate, and that the topics and treatment of the different language skills will be attractive. As a result the teacher will want to go ahead and use what is in the book. If, however, teachers have the time or inclination to amend parts of a coursebook (because the texts or activities don't seem appropriate for a particular group of students or a particular lesson, or because they want to tailor the material to match their own particular style), they have to decide what to do next.

There are four alternatives to consider if we decide that part of a coursebook is not appropriate. Firstly, we might simply decide to omit the lesson. That solves the problem of inappropriacy and allows us and our students to get on with something else.

There's nothing wrong with omitting lessons from coursebooks. Teachers do it all the time, developing a kind of 'pick and choose' approach to what's in front of them. However, if they omit too many pages, the students may begin to wonder why they are using the book in the first place, especially if they have bought it themselves.

Another alternative is to replace the coursebook lesson with one of our own. This has obvious advantages: our own material probably interests us more than the coursebook and it may well be more appropriate for our students. If we cover the same language or topic, the students can still use the book to revise that particular language/vocabulary. But as with omitting pages, if too much of the coursebook is replaced, both students and teacher may wonder if it is worth bothering with it at all.

The third option is to add to what is in the book. If the lesson is rather boring, too controlled, or if it gives no chance for students to use what they are learning in a personal kind of way, the teacher may want to add activities and exercises which extend the students' *engagement* with the language or topic. We are using the coursebook's strengths but marrying them with our own skills and perceptions of the class in front of us.

The final option is for teachers to adapt what is in the book. If a reading text is dealt with in a boring or uncreative way, if an invitation sequence is too predictable or teachers simply want to deal with the material in their own way, they can adapt the lesson by rewriting parts of it, replacing some of the activities (but not all), reordering activities or reducing the number of activities in the sequence.

Using coursebooks creatively is one of the teacher's premier skills. The way in which we get students to look at reading texts, do exercises or solve puzzles in the book is extremely important. At what point, for example, do we actually get the students to open the book? If they do so before we give our instructions, they often don't concentrate on what we have to say. Should the books always be on the students' desks, or should they be kept in a drawer or in the students' bags until they are needed? Furthermore, as we have said, many teachers do not go through the book line by line. Instead they use the parts that are most appropriate for their class, and make suitable changes to other material so that it is exactly right for their students.

Adding, adapting and replacing

In the following three examples, we are going to show how coursebook material can be used differently by teachers. However, it is not being suggested that any of these coursebook extracts have anything wrong with them. Our examples are designed only to show that there are always other ways of doing things even when the original material is perfectly good.

Example 1: adapting and adding (elementary)

In the following example, students are working with a coursebook called *New Cutting Edge Elementary* by Sarah Cunningham and Peter Moor. They have just read a text called 'Amazing facts about the natural world' which includes such statistics as the fact that we share our birthdays with about 18 million other people in the world, we eat about 8 kilos of dirt in our lifetimes, donkeys kill more people than plane crashes do, elephants can't jump, the Arctic Tern does a 22,000-mile trip to the Antarctic every year, etc. After discussing the text they make sentences with 'can' and 'can't' about these facts, e.g. 'Elephants can't jump', 'Pigs can't look at the sky', 'Kangaroos can't walk backwards', etc.

They now look at the following page (see page 148) which shifts the focus towards various question words (how long, how fast, etc), and not only includes a grammar description and a practice activity where students have to choose the right question word or phrase, but also a short quiz referring back to the 'amazing facts' text they have read (the unit continues with more question practice designed for pairwork).

There is absolutely nothing wrong with the page we are illustrating. On the contrary, it is bright and well conceived. But for whatever reason, we may decide to adapt what the authors have suggested, even adding more material of our own. We could, for example, adapt the quiz by having individual students each choose an animal (perhaps after looking up information in an encyclopedia or on the Internet). They don't tell their classmates which animal they have chosen. The class then tries to find out which animals different individuals have chosen by asking questions such as 'How fast can you run?', 'How big are you?', 'Which countries do you live in?', 'How far do you travel?', 'Is there anything you can't do?'

Language focus 2
Question words

1 a Work in pairs. How many questions in the Animal quiz can you answer without looking back at the text?

b Look back at the text and check your answers.

2 Circle the question word in each question.

Grammar

1 There are many two-word questions with *how*, *what* and *which*. Match the question words to the answers.

a How far ...?	Los Angeles.
b How tall ...?	Every day.
c How often ...?	Lions.
d How long ...?	Ten metres.
e How fast ...?	Forty kilometres an hour.
f Which city ...?	Ten kilometres.
g Which animals ...?	Rock and pop.
h What kinds of music ...?	Three hours.

2 **Do you remember? Choose the correct alternative.**
We use:
• *How many* with countable / uncountable nouns.
• *How much* with countable / uncountable nouns.

3 We use *what* when there are a large number of possible answers.
What is the population of China?
We use *which* when there are only a few possible answers.
Which continent has no active volcanoes?

▶ Read Language summary B on page 157.

Practice

1 Choose the correct question word.

a Which / What do kangaroos eat?
b How much / How many water do people need to drink every day?
c What / Which do you like best, dogs or cats?
d How much / How many pets have you got?
e How much / How long do elephants usually live?
f How far / How often do you need to feed a baby?
g How fast / How long does the average person walk?
h How far / How many can you swim?
i How long / How often do you go swimming?
j Which / What is your dog's name?

Animal quiz

1 How much dirt does the average person eat during their life?

2 What kind of animals can't jump?

3 Which continent has no active volcanoes?

4 How fast does the earth rotate?

5 How many ants are there in the world?

6 How long can snails sleep?

7 How do guide dogs know when to cross the road?

8 How far do Arctic Terns fly every year?

9 What is the present population of the world?

Alternatively, we might decide to get the students to look back at the text and write their own questions, and then divide the class into two teams. They fire their questions at the opposing team who have to give as many correct answers as possible within a time limit.

Another adaptation, which will appeal to those students who respond well to kinaesthetic stimuli (see page 16), is to write questions and answers on different pieces of paper. Students take a question card or an answer card and have to 'mill around' finding the student who has the answer to their question, or vice versa.

We could also adapt the quiz by turning it into the kind of 'interview' which can be found in many magazines. In this case, however, students are not interviewing a celebrity, but one of the animals from the text (elephants, kangaroos, ants, etc). Students write interview questions and send them to other students, who answer as if they were the animal they have chosen; they can answer as seriously, comically or facetiously as they want. They can write their questions on a piece of paper, leaving space for the answers, and then 'send' them to the student (animal) they wish to interview, they can use photocopies of blank 'email windows' to simulate a typical email exchange, or they can, of course, send their questions via email if this is available.

None of the activities suggested here are better than the ones in the coursebook; they are simply different. Indeed, these activities may not appeal to some teachers at all, which is exactly the point. It is up to individual teachers and their students to decide how and when to use different sections of a coursebook.

Example 2: adding (intermediate)

Most coursebooks have word lists, sometimes at the back of the book, sometimes at the end of a unit or a section. These are usually ignored, except by some students who often write inaccurate translations of the words. Teachers seldom touch them. Yet here is a chance to add to what the coursebook provides in enjoyable and useful ways.

The following word list occurs after three lessons of intermediate material.

admire	exciting	law	protection
attendance	experience	leader	record
attractive	factor	lovely	rugged
bad	fair-haired	lover	scenic
beautiful	fair-skinned	magnificent	sick
boring	fantastic	Melanin	skin cancer
cute	fascinating	memorable	song
dangerous	flight attendant	motorway	striking
dark-haired	freckles	moving	stunning
dark-skinned	gang	newscaster	sunburnt
die	good-looking	picturesque	suntanned
doctor	handsome	pig	trust
dramatic	impressive	place	ultraviolet
elegant	interesting	pretty	unmemorable
event	killer	professor	victim

There are a number of things that we can do with such an apparently static piece of text. They fall into three categories: personal engagement, word formation and word games.

Personal engagement: the teacher can ask students to discuss questions like 'Which words have a positive meaning for you?' and 'Which words have a negative meaning for you?' (Notice that we are asking them about their own personal reaction to these words.)

The teacher can ask students to list their five favourite words from the list – words that appeal to them because of their meaning, sound, spelling, etc. They then have to explain to the class why they have chosen those particular words. We can go further and ask students which five words they would most like to take to a desert island, and why. This demands that they think a bit laterally, but they might decide to take 'protection', for example, because of the sun or 'beautiful' because beautiful islands are better than ugly ones! We can ask students to predict which words will be most useful for them in the future. We can even hold a word auction where students have to bid for the words they most want to buy.

The teacher can ask whether any of the words look or sound like words in their language and whether they mean the same. This is especially useful for Romance languages.

We can ask students which words they find easy to pronounce and which they find difficult. The moment we ask them questions like this, we are, in a sense, saying that these words belong not to the teacher or the book, but to the students themselves.

Word formation: we can ask a number of questions about how the words (in any list) are constructed. Students can be asked to make a list of words which are stressed on the first, second or third syllables. They can be asked how many of the adjectives can be changed into verbs and/or what endings the verbs would need if they were changed into adjectives. They can be asked to identify compound words (made up from two words – e.g. 'dark-skinned', 'skin cancer', 'suntanned') and say how they are formed.

There are many other possible activities here: students can make contrary meanings by adding 'un-' or 'in-', for example, give adjectives a comparative form, decide which of the verbs are 'regular' and what sound their past tense endings make, etc. In each case, using a word list reminds students of some of the rules governing words and their grammar.

Word games: there is almost no limit to the games we can play with a collection of words from the wordlist. We can ask students to make tabloid headlines from the list (e.g. 'Attractive doctor in dramatic motorway experience!'). The word list can be used for 'expansion', too, by giving the students a sentence like 'The man kissed the woman' and asking them to expand it using as many words from the list as they can (together with any necessary grammar words). Can anyone make a longer sentence than 'The attractive fair-haired man with dramatic but elegant suntanned freckles kissed the fascinating pretty flight attendant in front of the dangerous woman on the motorway'?

The words can be written on cards which are then put into a hat. When a student pulls one of the cards out of the hat, they have to make up a good sentence on the spot with the word on the card. Students can write correct and incorrect definitions for the different words. Opposing teams then have to guess which are the correct definitions and which are false. We can ask students to design word bingo cards with some of the words. They then read out sentences, omitting a word and other students have to cross off the word on their cards which they think will go in the gap.

Some modern coursebooks include activities like this, but many do not. In such circumstances, there is almost no limit to the kinds of activity we can add to the list to make it dynamic and engaging. As a result, students have a good chance of remembering more of the words than they otherwise might have done.

Example 3: replacing (pre-intermediate)

In the following example (from a coursebook for teenagers), a reading text is part of a longer unit which concentrates on the past simple and includes biographical information, a functional dialogue about apologies ('I'm sorry I'm late') and listening and activity pages.

Students are asked to complete a chart with information about the dates 1870, 1883, 1886, 1890, 1892 and 1893 by reading the following text:

He photographed the world!

Go into the TV room and switch on the TV. Suddenly you are not at home any more: you are in another country thousands of miles away. Television has made the world a smaller place.

One hundred and fifty years ago it was different. There were no planes and people did not travel to different countries all the time. But one man did. His name was Burton Holmes and he was born in 1870 in Chicago, Illinois.

In 1883, Holmes bought his first camera and when he was sixteen he travelled to Europe with his grandmother. He took photographs and he loved it. Four years later, Holmes came back to the US with his pictures.

In 1892 Holmes went to Japan and one year later he started to give lectures with slides. He talked about the countries he had visited (in Europe and Asia) and showed slides. Many people came to see and hear. Most of his slides were in black and white, but Japanese artists had coloured some of them and they were very beautiful. Four years later he showed his first moving pictures.

Burton Holmes continued his lectures into the 1950s. He was famous all over the US as a great traveller, the man who photographed the world.

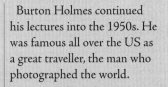

The coursebook then encourages the students to ask as many questions about Burton Holmes as possible.

There are a number of options for using this text. We could try to make it more engaging by having students work in pairs where one of them plays the role of Burton Holmes and the other is an interviewer. We could blank out words in the text, or cut the text up into paragraphs which students have to rearrange. Students could search the Internet for further information about Burton Holmes (although at their level this might prove difficult), or we could do a search ourselves and come up with more facts about the man.

But it is equally possible that we do not want to use this text because we do not think it has sufficient potential for interesting our students. We will need to replace it, then, with an appropriate text (or activities) that fits in with the coursebook unit. We could, for example, bring in some of our own photographs and then show students a text (photocopied, or on an OHT) which describes one of them. The students have to decide which one it is. We can ask students to bring in a photo of their own, for which they will have prepared a narrative (where it was taken, what happened, etc). We could show students famous 'event' pictures and ask them to say what they think is happening before giving them an oral or written description. Perhaps we could ask them to judge a competition for the best photograph from a set of four or five (for a full description of this activity see page 124), though this will be fairly demanding at this level.

Of course, it may be that we don't want to deal with the topic of photography. We could instead look for any biographical text or information that we think students will be interested in – a singer or other celebrity, or someone famous from the students' own culture – and offer material about that person.

There is almost no limit to the ways in which we can replace coursebook excerpts. However, as we have said above, we will need to decide how much and how often we wish to replace in this way.

Reasons for (and against) coursebook use

Some teachers have a very poor opinion of coursebooks. They say they are boring, stifling (for both teacher and students) and often inappropriate for the class in front of them. Such people would prefer to rely on their own ideas, snippets from reference books, pages from magazines, ideas from the students themselves and a variety of other sources.

Other teachers feel much more positive about coursebooks. For them, coursebooks provide good teaching material which is often attractively presented. The coursebook has been carefully researched and has a consistent grammar syllabus as well as providing appropriate vocabulary exposure and practice, together with pronunciation work and writing tasks. Good coursebooks have a range of reading and listening material and workbooks, for example, to back them up (to say nothing of Internet tie-ins and other extras). It takes less time to prepare a good coursebook lesson than to start from the beginning each time and prepare brand new material; however ideal such freshness might be, many teachers simply do not have the time to prepare and plan as much as they would like to. Most coursebooks have an accompanying **teacher's guide** to help teachers with procedure and give them extra ideas. And students often feel extremely positive about coursebooks, too. For them, the coursebook is reassuring. It allows them to look forward and back, giving them a chance to prepare for what's coming and review what they have done.

However, there is the ever-present danger that both teacher and students will get locked into the book, using its content as the only material which is taken into the classroom, and always teaching and learning only in the way the book suggests. In such circumstances, the book may become like a millstone around the necks of all concerned, endangering the *engagement* which a student-centred classroom might otherwise create. As a result, some teachers take the decision to do without coursebooks altogether, a decision which may well be of benefit to their students if, and only if, they have the experience and time to provide a consistent programme of work on their own, and if they have a bank of materials to back up their 'no-coursebook' decision.

Even teachers who are enthusiastic coursebook users, however, need to see them as **proposals for action**, rather than instructions for action. In other words, we can look at the possibilities the coursebook offers us and then decide between the options for coursebook use which we discussed at the beginning of this chapter. If teachers and students approach coursebooks in that light, and use them according to the criteria we suggested above, they will have a much more beneficial effect than if they are followed slavishly. However good a coursebook is, it only really comes to life when it is used by students and teachers, and it is they, not the book, who should determine exactly how and when the material is used.

Choosing coursebooks

At many stages during their careers, teachers have to decide what books to use. How should they do this, and on what basis will they be able to say that one book is better or more appropriate than another?

The first thing we need to do is **analyse** the books under consideration to see how they compare with each other. Probably the best way of doing this is to select areas that interest us (e.g. layout and design, methodology, topics, etc), write short descriptions of how our ideal coursebook would deal with such areas, and then use these descriptions to see whether the books we are looking at match up to them. Alternatively, we can turn our descriptions into questions, as in the checklist on page 154. It is important to note here that when teachers make their own questions, they may not be the same as those shown here. The questions will always depend on the specific priorities of those who are asking them. This checklist is, therefore, just an example of some possible questions.

Once we have analysed the competing merits of different materials, and chosen the one or ones that most interest us, it will be important to **pilot** it – or parts of it – with a class so that we can assess its strengths and weaknesses.

Before making our final choice, we will want to consult colleagues, and indeed anyone who has an opinion about the book(s) in question. We need to be aware, of course, of their differing teaching situations or competing publisher, author or methodology loyalties, but it is always worth listening to what other people have to say.

Lastly, it is always a good idea to let our students have a look at the two or three books we are considering and ask their opinion on what looks best to them. They may not make our decision for us, but their opinion can help us come to a final decision.

Possible areas for consideration	Possible questions for coursebook analysis
Price and availability	How much does the coursebook cost? Will students have to buy any extra material (workbook, etc)? Are all the components (coursebook, workbook, teacher's guide, audio, etc) available? What about other levels? Is this good value for money? How much does the whole package (with all the components) cost?
Add-ons and extras	Apart from a workbook, what other extras are offered with the course? Are there Internet sites with extra material (exercises, texts, etc), or with 'meeting places' for users? What else does the publisher offer to support the course? What value should we place on the extras that are available?
Layout and design	Is the book attractive? Is its design appropriate for (a) the students, and (b) the teacher? Does the design of the book make it easy to follow?
Instructions	Are the instructions clear and unambiguous? Are they written in language that the students will understand? Can the coursebook be used by students working on their own, or is a teacher necessary to show them how to use it?
Methodology	What kind of teaching and learning does the coursebook promote? Is there a good balance between *study* and *activation*? How do the authors appear to think that people learn languages and do we agree with them?
Syllabus	Is the syllabus appropriate for our students? Does it cover the language areas (grammar, vocabulary, functions, pronunciation, etc) that we would expect? Do we and our students like the sequencing of language and topics, etc? Does the coursebook build in a feeling of progress?
Language skills	Does the coursebook have the appropriate balance of skills? Is the skills work really designed to promote the skills (e.g. writing-for-writing, not writing-for-learning)? Are there possibilities for both *study* and *activation* in the skills areas? Are the skills activities likely to *engage* students?
Topics	Does the book contain a variety of topics? On balance, are the topics appropriate for the kind of students who will be using the coursebook? Are the topics likely to *engage* the students?
Cultural appropriacy	Is the material appropriate for the cultural situation that the students are in? Do the texts contain culturally insensitive material? Are the activities appropriate for the learning culture? Is the coursebook unprejudiced in the way it deals with different customs, ethnicities, races and sexes?
Teacher's guide	Does the coursebook have an accompanying teacher's guide? Is it easy to use? Does it explain things clearly? Does it offer alternatives to the coursebook activities? Does it have all the answers that teachers and students need? Does it provide differentiated activities for fast and slow learners?

Descriptions into questions: a possible coursebook analysis checklist

Conclusions | *In this chapter we have:*

- looked at four different options – omit, replace, add and adapt – for coursebook use when, for some reason, the teacher decides that (the lesson in) the coursebook is not appropriate for the class.

- said that creative coursebook use is one of a teacher's main skills.

- looked at examples of adding, adapting and replacing coursebook material.

- discussed the criticisms often levelled at coursebooks: that they are boring, inappropriate and lacking in variety, for example. But we have said that their advantages (clarity, solid progression, attractiveness) often outweigh these disadvantages, and that it is precisely because of some of their perceived defects that teachers need to use them creatively – provided they realise that coursebooks are proposals for action rather than obligatory instruction manuals.

- suggested that teachers should make decisions about which coursebook to use based on analysis, piloting, consultation and the gathering of opinions from students and colleagues – and that one way of doing this is to prepare a checklist of questions.

Planning lessons

- ■ **Reasons for planning**
- ■ **A proposal for action**
- ■ **Lesson shapes**
- ■ **Planning questions**
- ■ **Plan formats**

- ■ **Planning a sequence of lessons**
- ■ **After the lesson (and before the next)**

Reasons for planning

Some teachers with experience seem to have an ability to think on their feet, and this allows them to believe that lesson planning is unnecessary. However, most teachers do not share this view and prepare their lessons. The resulting lesson plans range from the very formal and elaborate to a few hurried notes. But even the notes are still a plan of a kind.

For students, evidence of a plan shows that the teacher has devoted time to thinking about the class. It strongly suggests a level of professionalism and a commitment to the kind of research they might reasonably expect. Lack of a plan may suggest the opposite of these teacher attributes, even if such a perception is unjustified.

For teachers, a plan gives the lesson a framework, an overall shape. It is true that they may end up departing from it at some stage of the lesson, but at the very least it will be something to fall back on. Of course, good teachers are flexible and respond creatively to what happens in the classroom, but they also need to have thought ahead, to have a destination which they want their students to reach, and some idea of how they are going to get there. In the classroom, a plan helps to remind teachers what they intended to do – especially if they get distracted or momentarily forget what they had proposed.

There is one particular situation in which planning is especially important, and that is when a teacher is to be observed as part of an assessment or performance review. Such plans are likely to be more elaborate than usual, not just for the sake of the teacher being observed, but also so that the observer can have a clear idea of what the teacher intends in order to judge how well that intention is carried through.

A proposal for action

Whatever lesson plans look like, they should never be thought of as instructions to be slavishly followed, but rather as *proposals for action* (in the same way as coursebook lessons – see page 153). We may have an idea of what the **learning outcomes** for the lesson should be (that is, what the students will have learnt by the end), but we will only really know what those outcomes are once the lesson itself has finished. How closely lesson plans are followed depends, in other words, on what happens when we try to put them to work.

Suppose, for example, that the teacher has planned that the students should prepare a dialogue and then act it out, after which there is a reading text and some exercises for them to get through. The teacher has allowed twenty minutes for dialogue preparation and acting out. But when the students start working on this activity, it is obvious that they need more time. Clearly the plan will have to be modified. A similar decision will have to be made if the class suddenly encounters an unexpected language problem in the middle of some planned sequence of activities. The teacher can bypass the problem and keep going, or they can realise that now is an ideal time to deal with the issue, and amend the plan accordingly.

Another scenario is also possible: all the students are working on preparing a dialogue except for two pairs who have already finished. The teacher then has to decide whether to tell them to wait for the others to catch up (which might make them bored and resentful) or whether to stop the rest of the class to prevent this (which could frustrate all those who didn't get a chance to finish).

There are other unforeseen problems too: the tape/CD player or computer program suddenly doesn't work; we forget to bring the material we were relying on; the students look at the planned reading text and say 'We've done that before'.

Good teachers need to be **flexible** enough to cope with unforeseen events, and it is because they know that they may have to adapt to changing circumstances that they understand that a lesson plan is not fixed in stone.

So far we have suggested that teachers need to be flexible when confronted with unforeseen problems. But a happier scenario is also possible. Imagine that during a discussion phase a student suddenly says something really interesting, something which could provoke fascinating conversation or suggest a completely unplanned (but appropriate and enjoyable) activity. In such a situation – when this kind of **magic moment** suddenly presents itself – we would be foolish to plough on with our plan regardless. On the contrary, a good teacher will recognise the magic moment for what it is and adapt what they had planned to do accordingly. Magic moments are precious, in other words, and should not be wasted just because we didn't know they were going to happen.

There will always be a tension between what we had planned to do and what we actually do when magic moments or unforeseen problems present themselves. It is the mark of a good teacher to know when and how to deal with unplanned events, and how to balance a proposal for action with appropriate flexibility.

Lesson shapes

A good lesson needs to contain a judicious blend of **coherence** and **variety**. Coherence means that students can see a logical pattern to the lesson. Even if there are three separate activities, for example, there has to be some connection between them – or at the very least a perceptible reason for changing direction. In this context, it would not make sense to have students listen to an audio track, ask a few comprehension questions and then change the activity completely to something totally unrelated to the listening. And if the following activity only lasted for five minutes before, again, something completely different was attempted, we might well want to call the lesson incoherent.

Nevertheless, the effect of having a class do a 45-minute drill would be equally damaging. The lack of variety, coupled with the relentlessness of such a procedure, would militate against the possibility of real student engagement. However present it might be at the beginning of the session, it would be unlikely to be sustained. There has to be some variety in a lesson period.

There are other methodological reasons why a 45-minute drill is inappropriate, too. Drilling concentrates only on the *study* aspect of our three ESA learning elements (see page 52). In effective lessons, the teacher has thought (and is thinking) carefully about the balance of *engagement, study* and *activation,* and how one can lead to the others in a variety of different sequences such as the *straight arrows, boomerang* and *patchwork* sequences we discussed in Chapter 4. The moment we think of lessons in this way, both variety and coherence are almost guaranteed.

The ideal compromise, then, is to plan a lesson that has an internal coherence but which nevertheless allows students to do different things as it progresses.

Planning questions

Unless teachers walk towards a class with absolutely no idea about (or interest in) what is going to happen when they get there, they will have thought about what they are going to do. These thoughts may be extremely detailed and formalised, or they may be vaguer and more informal. When we discuss plan formats on page 160, we will see differences between more and less formal thinking of this kind, but in every case teachers will be answering seven fundamental questions when they decide what activities to take to a lesson.

Who exactly are the students for this activity?
The make-up of the class will influence the way we plan. The students' age, level, cultural background and individual characteristics have to be taken into account when deciding what activities, texts or methodologies to use in the classroom. This includes an understanding of the kinds of individual differences in learning style, for example, that we discussed in Chapter 1.

What do we want to do and why?
We have to decide what we want to do in the lesson in terms of both activities, skills and language. We also need to know why we want to do it. It might be because we ourselves like the activity, or because we think it will be appropriate for a particular day or a particular group. There is nothing wrong with deciding to do an activity simply because we think it will make students feel good.

However, before deciding to use an activity just because we or the students might like it, we need to try to predict what it will achieve. What will students know, be able to do, understand or feel after the activity that they did not know, were not able to do, did not understand or feel before? What, in other words, is the learning outcome of the activity?

Examples of what an activity might achieve include giving students a greater understanding of an area of vocabulary, providing them with better listening strategies, teaching them how to construct conditional sentences, improving their oral fluency or raising the morale of the group through appropriate cooperative interaction.

How long will it take?
Some activities which, at first glance, look very imaginative end up lasting for only a very

short time. Others demand considerable setting-up time, discussion time, student-planning time, etc. The students' confidence in the teacher can be undermined if they never finish what they set out to do; students are frequently irritated when teachers run on after the bell has gone because they haven't finished an activity. Teachers, for their part, are made uncomfortable if they have overestimated the amount of time something might take and are thus left with time on their hands and no clear idea what to do. There is no absolute way of preventing such problems from occurring, of course, but we should at least try to estimate how long each activity will take (based on our experience and knowledge of the class) so that we can measure our progress as the lesson continues against our proposed 'timetable'. We can also plan for our material taking too little time by having some spare activities with us (see page 160). If we have built-in lesson stages in our plan, we can decide, as the lesson progresses, where we might want to veer away from the plan if we see that we have taken too much time over one particular element of it.

How does it work?

If we want to use the photograph-choosing activity on page 124, we need to know how we and our students are going to do it. Who does what first? How and when should students be put in pairs or groups? When do we give instructions? What should those instructions be? What should we be doing while the students are working in groups?, etc. Experienced teachers may have procedures firmly fixed in their minds, but even they, when they try something new, need to think carefully about the mechanics of an activity.

What will be needed?

Teachers have to decide whether they are going to use the board, a CD or tape player, an overhead projector, a data projector, some role-cards or a computer (or computers). It is important to think about the *best* way of doing something (in other words, the most effective piece of classroom equipment – see Appendix A on page 252), rather than automatically choosing the most technologically exciting option. It is also important to consider the physical environment of the classroom itself and how that might affect whatever teaching equipment we wish to use.

What might go wrong?

If teachers try to identify problems that might arise in the lesson, they are in a much better position to deal with them if and when they occur. This will also give the teacher insight into the language and/or the activity which is to be used. This isn't to say that we can predict everything that might happen. Nevertheless, thinking around our activities – trying to put ourselves in the students' minds, and gauging how they might react – will make us much more aware of potential pitfalls than we might otherwise be.

How will it fit in with what comes before and after it?

An activity on its own may be useful and engaging and may generate plenty of good language. But what connection, if any, does it have with the activities which come before and after it? How does it fit into our need for the three ESA lesson elements? Is there a language tie-in to previous or future activities? Perhaps two or three activities are linked by topic, one leading into the other (like the threads of a **multi-lesson sequence** – see page 163). Perhaps an activity has no connection with the one before it: it is there to break up the monotony of a lesson or to act as a 'gear change'. Perhaps we may decide to start our lesson with a short **icebreaker** (sometimes called a **warmer**) for no other reason than to get the students in a good mood for the lesson that is to follow. The point of answering this question for ourselves is to ensure that we have some reasonable vision of the overall shape of our lesson and that it is not composed of unrelated scraps.

Plan formats

When making plans, some teachers write down exactly what they are going to do and note down each sentence that the students are going to say. Others use note-form hints to themselves (e.g. 'T checks comprehension') or just write 'pairwork' or 'solowork' or 'whole class', for example, to describe how they are going to do something. Some teachers write down notes with ordered paragraph headings, whereas others produce flow diagrams or random notes. Some just write short headings like 'going to' or 'photograph activity' or 'Little Rock reading' to remind them what to do. And of course there are teachers who keep the whole plan in their heads. This may be completely appropriate for them, of course, but won't help anyone else (observers, possible substitute teachers, etc) to know what they had in mind.

When teachers are observed – or when an institution asks for formal plans – the exact format of the plan may depend on the personal preferences of trainers, exam schemes or institutions (schools, colleges, etc). However, in some form or other, the following elements (which match the kinds of questions we asked in the previous section) are usually included:

Description of the students: this includes anything from a general picture of the group (its level, age range, atmosphere, etc) to detailed descriptions of individual students (what they find easy or difficult, how they respond to different activities, etc).

Aims and objectives: we generally say what we hope to achieve; the more specific we are, the easier it will be for us – and anyone observing – to see whether or not we have achieved those aims. Broad aims like 'have a good time' are bound to be less useful than 'sensitise students to uses of pitch and intonation to indicate enthusiasm (or lack of it)'. Most lessons will have a series of primary and secondary aims.

Procedures: the meat of the plan is in the description of how it will be executed. The section on procedures can include patterns of interaction. We might write T → SS (for times when the teacher talks to the whole class), S → S (for pairwork) or SSS → SSS (for groupwork); or we could write 'groups', 'pairs', etc, or record these patterns in some other way.

Frequently we will include timings as well, so that we have some idea of how long we expect things to take. We will also include the actual procedures, such as 'students look through the pictures and match them with the phrases'.

Anticipated problems: teachers frequently make some kind of a list of potential difficulties – and suggestions about what to do if they arise. They might consider what they would do if a computer or other piece of equipment failed them – or if some other student-based eventuality occurred (such as the activity being a lot more difficult for the class than expected).

Extra activities/material (just in case): many teachers make a note of extra activities they could include if things go quicker than anticipated.

Material to be used in the lesson: especially when they are to be observed, teachers attach examples of the material they are to use with the students to their plan.

Group:	Date:	Time:	No. of students:
Recent topic work:		**Recent language work:**	

Aims: (stated in input terms, i.e. what the teacher intends to do)

Objectives: (stated in output terms, i.e. what the students are expected to do)

Assessment:

Materials:

Anticipated problems:

Timing	Teacher activity	Student activity	Success indicators	Aims of the stage

Additional possibilities:

Homework/Further work:

Lesson plan blank

The actual form of a plan becomes important for teachers in training, especially when they are about to be observed. In such circumstances, the plan format is dictated by the training program and the trainers who teach it. The plan blank above, for example, shows one such institutional template.

There are two elements in this template that we have not so far mentioned. Firstly, there is a column called *Success indicators* where the planner has to note down how they will be able to measure the success of what happens. This forces the planner to focus on exactly how both teacher and students will know if something has worked, in other words, if the learning outcomes have been met. There is also a final heading for *Homework/Further work* which will show the planner thinking ahead beyond the actual lesson to be taught.

The (first page of a) completed lesson plan on page 163 shows how a different plan blank (from a different institution) might be filled in.

Notice that, in contrast to the plan blank on page 161, there is no column here for success indicators, but there is a special column for *Interaction* (who's interacting with whom), since the trainer/designers perceive this as being of special significance.

Other trainers and schools may have their own formats, of course, and they may look significantly different from the two templates shown here. A lot will depend on the priorities of the training course – and perhaps the teaching qualification which the trainees are working towards. There is no one correct format, in other words, although, of course, trainees will almost certainly have to conform to the format that is used on their particular training course.

To sum up: the purpose of a plan is to be as useful as possible to the people who are going to use it (whether they are the teachers themselves, their observers or an examination board). This, in the end, is what should guide the form in which teachers put their thoughts down on paper.

Planning a sequence of lessons

We have stressed the need for variety in classroom activities and teacher behaviour as an antidote to student (and teacher) boredom. This means, as we have seen, that when teachers plan a lesson, they build in changes in pace and a variety of different activities. The same principles also apply to a sequence of lessons stretching, for example, over two weeks or a month. Once again, students will want to see a coherent pattern of progress and **topic-linking** so that there is a transparent connection between lessons, and so that they can perceive some overall aims and objectives to their program of study. Most find this preferable to a series of 'one-off' lessons.

However, two dangers may prejudice the success of a sequence of lessons. The first is **predictability**; if students know exactly what to expect, they are likely to be less motivated than if their curiosity is aroused. The second is sameness; students may feel less enthusiastic about today's lesson if it starts with exactly the same kind of activity as yesterday's lesson. Once again, however, thinking about the three **ESA** learning elements will help us to avoid such problems. We recognise that there are many different ways of combining and sequencing the three elements, and that our choice of how they should be sequenced will often depend upon the task, the level and age of the students and what exactly we want them to achieve.

According to Tessa Woodward in her book on planning (see the reference on page 265), an ideal multi-lesson sequence has **threads** running through it. These might be topic threads, language threads (grammar, vocabulary, etc) or skill threads (reading, listening, etc). Over a period of lessons students should be able to see some interconnectivity, in other words, rather than a random collection of activities. The need for both coherence and variety is just as necessary in multi-lesson sequences as it is in single lessons.

Seven Language and Culture SP Date: Length of class: 150 minutes Level: basic Book: World Link Intro A							
Class profile		There are 13 students in this group, 5 men and 8 women. Most of them are between 16 and 25 years old. They have had little exposure to spoken English. They have had few opportunities to speak English.					
Timetable fit		This is the second week of the course. Ss are being taken from a very basic level to the ability to manage simple conversation such as: asking about names, talking briefly about occupations, greeting, asking and giving phone numbers, describing people, talking about locations, informal phone conversations, and talking about current activities. In this class they will produce y/n questions with be, they will practise the vocabulary related to the family, which was introduced in the previous class, and they will be introduced to numbers and to the irregular form of the plural. Ss will also be provided with practice related to the new structures.					
Terminal objective(s)		1 Ss will review the vocabulary learned in the previous lesson. 2 Ss will learn new vocabulary and grammar. 3 Ss will learn to say thank you.					

TIME	STAGE	AIM	ANTICIPATED PROBLEMS AND SOLUTIONS	PROCEDURES	INTERACTION	MATERIAL
13'	Warm up	Review the adjectives learned in the previous lesson in a meaningful context	P: Ss might have a hard time filling in the slips. S: circulate a lot during the activity and check if Ss are on the right track. P: Ss might make mistakes during the practice. S: encourage to correct themselves.	1. tell Ss they have to fill in the chart with their idea of place, where it is and what it is like. 2. distribute the handout to Ss. 3. give then time to fill it in. 4. encourage each S to talk to another 3 Ss. 5. at the end, Ss report their findings as to what place they would like to go on their holiday.	T X sss Individual Cocktail	Slips for Ss to fill in
10'	Vocabulary presentation	Introduce personal items	P: Ss might not understand meaning of a new piece of vocabulary. S: encourage Ss to explain the definitions to each other.	1. give Ss the poster with the pictures and Ss to match the slips with the names of the items. 2. work on the pronunciation of each of the items (number of syllables, stressed syllables). 3. ask Ss to copy it into their notebooks by drawing as well.	group T X ssss Individual	Poster Slips Glue
10'	Grammar practice	Introduce the difference between a and an (indefinite articles)	P: Ss might not understand the instructions of the exercise. S: have a S who understood the instructions in English clarify the instructions in Portuguese to the others.	1. put the poster with the personal items on the floor and tell Ss they will have to put before each of them a or an. The group should agree on what to put where and they should be able to justify their choices. 2. elicit the rule and put it on the bb. 3. Ss copy the bb record.	Group T X sss	Poster Slips with the articles Board Glue

Page 1 of a completed lesson plan

The following lesson notes show how three such threads (topic, grammar (tense) and a skill (reading)) can be woven into five consecutive classes:

Threads	MONDAY	TUESDAY	WEDNESDAY	THURSDAY	FRIDAY
Animals vocabulary thread (10 mins each time)	Parts of cat's body	Review + cat words	Review + cat metaphors	Review and start fish vocab	Review and start fish verbs
Tenses thread (30 mins each time)	Regular past simple first person	Review + all persons	Review + all negatives	Review + some irregulars	Review and start 'Did you … ?' questions
Reading thread (20 mins each time)	Introduction of a graded reader	First two pages + comp. questions	Review and Chap. 1	Study of past forms in Chap. 1	Oral summary of Chap. 1 + vocab in notebooks

Lesson threads

Perhaps the most important thing to remember, however, is that a long teaching sequence (e.g. two weeks) is made up of shorter sequences (e.g. six lessons) which are themselves made up of smaller sequences (one or two per lesson perhaps). And at the level of a teaching sequence we have to ensure the presence of our three elements, *engage*, *study* and *activate* in their various permutations.

After the lesson (and before the next)

In the lesson plan blank on page 161 there was a column labelled *Success indicators*, so that teachers could work out how to judge if a lesson (or part of a lesson) had been a success. Evaluation of how well things have gone (for both teacher and students) is vital if our lessons are to develop in response to our students' progress. In other words, we need to plan future lessons on the basis of what happened in previous classes. Not only that, but our decision about whether to use an activity more than once (or whether we need to change the way we use that activity) will depend on how successful it was the first time we tried it.

When we evaluate lessons or activities, we need to ask ourselves questions such as, Was the activity successful? Did the students enjoy it? Did they learn anything from it? What *exactly* did they get from the activity? How could the activity be changed to make it more effective next time? Unless we ask ourselves such questions, we are in danger of continuing with activities and techniques that either do not work, or, at the very least, are not as successful as they might be with appropriate modification.

One kind of data which will help us evaluate lessons and activities is **feedback from students**. We might, for example, ask them simple questions such as, 'Did you like that exercise? Did you find it useful?' and see what they say. But not all students will discuss topics like this openly in class. It may be better to ask them to write their answers down and hand them in. A simple way of doing this is to ask students once every fortnight, for example, to write down two things they want more of and two things they want less of. The answers we get may prove a fruitful place to start a discussion, and we will then be able to modify what happens in class, if we think it appropriate, in the light of our students' feelings. Such modifications will greatly enhance our ability to manage the class.

We can also give students special evaluation forms where they have to rate different activities with a score, or put them in some kind of order and then add comments about what they thought. We might ask students to submit comments by email.

Another way of getting reactions to new techniques is to invite a colleague into the classroom and ask them to observe what happens and make suggestions afterwards. This kind of **peer observation** is most successful when both teachers discuss the content and practice of the lesson both before and after the observation. It is important that the colleague who comes into our classroom does so in order to offer constructive advice rather than to concentrate on our apparent failings. The lesson could also be videoed. This will allow us to watch the effect of what happened in the lesson with more objectivity than when we try to observe what is happening as it takes place.

Some teachers keep **journals** in which they record their thoughts about what happened as soon as possible after the lesson has finished. In that way they can read through their comments later and reflect on how they now feel about what happened.

Good teachers also need to assess how well their students are progressing. This can be done through a variety of measures including homework assignments, speaking activities where the teacher scores the participation of each student and frequent small progress tests (see Chapter 13).

Conclusions | *In this chapter we have:*

- discussed reasons for planning, showing its advantages both for student confidence in the teacher and also as a framework for teachers to work from. We said how important plans are for teachers in training.

- stressed that plans are proposals for action rather than the action itself. Teachers need to be receptive and flexible when unforeseen problems and magic moments turn up in a lesson.

- talked about the need for a blend of both coherence and variety in a lesson plan.

- said that whatever the format the plan takes, it should be based on who the students are, what we want them to do, how long each activity will take, how the activity actually works, what equipment will be needed, what might go wrong and how what we are planning will fit into what comes before and after it.

- discussed different plan formats, saying that there are many different ways of laying out the information. A lot will depend (especially on training courses) on who the plan is written for – apart from the teacher. However, we have suggested that most formal plans should include a description of the students, a statement of aims and objectives, a description of procedures (including who will be interacting with whom, and how long each activity will take), anticipated problems, extra materials and the material to be used in the lesson.

- talked about planning a sequence of lessons where topic-linking is important, but there are dangers of predictability and sameness. We introduced the concept of lesson threads which run through a sequence of lessons.

- said that it is important to plan future lessons on the basis of what has gone before, and using student feedback and our own observation to inform our future decisions.

13 | Testing

- Reasons for testing students
- Marking tests
- Good tests
- Designing tests
- Test types

Reasons for testing students

At various stages during their learning, students may need or want to be tested on their ability in the English language. If they arrive at a school and need to be put in a class at an appropriate level, they may do a **placement test**. This often takes the form of a number of discrete (indirect) items (see below), coupled with an oral interview and perhaps a longer piece of writing. The purpose of the test is to find out not only what students know, but also what they don't know. As a result, they can be placed in an appropriate class.

At various stages during a term or semester, we may give students **progress tests**. These have the function of seeing how students are getting on with the lessons, and how well they have assimilated what they have been taught over the last week, two weeks or a month.

At the end of a term, semester or year, we may want to do a final **achievement test** (sometimes called an **exit test**) to see how well students have learnt everything. Their results on this test may determine what class they are placed in next year (in some schools, failing students have to repeat a year), or may be entered into some kind of school-leaving certificate. Typically, achievement tests include a variety of test types and measure the students' abilities in all four skills, as well as their knowledge of grammar and vocabulary.

Many students enter for **public examinations** such as those offered by the University of Cambridge ESOL, Pitman or Trinity College in the UK, and in the US, the University of Michigan and TOEFL and TOEIC. These **proficiency tests** are designed to show what level a student has reached at any one time, and are used by employers and universities, for example, who want a reliable measure of a student's language abilities.

So far in this chapter we have been talking about testing in terms of 'one-off' events, usually taking place at the end of a period of time (except for placement tests). These 'sudden death' events (where ability is measured at a particular point in time) are very different from **continuous assessment**, where the students' progress is measured as it is happening, and where the measure of a student's achievement is the work done all through the learning period and not just at the end. One form of continuous assessment is the language **portfolio**, where students collect examples of their work over time, so that these pieces of work can all be taken into account when an evaluation is made of their language progress and achievement. Such portfolios (called *dossiers* in this case) are part of the **CEF** (Common European Framework), which also asks language learners to complete *language* *passports* (showing their language abilities in all the languages they speak) and *language biographies* (describing their experiences and progress).

There are other forms of continuous assessment, too, which allow us to keep an eye on how well our students are doing. Such **continuous recording** may involve, among other things, keeping a record of who speaks in lessons and how often they do it, how compliant students are with homework tasks and how well they do them, and also how well they interact with their classmates.

Some students seem to be well suited to taking progress and achievement tests as the main way of having their language abilities measured. Others do less well in such circumstances and are better able to show their abilities in continuous assessment environments. The best solution is probably a judicious blend of both.

Good tests

Good tests are those that do the job they are designed to do and which convince the people taking and marking them that they work. Good tests also have a positive rather than a negative effect on both students and teachers.

A good test is **valid**. This means that it does what it says it will. In other words, if we say that a certain test is a good measure of a student's reading ability, then we need to be able to show that this is the case. There is another kind of validity, too, in that when students and teachers see the test, they should think it looks like the real thing – that it has **face validity**. As they sit in front of their test paper or in front of the screen, the students need to have confidence that this test will work (even if they are nervous about their own abilities). However reliable the test is (see below) face validity demands that the students *think* it is reliable and valid.

A good test should have marking **reliability**. Not only should it be fairly easy to mark, but anyone marking it should come up with the same result as someone else. However, since different people can (and do) mark differently, there will always be the danger that where tests involve anything other than computer-scorable questions, different results will be given by different markers. For this reason, a test should be designed to minimise the effect of individual marking styles.

When designing tests, one of the things we have to take into account is the practicality of the test. We need to work out how long it will take both to sit the test and also to mark it. The test will be worthless if it is so long that no one has the time to do it. In the same way, we have to think of the physical constraints of the test situation. Some speaking tests, especially for international exams, ask not only for an examiner but also for an **interlocutor** (someone who participates in a conversation with a student). But this is clearly not practical for teachers working on their own.

Tests have a marked **washback/backwash effect**, whether they are public exams or institution-designed progress or achievement tests. The washback effect occurs when teachers see the form of the test their students are going to have to take and then, as a result, start teaching *for* the test. For example, they concentrate on teaching the techniques for answering certain types of question rather than thinking in terms of what language students need to learn in general. This is completely understandable since teachers want as many of their students as possible to pass the test. Indeed, teachers would be careless if they did not introduce their students to the kinds of test item they are likely to encounter in the exam. But this does not mean that teachers should allow such test preparation to dominate their lessons and deflect from their main teaching aims and procedures.

The washback effect has a negative effect on teaching if the test fails to *mirror* our teaching because then we will be tempted to make our teaching fit the test, rather than the other way round. Many modern public examinations have improved greatly from their more traditional versions, so that they often do reflect contemporary teaching practice. As a result, the washback effect does not have the baleful influence on teaching which we have been discussing.

When we design our own progress and achievement tests, we need to try to ensure that we are not asking students to do things which are completely different from the activities they have taken part in during our lessons. That would clearly be unfair.

Finally, we need to remember that tests have a powerful effect on student **motivation**. Firstly, students often work a lot harder than normal when there is a test or examination in sight. Secondly, they can be greatly encouraged by success in tests, or, conversely, demotivated by doing badly. For this reason, we may want to try to discourage students from taking public examinations that they are clearly going to fail, and when designing our own progress and achievement tests, we may want to consider the needs of all our students, not just the ones who are doing well. This does not mean writing easy tests, but it does suggest that when writing progress tests, especially, we do not want to design the test so that students fail unnecessarily – and are consequently demotivated by the experience.

Test types

When designing tests, we can either write **discrete items**, or ask students to become involved in more **integrative** language use. Discrete-item testing means only testing one thing at a time (e.g. testing a verb tense or a word), whereas integrative testing means asking students to use a variety of language and skills to complete a task successfully. A further distinction needs to be made between direct and indirect test items. A **direct test item** is one that asks students to do something with language (e.g. write a letter, read and reply to a newspaper article or take part in a conversation). Direct test items are almost always integrative. Indirect test items are those which test the students' knowledge of language rather than getting them to use it. **Indirect test items** might focus on, say, word collocations (see page 75) or the correct use of modal verbs (see page 69). Direct test items have more to do with *activation*, whereas indirect items are more closely related to *study* – that is the construction of language.

Indirect test items

There are many different ways of testing the students' knowledge of language construction. We will look at three of the most common.

Multiple choice

Multiple-choice questions are those where students are given alternatives to choose from, as in the following example:

> **Circle the correct answer.**
>
> You must _____ here on time.
>
> **a** to get   **b** getting   **c** to have get   **d** get

Sometimes students are instructed to choose the 'correct' answer (because only one answer is possible), as in the example above. But sometimes, instead, they can be told to choose the 'best' answer (because, although more than one answer is possible, one stands out as the most appropriate), e.g.

> **Circle the best answer.**
>
> Police are worried about the level of _____ crime.
>
> **a** juvenile   **b** childish   **c** young   **d** infant

Multiple-choice questions have the great advantage of being easy to mark. Answer sheets can be read by computer, or can be marked by putting a transparency over the answer sheet which shows the circled correct letters. Markers do not have to worry, then, about the language in the questions; it is simply a matter of checking the correct letters for each question.

One problem with multiple-choice questions lies in the choice of **distractors**, that is the three incorrect (or inappropriate) answers. For while it may not be difficult to write one obvious distractor (e.g. answer **a** 'to get' in the first example above), because that is a mistake that students commonly make, it becomes less easy to come up with three items which will all sort out those students who know how this piece of language works from the ones who don't. In other words, there is a danger that we will either distract too many students (even those who should get the question right) or too few (in which case the question has not done its job of differentiating students).

Multiple-choice questions can be used to test reading and listening comprehension (we can also use **true/false questions** for this: students circle 'T' or 'F' next to statements concerning material they have just read or listened to).

The washback effect of multiple-choice questions leads some people to find them unattractive, since training students to be good at multiple-choice questions may not help them to become better language learners. And there is a limit to how much we can test with this kind of indirect item. Nevertheless, multiple-choice questions are very attractive in terms of scorer reliability.

Fill-in and cloze

This extremely common form of indirect testing involves the examinee writing a word in a gap in a sentence or paragraph, e.g.

> Yesterday I went **a** _____ the cinema **b** _____ my friend Clare. I enjoyed the film **c** _____ she did not.

Gap-fill (or **fill-in**) items like this are fairly easy to write, though it is often difficult to leave a gap where only one item is possible. In such cases, we will need to be aware of what different answers we can accept. They also make marking a little more complex, though we can design answer sheets where students only have to write the required word against different letters, e.g.

a	_____
b	_____
c	_____

A variation on fill-ins and gap-fills is the **cloze** procedure, where gaps are put into a text at regular intervals (say every sixth word). As a result, without the test writer having to think about it too much, students are forced to produce a wide range of different words based on everything from collocation to verb formation, etc, as in the following example.

> All around the world, students **a** _____ all ages are learning to **b** _____ English, but their reasons for **c** _____ to study English can differ **d** _____. Some students, of course, only **e** _____ English because it is on **f** _____ curriculum at primary or secondary **g** _____, but for others, studying the **h** _____ reflects some kind of a **i** _____.

The random selection of gaps (every sixth word) is difficult to use in all circumstances. Sometimes the sixth word will be impossible to guess – or will give rise to far too many alternatives (e.g. gaps **c** and **d** above). Most test designers use a form of **modified cloze** to counteract this situation, trying to adhere to some kind of random distribution (e.g. making every sixth word into a blank), but using their common sense to ensure that students have a chance of filling in the gaps successfully – and thus demonstrating their knowledge of English.

Transformation

In **transformation items** students are asked to change the form of words and phrases to show their knowledge of syntax and word grammar. In the following test type they are given a sentence and then asked to produce an equivalent sentence using a given word:

> **Rewrite the sentence so that it means the same. Use the word in bold**
>
> Could I borrow five pounds, please?
>
> **lend** _____

In order to complete the item successfully, the students not only have to know the meaning of *borrow* and *lend*, but also how to use them in grammatical constructions.

A variation of this technique is designed to focus more exactly on word grammar. Here, students have to complete lines in a text using the correct form of a given word, e.g.

It was a *terrifying* performance.	*terrify*
The acrobats showed _____ no fear even though	*absolute*
their feats of _____ shocked the crowd into stunned silence.	*dare*

These kinds of transformations work very well as a test of the students' underlying knowledge of grammar and vocabulary. However, the items are quite difficult to construct.

There are many other kinds of indirect test item. We can ask students to put jumbled words in order, to make correct sentences and questions. We can ask them to identify and correct mistakes or match the beginnings and ends of sentences. Our choice of test item will depend on which, if any, of these techniques we have used in our teaching since it will always be unfair to give students test items unlike anything they have seen before.

Direct test items

In direct test items, we ask students to *use* language to do something, instead of just testing their knowledge of how the language itself works. We might ask our students to write instructions for a simple task (such as using a vending machine or assembling a shelving system) or to give an oral mini-presentation.

There is no real limit to the kinds of tasks we might ask students to perform. The following list gives some possibilities:

Reading and listening

Some reading and writing test items look a bit like indirect items (e.g. when students are given multiple-choice questions about a particular word in a text, for example, or have to answer T/F questions about a particular sentence). But at other times we might ask students to choose the best summary of what they have heard or read. We might ask them to put a set of pictures in order as they read or listen to a story, or complete a phone message form (for a listening task) or fill out a summary form (for a reading task).

Many reading and listening tests are a blend of direct and indirect testing. We can ask students direct language – or text-focused – questions as well as testing their global understanding.

Writing

Direct tests of writing might include getting students to write leaflets based on information supplied in an accompanying text, or having them write compositions, such as narrative and discursive essays. We can ask students to write 'transactional letters' (that is letters replying to an advertisement, or something they have read in the paper, etc). In transactional writing we expect students to include and refer to information they are given.

Speaking

We can interview students, or we can put them in pairs and ask them to perform a number of tasks. These might include having them discuss the similarities and differences between two pictures (see information-gap activities on page 129); they might discuss how to furnish a room, or talk about any other topic we select for them. We can ask them to role-play certain situations (see page 125), such as buying a ticket or asking for information in a shop, or we might ask them to talk about a picture we show them.

When designing direct test items for our students, we need to remember two crucial facts. The first is that, as with indirect tests, direct tests should have items which look like the kind of tasks students have been practising in their lessons. In other words, there is no point in giving students tasks which, because they are unfamiliar, confuse them. The result of this will be that students cannot demonstrate properly how well they can use the language, and this will make the test worthless.

Direct test items are much more difficult to mark than indirect items. This is because our response to a piece of writing or speaking will almost certainly be very subjective –

unless we do something to modify this subjectivity. We will now go on to look at how this can be done.

Marking tests

The marking of tests is reasonably simple if the markers only have to tick boxes or individual words (though even here human error can often creep in). Things are a lot more complex, however, when we have to evaluate a more integrative piece of work.

One way of marking a piece of writing, for example, is to give it an overall score (say A or B, or 65%). This will be based on our experience of the level we are teaching and on our 'gut-instinct' reaction to what we read. This is the way that many essays are marked in various different branches of education and sometimes such marking can be highly appropriate. However, 'gut instinct' is a highly subjective phenomenon. Our judgment can be heavily swayed by factors we are not even conscious of. All students will remember times when they didn't understand why they got a low mark for an essay which looked remarkably similar to one of their classmates' higher-scoring pieces.

There are two ways of countering the danger of marker subjectivity. The first is to involve other people. When two or three people look at the same piece of work and, independently, give it a score, we can have more confidence in the evaluation of the writing than if just one person looks at it.

The other way of making the marking more objective is to use marking scales for a range of different items. If we are marking a student's oral presentation, we might use the following scales:

	0	1	2	3	4	5
Grammar						
Vocabulary						
Pronunciation						
Coherence						
Fluency						

This kind of scale forces us to look at our student's speaking in more detail than is allowed by an overall impressionistic mark. It also allows for differences in individual performance: a student may get marked down on pronunciation, but score more highly on use of grammar, for example. As a result, the student's final mark out of a total of 25 may reflect his or her ability more accurately than a one-mark impression will do. But we are still left with the problem of knowing exactly why we should give a student 2 rather than 3 for pronunciation. What exactly do students have to do to score 5 for grammar? What would make us give students 0 for fluency? Subjectivity is still an issue here (though it is less problematic because we are forcing ourselves to evaluate different aspects of the students' performance).

One way of trying to make marking scales more objective is to write careful descriptions of what the different scores for each category actually represent. Here, for example, is a scale for assessing writing, which uses descriptions:

	5 Exemplary	4 Strong	3 Satisfactory	2 Developing	1 Weak
Ideas/Content	Original treatment of ideas, well-developed from start to finish, focused topic with relevant, strong supporting detail.	Clear, interesting ideas enhanced by appropriate details.	Evident main idea with some supporting details. May have some irrelevant material, gaps in needed information.	Some attempt at support but main topic may be too general or confused by irrelevant details.	Writing lacks a central idea; development is minimal or non-existent, wanders.
Organisation	Effectively organised in a logical and interesting way. Has a creative and engaging introduction and conclusion.	Structure moves the reader smoothly through the text. Well organised with an inviting introduction and a satisfying closure.	Organisation is appropriate but conventional. There is an obvious attempt at an introduction and conclusion.	An effort has been made to organise the piece, but it may be a 'list' of events. The introduction and conclusion are not well developed.	A lack of structure makes this piece hard to follow. Lead and conclusion may be weak or non-existent.
Voice	Passionate, compelling, full of energy and commitment. Shows emotion and generates an emotional response from the reader.	Expressive, engaging, sincere tone with good sense of audience. Writer behind the words comes through occasionally.	Pleasant but not distinctive tone and persona. Voice is appropriate to audience and purpose.	Voice may be mechanical, artificial or inappropriate. Writer seems to lack a sense of audience.	Writing tends to be flat or stiff. Style does not suit audience or purpose.
Word Choice	Carefully chosen words convey strong, fresh, vivid images consistently throughout the piece.	Word choice is functional and appropriate with some attempt at description; may overuse adjectives and adverbs.	Words may be correct but mundane; writing uses patterns of conversation rather than book language and structure.	Word choice is monotonous; may be repetitious or immature.	Limited vocabulary range.
Sentence Fluency	High degree of craftsmanship; control of rhythm and flow so the writing sounds almost musical to read aloud. Variation in sentence length and forms adds interest and rhythm.	The piece has an easy flow and rhythm with a good variety of sentence length and structures.	The writing shows some general sense of rhythm and flow, but many sentences follow a similar structure.	Many similar sentence beginnings and patterns with little sense of rhythm; sounds choppy to read aloud. May have many short sentences or run-ons.	No real sentence sense – may ramble or sound choppy to read aloud.
Conventions	The writing contains few, if any, errors in conventions. The writer shows control over a wide range of conventions for this grade level.	Generally, the writing is free from errors, but there may be occasional errors in more complex words and sentence constructions.	Occasional errors are noticeable but minor. The writer uses conventions with enough skill to make the paper easily readable.	The writing suffers from more frequent errors, inappropriate to the grade level, but a reader can still follow it.	Errors in conventions make the writing difficult to follow. The writer seems to know some conventions, but confuse many more.

A marking scale for writing

This framework suggests that the students' writing will be marked fairly and objectively. But it is extremely cumbersome, and for teachers to use it well, they will need training and familiarity with the different descriptions provided here.

When marking tests – especially progress tests we design ourselves – we need to strike a balance between totally subjective one-mark-only evaluation on the one hand, and over-complexity in marking-scale frameworks on the other.

Designing tests

When we write tests for our classes, we need to bear in mind the characteristics of good tests which we discussed on pages 167–168. We will think very carefully about how practical our tests will be in terms of time (including how long it will take us to mark them).

When writing progress tests, it is important to try to work out what we want to achieve, especially since the students' results in a progress test will have an immediate effect on their motivation. As a consequence, we need to think about how difficult we want the test to be. Is it designed so that only the best students will pass, or should everyone get a good mark? Some test designers, especially for public exams, appear to have an idea of how many students should get a high grade, what percentage of examinees should pass satisfactorily, and what an acceptable failing percentage would look like.

Progress tests should not work like that, however. Their purpose is only to see how well the students have learnt what they have been taught. Our intention, as far as possible, should be to allow the students to show us what they know and can do, not what they don't know and can't do.

When designing tests for our classes, it is helpful to make a list of the things we want to test. This list might include grammar items (e.g. the present continuous) or direct tasks (e.g. sending an email to arrange a meeting). When we have made our lists, we can decide how much importance to give to each item. We can then reflect these different levels of importance either by making specific elements take up most of the time (or space) on the test, or by *weighting the marks* to reflect the importance of a particular element. In other words, we might give a writing task double the marks of an equivalent indirect test item to reflect our belief in the importance of direct test types.

When we have decided what to include, we write the test. However, it is important that we do not just hand it straight over to the students to take. It will be much more sensible to show the test to colleagues (who frequently notice things we had not thought of) first. If possible, it is a good idea to try the test out with students of roughly the same level as the ones it is designed for. This will show us if there are any items which are more difficult (or easier) than we thought, and it will highlight any items which are unclear – or which cause unnecessary problems.

Finally, once we have given the test and marked it, we should see if we need to make any changes to it if we are to use some or all of it again.

It is not always necessary to write our own tests, however. Many coursebooks now include test items or test generators which can be used instead of home-grown versions. However, such tests may not take account of the particular situation or learning experiences of our own classes.

Conclusions | *In this chapter we have:*

- discussed the different reasons that students take tests, and detailed the differences between placement tests, progress tests, achievement tests, public examinations and proficiency tests.

- said that good tests are both valid and reliable – and that face validity ('looking good') is also important.

- mentioned the fact that test design may be influenced by physical constraints (e.g. time and money).

- talked about the washback effect which can sometimes persuade teachers to work only on exam preparation with their students while ignoring general language development. We have said this is not usually a good thing. We talked about the effect of success or failure in tests on students' motivation.

- looked at examples of different test types and items including discrete test items (one thing at a time) and integrative test items (where students use a variety of language and skills); direct test items (where students are asked to do things with the language – e.g. writing a report) and indirect test items (where they are tested about the language – e.g. grammar tests).

- discussed the issue of subjectivity when it comes to marking tests and shown how marking scales can counter such subjectivity – though if they are over-detailed they may become cumbersome.

- said that when preparing tests, we need to decide what we want to test and how important each part of a test is in relation to the other parts. We said that teachers should show their tests to colleagues and try them out before using them 'for real'.

What if?

- **What if students are all at different levels?**
- **What if the class is very big?**
- **What if students keep using their own language?**
- **What if students don't do homework?**
- **What if students are uncooperative?**

- **What if students don't want to talk?**
- **What if students don't understand the audio track?**
- **What if some students finish before everybody else?**

What if students are all at different levels?

One of the biggest problems teachers face is classes where the students are at different levels – some with quite competent English, some whose English isn't very good, and some whose English is only just getting started. Even if things are not quite so extreme, teachers of English – along with teachers of other curriculum subjects – regularly face **mixed-ability groups** where different individuals are at different levels and have different abilities. What then are the possible ways of dealing with the situation?

Use different materials/technology

When teachers know who the good and less good students are, they can form different groups. While one group is working on a piece of language study (e.g. the past continuous), the other group might be reading a story or doing Internet-based research. Later, while the better group or groups are discussing a topic, the weaker group or groups might be doing a parallel writing exercise, or sitting round a CD player listening to an audio track. This is an example of **differentiation** – in other words, treating some students differently from others.

In schools where there are self-study facilities (a study centre or separate rooms), the teacher can send one group of students off to work there in order to concentrate on another. Provided the self-study task is purposeful, the students who go out of the classroom will not feel cheated.

If the self-study area is big enough, of course, it is an ideal place for different-level learning. While one group is working on a grammar activity in one corner, two other students can be watching a DVD; another group again can be consulting an encyclopedia while a different set of students is working at a computer screen.

Do different tasks with the same material/technology

Where teachers use the same material with the whole class, differentiation can still take place. We can encourage students to do different tasks depending on their abilities. A reading text can have sets of questions at three different levels, for example. The teacher tells the students to see how far they can get: the better ones will quickly finish the first two sets and have to work hard on the third. The weakest students may not get past the first set.

In a language study exercise, the teacher can ask for simple repetition from some students, but ask others to use the new language in more complex sentences. If the teacher is getting students to give answers or opinions, she can make it clear that one word will do for some students whereas longer and more complex contributions are expected from others. In role-plays and other speaking or group activities, she can ensure that students have roles or functions which are appropriate to their level.

Ignore the problem

It is perfectly feasible to hold the belief that, within a heterogeneous group, students will find their own level. In speaking and writing activities, for example, the better students will probably be more daring; in reading and listening, they will understand more completely and more quickly. However, the danger of this position is that students may either be bored by the slowness of their colleagues or frustrated by their inability to keep up.

Use the students

Some teachers adopt a strategy of peer help and teaching so that better students can help weaker ones. They can work with them in pairs or groups, explaining things or providing good models of language performance in speaking and writing. Thus, when teachers put students in groups, they can ensure that weak and strong students are put together. However, this has to be done with great sensitivity so that students don't feel alienated by their over-knowledgeable peers or oppressed by their obligatory teaching role.

Many teachers, faced with students at different levels, adopt a mixture of solutions such as the ones we have suggested here. However, it is vitally important that this is done in a supportive and non-judgmental manner. Students should not be made to feel in any way inferior, but rather should have the benefits of different treatment explained to them. Furthermore, we should be sensitive to their wishes so that if they do not want to be treated differently, we should work either to persuade them of its benefits or, perhaps, accede to their wishes.

What if the class is very big?

In big classes, it is difficult for the teacher to make contact with the students at the back and it is difficult for the students to ask for and receive individual attention. It may seem impossible to organise dynamic and creative teaching and learning sessions. Frequently, big classes mean that it is not easy to have students walking around or changing pairs, etc. Most importantly, big classes can be quite intimidating for inexperienced teachers.

Despite the problems of big classes, there are things which teachers can do.

Use worksheets

One solution is for teachers to hand out worksheets for many of the tasks which they would normally do with the whole class, if the class was smaller. When the feedback stage is reached, teachers can go through the worksheets with the whole group – and all the students will get the benefit.

Use pairwork and groupwork

In large classes, pairwork and groupwork play an important part since they maximise student participation. Even where chairs and desks cannot be moved, there are ways of doing this: first rows turn to face second rows, third rows to face fourth rows, etc. In more technologically equipped rooms, students can work round computer screens.

When using pairwork and groupwork with large groups, it is important to make instructions especially clear, to agree how to stop the activity (many teachers just raise their hands until students notice them and gradually quieten down) and to give good feedback.

Use chorus reaction

Since it becomes difficult to use a lot of individual repetition and controlled practice in a big group, it may be more appropriate to use students in chorus. The class can be divided into two halves – the front five rows and the back five rows, for example, or the left-hand and right-hand sides of the classroom. Each row/half can then speak a part in a dialogue, ask or answer a question, repeat sentences or words. This is especially useful at lower levels.

Use group leaders

Teachers can enlist the help of a few group leaders. They can be used to hand out copies, check that everyone in their group (or row or half) has understood a task, collect work and give feedback.

Think about vision and acoustics

Big classes are often (but not always) in big rooms. Teachers should ensure that what they show or write can be seen and that what they say or play to the whole group can be heard.

Use the size of the group to your advantage

Big groups have disadvantages of course, but they also have one main advantage – they are bigger, so that humour, for example, is funnier, drama is more dramatic, a good class feeling is warmer and more enveloping. Experienced teachers use this potential to organise exciting and involving classes.

No one chooses to have a large group: it makes the job of teaching even more challenging than it already is. However, some of the suggestions above will help to turn a potential disaster into some kind of a success.

What if students keep using their own language?

In Chapter 3 we discussed situations in which using the students' L1 (their mother tongue) in class might be both sensible and beneficial. However, there are also occasions in which students use their native language rather than English to perform classroom tasks, such as having a discussion or doing an English-language role-play, and in such circumstances the use of the L1 is less appropriate. If we want students to activate their English, they won't be helped if they talk in a different language instead.

When students use their L1 in such circumstances, they often do so because they want to communicate in the best way they can and so, almost without thinking, they revert to their own language. But however much we sympathise with this behaviour, the need to have students practising *English* in such situations remains paramount, and so we will need to do something to make it happen. Here are some ways of doing this:

Talk to them about the issues

Teachers can discuss with students how they should all feel about using English and/or their own language in the class. Teachers should try to get their students' agreement that overuse of their own language means that they will have less chance to learn English; that using their own language during speaking activities denies them chances for rehearsal and feedback.

Encourage them to use English appropriately

Teachers should make it clear that there is not a total ban on the students' own language – it depends on what's happening. In other words, a little bit of the students' native language when they're working on a reading text is not much of a problem, but a speaking exercise will lose its purpose if not done in English.

Only respond to English use

Teachers can make it clear by their behaviour that they want to hear English. They can ignore what students say in their own language.

Create an English environment

Teachers themselves should speak English for the majority of the time so that, together with the use of listening material and video, the students are constantly exposed to how English sounds and what it feels like. Some teachers anglicise their students' names too.

Keep reminding them

Teachers should be prepared to go round the class during a speaking exercise encouraging, cajoling, even pleading with the students to use English – and offering help if necessary. This technique, often repeated, will gradually change most students' behaviour over a period of time.

What if students don't do homework?

We know that homework is good for students. After all, the more time they spend working with English, the better they get at it. Yet homework is often a dispiriting affair. Teachers sometimes give out homework tasks with no special enthusiasm, students don't always do it and teachers don't especially enjoy marking it.

In some schools, systems have been developed to deal with this situation. Students all have a homework 'diary' in which they have to write their homework tasks, and whether or not they have done them. Their parents have to sign off their homework diaries at the end of the week so there is some hope that they will ensure that their sons and daughters do the required tasks.

It is more difficult when students are older, however. Here we cannot rely on parents to help out.

Ask the students

We can ask the students what they think about homework and get their agreement about how much we should ask for. We can find out what their interests are, and try to ensure that we set homework tasks which are relevant to them (not only in terms of their interests, but also in terms of what they are studying).

Lesley Pointer recounted a situation in which she got her students to say what their ideas of useful and appropriate homework were. She then used the results to set homework assignments, and the outcome was that many more students did the homework tasks with something like enthusiasm – an enthusiasm she shared when correcting their work.

Make it fun

Some students think that homework will always be set by the teacher on a Friday afternoon, and it will always be the same kind of task (an exercise from a workbook, for example). Such students are much more likely to be engaged if the tasks are varied, and if the teacher tries to make them fun. We can give out homework tasks in envelopes or send them in emails. We can have students do some serious things, yes, but include some slightly crazy tasks too. Homework will then become something that students want to be involved in.

Respect homework

Some teachers have difficulty in working up any enthusiasm for setting and marking homework, and students sense this. It is especially inappropriate if they give homework in on time but the teacher keeps forgetting to mark it and hand it back. Students need to know that the effort they make in doing the tasks will be reciprocated by the teacher.

Make post-homework productive

Students are unlikely to develop much respect for the teacher's comments if, when marked homework is handed back, they are not encouraged to look at the feedback to see how they might make corrections. Left to their own devices, they may well just glance at the comments – or a grade they have been given – before putting the work into some folder, never to be looked at again.

We need to change this behaviour by ensuring not only that the feedback we give on homework is useful, but also that students are encouraged to correct their mistakes and learn from them before putting the returned homework away. We need to provide opportunities for them to react to suggestions we make on their homework or to discuss the task that was set in the light of our comments.

It is often a good idea to get students to correct each other's homework, provided that this is done in a supportive and cooperative way.

What if students are uncooperative?

As we saw on page 15, all teachers are nervous about the possibility that their students will start behaving badly. We need to have some idea about what to do when this happens.

Problem behaviour can take many forms: constant chattering in class, not listening to the teacher, disengagement from what's going on (a kind of passive resistance), blunt refusal to do certain activities or to do what they are told, constant lateness and even rudeness. These are the occasions when we, as teachers, need to draw on our reserves of professionalism in a clear and cool-headed way.

There are a number of ways teachers can react to problem behaviour.

Remember that it's 'just a job'

When students behave badly, especially when this involves rudeness or obstinacy, we often feel very hurt and tend to see their behaviour as a personal attack. This makes reacting to what is happening very difficult. But teaching is a job, not a lifestyle, and in order to act professionally, we need to be able to stand back from what is happening so that we can react dispassionately, rather than taking instant decisions in the heat of the moment. In other words, we need to *keep calm*, and respond as objectively as we can. Instead of interpreting the behaviour as an attack on us as people, we need to view it as something 'the teacher' has to deal with. Of course this is easier said than done, but some kind of emotional detachment will always be more successful than reacting emotionally.

Deal with the behaviour, not the student

When we lose our objectivity, it is sometimes easy to criticise the students who are exhibiting problem behaviour by using sarcasm or insults, or humiliating them in some other way. But this will not help the situation since it will only cause greater resentment. And anyway, it is not the student we want to stop, but the problem behaviour itself.

When problem behaviour occurs, therefore, we need to *act immediately* and stop it from continuing. As far as possible, we need to deal with the student or students who are causing difficulties by talking to them away from the whole class. Such face-to-face discussion has a much greater chance of success than a public confrontation in front of all the other students.

It is also helpful to find out why the student is behaving uncooperatively. For example, if students are always arriving late, we need to find out why they arrive late so often, and keep a check on how often this occurs. It may be necessary to impose some kind of sanction on persistent latecomers (such as excluding them from the lesson if they arrive more than, say, ten minutes late), or not allowing them to take part in some class activities or tests. However, our objective should always be to try to identify the problem and see if we can resolve it without having to take such measures.

Be even-handed

The way we deal with problem behaviour has an effect not just on the student who is causing trouble, but also on the whole class. All the students watch how we react to uncooperative students and come to their own conclusions about how effective we are. If the class sees sarcasm used as a weapon, their respect for the teacher's professionalism may be diminished. If they see one student getting away with behaviour which others are punished for, they will resent such favouritism.

For the same reason, students need to be clear about what action we will take if and when problem behaviour occurs. They then need to see such action being carried out when it happens. They will be confused if we react to the behaviour on some occasions but not others.

Go forward

The best way to deal with problem behaviour is to work out what will happen next. Rather than focusing only on what a student has done, we need to see how their behaviour can be improved in the future. We can change the activity, for example, or reseat students rather than discussing exactly who did what and when. We can ask for future good behaviour so that the student knows that what happens in the future is the most important thing.

Use any means of communication

We can talk to students individually. We can discuss the problem via email, or send a 'letter' to the class explaining the problem and asking them to reply if they have anything they need or want to say.

Enlist help

Teachers should not have to suffer on their own! They should talk to colleagues and, if possible, get a friend to come and observe the class to see if they notice things that the teacher him- or herself is not aware of. Finally, of course, they may need to rely on higher authority and the school or institute's behaviour policy.

Prevention or cure?

It is always better to preempt problem behaviour so that it never takes place than to have to try to react to it when it does. One of the ways of doing this is to agree on behaviour standards with the class at the beginning of a semester. This might involve making a **language-learning contract** in which both teacher and students say what they expect and what is unacceptable. If the students have had a hand in deciding what the rules should be (if they have some agency in the decisions – see page 21), they are much more likely to recognise problem behaviour when it occurs and, as a result, stop doing it when they are reminded of their original decisions.

What if students don't want to talk?

Many teachers have come across students who don't seem to want to talk in class. Sometimes this may have to do with the students' own characters. Sometimes it is because there are other students who dominate and may even intimidate. Sometimes it is because students are simply not used to talking freely in a classroom setting. Perhaps they suffer from a fear of making mistakes and therefore 'losing face' in front of the teacher and their colleagues.

Whatever the reason, it makes no sense to try forcing such students to talk. It will probably only make them more reluctant to speak. There are other much better things to try.

Use pairwork

Pairwork (and groupwork) will help to provoke quiet students into talking. When they are with one or perhaps two or three other students, they are not under so much pressure as they are when asked to speak in front of the whole class.

Allow them to speak in a controlled way at first

Asking quiet students for instant fluency will probably be unsuccessful. It is better to do it in stages. For example, the teacher can dictate sentences which the students only have to fill in parts of before reading them out. Thus, the teacher dictates 'One of the most beautiful things I have ever seen is …' and the students have to complete it for themselves. They then read out their sentences, e.g. 'One of the most beautiful things I have ever seen is Mount Fuji at sunset', etc.

In general, it may be a good idea, at first, to let students write down what they are going to say before they say it. And then once they have read out their sentences, the teacher or other students can ask them follow-up questions. Psychologically, they are more likely to be able to respond.

Use 'acting out' and reading aloud

Getting students to act out dialogues is one way of encouraging quiet students. However, acting out does not just mean reading aloud. The teacher has to work with the students like a drama coach, working out when the voice should rise and fall, where the emphasis goes, what emotion the actor should try to convey. When the student then acts out the role, the teacher can be confident that it will sound good.

Use role-play

Many teachers have found that quiet students speak more freely when they are playing a role, when they are not having to be themselves. The use of role-cards (see page 125) allows students to take on a new identity, one in which they can behave in uncharacteristic ways. It can be very liberating.

Use recording

If teachers have time, they can tell students to record what they would like to say, outside the lesson. The teacher then listens to the tape and points out possible errors. The student now has a chance to produce a more correct version when the lesson comes round, thus avoiding the embarrassment (for them) of making mistakes.

What if students don't understand the audio track?

Sometimes, despite the best judgment of the teacher (or the materials designer), listening material seems to be too difficult for students to understand. However many times the teacher plays the track, it just doesn't work. The teacher then abandons the activity and everyone loses face.

There are a number of alternatives to this scenario which can help.

Preview interview questions

Students can be given the questions of an interview and are encouraged to role-play what might be said before listening to it. This will have great predictive power.

Use 'jigsaw listening'

Different groups can be given different audio excerpts (either on tape or CD, or – for some of them – as **audioscripts**). When the groups hear about each other's extracts, they can get the whole picture by putting the 'jigsaw' pieces together.

One task only

Students can be given a straightforward task which does not demand too much detailed understanding. For example, we can get them to describe the speaker on the recording – the sound of the voice will suggest sex, age, status, etc. Such an activity offers the possibility of success, however difficult the listening passage.

Play a/the first segment only

Instead of playing the whole recording, teachers can just play the first segment and then let students predict what's coming next. Our third example in Chapter 10 (see pages 139–142) was a version of this.

Play the listening in chunks

Break the audio track into manageable chunks so that students understand the content of a part of it before moving on to the next one. This can make listening less stressful, and help students to predict what the next chunk will contain.

Use the audioscript

There are three ways of using the audioscript to help students who are having difficulty. In the first place, we can cut the script into bits. The students put the bits in the right order as they listen. Secondly, we can let the students see the first part of the audioscript before they listen. They will then know what the listening text is going to be about. Finally, the students can read the audioscript before, during and after they listen. The audioscript can also have words or phrases blanked out.

Use vocabulary prediction

We can give students 'key' vocabulary before they listen. They can be asked to predict what the recording will be about and, because they now know some of the words, they will probably understand more.

Have students listen all the time

Encourage students to carry listening extracts in their car or on their MP3 players. Get them to listen to the news in English on the radio or Internet as often as possible and to try to understand just the main points. Remind them that the more you listen, the easier it gets.

What if some students finish before everybody else?

When teachers put students in groups and ask them to complete a task – designing a poster, discussing a reading text, etc – they can be sure that some groups will finish before others. If the activity has a competitive element (for example, who can solve a problem first), this is not a worry. But where no such element is present, we are put in a quandary: should we stop the activity (which means not letting some finish) or let the others finish (which means boring the people who finished first)?

As in so many other cases, common sense has to prevail here. If only one group finishes way before the others, we can work with that group or provide them with some extra material. If only one group is left without having finished, we may decide to stop the activity anyway – because the rest of the class shouldn't be kept waiting.

One way of dealing with the problem is for the teacher to carry around a selection of spare activities – little worksheets, puzzles, readings, etc – which can be done quickly and which will keep the early-finishing students happy until the others have caught up. Another solution is to plan extensions to the original task so that if groups finish early, they can do extra work on it.

Conclusions | *In this chapter we have:*

- talked about the problem of teaching mixed-ability classes, suggesting either different material, different tasks, ignoring the problem or using the students themselves as ways of dealing with it.

- discussed the issue of large classes, suggesting ways of coping with them, such as using worksheets, using pairwork and groupwork, using chorus reaction, using group leaders, thinking about vision and acoustics and using the size of the group to your advantage.

- looked at solutions to the problem of students using their own language when we want them to be using English. We suggested talking to students about the issue, encouraging them to use English appropriately, only responding to English use, creating an English environment and continuing to remind them of the issue.

- studied the issue of uncooperative students, suggesting that where there is trouble, we have to deal with the behaviour rather than criticising the students themselves. We stressed the need for even-handedness and showed how we need to move on from the offending behaviour using any means of communication and, where appropriate, enlisting the help of others. We suggested a language-learning contract as a way of preempting behaviour problems.

- faced the problem of students who are reluctant to speak. Possible solutions included using pairwork, allowing students to speak in a controlled way first, using acting out and reading aloud, and using role-play.

- listed solutions for situations where students are having real trouble with listening material. Among many alternatives, we can give them interview questions before they listen (again), give them different bits of the listening text in a 'jigsaw' activity, concentrate on one simple listening task only, only play the (first) bit of the recording, use the audioscript in a variety of ways and, finally, get students to predict listening content by giving them key vocabulary.

- suggested that teachers should always have some spare activities 'up their sleeve' for situations where some groups finish long before others.

Introduction

- The exercises in this section all relate to topics discussed in the relevant chapter. Some expect definite answers, while others ask only for the reader's ideas and opinions.
- Tutors can decide when it is appropriate to use tasks in this section. Readers on their own can work on the tasks at any stage in their reading of the book.
- An answer key (pages 233–244) is provided after the Task File for those tasks where it is possible to provide specific or suggested answers. The symbol ✔ beside an exercise indicates that answers are given for that exercise in the answer key.
- The material in the Task File can be photocopied for use in limited circumstances. Please see the notice on the back of the title page for photocopying restrictions.

Two task types recur frequently in the task files:

The A & D chart: A & D (advantages & disadvantages) charts are often suggested to discuss the relative merits of a technique, idea or activity. Where the A & D charts refer to one topic (e.g. Using authentic listening texts at any level – see page 218), they should have two columns.

Advantages of using authentic listening texts at any level	Disadvantages of using authentic listening texts at any level

But where the A & D charts refer to different topics (e.g. different student groupings, such as 'whole class', 'pairwork', etc) they should have three columns.

	Advantages	Disadvantages
Whole-class grouping		
Groupwork		
Pairwork		
Solowork		

Jargon buster: Jargon busters ask you to say what you understand by certain terms and what their relevance is to teaching. You can then check in the appropriate chapter and/or check the glossary (pages 268–285), where you will find further explanations to compare with your own understanding.

	Your definition	Relevance for language learning/teaching
Neuro-Linguistic Programming (NLP)		
Multiple Intelligences theory (MI)		
Learning by rote		
Learning by doing		

Chapter 1: Learners

A Reasons for learning (pages 11–12)

Match the student needs on the left with the terms on the right.

a I have to be able to write projects (and my thesis) in English.

b I need to learn English so that I can work as a nurse in English-speaking contexts.

c I think English is an important international language and so I'd like to learn it in case I need it.

d We came to this country as refugees and we want to make a success of our lives here.

e We are trying to establish commercial links with international trading partners so I need to improve my English.

i General English

ii English for Academic Purposes

iii English for Specific Purposes

iv Business English

v Target-language community interaction

B Different contexts for learning (pages 12–14)

Read the following descriptions and say which learning context (in the box) they refer to.

English lessons at secondary school   In-company teaching   Large classes
One-to-one teaching   Private language school   Virtual learning

a Even though students may not be physically present, there are still issues of student motivation and learning management to be dealt with.

b It is vital to find out exactly what your student needs and enter into a dialogue with him or her about the content of the lessons.

c The job of the teacher is to ignore the fact that students have to be there and instead treat all lessons as something special.

d We have to find techniques which will allow students some individual work or pairwork to counteract the problem of numbers.

e We prefer teachers to come to us. That way our employees lose less time.

f We try to keep class sizes down to a maximum of ten. Our clients expect it.

C Learner differences (pages 14–20) 🔑

1 Make an A & D chart (see page 186) for teaching children, adolescents and adults.

2 Who do you think is being described in these examples? Put C = children, A = adolescents, Ad = adults or ? = don't know in the boxes.

   a A small group of students come to see you and say that they're finding learning English much more difficult than they had hoped. They want to stop the classes. ☐

   b After a lesson, a group of students come to see you and say, 'We don't like the way you're teaching. We want more grammar.' ☐

   c One of the students' favourite activities is the chanting of rhythmic sentences to develop good pronunciation. ☐

   d Students get really excited when you offer to let them sing a song. ☐

   e Students play tricks such as hiding under desks and giving the wrong names when you are taking the register. ☐

   f When you arrive late for class, some of the students are quietly getting on with their work. ☐

   g When you ask a student to come out to the front of the class to take part in a demonstration, he is extremely reluctant to do so because he is so nervous. ☐

   h You get students in groups to play a board game adapted from a general knowledge quiz. They are reluctant to play the game. ☐

   i You get students to write poems on the subject of friendship and you are surprised and moved by their work. ☐

3 What level are these activities appropriate for? Put B = beginner, I = intermediate or A = advanced in the boxes. Some may be appropriate for more than one level.

   a ☐ Students write and assemble the front page of an imaginary newspaper with stories you have given them and others they make up.

   b ☐ Students listen to a dialogue between a railway official and a tourist asking for information.

   c ☐ Students listen to an interview with an actor talking about how she got started.

   d ☐ Students practise introducing themselves with language such as 'Pleased to meet you', 'Hello, my name's Karen'.

   e ☐ Students practise repeating/saying words with the /æ/ sound, e.g. 'c<u>a</u>b', 's<u>a</u>nd', 'b<u>a</u>t', '<u>a</u>nd', '<u>a</u>t', etc.

   f ☐ Students put together a radio commercial for a new kind of shoe.

   g ☐ Students report back on an unsimplified work of English-language fiction.

   h ☐ Students role-play choosing a dress in a clothes store.

   i ☐ Students watch a video of a documentary about global warming.

Jargon buster

Copy the chart with your own definitions for the following terms (column 1) and explain their relevance to teaching (column 2).

	Your definition	Relevance to language learning/teaching
Neuro-Linguistic Programming (NLP)		
Multiple Intelligences theory (MI)		
Learning by rote		
Learning by doing		
Extrinsic motivation		
Intrinsic motivation		
Affect		
Agency		
Learner autonomy		

Chapter 2: Teachers

A Describing good teachers (page 23)

1 Think of two good teachers from your past. What personal qualities do/did they share?

2 Rate the following teacher qualities in order of importance (1–10).

- ☐ They are adaptable.
- ☐ They are even-handed in their treatment of students.
- ☐ They are good-looking.
- ☐ They care about their students.
- ☐ They dress well.
- ☐ They give interesting lessons.
- ☐ They know their subject.
- ☐ They listen to their students.
- ☐ They prepare well.
- ☐ They use new technology.

Add two more qualities that you think are important.

a ....

b ....

B Who teachers are in class (pages 23–25) ☞

1 Do you agree with the following paragraph? Why? Why not?

> 'Good teachers plan their classes minutely so that everything they do is prearranged. Once they are in the classroom, they follow their plan without deviation, always watching out for irrelevancies which the students may bring up and which would disrupt the plan.'

2 Match the descriptions on the left with the teacher roles on the right.

a	Students make appointments to talk to the teacher about their progress.	i	assessor
b	The teacher is explaining something to the class.	ii	controller
c	The teacher is telling students how correct (or incorrect) their language use is.	iii	prompter
d	The teacher makes herself available to answer any questions/supply information while students are working on a task in groups.	iv	resource
e	The teacher wants to help the students along during a fluency activity (where their conversation is faltering a bit).	v	tutor

C Rapport (pages 25–27)

Rewrite the following statement so that it accurately reflects your own opinion.

> 'It is easy to create good rapport with your students; all you have to do is to be entertaining and give them something interesting to do.'

D Teacher skills (pages 28–30)

Make an A & D chart (see page 186) for the following approaches to students' names.

   a Class seating plan

   b Name badges

   c Name cards on the desk

   d Not using students' names (because you can't learn them all)

   e Students always say their names when they ask a question or when you ask them to do something.

   f Write notes about appearance/attitude, etc against the students' names in the class register.

E Teacher knowledge (pages 30–32)

Complete the chart.

	In use when I was at school/ university	I use this in my daily life (give details)	I have never used this (or been taught using this)	Usefulness rating 0 (= useless) to 5 (= fantastic)
Black/whiteboard				
CD player				
Computer				
Data projector				
DVD player				
Interactive whiteboard				
Language laboratory				
Overhead projector				
Tape recorder				
Video machine				

Jargon buster

Copy the chart with your own definitions for the following terms (column 1) and explain their relevance to teaching (column 2).

	Your definition	Relevance to language learning/teaching
Magic moments		
Learning outcome		
Learner role		
Monolingual learners' dictionary (MLD)		
Podcast		
Blog		

Chapter 3: Managing the classroom

A The teacher in the classroom (pages 34–36)/
Using the voice (page 36)

Give a rating of 1 (= just right) to 5 (= absolutely terrible) for a teacher you remember well.

appearance		general presence in class	
audibility		movement	
clarity		vocal quality	

- In the case of a low score, explain your reasons.
- Now score yourself as you are or are likely to be.

B Talking to students (page 37)/
Giving instructions (pages 37–38) ✎

1 Put a tick (✓) in the boxes if you think the instructions are good.

☐ Teacher: Now I want you to work in pairs … yes (*gesturing*) … that's right … you two … you two … you two. Good. Now listen carefully. I want you to read this text (*holding up the book and pointing to it*) on page 26 and answer the questions … OK? Now then, Ilona, what's the page? … Good … What are you going to do, Danuta …?

☐ Teacher: OK, this is the deal – and I hope you really enjoy this 'cos I spent a lot of time planning it, you know, well in between some wild contests on my gameboy – and I was going to watch Sky Sports but I got, you know, sidetracked – anyway, where was I, yes, well, because I'm ideologically committed to cooperative work, I thought you could probably access this grammar problem yourselves, by looking it up in your book in groups. OK?

☐ Teacher: (*sitting at desk, looking at his/her notes*). Open your books on page 26. What's the answer to question 1?

☐ Teacher: (*holding up large picture*): Right, we're going to do something a bit different now. Fumiko … everybody … are you listening? Good. Right. Now ask me questions about the picture (*pointing to the picture, gesturing*) … questions with 'What' … Anybody? Yes, Fumiko?

2 What information would you have to get over if you wanted to explain how to

a change a tyre?
b use a cash machine?
c fry an egg?

Write the instructions you would give to a low-level group of students for one of these procedures.

C Student talk and teacher talk (page 38) ✎

1 In a class of twenty students (working as a whole group) and one teacher, how much speaking time will each student have in a fifty-minute language practice class.
2 Make an A & D chart (see page 186) for teacher talking time (TTT) and student talking time (STT) in an English lesson.

D Using the L1 (pages 38–39)

Rewrite the following statement so that it reflects your own opinion.

'Students and teachers should be discouraged from using the students' mother tongue (L1) in the classroom.'

E Creating lesson stages (pages 39–40)

Number the following ways of regaining the initiative in a noisy class in order of personal preference and give your opinion of their effectiveness.

a The teacher blows a whistle. ☐
b The teacher claps his or her hands. ☐
c The teacher raises his or her hand, expecting students to raise their hands, too, and quieten down. ☐
d The teacher shouts at students to be quiet. ☐
e The teacher stands on a table and shouts at students to be quiet. ☐
f The teacher speaks quietly in the hope that students will quieten down to listen. ☐
g The teacher stands in front of the class with arms folded, fixing the students with a baleful stare. The teacher waits. ☐

F Different seating arrangements (pages 40–43)

What is the best seating arrangement for the following situations?

a A team game with a class of forty
b A class discussion with fifteen students
c Pairwork in a group of thirty students
d A reading task in a group of ten
e Students design an advertisement in groups
f Students all listen to an audio track
g The teacher explains a grammar point

G Different student groupings (pages 43–45)

1 Make an A & D chart (see page 186) for whole class, groupwork, pairwork and solowork.
2 What is the best grouping for these activities, do you think? Put W = whole class, P = pairwork, G = groupwork or S = solowork in the boxes.

☐ a Students choose one of three alternatives when faced with an imaginary moral dilemma.
☐ b Students design a website for a school or special interest group.
☐ c Students listen to an audio recording of a conversation.
☐ d Students practise saying sentences with the present perfect ('I've lived here for six years', 'He's studied here for six months').
☐ e Students prepare a talk/presentation on a subject of their choice.
☐ f Students repeat words and phrases to make sure they can say them correctly.
☐ g Students work out the answers to a reading comprehension.
☐ h Students write a dialogue between a traveller and an immigration official.
☐ i Students write a paragraph about themselves.
☐ j The teacher explains the rule for the pronunciation of 's' plurals ('pins', 'cups', 'brushes').

Jargon buster

Copy the chart with your own definitions for the following terms (column 1) and explain their relevance to teaching (column 2).

	Your definition	Relevance to language learning/teaching
Gesture		
Expression		
Mime		
TTQ		
L1		
L2		
Mixed-ability class		
Collaborative writing		

Jeremy Harmer *How to Teach English* © Pearson Education Limited 2007
PHOTOCOPIABLE

Chapter 4: Describing learning and teaching

A Children and language (pages 46–47)

Complete the chart with as many differences as you can think of between babies/young children learning their mother tongue and schoolchildren/adults learning a second or foreign language.

Mother tongue	Second/Foreign language

B Acquisition and learning (pages 47–48)

How like or unlike natural language acquisition was your experience of learning a foreign language at school?

C Different times, different methods (pages 48–51)

Which methods/approaches in the box are being described in the following statements (sometimes more than one statement applies to an approach).

> Audio-lingualism   Communicative Language Teaching (CLT)   Grammar–translation
> PPP   Task-Based Learning (TBL)   the Lexical Approach   the Silent Way
> teaching language functions

a After students have been introduced to a situation which exemplifies the meaning and use of the new language (and had the language explained to them), they do some controlled practice before being asked to produce examples of the new language themselves.

b By repeated drilling of new language (coupled with appropriate rewards and encouragement), students learn correct language habits.

c Language consists of a number of lexical phrases (or chunks). These should form the basis of learning.

d Language learning is a process of working out the similarities and differences between the language you speak and the language you are learning.

e Students learn by being involved in communicating with each other.

f Students study how language is used – and what language to use to perform certain functions, such as requesting, agreeing, etc.

g The syllabus is organised into certain tasks; the students learn by trying to complete these tasks.

h The teacher says almost nothing; the students have to listen to each other, think and correct themselves as far as possible.

D ESA lesson sequences (pages 54–57)

1 What do the following letters stand for?

   1 CLT   2 PPP   3 TBL

   What connection (if any) is there between the letters above and the following:

   a Straight arrows lessons?   b Boomerang lessons?   c Patchwork lessons?

2 How would you describe the following lesson sequences in terms of ESA?

   A

   1 The teacher gives students a number of words and tells them they all come from a story. In groups, the students have to try to work out what the story is.

   2 The teacher reads the (ghost) story aloud and the students see if they were right. They discuss whether they like the story.

   3 The students now read the story and answer detailed comprehension questions about it.

   4 The students look at the use of the past continuous tense (e.g. 'They were sitting at the kitchen table') in the story and make their own sentences using the past continuous.

   5 The students talk about ghost stories in general: do they like them/are they scared by them?, etc.

   6 The students write their own ghost stories.

   B

   1 The teacher stands in front of the class and starts to look very unhappy. The students are clearly interested/concerned.

   2 The teacher mimes feeling ill. The students look as if they understand what's going on.

   3 The teacher says, 'I'm feeling ill'. The students repeat, 'I'm feeling ill'.

   4 The teacher mimes feeling frightened/sad/angry/depressed, etc, and says, 'I'm feeling sad', etc, and the students repeat the sentences.

   5 The teacher models the question 'What's the matter?' The students repeat the question.

   6 The students practise questions and answers, e.g. 'What's the matter?', 'I'm feeling depressed', etc.

   7 The students do a role-play in which two neighbours meet – and one has just had their car stolen.

   C

   1 The teacher asks students if they like photographs.

   2 The teacher shows students four photographs and puts them in groups to decide which should win a photographic competition.

   3 The students question each other about photography – Do they own a camera? Do they take a lot of photographs?, etc.

   4 The students look at a number of words (which will appear in stage 5) and have to decide which part of speech they are.

   5 The students look at a poem about a photograph with some of the words blanked out. They have to decide what parts of speech are missing.

   6 The students now put their words from stage 4 in the blanks. They listen to a reading of the poem to check that they've got it right.

   7 The teacher and the students discuss the meaning of the poem. What's the story? Did they like it?

   8 The students write their own poems on a similar theme.

Jargon buster

Copy the chart with your own definitions for the following terms (column 1) and explain their relevance to teaching (column 2).

	Your definition	Relevance to language learning/teaching
Rough-tuning		
Comprehensible input		
Monitor (v)		
Noticing		
Conditioning		
Cue-response drill		
Language function		
Task cycle		
Discovery activity		

Chapter 5: Describing language

A The elements of language (pages 60–63)

Grammar

1 Identify the elements in the following sentences in terms of S (subject), V (verb), O (object), C (complement) and A (adverbial).

a He left quickly.
b She is incredibly intelligent.
c She read the book very slowly.
d The school principal wrote a letter.
e They kissed each other.
f They will arrive in two hours.

2 Look at the underlined parts of the sentences. Are the verbs transitive or intransitive? What different kinds of object are there?

a Don't <u>break</u> the cup.
b He <u>fell</u>.
c He <u>gave me the letter</u>.
d It <u>broke</u>.
e Please <u>sing me that song</u> again.
f That aftershave <u>smells</u> terrible!
g They <u>sent the message to their family</u> by email.

Pronunciation

1 How many sounds are there in these words?

a activate
b arrangement
c classroom
d emotion
e learner
f overhead projector
g performance
h rapport
i teacher
j willingness

2 Write the following words and mark the stress using underlining, stress marks, squares or circles.

a activate
b adolescent
c classroom
d emotion
e export (noun)
f export (verb)
g learner
h procrastination
i stipulation
j willingness

3 How many different ways can you say the following sentences by changing the stress on the words? What different situations could the sentences be said in?

a It was only last night that you arrived.
b This is the best show I've ever attended.
c She's decided she loves you.

4 How many different meanings can you give the following words by changing the intonation?

a well
b no
c happy
d OK

B Forms and meanings (pages 63–64) 🔑

1 What different meanings can you think of for the following words, phrases and sentences? Check a dictionary to see whether you have thought of all the meanings possible.

a edge	d pick	g They're off.	j They're watching a DVD.
b end	e shadow	h I don't want to miss her.	
c flag	f twist	i It's a goal.	

2 What time is the present continuous referring to in the following sentences?

a They're living in Singapore.

b He's always leaving his keys behind.

c They're meeting up in ten days or so.

d So there I am. It's ten o'clock on a cold winter evening – about a year ago – and I'm waiting for the bus when suddenly …

e It's no use talking. I'm not listening, OK!

What different tenses could you use to mean roughly the same thing in each case?

C Parts of speech (page 64) 🔑

1 Read the following extract and then complete the chart on page 200 with at least two words from the text for each part of speech.

Matilda said goodnight and set out to walk home to her parents' house, which was about an eight-minute journey away. When she arrived at her own gate, she saw a large black Mercedes motor-car parked outside. She didn't take too much notice of that. There were often strange cars parked outside her father's place. But when she entered the house, she was confronted by a scene of utter chaos. Her mother and father were both in the hall frantically stuffing clothing and various objects into suitcases.

"What on earth's going on?" she cried. "What's happening, Daddy?"

"We're off," Mr Wormwood said, not looking up. "We're leaving for the airport in half an hour so you'd better get packed. Your brother's upstairs all ready to go. Get a move on girl! Get going!"

"Off?" Matilda cried out. "Where to?"

"Spain," the father said. "It's a better climate than this lousy country."

"Spain!" Matilda cried. "I don't want to go to Spain! I love it here and I love my school!"

"Just do as you're told and stop arguing," the father snapped. "I've got enough troubles without messing about with you!"

"But Daddy …" Matilda began.

"Shut up," the father shouted. "We're leaving in thirty minutes! I'm not missing that plane."

"But how long for, Daddy?" Matilda cried. "When are we coming back?"

"We aren't," the father said. "Now beat it! I'm busy!"

From *Matilda* by Roald Dahl

noun	
pronoun	
adjective	
verb	
adverb	
preposition	
article	
conjunction	

2 Look at the chart in Exercise 1. Add two more words to each category which are not from the text.

D The noun phrase (pages 64–68)

1 In the *Matilda* extract (Section C above), find:

    a some countable nouns   b some uncountable nouns

2 Which different kinds of noun (countable, uncountable, plural, collective) can you put in the blanks?

    a I'd like some . . . .
    b There are two . . . . in the story.
    c The . . . . is unbelievable.
    d Our . . . . are completely crazy!
    e . . . . is not only unavoidable, but a good idea, too!

Choose words to go in the blanks.

3 Explain what is wrong with these student sentences.

    a He bought a French designer red big plastic chair.
    b He himself washed.
    c I like often to play tennis.
    d I love the nature.
    e I'm crazy of French films.
    f The lady sat down beside me was beautiful.
    g She is more bright than her brother.
    h The inhumanity is a terrible thing in our world.
    i In spite of it was late but he started to revise for his exam.
    j I'll see you at Saturday at five o'clock.
    k I have seen him yesterday.

4 Expand this sentence from the *Matilda* extract (Section C above) using as many adverbs and adjectives as you can without the sentence becoming impossible. You can use commas, colons, semicolons and hyphens.

We're leaving for the airport in half an hour so you'd better get packed.

E The verb phrase (pages 68–73) 🔑

1 Look at the *Matilda* extract (Section C above) and answer the following questions.

    a How many contracted verb forms can you find? What would the full form be?

    b Can you find at least one example of:
        1 an auxiliary verb?   2 a main verb?   3 a phrasal verb?

2 What are the underlined verbs – auxiliary, main or phrasal?

    a I <u>don't want</u> to go to Spain.

    b We<u>'re leaving</u> in thirty minutes.

    c She <u>can't understand</u> all the fuss.

    d Matilda <u>was brought up</u> very badly by her parents.

    e I <u>might</u> not <u>mind</u>.

3 Look at the *Matilda* extract (Section C above) and find one example of each of the following.

    a past simple   c present simple

    b present continuous   d a passive verb

4 Describe the verb forms in these sentences.

    a I haven't seen him for a week.

    b He was being chased by a tiger.

    c I'm enjoying myself.

    d People are usually frightened by the unknown.

    e They were sitting in the early evening sunshine.

    f He had been practising for the game.

    g I get up at about six o'clock every morning – it's terrible!

    h Water! Water! I've been jogging.

    i He finished his drink and walked out of the bar.

F Hypothetical meaning (pages 73–74) 🔑

Give the 'if' conditions in the following sentences a label saying (a) whether they are 'real' or 'hypothetical', and (b) whether they refer to the present, future or past (e.g. 'real future', 'hypothetical past', etc).

    a If I finish the letter, I'll post it this evening.

    b I'd have helped you if you had asked me.

    c If you were at all interested, I would tell you about it.

    d If you get caught cheating, you have to leave. That's the rule.

    e I'll drop in on my way back if I have time.

    f If she hadn't fallen asleep, she wouldn't have missed her station.

    g If I was clever, I'd know the answer.

    h If I got a pay rise, I'd move to a nicer apartment.

G Words together (pages 74–76) 🔑

1 Which of these words go together? Tick the boxes.

	alert	asleep	awake	conscious
fast				
fully				
half				
semi				
sound				
wide				

2 Find the missing noun for the sentences in column A and the missing verb for the sentences in column B.

A		B	
1	Be a . . . . . and fetch me my gloves.	1	If you . . . . . the club code, they'll kick you out.
2	She fell in . . . . . with a Japanese guy.	2	Go on, ... the habit of a lifetime and take some exercise!
3	For the . . . . . of God be quiet!	3	We going to . . . . . our journey in Des Moines, Idaho.
4	When he saw her it was . . . . . at first sight.	4	She doesn't believe that she can . . . . . the record.
5	There is no . . . . . lost between them.	5	The more you . . . . . promises like this, the more people will distrust you.
6	They're head over heels in	6	I'm going to . . . . . the back of this report before I go to bed.

– what are the lexical phrases in each case?
– what other lexical phrases can you think of including the words for column A and column B?

H Language functions (page 76) 🔑

1 How many different ways can you think of for expressing the following language functions?

 a giving advice   c offering help
 b inviting someone   d giving your opinion

2 Which language function are the following phrases expressing. Put F (formal), I (informal) or N (neutral) in the boxes.

a ☐ Be a love and bring me the phone, would you?
b ☐ Rachel! The phone! Now.
c ☐ You couldn't possibly answer the phone, could you?
d ☐ I'd be most grateful if you could answer the phone.
e ☐ Somebody get that!
f ☐ Could you answer the phone, please?
g ☐ The phone's ringing, Lianli.

Can you think of any other ways of performing the same function?

I Text and discourse (pages 76–78)

Put these sentences from an article called 'Against the modern world' in order. The first one is done for you.

☐ a And if they're (a) not talking into phones, they have earphones pressed to their (b) ears as they (c) listen to thumping music which may well make them (d) deaf.

☐ b Everywhere you look, people are involved in their (e) own private worlds.

☐ c So we (f) will end up with a situation where people won't talk to each other anymore, and even if they (g) do, no one will hear them (h) because they'll (i) all be deaf! Oh, brave new world!

☐1 d We (j) live in an alienating culture.

☐ e When they (k) walk down the street they (l) have mobile phones pressed to their (m) ears, shrieking into them (n) as if no one else was on the street with them (o).

Now say what the pronouns mean:

a	they	....	i they	....
b	their	....	j we	....
c	they	....	k they	....
d	them	....	l they	....
e	their	....	m their	....
f	we	....	n them	....
g	they	....	o them	....
h	them	....		

J Language variables (pages 78–80)

1 Use the following sentence frame to make as many sentences as possible about the differences between speaking and writing.

Speaking is different from writing because ...

2 Record an informal conversation between (yourself and) friends in English. Transcribe what you hear on the tape and then complete these tasks.

a Take any two lines of the transcription and write them out in formal written English.

b Study the transcription and the formal version you have written. What words from the formal version are not included in the conversational version?

A Teaching specific aspects of language (pages 81–83) ☞

Put D (for deductive/explain and practise) or I (for inductive/discovery activity) in the boxes.

a ☐ The teacher models sentences using the present simple. Students repeat.

b ☐ The students read a text and in their groups discuss the different ways the writer refers to past time.

c ☐ Students watch a film of a job interview in preparation for an interview role-play. They pay particular attention to the way questions are asked.

d ☐ The students listen to a recorded dialogue. The teacher draws their attention to the invitation language being used, isolating parts of invitation models for the students' attention. Students practise using the same language.

e ☐ The teacher holds up flashcards with pictures of animals. For each one, he or she models the correct pronunciation and the students repeat. The teacher then holds up different flashcards for a cue-response drill and the students have to say the right words.

f ☐ The teacher shows students the position of lips and teeth for the sounds /w/ and /v/ before getting them to say words with the two sounds.

B Explaining meaning (pages 83–84)

1 How could you make sure that students understood the meaning of the following words?

a to count	c flower	e stagger	g to promise	i vehicle
b confused	d full	f teacher	h under	j very

2 How could you ensure that students understood the meaning of the following language items?

a Ordinal numbers (1st, 2nd, 3rd, etc)

b 'Do you like X?', 'Yes, I do/No, I don't.'

c going to future ('I'm going to see my grandmother next week.')

d the first conditional ('If it rains, we'll stay at home', 'If I finish work early, I'll call you')

e the past continuous ('She was waiting at the station', 'The government was preparing for war', etc)

C Explaining language construction (pages 84–85)

How would you explain the construction of the following structural items? (You can isolate, distort, use gesture, draw board diagrams, etc.)

a past tense negatives ('They didn't feel good', 'She didn't go to work', etc)

b present simple, 3rd person ('He sleeps', 'She takes', 'It hurts', etc)

c superlatives ('best', 'youngest', 'prettiest', 'most alarming', etc)

d past passives ('He was seen', 'They were contacted', 'It was designed by …', etc)

e compound words with participles ('walking stick', 'running shoes', 'laughing gas', etc)

D Practice and controlled practice (pages 85–87)

1 Write six model sentences which you could use to practise the following structures.

   a adverbs of manner ('wearily', 'happily', 'longingly', etc)

   b 'must' and 'mustn't' ('You must take off your shoes', 'You mustn't bring the dog', etc)

   c past simple ('They laughed', 'She cried', 'It happened', etc)

   d prepositions of place ('on', 'in', 'under')

   e the present perfect with 'never' ('He's never seen Mount Fuji', etc)

2 Number the following actions to put them in order to make part of an effective cue-response drill. (The order of the flashcards is headache, stomachache, toothache.)

   a ☐ Boris: He's got a toothache.

   b ☐ Boris: He's got some toothache.

   c ☐ Kim: She's got a headache.

   d ☐ Maria: He's got a stomachache.

   e ☐ (*Teacher holds up a picture of a man with a toothache.*)

   f ☐ (*Teacher holds up picture of a woman with a headache.*)

   g ☐ (*Teacher holds up picture of someone with a stomachache.*)

   h ☐ Teacher: Maria.

   i ☐ Teacher: Boris.

   j ☐ Teacher: Good.

   k ☐ Teacher: Kim.

   l ☐ Teacher: Some toothache?

   m ☐ Teacher: Well done, Kim.

   n ☐ Teacher: Yes, that's it. Good.

Write down the letters of the cues . . . .

Write down the letters where the teacher nominates students . . . .

Write down the letters of the student responses . . . .

E Examples of language system teaching (pages 87–96)

Grammar

Read the following text and answer the questions that follow:

Archery Target

When I opened my eyes that morning, I knew I should have stayed asleep. My head felt terrible and when I got up, it felt worse.

I lit a cigarette and dragged the electric razor across my chin. The noise it made hit the hangover in my brain like the 'Dies Irae' from Verdi's *Requiem* – that's the bit with the bass drum, the shrieking chorus, and the full orchestra for those of you who don't know their Verdi. I hadn't managed to sleep it off after all. It was going to be one hell of a day.

As I opened the door the sunlight blasted into my eyes like a searchlight. It hurt. So did the jogger who sprinted past me as I stumbled into the street. I should have realised then that something was wrong. We didn't get many joggers in our neighbourhood – certainly not ones with bright-green running suits.

I staggered down towards the coffee shop for my morning coffee. I was moving at a snail's pace, but even that was faster than Easy Eddie who I met shuffling along the sidewalk. He was always shuffling along the sidewalk and I had got used to him by now.

He gave me a cheerful greeting. I muttered 'Hi.'

Someone strode past me and hurried down the street. He wasn't wearing a running suit, he was wearing a morning suit – with a tail coat and a white bow tie. I reckoned I must be hallucinating. For the hundredth time I swore I'd never drink Bourbon again.

I turned into Mission Boulevard and there she was. She was sauntering along on the other side of the street, colored like an archery target, with head held high and that innocent look of hers. Then, from the corner of my eye I saw the running suit again and suddenly the fog blew right out of my head. *I knew what was going to happen!* I dashed across the road, weaving in and out of the early taxis and the garbage trucks as they hit their klaxons and shouted curses at me. But I was too late. I just had time to see the jogger stop her and the man with the morning suit touch her back – almost gently – and then they were gone.

"Lauren, Lauren," I called through dry lips. She seemed to hear. She turned her head in my direction and limped towards me and then she just kind of fell in a rustling heap right there on the sidewalk. By the time I reached her she was gone.

I pulled another cigarette from the crushed packet in my pocket. One day, I swore, I'd give them up, but not now. Especially not now.

   a What level could you use this text with?
   b How would you use this text to revise/teach different ways of talking about the past?
   c How would you introduce the text?
   d How would you get students to practise the different past tenses in the text?
   e What other activities would you use with this text?

Pronunciation: intonation

Look at these expressions of reaction to what people say and answer the questions which follow:

That's fantastic!   How interesting!   Really?   That's incredible!

   a How could you use the expressions to teach variations of pitch and intonation?
   b What level would this be appropriate for?

Pronunciation: sounds

   a Design an activity for elementary students to show how the letter 'a' is pronounced.
   b What is the best way to teach the sounds /æ/ c<u>a</u>t, /ʌ/ c<u>u</u>t, and /ɒ/ c<u>o</u>t to lower-intermediate students?

Vocabulary

Look at the following list of words and answer the questions which follow:

> attractive beautiful chubby emaciated fat flabby good-looking handsome hideous lean muscular nubile obese overweight plain pretty shapely sinewy skinny slender slight slim stout tanned thin ugly underweight voluptuous well-built

a At what level would it be appropriate for students to concentrate on these vocabulary items?
b How could you get students to understand the meaning and connotation of the words?
c What aspects of the pronunciation of these words would you draw students' attention to?
d What kind of situations can you think of to get students using the new words?

F Correcting students (pages 97–98)

Complete the blanks with an appropriate form of the correction in the following exchanges between a teacher and her elementary students.

a TEACHER: OK … question, Juan.
   JUAN: where the book is
   TEACHER: ………………………

b TEACHER: Olga?
   OLGA: He never has been see Paris.
   TEACHER: Can anyone help her?
   STUDENTS: He never has see/He never been/He never sees, etc.
   TEACHER: ………………………

c PAULA: He can to play tennis.
   TEACHER: ………………………

Jargon buster

Copy the chart with your own definitions for the following terms (column 1) and explain their relevance to teaching (column 2).

	Your definition	Relevance to language learning/teaching
Personalisation		
Deductive approach		
Model		
Isolate		
Inductive approach		
Check questions		
Elicitation		
Minimal pair		
Error		
Slip		
Attempt		
False friend		
Developmental error		

A Reasons for reading (page 99)

List the last five different reading tasks you have done (e.g. I looked at the TV guide to see what time a programme was on) in column 1, and then say if the same kinds of reading would be useful for your students or not. Give your reasons.

Type of reading	Useful? Why/why not?

B Different kinds of reading (pages 99–100) 🔑

Look at the following texts for elementary students and complete the table which follows.

TEXT A

Three and a half hours later on that same day I sat down with Inspector Portillo in the dining room.

"Good morning, Miss Biggleswade," he said.

"Good morning," I answered nervously. Why did he want to see me? Why were the police talking to everybody?

"I know about you," he said.

"You do?" I asked.

"Yes. You're the player with the double bass."

"Without the double bass," I said.

"Yes," he laughed, "but we're looking for it."

"Will you find it?" I asked.

"I hope so." He isn't cold at all, I thought. He's very nice. I like him. Then, suddenly, he changed. "Now, I have some questions for you."

"Why?" I asked.

"That is not an intelligent question, I think," he said, "someone has died. We always ask questions."

"So you think I'm stupid, do you?" I was angry and very, very tired.

"No, of course not. I am very sorry," he said. I looked into his face. He really *was* sorry.

"Forget it!" I said, "I'm just tired."

"Yes, so am I," he laughed, "now, can I ask you some questions?"

TEXT B

South America is one of the most beautiful places in the world.

It is a lot bigger than Europe and two times bigger than Australia.

The Amazon River is 6,448 kilometres long but it isn't the longest river in the world. The Nile in Africa is 6,695 kilometres long.

South America has got the biggest rain forest in the world (in Brazil) where twenty per cent of all the world's trees grow. It's also got the world's driest desert – the Atacama Desert in Chile.

Lake Titicaca – in the Andes between Peru and Bolivia – is the highest large lake in the world.

The Andes mountain range is the longest on Earth. It starts in the south of Chile and finishes in Venezuela. The Andes mountains are higher than any mountains in North America, Africa, Australia or Europe.

South America has got half of the world's animals and insects. It has also got the biggest spider – the goliath bird-eating spider. It is bigger than a page of this book and it really can eat small birds and snakes!

The tropical rattlesnake from Brazil is more dangerous than a spider (to humans). It is the most poisonous snake in South America!

Three of South America's biggest cities are in the top ten biggest cities in the world.

	Text A	Text B
a What level would the text be useful for?		
b Is the extract designed for extensive or intensive reading?		
c How would you describe the genre in which the text is written?		
d What would you get the students to do with the text?		

C Reading skills (pages 100–101) 🔑

Match the skills with the reading aims.

a	Reading for detailed comprehension	i	You are an 18-year-old history student. In a school history magazine you see an article about reassessing the Cold War in terms of Third World politics.
b	Reading for pleasure	ii	You are trying to decide what movie to take your 7-year-old niece to see. You check your local newspaper.
c	Scanning	iii	When you are in the dentist's waiting room, you see an article about your favourite singer in a magazine.
d	Skimming	iv	You have heard about a singer/artist and you are mildly interested in their life. You look them up on the Internet when you don't have much else to do.

D Reading sequences (pages 102–107) 🔑

Look at the reading text and answer the questions which follow.

Your sleep and you

Miriam Kellaway reports

How much beauty sleep do you need? According to Philip Sedgewick, research fellow at the Sleep Disorders Clinic at the Department of Mental Health at St George's Hospital, most of us need roughly eight hours a night if we want to stay healthy. And we need to have a regular routine too.

Problems for tired people:

- more chance of bugs and infections
- shift workers (people who work at different times of day and night) get more infectious diseases than the rest of us.
- more chance of stress
- more need for energy food like chocolate, coffee, etc. Students in the USA say tiredness causes overeating. In a survey of hospital nurses across the country, ninety per cent of those working on the night shift gained weight.
- irritability, grumpiness

REM & Non-REM

- REM stands for Rapid Eye Movement. That's the time we dream, when we sort out all the memories, thoughts and feelings in our head. Non-REM is often called Deep Sleep.
- without REM people become forgetful, irritable and less able to concentrate.
- deep sleep provides us with physical and mental recovery.

Things not to do in bed (according to sleep experts):

- eat
- read
- watch television
- work
- drink caffeine
- smoke cigarettes
- have alcohol (It interferes with REM sleep. It can make you tired and irritable the morning after the night before.)

Canadian sleep researcher Harvey Modofsky, at the Toronto Western Hospital took blood from sleeping people and he found that sleeping bodies were fighting infection better than those that were awake and in a recent study of 9,000 adults in the UK, those who slept between six and a half and eight and a half hours a night were more healthy than those who slept less.

---

a What level do you think it might be suitable for?

b What kind of comprehension tasks could you do with it?

c How would you get students *engaged* with the topic of the text?

d What language, if any, would you focus the students' attention on in the reading text for a *study* exercise?

e What would you do after the students had read the text?

Jeremy Harmer *How to Teach English* © Pearson Education Limited 2007

PHOTOCOPIABLE

E   Encouraging students to read extensively (pages 109–110)

Rewrite the following statement so that it reflects your own point of view:

> Students should always give detailed feedback on books which they have read for pleasure (e.g. readers).

Jargon buster

Copy the chart with your own definitions for the following terms (column 1) and explain their relevance to teaching (column 2).

	Your definition	Relevance to language learning/teaching
Genre		
Genre analysis		
Authentic text		
Graded reader		
Webquest		
Jigsaw reading		
Reassembling poems		

Chapter 8: Teaching writing

A Reasons for teaching writing (page 112) 🔑

Read the following task rubrics. Are the tasks designed for 'writing-for-learning' (L) or 'writing-for-writing' (W). Write L or W in the boxes.

a Expand the following sentence using as many adjectives as you can. ☐

b Interview a colleague and write up the interview for inclusion in a class website. ☐

c Write a paragraph about a member of your family. Say who they are, what they do, what languages they speak and what their favourite hobbies are. ☐

d Write a paragraph with the title 'Three things I would like to do before I'm thirty'. Use language from activities 32–35. ☐

e Write an essay with the title 'Charity is not the responsibility of individuals, but of governments'. ☐

f Write descriptions of the people in the photographs using the words in the box. ☐

g Write five sentences using the present perfect tense. ☐

h Write your own blog; update it every week. ☐

B Writing issues (pages 112–113)

Put these writing activities in an order of preference for you and a group of intermediate students (aged 14–16).

☐ autobiographical narrative
☐ construct a class website
☐ fill in a university application form
☐ imaginary 'agony column' letters
☐ magazine advertisement
☐ poems
☐ postcards
☐ poster for an imaginary amateur drama production
☐ report on eating – people's habits
☐ script for an imaginary soap-opera episode
☐ students rewrite statements to reflect their own views
☐ write an email to a mousepal/keypal

What were your reasons for your number 1 choice? What were your reasons for your last choice?

Jeremy Harmer *How to Teach English* © Pearson Education Limited 2007

PHOTOCOPIABLE

C Writing sequences (pages 114–118)

Look at these two writing activities for students and answer the questions which follow.

TASK A

> Report writing
> Work in groups and complete the following tasks:
>
> 1 Write a multiple-choice questionnaire to find out about people's attitudes to one of the following:
>   mobile phones
>   computers
>   housework
>   marriage
>
> 2 Do the questionnaire in class and collate the results.
>
> 3 Write a report to summarise your feelings. Use expressions from the survey highlights above.

8 Write

Write an answer to the problem.
Use these prompts to help you.
- not to worry
- see a dentist
- wear a brace
- talk to friends who wear one

You shouldn't worry ...

> Help! My teeth aren't very straight but I don't want to wear a brace. Everyone will stare at me. What can I do?
>
> *Jenny, 13 Hastings*

TASK B
a What age and level are they appropriate for?
b Would you feel confident using them as a teacher? Why? Why not?
c What problems, if any, can you anticipate with these activities?
d What would you need to do before starting the activities to ensure that they were a success?
e What do you think might have come before them and after them in the textbooks from which they were taken?

D Correcting written work (pages 120–121) 🔑

1 Rewrite the following paragraph so that it reflects your own opinions.

> Teachers should correct all the mistakes they find in a student's written work. They should underline the mistakes in red ink. Students should be made to write the work out again.

2 Write the correction symbols in the left-hand column of the chart on page 214 and the descriptions of the student error in the second column.

> Symbols: *C G ʌ S WO {} F/I ?M P T WW*

Descriptions:

a grammar mistake   a mistake in word order   a punctuation mistake
a spelling error   concord mistake (e.g. subject and verb agreement)
something has been left out   something is not necessary   the meaning is unclear
too formal or informal   wrong verb tense   wrong word

Symbol	Meaning	Example error
		The answer is _obvius_.
		I _like very much_ it.
		I am going to buy some furniture_s_.
		I _have seen him_ yesterday.
		People _is_ angry.
		He told‸that he was sorry.
		I am interested _on_ jazz music.
		He was not ⦃ too ⦄ strong enough.
		That is a _very excited photograph_.
		Do you like London_._
		_Hi_ Mr Franklin, Thank you for your letter ...

Jargon buster

Copy the chart with your own definitions for the following terms (column 1) and explain their relevance to teaching (column 2).

	Your definition	Relevance to language learning/teaching
Discourse community		
Guided writing		
Writing process		
Collaborative writing		
Dictogloss		
Mousepal		
Over-correction		
Responding		

Chapter 9: Teaching speaking

A Reasons for teaching speaking (pages 123–124)

1 What should the characteristics of a speaking activity be? Put a tick (✓) or a cross (✗) against the statements if you agree or disagree with them.

a ☐ It should be a *study* exercise.
b ☐ It should be an *activate* exercise.
c ☐ It should *engage* students.
d ☐ It should involve everyone.
e ☐ It should practise specific language structures.
f ☐ Students should concentrate on the accuracy of what they are saying.

2 Which is the odd one out? Why?

a a role-play   a discussion   a drill   a communication game   a questionnaire
b a letter   a speech   a poem   a grammar exercise   a play extract
c study   rehearsal   feedback   engagement   enjoyment

B Speaking sequences (pages 124–128)

1 Look at these two speaking activities for students and answer the questions which follow.

ACTIVITY 1
Find the differences between the two pictures. Do not look at each other's pictures.

ACTIVITY 2

a   What level could you use the activities with?

b   Would you feel confident using them as a teacher? Why? Why not?

c   What problems, if any, can you anticipate with these activities?

d   What would you need to do before starting the activities to ensure that they were a success?

e   What do you think might have come before them and after them in the textbooks from which they were taken?

2   **What kind of activity might be suitable for the following topics and levels?**

a   a visit to a travel agent (elementary)

b   the issue of gambling (intermediate)

c   two similar but slightly different pictures (beginners)

d   leisure activities (lower intermediate)

e   Should a pub be allowed to exclude women from one of its bars? (advanced)

Choose one of the activities a–e above and say how the teacher might organise it for the students.

a   Look at the activities below. For each, mark how dangerous you think it is on a scale of 0–3.

> 0 = I don't think it's dangerous at all
> 1 = I think it's quite dangerous
> 2 = I think it's very dangerous
> 3 = I think it's incredibly dangerous

☐ driving and talking on a mobile phone
☐ going out with someone you hardly know
☐ sunbathing
☐ walking alone in the hills or mountains
☐ hitchhiking
☐ travelling in the back of a car without a seatbelt
☐ cooking
☐ adventure sports like bungee-jumping or rafting
☐ swimming after a heavy meal
☐ doing home repairs
☐ travelling in a country where they don't speak your language or English

b   In groups of three, compare your marks. Use your own experiences to explain your opinions.

Jeremy Harmer *How to Teach English* © Pearson Education Limited 2007
PHOTOCOPIABLE

C More speaking suggestions (pages 129–131)

1 Read the following situation, which presents a 'moral dilemma'.

In a department store a woman (Perdita) is seen taking some bread and cheese without paying for it. It is known that she is very poor and that if she is charged and taken to court, she will probably get sent to prison and her children will be taken into care. In the department store a meeting has been quickly arranged to decide what to do about Perdita.

What five different roles could you assign students to provoke a role-play of the meeting?

2 Think of at least two different ways of using the following pictures.

Jargon buster

Copy the chart with your own definitions for the following terms (column 1) and explain their relevance to teaching (column 2).

	Your definition	Relevance to language learning/teaching
Rehearsal		
Speaking-as-skill		
Simulation		
Role-play		
Role-card		
Buzz group		
Describe and draw		
Story reconstruction		

Chapter 10: Teaching listening

A Reasons for listening (page 133)

List five different types of listening you have done in the last twenty-four hours and complete the chart.

Listening genre (e.g. play, conversation)	Listening delivery method (e.g. radio, face-to-face)	Useful for students to listen to? At what level?

B Listening levels (pages 134–135) 🔑

Make an A & D chart (see page 186) for using authentic listening texts at any level.

C Listening principles (pages 135–136)

Rewrite the following sentences so that they more accurately reflect your own opinion.

  a Students should get everything they need from one exposure to a listening text. Otherwise they may get bored.

  b The most important thing that students should get from a listening text is information about how language is used.

  c Students should only listen to listening texts in class where the teacher can help and guide them.

D Listening sequences (pages 136–142)

Read the following tapescript and answer the questions which follow it.

ASSISTANT:	Can I help you?
OLLIE:	Yes, please. I'm looking for some suncream.
ASSISTANT:	What kind do you want?
OLLIE:	I'm not really sure.
ASSISTANT:	Well, the thing to do is decide what factor you need.
OLLIE:	What factor?
ASSISTANT:	Yes. Choose the right factor and it'll protect you from UV rays.
OLLIE:	Ultra violet rays?
ASSISTANT:	Yeah. All you have to do is select the factor which fits your colouring and skin type.
OLLIE:	OK. I mean, I'm the kind of person who burns quite easily. But I tan in the end.
ASSISTANT:	Well, start with this Factor 15 and then when you've gone brown a bit, you can gradually reduce the strength to, I don't know, about 8.
OLLIE:	Oh, right. So I buy both of these?
ASSISTANT:	Yes. That would be a good idea.
OLLIE:	How much are they?
ASSISTANT:	Six pounds fifty.

Jeremy Harmer *How to Teach English* © Pearson Education Limited 2007
PHOTOCOPIABLE

OLLIE:	Each?
ASSISTANT:	Yes.
OLLIE:	That's really expensive. I wasn't expecting …
ASSISTANT:	You want to protect yourself against skin cancer or not?
OLLIE:	Yes, of course.
ASSISTANT:	Well …
OLLIE:	Oh, OK. Here you are.
ASSISTANT:	Thanks. That's seven pounds change.
OLLIE:	Thanks.
ASSISTANT:	Enjoy your sunbathing.
OLLIE:	If I can afford it!

a Based on what you have read so far, what level do you think this tapescript could be used with?

b How would you *engage* students with the topic? What preparation would you do with the students before they listened to this extract?

c What general listening task would be appropriate for this tapescript?

d What *study*/detailed listening activity would be appropriate for this activity?

e Can you think of an *activate* stage to follow this listening activity?

f Would you use this tape? Why? Why not?

E More listening suggestions (pages 142–144)

1 Find a song you think would be appropriate for students at or around the intermediate level. Think of at least four different things that you could do with the song.

2 You are going to write and record a conversation in which someone asks for (and gets) directions. The conversation is for elementary students to listen to. They should be able to understand it, but at the same time it should be as authentic as possible.

a Write the conversation.

b Say how you will use it when you play it to students.

Jargon buster

Copy the chart with your own definitions for the following terms (column 1) and explain their relevance to teaching (column 2).

	Your definition	Relevance to language learning/teaching
Regional variations		
Intensive listening		
Extensive listening		
Live listening		
Paralinguistic clues		
Follow-up questions		
Sound effects		
Radio genres		
Freeze frame		

Chapter 11: Using coursebooks

A Options for coursebook use (pages 146–147) 🔑

Complete the diagram with the following words:

> Adapt   Change   No   Replace

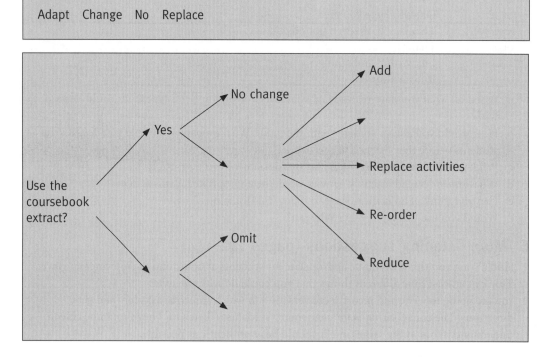

B Adding, adapting and replacing (pages 147–152) 🔑

Look at the coursebook lesson on page 221 and answer the following questions.

    a What is/are the aim(s) of the lesson?

    b What should/might students be able to do at the end of the lesson that they were not able to do at the beginning?

    c If you were going to replace any part of the lesson, which would it be?

    d What adaptations, if any, would you make to the material?

    e What additions, if any, would you make to the lesson?

C Reasons for (and against) coursebook use (pages 152–153) 🔑

1 Complete these sentences.

    a When I learnt a foreign language at school, the coursebook …

    b The best kind of coursebook for a language student …

    c If I wrote a coursebook, I …

2 Make an A & D chart (see page 186) for coursebook use.

3 Do/Will you use a textbook a lot, often, sometimes, rarely or not at all?

    Jeremy Harmer *How to Teach English* © Pearson Education Limited 2007

2 Communication

Holiday routines

1 Match the photos to the captions.

1 In the city ☐
2 In the mountains ☐
3 At the beach ☐

2 **a** Complete the questions in the questionnaire with words from the box.

do do get ~~go~~ go time what when ~~where~~ who

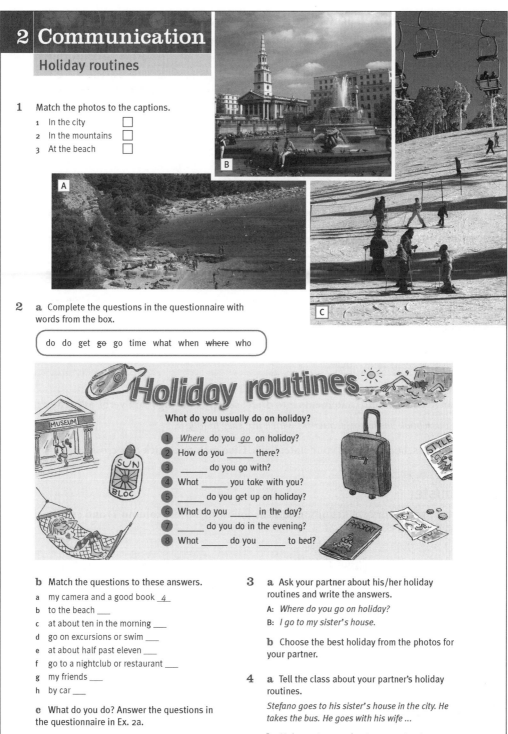

Holiday routines

What do you usually do on holiday?

1 *Where* do you *go* on holiday?
2 How do you _____ there?
3 _____ do you go with?
4 What _____ you take with you?
5 _____ do you get up on holiday?
6 What do you _____ in the day?
7 _____ do you do in the evening?
8 What _____ do you _____ to bed?

b Match the questions to these answers.

a my camera and a good book _4_
b to the beach ___
c at about ten in the morning ___
d go on excursions or swim ___
e at about half past eleven ___
f go to a nightclub or restaurant ___
g my friends ___
h by car ___

c What do you do? Answer the questions in the questionnaire in Ex. 2a.

3 **a** Ask your partner about his/her holiday routines and write the answers.

A: *Where do you go on holiday?*
B: *I go to my sister's house.*

b Choose the best holiday from the photos for your partner.

4 **a** Tell the class about your partner's holiday routines.

Stefano goes to his sister's house in the city. He takes the bus. He goes with his wife ...

b Make sentences about your partner's holiday routines.

D Choosing coursebooks (pages 153–154)

1 Complete the chart with three 'should' statements for each topic (as in the example).

Area	Comments
1 Layout and design	The coursebook should have lesson sequences which are easy to follow.
2 Instructions/rubrics	
3 Methodology	
4 Skills	
5 Syllabus	
6 Topics	
7 Cultural appropriacy	
8 Teacher's guide	

2 Now change your 'should' statements into direct sentences using main verbs as in the example.

The coursebook has lesson sequences which are easy to follow.

3 Look at a coursebook and use your statements. Give each one a tick or a cross.

Jargon buster

Copy the chart with your own definitions for the following terms (column 1) and explain their relevance to teaching (column 2).

	Your definition	Relevance to language learning/teaching
Pilot		
Consult		
Analyse		
Add-on		
Balance of skills		
Unprejudiced		
Syllabus		
Cultural appropriacy		

Chapter 12: Planning lessons

A Reasons for planning (page 156)

1 Write a list of any written or mental plans you make in your daily life apart from teaching (e.g. shopping lists).

    a What do you use your plans for?

    b How useful are the plans?

    c How much do you deviate from your plans as you carry them out?

2 Make an **A & D** chart (see page 186) for planning lessons.

B Plan formats (pages 160–162)

Study the plan on page 224 and complete the chart with your comments. In each case say whether you approve of the plan or whether, on the contrary, you think it is lacking something. Give reasons in each case.

Appropriacy of lesson plan format (For the teacher? For an observer?)	
Lesson details (Are they sufficient for the teacher? For an observer?)	
Lesson shape (e.g. Is the lesson coherent? Does it have variety?)	
Timings (e.g. Are they clear? Do you 'believe' them?)	
Who does what? (e.g. Do you approve of the patterns of interaction?)	
Is it a good plan? (e.g. What would you (a) leave out? (b) add to? (c) bring in? or (c) change completely?	

LESSON PLAN	Time [" = minutes]
Description of class Intermediate plus: 20 students Difficult to make them take part in speaking activities and things like that. They can be uncooperative, especially if they have been out the night before (because it's a morning class).	
Aims To get Ss reading in the fiction genre. To raise Ss' awareness of different conditional constructions. To get Ss talking in a relaxed and engaging way.	
Procedure 1 T tells Ss about their (teacher's) grandmother. Encourages Ss to ask questions.	5"
2 T tells Ss to read a text about a boy and his grandmother (see page 89*).	8"
3 T tells Ss to see how many differences they can think of between George's grandmother (in the text) and the T's grandmother they discussed earlier. Ss do this in pairs.	5"
4 T asks pairs for their conclusions and discusses with the class.	5"
5 T asks Ss to find sentences in text with the word 'if'. T discusses with class that these are conditional sentences, but combine grammar differently from the traditional 1st, 2nd and 3rd conditionals.	10"
6 T elicits sentences using equivalent grammar constructions to the four different grammar patterns. T writes sentences with mistakes on the board and corrects them.	12"
7 T shows Ss the picture of 'The Arnolfini Marriage' (see page 127*). In groups, Ss prepare questions for the man, the woman and the dog.	10"
8 T chooses three Ss to role-play the man, the woman and the dog. The other Ss ask their prepared questions.	10"
Comments Ss may be reluctant to speak at all stages. T will encourage them. SS may find it very difficult to produce equivalent conditional sentences (see stage 6). T will prepare sentences for prompting.	

* Page numbers refer to pages in this book.

Jargon buster

Copy the chart with your own definitions for the following terms (column 1) and explain their relevance to teaching (column 2).

	Your definition	Relevance to language learning/teaching
Coherence		
Variety		
Multi-lesson sequence		
Patterns of interaction		
Topic-linking		
Threads		
Peer observations		
Journal		

Chapter 13: Testing

A Reasons for testing students (pages 166–167) 🔑

Complete the sentences with a phrase from the box.

> achievement test   continuous assessment   exit test   placement test
> portfolio assessment   proficiency test   progress test

a .... is the name given to a situation where examples of students' work, taken over a term, semester or year, are collected together and used to decide the students' final grades.

b .... is the name given to a situation where marks for the students' work over a term, semester or year are collected, and are used for a final grade.

c A .... measures the students' knowledge at the time the test is taken. Most public exams are tests of this type.

d Students often take an .... to see how well they have learnt the subject(s) of recent lessons.

e Students take a .... to see how well they are getting on.

f Students take an .... at the end of a course.

g We give students a .... to decide which class/level will be most suitable for them.

B Good tests (pages 167–168) 🔑

Comment on the suitability of the following test items for students of general English.

a | Write a composition about the importance of DNA research in not more than 500 words. |

b | I didn't enjoy the book. I found it .... difficult.
   a very   b terrible   c un-   d rather |

c | Write ten words you have learnt recently. This is the only task for today's test. |

d | Write a poem about happiness. |

e | Complete the following sentences.
   Before I am thirty I ....
   I have never .... |

f | The human brain is (a) .... sensitive to any and (b) .... event: we cannot complacently (c) .... it as an article (d) .... faith that it will (e) .... inviolate and that ways (f) .... learning and thinking will (g) .... constant. A new idea (h) .... that there is room (i) .... improvement. So-called transhumanism, (j) .... as 'the world's most (k) .... idea', promotes the ability (l) .... science and technology to (m) .... beyond the 'norm' (whatever (n) .... is) for physical and (o) .... human enhancement. |

Jeremy Harmer *How to Teach English* © Pearson Education Limited 2007
PHOTOCOPIABLE

C Test types (pages 168–172)

1 Write multiple-choice items to test whether students know the following collocations.

   a clench + fist

   b heavy + traffic

   c shrug + shoulders

   What level could your test items be used with?

2 Use the following passage for a *cloze* test. Try it first deleting every sixth word, regardless of what word it is. Then do it again, deleting *roughly* every sixth word, but don't stick rigidly to the rule – e.g. you can select more appropriate words to delete if you want.

   a Which is better? Strict cloze (every sixth word) or *modified cloze* (you choose the words).

   b What level could you use this passage with?

   When you read a book, the author usually takes you by the hand and you travel from the beginning to the middle to the end in a continuous narrative of interconnected steps. It may not be a journey with which you agree, or one that you enjoy, but none the less, as you turn the pages, one train of thought succeeds the last in a logical fashion. We can then compare one narrative with another and, in so doing, start to build up a conceptual framework that enables us to evaluate further journeys, which, in turn, will influence our individualised framework. We can place an isolated fact in a context that gives it a significance. So traditional education has enabled us to turn information into knowledge.

3 Write transformation exercises to test whether students know the relationship between the following words:

   a divisive division   c honestly honesty

   b explain explanation   d inform information

D Marking tests (pages 172–174)

Read the activity on page 228 and mark the student's script using the following marking scale to produce a total mark out of 20.

	0	1	2	3	4	5
Grammar						
Vocabulary						
Coherence						
Fluency						

Get a friend or colleague to mark the work, using the same scale. Do you end up with the same mark?

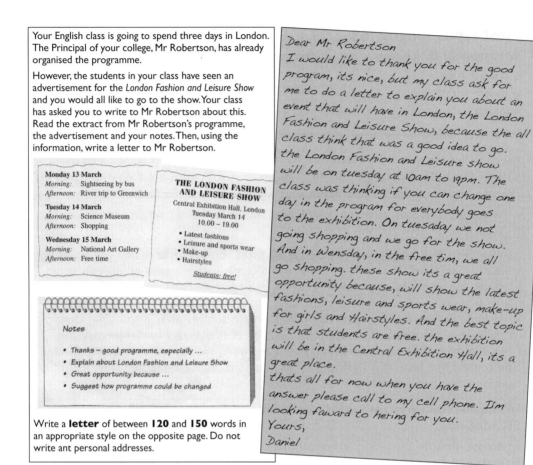

Your English class is going to spend three days in London. The Principal of your college, Mr Robertson, has already organised the programme.

However, the students in your class have seen an advertisement for the *London Fashion and Leisure Show* and you would all like to go to the show. Your class has asked you to write to Mr Robertson about this. Read the extract from Mr Robertson's programme, the advertisement and your notes. Then, using the information, write a letter to Mr Robertson.

Monday 13 March
Morning: Sightseeing by bus
Afternoon: River trip to Greenwich

Tuesday 14 March
Morning: Science Museum
Afternoon: Shopping

Wednesday 15 March
Morning: National Art Gallery
Afternoon: Free time

THE LONDON FASHION AND LEISURE SHOW
Central Exhibition Hall, London
Tuesday March 14
10.00 – 19.00
• Latest fashions
• Leisure and sports wear
• Make-up
• Hairstyles

Students: free!

Notes

• Thanks – good programme, especially ...
• Explain about London Fashion and Leisure Show
• Great opportunity because ...
• Suggest how programme could be changed

Write a **letter** of between **120** and **150** words in an appropriate style on the opposite page. Do not write ant personal addresses.

Dear Mr Robertson
I would like to thank you for the good program, its nice, but my class ask for me to do a letter to explain you about an event that will have in London, the London Fashion and Leisure Show, because the all class think that was a good idea to go. the London Fashion and Leisure show will be on tuesday at 10am to 19pm. The class was thinking if you can change one day in the program for everybody goes to the exhibition. On tuesaday we not going shopping and we go for the show. And in Wensday, in the free tim, we all go shopping. these show its a great opportunity because, will show the latest fashions, leisure and sports wear, make-up for girls and Hairstyles. And the best topic is that students are free. the exhibition will be in the Central Exhibition Hall, its a great place.
thats all for now when you have the answer please call to my cell phone. I'm looking faward to hering for you.
Yours,
Daniel

Jargon buster

Copy the chart with your own definitions for the following terms (column 1) and explain their relevance to teaching (column 2).

	Your definition	Relevance to language learning/teaching
Validity		
Reliability		
Face validity		
Backwash effect		
Interlocutor		
Discrete test item		
Integrative test item		
Direct test item		
Indirect test item		

Chapter 14: **What if?**

A Students are all at different levels (pages 176–177)

1 Rewrite these sentences so that they reflect your own opinion.

   a Mixed-ability classes present the teacher with insuperable problems.

   b The only thing you can do with a mixed-ability class is ignore the problem.

   c All classes are mixed-ability classes.

2 How would you approach these situations with a mixed-ability group?

   a You want to use the interview with Diana Hayden on page 141 with your students.

   b You want students to write a ghost story, having studied story telling, and having been given some 'ghost' vocabulary and phrases.

   c You want students to study ways of agreeing and disagreeing – and later use them, if possible, in some kind of discussion.

   d You have a poem which you want students to look at. You can refer to 'Fire and Ice' on page 108 if you want.

   e Three of your good students are making it clear that they're finding your classes too easy for them.

   f You want to hand back some written work and deal with the mistakes that you found when correcting.

B The class is very big (pages 177–178)

1 Complete the chart. In the first column write things you can do with small classes (ten or under) but you can't do with big classes (of forty plus). In the second column write things you can do with big classes which you can't do with small classes.

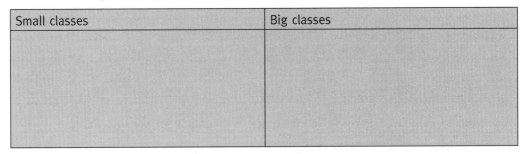

Small classes	Big classes

2 In big classes, what special considerations need to be taken into account for the following?

   a the teacher's voice

   b the teacher's place in the class

   c the teacher's board work/overhead projector use

   d using the tape recorder

C Students keep using their own language (pages 178–179)

1 What action can teachers take if students use their own language in class all the time? List as many things as you can think of.

2 In which of the following situations, if any, would you be happy (or at least not unhappy) for students to use their own language?

   a Students are working in pairs to practise a dialogue.

   b Students are debating the issue of whether birth control should be imposed on the world to prevent overpopulation.

   c Students are working in pairs to solve a reading puzzle.

   d Students are checking that they understand the instructions for an activity.

   e Students are doing a group writing task.

   f Students are taking part in a business meeting simulation.

D Students don't do homework (pages 179–180)

Write 1 (= most favourite) to 9 (= least favourite) in Column A: Me as the teacher.

A	B	Homework task
		Students do a fill-in exercise, choosing between 'going to' and 'will'.
		Students interview residents/tourists in the street and bring the results to the next lesson.
		Students learn a list of words by heart to be tested by the teacher in the next lesson.
		Students prepare a presentation which they will give (individually) in the next lesson.
		Students prepare roles for next week's role-play.
		Students read a text and answer multiple-choice questions.
		Students write six sentences using the past continuous.
		Students write a composition about the environment.
		Students write a publicity leaflet based on something in the coursebook.

Now write 1 (= most favourite) to 9 (least favourite) in Column B: Me as a student.

E Students are uncooperative (pages 180–182)

1 How many ways are there for students to be uncooperative in class? List them in order where the first one is most difficult for the teacher to deal with and the last is the least challenging for the teacher.

2 What might teachers and students write in this contract form?

THE LANGUAGE-LEARNING CONTRACT	
TEACHER	LEARNER
As your teacher I will ...	*As a learner I will ...*
As your teacher I expect ...	*As a learner I expect ...*

Jeremy Harmer *How to Teach English* © Pearson Education Limited 2007
PHOTOCOPIABLE

F Students don't want to talk (pages 182–183)

Copy and complete the chart with things you could do to make reluctant speakers talk – and say what the possible consequences are (both positive and negative).

Action	Consequences
Join in yourself in order to try to stimulate discussion.	It might relax students; on the other hand students may end up listening more than talking.

G Students don't understand the audio track (pages 183–184)

1 What problems do students have (in general) when listening to audio tracks in class? How can you help them to overcome these difficulties?

2 Look at this audioscript of an interview with an amateur musician (intended for use with intermediate students) and answer the questions below.

> SUSAN: Umm … went into a room where you could practise and then the accompanist came in and had a quick run-through … umm … and so you're waiting in a little room and you can hear other people auditioning who sound ten times better than you, which then makes you even more frightened because you wonder what – you know – I wondered, 'What on earth am I doing here?' I thought, 'I may as well go home now' … umm … but I thought, 'No, I'm here I may – you know, I've I've got this far, I may as well just see it through another 15 minutes and I can be out of here then, you know if it goes all horribly wrong, I never have to see these people again.' … umm … So then went into a room where there was two people who were auditioning you and the accompanist and you sat down with the music and played, the accompanist accompanied piece … umm … and, er …
>
> INTERVIEWER: How did that go?
>
> SUSAN: Some mistakes I was just –
>
> INTERVIEWER: Because I bet you can remember just about every minute of it.
>
> SUSAN: Oh, it was horrible. I hated it. Absolutely dreadful. I, I made mistakes. And I think because I was nervous I made mistakes … umm … and I wasn't used to playing with an accompanist because I don't have anybody to just practise with at home … umm … and any little mistake you make, you think they're gonna, they know that you've made a mistake, they're very good musicians, they are going to be thinking 'Oh, she's dreadful, what on earth is she doing?' and I sort of breathed a huge sigh of relief when I ground to a – the end and nearly nearly felt like crying – I don't know, out of relief or just nerves that you've got to the end, yeah, just absolutely … er … it's w – a horrible moment moment … erm … and then they gave a piece of sight-reading to do which wasn't too bad, actually it was better than I'd – had thought, and then a scale, I played a scale – I was so relieved when I played it in tune … which is always a bit of a bonus when playing a scale, and then and then they said to me, they said,

'Oh … umm … will you be at orchestra on Monday?' because this was on a Saturday and I said, 'Well, kind of depended on today really,' and they said, I said, 'When will I get to know?' and they said that the person who sorts out the auditions would phone me … umm …and so they said, 'Oh come along on Monday,' so I thought, well, do I take that as a 'yes' or do I take that as … umm …? You know, you just don't know, so I went home and I was actually going out that evening and quickly phoned my parents and said, 'Er, dreadful! Horrible! They'll ring me,' and nobody phoned me for the rest of the weekend. Monday evening ca – time to go to orchestra, nobody had phoned me so I thought, well I'd better go because nobody's told me not to go, and … umm … they – someone came up to me just before we started and – no, actually, I think it was in the interval – and said, 'Oh I'm pleased you got in,' which after all that, you know to me it was such a big thing – you know, I'd been practising for a long time – when it's something that you want to do and just suddenly, erh, you're in.

a   What problems, if any, would you expect students to have with this tape? (The speaker uses a 'British northern English' variety of English; she speaks reasonably clearly, but with many topic shifts, etc.)

b   What action would you take to counter these problems?

H Some students finish before everybody else (pages 184–185)

1   What kind of activity could you have 'up your sleeve' to give to groups of students who finish before some of the other groups in the class? Can you think of examples?

2   Look at the photographic competition activity on pages 124–125. What would you do in these situations?

a   One group decide on the winner before the others.

b   One group still haven't decided on the winner even after the rest have.

c   One group don't seem to be concentrating on the activity; they are talking about something else.

d   One group keep asking you for help to do the activity.

e   One group say 'We did a photographic competition with the last teacher' when you give them the sheets of paper.

NOTE: No answers are given for the Jargon buster tasks. Readers should check their answers by looking back at the chapter and/or consulting the glossary on pages 268–285.

Chapter 1

A

a ii b iii c i d v e iv

B

a virtual learning b one-to-one teaching c English lessons at secondary school d large classes e in-company teaching f private language school

C

1 Some of the possible advantages and disadvantages of the different age groups – from a teacher's point of view – are:

	Advantages	Disadvantages
Children	• Respond well to individual attention • Curious about almost everything • Respond well to involving activities • Have an unlimited acquisition potential (depending on age)	• Shortish attention span • Inability to deal with abstract thought • Ability to forget languages as quickly as they acquire them (depending on age)
Adolescents	• Developing capacity for abstract thought • Understand the need for learning • Largely untapped creative potential • Passionate commitment	• Search for identity can make them awkward • Need for self-esteem can make them awkward • Peer group is highly influential
Adults	• Wide range of life experiences to draw on • Good at application to learning • Clear understanding of learning purposes • Disciplined	• Fear of failure • Previous (negative) learning experiences • (Sometimes) out of the habit of classroom learning • Strong ingrained views about teaching

2 a Ad b Ad c ? d C (most likely) e A f Ad (most likely) g ? h Ad (most likely) i ?

3 a A b B/I c I/A d B e B/I (and maybe A for remedial practice) f I/A g A h B/I/A i I/A

Chapter 2

B

2 a v b ii c i d iv e iii

D

	Advantages	Disadvantages
Class seating plan	• In the teacher's hands • Easy to refer to during a lesson	• Students always have to sit in the same place • Some students may deliberately sit in different places
Name badges	• Easy to see • Students 'carry' them with them • Easy and quick to make	• Have to be re-made each class unless they are durable, and then (a) they cost money and (b) students will forget them • Students may not like them
Name cards on the desk	• Clear • Creates nice formal-but-friendly atmosphere	• Need good stiff paper/cardboard • Difficult to see in a big classroom • They get knocked off desks
Not using students' names	• Takes pressure off the teacher • All students treated equally	• Students want the T to 'know their names' • Encourages T pointing • Makes the class less personal • May look as if the T doesn't care
Students always say their names when they ask a question or when you ask them to do something	• Takes pressure off the teacher • Lots of repetition of the students' names so everyone gets to remember them	• Makes classroom interaction very unnatural • Makes the classroom seem a bit military • Students think the T can't remember names (!)
Write notes about appearance/attitude, etc against the students' names in the register	• A very good way to remember who students are • Makes us concentrate on different student identities	• Difficult to think of something to say about every student • Takes up a lot of space/messes up register • T always has to look at notes

(You can add your own feelings about the different naming schemes.)

Chapter 3
B
1 The first instruction is clear, uses gesture and repetition, and then checks that students have understood what is going on.

The second instruction uses complex language, is full of non sequiturs and includes information that is completely unhelpful to the students.

The third instruction is perfectly efficient, but doesn't actually 'include' students in any way.

The fourth instruction works in a number of ways. The teacher announces a change of direction/a new stage. She makes sure even the student who is currently distracted is listening, and then starts to elicit questions.

C
1 Supposing that the teacher speaks for about twenty-five minutes in total (including taking the register, etc), the maximum time any one student could talk would be one minute and fifteen seconds.

2

	Advantages	Disadvantages
Teacher talking time (TTT)	• T is a good language model. • Good Ts are good 'rough-tuners' – so their language is useful for the students' acquisition. • SS like listening to the T. • T can focus the attention and energy of the whole group.	• SS need speaking practice, not the teacher. • It can be very boring if it goes on too long. • It means SS are usually working only as a whole group. • It means SS are only listening – which cuts out the learning potential that speaking, reading and writing offer.
Student talking time (STT)	• SS need the practice! • STT can provide rehearsal (see Chapter 9). • STT gives T and SS good information about how well the SS are doing.	• It can be very chaotic – especially in groups, etc. • It may be less efficient than TTT for getting across specific information. • It is easy for individual SS to dominate.

F
a probably orderly rows with the aisle (if there is one) dividing the teams, or two sides of a horseshoe; in smaller groups, each team could be at a separate table b sitting in a circle (or horseshoe seating) c orderly rows (unless you can have two or three pairs at each separate table) d separate tables e separate tables f just about any seating arrangement g orderly rows (although any seating arrangement will do if they can all turn to the front)

G

1 These are among the advantages and disadvantages:

	Advantages	Disadvantages
Whole class	• Creates a sense of group identity. • Suitable for T-as-controller activities. • Ideal for showing things.	• Favours groups over individuals. • Does not encourage SS to take responsibility for their own learning. • Is not good for decision-making, discussion, etc.
Groupwork	• Increases speaking time for individuals (in contrast to whole-class grouping). • Opportunities for lots of different opinions. • Encourages learner self-reliance through group decision-making.	• Can be noisy. • Some students get 'lost' in groups. • Some students end up always fulfilling the same group role. • Can be difficult to organise. • Some SS prefer whole-class grouping.
Pairwork	• Dramatically increases speaking time in contrast to whole-class grouping. • Students work/interact independently. • Two heads are better than one! • Easy to organise.	• Can be very noisy. • SS may veer off the point of the activity. • SS are not always keen on pairwork. • It depends who individuals are paired with.
Solowork	• Allows SS to work at their own pace. • Less stressful than whole-group 'performance'. • Quiet.	• Doesn't necessarily help group solidarity. • More work for the teacher.

2 a G b G c W/S d W/P e S f W g P h P i S j W

Chapter 4
A

Some of the many differences are:

Mother tongue	Second/foreign language
• Massive exposure to language. • The mother tongue is a bonding language. • Input usually very comprehensible ('motherese' is subconsciously designed for babies and children and usually highly effective). • Input is 'rough-tuned' rather than selected precisely – so it's rich in acquisition terms. • Focus usually on activation rather than study (though parents do correct children and, especially, involve them in repetitive routines which look a little like study). • Language is generated by need (the baby/child's) and the positive aspect of human–human interaction. • Massive positive reinforcement of language production (the baby/child gets what it wants/a [positive] reaction).	• Exposure is often limited to lessons only. • Language is often carefully selected – and can therefore be poor in terms of acquisition potential, but highly appropriate in terms of learning. • The comprehensibility of the input depends on the teacher's skill. • Teachers help students to focus precisely on important language issues. • Teachers can control the amount of input. • Depending on age, students have the experience of L1 acquisition to help them with the second language. • L1 and L2 contrast can be both insightful but (sometimes) confusing. • There is not the same 1–1 contact between the knower (mother/teacher) and the student (or child).

C

a PPP **b** Audio-lingualism **c** the Lexical Approach **d** Grammar–translation **e** Communicative Language Teaching (CLT) **f** teaching language functions **g** Task-Based Learning (TBL) **h** the Silent Way

D

1 1 Communicative Language Teaching – many CLT lessons will be patchwork lessons involving a number of different E, S and A sequences.

2 Presentation, Practice and Production – most PPP lessons are equivalent to straight arrows lessons.

3 Task-Based Learning – most TBL lessons are like boomerang lessons in that doing the task is the thing that prompts later study of language that needs more work.

2 A E → A → S → S → A → A

B E → S → S → S → S → S → A

C E → A → A → S → S → S → E → A

Chapter 5
A

Grammar

1 **a** SVA **b** SVC **c** SVOA **d** SVO **e** SVO **f** SVA

2 **a** transitive, direct object **b** intransitive **c** transitive, indirect object (me), direct object (the letter) **d** intransitive **e** transitive, indirect object (me), direct object (that song) **f** intransitive **g** transitive, direct object (the message) indirect object (their family)

Pronunciation

1 **a** 6 **b** 9 **c** 7 **d** 6 **e** 4 **f** 14 **g** 8 **h** 4 **i** 4 **j** 8

2 **a** 'activate **b** adol'escent **c** 'classroom **d** e'motion **e** 'export **f** ex'port **g** 'learner
h procrastin'ation **i** stipu'lation **j** 'willingness

3 **a** It <u>was</u> only last night that you arrived (= don't contradict me. I'm sure of my facts), It was
only <u>last</u> night that you arrived (= surely. You didn't arrive the night before that or the one
before that), It was only last <u>night</u> that you arrived (= well you didn't arrive in the morning or
the afternoon), It was only last night that <u>you</u> arrived (= other people arrived at different times,
but you arrived last night), It was only last night that you <u>arrived</u> (= surely you're not thinking
of going already)

b <u>This</u> is the best show I've ever attended (= not some of the other ones you're talking about),
This is the <u>best</u> show I've ever attended (= not the worst or the second best, etc), This is the best
<u>show</u> I've ever attended (= it's not necessarily the best concert or play, but it is the best show),
This is the best show <u>I've</u> ever attended (= other people may have been to better ones, but not
me), This is the best show I've <u>ever</u> attended (= in my whole, whole life), This is the best show
I've ever <u>attended</u> (= not the best one I've ever seen, e.g. on the TV, or heard, e.g. on the radio,
but the best one I've actually been to)

c <u>She's</u> decided she loves you (= nobody else has decided but her), She's <u>decided</u> she loves you
(= she took the decision), She's decided <u>she</u> loves you (= not anyone else, but her), She's decided
she <u>loves</u> you (= she doesn't like you, she actually loves you), She's decided she loves <u>you</u> (= she
thought it was someone else, but actually it's you)

B

2 **a** This refers to a (present) temporary state of affairs.
b This refers to a pattern of repeated actions which is in some way irritating.
c This refers to an arrangement that has already been made for the future.
d The present continuous is being used here to tell a story in the past – but by using present
tenses it has a special immediacy.
e This is slightly ambiguous. It either refers to a present temporary state of affairs or it might
mean 'I'm not going to listen'.

C

1

noun	Matilda, parents, house, journey, gate, Mercedes, motor-car, etc
pronoun	she, we, I, you, etc
adjective	eight-minute, large, strange, better, lousy, etc
verb	said, walk, arrived, saw, take, were, etc
adverb	home, frantically, in half an hour, etc
preposition	at, outside
article	a, the
conjunction	but, and

D

1 **a** parent, journey, gate, motor-car, place, scene, hall, object, etc **b** notice, clothing
2 **a** all categories of noun can go here **b** countable noun **c** singular countable noun, uncountable

noun, collective noun **d** plural countable noun, collective noun **e** singular countable noun, uncountable noun

3 **a** adjective order (It should be 'big red French plastic designer chair'.)

   b word order (It should be 'He washed himself'.)

   c position of 'often' (It could be 'Often I like to play tennis' or 'I like to play tennis often'.)

   d we don't use an article when expressing general concepts (It should be 'I love nature'.)

   e the wrong particle is attached to the verb (It should be 'I'm crazy about French films'.)

   f the clause is in the wrong place and there's no relative pronoun (It should be 'The lady who sat down beside me was beautiful'.)

   g the comparative form is incorrect (It should be 'She is brighter than her brother'.)

   h general concepts do not have an article (It should be 'Inhumanity is a terrible thing in our world'.)

   i 'in spite of' must be followed by a noun or noun phrase (It should be 'In spite of the fact that it was late/In spite of the time/lateness of the hour …'.)

   j the wrong preposition is used (It should be 'I'll see you on Saturday …'.)

   k we don't use the present perfect with a past time adverbial (It should be 'I saw him yesterday'.)

E

1 **a** didn't take (= did not take), what on earth's going on? (= what on earth is going on?), What's happening (= what is happening), We're off, we're leaving, (= we are), You'd better get packed (= you had), Your brother's upstairs (= your brother is), It's a better climate (= it is), I don't want to (= I do not), do as you're told (= you are), I've got enough troubles (= I have got), I'm not missing that plane (= I am), We aren't (= are not)

   b 1 didn't (take), what's (happening), we're leaving, your brother's upstairs, etc **2** said, was (an eight-minute journey), arrived, saw, take, were (often strange cars …), etc **3** set out, shut up

2 **a** don't (auxiliary) want (main) **b** 're (auxiliary), leaving (main) **c** can't (modal auxiliary), understand (main) **d** was (auxiliary), brought up (phrasal verb) **e** might (modal auxiliary), mind (main)

3 **a** said, set out, was, arrived, saw, etc **b** What's happening? We're leaving, I'm not missing **c** We're off, your brother's upstairs, It's a better climate, I love it here, etc **d** she was confronted by a scene

4 **a** present perfect simple **b** past continuous passive **c** present continuous **d** present passive **e** past continuous **f** past perfect continuous **g** phrasal verb **h** present perfect continuous **i** past simple (both verbs)

F

a real, future **b** hypothetical, past **c** hypothetical, present **d** real, timeless present **e** real, future **f** hypothetical, past **g** hypothetical, present **h** hypothetical, future

G

1 fast asleep fully alert/awake/conscious half asleep/awake/conscious semi-alert/conscious sound asleep wide awake

2 **A:** love **B:** break

H

1 **a** (includes) If I were you, I'd study more, How about studying more? Why not study more? Study more, I reckon, Perhaps you should study more, etc

   b Would you like to come to dinner? D'you fancy coming to dinner? I was wondering if you might be interested in coming for dinner? How about coming for dinner? Dinner at my place?, etc

c Can I help you? Would you like some help? I'll help you, let me help you, etc

d In my opinion …, the way I see it …, it's a fact that …, you've got to admit that …, as far as I can see …, etc

2 All the sentences are requesting someone to do something. In terms of formality, they can be described as **a** I, **b** I, **c** F, **d** F, **e** I, **f** N, **g** N. Remember, a lot depends on pitch and tone of voice.

I

The order is **d, b, e, a, c.**

Pronoun reference: **a** people – from sentence 2 **b** people's – ditto **c** people – ditto **d** people – ditto **e** people – from this sentence **f** all of us, society **g** people – the ones who aren't talking to each other **h** people – ditto **i** people – ditto **j** all of us – society in general **k** people – from sentence 2 **l** people – ditto **m** people's – ditto **n** mobile phones **o** the people talking into their mobile phones

Chapter 6

A
a D **b** I **c** I **d** D **e** D **f** D

D
2 The correct order is **f, k, c, m, g, h, d, j, e, i, b, l, a, n**

Cues: **e, f** and **g**

Teacher nominating: **h, i, k**

Student responses: **a, b, c** and **d**

F
a possibilities: 'where the book is?' (with rising intonation), 'Is that a question, Juan?', 'Question, remember', 'Try again', etc

b Possible T response: 'OK, listen everyone. Look (writes on the board) He's never been … he's … he has … he has … he's … he's never been … OK?'

c 'Can to?' or 'to?' with rising intonation, 'Do we need "to"?'

Chapter 7

B
a Both texts seem to be at the elementary to pre-intermediate level.

b Text A is designed for extensive reading. We can tell this because it is clearly written and is obviously part of a longer piece. Text B is designed for intensive reading. We know this because it is packed full of facts and figures, is short, and is clearly designed for some kind of post-reading exercises about comparative/superlative adjectives.

c Text A seems to be a fiction genre, perhaps a detective novel/thriller. Text B is an imitation of the information/encyclopedia genre – but is clearly from some kind of a coursebook.

d You decide!

C
a i **b** iii **c** ii **d** iv

D
a This text could be used with intermediate students and above. **b** You decide. **c** You decide.

d You decide, though – amongst many other language features – there is a lot of good present simple use, the 'Canadian sleep researcher' paragraph is good on formal uses of past tenses, and the use of bullet points to list things (especially with 'more') is interesting. There are also many nouns: stress, tiredness, sleep, overeating, irritability, grumpiness, infection, etc, which might lead into a good word 'field' – and we could do some word formation exercises on the different adjective-noun-adverb-verb forms. **e** You decide.

Chapter 8

A

a L b W c L d L e W f L g L h W

D

2

Symbol	Meaning	Example error
S	A spelling error	*The answer is <u>obvius</u>.*
WO	A mistake in word order	*I <u>like very much</u> it.*
G	A grammar mistake	*I am going to buy some furniture<u>s</u>.*
T	Wrong verb tense	*I <u>have seen him</u> yesterday.*
C	Concord mistake (e.g. subject and verb agreement)	*People <u>is</u> angry.*
ʌ	Something has been left out.	*He told˅that he was sorry.*
WW	Wrong word	*I am interested <u>on</u> jazz music.*
ξ ϡ	Something is not necessary.	*He was not ξ too ϡ strong enough.*
?M	The meaning is unclear.	*That is a <u>very excited photograph</u>.*
P	A punctuation mistake	*Do you like London<u>.</u>*
F/I	Too formal or informal	*<u>Hi</u> Mr Franklin, Thank you for your letter ...*

Chapter 9

A

1 a ✗ b ✓ c ✓ d ✓ e ✗ f ✗

2 **a** drill – because it is a controlled practice exercise, not a 'speaking-as-skill' exercise
  b a grammar exercise – because all the others are examples of language genres, rather than studying the language itself
  c study – because all the others are about person–person interaction, whereas study is about person–language

Chapter 10
B

Advantages of using authentic listening texts at any level	Disadvantages of using authentic listening texts at any level
• Motivating (because it's the real thing). • Gives students exposure to real language use instead of concocted examples. • There's a much greater variety of authentic listening texts. • Students respond in different ways; authentic listening may bring some of them on very quickly.	• Demotivating (because students can't understand it). • Speed, accent and colloquialism may make it inappropriate. • Complex speech patterns (in regional variety informal conversation) may not be useful for students of international English. • May not have repetition of language patterns/lexis, which makes some non-authentic material very good for study activities. • Not geared or designed for a specific audience of language learners.

Chapter 11
A

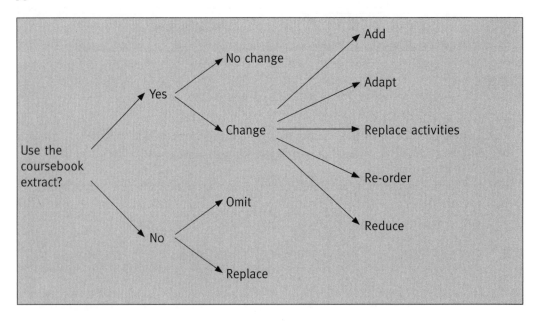

B

a The aims of the lesson appear to be (1) to recycle/practice/teach holiday topic vocabulary, (2) to recycle/practise/teach present simple questions and answers, and (3) to use the present simple to talk about routines, using holiday language. **b** Students should be able to use the present simple confidently to talk about holidays. **c** You decide. **d** You decide. **e** You decide.

C

2

Advantages of using coursebooks	Disadvantages of using coursebooks
• Systematically written • Colourful • Full of solid ideas that work (ideal for busy teachers) • A cumulative syllabus and good sequencing • Students feel secure • Something for students and teachers to use to see progress, and check on past learning	• Often have an unvaried format • Not written especially for your class • May perhaps stifle teacher creativity • Often have topics which are not especially interesting for your students • Create a kind of 'book-dependency' in students

Chapter 12

A

2

Advantages of planning lessons	Disadvantages of planning lessons
• T has thought about what will be appropriate for the lesson. • T has some idea of what s/he wants the students to achieve. • T has thought about how the lesson fits into a sequence. • SS like to see that the T has planned the lesson.	• Plans straightjacket a lesson. • Plans are uncreative – because everything depends on the T's ability to react to the 'here-and-now'. • Plans can discourage Ts from reacting to magic moments and unforeseen circumstances.

B

Individual readers will have different responses to the plan. Below are a few possible reactions:

Appropriacy of lesson plan format (For the teacher? For an observer?)	The format is clear and easy to follow. Some plan formats have a separate column for interaction patterns (e.g. T–SS, S–S, etc). This makes them easier to follow in some ways.
Lesson details (Are they sufficient for the teacher? For an observer?)	Some of the information is not very detailed (for example, the description of the class – it would be nice to know more about individual students). The third aim is rather general. There is nothing in this plan about possible extra activities.

Lesson shape (e.g. Is the lesson coherent? Does it have variety?)	There's a good variety of activities (listening, reading, discussion, study, speaking, etc). There's a question about why the plan suddenly switches from the grandmother topic to a not-very-related speaking activity. It might be better to have a more topic-linked speaking activity – although this itself might not be ideal!
Timings (e.g. Are they clear? Do you 'believe' them?)	Many of the timings seem a little optimistic (e.g. procedures 2 and 6), especially since there are 20 students here. But everything depends on the actual students and how the lesson progresses.
Who does what? (e.g. Do you approve of the patterns of interaction?)	There seems to be a good range of interaction patterns in this plan (e.g. T–SS, S–S, SS–SS, etc).
Is it a good plan? (e.g. What would you (a) leave out? (b) add to? (c) bring in? or (d) change completely?)	You decide.

Chapter 13
A
a portfolio assessment b continuous assessment c proficiency test d achievement test e progress test f exit test g placement test
B
a This test is not valid since it not only tests the students' writing ability, but also presupposes (and therefore is testing) their knowledge of issues surrounding DNA. It might, however, be valid in an 'English-for-science' class, where DNA research had been a topic – but even in that case it is testing more than just the language.

b This item doesn't work because both answer **a** and answer **d** are possible.

c This item/test fails on the grounds of face validity. Students would wonder why such a short test was given.

d This might be invalid for those students who are not natural poets – especially since it gives so little guidance about how the task is to be done.

e This test item is perfectly feasible, except that it gives very few parameters and so different students might write answers of wildly differing lengths and complexity. There is then an issue of both validity and reliability.

f This is a strict 'every-5th-word' cloze test. There are many blanks that are fillable by a number of different words (e.g. **a, j, k**) whereas others are highly predictable (e.g. **c, d, f**). Perhaps it would be better to use a modified cloze procedure so that we could ensure good answers to the questions.

DVD TASK FILE

Introduction

The DVD provides real-life illustrations of a number of key teaching activities and techniques through extracts from classes and interviews with teachers.

There are ten sections on the DVD, and each section consists of two parts. First, a short film sequence that focuses on a particular activity or technique, with extracts taken from one or more classes. This is followed by a discussion on the topic of the film sequence between the author and one (or two) of the teachers who appeared in the extract(s).

Each DVD section is accompanied by a series of tasks in the following pages. Some of these tasks should be used while viewing the DVD material; others can be used for further discussion and analysis of the topic. We recommend that you watch the film sequence and do the tasks before you watch the discussion with the teacher(s).

An answer key (page 251) is provided after the DVD Task File for those tasks where it is possible to provide specific or suggested answers. The symbol ☛ beside an exercise indicates that answers are given for that exercise in the answer key.

The material in the DVD Task File can be photocopied for use in limited circumstances. Please see the notice on the back of the title page for photocopying restrictions.

1 Student levels
2 The teacher in the classroom
3 Giving instructions
4 Organising student groupings
5 Different seating arrangements
6 Teaching vocabulary
7 A reading sequence
8 Speaking tasks
9 Beginning the lesson
10 Games

1: Student levels (2:44)

1 Match the levels on the left with the teachers' names on the right. ✔

  a beginner   **i**   Louise
  b intermediate   **ii**   Mark
  c advanced   **iii**   Pip

2 Read these extracts from the classroom transcripts. Match them to the levels in Task 1. ✔

  a STUDENT: Because if you don't have to go to lessons, you will just choose the lessons you – you like and then you will miss …

  b STUDENT: I – I worked er teacher.

  c STUDENT: I've never heard about a free school in Switzerland, but I'm not sure if I would like to go there.

  d STUDENT: I – I read most my dictionary.

  e TEACHER: Okay, you can close your books for a second. Um, let's see … Fionetta, in Italy do you have anything similar to a free school?

  f TEACHER: What did you do? What did you do? Um, so what do you do?

  g STUDENT: Er yes I, I usually read in the afternoon too, but recently I don't read, I didn't read …

3 How would you expect student and teacher language to be different at beginner, intermediate and advanced levels?

2: The teacher in the classroom (4:03)

1 Match the following events with where the teachers were in the classroom. ✔

Events	Teacher's position
a Giving instructions for an exercise/game (x 2)	**i** Crouching on the floor next to a group
b Going through answers (x 2)	**ii** Kneeling on the floor next to a group
c Monitoring a small group (e.g. discussing the tasks, suggesting, checking answers, etc) (x 4)	**iii** Sitting at a group table
	iv Sitting at the front of the class (x 2)
d Talking about a topic (different kinds of reading)	**v** Sitting casually on the edge of a table
	vi Standing at a group table
	vii Standing at the front of the class (x 2)

2 Which of the teacher–student interactions shown in the extracts would you feel most/least comfortable with as: (a) a teacher? (b) a student?

Jeremy Harmer *How to Teach English* © Pearson Education Limited 2007

PHOTOCOPIABLE

3: Giving instructions (4:15)

1 Which of the different techniques listed below do you see being used by the teachers? ✔

   a The teacher asks a student to summarise the task for the class. ☐

   b The teacher asks a student to translate the instructions into the class' L1. ☐

   c The teacher asks two students to demonstrate the task for the class. ☐

   d The teacher demonstrates the task by doing one item with the whole group. ☐

   e The teacher explains (verbally) what the students are going to do. ☐

   f The teacher gives the students written instructions for the task. ☐

   g The teacher makes sure the students have the language they need to do the activity. ☐

   h The teacher shows the students the material they are going to be working with. ☐

   i The teacher accompanies instructions with gestures. ☐

2 Look at the list of techniques in Task 1. Are there any situations in which any of them might *not* be appropriate?

4: Organising student groupings (3:43)

1 Read the list of techniques below. Write the name of the teacher next to the technique/s he or she uses (Pip, Mark, Philip). Some of the teachers use more than one technique. ✔

a	explanatory pictures/diagrams	....	....	....
b	gesture	....	....	....
c	moving individual students	....	....	....
d	moving the furniture	....	....	....
e	verbal instructions	....	....	....

   Which teacher does not reorder the pairs or groups?

2 Put the teachers in order, where 1 = the shortest/simplest instructions and 3 = the longest/ most complex instructions. What makes the instructions simple or complex?

3 What reasons (apart from the ones on the film clips) can you think of for the teacher to:

   a leave the students sitting where they are (and so form pairs or groups with the people next to them)?

   b move the students around so that they sit/work with other people?

5: Different seating arrangements (1:28)

1 Describe the seating arrangements for the following events from the film clips. ✔

   a   The students are working individually.
   b   The teacher is explaining some pronunciation.
   c   The teacher is explaining something using the board.
   d   The teacher is handing out a worksheet and explaining a task.
   e   The students are listening to a tape.
   f   The teacher uses the board to explain vocabulary and then sets up groupwork.

2 Which of the seating arrangements you noted would you use in the following situations?
   a   The teacher is explaining a grammar point to the class.
   b   Students are writing group stories.
   c   The class is having a formal debate.
   d   All students are reading individual graded readers for a ten-minute reading period.
   e   Students are helping each other to do an exercise from a workbook.
   f   Students are acting out a dialogue in front of their classmates.
   g   Students are playing a teacher-directed team game.

3 What are the advantages and disadvantages of the seating arrangements you have seen, in your opinion? NOTE: think of what the teacher or the students is/are actually doing in the clips.

6: Teaching vocabulary (5:38)

1 Match the word or phrase on the left with the techniques on the right that the teacher used to explain/elicit it. Some words or phrases are explained in more than one way. ✔

poetry	a The teacher asks students to supply alternatives and discusses them.
frying pan	b The teacher draws the object.
stir	c The teacher explains the vocabulary with words.
scramble	d The teacher explains what it does, or what you do it with.
slice	e The teacher gives students the beginning of a word to try to elicit it.
chop	f The teacher mimes/gestures.
beat	g The teacher shows an object (realia) to explain the meaning.
grate	h The teacher uses facial expression.
bitter	i The teacher uses sound effects.
sour	
uncertain	
it seems	
increasing	

2 Which of the techniques in Task 1 do you think you would find easiest/most challenging?

3 Take any two of the words from Task 1 and think of two other ways you could explain them.

Jeremy Harmer *How to Teach English* © Pearson Education Limited 2007
PHOTOCOPIABLE

7: A reading sequence (8:42)

1   Match the two reading tasks on the left with their purpose on the right. ☞

   a   The students find the information they   i   quick reading for gist
       discussed at the beginning of the sequence.

   b   The students find out what the caption   ii   reading for more detailed information
       means.

   Where does Pip get the questions for activity b from?

2   Put the following events in order. ☞

   a   ☐   The students read the text again in pairs.
   b   ☐   The students read the text to find out what the title of the text means.
   c   ☐   The teacher asks the students to predict what the title of the text means.
   d   ☐   The teacher checks the answer to the first comprehension task.
   e   ☐   The teacher holds up a photocopy of the text the students are going to read.
   f   ☐   The teacher shows the students a picture of JK Rowling.
   g   ☐   The teacher tells the students to read the text again in more detail.
   h   ☐   The teacher asks students to say what they know about JK Rowling.
   i   ☐   The teacher goes through the answers with the students.

3   Why does Pip spend some time getting students to: (a) think of what they know about JK
    Rowling? (b) think about what the text caption might mean?

8: Speaking tasks (8:48)

1   Who does the following, Pip or Philip? ☞

   a   The teacher answers a student's question in a demonstration by talking about him/herself.
   b   The teacher demonstrates exactly how the activity should proceed.
   c   The teacher engages the students with an amusing technique.
   d   The teacher gives very precise instructions about the activity.
   e   The teacher wants to make sure that the activity works exactly as it should.
   f   The teacher gives general instructions about what the students should do.
   g   The teacher is sure the activity will work as it should without too much explanation.

2   Answer the following questions.

   a   Why does Pip prompt Ines (the student doing the demonstration) to ask her (Pip) a
       question during the demonstration?
   b   Why does Pip say, 'ready, steady, go'?
   c   Why does Pip say, 'well done, everyone, really good'?
   d   Why do you think Philip organises a speaking activity at the end of his lesson?
   e   Why does Philip pretend he cannot write vowels?

3   What are the reasons for the differences between the two teachers' approaches, in your
    opinion? NOTE: you can hear how the teachers themselves answered this question in the
    discussion with the teachers.

9: Beginning the lesson (2:48)

1 Match the teachers with the way they start their lessons. ✏

   Mark   a After a quick greeting, the teacher launches straight into the lesson.

   Pip   b The teacher gives a detailed explanation of what the lesson will be about.

   Philip   c The teacher introduces the lesson and then gets students to brainstorm ideas.

   Chris   d The teacher organises a quick warm-up game.

2 Why might it be a good idea to:
   a explain the order of the lesson?
   b start straightaway with a game?
   c get students to brainstorm ideas at the start of a lesson?
   d start the lesson with an activity which introduces the topic of the lesson?

3 What, in your opinion, is the best way to start a lesson if:
   a you want students to get a clear idea of the lesson contents?
   b students are tired and need animation?
   c you want to engage the students' curiosity?
   d the students are very noisy when you come into the lesson?
   e it is late in the evening and the students are tired?

10: Games (7:07)

1 Which game (Mark's or Louise's – or both): ✏
   a is competitive?
   b involves a change of classroom seating?
   c involves student conversation as part of the game?
   d has a winner in each group?
   e involves movement as well as speech?
   f depends on the students' speed?
   g ends when the teacher says so?
   h ends when the game task is complete?
   i puts different individual students in prime position as the game continues?

2 Which game (Mark's or Louise's), in your opinion:
   a provokes more student interaction?
   b is more fun?
   c is easier to use at lower levels?
   d is the easiest for the teacher to organise and manage?

3 Which games from 'ordinary' life (e.g. *Charades, Noughts and crosses*) could be adapted for use in the English-language classroom, do you think?

1: Student levels

1 **a** ii **b** iii **c** i
2 **a** advanced
  b beginner
  c advanced
  d intermediate
  e advanced
  f beginner
  g intermediate

2: The teacher in the classroom

1 **a** v, vii **b** iv, vii **c** i, ii, iii, vi **d** iv

3: Giving instructions

1 c, d, e, g, h, i

4: Organising student groupings

1 **a** Mark
  b Pip, Mark, Philip
  c Mark, Philip
  d Mark
  e Pip, Mark, Philip

5: Different seating arrangements

1 **a** whole class horseshoe
  b whole class horseshoe
  c small groups at three separate tables
  d students sitting round a single big table
  e small groups at two separate tables
  f small groups at four separate tables

6: Teaching vocabulary

1 Poetry: c, g
  Frying pan: b, c, d, f, i
  Stir: c, d, f
  Scramble: c, d, f
  Slice: f
  Chop: f
  Beat: d, f
  Grate: c, f
  Bitter: c, h, i
  Sour: c, h

Uncertain: e
It seems: a
Increasing: a

7: A reading sequence

1 **a** ii **b** i
2 **a** 8 **b** 5 **c** 4 **d** 6 **e** 3 **f** 1
  g 7 **h** 2 **i** 9

8: Speaking tasks

1 **a** Pip
  b Pip
  c Philip
  d Pip
  e Pip
  f Philip
  g Philip

9: Beginning the lesson

1 **a** Philip
  b Pip
  c Chris
  d Mark

10: Games

1 **a** Mark, Louise
  b Louise
  c Louise
  d Mark
  e Mark
  f Mark
  g Louise
  h Mark
  i Louise

APPENDIX A

Classroom equipment, classroom technology

Different classrooms

Twenty-first century classrooms around the world have a wide range of equipment and technology available to them. Picture 1 shows an arrangement which is still the norm in many countries and which has not (with the exception of the tape recorder and the OHP) changed much for the last 200 years or so.

In this classroom there is a **board** which the teacher and the students can write on using chalk, and the students have books to work with. The teacher has a tape recorder to play conversations and songs. There is also an **overhead projector** (OHP) which the teacher can use to project images and text.

Picture 2, on the other hand, shows a classroom equipped with modern technology. Here, the board is an **interactive whiteboard** (**IWB**) (a) which has a number of special features. In the first place, anything the teacher or the students write can be saved or printed because the board acts as a large computer monitor. Because the board is hooked up to a computer (b) (and there is a fixed **data projector** (c) which shines on to it), teachers and students can not only show computer-generated images (and use presentation programs such as PowerPoint and Flash player), but they can also access the **Internet** and project web pages for the class as a whole. In addition, they can show film from DVDs or computer movie files. The students have individual **IWBs** (d) at their desks as well as **wireless keyboards** (e) so that they too can project their work onto the main IWB at the front of the class. **Audio** files are stored on the computer and can be played either through the speaker system (f) or via individual headphones at the different desks.

We will now look at various items of classroom equipment and technology, which can be used in a number of different situations.

The board

Whether chalk-based or for use with marker pens, the board is one of the most important pieces of classroom technology.

- Boards (especially whiteboards) can be used for anything: writing, drawing, sticking things on, projecting overhead transparencies, etc.
- The two things to remember about boards are (a) that your writing needs to be visible and legible to all the students in the class, and (b) that organised boards are better than chaotic ones! Some teachers divide their boards so that a column is kept for new words, etc. Many teachers use different coloured pens or chalk to highlight grammar or pronunciation. Some teachers have different areas of the board for different subjects – e.g. pronunciation, homework, etc.

Picture and word cards

Even in an increasingly technological age, there is still good value to be had from pictures of all shapes and sizes. Cards (often called flashcards) can be used with either pictures or words for cue-response work or as aids in pairwork and groupwork.

- Pictures can come from a variety of sources: drawings, magazines, professionally published material, postcards, photographs, etc.
- Teachers can use pictures as prompts for controlled language work – as an alternative to bringing in objects that would be difficult to have in a classroom – as aids for speaking activities or writing tasks, or as a focus for description and discussion (teasing meaning out of a painting, for example).
- Cards with pictures and/or words can be used in a variety of activities. For example, we can write words on cards which the students then have to put into the correct sequence. Cards can have a picture on one side and the word for that thing on the other side – for use in team-based word games.

Cards should be durable – tough and properly covered with some kind of laminate (where this is possible) so that they can be reused. They should look good – there's nothing worse than a tatty torn picture from an old magazine.

Flip charts

A flip chart is a pad of outsize paper on a frame like an artist's easel. The paper can be written or drawn on, of course, but crucially the individual sheets can be torn off for people to keep and work with and/or look at later. As a result, flip charts are good for brainstorming ideas. Some teachers are lucky enough to have more than one flip chart in a classroom so that different groups can write their different thoughts up in different areas of the room. Sheets of paper can be torn off the easel and kept by the teacher – or by a representative of a group, for example. Individual students can take the sheets of paper away in turn to work with them/copy them down.

Cuisenaire rods

Cuisenaire rods are small blocks of wood of different lengths and colours. They are useful for a wide range of activities: we can say a particular rod is a vocabulary item (say a dog, or a key, or even the pronoun 'he' or 'she'). By arranging the rods in various sequences, we can use them to tell a story. Or they can be put in sequences to demonstrate grammatical sentences. We can use the rods' varying sizes to show where main stress occurs in a word or a sentence, or – by putting the rods in various positions – what prepositions mean.

The overhead projector

Overhead projectors (OHPs) allow us to project transparencies (OHTs) which can be either prepared in advance, written on in class, or a combination of the two – as in the following example, where the teacher has typed up some student writing and the students have then tried to correct it with marker pens (as part of their writing-correction training).

> Once upon a time, a *beautif* princess lived in a castle by a river. *Sp*
>
> She was very clever.
>
> She always read and studied. *T/WW*
> However, she hasn't seen the gergous nature around her, where she was living, *Sp*
> she had a stemother that hate her very much. *Sp T*
>
> She had a lovely dog.
>
> It was very loyalty. *Gr*
>
> One day, her stepmother bought a basket of apples from the local market. *WW*
> The stepmother putted poison in apples. *WW T*
> Her dog saw what the stepmother do, so, when the stepmother gave the apple to her, *P*
> her dog jumped and ate the apple. Then, the dog died.

When using OHPs, we need to be sure that (a) the writing/designs on the OHTs are big enough and clear enough for everyone to see and (b) there should be some surface to project on (a screen, the wall, a board) which is not bleached out by direct sunlight, etc.

One of the main advantages of OHTs is that we can mask them with pieces of paper or card – and we can then reveal things gradually.

Six Listening Principles
- Principle 1: Encourage students to listen as often and as much as possible.

Six Listening Principles
- Principle 1: Encourage students to listen as often and as much as possible.
- Principle 2: Help students prepare to listen.
- Principle 3: Once may not be enough.
- Principle 4: Encourage students to respond to the content of a listening, not just to the language.
- Principle 5: Different listening stages demand different listening tasks.
- Principle 6: Good teachers exploit listening texts to the full.

Computer-based technologies and programs

The big revolution in classroom technology has been in the development of computers and associated hardware and software. We will look at three areas in which computers are most commonly used: presentation, information getting and composing.

Using computer-based technology for presentation

- When hooked up to data projectors, computers can show a variety of presentation media including pictures, both still and animated. By using programs such as PowerPoint™, they can offer animated and highly attractive presentations using a combination of text, pictures and slide animation.
- When computers are hooked up to interactive whiteboards, not only can we project anything we want (e.g. word-processed text, PowerPoint presentations, film footage) from the computer's hard disk, but we can also save onto that hard disk anything that has been written or drawn on the board.
- Where students have wireless keyboards, for example, they can put their own work on the IWB, and also access the Internet, etc from where they sit – and it will appear on the main board.
- As with other visual technology, clarity and size are vital. And as data projectors use a light beam, teachers have to be careful not to have the beam shining in their eyes every time they turn to face the class.

Using computer-based technology for information-getting

Computer-based technology has allowed users to access an extraordinary wealth of information in ways that were impossible before.

- Whether we use the Internet or specially designed CD-ROMs or DVDs, computers are fantastic reference tools. We can use search engines such as **Google** to find information, and many dictionaries and encyclopedias are now available – either online (e.g. Internet-based), or on CD-ROMs. Good **MLDs** (monolingual learners' dictionaries) are an invaluable tool for students, and when offered electronically have impressive features including visuals, audio, etc and sophisticated referencing.
- The Internet is an endless source of activity and information. Whether students are researching a project on their own or following a **webquest** we have designed (see page 105), the information they can find on the web is extremely rich and varied, and dissolves the walls of the classroom. The possibilities are limitless.

Using computer-based technology for composing

- **Word processing** is still one of the most important uses for computers in the classroom. Pairs and groups of students can work at the same screen, constructing a piece of writing together. And their writing can be corrected using editing software (such as Track Changes in Microsoft Word, for example).
- Teachers and students also use the Internet and emailing for **chatting** (holding text-based conversations with other users, whether in the same school, or in different cities or countries). Teachers can encourage students to become **keypals** or **mousepals** (i.e. using the computer as a more efficient way of having pen pals.) Here, we need to be sure that students are familiar with chatting etiquette – and the difference between computer chat and other written and spoken forms – and that initial keypal enthusiasm is not dissipated through lack of teacher support.

When we encourage the students to use computers, we need to make sure that they do not waste their time in fruitless and undirected searching, for example, or use its great potential for other non-related activities.

It is also important for students (and teachers) to know the rules about **copyright** and understand the pitfalls of **plagiarism**. Copyright laws prohibit people from reproducing other people's original work; if they do, they are liable to prosecution. Plagiarism is where people use other people's work and pass it off as their own. It is the teacher's job to remind students that both infringing copyright, and plagiarising other people's work are unacceptable in an academic environment.

Audio and video

A lot of classroom technology is designed so that teachers and students can listen to audio and watch film and video.

- Tape recorders – especially the small portable kind – are still the mainstay of many teachers and students. We can bring cassettes to class with recorded music, coursebook dialogues, pronunciation exercises, broadcast excerpts or homemade texts. Good tape recorders are clearly audible, but not too expensive or unwieldy. They should have efficient **tape counters** so that we can find our place easily.

  CD players have all the advantages of tape recorders and are in some ways easier to use (and CDs are easy to carry around). However, some teachers stick with tape recorders because they prefer tape counters to CD information.

- Video and DVD players allow us to show students film, TV programmes, coursebook excerpts and home-produced efforts. Once again, the quality of the machines and the monitors we use is vitally important. It is important to make sure that students do not watch passively (as they may watch TV and DVDs at home); we need to ensure there is a good reason for watching, and appropriate tasks for them to undertake.

- Modern **language laboratories** have both audio machines and computer monitors and keyboards. This allows teachers and students to listen, word process, watch video clips or other presentation programs. Teachers can have students work individually, individually with the teacher, in small groups (we can hook up different student workstations from the teacher's computer console), or in **lockstep** – that is, the whole class working with the same material at the same time. Care needs to be taken, however, in case overuse of the laboratory makes teaching and learning too machine-based. Nevertheless, modern language labs have come a long way from the drill-only booths that once characterised them.

- Where possible, we should encourage students to download podcasts or record English-learning material onto their MP3 players, or have CDs (or tapes) with material which they can listen to on the way to and from school or work, or whenever they have a moment free. Watching English-language films with subtitles is also a very good way of getting appropriate listening practice.

- It often helps if students record themselves on audio or video. This can add realism to a role-play of a news studio or television discussion programme, for example, and teachers and students can watch videos (or listen to audio tracks) to analyse their language performance and to see how much progress they are making.

Dictionaries

Perhaps the most useful piece of 'equipment' a student can ever own or use is a good dictionary. Modern dictionaries are clearly designed, have a wealth of information, and help students to understand what words mean, how they are used, how common they are, and what phrases they occur in.

Bilingual dictionaries

Most students start, quite rightly, by using a bilingual dictionary, such as the example here from a Polish–English dictionary.

It is important that students choose a dictionary that gives good information, including accurate translations, examples and collocational information.

Monolingual learners' dictionaries (MLDs)

Good MLDs are now designed better than ever before. The data is clearly presented, with information about frequency (how common a word is in speaking and writing), appropriate definitions, authentic examples, and most importantly, information about how the word operates and what other words it collocates with. The example here shows how, for the second meaning of 'heavy', the phrases the word occurs in are highlighted immediately. This is extremely useful information since it is usually in these phrases that the word – with this particular meaning – is found.

Dictionaries and technology

Non-book/paper dictionaries come in three forms: on the Internet, on CD-ROMs, or as separate pocket **electronic dictionaries**. The great advantage of all three is that users no longer have to worry about alphabetical order. They can find what they want just by typing in a word or phrase. Especially on CD-ROM-based dictionaries, users can go from words to phrases and associated language at the click of a mouse rather than having to turn pages backwards and forwards. Modern portable electronic dictionaries are now much more impressive than the originals since they have bigger windows, better navigation systems, and often two or more dictionaries bundled into the same device.

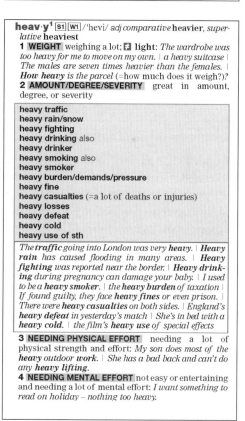

choice¹ /tʃɔɪs/ *n* **1** [C,U] wybór: *If you had a choice, where would you want to live?* | *The prizewinner was given a choice between* (=zwycięzcy dano do wyboru) *£10,000 and a cruise.* | *It was a difficult choice* (=wybór był trudny), *but we finally decided Hannah was the best.* | **+ of** *The supermarket offers a choice of different foods.* | **have no choice** *He had no choice but* (=nie miał innego wyjścia niż) *to move back into his parents' house.* | **have a choice of sth** *You will have a choice of* (=będziecie mogli wybierać spośród) *five questions in the test.* | **a wide choice** (=duży wybór) *There is a wide choice of hotels.* | **make a choice** (=dokonać wyboru) *I hope I've made the right choice.* **2 by choice** z wyboru: *Do you really believe that people are homeless by choice?*

choice² *adj* wyborowy: *choice plums*

heav·y¹ [S1] [W1] /'hevi/ *adj comparative* **heavier**, *superlative* **heaviest**
1 WEIGHT weighing a lot; 🔒 light: *The wardrobe was too heavy for me to move on my own.* | *a heavy suitcase* | *The males are seven times heavier than the females.* | *How heavy is the parcel* (=how much does it weigh?)*?*
2 AMOUNT/DEGREE/SEVERITY great in amount, degree, or severity

> heavy traffic
> heavy rain/snow
> heavy fighting
> heavy drinking also
> heavy drinker
> heavy smoking also
> heavy smoker
> heavy burden/demands/pressure
> heavy fine
> heavy casualties (=a lot of deaths or injuries)
> heavy losses
> heavy defeat
> heavy cold
> heavy use of sth

*The **traffic** going into London was very **heavy**.* | ***Heavy** rain has caused flooding in many areas.* | ***Heavy** fighting was reported near the border.* | ***Heavy** drinking during pregnancy can damage your baby.* | *I used to be a **heavy smoker**.* | *the **heavy burden** of taxation* | *If found guilty, they face **heavy fines** or even prison.* | *There were **heavy casualties** on both sides.* | *England's **heavy defeat** in yesterday's match* | *She's in bed with a **heavy cold**.* | *the film's **heavy use** of special effects*

3 NEEDING PHYSICAL EFFORT needing a lot of physical strength and effort: *My son does most of the **heavy** outdoor work.* | *She has a bad back and can't do any **heavy lifting**.*
4 NEEDING MENTAL EFFORT not easy or entertaining and needing a lot of mental effort: *I want something to read on holiday – nothing too **heavy**.*

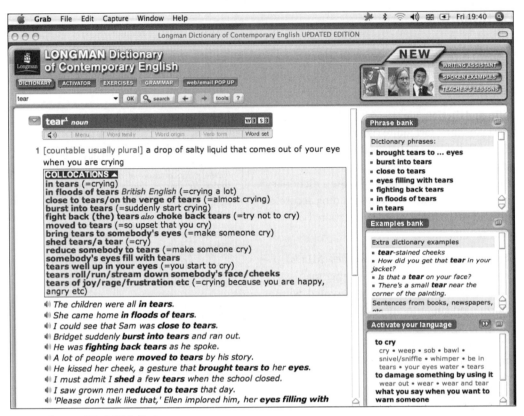

Screen from a CD-ROM dictionary

All students and all classrooms should have access to good bilingual dictionaries or MLDs. However, it is frequently the case that students buy dictionaries and then never use them – or use them inappropriately – because they are unfamiliar with the riches contained within them and have never been trained in how and when to use them. It is vitally important, therefore, that teachers not only show students how dictionaries work, but also give guidance in the best ways to access the information in them. We then need to include dictionary use as part of our normal classroom routines.

APPENDIX B

Useful organisations and websites

Websites on the Internet are evolving all the time so this list could already be out of date. However, the following (very small selection of) sites all offer something for teachers of English.
Note: for a more complete list of websites and other online and technical resources, see *How to Teach English with Technology* in this series.

How to ... – Readers who wish to follow up issues in *How to ...* books – and find extra methodological articles, tips and materials, should go to our methodology site (longman.com/methodology).

Teachers' associations – Most teachers' associations have their own website which you can find by searching (see below) on a search engine like Google. IATEFL in the UK (iatefl.org) and TESOL in the US (tesol.org) are the sites for two important organisations.

Searching – Google (Google.com) is still the most complete search engine on the web. However, it is worth remembering that there is more to Google than just searching for words (though what is available depends on which country Google is being offered in). Click on *Images* and you will find pictures of what you are looking for (though from a wide variety of more or less relevant sites). Click on *Groups* and you will be directed to areas of interest. Click on *Froogle* and you can access a smart shopping site. Clicking on *More* takes you to some extra Google sites (e.g. 'University Search' in the UK, for example, and 'Scholar' which allows you to search a vast array of academic papers and publications).

Teachers – Teaching English (teachingenglish.org.uk) is an invaluable site which is full of articles, teaching tips, advice on methodology, etc. It is run by the BBC and the British Council.
Another useful site is the Macmillan Heinemann One stop English site (onestopenglish.com).

The Guardian newspaper has a lively TEFL news section with a variety of archived articles and blogs at its Education TEFL site (http://education.guardian.co.uk/tefl/). Despite its occasional UK bias, it is well worth visiting.

An early pioneer for ESL websites, and still well worth a visit, is Dave's ESL Café (eslcafe.com). Many of its links are 'sponsored', but there's still a lot of good material for teachers and some lively chat and debate.

Learners – a BBC site called Learning English (bbc.co.uk/worldservice/learningenglish) has the same breadth of ideas as its equivalent teachers' site (see 'Teaching English' above).

Dave's ESL Café (eslcafe.com) also has a lot of material for students.

Online journals – Many journals have online presences where you can read articles, see correspondence and join in the fun. One of the most interesting is *Humanising Language Teaching* (hltmag.co.uk) which is not only free but also has a wonderfully eclectic mix of the academic, practical and downright opinionated. The magazine *Modern English Teacher* (onlinemet.com) and its sister publication *English Teaching professional* (etprofessional.com) have all the articles that grace their printed publications – that is to say, really good down-to-earth discussions of ideas and techniques. You have to be a subscriber to these as you do to the *ELT Journal* (eltj.oxfordjournals.org), where the practical nature of the articles is augmented by their more theoretical content. All three journals are absolutely worth their weight in gold.

Two of the ways that teachers can stay in touch with what is happening in the world of English language teaching are through teachers' associations (which hold local and national conferences and which publish magazines and newsletters), and via subscriptions to journals. The Internet is also a major source of information, articles and activities (see Appendix B on page 259).

Most countries have their own teachers' associations (e.g. JALT in Japan, SPELT in Pakistan). The best way to find them is to conduct an Internet search.

In Britain, the main teachers' association is IATEFL (International Association of Teachers of English as a Foreign Language) which can be found at www.iatefl.org. In the United States, TESOL (Teachers of English to Speakers of Other Languages) can be found at www.tesol.org. Both organisations have affiliates in many other countries (e.g. TESOL Greece, IATEFL Chile).

The *How to ...* series

This book is informed by the titles so far produced in the *How to ...* series, all published by Pearson Education. The books are:

Burgess, S and Head, K (2005) *How to Teach for Exams*

Dudeney, G and Hockly, N (2007) *How to Teach English with Technology*

Frendo, E (2005) *How to Teach Business English*

Harmer, J (2004) *How to Teach Writing*

Kelly, G (2000) *How to Teach Pronunciation*

Thornbury, S (1999) *How to Teach Grammar*

Thornbury, S (2002) *How to Teach Vocabulary*

Thornbury, S (2005) *How to Teach Speaking*

In the chapter notes these books will be referred to only by author and date, e.g. Thornbury (2005).

Throughout these chapter notes reference will be made to my book *The Practice of English Language Teaching* (2007) (4th edn) Pearson Education, which deals with many of the topics here in greater detail. The book will be referred to simply as *PELT*.

Chapter 1

See *PELT* Chapter 5

Business English: see Frendo (2005).

EFL, ESL, ESOL, etc: on the changing face of English and English Teaching see Graddol, D (2006) *English Next*, The British Council.

Large classes: see Hess, N (2001) *Teaching Large Multilevel Classes*, Cambridge University Press.

One-to-one teaching: see Osborne, P (2006) *Teaching English One to One*, Modern English Publishing.

Virtual learning environments: see Dudeney and Hockly (2007); and Smith, D and Baber, E (2006) *Teaching English with Information Technology*, Modern English Publishing.

Learners/learner differences: see Scrivener, J (2005) *Learning Teaching* (2nd edn) Macmillan, Chapter 4.

Neuro-Linguistic Programming: see Baker, J and Rinvolucri, M (2004) *Unlocking Self-expression through NLP*, DELTA Publishing; and Revell, J and Norman, S (1997) *In Your Hands*, Saffire Press.

Multiple Intelligences: see Christison, M (2005) *Multiple Intelligences and Language Learning: A Guidebook of Theory, Activities, Inventories, and Resources*, Alta Books; and Puchta, H and Rinvolucri, M (2005) *Multiple Intelligences in EFL: Exercises for Secondary and Adult Students*, Helbling Languages.

Motivation: see *PELT* Chapter 5.

Agency/learner autonomy: see Scharle, A and Szabo, A (2000) *Learner Autonomy*, Cambridge University Press; Hedge, T (2000) *Teaching and Learning in the Language Classroom*, Oxford University Press, Chapter 3; Harmer, J (2006) 'Engaging students as learners' (*English Teaching professional* 42), and *PELT* Chapter 5.

Dictionaries: see Bruton, A and Broca, A (2004) 'Dictionaries in use' (*English Teaching professional* 31); Harmer, J (2003) 'Best friend: How to help students use and understand their dictionaries' at www.eltforum.com/topic_arch.asp; and Wright J (1998) *Dictionaries*, Oxford University Press. See also the dictionary list in the notes for Chapter 5.

Adults: see McKay, H and Tom, A (2000) *Teaching Adult Second Language Learners*, Cambridge University Press.

Adolescents/teenagers: see Linstromberg, S (ed) (2004) *Language Activities for Teenagers*, Cambridge University Press; Damin, C, Peixoto, M and Wasenkeski, W (2002) 'Teaching teenagers' (*English Teaching professional* 23); and Leiguarda, A (2004) 'Teenagers! Motivating the Teenage Brain' (*Modern English Teacher* 13/4).

Young learners: see Cameron, L (2001) *Teaching Languages to Young Learners*, Cambridge University Press; Moon, J (2000) *Children Learning English*, Macmillan Education; and Rixon, S (2005) *Teaching English to Young Learners*, Modern English Publishing. See also Lewis, G (2004) *The Internet and Young Learners*, Oxford University Press.

Common European Framework and ALTE levels: for more information go to http://www.alte.org/about_alte/index.php.

Mixed ability: see Bowler, B and Parminter, S (2000) 'Mixed-level tasks' (*English Teaching professional* 15); and Hess, N (2001), *Teaching Large Multilevel Classes*, Cambridge University Press.

Chapter 2

See *PELT* Chapter 6.

Describing good teachers: a book still well worth reading is Brown, S and McIntyre, D (1993) *Making Sense of Teaching*, Open University Press.

Teacher roles: see Hedge, T (2000) *Teaching and Learning in the Language Classroom*, Oxford University Press, pages 26–34; and Scrivener, J (2005) *Learning Teaching* (2nd edn) Macmillan, pages 22–26.

Rapport: see Petty, G (2004) *Teaching Today* (3rd edn) Nelson Thornes, pages 96–100. See also *PELT* Chapter 6.

Learner roles: see Hedge, T (2000) *Teaching and Learning in the Language Classroom*, Oxford University Press, pages 34–36.

MLDs: see 'Dictionaries' reference for Chapter 1, and the list of dictionaries in notes for Chapter 5.

Classroom equipment: see Appendix A.

Keeping up to date: see Appendix B.

Chapter 3

On classroom management in general see Petty, G (2004) *Teaching Today* (3rd edn) Nelson Thornes, Chapter 8; and Scrivener, J (2005) *Learning Teaching* (2nd edn) Macmillan, Chapter 5.

Response-ability: this remark is quoted in Lewis, M (1993) *The Lexical Approach*, Language Teaching Publications, page iii.

Teacher's voice: see Maley, A (2000) *The Language Teacher's Voice*, Macmillan.

Chapter 4

Noticing: see Harmer, J (2003) 'Do your students notice anything?' (*Modern English Teacher* 12/3).

The Lexical Approach: see Lewis, M (1993) *The Lexical Approach*, Language Teaching Publications; but see also Thornbury, S (1998) 'The Lexical Approach: a journey without maps?' (*Modern English Teacher* 7/4).

Silent Way, **Community Language Learning**: these now somewhat outdated methods are described in Richards, J and Rodgers, T (2001) *Approaches and Methods in Language Teaching* (2nd rev edn) Cambridge University Press.

Harold Palmer's book: Palmer, H (1921) *The Principles of Language Study*, World Book Company.

Grammar–translation: see Howatt, A (2004) *A History of English Language Teaching* (2nd edn) Oxford University Press, pages 151–158.

Behaviourism, **Audio-lingualism**: see Howatt, A (2004) *A History of English Language Teaching* (2nd edn) Oxford University Press, Section 2.

CLT (**Communicative Language Teaching**): see Hedge, T (2000) *Teaching and Learning in the Language Classroom*, Oxford University Press, Chapter 2; and see *PELT* Chapters 3 and 4.

TBL (**Task-Based Learning**): see Nunan, D (2004) *Task-Based Language Teaching*, Cambridge University Press; and Willis, J (1996) *A Framework for Task-Based Learning*, Longman.

Personalisation: on personalising language learning in general see Griffiths, G and Keohane, K (2000) *Personalizing Language Learning*, Cambridge University Press.

Chapter 5

See *PELT* Chapter 2.

Grammar: here are a few of the multitude of grammar books on offer. I hope I haven't missed out your favourites!

For the serious researcher/teacher/student

Cambridge Grammar of English (2006) by Ronald Carter and Michael McCarthy, Cambridge University Press.

Longman Student's Grammar of Spoken and Written English (2002) by Douglas Biber, Geoffrey Leech and Susan Conrad, Longman.

For teachers/students/researchers at various levels

An A–Z of English Grammar and Usage (2001) (new edn) by Geoffrey Leech, Bentia Cruickshank, and Roz Ivanic, Longman.

Longman Student's Grammar of Spoken and Written English (2002) by Douglas Biber, Geoffrey Leech and Susan Conrad, Longman.

Practical English Usage (2005) by Michael Swan, Oxford University Press; and *Grammar for English Language Teachers* (2000) by Martin Parrott, Cambridge University Press.

For students (containing brief explanations and practice exercises)

English Grammar in Use (2004) by Raymond Murphy, Cambridge University Press.

Grammar Practice for Elementary Students, Pre-Intermediate Students (etc) by Elaine Walker and Steve Elsworth, Longman.

Real English Grammar by Hester Lott, Marshall Cavendish ELT.

For an overview of what grammar is all about see Swan, M (2005) *Grammar*, Oxford University Press.

Vocabulary: see Thornbury (2002); Morgan, J and Rinvolucri, M (2002) *Vocabulary* (2nd edn) Oxford University Press; Schmitt, N (2000) *Vocabulary in Language Teaching*, Cambridge University Press; and Gairns, R and Redman, S (1986) *Working with Words*, Cambridge University Press.

For **vocabulary practice** there are many books such as *Vocabulary Games* (at various levels) by Jill and Charles Hadfield, Longman; and the series *English Vocabulary in Use* (mostly by Mike McCarthy and Felicity O'Dell), Cambridge University Press.

The best vocabulary resources are, of course, **dictionaries**. Modern monolingual learners' dictionaries are extraordinary in their breadth and design, especially now that they have CD-ROM-based resources and web presences. My personal list of favourites includes the *Longman Dictionary of Contemporary English*, Longman; and the *Macmillan English Dictionary*, Macmillan Education. But Oxford University Press, Cambridge University Press and Collins Cobuild also publish much-loved dictionaries for students. There are other dictionary resources, too, such as the *Longman Language Activator* (a thesaurus-type production dictionary) from Pearson Education; and the *Oxford Learner's Wordfinder Dictionary* from Oxford University Press.

Pronunciation: see Kelly (2000), and Underhill, A (2005) *Sound Foundations* (2nd edn) Macmillan. See also Wells, J C (2000) *Longman Pronunciation Dictionary*, Pearson Education.

Collocations: The quotation on page 77 is from the novel *Small Island* by Andrea Levy, Review Publishing, 2004.

Language varieties: see Crystal, D (2003) *The Cambridge Encyclopedia of the English Language* (2nd edn) Cambridge University Press, Chapter 7.

Chapter 6

Teaching grammar: see Thornbury (1999); and *PELT* Chapter 13.

Teaching vocabulary: see Thornbury (2005); and *PELT*, Chapter 14.

Teaching pronunciation: see Kelly (2000); Hewings, M (2004) *Pronunciation Practice Activities*, Cambridge University Press; and *PELT* Chapter 15.

The text on page 89 is from *George's Marvellous Medicine* by Roald Dahl, Puffin Books.

Chapter 7

On **reading** see Nuttall, C (2005) *Teaching Reading Skills in a Foreign Language* (2nd edn) Macmillan ELT. On teaching **reading for exams** see Burgess and Head (2005), Chapter 3. See also *PELT* Chapter 16.

Extensive reading: see Day, R and Bamford, J (1998) *Extensive Reading in the Second Language Classroom*, Cambridge University Press; and Bamford, J and Day, R (2004) *Extensive Reading Activities for Teaching Language*, Cambridge University Press.

The text and exercise on pages 104–105 are from *Energy 4*, Student's Book by Steve Elsworth and Jim Rose, Longman.

Gavin Dudeney and Nicky Hockly's article on **webquests** is at http://www.teachingenglish.org.uk/think/resources/webquest.shtml . See also their book *How to Teach with Technology*, Chapter 4. JoAnn Miller's UFO webquest is at http://www.kn.pacbell.com/wired/fil/pages/webufosjo.html . 'Fire and Ice' (see page 108) is taken from *The Poetry of Robert Frost*, edited by Edward Connery Latham, Henry Holt & Co, 1951.

Chapter 8

For more on the theory and practice of **writing** see Harmer (2004). For a wealth of writing activities see Hedge, T (2005) *Writing* (2nd edn) Oxford University Press. On teaching writing for exams see Burgess and Head (2005) Chapter 4. See also *PELT* Chapter 18.

Process: see Harmer (2004) Chapter 1.

Genre: see Harmer (2004) Chapter 2.

The postcards activity on page 114 is taken from *Cutting Edge* Workbook Intermediate by Jane Comyns Carr and Frances Eales (2005), Pearson Education.

The interview on page 116 (compiled by Rosanna Greenstreet) is taken from 'Guardian Weekend' (the colour supplement of *The Guardian* newspaper), 18 June 2005.

The report writing sequence on page 117 is from *Opportunities* Upper Intermediate Students' Book by Michael Harris, David Mower and Anna Sikorzynska (2002), Pearson Education.

Music: the best book on using music – now sadly out of print – was Cranmer, D and Laroy, C (1991) *Musical Openings*, Longman. See also Walker, R (2006) 'Going for a song' (*English Teaching professional* 43); and Wingate, J (2005) 'The power of music' (*English Teaching professional* 36).

Pictures: see Wade, J (2002) 'Fun with flashcards' (*English Teaching professional* 23).

Poetry: see Holmes, V and Moulton, M (2001) *Writing Simple Poems*, Cambridge University Press.

Dictogloss: see Thornbury (1999), pages 82–85; and Harmer (2004), pages 74–76.

Correcting writing: see Harmer (2004) Chapter 7.

Handwriting: a useful website where you can make your own handwriting worksheets is http://www.handwritingworksheets.com.

Chapter 9

For more on the theory and practice of classroom **speaking** see Thornbury (2005). On teaching speaking for exams see Burgess and Head (2005) Chapter 7. See also *PELT* Chapter 20.

Speaking as skill: see Thornbury (2005), page iv. He ends his book with the comment about a culture of speaking (on page 131).

Automaticity and autonomy: see Thornbury (2005) Chapter 6.

'The Arnolfini Marriage': Jan van Eyck's painting is in the National Gallery in London. This activity is an adapted version of the one in *Motivating High Level Learners* by David Cranmer (1996) Longman – sadly now out of print.

Favourite objects: an extended (and clearly sequenced) version of this activity can be found in *New Cutting Edge Intermediate* by Sarah Cunningham and Peter Moor (2005), Pearson Education.

Correcting speaking: see Thornbury (2005), pages 91–93; and *PELT* Chapter 9.

Chapter 10

For an introduction to **listening** see Hadfield, J and Hadfield, C (1999) *Simple Listening Activities*, Oxford University Press. On listening in general see *PELT* Chapter 18. On teaching listening for exams see Burgess and Head (2005) Chapter 6.

The ticket-buying activity on pages 137–139 is from *Total English* Pre-intermediate Student's Book by Richard Acklam and Araminta Crace (2005), Longman.

The interview with Diana Hayden on pages 140–142 is from *Just Right* Upper Intermediate Students' Book by Jeremy Harmer and Carol Lethaby (2005), Marshall Cavendish ELT.

Music: see the references for Chapter 8.

Stories: see Wajnryb, R (2003) *Stories*, Cambridge University Press.

Chapter 11

See *PELT* Chapter 22.

Options for coursebook use: see Rinvolucri, M (2002) *Humanising your Coursebook*, DELTA Publishing.

The animal quiz on page 148 is from *New Cutting Edge Elementary* Student's Book by Sarah Cunningham and Peter Moor (2005), Pearson Education.

'He photographed the world' on page 151 is from *Touchdown for Mexico* Student Book 2 by Jeremy Harmer with D'Arcy Adrian Vallance and Olivia Johnston (1994), Pearson Education.

Pro and anti coursebook: see Harmer, J (2001) 'Coursebooks: a human, cultural and linguistic disaster?' (*Modern English Teacher* 10/3); and Thornbury, S and Meddings, L (2001) 'Coursebooks: the roaring in the chimney' (*Modern English Teacher* 10/3).

Chapter 12

On **planning** in general see *Planning Lessons and Courses* by Tessa Woodward (2001), Cambridge University Press. See also *PELT* Chapter 21; and Scrivener, J (2004) *Learning Teaching* (2nd edn) Macmillan, Chapter 2.

The plan template on page 161 has been supplied by Gabriel Diaz in Uruguay.

The extract on page 163 is from a plan by Adriana Gil prepared at the Seven Language School (Brazil).

Chapter 13

On **testing** see Hughes, A (2002) *Testing for Language Teachers* (2nd edn) Cambridge University Press; McNamara, T (2000) *Language Testing*, Oxford University Press; and Rea-Dickins, P 'Classroom Assessment' in Hedge, T (2000) *Teaching and Learning in the Language Classroom*, Oxford University Press. See also *PELT* Chapter 23.

Chapter 14

Students at different levels: see Hess, N (2001) *Teaching Large Multilevel Classes*, Cambridge University Press.

Big classes: see Hess (above); and Baker J and Westrup, H (2000) *The English Language Teacher's Handbook: How to teach large classes with few resources*, Continuum International Publishing Group.

Students use their own language: on the uses of the students' mother tongue see Deller, S and Rinvolucri, M (2002) *Using the Mother Tongue*, First Person Publishing.

Homework: Lesley Painter's article about homework is in Painter, L (1999) 'Homework' (*English Teaching professional* 10). She has expanded this into an excellent collection of homework activities in the book *Homework* (2003) Oxford University Press. See also Stirling, J (2005) 'The dog ate my homework' (*English Teaching professional* 38).

Uncooperative students: see Petty, G (2004) *Teaching Today* (3rd edn) Nelson Thornes, Chapter 9. See also *PELT* Chapter 7.

Appendix A

The board: see Dobbs, J (2001) *Using the Board in the Language Classroom*, Cambridge University Press.

Cuisenaire rods: see Scrivener, J (2004) *Learning Teaching* (2nd edn) Macmillan ELT, pages 308–312.

Computer-based technologies and programs: see Dudeney and Hockly (2007). See also Lewis, G (2004) *The Internet and Young Learners*, Oxford University Press.

Dictionaries: see the references for Chapter 1 and the list of dictionaries in the notes for Chapter 5.

APPENDIX D

Phonemic symbols

Consonants

p	pen, happy, publish
b	bed, cab, blackboard
t	time, little, watched
d	dance, played, advance
k	cup, kind, pack
g	good, mug, toggle
tʃ	chin, chatter, arch
ʒ	pleasure, vision, decision
dʒ	July, geometry, judge
f	fan, life, photograph
v	very, live, advance
θ	think, path, thank
ð	then, mother, that
s	sail, cell, boats
z	zen, lens, lends
ʃ	shell, mesh, ship
h	he, hymn, hand
m	meet, bomb, immense
n	no, can, another
ŋ	ring, singer, playing
l	let, sell, lullaby
r	ring, wring, tomorrow
j	yes, yacht, opinion
w	when, what, wait

Vowels

iː	sheep, breathe, these
ɪ	ship, bit, started
e	when, breath, any
æ	pat, back, marry
ɑː	arm, rather, heart
ɒ	clock, what, because
ɔː	floor, law, caught
ʊ	wood, would, woman
uː	shoe, school, July
ʌ	uncle, son, rough
ɜː	first, journey, earth
ə	again, photograph, teacher
eɪ	play, rage, great
əʊ	ago, tow, though
aɪ	climb, kite, buy
aʊ	house, mouth, clown
ɔɪ	spoil, buoy, enjoy
ɪə	cheer, clear, weird
eə	chair, where, their
ʊə	pure, lure, fewer

GLOSSARY

This glossary contains entries for all the terms cited in bold in *How to Teach English*. In the case of Chapter 5, however, only main entries (e.g. noun, verb) are given.

Explanation

In the following entry the main heading (appropriacy) is in **bold**. Because proximity and formal are written in small capitals, this means there are entries for them in the glossary too. The symbol → means that you should (also) look at that entry – in this case 'proximity'.

appropriacy (**1**) – establishing the right professional relationship with students in classrooms → PROXIMITY. (**2**) – choosing language that is not just correct but also appropriate to the situation (in terms of who we are talking to, how FORMAL or INFORMAL we want to be, etc).

Where you see this → Chapter 5 pages 59–80, it means you will find more details in Chapter 5.

A

accuracy is the degree of correctness which a student achieves when using grammar, vocabulary and pronunciation.

achievement test – a test taken at the end of a course of study to see how well students have learnt what they have been studying. See also EXIT TEST.

acquisition is a subconscious process; the effortless mastery of language through being exposed to it, rather than consciously LEARNING it.

acting out is when students perform DIALOGUES, etc as if they were in a play.

activate/activation is what happens when students try to use all and/or any language to complete some kind of a task. It is putting their ACQUISITION and LEARNING into action. → ESA

active sentences → VERBS

adaptability is the teacher's ability to respond to unforeseen events in a lesson; the ability to adapt lessons to suit particular individuals or groups.

adjectives are words like 'big', 'old', 'exciting', 'expensive', 'lovely' which are used to describe things, places, people, events, etc. Used with NOUNS ('a lovely concert') and PRONOUNS ('It's very big'). Adjectives have comparative forms ('bigger', 'more expensive') and superlative forms ('biggest', 'most exciting'). → Chapter 5 page 68

adult is a word generally used to mean anyone who is over 18, though in ELT terms some material is designed for 'adults and young adults' which tends to mean anyone from 16 onwards.

advanced is the level students get to usually after about 500+ hours of classroom English. It is equivalent to ALTE levels C1 and C2.

adverbs are words used to say when or how something happens. Adverbs of time say when something happens ('tomorrow', 'at ten o'clock', 'in three minutes'); adverbs of manner say how something happens ('quickly', 'languidly', 'in a flash'); adverbs of place say where something happens ('at home', 'in Australia', 'three doors away'). There are many other kinds of adverb, too. → Chapter 5 pages 72–73

affect – the emotional factors which influence language learning.

agency – we say an individual has agency when they take responsibility for their decisions or have some LEARNER AUTONOMY or decision-making power.

aims are what teachers hope the students will achieve as a result of their teaching; they are usually indicated/detailed at the beginning of a lesson plan. The term is often used synonymously with OBJECTIVES.

ALTE/ALTE – Association of Language Testers of Europe. There are six ALTE levels from A1 (equivalent to beginners) to C2 (equivalent to higher advanced).

analyse coursebook → COURSEBOOK ANALYSIS

anaphoric reference is when we use words to refer to something that has already been mentioned (e.g. 'He picked up the stick and threw <u>it</u> for the dog'). → Chapter 5 page 77

anticipated problems – these are the potential difficulties which teachers think may arise in a lesson. Usually included in a lesson plan, especially to show observers that the teacher has thought carefully about what might happen in the lesson.

antonyms are words with opposite meanings (e.g. 'hot' – 'cold'). Different from SYNONYMS. → Chapter 5 page 61

appropriacy (**1**) – establishing the right professional relationship with students in classrooms → PROXIMITY. (**2**) – choosing language that is not just correct but also appropriate to the situation (in terms of who we are talking to, how FORMAL or INFORMAL we want to be, etc).

articles can be definite ('the'), indefinite ('a', 'an') or 'zero' articles (that is, we don't use them in sentences like 'People are becoming suspicious'). → Chapter 5 page 67

aspect describes whether the action of a verb is ongoing or complete. We talk about continuous, perfect or simple aspect. → VERBS/ VERB TENSES → Chapter 5 pages 68–72

assessor – a role in which the teacher judges students' performance and tells them how well they have done, either orally in class or by giving them written grades.

attempt is a term used to describe the kind of MISTAKES students make because they are trying to say something they do not yet quite know how to say.

audio/audio track is any individual sound file (such as a song or DIALOGUE) on, say, a CD or a tape.

Audio-lingualism was a methodology, popular in the 1940s–1970s, which relied on avoidance of error and used repeated and extensive DRILLING.

audioscript – the written version of what is recorded on a tape, CD or other sound format.

authentic – the term used to describe texts or language written for native or competent speakers of a language (i.e. with no concessions for a foreign-language speaker). An English novel might be considered authentic, whereas a SIMPLIFIED READER, adapted for students of ESOL often wouldn't be regarded in this way.

autonomous language learners are those who can organise their own learning without necessarily needing a teacher to guide them.

awareness – the teacher being aware of students, their reactions, responses, etc.

B

back-chaining is when teachers get students to repeat sentences bit-by-bit, starting from the back, e.g. 'known … I'd known … if I'd known … come if I'd known … have come if I'd known … I would have come if I'd known.'

backwash effect → WASHBACK EFFECT

balloon debate – an activity where the speakers are all supposed to be in the basket of a hot-air balloon which is leaking air. Only one can survive. Speakers have to argue their case and are voted out of the balloon one by one until only the 'winner' remains.

base forms of verbs are the infinitive form (e.g. 'go', 'walk', 'play', etc) without 'to'. → Chapter 5 pages 68–72

beginner – someone who knows little or none of the language they are going to study.

behaviourism is the idea that behaviour can be CONDITIONED through the use of STIMULUS– RESPONSE–REINFORCEMENT procedures so that people will learn good habits through constant reinforcement.

bilingual dictionary – a dictionary which deals with two languages, offering definitions and examples in both. Usually, bilingual dictionaries are divided into two halves. In the first half, words in one language (say Arabic) are defined in the other (say English). Then in the second half, the words are in the other language (say English) and defined in the first language (say Arabic). Different from MLD.

blog – a diary (or weblog) which can be accessed via the Internet.

board – blackboards (used with chalk) or whiteboards (used with marker pens) are found on the front wall of most classrooms. Teachers and students write, draw or project images on them. → INTERACTIVE WHITEBOARD

boomerang – the name for a lesson sequence which goes in the order ENGAGE–ACTIVATE–STUDY → ESA

brainstorming is when we ask students to get into pairs or groups to prepare a TOPIC and come up with as many ideas as possible in the shortest possible time.

business English – students of business English study the language needed for a life in the world of business (finance, banking, service industries, manufacturing, etc). They may do this before they enter the world of business, as part of a business studies course, or while they are working in a business environment.

buzz groups are impromptu groups of students which are formed to BRAINSTORM ideas before, say, discussion with the whole class.

C

CEF (**Common European Framework**) – a document setting standards for language competences necessary for communication, the skills needed for that communication and the situations in which these competencies are performed. Used in conjunction with ALTE LEVELS, it helps students and teachers design courses and measure their knowledge in a range of different languages

chants – when students repeat lines and lyrics in a rhythmic way as if (almost) singing. Useful for establishing stress and rhythm.

chatting → LIVE CHAT.

check questions are asked by the teacher to make sure that students have understood a new situation, concept, piece of grammar or vocabulary item.

choral repetition is when the teacher gets all the students to repeat a short phrase or sentence at the same time and with the same rhythm.

chorus is the word used to describe any situation (such as in a drill) when the class speak together using the same words, rhythm, stress, etc.

chorus reaction – when the teacher divides the class into, say, two halves and each half, speaking in chorus, takes one part of a dialogue or responds in some other way separately from the other half.

circle seating – a situation where students and the teacher sit in a circle.

class-to-class is when one class works with another, doing surveys and questionnaires, for example.

clauses are parts of sentences with a subject and a verb. They are often joined together by conjunctions. → Chapter 5 pages 60–61

cloze – a test in which every nth word is randomly replaced by a gap/blank for the students to FILL IN. Different from MODIFIED CLOZE.

cognitive effort is when students are encouraged to think about what they are seeing, hearing or working on – rather than, say, just repeating mindlessly.

coherence (**1**) – in a lesson plan, coherence is where the pattern or 'shape' of the lesson makes sense. Instead of being a chaotic mess,

there is some sensible sequence or THREAD/S to the lesson. (**2**) – in writing, coherence is when writers organise their ideas in a logical (or coherent) way. → Chapter 5 pages 76–78

cohesion is how things stick together in texts. This can be achieved through devices such as ANAPHORIC REFERENCE, lexical or grammatical cohesion. → Chapter 5 pages 76– 77

collaborative writing is where students (usually in groups) work together to produce a piece of writing.

collocation is where two or more words often occur together (collocate), e.g. 'fast asleep', 'shrug your shoulders'. → Chapter 5 pages 75–76

communicative activities are those where students use (ACTIVATE) language to communicate real meaning, rather than just practising language.

Communicative Language Teaching (**CLT**) is that which encourages students to communicate real meaning as a way of learning, and which emphasises language use, especially through concentrating on LANGUAGE FUNCTIONS.

Community Language Learning was a methodology developed in the 1960s (with links to counselling) where bilingual teachers help students to say what they want to say in the language they are learning.

complements are sentence elements that give more information about the subject with verbs like 'appear', 'seem', 'be' (e.g. 'She appears tired', 'They're annoyed', 'He seems old'). → Chapter 5 page 60

comprehensible input is a term used to describe language which the students see or hear and which they more or less understand, even though it is slightly above their own language level. Helpful for ACQUISITION. → ROUGH-TUNING

conditional sentences generally use 'if' to specify what condition has to apply if something else happens. First conditionals typically talk about the future ('If it rains, I won't go out'). Second conditionals often talk about the present ('If you weren't my brother, I'd never speak to you again') and third conditionals often refer to the past ('If I'd been in town, I would have bought a book'). We talk about real and hypothetical conditional sentences. There is a 'zero' conditional which states what is always true if certain conditions are met (e.g. 'If you prick us, do we not bleed?' – Shylock speaking in Shakespeare's *Merchant of Venice*). → Chapter 5 pages 73–74

conditioning is the process in BEHAVIOURISM where subjects are 'conditioned' through STIMULUS, RESPONSE and REINFORCEMENT to always behave in a certain way.

conjunctions are words like 'and', 'or' and 'but' which join sentences together. → Chapter 5 page 73

connotation is the impression that a word gives beyond its literal meaning. For example, 'slim' and 'thin' both mean more or less the same thing, but 'slim' has the more positive connotation.

conservation (**of voice**) refers to the ways in which teachers can try to take care of their voices.

consonants are sounds like /p/ – people, /dʒ/ – judge, or /ð/ – that, which are formed when something (lips, tongue, palate, teeth, etc) obstructs the passage of air from the lungs. (See page 267 for a list of phonemic symbols.) Different from VOWELS.

construction is the term used to refer to the way language items (verb tenses, intonation patterns, sentences or paragraphs) are put together.

content (**of a text or task**) – the information and meaning in a text/task, rather than the language, text CONSTRUCTION, etc.

content words are words which carry meaning (such as 'blue', 'write', 'environment', 'push'). Different from FUNCTION WORDS. → Chapter 5 page 79

context describes the environment (topic and linguistic) in which a word or phrase occurs. → Chapter 5 pages 59–60

contexts for learning are the situations in which learning takes place (e.g. whether students are studying in a school or are the recipients of IN-COMPANY TEACHING; whether they are learning EFL or ESOL; whether they are learning in a classroom or in a virtual learning environment.

continuous assessment happens when teachers mark a student's work at frequent intervals and use the marks to build into that student's final results. Different from an EXIT TEST, where

a final exam determines a student's grade. In some continuous assessment schemes, students build up a PORTFOLIO of their work.

continuous recording takes place when the teacher keeps a continuous record not only of the students' work but also their participation in lessons, etc. → CONTINUOUS ASSESSMENT

controlled practice is practice where students are expected to concentrate on specific language items, often in the context of CUE-RESPONSE DRILLS.

controller is a role in which the teacher is in charge of what is going on – for example, when he or she is conducting a DRILL, getting all the students to listen to an audio track or discussing ERRORS that he or she has heard in a COMMUNICATIVE ACTIVITY.

cooperative activity – one where students have to work together to make it succeed.

copyright is the protection given to someone's written work so that it may not be copied or PLAGIARISED.

corpora/computer corpora – a formal plural of CORPUS.

corpus/language corpus – a large collection of written and spoken material (taken from books, magazines, notices, conversations, radio programmes, etc) which is put onto a computer hard disk and which is then available for language research through the use of concordancing software.

correction/correcting students happens when students make MISTAKES (SLIPS, ERRORS or ATTEMPTS). There are various ways of telling students they are wrong so that they can get it right. Different from RESPONDING → ECHO CORRECTION, GENTLE CORRECTION, SELF-CORRECTION.

coursebook – the main book used by teacher and students for a term, semester or year. Often used as the basis for the SYLLABUS.

coursebook analysis is when teachers look at a coursebook in detail in order to decide whether or not to consider it for adoption.

coursebook unit – coursebooks are usually divided into a number of units (say 16, 20 or 24). These each concentrate on different structures, VOCABULARY or TOPICS.

cue – the first stage in a CUE-RESPONSE DRILL.

cue-response drills are when a teacher gives a cue (or STIMULUS) such as 'question … where

...', NOMINATES a student, and the nominated student offers a RESPONSE such as 'Where's the station?'

Cuisenaire rods are small blocks of wood of different sizes and colours used to demonstrate things like stress patterns and word order.

cultural appropriacy is when a topic, exercise or methodology suits the culture or CULTURAL BACKGROUND of the students and/or teacher.

cultural background is the culture that a student has grown up or lived in (culture here means country, region or social group).

D

data projector – a projector that allows you to project what is on a computer screen onto a big screen or INTERACTIVE WHITEBOARD.

debate is the name for a number of activities in which students are asked to discuss or argue different points of view. → BALLOON DEBATE

deductive approach is a name given to procedures where students first learn rules and then try to make sentences on the basis of those rules (see for example PPP). → INDUCTIVE APPROACH

demonstrating is when teachers show students how an activity works by doing it – so that they will then do it correctly.

describe and draw – an activity where one student gives another student instructions so that they can draw a picture (often the same picture that the instructing student has, but which they do not show to their partner while the activity is taking place). → INFORMATION-GAP ACTIVITIES

description of students (sometimes called 'student profile') – an integral part of many lesson plans, especially where a lesson is to be observed by an outsider. The description gives an idea of individual student strengths and weaknesses as well as a picture of how the group behaves *as a group*.

determiners are words or phrases that are used at the beginning of NOUN phrases. They include ARTICLES, QUANTIFIERS, etc. → Chapter 5 page 65

developmental errors are errors that occur naturally as learners gain more insight into the language system (e.g. saying 'I seed' instead of 'I saw' because they have learnt the '-ed' past tense rule). → MISTAKE

dialogue – when two people talk to each other. We often get students to listen to, write or practise dialogues.

dictogloss – a technique where students try to write down exactly what they have heard (delivered at a faster speed than a dictation) – and then compare their versions with the original in order to see how they differ.

differentiation is when teachers give students in the same class different tasks to do because they are at different levels. → MIXED ABILITY

direct test item – an item which tests the students' ability to do something, such as write a letter or make a speech rather than testing individual language points. Different from INDIRECT TEST ITEM.

discourse is a term used to describe any stretch of text (whether written or spoken) bigger than a sentence or, usually, paragraph or utterance. → Chapter 5 pages 76–78

discourse communities are any groups that share ways of communicating in terms of established routines, writing formats, etc.

discourse markers are items of language that explain the relationship between what went before and what comes after (e.g. 'Yeah, as I was saying ...', 'Hold on a second', 'Furthermore', etc). → Chapter 5 page 78

discovery activities are those where students are shown language and asked to try to work out how it works (rules, etc) for themselves rather than being told by the teacher. → INDUCTIVE APPROACH

discrete test item – an item that tests only one thing (e.g. a verb form or the use of an ARTICLE) at a time. Different from INTEGRATIVE TEST ITEM.

discursive essay – a written composition in which students argue the case in favour of and/ or against a certain point of view.

discussion – an activity in which students are asked to give opinions about a TOPIC or DEBATE it.

distractors are the two or three wrong answers in a MULTIPLE-CHOICE item.

drafting – the stage in the WRITING PROCESS where we write out our first version of something, knowing that we are probably going to amend it later.

drill – a technique where the teacher asks students to repeat words and phrases, either in

CHORUS or individually, and then gets them to practise substituted (but similar) phrases, still under the teacher's direction.

E

EAP (English for Academic Purposes) – English studied specifically for use in, for example, university courses.

echo correction – a technique whereby the teacher repeats what a student has just said (often in a questioning way) to indicate that something isn't quite right.

editing – the stage in the WRITING PROCESS where we look at what we have DRAFTED and make corrections and changes to it.

educational background refers to the way students were previously taught and how much they achieved in their previous education.

EFL (English as a Foreign Language) – a term that has been used to describe the language that people study so that they can speak English around the world. Different from ESL (but see ESOL).

elementary – an elementary student is one who is not a BEGINNER (because they know a little bit of English), but has not yet reached an INTERMEDIATE level.

elicit – when we try to get information and language from students rather than telling it to them (e.g. 'Can anyone tell me what you can say in this situation?').

ellipsis means leaving out words (and so saying something much shorter) because we assume that our listeners/readers will understand what we are saying (e.g. 'Biscuit?' meaning 'Would you like a biscuit?'). → Chapter 5 page 78

engage/engagement is the involvement of the students through curiosity or emotion that means their 'hearts' (as well as their minds) are switched on. → ESA

errors are MISTAKES that students make because they have not learnt some language correctly.

ESA stands for ENGAGE, STUDY and ACTIVATE: the three elements that should be present in a teaching sequence.

ESL (English as a Second Language) – a term that has been used to describe the type of language that students learn when they live and work in the target-language community (e.g. immigrants). Different from EFL (but see ESOL).

ESOL (English for Speakers of Other Languages) – the term now generally used to describe the English that people learn whether it is as a foreign language (EFL) or as a second language (ESL).

ESP (English for Specific Purposes) – in contrast to general English, ESP students study a particular kind of language (e.g. BUSINESS ENGLISH, nursing English, English for tourism, etc).

exit test – a test taken at the end of a course of study (same as ACHIEVEMENT TEST).

explain and practise – teaching sequences where the teacher first shows how language works, through explanation of meaning and form, before going on to a controlled practice session. → DEDUCTIVE APPROACH

exponents/language exponents – the different language formulations for performing a LANGUAGE FUNCTION. 'If I were you, I would …', 'Why don't you …?' and 'I think if I was in your position, I would …' are all exponents of the function of advising.

exposure – when students hear or listen to language, they are exposed to it.

extensive listening – listening material which is longer than a typical classroom listening text, and which students often listen to for pleasure. Often sourced from PODCASTS, etc. Different from INTENSIVE LISTENING.

extensive reading – reading where the students read, often for pleasure, texts which are longer than typical classroom passages. Often done outside the class using GRADED READERS. Different from INTENSIVE READING.

extra activities are any activities we take into a lesson with us to use in case we get through what we had intended quicker than expected. Teachers often have extra activities with them at all times, just in case.

extrinsic motivation – MOTIVATION that comes from outside the classroom and the learning experience. Extrinsic motivation might be the result of a student's desire to get a new job or to be able to use English for travel, for example.

F

face validity is achieved when a test looks as if it probably has TEST VALIDITY.

false beginners – although false beginners are hardly able to use any English to express themselves, it turns out that they already know quite a few words and phrases. False beginners are usually somewhere in the A1 ALTE level.

false friends are words which sound the same in two languages but actually mean something different, e.g. 'librería' in Spanish means 'bookshop' in English, not 'library'.

feedback is what teachers tell students about how well they have done in terms of the language they have used or a task they have performed. Can involve CORRECTION, praise, etc.

feedback from students is where students give their reactions to lessons, activity types, etc, especially at the invitation of teachers who want to know if it is necessary to modify the things they are doing in class.

fill-in – an exercise (often in a test) where students have to write a word or phrase in blanks/gaps in a sentence or text.

fixed lexical phrases → LEXICAL CHUNKS

flashcards are cards which teachers can hold up, one-by-one, when conducting a CUE-RESPONSE DRILL.

flexibility is the teacher quality of being able to adapt what they do in a lesson, especially when faced with MAGIC MOMENTS and unforeseen problems.

flip chart – a large pad of tear-away paper mounted on an easel, which can be used in classrooms instead of a BOARD.

follow-up questions are questions students are encouraged to ask after someone has answered their previous question. Follow-up questions keep the conversation going.

for and against composition → DISCURSIVE ESSAY

formal is a term used to describe language which is often slightly more elaborate because it is used in situations where politeness or tentativeness is expected. → Chapter 5 page 79

freer practice – the stage beyond CONTROLLED PRACTICE where students try to use 'new' language in their own sentences or conversations.

functions/language functions are ways in which we do or perform certain things such as apologising, inviting, suggesting, etc. Language functions are realised through a number of different LANGUAGE EXPONENTS.

function words are words that make the text work but do not have any topic meaning (e.g. 'any', 'the', 'of', etc). Different from CONTENT WORDS. → Chapter 5 page 79

G

gap-fill → FILL-IN

general English is the type of English taught and learnt in the majority of the classrooms in the world. Students have no specific reason for learning (ESP), but instead want the language for a wide variety of possible future uses.

general understanding – reading or listening for general understanding is similar to SKIMMING and describes situations where we listen or read to get the gist of what we are hearing/seeing. Different from SPECIFIC INFORMATION.

genre – a style or type of DISCOURSE which is often identified by discourse features, REGISTER and layout, e.g. advertisement, letter, lecture, etc.

genre analysis is when students STUDY different examples within a GENRE in order to find out how texts are constructed within that genre.

gentle correction is a term used to describe situations where the teacher indicates that something has gone wrong with a hint or a nod but does not press students to correct it immediately. REFORMULATION is often used in this way.

gestures – the various arm and hand movements that teachers make to indicate concepts such as verb tense, direction, position, etc.

gist – the general idea of a text, whether written or spoken.

giving instructions takes place when teachers tell students what they are going to do, where to sit, how they are to participate in an activity, etc.

graded (reader) → SIMPLIFIED READER

grammar – the way in which different elements (e.g. subject, verb, object) are put into correct sequences. → Chapter 5 pages 60–61

Grammar–translation method – a popular method in the first half of the twentieth century which relied on translation between the TARGET LANGUAGE and the L1 together, usually, with DRILLING for learning.

grammatical cohesion is when the use of grammar in a text helps to bind it together (e.g. repeated use of the past tense). → Chapter 5 page 77

group leader – the student in a group of, say, five who is chosen to be in charge of the group.

groupwork is when students work together in groups. Groups larger than seven or eight students are often less effective than a group of five. Odd numbers are always better if there is a decision to be made. When students work in groups of two, we call it PAIRWORK.

guided discovery is where the teacher points the students in the direction of the language they are being asked to understand in DISCOVERY ACTIVITIES – i.e. language that they are to find out or NOTICE for themselves.

guided writing is where we give students the shape and sequence of a piece of writing (and some of the language they might need) in order to help them to do it.

H

homework is work which a teacher usually asks the students to do out of class – which is then usually (but not always) handed in and marked or commented on by the teacher. Homework can be a writing task, pre-lesson reading or any other kind of investigation (say, on the Internet).

horseshoe seating is where students and the teacher sit on chairs arranged in the shape of a horseshoe.

I

icebreakers – short activities which some teachers use at the beginning of a lesson to 'warm up' their students. They are often spoken activities and may involve PAIRWORK or GROUPWORK (same as WARMERS).

idioms are sayings that are commonly used by a cultural group. Even though we know the meaning of every individual word, we can only understand the idiom if we know the meaning of the whole phrase (e.g. 'as plain as the nose on your face', 'She thinks she's the cat's whiskers'). → Chapter 5 pages 75–76

impressionistic mark – a mark given on the basis of a feeling for a student's overall performance. → MARKER SUBJECTIVITY

in-company teaching is where teachers (especially of BUSINESS ENGLISH) go to a company's office to give lessons rather than have the students come to a language school or college.

indirect test item – an item that tests knowledge of the language (grammar and vocabulary) rather than measuring the students' ability to do things such as write a letter, make a speech, etc. Different from DIRECT TEST ITEM.

inductive approach – the name given to procedures where students come into contact with examples of the language and try to work out how it is constructed, rather than having it told to them. → DISCOVERY ACTIVITIES. Different from DEDUCTIVE APPROACH.

inference – this is the meaning we get from someone's words (spoken or written) even though that is not exactly what they say. It is the meaning 'behind the words'.

informal is a term used to describe language which is relaxed and often used between friends or in situations where politeness and/or tentativeness are not expected. Different from FORMAL. → Chapter 5 page 79

information-gap activities are those where students have different pieces of information about the same subject and have to share this information (usually without looking at what their partner has got) in order for them both to get all the information they need to perform a task. → DESCRIBE AND DRAW, JIGSAW LISTENING/READING

instant writing is where we provoke students to write things (words and sentences) immediately, rather than giving them time to think about it. Designed to give them writing confidence.

instructions are the words which tell students what they are expected to do. → GIVING INSTRUCTIONS

integrative test item – an item which tests more than one thing at a time (e.g. a writing task tests the students' grammar, vocabulary, punctuation, spelling, etc). Different from DISCRETE TEST ITEM.

intensive listening is when students listen to a listening text – usually on tape or a CD – and discuss detailed aspects of meaning as well as STUDYING language and text CONSTRUCTION, usually with the help of the teacher. Different from EXTENSIVE LISTENING.

intensive reading is when students read texts – usually in class – and discuss detailed aspects of meaning as well as STUDYING language and text CONSTRUCTION, usually with the help of the teacher. Different from EXTENSIVE READING.

interactive whiteboard (IWB) – a kind of board which is connected up to a computer so that any computer images (including current Internet sites, for example) can appear on the board thanks to a DATA PROJECTOR. IWBs can be written on too, and the contents of the board can be printed out.

interlocutor – a person who engages a candidate in conversation in an oral test, but who does not mark the candidate (that is done by someone else).

intermediate – a level usually reached after students have studied for about 200 class hours, roughly approximate to ALTE levels B1 and B2.

intonation is when pitch changes to convey meaning or functionality. Saying 'yes' in a doubting way has different intonation (a different tune) from saying 'yes' in an enthusiastic (agreeing) way.

intonation patterns are the different directions that INTONATION takes.

intrinsic motivation is the motivation that happens as a result of what goes on in the classroom – what the students do and experience, and what the teacher does.

isolation is where the teacher picks out a specific part of a MODEL (e.g. '-ing' when modelling 'he's swimming') and focuses the students' attention on it.

IT (information technology) – computers, INTERACTIVE WHITEBOARDS, education software and other communication devices which rely on microchips and display software (and, frequently, have access to the Internet).

J

jigsaw listening/reading is where different students listen to or read different excerpts from a whole and then have to share what they have heard or read in order for everyone to get all the information.

journals/teacher journal – some teachers keep a journal (a kind of diary) about what happens in their lessons. It helps them to reflect on their teaching and the students' reactions to it.

K

keypal – someone who emails people in other countries to establish a connection, and give

opportunities for writing practice. Same as mousepal. Different from PEN PAL.

kinaesthetic learners are students who learn best through movement and physical manipulation of items.

L

L1 (first language) – a speaker's main language, usually their MOTHER TONGUE, although some people have more than one 'first language'.

L2 (second language) – a term often used to describe the language which the students are learning.

language chunk – a group of individual words which operate as a common meaning unit, e.g. 'See you later' and 'No way' (where you can't substitute any of the words) or, 'Sounds awesome!' (where different words other than 'awesome' can be used). → LEXICAL CHUNK/PHRASE

language exponents → EXPONENTS

language focus – concentrating on a particular language feature.

language functions → FUNCTIONS

language laboratory – a place where a number of students can work with tape recorders or computers at the same time using headphones and microphones. They can work in LOCKSTEP (that is, all together at the same time) or individually. Modern language laboratories also allow students to watch things (video, etc) all at the same time and/or work on the computer screen. A teacher can control everything that goes on from a console.

language-learning contract – a document (or a verbal agreement) drawn up by teacher and students to set class behaviour standards.

language processing is when students think about language they are producing or being exposed to so that they understand its construction better.

large class – the definition of a large class is variable. Most people would say that twenty plus students in a group makes a large class, but English is also taught to, say, forty-five students at a time and sometimes to more than a hundred. That's a large class!

layout – the design on a coursebook page – where the exercises and visual material are placed and how they are presented. → PLAN FORMAT

learner autonomy – the stage when students are capable of taking their own learning decisions, using study skills and different learning resources on their own without the help of the teacher. → AUTONOMOUS LANGUAGE LEARNERS

learner roles are the different things students are asked to do, especially in GROUPWORK – for example scribe, GROUP LEADER, etc.

learning – in its technical sense, learning is the conscious focusing in on the construction of language, and is thus seen as different from ACQUISITION.

learning by doing is the idea that students will learn language when they use it to do something rather than studying it as a language. This is the basic concept behind COMMUNICATIVE LANGUAGE TEACHING and TASK-BASED LEARNING.

learning by rote is learning things automatically – e.g. learning lists of words or memorising sentences.

learning outcome – a term used both to describe what we hope the result of the lesson will be (what the students will have learnt, experienced or felt by the time the lesson is over) and also to say what the students actually did learn, etc when the lesson had finished.

learning resources are any items (dictionaries – MLDs, bilingual dictionaries – worksheets, supplementary books, DVDs, etc) which both teacher and students can use to learn either in class or in places such as SELF-ACCESS CENTRES.

learning styles are the ways that different people approach learning, for example, whether they are prepared to try for LEARNER AUTONOMY or not, or which of their MULTIPLE INTELLIGENCES they will use or how they respond to different stimuli.

lesson planning → PLANNING

lesson stages – the different parts of/activities in a lesson.

level – the standard of English that a student has reached (e.g. BEGINNER, ALTE level B1, etc).

level of challenge – the degree of difficulty students are likely to encounter when doing a task or learning some new language.

Lexical Approach – a way of looking at language and language learning which suggests that vocabulary and the way it collocates (and the LEXICAL CHUNKS that are formed) are perhaps a more proper subject for learning than focusing on GRAMMAR.

lexical chunks are collections of words which occur together – and the collection operates more or less as a unit of meaning, e.g. 'If I were you …', 'Mustn't grumble', 'D'you fancy …', 'out of the ordinary'. Fixed lexical phrases are those where you can't change any of the words in them and still hope to use the phrase (e.g. 'sick as a parrot' in British English), whereas in semi-fixed lexical phrases we can change some of the words and still use the phrase (e.g. 'It's amazing/extraordinary how …', 'See you later/this afternoon/tomorrow'). → Chapter 5 pages 75–76

lexical cohesion is when words are used to bind a text together – as when a series of similar topic words (e.g. 'children', 'adults', 'grandparents', 'grandchildren') are all used in a text, making the connections between them clear. Different from GRAMMATICAL COHESION. → Chapter 5 pages 76– 77

lexical phrase is the same as LEXICAL CHUNK.

lexis/lexical – anything to do with vocabulary. A lexical item may be a word, but it can also be a phrase treated as a LEXICAL CHUNK.

linkers are words or phrases which connect ideas, e.g. 'for', 'furthermore', 'for instance', 'for example'. → Chapter 5 page 77

listening for general understanding is the listening equivalent of SKIMMING in reading.

listening for specific information – times when we listen because we want to hear a particular item of information (such as a platform number, the time of a programme, etc). Similar to SCANNING (when reading).

live chat is when people 'talk' to each other in real time on the Internet by emailing a website to which all the other 'chatters' are also connected.

live listening is where students are listening to people in a face-to-face situation – or whom they can physically see (such as in the theatre, etc). Different from listening to RECORDED EXTRACTS.

lockstep is when all the students are 'locked into' the same procedure, for example, in a language laboratory or in a classroom DRILL.

long-term memory is where we store things which we remember permanently. Different from SHORT-TERM MEMORY.

M

magic moments are events which happen in a lesson which the teacher did not expect and/but which may well be extremely beneficial for the students even though they were not part of the original PLAN.

marker subjectivity occurs when someone marking a test does so using their own opinions and judgment rather than relying on a more objective measure.

marking scale – a series of descriptions of different abilities which allow us to say which description fits a student's abilities, and thus what grade they should be awarded in a test.

matching exercises – those where students have to match (for example) words from column A with meanings from column B.

minimal pairs are pairs of words which are only different in one sound (e.g. 'ship' and 'sheep').

mistakes occur whenever students produce language that is not correct. → ATTEMPTS, ERRORS, SLIPS

mixed-ability classes/groups are those where students have different LEVELS of English knowledge and ability. → DIFFERENTIATION

MLD (monolingual learner dictionary) – a dictionary written in English for learners of English as a foreign language. Modern MLDs have a wealth of material from definitions to examples, and information about collocations and other language features. Such MLDs now have CD-ROMs with a wide variety of extra material, including pronunciation help, etc. Different from BILINGUAL DICTIONARY.

models are well-said or written examples of language, often given by the teacher, for students to imitate. Also used when a teacher 'models' a sentence.

modified cloze – a test type where words are replaced by gaps/blanks for the students to FILL IN, but unlike CLOZE tests where the blanks occur every nth word whatever the original words were, in modified cloze tests, the test designer decides exactly which words should be replaced by gaps.

monitor – this describes when we evaluate our own language output, trying to gauge whether it is right. LEARNING allows us to monitor our own language use.

monologue – a spoken event in which only one person speaks (as in a speech or one-woman show in the theatre).

morphology is the study of the structure of words and how they can be changed, for example, through inflection (e.g. adding '-ed' for the past tense) or by addition (e.g. 'town hall', 'midwife', etc. → Chapter 5 page 61

mother tongue is the language that people grow up speaking: their first language. This concept is complicated by the fact that some children grow up bilingually (speaking two or more languages). Nevertheless, we refer to the mother tongue as being a speaker's main first language.

motivation is the degree to which students, perceiving some goal, have a desire to do something. → EXTRINSIC MOTIVATION, INTRINSIC MOTIVATION, SUSTAINING MOTIVATION

multi-lesson sequences are sequences where teachers plan a series of lessons so that a two-week period, for example, has some COHERENCE, which may be partly the result of various lesson THREADS running through the sequence.

multilingual classes are those where the students probably come from different countries and so have different MOTHER TONGUES.

multiple choice is when students choose between three or four possible answers – and only one of these is correct.

Multiple Intelligences – a theory developed originally by Howard Gardner which says that rather than thinking of people as 'intelligent' or 'unintelligent' we should recognise that we have a number of intelligences (musical, mathematical, interpersonal, etc), and that different people function more or less efficiently in these different spheres.

murmuring is when teachers tell their students to practise saying things 'under their breath' – so they all try out saying something new very quietly and in their own time.

N

narrative is the word used to describe writing or speaking that tells a story.

NLP (Neuro-Linguistic Programming) – a theory developed by Richard Bandler and John Grinder which says that everyone has a preferred stimulus (visual, auditory, kinaesthetic, olfactory or gustatory) which they respond to above all others.

nominating is when the teacher chooses who to speak (for example), especially in a CUE-RESPONSE DRILL.

noticing is what happens when we become conscious of a language feature so that the next time we see or hear it we recognise it. Some people think that it is impossible to LEARN or ACQUIRE anything unless we have noticed it first.

nouns are words like 'town', 'glossary', 'sun', which can be used with articles (e.g. 'the sun'). They describe people, things, concepts, feelings and events, etc. They often occur in noun phrases (which can include articles, adjectives, etc), e.g. 'the intelligent editor', 'the girl with a lopsided grin'. Proper nouns (i.e. names) usually don't have an article (e.g. 'Cambridge', 'Spain', 'Clare', 'Sebastian'). There are many different kinds of noun, but a distinction worth noting is between countable nouns like 'chair' (which can be made plural) and uncountable nouns like 'furniture' (which generally can't). → Chapter 5 pages 64–66

O

objects are things which generally occur after verbs because the verb has affected them in some way, e.g. 'The cat killed the bird', 'He wrote a letter'. Objects can be direct or indirect, e.g. 'She sent him (indirect object) a letter (direct object)'. → Chapter 5 page 60

objectives are what we hope to achieve – or what we hope the students will achieve as the result of what we ask them to do – especially in a lesson plan. Often used synonymously with AIMS.

one-to-one teaching is when a teacher works with just one student.

orderly rows – the traditional classroom organisation where students sit in rows, often behind desks, sometimes with the furniture fixed to the floor.

over-correction is when teachers indicate every mistake that students make (especially in writing) and thus demotivate the students.

overhead projector (**OHP**) – a device that allows us to project images written or drawn on an OVERHEAD TRANSPARENCY.

overhead transparency (**OHT**) – a transparent sheet which we can draw or write on (or

photocopy/print on) which when put onto an OVERHEAD PROJECTOR, projects that image onto a screen (or the board/wall, etc).

P

pairwork is when two students work together. → GROUPWORK

paragraph organisation – the order in which sentences (e.g. topic sentences, conclusions, example sentences) are put together within a paragraph.

paralinguistic – a reference to times when we convey meaning without using verbal language (e.g. by shrugging our shoulders, showing with the PITCH of our voice how we feel, etc).

paralinguistic clues – the way someone looks, gestures or adopts a particular tone of voice, which tells us a lot about how they feel or what they actually mean.

participating is when teachers take part in an activity at the same time as (and in the same way as) the students.

passive → VERBS

patchwork – the name for a lesson sequence in which the ESA elements occur and recur in different orders. → ESA

patterns of interaction are indications (in a lesson plan) of who talks to or works with whom (e.g. T → SS means the teacher working with the whole class, but S → S indicates pairwork).

peer observation is where two colleagues of the same seniority observe each other; they often plan a lesson together and then one teaches while the other observes. Very different in character from when an examiner, manager or other outsider watches a lesson.

peers are people at the same level, of e.g. seniority, who work or study together.

pen pal – a person who sends letters to (and receives letters from) people in other countries to establish a connection, and give opportunities for writing practice. Different from KEYPAL.

personal engagement is when we encourage students to make some personal relationship between themselves and various vocabulary items (e.g. by asking them which words they like best, for example).

personal pronoun → PRONOUN

personalisation is the stage where students use the language they are studying to talk about themselves and their lives.

personality/teacher personality – the personality which the teacher shows to the students (which may be different from their behaviour outside class).

phonemes are the sounds of the language; they are represented differently from regularly written letters because there are many more sounds and sound combinations than there are letters of the alphabet.

phrasal verbs are verbs of more than one word created by a verb and a particle, e.g. 'take off' (an aeroplane), 'look into' (investigate). Like IDIOMS, it is often difficult to understand their meaning even if you understand all the individual words. → Chapter 5 pages 69–70

phrases are two or more words that join together and function as a group – but do not go so far as to make a sentence. → UTTERANCE/LEXICAL PHRASE

pilot – to use coursebooks or other materials for a trial period to see whether it is a good idea to adopt them (and/or modify them) for permanent use.

pitch describes how high or low the sound of the voice is. We call changes in pitch INTONATION. → Chapter 5 pages 61–63

placement test – a test (or series of tests) that students take, usually at the beginning of a semester or term, to find out which class they should be placed in.

plagiarism is when someone copies another person's written work and tries to suggest that it is their own.

plan format is the actual form in which a lesson plan is written. Different teachers use different formats and page layouts when PLANNING. Especially in training, teachers usually adopt the format favoured by their trainers or institution.

plan/planning (1) – when teachers decide roughly what they are going to do in a lesson before they teach it. The PLAN FORMATS may vary from highly technical to very scrappy, depending on teachers and their circumstances. (2) – the name given to the part of the WRITING PROCESS where writers think about what they are going to write (and the order they are going to write it in) so that they can write their first draft.

plateau effect – when students reach a stage where they think consciously or unconsciously that their English is good enough and so find it difficult to learn more sophisticated language.

podcast – a sound file which can be downloaded onto a portable MP3 player such as an iPod. Commercial podcasts often come from radio programmes, for example, and can be found on the Internet. Teachers can provide similar files for their students to listen to on their own players.

portfolio – a collection of a student's work which he or she gradually adds to and which can be used to give a grade at the end of a semester or as part of a scheme of CONTINUOUS ASSESSMENT.

PPP – a teaching procedure which grew out of STRUCTURAL-SITUATIONAL TEACHING in which the teacher PRESENTS a situation and the language; the students then PRACTISE the new language (often through DRILLING), before they go on to PRODUCE the language for themselves, making their own original sentences, etc.

practice → PPP, CONTROLLED PRACTICE

predictability describes a situation when students know exactly what the teacher is going to do (because they never vary their teaching). It can be very un-ENGAGING.

prediction – the process of students trying to anticipate what they will hear or see in reading and listening texts.

preparation – the time which teachers spend PLANNING their lessons.

prepositions are words like 'off', 'in' and 'on' which are usually followed by a noun and which express time and spatial relationships between words. → Chapter 5 page 73

presentation → PPP, EXPLAIN AND PRACTISE

pre-task – the stage of preparation, planning, etc before students perform a task in TASK-BASED LEARNING.

principled eclecticism – using a variety of techniques and approaches rather than sticking rigidly to one approach – specifically as a result of beliefs about teaching, rather than just as a product of carelessness.

procedure – the part of a PLAN where teachers describe what is going to happen, and in what order.

process writing/the writing process – the various stages (PLANNING, DRAFTING, EDITING, etc) that writers go through in a variety of sequences in order to compose written text.

production → PPP, ACTIVATE

proficiency test – a test taken to assess a candidate's language knowledge, irrespective of where the student has studied. Proficiency tests are often PUBLIC EXAMINATIONS.

progress test – a test given after a period of time (e.g. three weeks, two months, etc) to see how well students have been learning the curriculum they have been following.

prompter (**prompt**) – a role in which the teacher encourages students to speak or carry on speaking despite the fact that they seem to have run out of ideas or the language to express them.

pronouns are words that stand in for longer noun phrases, e.g. 'he' (instead of 'the man in the black coat'), or 'their' (instead of 'belong to the people by the bus stop'). They can be personal ('I', 'you', 'she', etc), object pronouns ('me', 'him', etc) relative ('who', 'which', 'that', etc), possessive ('mine', 'ours', etc) or reflexive ('myself', 'herself', etc). → Chapter 5 pages 66–67

pronunciation – the way we make the SOUNDS of the language, how and where we place STRESS, and how we use PITCH and INTONATION to show how we are feeling and what we mean.

proposal for action – a term used to describe plans or coursebook extracts or units as possible lessons, but which can and will be modified in the light of what happens in the lesson.

proximity – how close teachers get to students in the classroom.

public examination – an examination that anyone can enter for (and so different from, say, an internal school test).

purpose – the aim, the end point, the destination of a speaking or writing activity.

Q

quantifiers are words which say how much of something or how many things we are talking about – e.g. the quantity of NOUNS. Examples are 'many', 'some', 'a lot of', etc. → Chapter 5 page 66

R

rapport – the successful relationship between teachers and their classes; the way in which the students 'get on with' their teacher, and vice versa.

reading for detailed comprehension means going through a text to focus in on language, meaning or text construction, often for the purpose of STUDY. → INTENSIVE READING

reading for pleasure is reading which is done for fun rather than study (see also EXTENSIVE READING).

reading puzzles are designed to motivate students to read. There are many types of puzzle, such as giving students bits of text which have to be reassembled or messages which have to be put in the correct sequence.

reassembling a poem/text – a type of activity where students are given, say, lines of a poem on different cards. They have to reassemble the poem by putting the cards in the correct order.

record keeping is when we write an account of what happened in lessons so that we and/or a coordinator can trace the progress of a year or semester.

recorded extracts are any stretches of film or audio which students hear via a tape recorder, CD player, DVD or MP3 file.

reformulation is a way of CORRECTING where the teacher reformulates what a student has just said (incorrectly). In other words, the teacher says it correctly, but does not then insist on the student repeating the correct version. → GENTLE CORRECTION

regional varieties/variations are those particular accents and grammars of a language (e.g. British English) used exclusively in a particular geographical location (e.g. Cornish English or British English from the north-east of England).

register describes the choice of words in a text or conversation on the basis of topic or tone. → Chapter 5 page 79

rehearsal is when students do SPEAKING-AS-SKILL activities which are very much like the kind of speaking tasks they will have to do in real life. Similar to WRITING-FOR-WRITING.

reinforcement is when students are given tasks (e.g. WRITING-FOR-LEARNING) whose aim is to help them to remember language that they have been STUDYING.

relative clauses are clauses introduced by relative PRONOUNS and which say something more about the NOUNS or noun phrases they refer to (e.g. 'The man who came to tea stayed for supper').

reliability → TEST RELIABILITY

repetition is when students are asked to repeat a sound, word or phrase, either individually or in CHORUS.

resource – a role in which the teacher is on hand to supply information about language (or other information) if and when students ask for it as they complete some kind of learning TASK.

responding – the way teachers react to student work (especially during the WRITING PROCESS). Unlike CORRECTION, the aim of which is to make students get things right, responding is designed to be supportive and suggest future courses of action.

response is what happens when a student reacts to a STIMULUS or a CUE or PROMPT from the teacher by saying or doing something. In BEHAVIOURISM, part of the CONDITIONING cycle.

retelling stories is when we get students to tell a story they've heard or read more than once so that they get better at it each time they do so.

reviewing is the part of the WRITING PROCESS where we look at what we have written to see if it needs (further) EDITING.

reward is a stage in the theory of BEHAVIOURISM where the subject is given a present (which could take the form of praise from the teacher) because their RESPONSE was satisfactory.

rhythm is the regular patterning of sounds.

role-card – a card with information on it which is given to individual students who are going to take part in a ROLE-PLAY. It tells them what role they are playing, how their character feels, etc.

role-play – an activity in which students are asked to imagine themselves in a situation and are given roles to play in that situation (e.g. a check-in clerk and a passenger at an airport). → SIMULATIONS

rough-tuning is when teachers adjust their language use to the comprehension abilities of their students. This is not done precisely, but rather in a 'more-or-less' kind of way so that students receive COMPREHENSIBLE INPUT.

S

scan – to look over (or listen to) a text, trying to find some specific information. Different from SKIM.

seating plan – a plan made by the teacher showing where each student is sitting in the classroom.

self-access centres (**SACs**) are places where students can go to work on their own. Such centres normally have a wide variety of resources including books, tapes, films, CD-ROMs, computers (with Internet access), etc.

self-correction is when students can correct their own SLIPS once it has been indicated that something is wrong.

semi-chorus is where the teacher divides the class in half so that each half takes part in different episodes of CHORAL REPETITION.

semi-fixed lexical phrases → LEXICAL CHUNK

short-term memory – the ability to remember things (e.g. house and phone numbers) for a temporary period only, because they do not get transferred to our LONG-TERM MEMORY.

Silent Way – a methodology developed in the 1970s where the teacher tries to remain as silent as possible, directing students themselves to find answers, make corrections, etc.

simplified reader – a book (fiction or non-fiction) where the language has been specially chosen so that students at a certain level can read and understand it.

simulations are activities where students pretend (or simulate) a real-life event in the classroom, such as checking in at an airport, ringing a helpline, etc. When students have ROLE-CARDS, simulations become ROLE-PLAYS.

skim – to read a text to get the general meaning or gist. Different from SCAN.

slips are small MISTAKES of production which students can usually SELF-CORRECT if they are pointed out (i.e. they actually know the right way of saying it, but have just 'slipped up').

solowork is when students work on their own, individually.

sound effects are any non-verbal sounds on recorded extracts which tell us what is going on (e.g. a creaking door).

sounds → PHONEMES

speaking-as-skill describes activities where students are practising real speaking events rather than just using speaking to practise specific language points. → WRITING-FOR-WRITING, REHEARSAL

specific information → SCAN

stimulus is the first stage in the CONDITIONING cycle where the subject is encouraged/prompted to do something specific in order to get a REWARD if they give the correct RESPONSE.

story circle – an activity where students sit in a circle and pass their stories round, in sequence, so that each student adds to each other student's story.

story reconstruction is when different students are given different pieces of information (often in the form of pictures) and then, working together without the pictures, have to work out what story the different information tells → INFORMATION GAP.

straight arrows – a lesson sequence which goes in the order ENGAGE–STUDY–ACTIVATE. → ESA

stress is the degree of emphasis that is given to different syllables or words (e.g. in the word 'glossary', the first syllable is stressed, whereas the next two have less stress).

structural-situational teaching was a (1950s–1960s) way of marrying the habit formation of AUDIO-LINGUALISM to realistic situations, showing how the language is used and what it means.

STT stands for *student talking time*, the amount of time in a lesson when the students speak. Different from TTT, TTQ.

student differences are the differences between students in terms of age, LEVEL, LEARNING STYLES, etc.

student presentations – mini-lectures given by students to the rest of the class.

study is any stage of a teaching sequence where students focus on the construction of something (GRAMMAR, PRONUNCIATION, DISCOURSE, etc). Similar in meaning to LEARNING. One of the elements of ESA.

subjects are nouns or pronouns which come before verbs in active sentences. They say who or what does the action. → Chapter 5 page 60

sustaining motivation – nurturing and encouraging initial MOTIVATION (probably EXTRINSIC MOTIVATION) over a period of time so that it does not dissipate. → INTRINSIC MOTIVATION

syllabus – a list of items which show what students will study (and are expected to learn) over a period of time. Syllabuses can be, for example, lists of GRAMMAR items, VOCABULARY areas, LANGUAGE FUNCTIONS or TOPICS. Many syllabuses are mixtures of these and other elements.

synonyms are words that more or less mean the same (e.g. 'tolerate' – 'stand'). Different from ANTONYMS. → Chapter 5 page 61

T

target-language community – a community which the student lives or wants to live in, and where the main language is the one the student wishes to learn. For a learner of English, therefore, places in Britain, Australia or the US would be target-language communities.

task – something we ask students to do, such as solving a problem (in English), making a presentation or creating an advertisement. This is seen as different from, say, studying an item of language. → SPEAKING-AS-SKILL, WRITING-FOR-WRITING

Task-Based Learning (TBL) – an approach where students have to learn language to complete tasks, rather than just learning language 'because it is there'.

task cycle – the stages that students go through in a TASK-BASED LEARNING sequence.

teacher roles are the different functions/personalities the teacher takes on at different times (e.g. CONTROLLER, RESOURCE, etc) in order to help students engaged in different kinds of learning task.

teacher's guide – the manual that normally comes with a COURSEBOOK and is full of ideas and notes about how to use the material.

tense → VERB TENSES

TESOL (Teaching English to Speakers of Other Languages) – the acronym for the TESOL organisation of teachers in the United States with branches all over the world (see www.tesol.org).

test reliability is achieved when a test gives consistent results whoever is marking it.

test validity is achieved when the test does what it says it will – and when it is a good measure of what it is testing. → FACE VALIDITY

test–teach–test is a procedure where students first try out the language, are taught what they were unable to do (if they were), and are then tested (e.g. they try to use the language again on the basis of the 'teach' session). Similar to BOOMERANG sequences.

threads/lesson threads are TOPICS, activities or language areas that crop up more than once in a LESSON SEQUENCE.

time lines are used to represent verb tenses diagrammatically.

timings are teachers' estimates of how long individual activities will take when they are planning lessons.

tone means the attitude conveyed by the choice of words you use (but see also TONE OF VOICE). → Chapter 5 pages 79

tone of voice means the way our voices sound – and the attitude we convey as a result (e.g. whispering, shouting, etc).

topic – the subject or theme of a reading text, a TASK, a lesson or a lesson sequence. → SYLLABUS

topic-linking is where we use similar topics to join different parts of lessons or lesson sequences. → THREADS

topic sentence – the sentence within a paragraph (usually at the beginning) which tells the reader what the paragraph is about.

transformation items are items (often in a test) where students are asked to rewrite sentences, etc using different (or modified forms of) given words.

translation process – what happens when students come up with L1 equivalents for what they are doing in English, and vice versa.

triphthongs are three VOWELS occurring together (e.g. /aʊə/ = 'hour'). → Chapter 5 page 62

true/false questions are those where students have to say whether a statement is true or false. Used especially in INTENSIVE LISTENING and INTENSIVE READING, but also tests.

TTQ stands for *teacher talking quality*, the actual content of what the teacher says in a lesson (how interesting it is, and how useful for students).

TTT stands for *teacher talking time*, the amount of time in a lesson where the teacher is speaking.

tutor – a role in which the teacher advises the students about what to do (next).

U

use – a word to describe what language actually does. For example, the present continuous can have a number of different uses (commenting on what's happening, talking about what we will be doing tomorrow, etc).

utterances are spoken PHRASES, i.e. a word or group of words that form a unit before the next speaker says something. → Chapter 5 pages 76

V

valid → TEST VALIDITY

variety – the degree of variety depends on how many different activities we use in a lesson (or in a series of lessons), on how often we change student groupings, or on how often we change the topic or skill focus in a lesson (or series of lessons).

variety of the tone of voice means that teachers modify the voice they use throughout a lesson, not always speaking in exactly the same way.

verbs generally refer to actions ('play', 'listen', 'read', 'agree') or states ('be', 'seem', 'have'). Main verbs carry meaning ('She read a book'), whereas auxiliary verbs have to be used with a main verb to make TENSES, passive forms, etc ('She is reading a book', 'Did she read a book?'). Verbs can be transitive (they take an OBJECT) or intransitive (they don't take an OBJECT). They can be active ('She read the book') or passive ('The book was read by her'). → Chapter 5 pages 68–72

verb complementation refers to what grammatical patterns follow certain verbs. For example, 'like' can be followed by 'to' + infinitive or '-ing' ('I like to dance/I like dancing') whereas 'enjoy' can only be followed by '-ing' ('I enjoy dancing') → Chapter 5 page 72

verb tenses show the time of an action or event, e.g. past tense ('He sent an email', 'He was relieved'), present tense ('She teaches children', 'They are rehearsing for a concert'). → ASPECT

virtual learning means learning over the Internet, e.g. where learners and teachers are not in the same physical space, but can nevertheless communicate and read each other's work.

vocabulary includes not only all the words in a language, but also the way words collocate (join together) into lexical phrases and chunks. → Chapter 5 pages 61 and 75–76

vocabulary prediction is where we give students some vocabulary before they listen or read so that they can try to predict what they are going to hear or see.

vocal cords are the two flaps of muscle which lie horizontally across the throat behind the Adam's apple. They can either be wide open for VOICELESS SOUNDS, or pressed together for VOICED SOUNDS.

voiced sounds are all vowels and some consonants which are distinctive because air from the lungs is forced to pass through the nearly closed vocal cords. The vibration of these cords causes the voice to sound.

voiceless sounds/consonants (also sometimes called 'unvoiced') are sounds made when the vocal cords are wide open. As a result the air from the lungs can pass through without any obstruction – and therefore without vibrating. Thus the voice doesn't sound.

vowels are the written letters A, E, I, O and U. Vowel sounds (of which there are many more than written vowels – see page 267) are made when the air coming from the lungs is not obstructed by any part of the mouth (tongue, palate, teeth, lips, etc). Different from CONSONANTS. → Chapter 5 pages 62–63

W

warmers → ICEBREAKERS

washback effect is the influence that a test has on the way students are taught (e.g. the teaching mirrors the test because teachers want their students to pass).

webquest – the name for a project where students get various kinds of information from the Internet (web) in order to complete a task. The websites they visit have often been pre-selected by the teacher.

whole-class grouping is where the teacher is using/teaching the whole class as one group.

workbook – a book full of practice exercises and other material to back up the things that are taught in a COURSEBOOK.

worksheets are any pages of exercises which students have to fill in or write on to complete a task.

writing-for-learning describes activities where students write in order to learn language better, e.g. in order to REINFORCE something they have been studying. Different from WRITING-FOR-WRITING.

writing-for-writing describes activities which are designed to train students to be better writers. The tasks reflect real writing tasks. Different from WRITING-FOR-LEARNING.

writing process → PROCESS WRITING

written correction symbols (sometimes called 'correction code') These are marks (e.g. Λ and ?M) which we put on students' written work when CORRECTING it to tell them that they have made a mistake.

INDEX

Note: References in italic are to the Task File and Key, and to the DVD Task File.

activation 53, 95–6, 123–4, 138–9
adjectives 65, 67–8, 150
adolescents 14, 15, 47, 103–5
adults 15–16, 47
adverbial phrases 60, 65, 72
adverbs 65, 68, 72–3
ALTE 17–18
anaphoric reference 77
antonyms 61
appropriacy 18, 35, 37, 50, 146
assessment 19, 25, 166–7
attempts 96, 97
audio 134, 144, 183–4, *231–2*, 252, 256–7
Audio-lingualism 49
auxiliary verbs 68–9

back-chaining 95
behaviourism 49
blogs 31
boards 252, 253
brainstorming 120, 128
business English 11

children 14–15, 46–7, 91–2, *195, 237*
chorus 86, 178
class-to-class 44
classes 12–14, *187*
  large classes 13, 177–8, *229*
  mixed-ability 42–3, 176–7
  multilingual 20, 39
classroom management 28–9, 34–45, *192–4, 246–8*
  appropriacy 35, 37
  awareness 35–6
  getting attention 40
  groupings 43–5, 176–7, *193, 236, 247*
  instructions 37–8, 39, *192, 235, 247*
  L1 use 38–9, 44, 178–9, *193, 230*
  lesson stages 39–40, *193, 250*
  movement 35
  proximity 34–5, *246*
  seating 40–3, 178, *193, 235, 248*
  talking 37, 38, *192, 235*
  voice 36, *192*
clauses 60–1, 67
coherence 77, 157, 162
cohesion 76–7
collective nouns 66
collocations 75, 82
Common European Framework (CEF) 17, 166–7
communicative activities 50
Communicative Language Teaching (CLT) 50
Community Language Learning 48
comparative and superlative 68, 73
complements 60, 72
compound nouns 66
comprehensible input 47, 100

computers 255–6
conditional sentences 74, 88–90
conditioning 49
conjunctions 65, 73
connotation 18, 64
consonants 62–3
content 101, 136
content words 79
contractions 78
copyright 256
corpus/corpora 75
correction 26–7, 97–8, 120–1, 131, *207, 213–14, 240, 241*
countable/uncountable nouns 64, 66
coursebooks 146–55, *220–2*
  adapting/adding/replacing 57, 146–52, *220, 242*
  analysis 153, 154
  choosing 153, *222*
  options for use 31, 146–7, *220, 242*
  reasons for 152–3, *220, 243*
  teacher's guides 152
  tests 174
cue-response drills 49, 52, 82, 86–7, 95
Cuisenaire rods 84, 254

data projectors 252
deductive approach 81–2
definite article 67
determiners 65, 67
dictionaries 21–2, 255, 257–8
dictogloss 120
differentiation 176–7
diphthongs 62
direct objects 60
discourse 76–8, *203, 240*
discourse communities 113
discourse markers 78
discovery activities 52–3, 82–3, 88–90
drills 29, 49, 158
DVD Task File *245–51*

EAP (English for Academic Purposes) 11
echoing 97
EFL (English as a Foreign Language) 12
eliciting 88
ellipsis 77, 78
engagement 52, 101, 135
English as an International Language 80, 139
equipment 31–2, 159, 252–8
errors 96, 97
ESA (engage, study, activate) 51–4
  lesson sequences 54–7, 162, *196, 237*
  planning 57, 158, 162
ESL (English as a Second Language) 12
ESOL (English for Speakers of Other Languages) 12
ESP (English for Specific Purposes) 11

explain and practise 82, 88, 95–6

false friends 96
feedback 25, 121, 131, 178, 180
  from students 102, 110, 123, 164–5
fixed lexical phrases 75–6
flashcards 93, 253
flip charts 253
formal language 79
function words 79
future 63–4

games *250*
general English 11
genre analysis 109, 113, 119
genres 100, 113, 120, 134, 143
gestures 37, 78, 83, 84
grammar 60–1, 88–90, *198, 205–6, 237*
Grammar–translation method 48–9
grammatical cohesion 77
groupwork 13, 43–4, 176–7, 178, 182, 184–5, *193, 236*

handwriting 121
homework 16, 21, 28, 162, 165, 179–80, *230*

icebreakers 159
idioms 75–6, 94
in-company teaching 13
indefinite article 67
indirect objects 60
inductive approach 82–3
inference 18
informal language 79, 82
instructions
  checking understanding 38
  giving 37–8, 39, *192, 235, 247*
  reading 108
interactive whiteboards 84, 252
Internet 12, 13–14, 32, 105–7, 252, 255
intonation 46, 61–2, 84, 90–1, 93
isolation 82

keypals 120, 255

L1 use 38–9, 44, 178–9, *193, 230*
language 59–80, *198–203*
  chunks 48
  elements 60–3, *198, 237–8*
  exponents 50, 76
  focus 51
  functions 50, 59, 76, 95–6, *202–3, 239–40*
  levels 19
  meaning 59–60, 63–4, 73–4, *199, 201, 238, 239*
  parts of speech 64–73, *199–200, 238*
  register 76, 78, 79, 134
  speaking and writing 78–9, *203*
  text and discourse 76–8, *203, 240*
  varieties 79–80, 133

word groupings 74–6, *202, 239*
see also language system teaching
language acquisition 46–8, *195*
language laboratories 49, 256
language-learning contracts 182, *230*
language schools 12
language system teaching 30–1,
81–98, *204–7*
   construction 84–5, *204*
   correction 97–8, *207, 240*
   deductive approach 81–2
   functions 95–6
   grammar 88–90, *205–6*
   inductive approach 82–3
   meaning 83–4, *204*
   mistakes 96
   practice 85–7, *205, 240*
   pronunciation 90–3, *206*
   specific aspects 81–3, *204, 240*
   vocabulary 93–5, *206–7, 248*
learner autonomy 21, 27, 123
learning
   and acquisition 47–8
   by doing/by rote 20
   contexts 12–14, *187*
   ESA (engage, study, activate) 51–7
   objectives 160
   outcomes 28, 30, 57, 156–7, 158
   styles 16, 55
lesson sequences 162–4
   boomerang 55–6, 82–3, 116, 123
   multi-lesson 159, 162
   patchwork 56–7
   straight arrows 54–5, 82
lesson stages 39–40, *193*
level of challenge 20, 102
Lexical Approach 48
lexical chunks/phrases 75–6
lexical cohesion 76–7
linkers 77
listening 133–45, *218–19*
   activities 142–4, *219*
   audio and video 144
   authentic speech 134–5
   extensive 134, 135, 184
   for general understanding 135, 136
   genres and registers 134
   intensive 134, 135–6
   levels 134–5, 183–4, *218, 242*
   live listening 134, 135, 137
   principles 135–6, *218*
   reasons for listening 133, *218*
   sequences 136–42, *218–19*
   skills 135, 183–4
   sources 134
   for specific information 135
   to students 26
   testing 171
   see also pronunciation
live chat 13, 120, 255

magic moments 157
marking 167, 169, 172–4, *227–8*
meaning

in context 59–60, 63
   explaining 83–4, *204*
   and forms 63–4, *199, 238*
   hypothetical meaning 73–4, *201,
   239*
memory 85
mime 83
minimal pairs 92
mistakes 96
modal verbs 69, 73–4
models 81, 91, 92, 93
morphology 61
mother tongue 46, 49, *195, 237*
   see also L1 use
motivation 20–1, 168
Multiple Intelligences 16
murmuring 86

NLP (Neuro-Linguistic
Programming) 16
nominating 86
noticing 48
noun phrases 64, 65, *200, 238–9*
nouns 64, 65, 66

object pronouns 66
objects 60
one-to-one teaching 12–13
online learning 13–14
overhead projectors (OHP) 84, 252,
254

pairwork 13, 43–4, 178, 182, *193, 236*
paralinguistic clues 78, 135
participles 70
parts of speech 64–73, *199–200, 238*
peer observation 165
peer teaching 97, 177
pen pals 120, 255
personal pronouns 66–7
personalisation 53, 81, 87, 150
phonemes 62, 92, 93
phonemic symbols 267
phrasal verbs 69–70
phrases 61, 65, 68
pictures 253
pitch 61–2
plagiarism 256
planning lessons 156–65, *223–5*
   coherence 157, 162
   evaluation 164–5
   formats 160–2, 163, *223–4, 243–4*
   learning outcomes 156–7, 158
   lesson sequences 57, 162–4
   proposals for action 156–7
   questions 158–60
   reasons for 156, *223, 243*
   success indicators 161–2, 164
   threads 162–4
   variety 157–8, 162
plateau effect 18
plural nouns, singular verbs 66
podcasts 31, 134, 256
portfolios 166

possessive pronouns 67
PPP (present, practise, produce)
49–50
practice 85–7, *205, 240*
   controlled practice 50, 52, 81, 86–7
   freer practice 87
praise 98
predictability 162
prediction 52, 101–2, 109, 143, 183
prepositional phrases 65
prepositions 65, 68, 73
principled eclecticism 51
problems and solutions 159, 160,
176–85, *229–32*
pronouns 65, 66–7
pronunciation 39, 50, 61–3, 90–3,
133, *198, 206, 238*
proposals for action 153, 156–7
punctuation 78–9, 91, 143

quantifiers 66
questions
   check questions 83, 84
   follow-up questions 136–7
   true/false questions 169

rapport 25–7, 32, 37, 42, 180, 181,
190
reading 99–111, *208–11, 249*
   activities 107–9
   authentic texts 100
   choice 99, 110
   for detailed comprehension 101
   extensive 99, 101, 109–10, *208–9,
   211*
   feedback 102, 110
   genres 100, *208–9, 240*
   graded readers 100
   intensive 99–100, 102, *208–9*
   levels 100, 102, *208–9*
   library 110
   for pleasure 16, 99, 100
   predicting 101–2, 109
   principles 101–2
   reasons for reading 99, *208*
   sequences 102–7, *210, 240*
   simplified readers 100, 134
   skills 100–1, *209, 240*
   testing 171
   time 110
record keeping 28, 167
reflexive pronouns 66
regional varieties 133
register 76, 78, 79, 134
relative clauses 67
relative pronouns 67
repetition 81, 85–6
resources 22, 31, 259, 260–66
respect 26–7, 180
responses 49, 109
rewards 49
rhythm 91–2
role-cards 125, 126, 183
role-plays 19, 105, 125–8, 134, 183

rough-tuning 37, 38, 46

scanning 100
schools 12, 13
self-access centres (SACs) 22
Silent Way 48
simulations 125, 126–7
skimming 101
slips 96, 97
solowork 44, *193, 236*
sounds 62, 92–3
speaking 123–32, *215–17, 249*
  activities 129–31, *217*
  conversation 77–8
  correction 131
  discussion 99, 124–5, 128
  marking 172
  purpose 123
  reasons for teaching 123–4, *215,
  241*
  rehearsal 123, 128
  reluctant speakers 182–3, *231*
  role-play 19, 125–8, 183
  sequences 124–8, *215–16*
  speaking-as-skill 123, 129
  teacher participation 132
  testing 171
  time 38, *192, 235*
  turn-taking 77, 78
  and writing 78–9, *203*
spelling 92–3
stimulus 49
stress 62, 84, 91, 93, 150
structural-situational teaching 49
STT (Student Talking Time) 38, *192,
235*
students 11–22
  age 14–16, *188, 233*
  agency 21, 25, 43
  behaviour 15–16, 27, 180–2, *230*
  cultural/educational background
  19–20, 21
  fast finishers 157, 184–5, *232*
  learning styles 16, 55
  levels 16–19, 176–7, *188, 229, 246*
  reasons for learning 11–12, *187,
  233*
  responsibility 19, 21–2, 43
study 52–3, 81, 123
subjects 60, 66
synonyms 61, 64

target-language community 11, 12
Task-Based Learning (TBL) 51
teachers 23–33, *190–1*
  adaptability 24–5
  behaviour 19, 23–4, 34–6
  flexibility 25, 45, 157
  good teachers 23, 32, *190*
  journals 165
  knowledge 30–2, *191*
  personality 24
  preparation 28
  record-keeping 28, 167

reliability 27
responsibility 35
roles 25, 132, *190, 233*
skills 28–30, *191, 234*
talking 36–7, 38, *192, 235*
  see also classroom management;
  rapport
teaching
  art or science? 32–3
  ESA (engage, study, activate) 51–7
  methods 48–51, *195, 237*
  see also language system teaching;
  listening; planning lessons; reading;
  speaking; writing
technology 252–8
TESOL (Teaching English to Speakers
of Other Languages) 18
testing 166–75, *226–8*
  achievement tests 166, 167, 168
  cloze procedure 170, *227*
  continuous assessment 166–7
  designing tests 167, 168, 174
  direct test items 168, 171–2
  discrete test items 168
  distractors 169
  exit tests 166
  ace validity 167
  fill-in items 169–70
  good tests 167–8, *226, 244*
  indirect test items 168–71
  integrative test items 168
  interlocutors 167
  listening 171
  marking 167, 169, 172–4, *227–8*
  and motivation 168
  multiple choice 168–9, *227*
  placement tests 166
  proficiency tests 166
  progress tests 165, 166, 167, 168,
  174
  public exams 166, 168, 174
  reading 171
  reasons for testing 166–7, *226, 244*
  reliability 167
  speaking 171
  transformation 170, *227*
  true/false questions 169
  validity 167
  washback effect 167–8, 169
  writing 171
time lines 83
timings 110, 158–9, 160
tone 76, 79
tone of voice 78
topics 79, 99, 162
translation process 39, 83–4
triphthongs 62
TTQ (Teacher Talking Quality) 38
TTT (Teacher Talking Time) 38,
192, 235

utterances 76

variety 29–30, 36, 157–8, 162

verb phrases 68, *201, 239*
verbs 65, 68–72
  active 71
  aspect 68, 83
  auxiliary verbs 68–9
  base form 70
  complementation 72
  continuous 70, 71
  future perfect 71
  intransitive 60, 69
  main verbs 69
  modal verbs 69, 73–4
  participles 70
  passive 72
  past continuous 70
  past perfect 71
  past simple 70
  phrasal verbs 69–70
  present continuous 63, 70
  present perfect 71
  present simple 63, 70, 88
  progressive 70, 71
  regular and irregular 70
  simple 70, 71
  tense 63, 68, 83
  transitive 60, 69–70
video 144, 256–7
virtual learning 13–14
vocabulary 61
  context 63, 109
  meanings 63
  teaching 93–5, 149–51, *206–7, 248*
  word games 150–1
  word groupings 74–6, *202, 239*
vocal chords 62–3
voice 36, *192*
voiced/voiceless sounds 62–3, 92
vowels 62, 63

webquests 105–7, 255
whole-class grouping 43, *193, 236*
wireless keyboards 252
word cards 84, 253
worksheets 178
writing 112–22, *212–14*
  activities 118–20
  collaborative 43, 119–20, 255
  correction 120–1, *213–14, 241*
  discursive essays 120
  genres 113, 120, *212*
  guided writing 113
  habit 113, 118
  handwriting 121
  marking 172–4
  process 113
  reasons for teaching 112, *212, 241*
  sequences 115–18, *213*
  and speaking 78–9, *203*
  testing 171
  transactional writing 170
  writing-for-learning 112
  writing-for-writing 112, 113

zero article 67